UNDERSTANDING COMPUTERS
& INFORMATION PROCESSING

Today and Tomorrow

FIFTH EDITION

Understanding Computers & Information Processing

Today and Tomorrow

FIFTH EDITION

WITH BASIC

Charles S. Parker

The College of Santa Fe, New Mexico

The Dryden Press
Harcourt Brace & Company College Publishers

Forth Worth   Philadelphia   San Diego   New York   Orlando   Austin   San Antonio
Toronto   Montreal   London   Sydney   Tokyo

To Mom and Dad

Publisher	Liz Widdicombe
Acquisitions Editor	Richard J. Bonacci
Developmental Editor	Elizabeth Hayes, Michele Tomiak
Project Editor	Michele Tomiak
Art Directors	Jeanette Barber, Nick Welch
Production Manager	Mandy Manzano
Photo Editor	Sandra Lord
Copy Editors	Karen Carriere, Marne Evans
Indexer	Linda Webster
Compositor	Monotype Composition Company, Inc.
Art Program	Marco Ruiz
Text Type	11/12 Bodoni Book
Cover Image	Jack Zeman

Address for Editorial Correspondence
The Dryden Press, 301 Commerce Street, Suite 3700, Forth Worth, TX 76102

Address for Orders
The Dryden Press, 6277 Sea Harbor Drive, Orlando, FL 32887
1-800-782-4479, or 1-800-433-0001 (in Florida)

ISBN: 0-03-097905-6

Library of Congress Catalog Number: 92-075746

Printed in the United States of America

3 4 5 6 7 8 9 0 1 2   032   9 8 7 6 5 4 3 2 1

The Dryden Press
Harcourt Brace College Publishers

See the "Credits" section in the back matter for photo credits.

THE DRYDEN PRESS SERIES IN INFORMATION SYSTEMS

Parker
Understanding Computers and Information Processing: Today and Tomorrow
Fifth Edition

Parker
Understanding Computers and Information Processing: Today and Tomorrow with BASIC
Fifth Edition

Robertson and Robertson
Microcomputer Applications and Programming: A Complete Computer Course with DOS, WordPerfect 5.1, Lotus 1-2-3, dBASE III PLUS (or dBASE IV) and BASIC

Robertson and Robertson
Using Microcomputer Applications
(A Series of Computer Lab Manuals)

Roche
Telecommunications and Business Strategy

Simpson and Tesch
Introductory COBOL: A Transaction-Oriented Approach

Sullivan
The New Computer User

Swafford and Haff
dBASE III PLUS

The Harcourt Brace College Outline Series

Kreitzberg
Introduction to BASIC

Kreitzberg
Introduction to Fortran

Pierson
Introduction to Business Information Systems

Veklerov and Pekelny
Computer Language C

P R E F A C E

We are living at a time when the key to success in virtually every profession or career depends on the skillful use of information. Whether one is a teacher, lawyer, doctor, politician, manager, or corporate president, the main ingredient in the work involved is information—knowing how to get it, how to use it, how to manage it, and how to disseminate it to others.

At the root of all of these information-based work activities are computers and the systems that support them. Currently there are millions of computer systems in the world, and collectively, they are capable of doing thousands of different tasks. Some of the tasks that computer systems can now handle—such as making movies and creating art, or "speaking," "seeing," and "listening"— were thought impossible not too long ago. Few professions remain untouched by computers today or will remain so in tomorrow's world. No matter who you are or what you do for a living, it is highly likely that computers somehow affect the way you work.

The importance of computers in virtually every profession brings us to the purpose of this book. *Understanding Computers and Information Processing: Today and Tomorrow*, fifth edition, has been written with the end user of computers in mind. This nontechnical, introductory text explains in straightforward terms the importance of learning about computers, the types of computer systems and their components, the principles by which computer systems work, practical applications of computers and related technologies, and the ways in which the world is being and will be changed by computers. The goal of the text is both to provide knowledge of computer basics and to impart a perspective for using this knowledge effectively in the workplace.

The textbook is available in two versions—one with a guide to BASIC programming and one without. However, the textbook is but one component of a complete and flexible instructional package—one that can easily be adapted to virtually any teaching format. Supplementing the textbook is a comprehensive set of student and teacher support materials.

The Textbook

Understanding Computers and Information Processing: Today and Tomorrow, fifth edition, is designed for students taking a first course in computers and information processing. The text meets the requirements proposed for the first course in computing by both the Data Processing Management Association (DPMA) and the Association for Computing Machinery (ACM). Although it provides a comprehensive introduction to the world of computers, the text is not overly technical. Coverage is given to both commercial and personal applications of computers and large and small computer systems.

Key Features

Like previous editions, the fifth edition of *Understanding Computers and Information Processing: Today and Tomorrow* is current and comprehensive. It offers a flexible teaching organization and a readable and engaging presentation.

Learning tools in each chapter help students master important concepts. Tomorrow boxes, Feature boxes, and User Solution boxes provide insight on current issues of interest. The eight thematic "Windows," each of which highlights a major aspect of information processing, bring the world of computers to life. A marginal glossary and a glossary at the end of the book give concise definitions of important terms. The guide to BASIC, for those who adopt the version of the text that contains it, provides a comprehensive introduction to the BASIC programming language in a style students will find easy to use.

Currency.   Perhaps more than texbooks in any other field, computer texts must reflect current technologies, trends, and classroom needs. The state-of-the-art content of this book and its support package reflects these considerations. Before the fifth edition was started, reviews were commissioned and meetings were held to identify key areas of change for the text and support package. Also, throughout the writing and production stages, enhancements and new developments were continually being made to ensure that the final product would be as state-of-the-art as possible throughout its life. A glance at the Windows, Tomorrow boxes, Feature boxes, User Solution boxes, and chapter outlines should illustrate why this text has been and will continue to remain a market leader.

Comprehensiveness and Depth.   In planning for the fifth edition of this book, the publisher conducted several extensive research studies to determine the selection of topics, degree of depth, and other features that instructors of introductory information processing courses most want to see in their texts. As the manuscript evolved, instructors at a variety of institutions around the country were asked for their comments. The resulting textbook accommodates a wide range of teaching preferences. It not only covers traditional topics thoroughly but also includes the facts every student should know about today's "hot" topics, such as multimedia, wireless communications, microcomputers, global computing issues, desktop publishing, decision support and expert systems, object-oriented-language products, image processing, virtual reality, user and programmer productivity tools, office automation, computer graphics, and nontraditional approaches to systems development.

Flexible Organization.   A textbook locked into a rigid organization, no matter how thorough, will inevitably find its uses limited. To appeal to a wide audience, this book is designed to be flexible. Its sixteen chapters are grouped into six modules: Introduction (Chapters 1 and 2), Hardware (Chapters 3–5), Support Systems (Chapters 6 and 7), Productivity Software (Chapters 8–10), Information Systems (Chapters 11–14), and Computers in Society (Chapters 15 and 16). Every effort was made to have each chapter as self-contained as possible, making it easy for one to skip chapters or learn them in a sequence other than the one in the book. Each chapter is organized into well-defined sections, so you can assign parts of a chapter if the whole provides more depth than you need.

Readability.   We remember more about a subject if it is presented in a straightforward way and made interesting and exciting. This book is written in a conversational, down-to-earth style—one designed to be accurate without being intimidating. Concepts are explained clearly and simply, without use of overly technical terminology. Where technical points are presented, they are made understandable with realistic examples from everyday life.

Chapter Learning Tools.   Each chapter contains a number of learning tools to help students master the materials.

1. **Outline** An outline of the heading in the chapter shows the major topics to be covered.
2. **Learning Objectives** A list of learning objectives is provided to serve as a guide while students read the chapter.
3. **Overview** Each chapter starts with an overview that puts the subject matter of the chapter in perspective and lets students know what they will be reading about.
4. **Boldfaced Key Terms and Marginal Glossary** Important terms appear in boldface type as they are introduced in the chapter. These terms are also defined in the margin of the page on which they appear and in the end-of-text glossary.
5. **Tomorrow Boxes** These special elements, one in each chapter, provide students with a look at possible future developments in the world of computers and serve as a focus for class discussion.
6. **Feature Boxes** Each chapter contains one or more Feature boxes designed to stimulate interest and discussion about today's uses of information processing technology.
7. **User Solution Boxes** User Solution boxes describe how real-world organizations are using technology to solve business-related problems. Each chapter contains at least one of these features.
8. **Photographs and Diagrams** Instructive, full-color photographs and diagrams appear throughout the book to help illustrate important concepts. The use of color in the diagrams is a functional part of the book.
9. **Summary and Key Terms** This is a concise, section-by-section summary of the main points in the chapter. Every boldfaced key term in the chapter also appears in boldface type in the summary. Students will find the summary a valuable tool for study and review.
10. **Review Exercises** Every chapter ends with a set of fill-in, matching, discussion, and critical thinking questions.

Windows.   The book contains eight photoessays. Each of these "Windows" on the world of computers is organized around a major text theme and vividly illustrates state-of-the-art uses of computer technology.

End-of-Text Glossary.   The glossary at the end of the book defines approximately 500 important computer terms mentioned in the text, including all boldfaced key terms. Each glossary item has a page reference indicating where it is boldfaced or where it first appears in the text.

Appendix A: Number Systems.   At the end of the book is an appendix that covers number systems. Contained in it are explanations of the binary, octal, decimal, and hexadecimal numbering systems, as well as rules for converting numbers from one system into another.

Appendix B: A Brief History of Computers and Information Processing.   This appendix covers the history of computers, from the earliest calculating machines of the 1600s to today. Most of the appendix is devoted to the five generations of modern commercial computing and the developments by which each is best remembered.

A Beginner's Guide to BASIC.   The version of this book that contains a guide to BASIC provides a comprehensive introduction to that language. Much more than a list of rules and procedures, it is an engaging, easy-to-read tutorial that encourages students to begin creating programs immediately. Systematic program development techniques and the honing of debugging skills are also an integral part of the presentation. An added feature to the guide is its appendix describing QBASIC, for those who wish to introduce their students to this version of the BASIC language.

Changes from the Fourth Edition

Although the fourth edition of this text was one of the most successful textbooks published two years ago, the pace of technological advances has necessitated a number of key changes. Among the noteworthy differences between the fourth and fifth editions of *Understanding Computers* are the following:

1.   The text has been shortened from 17 to 16 chapters. To make this change possible, the chapters on programming languages and program development have been collapsed into a single chapter.
2.   A large number of business and problem-solving examples have been added to the text, giving it a much more applications-oriented flavor. Some of these examples are highlighted in User Solution boxes throughout each chapter. Each of these boxes shows how a real-world organization is using state-of-the-art technology to creatively solve business problems.
3.   Each chapter in the last two modules of the text—Module E (Information Systems) and Module F (Computers in Society)—contains a boxed feature and a Critical Thinking Question that address some international aspect of computers and/or communciations. (Each such feature or question is identified with a small globe icon.) This coverage reflects the increasing role of global issues in the technology field, as they relate to business, economic development, and the workplace.
4.   Most of the line illustrations and photos are new, reflecting the most recent advances in technology and applications.
5.   There is increased emphasis on microcomputer-based processing in this edition of the text. This shift reflects the trend in business toward downsizing computing operations from larger machines as well as the social trend of more and more people getting involved with microcomputers—both on the job and at home.
6.   A number of topics have emerged in importance since the text was last published and have received greater attention in this edition. Among these topics are personal digital assistants (PDAs), virtual reality, flash memory,

RAID and parallel processing systems, pen-based computing, object-oriented languages, global and international issues, beta testing of software, multimedia applications, graphical user interfaces (GUIs), wireless networks, global positioning systems, 32-bit operating systems for microcomputers, and optical-disk applications.

7. Coverage of presentation graphics and communicating with information utilities has been increased substantially.

8. The BASIC supplement now includes an appendix on QBASIC.

Student and Teacher Support Materials

Understanding Computers and Information Processing: Today and Tomorrow is available with a complete package of support materials for instructors and students. Included in the package are a student *Study Guide,* an *Instructor's Manual* with transparency masters, *Transparency Acetates,* a *Test Bank* in hardcopy and computerized form, videotapes from Dryden's Information Processing Video Library (including the acclaimed series "The Machine that Changed the World"), and a variety of productivity software manuals to meet lab needs.

Study Guide

The *Study Guide* is designed to help students master the material in the text through self-testing. For each of the sixteen chapters in the text, the *Study Guide* provides

1. An **Outline** and list of **Learning Objectives.**
2. A **Pretest** that lets students test their knowledge of the chapter before they begin to study it intensively.
3. A **Summary** that puts the subject matter of the chapter in perspective.
4. A **Learning Outline** that summarizes the main points in the chapter and that corresponds to the instructor's Teaching Outline.
5. A list of the chapter **Key Terms,** with space for filling in the proper definition.
6. **Study Exercises** that require recall of chapter material.
7. A **Crossword Puzzle,** using many chapter key terms to reinforce vocabulary.
8. Five types of **self-test questions:** matching, true/false, multiple-choice, fill-in, and short answer.
9. An **Answer Key.**

The *Study Guide* also covers the numbering-systems appendix, the computer-history appendix, and the guide to BASIC programming. For each section of the guide to BASIC, the *Study Guide* provides a brief summary, a review of BASIC commands, multiple-choice questions, and new programming problems.

Instructor's Manual

In the *Instructor's Manual* I draw on my own teaching experience to provide instructors with practical suggestions for enhancing classroom presentation. The *Instructor's Manual* contains suggestions for adapting this textbook to various course schedules, including one-quarter, two-quarter, one-semester, two-semester, and night courses. For each of the sixteen chapters of the text the *Instructor's Manual* provides

1. A list of **Learning Objectives.**
2. A **Summary,** oriented to the instructor, with teaching suggestions.
3. A list of the **Key Terms** in the chapter and their definitions.
4. A **Teaching Outline** that gives a detailed breakdown of the chapter, with all major headings and subheadings, as well as points to cover under each. References to the Transparency Acetates and Transparency Masters are keyed in to this outline. In addition, the Learning Outline in the *Study Guide* corresponds to this outline.
5. **Teaching Tips,** with recommended topics for class discussion, important points to cover on the transparency acetates, and mention of additional instructor resources.
6. **Lecture Anecdotes** providing additional stories, news items, and information specific to chapter content to liven up lectures.
7. **Transparency Scripts** for each transparency acetate and transparency master in the instructional package.
8. **Answers to Discussion Questions** that appear at the end of the chapter.
9. **Additional Discussion Questions,** for in-class discussion or testing, and their answers.
10. **Answers to Critical Thinking Questions** that appear at the end of the chapter.
11. **Transparency Masters** covering the chapter outline, chapter objectives, and other key topics for classroom discussion.

The *Instructor's Manual* also covers the numbering-systems appendix, the computer-history appendix, and the guide to BASIC programming. A brief teaching summary and suggested solutions to the Programming Exercises and Programming Problems are included for each section of the guide to BASIC. A BASIC program, a flowchart, and pseudocode are provided for each programming problem.

Transparency Acetates

A set of 116 *Transparency Acetates* for use with an overhead projector is available to help explain key points. Included among the acetates are figures derived from selected text diagrams and new pieces of art. The Teaching Outlines in the *Instructor's Manual* indicate when to show each of the acetates (as well as the Transparency Masters), and the Transparency Scripts in the *Instructor's Manual* list points to make about each.

Test Bank

The *Test Bank* contains over 3,200 test items in various formats, including true/false, multiple-choice, matching, fill-in, and short-answer questions. Answers are provided for all but the short-answer questions. The *Test Bank* is available in both hard-copy and computerized forms. The electronic versions—available for use with IBM and Macintosh microcomputers—allow instructors to preview, edit, or delete questions as well as to add their own questions, print scrambled forms of tests, and print answer keys.

A key indicating the chapter section from which each question was taken is also provided as part of the *Test Bank*. Keys are included with each question, except for the matching questions. Also provided is a ten-question, ready-to-copy-and-distribute multiple-choice quiz for every chapter, which tests students on a representative sample of important topics.

Interactive Multimedia Tutorial Software with User's Manual

The tutorial software, available for IBM PC-compatible computers on both 5¼- and 3½-inch diskettes, helps students review important concepts presented in classroom lectures. Audio clips and animated segments are included to help clarify complex topics and add interest to the learning environment.

Multimedia Presentation Software with User's Manual and Laser Disk

This supplement features a laser disk and software for use in classroom presentations. The laser disk includes video segments, hundreds of full-color electronic transparencies, and bulleted lecture outlines for display in the classroom. The laser disk is driven by LectureActive, a user-friendly software program which allows the instructor to organize lectures in advance, using electronic notecard prompts to assure a smooth presentation. It is available for MS-Windows and Macintosh platforms.

Videotapes

Videotapes from Dryden's Information Processing Video Library will be available to adopters of *Understanding Computers and Information Processing: Today and Tomorrow,* fifth edition. Videos focus on applications and cutting-edge technology involving computers, and illustrate concepts such as hardware, software, and systems; database management; graphics; and telecommunications. Adopters will have immediate access to professional-quality videotapes that explore such landmarks of technology as the electrical digital computer, the laser, and communications satellites; information theory; and the role of computers at Florida's Sea World theme park. Also available are "The New Literacy" series from the Annenberg foundation and the series "The Machine That Changed the World."

Productivity Software Options

Understanding Computers and Information Processing: Today and Tommorrow is available with productivity software modules in a number of shrink-wrap and binding configurations. The modules cover such software packages as MS-DOS, Microsoft Windows, WordPerfect, Lotus 1-2-3, Quattro, dBASE, Paradox, and a number of popular packages running under Windows. One set of modules covers these software packages briefly—Dryden's *Productivity Software Guide* series. Another set—the *Mastering Today's Software* series—covers the packages in greater depth. Individual modules on DOS, WordPerfect, Windows, Excel for Windows, Word for Windows, PageMaker for Windows, and Harvard Graphics for Windows are available in the series from Electronic Learning Facilitators (ELF). Check with your Dryden sales representative about the configuration options currently available.

Acknowledgments

I could never have completed a project of this scope alone. I owe a special word of thanks to the many people who reviewed the text—those whose extensive suggestions on the first four editions helped define the fifth, those whose comments on drafts of the fifth helped mold it into its final form, and those who reviewed the instructional package.

Fifth Edition.   Robert Andree, *Indiana University Northwest;* Thomas Case, *Georgia Southern University;* Mario E. Cecchetti, *Westmoreland County Community College;* Cynthia Corritore, *University of Nebraska at Omaha;* William Dorin, *Indiana University Northwest;* James H. Finger, *University of South Carolina at Columbia;* Timothy Gottleber, *North Lake College;* Robert Kirklin, *Los Angeles Harbor Community College;* Judith A. Knapp, *Indiana University Northwest;* Fran Kubicek, *Kalamazoo Valley Community College;* Robert Landrum, *Jones Junior College;* Donald Nielsen, *Golden West College;* Nicholas John Robak, *Saint Joseph's University;* Benito R. Serenil, *South Seattle Community College;* Fred J. Wilke, *Saint Louis Community College;* Roseanne Witkowski, *Orange County Community College;* Robert D. Yearout, *University of North Carolina at Asheville.*

Fourth Edition.   Virginia Anderson, *University of North Dakota;* Linda Armbruster, *Rancho Santiago College;* Jerry Booher, *Scottsdale Community College;* Curtis Bring, *Moorhead State University;* Cathy Brotherton, *Riverside Community College;* Gena Casas, *Florida Community College, Jacksonville;* Thomas L. Case, *Georgia Southern University;* John E. Castek, *University of Wisconsin—La Crosse;* Marvin Daugherty, *Indiana Vocational Technical College;* Donald L. Davis, *University of Mississippi;* Mark Dishaw, *Boston University;* Eugene Dolan, *University of the District of Columbia;* Hyun B. Eom, *Middle Tennessee State University;* Michael Feiler, *Merritt College;* Gene Garza, *University of Montevallo;* Donald Hall, *Manatee Community College;* Hank Hartman, *Iowa State University;* Richard Hatch, *San Diego State University;* Mary Lou Hawkins, *Del Mar College;* Elizabeth Swoope Johnson, *Louisiana State University;* Shelly Langman, *Bellevue Community College;* Alden Lorents, *Northern Arizona University;* Ed Martin, *Kingsborough Community College;* Mary Meredith, *University of Southwestern Louisiana;* Marilyn Meyer, *Fresno City College;* Marilyn Moore, *Purdue University;* George Novotny, *Ferris State University;* Bob Palank, *Florissant Community College;* James Payne, *Kellogg Community College;* Ken Ruhrup, *St. Petersburg Community College, Clearwater;* Harold Smith, *Brigham Young University;* Sandra Swanson, *Lewis & Clark Community College;* Jane M. Thompson, *Solano Community College.*

Third Edition.   Virginia Anderson, *University of North Dakota;* Gary E. Baker, *Marshalltown Community College;* Luverne Bierle, *Iowa Central Community College;* Curtis Bring, *Moorhead State University;* Carl Clavadetscher, *California State Polytechnic University;* J. Patrick Fenton, *West Valley Community College;* William Fink, *Lewis and Clark Community College;* Kay H. Gray, *Jacksonville State University;* Rosemary C. Gross, *Creighton University;* Stanley P. Honacki, *Moraine Valley Community College;* L. Wayne Horn, *Pensacola Junior College;* Joan Krone, *Ohio State University;* Liang Chee Wee, *University of Arizona;* Richard W. Manthei, *Joliet Junior College;* Donavan J. Nielsen, *Golden West College;* Kenneth R. Ruhrup, *St. Petersburg Junior College;* Larry Schwartzman, *Trident Technical College;* Sue Traynor, *Clarion University of Pennsylvania;* James R. Walters, *Pikes Peak Community College;* James D. Woolever, *Cerritos College.*

Second Edition.   Richard Batt, *Saint Louis Community College at Meremec;* James Buxton, *Tidewater Community College, Virginia;* Vernon Clodfelter, *Rowan Technical College, North Carolina;* Robert H. Dependahl, Jr., *Santa Barbara College, California;* Eugene T. Dolan, *University of the District of Columbia;* J. Patrick Fenton, *West Valley Community College, California;* William C. Fink, *Lewis and Clark Community College, Illinois;* George P. Grill, *University of North Carolina, Greensboro;* David W. Green, *Nashville State Technical Institute, Tennessee;* Dennis Guster, *Saint Louis Community College at Meremec;* L. D. Harber, *Volunteer State Community College, Tennessee;* Sharon A. Hill, *Prince George's Community College, Maryland;* J. William Howorth, *Seneca College, Ontario, Canada;* Richard Kerns, *East Carolina University, North Carolina;* Gordon C. Kimbell, *Everett Community College, Washington;* James G. Kriz, *Cuyahoga Community College, Ohio;* Alden Lorents, *Northern Arizona University;* James McMahon, *Community College of Rhode Island;* Don B. Medley, *California State Polytechnic University;* Marilyn D. Moore, *Indiana University Northwest;* Kenneth R. Ruhrup, *Saint Petersburg Junior College, Florida;* Sandra Swanson, *Lewis and Clark Community College, Illinois;* Joyce V. Walton, *Seneca College, Ontario, Canada.*

First Edition.   James Ambroise, Jr., *Southern University, Louisiana;* Richard Batt, *St. Louis Community College;* James Bradley, *University of Calgary;* Laura Cooper, *College of the Mainland, Texas;* John DiElsi, *Marcy College, New York;* William Hightower, *Elon College, North Carolina;* Peter L. Irwin, *Richland College, Texas;* Richard Kerns, *East Carolina University, North Carolina;* Glenn Kersnick, *Sinclair Community College, Ohio;* Wayne Madison, *Clemson University, South Carolina;* Gary Marks, *Austin Community College, Texas;* Robert Ralph, *Fayetteville Technical Institute, North Carolina;* Alfred C. St. Onge, *Springfield Technical Community College, Massachusetts;* John J. Shuler, *San Antonio College, Texas;* Michael L. Stratford, *Charles County Community College, Maryland;* Joseph Waters, *Santa Rosa Junior College, California;* Charles M. Williams, *Georgia State University;* A. James Wynne, *Virginia Commonwealth University.*

I am indebted to scores of people at dozens of organizations for the photographs they provided for this text. I would especially like to thank Jessie O. Kempter at IBM, Betty Sinkoff at Prodigy, Candice Clemens at Lotus Development, Kayla Wilhelm at Intergraph, Gina Rubbatino at Pixar, Peter Heyne of Compaq, Bruce Fox of Evans and Sutherland, Carol Parcels of Hewlett-Packard, and computer artists Clifford Pickover, Karl Sims, David Rickerd, and James Dowlen for the particularly outstanding contributions they made. Also, I extend heart-felt thanks to Jeff Glickman and Lew Witz at The College of Santa Fe (CSF) for the help they provided in preparing the computer programs that are contained in this text. Additionally, I deeply appreciate the continuing help and support on this textbook from my departmental colleagues and good friends at CSF, Dan Breheny and Pat Donahoe.

At The Dryden Press, a special word of thanks to my publisher, Liz Widdi-combe, to my acquisitions editor, Richard Bonacci, to Michele Tomiak, who served as both developmental and project editor, and to Elizabeth Hayes, assistant editor, for the suggestions and accommodations they made to produce a better manuscript. Also I would like to thank Nick Welch, Jeanette Barber, Mandy Manzano, Sandra Lord, Sheryl Nelson, Trisha Dianne, Kevin Cottingim, Scott Timian, and the many others who worked hard on behalf of this book.

Charles S. Parker

B R I E F
C O N T E N T S

W I N D O W S

C O N T E N T S

MODULE D

Productivity Software — 255

Understanding Computers & Information Processing

Today and Tomorrow

FIFTH EDITION

M O D U L E

A

INTRODUCTION

We are living in an age of computers. Businesses, government agencies, and other organizations use computers and related technologies to handle tedious paperwork, provide better service to customers, and assist managers in making better decisions. As the benefits to using computers continue to mount, and as the costs of computing resources continue to decrease relative to the price of everything else, computer technology will become even more widespread in our society. It is therefore essential to know something about it.

The chapters in this module introduce you to computers and some of their uses. Chapters 1 and 2 orient you to what computer systems are, how they work, and how they're used. These chapters also present some key terminology that you will see repeatedly throughout the text.

INTRODUCTION TO THE WORLD OF COMPUTERS

1

Why are managers increasingly hitting the road with their computers? As you'll learn in this chapter, computers that can be toted about can be used to make presentations to clients, enter and check the status of orders, prepare field reports . . . and so much more.

LEARNING OBJECTIVES

After completing this chapter, you will be able to:

1. Understand why it's especially important to learn about computers today.

2. Identify some of the major components in a computing environment and their relationships to one another.

3. Describe several applications in business and other areas of society in which computers play an important role.

4. Define several terms that are useful to know when reading about or discussing computers.

5. Appreciate the social impact of computers.

Overview

Unless you plan to spend your life living off the land in the upper reaches of the Yukon, computers and other forms of high technology will probably have an important impact on your life.

Computer systems keep track of our bank accounts and credit card purchases. They, along with sophisticated communications systems, are the cornerstones of the airlines' massive reservations systems. Computers perform the millions upon millions of computations needed to send astronauts into outer space and bring them back safely. Computers also direct production in our factories and provide executives with the up-to-date information they need to make decisions. Computers are embedded in watches, microwave ovens, television sets, phones, fax machines, automobiles, and probably even the stationary workout bike at your local gym. The applications are almost endless. Fifty short years ago, computers were part of an obscure technology of interest to only a handful of scientists. Today they are part of almost everyone's daily life.

Computers are very much like cars in that you don't need to know everything about them to use them effectively. You can learn to drive a car without knowing about internal combustion engines, and you can learn to use a computer without knowing about technical details such as logic circuits. Still, with both cars and computers, a little knowledge can give you a big advantage. Knowing something about cars can help you make wise purchases and save money on repairs. Likewise, knowing something about computers can help you use them for maximum benefit.

This book is about computers—what they are, how they work, and what they do. It is intended to give you the knowledge you need to use them effectively today and, through the Tomorrow boxes, give you a look into the future. Other boxed features throughout the text provide additional insights into the dynamic world of computers.

This book is not designed to make you a computer expert. It's a beginner's guide. If you're considering a career as a computer professional in business, this book will give you a comprehensive introduction to the field. If you're not, it will give you the basic knowledge you need to understand and use computers in school and on the job.

In this chapter, we'll first take a look at how computers are reshaping the workplace in the 1990s. From there, we turn to what computers are and how they work. Then we'll look at the various sizes in which computers come. Finally, we'll examine several examples of computer systems in action. Window 1, which follows Chapter 1, gives you a glimpse of the myriad applications of computers in today's world.

Computers in the 1990s Workplace

Prior to 1980, it was not critical for an ordinary person to know how to use a computer in his or her job. Computers were expensive, and few people had access to them. Furthermore, the use of computers generally required a lot of technical knowledge. Worse yet, most business computers were equipped to do little but carry out high-volume paperwork processing, such as issuing bills and keeping track of customer-account and inventory balances. Not only were most

FIGURE 1-1

Computers shaping the 1990s workplace. (a) Personal desktop workstations are rapidly becoming a necessity for office work. (b) Portable computers enable data to be electronically gathered out in the field. (c) People are increasingly buying computers for personal use, making it easier than ever before to run home-based businesses.

(a)

(b)

(c)

ordinary working people afraid of computers, but also there were few good reasons for getting familiar with them.

Then, suddenly, things began to change. Microcomputers—small, inexpensive computers that you will read about later in this chapter—were created. Consequently, today there are thousands of times more computers and hundreds of times more people involved with computers than just a couple of decades or so ago. This has resulted in a flood of high-quality, high-technology products in the marketplace. It has also changed the way many companies do business and the type of skills they seek in the people they hire.

Today, we are living in an era when most skill-based jobs heavily depend

U s e r   S o l u t i o n   1 – 1

Selling Smart with Laptops

Champion Products sportswear is a familiar item in the locker rooms of schools and professional sports teams. These days, when Champion salespeople go calling on customers—such as retail stores, college bookstores, and athletic departments—they go equipped with a laptop computer. In pre-laptop times, it used to take as long as two weeks to get a handwritten order from the field entered into the sales system. Now the salesperson can key in the order on the spot, as the customer is giving it, and automatically transmit it to headquarters for confirmation and immediate processing. This way, the customer has a guaranteed delivery date before the salesperson ever leaves the premises. The laptop can also be used to check on the status of any previously placed orders and the amount of stock on hand. Champion says that not only have the laptops provided better service, but they have also reduced errors, labor costs, and returned goods.

on the collection, use, creation, and dissemination of information. Whether you become a teacher, lawyer, doctor, professional athlete, executive, or blue-collar worker, your performance will largely depend on information and your use of it. Because computer systems can process facts at dizzying speeds, their availability may be equivalent to having an army of clerks at your disposal.

Following are several examples of how computers are being used in the workplace to enhance personal productivity (see also Figure 1-1):

■ Virtually everyone who needs to type in a job uses a computer system or electronic typewriter to do word processing. *Word processing*—which enables keystrokes to be stored and edited electronically—produces documents such as letters and books faster and better than an ordinary typewriter.

■ Managers and professionals at all levels of the business world use computing products called electronic *spreadsheets*—which in essence are powerful calculators—to perform analytical tasks in minutes that once took hours or days to do by hand. Not only can these people assemble information faster than they did before, they also can do tasks that once were impossible to perform manually. By being able to study "all the angles" of strategies or propositions, these individuals often find that they make better decisions.

■ Executives are relying increasingly on *database management systems*—tools that provide instant access to local or remote banks of information—to learn about business conditions. Many of these systems are so easy to use that even the most computer-shy executives are being won over to their use, knowing that failure to keep up will give competitors an edge. Worker groups such as lawyers, doctors, and stockbrokers, who need to search through mounds of data to draw conclusions, have also found that database technology has improved their performance.

■ Many companies have given thousands of *laptop computers*—computers the size of a notebook—to their field sales forces. These devices often give salespeople an advantage when dealing with clients, because the salesperson can analyze a client proposal on the spot, while he or she is in a receptive mood (see User Solution 1-1). The laptop can also be used to access remote data—possibly supplying information that will help close the sale. And, at the end of a day, it can be used to quickly prepare sales reports to send to headquarters.

■ At all levels of business, computers are helping workers put *presentation materials* together by creating stunning charts and slides to help sway a live audience and by enhancing the look of handout materials. Researchers have found that people who use computers in this manner often are considered by others to be more "professional."

■ In fields such as design and publishing, computers have completely revolutionized the way people work. Products such as cars, packages, buildings, shoes, and fabrics are often designed today with *computer-aided design (CAD)* systems. The rise of powerful *desktop publishing systems*—computer systems that fit on a desktop and enable ordinary people to produce work that looks as if it came from a professional printing press—has altered the structure of the entire publishing industry.

■ Many businesses are now using some form of modern *communications system* to get faster and better information. For instance, facsimile (fax) machines are today widely used to transmit documents between sites almost instantaneously. This allows people to complete within a few hours a task that could stretch out over days or even weeks with just a physical delivery system at hand. Also, electronic mailbox and messaging systems enable people to work in groups more easily, even though they may be at different locations.

These applications only scratch the surface in demonstrating how computers are affecting the workplace in the 1990s. As you read further in this text, you will learn about dozens of others.

What's a Computer and What Does It Do?

Four words sum up the operation of a computer system: **input, processing, output,** and **storage.** To see what these words mean, let's look at something you probably have in your own home—a stereo system.

A simple stereo system often consists of a compact disk (CD) player and/or turntable, an amplifier, and a pair of speakers. To use the system, you place a CD or record on the CD player or turntable and turn the system on. The CD player or turntable converts the patterns in the tracks or grooves into sounds and transmits them to the amplifier as electronic signals. The amplifier takes the signals, strengthens them, and transmits them to the speakers. The result is music. In computer terms, the CD player or turntable sends signals as *input* to the amplifier. The amplifier *processes* the signals and sends them to the speakers, which produce a musical *output*. The CD player and turntable are **input devices,** the amplifier is a *processing unit,* and the speakers are **output devices.** The amplifier is the heart of the system, whereas the CD player, turntable, and speakers are examples of **peripheral equipment.**

Input.
What is supplied to a computer process.

Processing.
The conversion of input to output.

Output.
The results of a computer process.

Storage.
An area that holds materials going to or coming from the computer.

Input device.
A machine used to supply materials going to the computer.

Output device.
A machine used to accept materials coming from the computer.

Peripheral equipment.
The machines that work with the computer.

Most stereo systems have a variety of other peripheral equipment. An antenna, for example, is another kind of input device. Headphones are another type of output device. A tape recorder is both an input and output device—you can use it to send signals to the amplifier or to receive signals from it. The tapes, compact disks, and records in your collection are, in computer terms, **input/output (I/O) media**. They *store* music in a **machine-readable** form—a form that the associated input device (tape recorder, CD player, or record turntable) can recognize (that is, "read") and convert into signals for the amplifier to process.

Computer Systems

All the elements in a stereo system have their counterparts in a computer system. A **computer system** consists of the computer itself, all the peripheral equipment, and the machine-readable instructions and facts it processes, as well as operating manuals, procedures, and the people who use the system. In other words, all the components that contribute to making the computer a useful tool can be said to be parts of a computer system.

At the heart of any computer system is the **computer** itself, or **central processing unit (CPU).** The CPU is the equivalent of the stereo amplifier. Like its counterpart, the CPU can't do anything useful without peripheral equipment for input and output and I/O media for storage. Computer input and output devices include, to name just a few, keyboards, display devices, disk units, tape units, and printers. I/O media include disks, tapes, and paper. We will discuss these and many other items in Chapters 2, 4, and 5.

A computer system, of course, is not a stereo system, and a computer is much more versatile than a stereo amplifier. For example, a computer system can perform an enormous variety of processing tasks and a stereo system only a few. Also, a computer can support a much greater variety of input and output devices than can a stereo amplifier.

What gives a computer its flexibility? The answer, in a word, is *memory*. A computer has access to a memory, or "workspace," that allows it to retain whatever inputs it receives and the results it produces from these inputs. An ordinary home stereo system has no such memory; what's playing on the compact disk player, tape recorder, or turntable passes directly through the amplifier to the speakers. Because computers can hold materials in such a workspace, they can be directed by *programs* to rearrange or recombine those materials in an amazing variety of ways before sending them along as output.

Data and Programs

The material that a computer receives as input is of two kinds: data and programs. **Data** are essentially raw, unorganized facts. **Programs** are instructions that tell the computer how to process those facts to produce the results that you, the computer system user, want. Let's discuss these important terms in a little more detail.

Data Almost any kind of fact can become computer data—facts about a company's employees, facts about airline flight schedules, or facts about baseball

---

Input/output (I/O) media. Objects used to store computer-processed materials.

Machine-readable. Any form in which data are represented so that they can be read by a machine.

Computer system. A collection of elements that includes the computer as well as all the components that contribute to making it a useful tool.

Computer. The piece of hardware, also known as the **central processing unit (CPU),** that interprets and executes program instructions and communicates with support devices.

Data. A collection of raw, unorganized facts.

Program. A set of instructions that causes the computer system to perform specific actions.

batting averages. Even pictures and sounds can become data. When we input data into a computer system, we usually aren't interested in getting them back just as we entered them. We want the system to process the data and give us new, useful *information.* **Information,** in the language of computers, refers to data that have been processed into a *meaningful* form.

We might want to know, for example, how many employees earn over $15,000, how many seats are available on Flight 495 from Los Angeles to San Francisco, or what Rickey Henderson's batting average was during last year's regular baseball season. The difference between data and information lies in the word "meaningful." Rickey Henderson's batting average may be meaningful to you because it will enable you to make a prediction about an upcoming game or merely because it will make watching the game more interesting. To a friend who doesn't follow baseball, however, Rickey Henderson's batting average may be meaningless—just ordinary data, not information. Thus, information is a *relative* term; it is something that has meaning for a specific person in a specific situation. Like beauty, the difference between data and information is strictly in the eye of the beholder.

Of course, you don't necessarily need a computer system to get information from a set of facts. For example, anyone can go through an employee file and make a list of people earning a certain salary. But to do so would take a lot of time, especially for a company with thousands of employees. In contrast, with their electronically fast speeds, computers can do such jobs almost instantly. Computer processing of data into information is called by a variety of terms, one of which is **information processing.**

Information processing has become an especially important activity in recent years because most jobs depend heavily on the wise use of information. Because better information often means better decisions, many companies today regard information as one of their most important assets.

Feature 1-1 describes the use of multimedia kiosks in providing information to an increasingly computer-literate and information-hungry public.

Programs   Like many other machines, the amplifier in your home stereo system is a *special-purpose* device. It is designed to support only a few specific tasks—play a CD, make a recording on tape, play music into speakers or headphones, and so forth. These functions are built into its circuitry. To put it another way, it is "hardwired" to perform a very limited number of specific tasks.

Most computers, in contrast, are *general-purpose* devices. They are able to perform an enormous variety of tasks—for instance, preparing letters to clients, analyzing sales figures, and creating slide presentations, to name just a few. Because most computers must be flexible, they can't be hardwired to do all the tasks they may be required to do. Instead, they rely on program instructions for guidance. As each program is read into the computer system, it is provided data by the user to process. The program then directs the circuits in the computer to open and close in the manner needed to do whatever task needs to be done with these data.

Programs cannot yet be written in ordinary English. They must be written in a **programming language**—a code the computer system can read and translate into the electronic pulses that make it work. Programming languages

Information.
Data that have been processed into a meaningful form.

Information processing.
Computer operations that transform data into meaningful information.

Programming language.
A set of rules used to write computer programs.

F e a t u r e   1 – 1

Self-Service Computing

Multimedia kiosks are making their move

It's a trend that actually began over 25 years ago, when the first automatic teller machines (ATMs) from the banking industry hit the scene.

Now that people are comfortable with ATMs, and technology has advanced by leaps and bounds in a number of related areas, a new breed of product has evolved—the multimedia kiosk. A *kiosk* is a self-service station, equipped with its own computer and storage bank, that users can go to for specific information or to make specific transactions. *Multimedia* means that the kiosk can handle a variety of data types—text, still pictures, animated images, and/or sound. Often, kiosks are housed in plastic consoles or glass-and-wood enclosures and equipped with easy-to-work touch-screen menus.

Increasingly, kiosks are popping up in airports, stores and supermarkets, auto showrooms, schools, museums and exhibitions, government

Kiosk. Information dissemination 1990s style.

come in many varieties—BASIC, Pascal, and C are three with which you may be familiar. In the early days of computers, programming languages consisted of strings of numbers that only experts could comprehend. Over the years, they have become easier for ordinary mortals to understand and use. We will discuss programs and programming languages in detail in Module E.

A Look at Computer Storage

So far we've seen that if you want to get something done on a computer system, you must supply it with both facts (data) and instructions (a program) specifying how to process those facts. For example, if you want the system to write payroll checks, you must supply such data as employees' names, social security numbers, and salaries. The program instructions must "tell" the system how to compute taxes, how to take deductions, where and how to print the checks, and so forth. Also, the computer relies on a memory (storage) to remember all these details as it is doing the work.

Actually, computer systems contain two types of storage. A **primary (internal) storage**—often called **memory**—holds the data and programs that the computer is currently processing. When data are "captured" in the computer's

Primary (internal) storage.
Also known as **memory,** this section of the computer system temporarily holds data and program instructions awaiting processing, intermediate results, and processed output.

offices, malls, restaurants, and even offices. In a word, everywhere.

In California, state and local governments are using kiosks for a variety of purposes. In San Diego and Sacramento, for instance, kiosks help local residents find employment and get health-care information. In South Central Los Angeles, where rioting occurred in 1992, a kiosk was installed to help residents hook up with community-assistance programs. Kiosks are also widely used in California and other states to assist with quizzing in the driver-licensing process.

A large Connecticut company decided to go the kiosk route when it searched for a convenient way to provide its employees with up-to-date information about health benefits. A multimedia kiosk was chosen over other computerbased alternatives because many people in the company were intimidated by conventional computer systems and did not know how to use them. Moreover, not everyone had access to a networked, desktop computer readily available.

Hotels are also beginning to seriously consider kiosks in a big way. Professionals in the hotel industry have avoided such technologies in the past because they felt machines violated the warm, friendly feeling that they wanted to project. However, a number of hotels are now pilot-testing self-service checkout stations to cut down lines at the front desk. Hotel kiosks are likely to prove most useful to the frequent business traveler who is in a rush.

One firm has even developed a kiosk that sells sheet music in music stores. A customer uses a touch screen to select from hundreds of titles. After a selection is made, the kiosk plays a few bars while the score is displayed on a screen. Once the score is purchased, the kiosk can also print the score in any key.

Many computer-industry experts feel that the multimedia kiosk business is poised to take off. Some even go so far as to say that these high-tech self-service stations will be more numerous than gasoline pumps within a few years. Businesses like kiosks because they cut down on labor costs and can be used as powerful selling tools, by providing information to which a clerk does not have access. They can even help businesses get a leg up on low-tech competitors. Customers like kiosks because they often provide better service than humans. Not only that, but many people are discovering that kiosks can be fun to use.

memory or "workspace," they can be rearranged or recombined by the instructions in the program. Memory is contained in the unit that houses the computer.

Data and programs the computer doesn't need for the job at hand are stored in **secondary (external) storage.** In large computer systems, secondary storage is usually located in a device separate from the computer itself. In smaller computer systems, secondary storage is usually implemented by a device that is fitted into the unit containing the computer. Whatever the case, this piece of equipment is called a *secondary storage device.* It enables us to conveniently save large quantities of data and programs in machine-readable form so that we need not rekey them into the system every time we use them. Some secondary storage devices are capable of storing thousands of programs and billions of pieces of data.

When the CPU needs a certain program or set of data, it requests it from the secondary storage device—much as you might request a particular song from a jukebox—and reads them into its memory for processing. Unlike the jukebox turntable, however, which puts the original record in play, the CPU puts only a copy of the original program or data into memory for use. It is often useful to think of secondary storage as a large "library" of programs and data resources on full-time call to the CPU.

Secondary storage. Storage on media such as disk and tape that supplements memory. Also called **external storage.**

FIGURE 1 – 2

Input, processing, output, and storage. Often, the computer fetches most of the programs and data it needs from secondary storage and from instructions given to it by a user at an input device. While it is working on specific programs and data, the computer uses primary storage as a "scratchpad" area. When finished, results are transferred from primary storage to an output device.

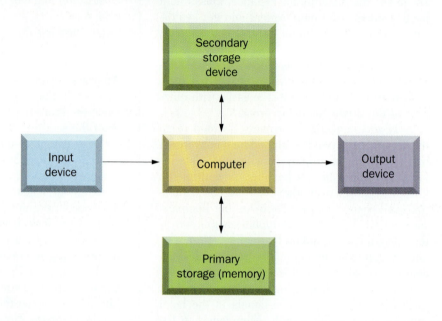

Figure 1-2 illustrates the relationships among input, processing, output, memory, and secondary storage.

Hardware and Software

Hardware.
Physical equipment in a computing environment, such as the computer and its peripheral devices.

Software.
Computer programs.

In the world of computers, it is common to distinguish between hardware and software. The word **hardware** refers to the actual machinery that makes up a computer system—for example, the CPU, I/O devices, and storage devices. The word **software** refers to computer programs.

Virtually all of the software you buy today in a computer store or through the mail is in "package" form (see Figure 1-3). Typically, such a *software package* consists of program disks, operating instructions, training tutorials, a warranty, and reference manuals inside of a shrink-wrapped box. All of the program disks have been written in some programming language, such as C or assembly language.

Users and the Experts

In the early days of computing, there was a clear distinction between the people who made computers work and those who used the results computers produced. This distinction still exists, but as computers become more available and easier to use, it is breaking down.

End users, or *users,* are the people who need the output computer systems produce. They include the accountant who needs a report on a client's taxes, the secretary who is word processing a letter, the engineer who needs to know whether a bridge will be structurally sound, the shop-floor supervisor who needs to know whether the day's quotas were met, and the company president who needs a report on the firm's profitability over the last ten years.

Programmers, on the other hand, are the people who write the programs that produce such outputs. Programming is their primary job responsibility. Thus, although end users may do modest amounts of programming with the packaged software on their desktop computer systems, the distinction between an ordinary end user and a professional programmer is based on what the person has actually been hired to do.

Organizations employ many other types of computer professionals. For instance, *systems analysts* are hired to build large computer systems within a company. *Computer operations personnel,* in contrast, are responsible for the day-to-day operation of large computer systems.

End user.
A person who needs the results computers produce in order to perform his or her job.

Programmer.
A person whose job is to write, maintain, and test computer programs.

FIGURE 1 – 3

Software package. A software package normally consists of program disks, operating instructions, training tutorials, a warranty, and reference manuals inside of a shrink-wrapped box.

FIGURE 1 – 4

Four microcomputer systems. (a) Apple Macintosh Quadra 150 desktop computer. (b) IBM PS/2 Model P75 portable computer. (c) Macintosh Powerbook laptop computer. (d) Sharp Travel Organizer hand-held computer.

(a)

(b)

(c)

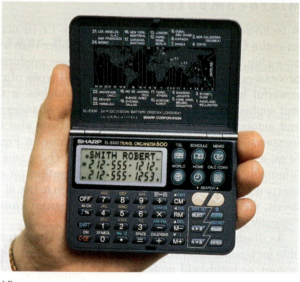

(d)

and compact (able to fit into a carrying case). Technically speaking, the most lightweight portable computers—which can be used on a person's lap, if desired—are called *laptop computers* or *notebook computers* (see Figure 1-4c). Although many portables are just as powerful as their larger desktop cousins, they tend to be more expensive, have small and hard-to-read screens, and have a dense arrangement of keys. These disadvantages notwithstanding, portability is "in" these days, and laptop computers currently are one of the fastest-growing segments of the microcomputer industry.

Hand-held Units *Hand-held computers*—or *palmtop computers*—look and behave a lot like standard pocket calculators. You can generally hold the entire computer system in your hand while operating it. Today, most hand-held computers are relegated to specialized tasks—keeping track of golf or bowling scores, translating words into foreign languages, checking the spelling of words, providing synonyms and antonyms for words, and organizing appointments (see Figure 1-4d). In the next several years, the market for hand-held computers is expected to grow explosively. Hand-held devices called *personal digital assistants,* or *PDAs,* which can be used to carry out such tasks as computing, messaging, form-filling, and faxing are becoming increasingly available (see Tomorrow box).

Micros are widely used in both small and large businesses. Small businesses use them to keep track of merchandise, prepare correspondence, bill customers, and do routine accounting. Large businesses use them as productivity tools for secretaries and as analysis tools for decision makers, to name just two important applications. Also, laptops are popular with salespeople making presentations at client sites and with managers who need a computer as they travel about. Microcomputers are increasingly being networked into large communications systems where they are used as data-entry devices or as general-purpose workstations.

Minicomputers

Minicomputers, or *minis,* generally are regarded as medium-sized computers (see Figure 1-5). Most of them fall between microcomputers and mainframes in their processing power. The very smallest minicomputers, however, are virtually

Minicomputer.
An intermediate-sized and medium-priced type of computer.

FIGURE 1 – 5

Minicomputers. Minicomputers are particularly useful where several people need to share a common system, such as in small companies or in departments of larger companies.

The PDAs Are Coming!
The PDAs Are Coming!

Is a New Major Industry on Its Way?

Some very credible people are saying it could produce the biggest revolution in technology since the personal computer. In fact, Apple Computer president, John Scully, is so bullish about it that he's formed a new spinoff company to develop products that hardly anybody's ever used in practice. Scully predicts a trillion-dollar industry by the end of the decade.

What we're talking about here is the *personal digital assistant,* or *PDA.*

PDAs are hand-held computers that are specially designed for people who don't like to interact with computers all that much. Newton, Apple's initial product, is a 6-by-8-inch device targeted to business users. It does calculations, keeps track of phone numbers, and manages personal schedules and to-do lists. Not only that, but it is also a communications device that can send and receive faxes and tap into data in larger computers at remote locations.

One of Newton's most compelling advantages is its ease of use. There are no keyboards to confuse you or complicated syntax to remember. You just write your commands onto the PDA or choose from menus with a penlike stylus. So if you want to send a message to Bob, you just write it out, along with the instruction "Fax to Bob." The PDA will then look up Bob's fax number and send the message automatically.

One of the most successful PDAs to date has been Sharp's Wizzard. At Brooklyn Union Gas Company, the Wizzard assists with customer service operations by guiding service representatives through the maze of regulatory data they need to have on hand when helping customers set up accounts. PDAs were chosen because they were the least costly way to conveniently provide every service representative with the tools needed to do his or her job. At Merck & Company, the Wizzard is used as a personal organizer for office managers and to help sales managers easily gain access the information needed to run territories. Merck reports that the approachable, toylike appearance of the PDA generates interest and use among people who find conventional computers frightening.

At Northern Telecom, the PDA of choice has been Sony's Data Discman. When a repair technician makes a call, he or she brings along a hand-held electronic service manual the size of a paperback book—one that includes the equivalent of 18,000 printed pages of data. By typing keywords on a compressed keypad, the technician can quickly access the required repair procedure on a small display. A PDA of this sort that can also communicate with the home office could conceivably access scores of electronic manuals, all with the latest updates, within seconds.

indistinguishable from the largest microcomputers, and the largest (sometimes called *superminis*) closely resemble small mainframes. Minicomputers usually are far more expensive than microcomputers and are unaffordable for most individuals.

Any of several factors might lead an organization to choose a minicomputer over a micro or mainframe. A small or medium-sized company may simply find microcomputer systems too slow to handle its current volume of processing. Or a company may need a computer system that can do several jobs at once and interact with multiple users at the same time. Many microcomputer systems lack sufficient power for handling such complex applications. Mainframes, of course, can handle these applications, but they are much larger and more expensive than minis.

Wallet power. PDAs and the mobile user (left, Sharp Wizzard; right, SkyTel Message Card).

At Xerox's Palo Alto Research Center (PARC), a PDA developed in the form of an electronic badge can be used for several purposes. For instance, if Judy Smith is away from her office and someone is trying to call her, the phone nearest to Judy will ring with a personalized jingle. Also, the badge can be used to automatically record Judy's daily whereabouts.

SkyTel's credit-card-sized Message Card is ideal if you travel a lot. When callers access a toll-free station with your personal identification number, they can leave their phone number or a complete voice message. Within seconds, the number to call is routed to your card.

The PDA is predicted to go well beyond business, into consumer electronics, as well. PDAs will come in the form of electronic books and entertainment gadgets, and devices that help us better manage the devices we now have. People may even have electronic art in their homes—flat-screen wall hangings that can be programmed to display almost anything you want, if, say, you press the right buttons.

The big unknown with PDAs at this point is whether consumers and businesses will buy them in droves. So far, acceptance has been slow, leaving some industry skeptics to caution that PDA may come to stand for "probably disappointed again." But people are typically cautious about accepting technology and changing the way they do things. Eventually, if a product is useful and exciting enough, and if the price is right, it's sure to be a winner.

Mainframes

The **mainframe** (see Figure 1-6) is the standard for almost all large organizations. It often operates 24 hours a day, serving hundreds of users on display devices during regular business hours and processing large jobs such as payroll and billing late at night. Many large organizations need several mainframes to complete their computing work loads. Typically these organizations own or lease a variety of computer types—say, mainframes, minis, and micros—to meet all their processing needs.

Most mainframes are employed to handle high-volume processing of business transactions and routine paperwork. For most businesses, this includes tasks such as keeping track of customer purchases and payments, sending out bills

Mainframe.
A large, transaction-processing-oriented computer.

FIGURE 1 - 6

IBM ES/9000 mainframe. IBM's ES/9000 series sets the standard for today's mainframes. IBM accounts for close to 75 percent of all mainframes sold.

and reminder notices, paying employees, and maintaining detailed tax records. These operations were some of the earliest applications of computers in business and have been the responsibility of mainframes from day one.

Supercomputers

Some organizations, such as large scientific and research laboratories, have extraordinary information processing needs. Applications such as sending astronauts into outer space and weather forecasting, for example, require extreme degrees of accuracy and a wealth of computations. High-quality animation, which produces the special effects you see in computer-generated movies and commercials, also demands enormous amounts of high-speed computation. To meet such needs, a few vendors offer very large, sophisticated machines called **supercomputers** (see Figure 1-7). These machines are very expensive, often costing several millions of dollars.

Supercomputer.
The fastest and most expensive type of computer.

Using Computers: Some Examples

Now that we've briefly seen how a computer system works, let's "walk through" a few applications within a typical organization to put many of the concepts you've just read about into sharper focus.

Large System   Paradise Beach Resort is a large hotel on the Florida coast. It uses a *mainframe* computer system to keep track of such matters as guest reservations, bills, and employees. Without the mainframe, the hotel would never be able to accommodate the number of guests it handles with its current staff, nor would it be able to provide the high level of service its guests expect.

In the precomputer days, operations were far less sophisticated. For instance, it was common for bills to be incorrect, misplaced, or mismanaged. Frequently, if a reservation was improperly recorded, the guest was detained in the lobby. In fact, often two desk clerks would be in the process of booking different guests for the same room—an embarrassing mishap for the hotel and one that sometimes resulted in lost business.

Today, with a computer keeping track of guests, these types of problems occur very infrequently. The mainframe also handles various other types of accounting tasks—paying employees and preparing comprehensive reports for management and taxing agencies, for instance. It does these tasks much more quickly and accurately—that is, more efficiently—than was possible in the precomputer days. Some of the information that management now routinely receives was impossible to obtain before the computer arrived. Consequently, managers now can be more effective at doing their jobs.

FIGURE 1-7

Cray supercomputer. Supercomputers are faster than conventional computers because they pack circuits much more tightly. Cray produces more than half of the supercomputers sold worldwide.

FIGURE 1 – 10

A screen menu. Screen menus beckon a user to choose a specific course of action. Using them effectively requires neither typing skills nor an extensive knowledge of computers.

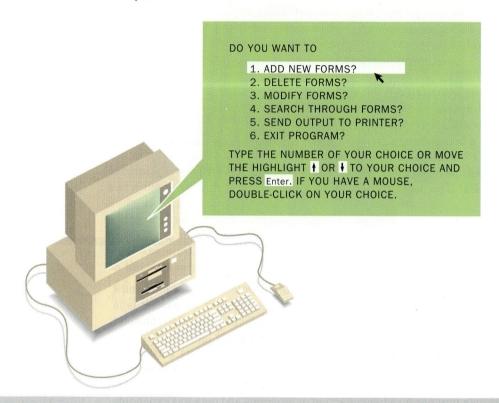

DO YOU WANT TO

1. ADD NEW FORMS?
2. DELETE FORMS?
3. MODIFY FORMS?
4. SEARCH THROUGH FORMS?
5. SEND OUTPUT TO PRINTER?
6. EXIT PROGRAM?

TYPE THE NUMBER OF YOUR CHOICE OR MOVE THE HIGHLIGHT ↑ OR ↓ TO YOUR CHOICE AND PRESS Enter. IF YOU HAVE A MOUSE, DOUBLE-CLICK ON YOUR CHOICE.

three separate types, or fields, of data—the name of the dish, its ingredients, and a few remarks.

If Lydia is helping a client plan a Saturday night banquet over the phone, she can summon the database program to search for all forms on her entrees disk file in which "ingredients" contains "beef" and "remarks" contains "dinner." Then she can have the names of these dishes directed to her display screen.

Of course, Lydia can rely on recall, but having the computer system make the search for her often turns up good alternatives that didn't cross her mind. Also, she can save a lot of phone time by having her computer system do the searching while she attends to other matters with the client. Lydia's database manager lets her add new forms to the file when she wants them, delete forms, and modify forms. She does this with a *screen menu* of processing alternatives (not to be confused with a food menu) that the database manager sends to her display screen, asking her what she wants to do (see Figure 1-10).

To make a screen menu selection, Lydia can use her keyboard or *mouse,* according to the instructions on the screen. Typically, she uses her mouse for this type of selection operation. As she moves the mouse along her desktop, the onscreen arrow—called a *pointer*—moves accordingly. When she activates a button on the mouse, the computer system will execute, or select, that choice.

Lydia also has a *communications interface,* which enables her computer to interact with other computers located miles away. For instance, Lydia uses her computer to automatically place food and beverage orders with a distributor located across town. The communications interface is made up of hardware and software elements that enable Lydia's computer to call up the distributor's computer and transfer a food and beverage order, electronically, over regular telephone lines. The distributor's computer will even relay back a confirmation of the order.

One reason for Lydia's success at her job is her skill at quickly pulling together key information when dealing with clients, managers, and suppliers. The database management system and word processor allow Lydia to give clients first-class service. Hotel management appreciates the value of this; a $50,000 booking can easily be won or lost on the quality of service. The spreadsheet allows her to quickly prepare important financial information for management, and to analyze that information in ways that would not be feasible if she had to do it by hand. Also, the communications interface enables Lydia to place orders more efficiently, saving time and lowering costs.

Computers and Society

The example we've just presented should give you some idea of why computer systems have become such an important part of modern life. Their ability to sort through massive amounts of data and quickly produce useful information for almost any kind of user—from payroll clerk to president—makes them indispensable in a society like ours. Without a computer, the catering manager in our example could not possibly provide the level of service she now extends to clients. The government would be unable to tabulate all the data it collects for the census every ten years. Banks would be overwhelmed by the job of tracking all the transactions they must process. The efficient airline and telephone service we are used to would be impossible. Moon exploration and the space shuttle would still belong to science fiction. The list is virtually endless.

But along with the benefits computers bring to society have come some troubling problems, ranging from health to personal security and privacy to ethics. The catering manager in our example, for instance, spends many hours in front of a display screen. Do the radiation and glare emanating from the screen impair her health? Banks keep data on customers' accounts on external storage devices. Can they prevent clever "computer criminals" from using their computer systems to steal from those accounts? The Internal Revenue Service has confidential information about every American taxpayer. Can it protect that information from unauthorized use? Because commercial software exists in electronic form, it can be easily copied. What restrictions should be placed on who can copy and use this software?

These are serious issues, but we can only mention them briefly in this chapter. In Chapter 16, we will discuss the costs and benefits of computers at length. Feature 1-2 discusses a relatively new use of computers that could change the way we interact socially—teledemocracy. A Critical Thinking question at the end of the chapter asks you to consider ways to keep such technology free from abuse.

F e a t u r e   1 – 2

Teledemocracy

A high-tech way to reflect your opinion

It's an old idea waiting for new ways to happen.

Teledemocracy refers to using home-based computer keyboards and other types of data-entry devices to do such things as voice opinions and cast votes. Perhaps the ultimate teledemocratic society is one in which there is a computer system in virtually every home with the ability to communicate with the outside. Everyone at home would then have the ability to tap into a common point that provides some reliable way of collecting or passing out survey or voting information.

We are still quite far away from such a scenario. But we are making progress.

Today, perhaps as many as a few million people participate in a limited form of teledemocracy through subscription-based information services, such as Prodigy and CompuServe, on home computers. A subscriber to one of these services might be able to access an *electronic bulletin board* and express an opinion on issues like taxing the rich or ways to cut the budget deficit. Subscribers can often also post notes and read what other subscribers have to say. Other available forms of teledemocracy include taking part in debates and asking questions to political candidates.

But subscriber information services currently have their limitations. First, many people find such services too expensive or not useful enough to buy into, even though they own a computer. Second, not everyone who has the ability to express an opinion is computer literate—not to mention just plain literate, which you have to be to read a computer screen. Third, the subscriber-based information services often avoid involvement in unpopular and politically incorrect matters. Recently, one person who advocated overthrowing the federal government was allegedly barred from promoting a discussion of this subject on an electronic bulletin board.

Today, only about one percent of Americans subscribe to computerized information services.

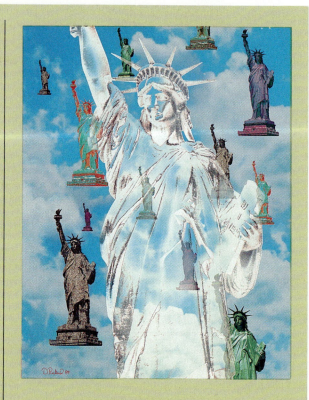

However, teledemocracy can be implemented in other ways, like interactive cable television. For instance, it's possible to have an "issues channel," where viewers are regularly asked to cast votes with a hand-held keypad. About a decade ago, such a system was tested in Columbus, Ohio, as an alternative for conventional political meetings. The company running the test discovered that citizens participated about ten times more than they did through conventional, face-to-face town meetings. Unfortunately, many of the problems that plague interactive cable TV as a vehicle for teledemocracy—such as viewer expense and issue censorship—are the same as those that affect the computer-based information services.

While the benefits of teledemocracy are enormous, many questions remain unanswered. Would instant audience feedback make it harder than ever for politicians to stand up for what's right rather than for what's popular? Would it become more difficult for any types of sweeping change or progress to take place? And consider this: Who would ultimately decide whether a vote held opposite *Monday Night Football* was biased?

Computers in Action

Where would you expect to find computers? In our discussion so far, we've seen some of the amazing variety of ways in which computers have become part of our lives. As you read through this book, you should get a good idea of what computer systems can and cannot do and where they do and do not belong. Window 1 presents an extensive picture essay of computers in just a few of the many settings in which you are likely to encounter them.

Summary and Key Terms

Computers appear almost everywhere in today's world. They're embedded in consumer products, used to run businesses, and employed to direct production in our factories, to name just a few applications.

Computers in the 1990s Workplace   Computers abound in today's workplace largely because we are living in an era when most jobs heavily depend on the collection, use, creation, and dissemination of information.

What's a Computer and What Does It Do?   Four words summarize the operation of a **computer system: input, processing, output,** and **storage.**

The processing function is performed by the **computer** itself, which is sometimes called the **central processing unit,** or **CPU.**

The input and output functions are performed by **peripheral equipment,** such as **input devices** and **output devices.** Just as your stereo amplifier would be useless if it had no speakers, headphones, tape deck, or turntable to supplement it, the computer would be helpless without these peripheral devices.

Mounted on some of the peripheral equipment are **input/output (I/O) media.** Many of these media *store* materials in **machine-readable** form, which the computer system can recognize and process.

The material that a computer receives as input is of two kinds: data and programs. **Data** are facts the computer has at its disposal; **programs** are instructions that explain to the computer what to do with these facts. Programs must be written in a **programming language** that the computer can understand.

Data that have been processed into a useful form are called **information.** The processing of data into information on computers is called **information processing.**

Computer systems have two types of storage. **Primary storage** (sometimes called **memory** or **internal storage**) is often built into the unit housing the computer itself; it holds the programs and data that the system is currently processing. **Secondary (external) storage** holds other programs and data. In many systems, secondary storage is located in a separate hardware device.

In the world of computers, it is common to distinguish between hardware and software. **Hardware** refers to the actual machinery that makes up the computer system, such as the CPU, input and output devices, and secondary storage devices. **Software** refers to computer programs.

End users are the people who need the output that computer systems produce. In a computing environment, there are many types of experts who help users meet their computing needs; for example, **programmers** are responsible for writing programs.

Virtually every benefit provided by computers boils down to making people do work either more efficiently or more effectively.

Computer Systems to Fit Every Need and Pocketbook   Small computers are often called **microcomputers (microcomputer systems)** or **personal computers** *(personal computer systems)*, medium-sized computers are called **minicomputers,** and large computers are called **mainframes.** The very largest computers, which are used for applications that demand the most in terms of speed and power, are called **supercomputers.** Although categorizing computers by size can be helpful, in practice it is sometimes difficult to classify computers that fall on the borders of these categories.

Using Computers: Some Examples   The hotel industry is but one example of an environment where computers—from mainframes to microcomputers—serve a variety of uses.

Computers and Society   Although computer systems have become an indispensable part of modern life, their growing use has created troubling problems, ranging from health to personal security and privacy to ethics.

Computers in Action   As you read through this book, you should get a good idea of what computer systems can and cannot do and where they do and do not belong. Window 1 presents an extensive picture essay of computers in just a few of the many settings in which you are likely to encounter them.

Review Exercises

Fill-in Questions

1. Four words sum up the operation of a computer system: input, output, _____, and storage.

2. When programs and data are being processed, they are stored in _____ storage.

3. Processed data that are in a useful form are called _____.

4. Another name for computer programs is _____.

5. When programs and data are not being processed but need to be "at the fingertips" of the computer, they are stored in _____ storage.

6. A term used for the equipment in a computing environment is _____.

7. A series of instructions that direct a computer system is known as a(n) _____.

8. The hardware, software, data, procedures, and personnel needed to process data successfully are called a(n) _____.

Matching Questions

Match each term with the description that fits best.

a. minicomputer
b. input device
c. mainframe
d. supercomputer
e. hardware
f. microcomputer

____ 1. The equipment that makes up a computer system.

____ 2. Another name for personal computer.

____ 3. A medium-sized computer.

____ 4. A large computer used to process business transactions in high volume.

____ 5. Any piece of equipment that supplies programs and data to a computer.

____ 6. The most powerful type of electronic computer.

Discussion Questions

1. Name several ways in which computers are used in today's workplace.

2. Provide some examples of input devices, output devices, processing devices, and input/output media that are found in the average household and are not necessarily computer related.

3. What is the difference between a computer and a computer system?

4. Name as many peripheral devices as you can. What is the purpose of each?

5. What are the major differences between primary storage and secondary storage?

6. What is the difference between programs and data?

7. Define and give some examples of end users of a computer system.

8. Identify some social problems created by the existence of computer systems.

Critical Thinking Questions

1. Should everyone getting a degree from a college or university today be required to take an introductory computer course? Defend your response.

2. The section on the workplace of the 1990s provides several examples describing how computers are changing the way ordinary people work. Can you think of any additional examples not mentioned in this section?

3. The term "computer literacy"—knowing something about computers—is widely used today. In your opinion, what types of computer knowledge should people such as yourself be literate about?

4. Feature 1–2 discusses ways in which teledemocracy can be implemented. What problems need to be worked out in this technology to make it possible for people to elect a president over the phone?

Computers in Our World

A Visual Portfolio of the Widespread Use of Computers

Computers rapidly have become an important force in almost every segment of our society. This first "window to the world of computers" presents a small sample of the many tasks to which computers may be applied. Included are examples from the fields of business, entertainment, design, advertising, art, education, the environment, health care, and science.

1. Computers are frequently used to alter images in fantastic ways. Here, four faces of Elvis have been read into the computer system and "chiseled" into a high-tech monument.

1

Business

2

2–3. In factories and plants, computers are widely used to control industrial processes and to support various types of engineering field work.

3

4–5. The computer has become a commonplace fixture in retailing, both for interacting with customers and for performing back-office accounting functions.

4

5

Entertainment

6

6. Virtual-reality games enable players wearing special goggles to enter their own computer-generated environments. In the game shown here, participants assume active roles in a medieval fantasy game.

7

7–9. Through the use of computers, the villain in *Indiana Jones and the Last Crusade* is spectacularly metamorphosized into a mummy before the movie-goer's eyes.

8

9

Design

10–11. Today, computers are widely used to design structures of all types, from homes to industrial facilities. In many cases, the designs are rendered in three dimensions, thereby making it possible to "walk through them" on the computer's display screen.

10

11

12. By using computers to create package designs electronically, both the designer and client can see on a computer screen how the packages look filled with food contents, standing in front of other food (as shown here), or sitting on the store shelf with other products.

12

13. Today, both cars and highways are "built" and "tested" by computer—often before physical building and testing ever take place.

13

Advertising and Art

14

14–15. Computers are commonly used to create advertising images that appear on film and in print. Many of the ads you see on television are either completely computer created or enhanced by the computer in some way.

15

16

16. The field of computer art is rapidly emerging as a serious art medium, with its own contests and shows.

Education and Training

17–18. Computers are often used as in-classroom tools to teach courses and as out-of-classroom tools to complete homework assignments.

17

18

19. At many museums and exhibitions, and even on business sites, computer-controlled booths called "kiosks" disseminate information.

19

20

20–21. A computerized laboratory cockpit, equipped with computer-graphics screens as windows, enables pilots to practice flying before actually getting in a plane.

21

Society and Government

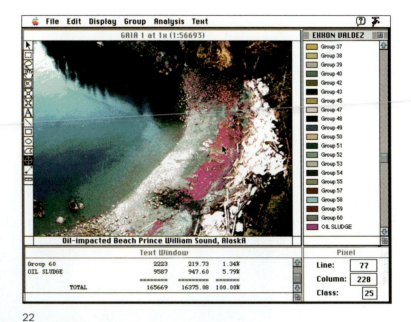

22. Technology regularly assists scientists as they study the environment. Here, a computer-enhanced photo of Alaska's Prince William Sound shows in pink the oil sludge left by the Exxon *Valdez* spill.

22

23. Controllers review computer-controlled communications systems at the Johnson Space Center in Houston, Texas.

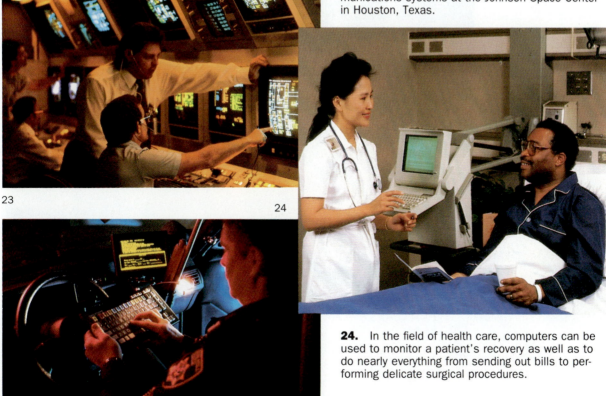

23

24

24. In the field of health care, computers can be used to monitor a patient's recovery as well as to do nearly everything from sending out bills to performing delicate surgical procedures.

25. Technology is employed at virtually all levels today in the fight against crime.

25

COMPUTER SYSTEMS AND INFORMATION PROCESSING

2

How do computers process data into useful outputs? In this chapter we'll look at some of the ways, and, also, examine types of hardware and software found in a typical computer system.

OUTLINE

LEARNING OBJECTIVES

After completing this chapter, you will be able to:

1. Identify several major classes of input, output, processing, and storage hardware.

2. Explain how data are organized in a computing environment.

3. Distinguish between applications and systems software.

4. Describe some of the ways in which computer systems process data into useful information.

5. Define several more key terms that are useful to know when reading about or discussing computers.

Overview

As you learned in Chapter 1, input, processing, and output, together with storage, are the major components of any computer system. In this chapter, you will see how they work together in more detail.

First, we'll take a look at computer system hardware. We'll cover some basic hardware concepts and discuss some of the most important kinds of input, output, and storage equipment. Then we'll see how this equipment can be linked, first in a small computer system and then in a large one. This section will prepare you for the detailed discussion of hardware in Module B.

From there, we'll take up the subject of data, specifically how data must be organized for processing on a computer system. Study the terms introduced in this section carefully, because you will encounter them frequently throughout the rest of the book.

Then we'll go on to a discussion of program software to introduce you to a subject we cover extensively later in the text.

Following this, we'll discuss information processing on computer systems. We'll examine representative examples of some of the most common types of processing to see how hardware, data, software, procedures, and users interact to do useful work.

Finally, to integrate many of the chapter materials, we'll look at how the hardware, software, data, and information-processing procedures you read about in earlier sections combine with people to form a sophisticated computer system.

The ways in which computers can provide useful information are too numerous to catalog in any textbook. While the bulk of the chapter covers some of the most widespread uses of computers, Feature 2-1 touches on a more exotic application—helping historians unravel the century-old mystery of Billy the Kid.

Computer Hardware

Computer.
A device that can perform arithmetic, make comparisons, and store and retrieve facts. Also called the **central processing unit (CPU).**

System unit.
The hardware unit that houses the computer and its memory, as well as a number of other devices.

Peripheral equipment.
The machines that work with the computer.

All computer systems consist of some combination of computers and peripheral equipment. The main **computer,** often called the *central processing unit,* or *CPU,* is the heart of the system; it controls the actual processing of data and programs. Closely tied to the CPU is its *memory,* which is almost always housed in the same hardware device, called the **system unit.** Many people, in fact, refer to the system unit as the computer, but strictly speaking it is merely the "box" that contains the computer. **Peripheral equipment** consists of all the machines that make it possible to get data and programs into the CPU, retrieve processed information, and store data and programs for ready access to the CPU.

Peripheral Equipment

Peripheral equipment for computer systems can be classified in a number of ways. One of the most basic classifications is by function: Is the device predominantly for input, output, or storage? Another is by medium: Does it use tapes or disks? A third is by its relation to the CPU: Is it online or offline? Let's consider each of these in turn.

F e a t u r e   2 – 1

Debunking the Billy the Kid Legend

Have computers put to rest an unsolved mystery?

One of the most famous symbols of the Old West is Billy the Kid. History books tell us that this notorious outlaw was shot and killed by Sheriff Pat Garrett—in Fort Sumner, New Mexico Territory—on the night of July 14, 1881. But many people insist that the shooting was a hoax and that the real Billy actually left Fort Sumner alive, managing to live out a long life elsewhere.

One of the most famous of these claims centers around a character named Brushy Bill Roberts, who passed away in Texas in 1950. Prior to his death, Brushy Bill insisted that he was the real Billy the Kid. He even asked the governor of New Mexico to pardon him for his alleged seventy-year-old crimes. Was Roberts the real Kid, or just a misguided publicity hound?

The latter, say some highly reputable computer-imaging researchers at the University of Chicago.

A few years back, computer experts developed a way to create updated pictures of missing children by electronically altering old photographs. Using many of the same computational techniques, the researchers compared photos of the real Billy the Kid to those of Brushy Bill Roberts and other claimants to the legend. The computer software works on the principle that certain facial structures of a person remain the same throughout time, despite the effects of aging. Consequently, by comparing distances, angles, and ratios between certain facial points—about 15 such measurements, say the researchers—it can be reasonably determined whether the person in one photograph is the same as the person in another.

The photographs to be compared are first "read" into the computer system with a scanning device and are then stored. When the images are later sent to the display screen, a skilled operator marks with a mouse the 15 predetermined facial

The Kid. Computer technology is proving the history books right.

points on each image. Then, the images are fed to a program that calculates a single statistic, reflecting the result of the comparisons. A 1.0 is a perfect match. Anything below a 0.8 essentially rules out the likelihood of the two people being the same individual.

The highest that any of the wannabe Billys scored was 0.57—far below the range that certifies authenticity. During the time it was being built, the program was tested on hundreds of people and is widely felt to be reliable.

Today, the same types of computer-imaging principles developed in the Billy-the-Kid project are being applied for another purpose—detecting matches from criminal mug-shot files. So, who knows? Maybe the hoodlum whom many feel was not worth much during his lifetime will wind up contributing some good after all.

Input, Output, or Storage?

Input device.
A machine used to supply materials going to the computer.

Output device.
A machine used to accept materials coming from the computer.

Secondary storage device.
A machine, such as a tape or disk unit, that supplements memory.

Input devices are machines that convert data and programs into a form that the CPU can understand and process. **Output devices** are machines that convert processed data into a form that users can understand. **Secondary storage devices** are machines that make frequently used data and programs readily available to the CPU. These functions often overlap in a single machine. Some machines, for example, work as both input and output devices, and all secondary storage devices also function as both input and output devices. Now let's discuss some of the most common kinds of support equipment in terms of these three functions.

Computer *keyboards* (see Figure 2-1) are input devices that closely resemble typewriter keyboards. They are used to type in programs and data and to interactively issue instructions to the computer system. Figure 2-1 also shows a *mouse,* a screen-pointing device that people are increasingly using to supplement

FIGURE 2-1

Input devices. The keyboard (top) is the most widely used input device for entering instructions and data into a computer system. The mouse (bottom) is useful for rapidly moving a pointer around the display screen, for making menu selections, and for moving and resizing objects on the screen.

Output devices (a) Display devices show both the input users type at the keyboard and the resulting output the computer produces. (b) Printers provide output in a form that can be carried around and later discarded.

(a)

(b)

keyboard operations. While mice aren't absolutely essential for most business uses, they are easier to use than keyboards for certain types of work. The current trend is for display-screen images to mimic office desktops, with several documents onscreen concurrently. Mice are especially handy to have in this type of applications environment because they make it easy to arrange and resize screen documents.

Display devices (see Figure 2-2a), which appear in almost all computer systems, are used for output. The operator enters commands to the computer system through a keyboard or mouse; then both the input the operator enters and the output the CPU produces appear on the screen. A *display terminal* is a display device and a keyboard that are packaged together and used as a communications workstation to a large computer. The local display devices commonly found with microcomputers are generally referred to as *monitors*.

Printers also produce output (see Figure 2-2b). Printers come in a variety of different sizes and capabilities. The printers found in microcomputer systems might cost only a few hundred dollars, print very limited graphics, and output only a page or two a minute. Printers used with large computers, on the other hand, may cost several hundred thousand dollars or more and output several hundred pages per minute.

Secondary storage devices hold frequently used data and programs for ready access to the CPU. They also function as both input and output devices; that

FIGURE 2 – 3

Microcomputer secondary storage devices. (a) A system unit with two diskette units. (b) A hard-disk unit designed for a notebook or hand-held computer. (c) An optical disk unit with an optical disk cartridge. (d) A tape unit.

(a)

(b)

(c)

(d)

is, they contain stored data and programs that are sent to the CPU as input, and the CPU transmits new data and programs to them as output. The most common types of secondary storage devices are disk units and tape units. Figure 2-3 shows several secondary storage devices designed for microcomputers.

Disk units read and write data and programs to or from disks. Most disk units work by either magnetic or optical means. The most common types of *magnetic disk units* are *diskette units* (Figure 2-3a) and *hard-disk units* (Figure 2-3b). *Optical disk units,* which permit much greater amounts of storage than magnetic disks, are also becoming popular in office and home use (Figure 2-3c).

Tape units are designed to read from or write to tapes—either those in detachable-reel form or those packaged in cartridges (see Figure 2-3d). On microcomputers, tapes are commonly used to "back up" a hard disk; that is, to make a duplicate copy of the hard disk's contents as a measure of security. The tape unit shown in Figure 2-3d can accept tape cartridges that store 250 million characters of data, which is more than the capacity of many hard disks.

Disk and tape units can be built directly into the system unit or can exist as separate, "external" devices that you plug into the system unit like you do a keyboard or printer. On most microcomputer systems the diskette and hard-disk units are built in.

Input/Output Media

Input and output devices are, respectively, machines used to get data and programs into a computer and machines used to get the results out in a usable form. Often, however, data and programs are not permanently stored in a particular device. Instead they are recorded on **input/output (I/O) media** in a form the associated device can read and transmit to the CPU. In other words, just as the tape deck on your home stereo system works with tape cassettes, input/output devices work with specific input/output media. Five of the most common input/output media in use today are *hard magnetic disks, diskettes, optical disks, detachable-reel magnetic tapes,* and *magnetic tape cartridges.* The magnetic media are illustrated in Figure 2-4; an optical disk is shown in Figure 2-3c. All of these media will be discussed in detail in Chapter 4.

Input/output (I/O) media. Objects used to store computer-processed materials.

FIGURE 2–4

Disks and tapes. (left) Hard disks. (right) Magnetic tape cartridge (left background), detachable-reel tape (right background), and diskettes (foreground).

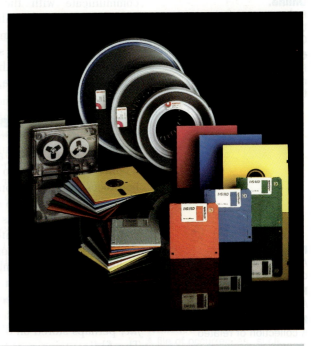

A student database. Databases, such as the one shown here, enable data that might otherwise exist in several separate files to be easily interrelated. Database technology has made it possible for users to ask the computer system complex questions—questions that require data to be drawn from multiple sources within the database.

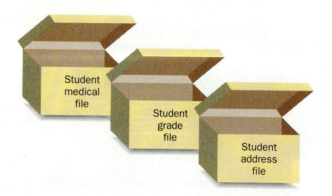

As mentioned previously, data from related files often are stored in databases. For example, data that normally would appear in the customer transaction file and customer master file might be collectively stored in a customer database.

Whatever the medium on which they are stored, entities such as files and databases always have names. The computer system uses these names to identify the files or databases when it needs to access them. For example, "CUSTOMER-MASTER-DATA" may be the name of a customer master file.

A Brief Introduction to Software

As mentioned earlier, the word *software* refers to computer programs. Programs direct the computer system to do specific tasks, just as your thoughts direct your body to speak or move in certain ways. Software comes in two varieties: applications software and systems software.

Applications software.
Programs that do the type of work that people acquire a computer system to do.

Applications Software   **Applications software** is designed to perform tasks such as computing the interest on or balance in bank accounts, preparing bills, creating documents, preparing and analyzing budgets, managing files and databases, playing games, scheduling airline flights, or diagnosing hospital patients' illnesses. In other words, applications software makes possible the types of "computer work" end users have in mind when they acquire a computer system. You can buy applications software prewritten or write it yourself. If you write it yourself, you must be familiar with a specific programming language.

Productivity software, which we will discuss in detail in Module D, is the class of easy-to-learn, easy-to-use applications software designed to make workers more productive at their jobs. Some important types of productivity software are described in Figure 2-7.

Systems software.
Computer programs, such as the operating system, that enable application programs to run on a computer system's hardware.

Systems Software   **Systems software** consists of "background" programs that enable applications software to run on a computer system's hardware devices. One of the most important pieces of systems software is the *operating system*, a set of control programs that supervise the computer system's work. Many recent Hollywood movies have portrayed the role of the operating system in an overly exaggerated manner—for example, as a demon master-control program that tries to take over the world. Fortunately, operating systems don't control people; rather, people control operating systems. We'll address operating systems and other types of systems software in more depth in Chapter 7.

Information Processing

Computer systems process data into information. When we talk about information processing, however, what kinds of processing do we have in mind?

The number of ways in which a full-fledged computer system can turn data into useful information is truly staggering and defies a simple, systematic enumeration at this early stage in the book. So rather than trying to look at all of them, let's focus on just a few commonly encountered information-processing tasks. This will help you appreciate the types of work you will likely need a computer system to do.

FIGURE 2 – 7

Types of productivity software. Productivity software packages are designed to make both ordinary users and computer professionals more productive at their jobs.

Package Type	Description
Word processor	Turns the computer system into a powerful typewriting tool
Spreadsheet	Turns the computer system into a sophisticated electronic calculator and analysis tool
Presentation graphics	Turns the computer into a tool that can be used to prepare overheads, slides, and presentation materials for meetings
File manager and database management system	Turns the computer system into an electronic research assistant, capable of searching through mounds of data to prepare reports or answer queries for information
Communications software	Enables users to call up remote computers for such things as financial information, marketing information, and news
Desktop publishing	Turns the computer system into a tool that can produce documents that look as if they were produced at a professional print shop
Desk accessory	Provides the electronic equivalent of tools commonly found on an office desktop—calendars, address files, and calculators, for instance
CASE (computer-assisted software engineering)	Automates and integrates many of the tasks performed by computer professionals, thus enabling them to develop systems and software far more effectively
Expert system	Enables workers to tap into expert knowledge to support their work
CAD (computer-aided design)	Gives people like architects and product designers the ability to bring products to market faster.

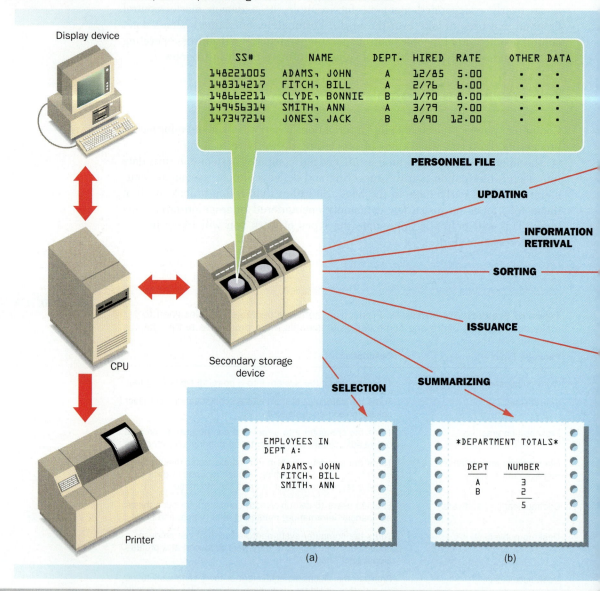

FIGURE 2-8

Information processing. Depicted are six fundamental ways in which computers are capable of processing data into useful information.

SS#	NAME	DEPT.	HIRED	RATE	OTHER DATA
148221005	ADAMS, JOHN	A	12/85	5.00	• • •
148314217	FITCH, BILL	A	2/76	6.00	• • •
148662211	CLYDE, BONNIE	B	1/70	8.00	• • •
149456314	SMITH, ANN	A	3/79	7.00	• • •
147347214	JONES, JACK	B	8/90	12.00	• • •

Display device

PERSONNEL FILE

UPDATING

INFORMATION RETRIVAL

SORTING

ISSUANCE

CPU

Secondary storage device

SUMMARIZING

SELECTION

Printer

```
EMPLOYEES IN
DEPT A:

    ADAMS, JOHN
    FITCH, BILL
    SMITH, ANN
```
(a)

```
*DEPARTMENT TOTALS*

DEPT    NUMBER

  A        3
  B        2
          ___
           5
```
(b)

Some common information-processing tasks are

- Selection
- Summarizing
- Issuance
- Sorting
- Information retrieval
- Updating

We will discuss each of these in turn and illustrate each with an example. All of our examples will use the personnel file in Figure 2-8. This file is housed in a secondary storage device, such as the hard-disk unit shown in the figure. We've used a small, five-record file here to simplify the examples (in reality,

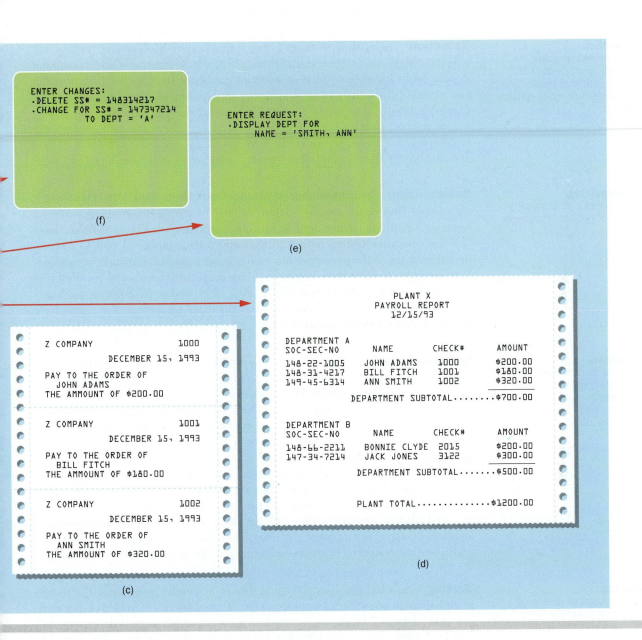

```
ENTER CHANGES:
.DELETE SS# = 148314217
.CHANGE FOR SS# = 147347214
            TO DEPT = 'A'
```

(f)

```
ENTER REQUEST:
.DISPLAY DEPT FOR
       NAME = 'SMITH, ANN'
```

(e)

```
             PLANT X
          PAYROLL REPORT
            12/15/93

DEPARTMENT A
SOC-SEC-NO      NAME      CHECK#      AMOUNT
148-22-1005  JOHN ADAMS    1000      $200.00
148-31-4217  BILL FITCH    1001      $180.00
149-45-6314  ANN SMITH     1002      $320.00
                                     _____
          DEPARTMENT SUBTOTAL........$700.00

DEPARTMENT B
SOC-SEC-NO      NAME      CHECK#      AMOUNT
148-66-2211  BONNIE CLYDE  2015      $200.00
147-34-7214  JACK JONES    3122      $300.00
                                     _____
          DEPARTMENT SUBTOTAL.......$500.00


          PLANT TOTAL..............$1200.00
```

(d)

```
Z COMPANY              1000
             DECEMBER 15, 1993

PAY TO THE ORDER OF
   JOHN ADAMS
THE AMMOUNT OF $200.00


Z COMPANY              1001
             DECEMBER 15, 1993

PAY TO THE ORDER OF
   BILL FITCH
THE AMMOUNT OF $180.00


Z COMPANY              1002
             DECEMBER 15, 1993

PAY TO THE ORDER OF
   ANN SMITH
THE AMMOUNT OF $320.00
```

(c)

many personnel files contain thousands of such records). Also, each record shown contains only five fields. The sixth column, "Other Data," indicates that we could have added many more fields had we wanted to.

Each of the information-processing operations we'll describe should be located in a program somewhere in secondary storage. For example, if we want to sort our data file, we will need a program that will enable us to sort data records.

In each of our examples, output can be directed to one or more output devices in the system—the display, the printer, or secondary storage. Again, to make things straightforward, we've shown output directed to only one device in each of the six example applications in Figure 2-8.

Selection.
The process of going through a set of data and picking out only those data elements that meet certain criteria.

Selection Selection involves going through a set of data and picking out only those items that meet certain criteria. Figure 2-8a illustrates how a computer system could handle one type of selection problem. In this case the computer had to select the names of all employees in department A and print out those names. Naturally, if we wished, we could have directed the names to the display screen instead (and saved paper, too). Selection criteria can be either simple or complex. For example, we could have asked the computer system to extract and display the names of all department A employees who were hired last year.

Summarizing.
The process of reducing a mass of data to a manageable form.

Summarizing Summarizing involves reducing a mass of data to a manageable form. This could require making a tally of items, determining sums for items in a particular class, and so forth. For example, in Figure 2-8b we have had the computer system output to the printer the number of people in each department and in the personnel file. Still another possible summarizing application would be to have the computer system output the number of people hired in each of several years, such as 1992, 1993, 1994, and so on. Software packages such as spreadsheets, file managers, and database management systems have strong facilities for summarizing data.

Issuance.
The use of computers to produce transaction-oriented documents such as paychecks, bills, and customer reminder notices.

Issuance Computer systems are also widely used to input records, perform a series of calculations on each record, and prepare a document for each record based on these computations. This process is sometimes called **issuance,** since the end result is the issuing of documents. In billing operations, for example, the computer system reads a record of payments and purchases for each customer, computes the amount due, and prepares a bill. Payroll processing, illustrated in Figure 2-8c, is another example.

Checks such as those shown in figure 2-8c cannot be generated from the personnel file alone. After all, how is the computer system to know how much to pay each employee? Therefore, to produce paychecks, the payroll program may consult two other files, one with the hours worked by each employee and another consisting of employee pay rates. Then, for each employee, the computer multiplies hours worked by a corresponding pay rate to produce the earnings due.

Sorting.
The process of arranging data in a specified order.

Sorting Sorting involves arranging data in a specific order—a list of names in alphabetical order, for example, or a list of numbers in ascending or descending order. Figure 2-8d shows a computer report in which payroll data are sorted first by department and then by name within each department. The report in Figure 2-8d is also an example of *control-break reporting*. As illustrated, the computer breaks after processing each department to print a subtotal and breaks again at the end of the report to print a final total.

Information retrieval.
Online inquiry to computer files or databases.

Information Retrieval Programs created for **information retrieval,** or *query*, enables users to enter a series of questions at the keyboard for the purpose of extracting information from a database or from many different data files. For example, a bank manager may want to check a customer's credit rating. The checking, savings, trust, and loan data needed to determine credit ratings are contained in a customer database. An information-retrieval program that responds to the manager's request for a credit check could extract all the needed information from the database and calculate the customer's credit rating automatically. Figure 2-8e illustrates a query to the personnel file, in which the operator is trying to determine the department in which Ann Smith works.

Updating   **Updating** involves changing the data in a file to reflect new information. Credit card companies, for example, update their customer files regularly to reflect customers' payments and purchases. Updating is done on either a batch or a realtime basis.

■   **BATCH PROCESSING**   **Batch processing** involves accumulating (batching) transactions over time in a separate transaction file and processing them all at once against a master file. For example, if you update your checkbook at the end of the month using data from the checking transactions made throughout that month, you are updating on a batch basis.

   Many issuance tasks, such as payroll, are done by processing work in a batch. For example, many companies pay employees at the end of the month. Billing is another operation that is often done in the batch mode. A company may maintain a file of customer transactions, which include purchases and payments. At a certain time of the month, this transaction file is processed against a master file of all customer balances. The computer system updates

Updating.
The process of bringing something up to date by making corrections, adding new data, and so forth.

Batch processing.
Processing transactions or other data in groups, at periodic intervals.

FIGURE 2 – 9

Realtime processing. Instantaneous updating of master files is absolutely critical for such applications as (left) managing passenger reservations for the airlines and (right) keeping track of customer withdrawals at banks.

Virtual Reality

Hanging Out in Cyberspace

You're lazing away on a warm beach in Mexico when the sun begins to nudge toward the horizon. The hills to your left take on an orange glow, gulls are diving for fish, and each harmless cloud in the sky looks wildly three-dimensional and painted with its own special color. "If only this could go on for another hour," you think. It does ... and not because it's actually happening. You've used a computer system to create a virtual reality.

Virtual reality refers to the use of computers to create special, customized environments that seem, to the computer operator, as if they were real. Although we are still far from the virtual reality that science fiction writers tell us about, there are many who believe that computer technology will someday make it possible to create such illusions. Several pioneering virtual-reality applications are visible in the marketplace today.

In architecture, for instance, it is now possible to take "tours" of buildings whose foundations are yet to be poured. How? A computer model

Steven King's CyberJobe. Virtual reality gone awry.

of the building is made in three dimensions. Once the building is mathematically specified, what a person can see if standing at any specific point in the building, looking in any specific direction, can be mathematically determined.

Let's say the client taking the tour wants to look at the top floor first and see the lounge before the offices. The tour can be taken in real time, which enables the client to move as he or she so chooses, deciding which facilities to view before

---

the balance in each account and issues statements that are sent to the customers.

Realtime processing.
Updating data immediately in a master file as transactions take place.

■ **REALTIME PROCESSING**   **Realtime processing** involves entering transaction data into a computer system as they take place and updating master files immediately (see Figure 2-9). All realtime processing is performed online.

A prime example of realtime processing occurs in banking. Tellers with terminals can update an account as soon as a customer makes a withdrawal. If the customer makes a withdrawal at an automatic teller machine, the machine updates the account immediately. The ability to check and update accounts on the spot protects the bank from overwithdrawals. Deposits, however, usually are not recorded in a customer's balance until the end of the day, when all deposits made by all customers that day are processed together. In other words, deposits typically are processed in the batch mode.

Figure 2-8f illustrates an update to the personnel file to show that Bill Fitch has left the company and Jack Jones has moved to department A. If changes such as these are immediately reflected in the computer system, realtime processing is

others, how much time to spend at each facility, and what to see there. Lighting routines are available that can show how natural light falls in the building on a sunny or rainy day and how artificial light changes a room. Does the client hate the look and size of the lounge? No problem. With a remodeling software package, it can be reshaped, repainted, relighted, refurnished, and ready for reinspection—in just a few minutes.

In the field of business, virtual reality techniques are now being applied to the analysis of securities. One of the problems inherent in conventional analysis is that it's often difficult to tell when a group of securities is moving relative to the market as a whole. With virtual reality, stocks belonging to a certain group—say, technology stocks—can each be given a characteristic color. When general stock movements are viewed in three dimensions over time, which is simulated by animation techniques, the analyst can more clearly visualize how the technology group, or any other group, is behaving.

In addition to benefitting fields such as architecture and business, virtual reality may someday enable the exploration of planets without actually going there, make possible educational and therapeutic experiences in which human confrontation is realistically simulated, help to recreate crime scenes, and allow people to take virtual vacations.

Expect virtual reality applications to arrive in full force in the entertainment industry, where illusion is the principal product. In some cities, shops have already sprouted up that feature virtual reality games in which players can battle demons on a realistic, computer-generated landscape. In many cases, the virtual-reality participant must don special goggles, which project computer-generated images directly toward the eye, and wear gloves with built-in sensors, which change the goggle images when the hands are moved. A golf game has also been developed in which budding Jack Nicklauses can swing away at the best holes on some of the world's greatest courses without ever leaving the local spa.

Perhaps it was the public's increasing curiosity about virtual reality that led to a major film using the topic as its centerpiece. *Lawnmower Man*, based on a Stephen King short story, is about a doctor who conducts virtual-reality experiments on chimps and, later, on a young man named Jobe. But the doctor has the same type of luck Dr. Frankenstein did with his own monstrous creation—science goes awry and CyberJobe (see photo), a being who exists entirely within the computer and who threatens to produce chaos, evolves. The film's creator's argue that much of what moviegoers see will soon be available. Coming next to your town: virtual-reality theatres.

in effect; if they are done at the end of a day or week, batch processing is taking place.

The Tomorrow box features *virtual reality*, perhaps the ultimate in realtime processing. User Solution 2-2 describes the use of wireless technology to update computer databases in real time. Wireless terminals can also be used to retrieve database data.

Getting It All Together: Combining Elements into a Complete Computer System

Now that you understand a few concepts about hardware, software, and data, it's time to learn how these elements interact with people and procedures to form a complete computer-based information processing system. Along the way, you'll be introduced to a few new concepts, ones that you will read about in detail in the text.

FIGURE 2 - 11

Recording transactions. When the label attached to each purchased item is read with a hand scanner connected to the computer system, valuable sales data are collected quickly and virtually without error. These data can be used to prepare customer receipts and are sent daily to headquarters for rapid management analysis.

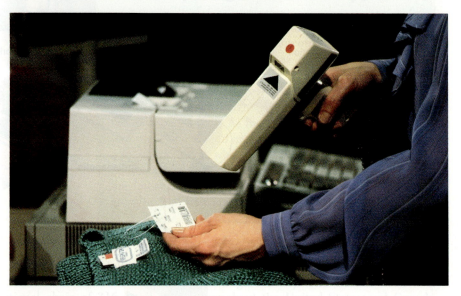

in separate files that couldn't be interrelated and the Dallas mainframe couldn't communicate daily with each of the stores, it took two or three weeks of intensive research to get answers. Most of the time, managers didn't bother.

Output   Computer output occurs at several levels in this sales information system.

At headquarters, sales executives are most concerned with how the stores and product lines are performing on the whole and in relation to competitive products. Every evening, computer data reflecting the day's activity are summarized into graphs and reports that sales executives can summon on display screens as soon as they arrive for work in the morning. Executives can also electronically browse through any other facts in the sales database to answer questions that go beyond the information available in the graphs and reports.

An *electronic mail* system enables sales executives and store owners to communicate over ordinary phone lines. If, for instance, an executive has important news to announce to store owners, it is typed as a memo and routed, in seconds, to the hard disks of individual store computers. At each store, a small symbol called a "message icon" shows up on the display screen, indicating a message has been sent. Store owners can also send memos to headquarters over the electronic mail system.

At the store level, details of each purchase are output in the form of a receipt given the customer and in the form of a transaction entry that is written to the hard disk.

Sales reports are sent daily to individual store managers. These reports are automatically routed by headquarters through the electronic mail system and are available to each store owner when stores open for business. These reports show owners how well their store has performed relative to expectations, show goods that will be delivered during the next few weeks, make suggestions for purchasing, and provide interesting news items about other stores in the chain and about trends in the industry. The reports are intended to be both informational and motivational, and store owners are free to make their own decisions. Store owners do not have access to the full sales database at headquarters, however.

Storage   Casual Look uses two types of electronic storage in its sales information system: disk and tape.

Both locally and at headquarters, sales data are stored and processed on hard disk. Today, magnetic disk is the most popular means of online secondary storage because it is relatively fast, capacious, and inexpensive. Hard disk, however, is not so capacious that it doesn't get filled over time. Rather than add more hard-disk capacity online, many organizations, including Casual Look, store hard-disk data they no longer need on tape and then store these tapes offline. For instance, because few managers are interested in looking at raw, detailed sales data from two or three years past, such data are put on tape.

Summary and Key Terms

Chapter 2 explains how input, processing, output, and storage work together to produce useful information.

Computer Hardware   All computer systems consist of some combination of **computers,** their memories, and **peripheral equipment.** The computer and its memory often are housed in the same hardware device, called the **system unit.** The most common types of support equipment are **input devices, output devices,** and **secondary storage devices.**

Input and output devices include keyboards, display devices such as display terminals and monitors, and printers.

Secondary storage devices include hard-disk units, diskette units, optical disk units, detachable-reel tape units, and cartridge tape units. These devices use, respectively, hard disks, diskettes, optical disks, detachable tape reels, and cartridge tapes as their **input/output (I/O) media.**

Support equipment may be either **online** or **offline** to the CPU at any point in time.

Organizing Data for Computer Systems   Data are commonly organized into fields, records, files, and databases. A **field** is a collection of individual characters, such as digits and letters of the alphabet. A **record** is a collection of related fields. A **file** is a collection of related records. As transaction data are generated, they are stored as records in a **transaction file;** a **master file** contains more permanent types of data. A **database** contains the contents of several files.

A Brief Introduction to Software   Software falls into one of two categories: applications software and systems software. **Applications software** does the "computer work" most end users have in mind when they buy a computer system. **Systems software** consists of support programs that enable applications software to run on a given set of hardware devices.

Information Processing   Six common information-processing tasks are selection, summarizing, issuance, sorting, information retrieval, and updating. **Selection** involves extracting from files only those fields or records that meet certain criteria. **Summarizing** consists of reducing a mass of data to a manageable form. **Issuance** involves inputting records, performing a series of calculations on each record, and preparing a document for each record based on the computations. **Sorting** means arranging data in some specified sequence, such as alphabetical order or numeric order. Summarizing, sorting, and issuance often are combined to do *control-break reporting*. **Information retrieval,** or *query*, enables users to extract information from data files. **Updating,** which involves changing data in a file to reflect new information, can be done on a periodic or immediate basis. These types of updating are called **batch processing** and **realtime processing,** respectively.

Getting It All Together: Combining Elements into a Complete Computer System   The case study featuring The Casual Look shows how the hardware, software, data, and information-processing procedures you read about in earlier sections combine with people to form a sophisticated computer system.

Review Exercises

Fill-in Questions

1. To be read by a computer system, data must be recorded in machine-readable form on some type of _____.

2. A file containing relatively permanent data is called a _____ file.

3. Any device that is set up to communicate with the CPU is said to be _____.

4. _____ software is written by users or programmers to perform tasks such as computing the interest or balance in bank accounts.

5. _____ software consists of programs that enable applications software to run smoothly on a given set of hardware.

6. A(n) _____ is a collection of characters that represents a single type of data.

7. _____ processing refers to collecting transactions until the end of the day or week and processing them all at once.

8. The method of updating that the airline industry uses for passenger reservations is called _____ processing.

Match each term with the description that fits best.

Matching Questions

a. information retrieval
b. issuance
c. batch processing
d. realtime processing
e. control-break reporting
f. sorting

____ 1. A company prepares a reminder notice for a customer whose payment deadline has passed.

____ 2. A company produces an employee phone book with names in alphabetical order.

____ 3. A bank records all deposits made to customer accounts at the end of each day.

____ 4. A report shows information on the sales of a single product, with three subtotals and a grand total.

____ 5. A librarian keys in the title of a book on a display terminal to see whether it has been checked out.

____ 6. Jane Williams withdraws $100 from her checking account, and that amount is immediately subtracted from her account balance.

Discussion Questions

1. Name some common types of peripheral equipment, and state whether each is used for input, output, storage, or some combination of these functions.

2. Name some common types of secondary storage devices and the I/O media each uses.

3. Create a small file of data. Can you identify the records and fields?

4. What is the difference between applications software and systems software?

5. What is the difference between a master file and a transaction file?

6. Identify and define the types of information processing discussed in this chapter. Can you think of any other examples of information processing?

Critical Thinking Questions

1. At a recent campus computer club meeting, you agreed to conduct a survey on how members feel about tours the club may make of local businesses next semester. You've designed a questionnaire that consists of seven to eight questions. Answers to most questions will be in the form of ideas or opinions that will likely run about two or three sentences. The thought has crossed your mind that the computer might be of some help in tabulating the results. Will it?

2. In the Casual Look example, it is mentioned that store owners do not have unlimited access to mainframe data. Do you think this is a mistake?

3. Virtual reality, covered in the Tomorrow box, is expected to help eliminate unnecessary animal experimentation in medical research. How do you see virtual reality techniques assisting in this area?

HARDWARE

When most people think of computers or computer systems today, hardware most readily comes to mind. Hardware comprises the exciting pieces of equipment delivered in crates or boxes when you buy a computer system. As you'll learn in this module, a rich variety of computer hardware is available in today's marketplace. But as you'll see later in this book, hardware needs a guiding force—namely, software—to be of any use. Hardware without software is like a human without the ability to reason and manipulate thoughts.

The hardware discussed in this module is divided into three areas. Chapter 3 describes the use of the CPU—the computer itself. Chapter 4 discusses the class of hardware that provides an indispensable library of resources for the CPU—secondary storage devices. Chapter 5 delves into input and output equipment.

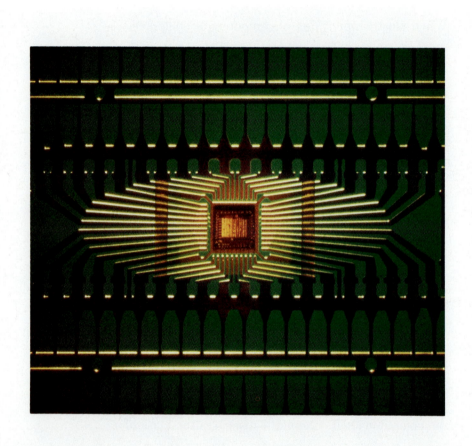

THE CENTRAL PROCESSING UNIT AND MEMORY

3

How sophisticated can a fingernail-sized CPU chip be? Very, as you'll learn in Chapter 3. Hard as it is to believe, the most powerful CPU chips made today contain millions of microscopic circuits and are capable of executing over 100 million instructions every second.

LEARNING OBJECTIVES

After completing this chapter, you will be able to:

1. Describe how the CPU and its memory process instructions and data.

2. Identify several binary-based codes used in a computing environment.

3. Explain the function of the various pieces of hardware commonly found under the cover of the system unit.

4. Name several strategies for making computers speedier.

Overview

So far we've considered the system unit, which houses the CPU and its memory, to be a mysterious "black box." In this chapter, we'll demystify that notion by flipping the lid off the box and closely examining the functions of the parts inside. In doing so, we'll try to get a feel for how the CPU, memory, and other devices commonly found in the system unit work together.

To start, we'll examine how a CPU is organized and how it interacts with memory to carry out processing tasks. Next, we'll discuss how data and programs must be represented in the computer system. Here we'll talk about the codes developed for translating back and forth from symbols the CPU can understand to symbols people find meaningful. These topics lead us into a discussion of how the CPU and its memory are packaged with other computing and storage devices inside the system unit. Finally, we look at strategies used to speed up the work of the CPU.

Since the first, room-sized electronic computers were sold to businesses almost 50 years ago, computers have been getting cheaper, faster, smaller (see User Solution 3-1), and able to support more storage. If the cost of other things had decreased as fast as that of computers has, you'd be able to pay for both an around-the-world trip and a Rolls Royce with a $5 bill . . . and receive change!

FIGURE 3-1

The CPU and its memory. Memory temporarily stores the program on which the computer is currently working, as well as input data, intermediate computations, and output. Each location in memory has an address, and often a single address can store a single character. Although only 20 locations are shown, memories typically contain from a few thousand addresses to several billion. All "figuring" done by the computer is accomplished in the arithmetic/logic unit (ALU). Data are transferred between memory and the ALU under supervision of the control unit.

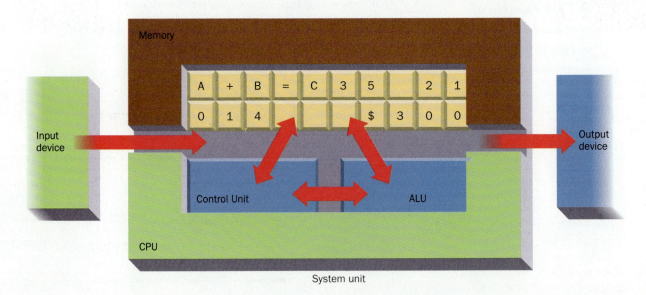

U s e r   S o l u t i o n   3 - 1

Honey, Phone Home

One of the worst fears of any parent is losing a child in a playground or shopping center. Now, a tiny technology product called Phone Home has taken a step toward preventing such a scenario. The device is about the size of a deck of cards and has a special chip that contains a phone number and the ability to dial it. In other words, a memory and processor. A lost child, or any other user, has only to hold the device to a phone mouthpiece and press its "smart button." Phone Home will automatically call the preset number, collect. If the caller is too young to understand or follow detailed directions, the recipient of the call can ask the operator for the phone number and have the police track down the location.

How the CPU Works

Every CPU is basically a collection of electronic circuits. Electronic impulses enter the CPU from an input device. Within the CPU, these impulses are sent under program control through circuits to create a series of new impulses. Eventually a set of impulses leaves the CPU, headed for an output device. What happens in those circuits? To begin to understand this process, we need to know first how the CPU is organized—what its part are—and then how electronic impulses move from one part to another to process data.

The CPU and Its Memory

The CPU works closely with its memory to carry out processing inside the system unit. This relationship is described in the next sections and illustrated in Figure 3-1.

The CPU   The CPU has two principal sections: an arithmetic/logic unit and a control unit.

The **arithmetic/logic unit (ALU)** is the section of the CPU that performs arithmetic and logical operations on data. In other words, it is the part of the computer that does the computing. *Arithmetic* operations include tasks such as addition, subtraction, multiplication, and division. *Logical* operations involve comparing two items of data to determine whether they are equal and, if not, which is larger. As we'll see, all data coming into the CPU, including nonnumeric data such as letters of the alphabet, are coded in digital (numeric) form. As a result, the ALU can perform logical operations on letters and words as well as on numbers.

Arithmetic/logic unit (ALU).
The part of the computer that contains the circuitry to perform arithmetic and logical operations.

The basic arithmetic and logical operations just described are the only ones the computer can perform. That might not seem very impressive. But when combined in various ways at great speeds, these operations enable the computer to perform immensely complex and data-intensive tasks.

The **control unit** is the section of the CPU that directs the flow of electronic traffic between memory and the ALU and between the CPU and input and output devices. In other words, it is the mechanism that coordinates or manages the computer's operation.

Control unit.
The part of the CPU that co-ordinates the operation of the computer.

Memory Memory—also called **primary (internal) storage**—holds the following:

■ The programs and data that have been passed to the computer for processing
■ Intermediate processing results
■ Output that is ready to be transmitted to secondary storage or to an output device

Memory.
The section of the computer system that holds data and program instructions awaiting processing, intermediate results, and processed output. Also called **internal (primary) storage.**

Once programs, data, intermediate results, and output are stored in memory, the CPU must be able to find them again. Thus, each location in memory has an *address.* In many computer systems, a table is automatically set up and maintained that provides the address where the first character of each stored program or data block can be found. Whenever a block of data, an instruction, a program, or the result of a calculation is stored in memory, it is assigned an address so that the CPU can find it again when it is needed.

The size of memory varies among computer systems. The smallest computers can accomodate a memory of only a few thousand characters and the largest a few billion. Because memory is relatively expensive, it is usually limited in size and used only temporarily. Once the computer has finished processing one program and set of data, another program and data set are written over them in the storage space they occupy. Thus, the contents of each storage location are constantly changing. The address of each location, however, never changes. This process can be compared with what happens to the mailboxes in a post office: The number on each box remains the same, but the contents change as patrons remove their mail and new mail arrives.

Sometimes the term *main memory* is used to distinguish conventional memory from products that merely have memory characteristics—such as *read-only memory (ROM)*, covered later in the chapter, and flash memory. *Flash memory*, discussed in Feature 3-1, is a recent development that combines the advantages of main memory and disk in a single product (see Feature 3-1).

Registers

To enhance the computer's performance, the control unit and ALU contain special storage locations that act as high-speed staging areas. These areas are called **registers.** Since registers are actually a part of the CPU, their contents can be handled much more rapidly than can those of memory. Program instructions and data are normally loaded (that is, staged) into the registers from memory just before processing. Registers play a crucial role in making computer speeds extremely fast.

Register.
A high-speed staging area within the computer that temporarily stores data during processing.

F e a t u r e   3 – 1

Flash Memory

A new storage solution for PCs

Memory has some hefty advantages over disks. Data can be written and retrieved more quickly. And unlike spinning disks—with their comparatively bulky and power-comsumptive disk units—memory contains no moving parts, is extremely lightweight and compact, and has low power requirements.

But one of the major problems with conventional memory is that it loses its contents when the computer is shut off. That's where *flash memory*—a new type of solid-state, credit-card-sized brand of memory technology—comes in handy.

Flash memory is packaged in cartridges that you insert into a computer system just as you would insert a diskette. A cartridge may hold 20 or 40 million characters or more of data, giving it the capacity of a low-end hard disk. But unlike conventional memory, data held in flash memory are retained when power is zapped. This property makes it an ideal storage medium for notebook and hand-held computers and in situations for which disk technology is too fragile—such as use in cars and out in the field. Flash memory is also expected to see widespread use in laser printers, photocopiers, and fax machines.

But along with its advantages, flash memory still has a couple of drawbacks, the most im-

Flash memory. Hard-disk capacity in a removable, solid-state cartridge.

portant of which is cost. Although prices are dropping rapidly, flash memory is roughly two or three times the cost of a hard disk, per character stored. Other disadvantages include its lower capacity and limited software support.

Nonetheless, many industry observers feel that the trend toward flash memory is unstoppable. It is likely we'll be seeing a lot of this product by the end of this decade.

Registers are available in several types, including the following:

■ **INSTRUCTION REGISTER AND ADDRESS REGISTER** Before each instruction in a program is processed, the control unit breaks it into two parts. The part that indicates what the ALU is to do next (for example, add, multiply, compare) is placed in the **instruction register.** The part that gives the address of the data to be used in the operation is placed in the **address register.**

■ **STORAGE REGISTER** The **storage register** temporarily stores data that have been retrieved from memory prior to processing.

■ **ACCUMULATOR** The **accumulator** temporarily stores the results of ongoing arithmetic and logic operations.

Instruction register.
The register that holds the part of the instruction indicating what the computer is to do next.

Address register.
A register containing the memory location of data to be used.

Storage register.
A register that, prior to processing, temporarily stores data that have been retrieved from memory.

Accumulator.
A register that stores the result of an arithmetic or logical operation.

Microcode.
Instructions that are built into the CPU to control the operation of its circuitry.

System clock.
The timing mechanism within the computer system that governs the transmission of instructions and data through the circuitry.

Machine cycle.
The series of operations involved in the execution of a single machine-level instruction.

I-cycle.
The part of the machine cycle in which the control unit fetches an instruction from memory and prepares it for subsequent processing.

E-cycle.
The part of the machine cycle in which data are located, an instruction is executed, and results are stored.

Millisecond.
One thousandth of a second.

Microsecond.
One millionth of a second.

The instruction and address registers are often located in the control unit, whereas the storage register and accumulator are frequently found in the ALU.

Machine Cycles

Now that we've described the CPU, memory, and registers, let's see how these elements work together to process an instruction.

Every instruction that you issue to the computer, whether it is in the form of a command that you type or an icon that you point to with a mouse, is broken down by your computer system into several smaller machine-level instructions called **microcode.** Each piece of microcode corresponds directly to a set of the computer's circuits.

The computer system has a built-in **system clock** that synchronizes its operations, just as a metronome can synchronize work for an orchestra. During each clock tick, a single piece of microcode can be executed, a single piece of data can be moved from one part of the computer system to another, and so on. Microcode instructions are coded in *machine language*, which will be covered later in the chapter.

The processing of a single, machine-level instruction is called a **machine cycle.** A machine cycle has two parts: an *instruction* cycle (I-cycle) and an *execution* cycle (E-cycle). During the **I-cycle,** the control unit fetches a program instruction from memory and prepares for subsequent processing. During the **E-cycle,** the data are located and the instruction is executed. Let's see how this works in a little more detail, using simple addition as an example.

I-cycle

1. The control unit fetches from memory the next instruction to be executed.
2. The control unit decodes the instruction.
3. The control unit puts the part of the instruction that shows what to do into the instruction register.
4. The control unit puts the part of the instruction that shows where the associated data are located into the address register.

E-cycle

5. Using the information in the address register, the control unit retrieves data from memory and places them into the storage register.
6. Using the information in the instruction register, the control unit commands the ALU to perform the required operation.
7. The ALU performs the specified operation, adding together the values found in the storage register and in the accumulator.
8. The result of the operation is placed back into the accumulator, destroying the value that was there previously.

Figure 3-2 depicts how the machine cycle works.

All this may seem like an extremely tedious process, especially when a computer must go through thousands, millions, or even billions of machine cycles to process a single program fully. But computers are *very* fast. In the slowest of them, cycle times are measured in **milliseconds** (thousandths of a second). In others, they are measured in **microseconds** (millionths of a second).

The machine cycle. Each command that you give to the computer system must be broken down into several machine instructions, or cycles.

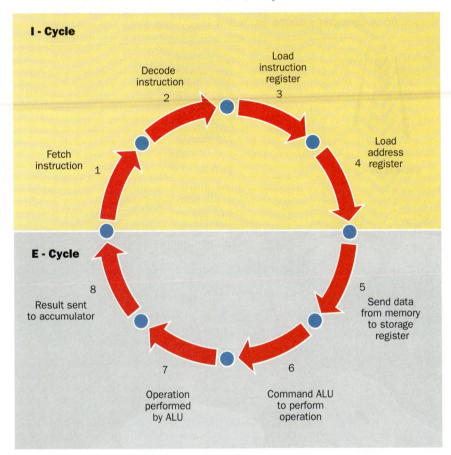

I - Cycle

Decode instruction
2

Load instruction register
3

Fetch instruction
1

Load address register
4

E - Cycle

Result sent to accumulator
8

Send data from memory to storage register
5

Operation performed by ALU
7

Command ALU to perform operation
6

In the fastest computers, they are measured in **nanoseconds** (billionths of a second) or in **picoseconds** (trillionths of a second).

Different terms are used to rate speeds in different types of computers. In the microcomputer world, speeds are rated in *megahertz (MHz)*. Each MHz represents a million clock ticks per second. While the original PC ran at 4.77 MHz, today's desktop microcomputers often push 50 MHz or more. In the mainframe world, speeds are rated in *mips* (each mips represents a million instructions per second); in the supercomputer world, it's *mflops* (each mflops represents a million floating-point operations per second).

Data and Program Representation

The electronic components of most computer systems work in two states. For example, a circuit is either open or closed; a magnetic spot is either present or absent; and so on. This two-state, or **binary,** nature of electronics is illustrated

Nanosecond.
One billionth of a second.

Picosecond.
One trillionth of a second.

Binary.
The number system with two possible states.

FIGURE 3-3

The binary nature of electronics. Circuits are either open or closed, a current runs one way or the opposite way, a charge is either present or absent, and so forth. The two possible states of an electronic component are referred to as *bits* and are represented by computer systems as 0s and 1s.

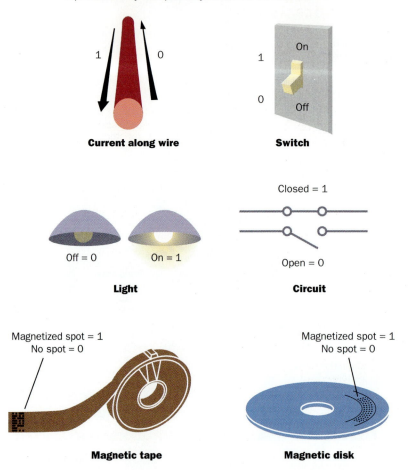

Bit.
A binary digit, such as 0 or 1.

in Figure 3-3. It is convenient to think of these binary states as the *0-state* and the *1-state*. Computer people refer to such zeros and ones as **bits,** which is a contraction of the words *BInary digiTS*. Being primarily electronic, computers do all their processing and communicating by representing programs and data in bit form. Binary, then, is the symbol set that forms the computer's "native tongue."

People, of course, don't speak binary. You're not likely to go up to a friend and say,

"0100100001001001"

which in one binary-based coding system translates as "HI." People communicate with one another in *natural languages,* such as English, Chinese, and Spanish. In our part of the world, we speak mostly English. Also, we write with a 26-character alphabet, and we use a number system with 10 rather than just 2 digits. Computers, however, understand only 0 and 1. So in order for us to interact with a computer, our messages to it must be translated into binary form and its messages to us must be translated from binary into a natural language.

The languages most people use to interact with computer systems consist of a wide variety of natural-language symbols. When we type a message such as

DISPLAY NAMES

at a keyboard, the computer system must translate all the natural-language symbols in the message into 0s and 1s. After processing is finished, the computer system must translate the 0s and 1s it has used to represent the program's results into natural language. This conversion process is illustrated in Figure 3-4. (If, incidentally, a mouse rather than a keyboard is being used for input, the conversion process remains unchanged. That is, any selections made by the user are automatically translated into 0s and 1s by the computer system.)

FIGURE 3 – 4

Conversion to and from binary-based form. (1) The user types in a message in natural-language symbols. (2) The computer system translates the message into binary-based form (this conversion often takes place in the input device). (3) The CPU does all the required processing in binary-based form. (4) The computer system translates the output back into natural-language symbols (this conversion usually takes place in the output device). (5) The user is able to read the output.

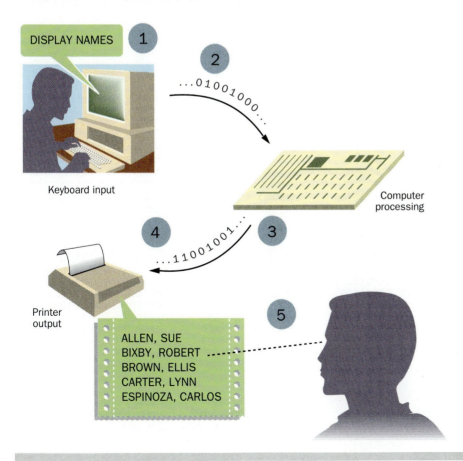

Computer systems use a variety of binary-based codes to represent programs and data. For example, when data and programs are being sent to or from the CPU (steps 2 and 4 in Figure 3-4), a fixed-length, binary-based code such as ASCII or EBCDIC is often used to represent each character transmitted. We will cover these two codes shortly.

Once data and programs are inside the CPU (step 3 of Figure 3-4), other types of binary-based codes typically handle them. For example, when a program is about to be executed, it is represented by a binary code known as machine language. Data, in contrast, may be represented by several different binary-based codes when being manipulated by the computer. One such code, which everyone learning how computers store numbers should know, is *true binary representation*. This code, as well as some fundamentals of number systems, is covered in Appendix A.

ASCII.
A fixed-length, binary-based code widely used to represent data for processing and communications.

EBCDIC.
A fixed-length, binary-based code widely used to represent data on IBM mainframes.

ASCII and EBCDIC

As mentioned earlier, when data or programs are being sent between the computer and its peripheral equipment, a *fixed-length*, binary-based code is commonly used. With a fixed-length code, the machines that are in communication can easily tell where one character ends and another begins. Such codes can be used to represent digits, alphabet characters, and other symbols.

Among the most popular of these codes are **ASCII** (American Standard Code for Information Interchange) and **EBCDIC** (Extended Binary-Coded Decimal

---

FIGURE 3 – 5

ASCII and EBCDIC. These two common fixed-length codes represent characters as unique strings of bits.

Character	Standard ASCII-8 Bit Representation	EBCDIC Bit Representation	Character	Standard ASCII-8 Bit Representation	EBCDIC Bit Representation
0	00110000	11110000	I	01001001	11001001
1	00110001	11110001	J	01001010	11010001
2	00110010	11110010	K	01001011	11010010
3	00110011	11110011	L	01001100	11010011
4	00110100	11110100	M	01001101	11010100
5	00110101	11110101	N	01001110	11010101
6	00110110	11110110	O	01001111	11010110
7	00110111	11110111	P	01010000	11010111
8	00111000	11111000	Q	01010001	11011000
9	00111001	11111001	R	01010010	11011001
A	01000001	11000001	S	01010011	11100010
B	01000010	11000010	T	01010100	11100011
C	01000011	11000011	U	01010101	11100100
D	01000100	11000100	V	01010110	11100101
E	01000101	11000101	W	01010111	11100110
F	01000110	11000110	X	01011000	11100111
G	01000111	11000111	Y	01011001	11101000
H	01001000	11001000	Z	01011010	11101001

Interchange Code). ASCII, developed largely through the efforts of the American National Standards Institute, is used on virtually all microcomputers. It is also widely adopted as the standard for data communications systems. EBCDIC, developed by IBM, is used primarily on IBM mainframes.

Both ASCII and EBCDIC represent each printable character as a unique combination of a fixed number of bits (see Figure 3-5). EBCDIC uses 8 bits to represent a character. A group of 8 bits has 256 (2^8) different combinations; therefore, EBCDIC can represent up to 256 characters. This is more than enough to account for the 26 uppercase and 26 lowercase characters, the 10 decimal digits, and several special characters.

ASCII originally was designed as a 7-bit code that could represent 128 (2^7) characters. Several 8-bit versions of ASCII (called ASCII-8 codes) have also been developed because computers are designed to handle data in chunks of 8 bits. Many computer systems can accept data in either coding system—ASCII or EBCDIC—and perform the conversion to their native code. The 8 (7) bits used to represent a character in ASCII or EBCDIC are collectively referred to as a *byte*.

A **byte** represents a single character of data. For this reason, many computer manufacturers use the byte measure to define their machines' storage capacity. As you may have noticed, computer advertisements are filled with references to kilobytes, megabytes, gigabytes, and terabytes. One **kilobyte** (**K-byte** or **KB**) is equal to a little over 1,000 bytes (1,024, to be precise), one **megabyte** (**M-byte** or **MB**) equals about 1 million bytes, one **gigabyte** (**G-byte** or **GB**) equals about 1 billion bytes, and one **terabyte** (**T-byte** or **TB**) equals about 1 trillion bytes.

The conversion from natural-language words and numbers to their ASCII (or EBCDIC) equivalents and back again usually takes place on an input/output device. For example, when a user types in a message such as

RUN

at a keyboard, an encoder chip inside the keyboard usually translates it into ASCII and sends it as a series of bytes to the CPU. The output that the CPU sends back to the display or to some other output device is also in ASCII, which the output device—with the aid of another encoder chip—translates into understandable words and numbers. Therefore, if the CPU sent the ASCII message

0100100001001001

to your display device, the word 'HI" would appear on your screen.

Computers usually handle data in byte multiples. For instance, a 16-bit computer is built to process data in chunks of two bytes; a (faster) 32-bit computer processes data in chunks of four bytes. These byte multiples are commonly called *words*. We'll look at words in more detail later in the chapter.

The Parity Bit   Suppose you are at a keyboard and press the *B* key. If the keyboard encoder supports ASCII coding, it will transmit the byte "01000010" to the CPU. Sometimes, however, something happens during transmission and the CPU receives a garbled message. Interference on the line, for example,

Byte.
A configuration of seven or eight bits used to represent a single character of data.

Kilobyte (K-byte or **KB).**
Approximately 1,000 (1,024, to be exact) bytes.

Megabyte (M-byte or **MB).**
Approximately 1 million bytes.

Gigabyte (G-byte or **GB).**
Approximately 1 billion bytes.

Terabyte (T-byte or **TB).**
Approximately 1 trillion bytes.

FIGURE   3 – 6

The parity bit. If the system used supports even parity, as shown here, the 1-bits in every byte must always add up to an even number. The parity bit is set to either 0 or 1 in each byte to force an even number of 1-bits in the byte.

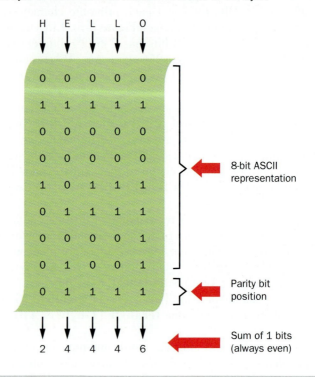

8-bit ASCII representation

Parity bit position

Sum of 1 bits (always even)

Parity bit.
An extra bit added to the byte representation of a character to ensure that there is always either an odd or an even number of 1-bits transmitted with every character.

might cause the sixth bit to change from 0 to 1 so that the CPU receives the message "01000110." Unless the CPU had some way of knowing that a mistake was made, it would wrongly interpret this byte as the letter *F*.

To enable the CPU to detect such transmission errors, EBCDIC and ASCII have an additional bit position. This bit, called the **parity bit,** is automatically set to either 0 or 1 to make all the bits in a byte add up to either an even or an odd number. Computer systems support either an even or an odd parity. In *odd-parity* systems, the parity bit makes all the 1-bits in a byte add up to an odd number. In *even-parity* systems, it makes them add up to an even number. Figure 3-6 shows how the parity bit works for the ASCII representation of the word "HELLO" on an even-parity system.

The parity bit is automatically generated by the keyboard's processor. Thus, if you typed the *B* character on an even-parity system, "010000100" would be sent up the line to the CPU. If the message were garbled so that the even-parity computer received "010001100" (an odd number of 1-bits), the CPU would sense the error immediately.

The parity check is not foolproof. For example, if two bits are incorrectly transmitted in a byte, they will self-cancel. A two-bit error, however, will rarely occur.

Machine Language

Before any program instruction can be executed by your computer, it must be converted into a binary-based code known as **machine language.** An example of a typical machine-language instruction appears below:

010110000111000000000000010000000010

A machine-language instruction may look like a meaningless string of 0s and 1s, but it actually consists of groups of bits that represent specific storage locations and operations. The instruction shown here for an IBM mainframe, for instance, transfers data between two specific memory locations.

In the earliest computers, including even the first microcomputers, all programs were written in machine language. Today, although it is still possible to write in machine language, hardly anybody does. Instead, most people rely on *language translators,* special systems programs that convert instructions automatically into machine language. The translation is so transparent that most users aren't even aware that it is taking place.

Each computer has its own machine language. A code used on an IBM PS/2 computer will be totally foreign to an Apple Macintosh. Incidentally, this is why when you buy a program package, such as a word processor or spreadsheet, you must get the version intended for your specific type of computer system. You don't want the program package translating all of your commands to Macintosh machine language if you have an IBM PS/2 computer that understands only PS/2 machine language.

Machine language.
A binary-based programming language that the computer can execute directly.

The System Unit

Now that we've talked conceptually about how the CPU and memory work, let's consider how they're realized in hardware and how they relate to other devices inside a system unit of, say, a typical microcomputer.

Almost all computers sold today use a modular hardware approach; for example, related circuitry is etched onto memory or processor chips, the chips are mounted onto carrier packages that are plugged into boards, and the boards are fitted into slots inside the system unit.

The **system unit** often consists of at least one CPU chip, specialized processor chips, memory (RAM and ROM) chips, boards on which these and other chips are mounted, ports that provide connections for external devices, a power supply, and internal circuitry to hook everything together (see Figure 3-7). Here we'll be discussing these devices. System units also often have built-in diskette and hard-disk units and sometimes even a tape drive. Disks and tapes will be covered in detail in Chapter 4.

System unit.
The hardware unit that houses the computer and its memory, as well as a number of other devices.

CPU Chip

Every microcomputer system unit contains a specific microprocessor chip as its CPU. This chip is put into a carrier package, as shown in Figure 3-8, and the carrier package is mounted onto a special board—called the **system board,**

System board.
A board that contains the computer.

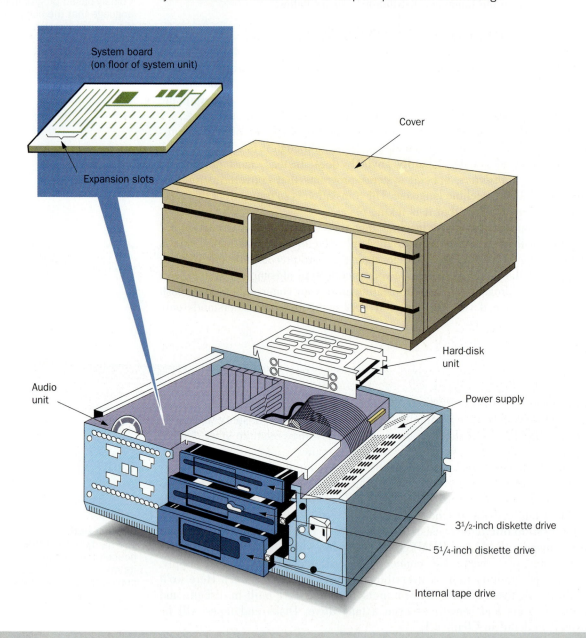

FIGURE 3-7

The inside of a system unit. With the cover of the system unit removed, you can see the parts inside. Generally, the system board is located on the floor. Most system units also contain a fan to keep the parts from overheating.

System board
(on floor of system unit)

Expansion slots

Cover

Hard-disk unit

Audio unit

Power supply

3½-inch diskette drive

5¼-inch diskette drive

Internal tape drive

or *motherboard*—that fits inside the system unit (see Figure 3-9). This board is located on the floor of the system unit shown in Figure 3-7.

Most microcomputer systems made today use CPU chips that are manufactured by either Intel or Motorola. The Intel line of chips—such as the 8086; 8088, 80286, 80386, 80486, and Pentium chip—is used on the microcomputer

FIGURE 3-8

CPU chip. (left) A chip itself, alongside a ruler. (right) The Intel Pentium chip mounted in a carrier package, which is plugged into a system board. The Pentium chip packs over three million circuits into a fingernail-sized area.

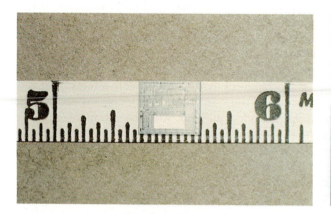

FIGURE 3-9

System board. The system board contains the CPU chip, RAM, ROM, and circuitry for a number of other functions.

systems made by IBM as well as by Compaq, Dell, Tandy, and scores of other companies that make "IBM-compatible" microcomputer systems. Many Intel chips are commonly referred to by their last three digits—for example, a '486 refers to an 80486 chip. Sometimes the chip numbers come with special suffixes—for instance, "DX" (or no suffix) is the standard chip, whereas "DXZ" is a twice-as-fast version of the chip, "SX" is an economy version, and "SL" is a low-power-consumptive version. The Motorola line of chips—including the 68000, 68020, 68030, and 68040—is used primarily on the Apple Macintosh line of computers.

The type of CPU chip in a computer's system unit greatly affects what you can do with the computer system. Software is written to work on a specific chip, and a program that works on one chip may not function on another unless modified. For instance, software is not very portable between Intel and Motorola chips, as these chips employ a somewhat dissimilar design philosophy. Also, a program designed for an Intel 80486 chip may not work on the earlier 80286 chip, which is less capable. And, even though a program designed for an 80286 chip may work on an 80486 chip, some of the 80486's power will be wasted.

CPU chips differ in many respects, one of the most important of which is word size. A computer **word** is a group of bits or bytes that may be manipulated and stored as a unit. It is a critical concept, because the internal circuitry of virtually every computer system is designed around a certain word size. The Apple Macintosh Quadra series and IBM PS/2 95 computers, for example, use the Motorola 68040 and Intel 80486 chips, respectively. Both the 68040 and 80486 chips have a 32-bit-word internal architecture, which means that data are transferred within each CPU chip itself in 32-bit chunks. Both chips also have a 32-bit-word I/O bus, meaning that there is a 32-bit-wide data path from each CPU to external devices. Often, the greater the word size, the faster the computer system.

Specialized Processor Chips

Working alongside the CPU chip in many system units are *specialized processor chips,* such as numeric coprocessors and graphic coprocessors. The role of these "slave chips" is to perform specialized tasks for the CPU, thereby enhancing overall system performance. For instance, a *numeric (math) coprocessor* chip helps the CPU perform arithmetic; a *graphic coprocessor* chip helps the CPU with the computationally intensive chore of creating complex screen displays. It is not unusual to boost the speed of a computer system several times over by using specialized chips such as these.

RAM

RAM (for **random access memory**)—the computer system's *main memory*—is used to store the programs and data on which the computer is currently working. Like the microprocessor, the RAM of a microcomputer system consists of circuits etched onto silicon-backed chips. These chips are mounted onto carrier packages, just as the CPU is, and the packages are plugged into the system board. Most desktop microcomputer systems in use today have enough RAM to store 256 thousand to several billion bytes of data. Many computer systems allow memory expansion (within limits) directly on the system board or through an add-in board (which we will discuss shortly) when RAM is

Word.
A group of bits or characters that are treated by the computer system as a unit.

Random access memory (RAM).
The computer system's main memory.

insufficient. RAM is *volatile,* meaning that the contents of memory are lost when the computer is shut off.

ROM

ROM, which stands for **read-only memory,** consists of nonerasable hardware modules that contain programs. Like RAM, these software-in-hardware modules are mounted into carrier packages that, in turn, are plugged into one or more boards inside the system unit. You can neither write over these ROM programs (that's why they're called read-only) nor destroy their contents when you shut off the computer's power (that is, they're nonvolatile). A program stored in ROM can be fetched more quickly by the CPU than if it were stored on disk, where it would have to be loaded into memory before the computer could work on it. Key pieces of systems software are often stored in ROM.

ROM is an example of **firmware,** software-in-hardware modules that are available in several other forms. For instance, *programmable read-only memory (PROM)* is identical to ROM except that the module is blank and the buyer writes the program. Special equipment is needed to write a program onto a PROM module, and once the program is on, it can't be erased. *Erasable programmable read-only memory (EPROM),* on the other hand, is like PROM except that its contents can be erased and a new program written. Firmware is usually supplied when a computer system is purchased, but it can also be bought separately.

Add-in Boards

Many microcomputer-system vendors enable you to customize your system by choosing your own **add-in boards.** These boards are cardlike pieces of hardware that contain the circuitry for performing one or more specific functions. They plug into *expansion slots* within the computer's system unit (refer back to Figure 3-7), thereby enabling you to either interface with specific types of peripheral devices or add new capabilities. For example, if you want a certain model of display unit attached to your computer, you may need a special *display adapter board* that contains the proper software routine for establishing the connection. Similarly, you can get your computer system to communicate with fascimile (fax) machines by getting a *fax board.*

Many types of add-in boards currently are available in the markeplace. Most of these boards provide either a basic function that is unavailable with the system unit or a "value-added" capability that enhances an existing function. With new machines and new capabilities being announced regularly, the number of types of add-in boards is increasing rapidly. Figure 3-10 lists several types of these boards and the functions they perform.

Ports

Most system units contain built-in sockets that enable you to plug in external hardware devices. These sockets, which often are found on the exterior of the system unit, are known as **ports.** Printers, for instance, generally hook up to microcomputers through either *parallel* ports or *serial* ports. IBM microcomputers and similar devices typically connect printers with parallel ports, whereas Apple

Read-only memory (ROM).
A software-in-hardware module that can be read but not written on.

Firmware.
Software instructions that are written onto a hardware module.

Add-in-board.
A board that may be inserted into the computer's system unit to perform one or more functions.

Port.
An outlet on the computer's system unit through which a peripheral device may communicate.

T O M O R R O W

The Coming Chip Technologies

What Will Be the Next Major Challenger to Silicon?

Since the beginning of modern computing, researchers have constantly searched for new types of circuit technologies to hold data and to manipulate them faster. The earliest computers used hardware such as vacuum tubes, magnetic drums, and core planes as their principal circuit components. In the 1970s, when it was possible to etch circuitry into an area the size of the head of a pin, another major medium evolved: silicon-backed chips. Silicon became popular because it is an unusually pure substance and will not interfere with the metal circuitry etched onto its surface.

Today, although it is possible to place more than a million microminiaturized circuit elements onto a silicon chip, that may not be enough. So researchers are pressing forward with other approaches. Five of the leading challengers to silicon are the following:

Gallium Arsenide Probably the most promising new computer chip technology involves gallium arsenide (GaAs). GaAs chips are superior

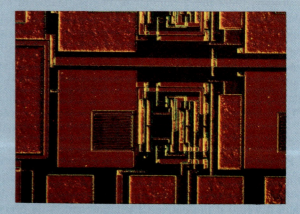

GaAs chip. Enough power to transmit 40 encyclopedia volumes every second.

to those made of silicon because:

- They move electronic impulses around several times faster (see photo).

- They enable optical transmission, something silicon can't do.

- They can operate at much higher temperatures and emit less heat, enabling circuits to be packed closer together.

Gallium arsenide products are already moving into the marketplace. Some of the more critical components of large computers now consist of GaAs chips, and GaAs is rapidly taking hold in areas such as high-speed communications.

Making Computers Speedier

Over the years, a number of strategies have been used to make computers faster. Four of these are moving circuits closer together, finding new materials with which to make computers, developing reduced instruction set computers (RISC), and using parallel processing.

Moving Circuits Closer Together As complex as computers seem sometimes, all must follow one intuitive natural law: the shorter the length of the circuit paths, the shorter the time it takes to move programs and data along them. During the last several decades, computer manufacturers have been able to pack circuitry ever closer together. Today, it is now possible to fit more than a million circuits on a single fingernail-sized chip.

Unfortunately, when the circuits are in use, they generate heat. And, when circuits are placed too close together, they melt. To circumvent this problem,

But gallium arsenide has some drawbacks. GaAs chips are still often several times more expensive than those made of silicon. And because the newer technology is still in its infancy, GaAs designers can currently squeeze far fewer circuits onto a single chip.

Superconductors One of the problems with conventional circuitry is that it heats up. When circuits get hot, their electrical resistance increases, impeding the flow of message-bearing electrons. If circuits are placed too close together, they can melt. Superconductive materials are those that can transfer electrons without the worry of electrical resistance or heat buildup.

Every year new materials are being discovered that more closely approach the ideal of superconductivity. While most of the superconductors of today must be cooled in order to lose resistance and avoid a meltdown, the search continues for materials that are superconductive at room temperature. If and when naturally superconductive materials emerge from the laboratories and are successfully implemented in products, they may result in circuitry that's 100 times faster than today's silicon-backed chips.

Optical Processing Optical processing uses light waves to do the work of the silicon-backed chip's electrons. Optical chips currently available in the marketplace can move data around about ten times faster than silicon-backed chips. Theo-retically, an optical processor would be capable of speeds hundreds of times faster than silicon—if data could be gotten into and out of it fast enough. Optical chips are today surfacing in such applications as collision-avoidance systems for cars, artificial vision systems for robots, and sensors for image processing.

Biotechnology Biotechnology offers yet another compelling alternative to today's silicon chip. Scientists have shown that tiny molecules can be grown and shaped to act as circuits. With such a technology, electrons are passed from molecule to molecule. Some scientists believe that if such a technology is ever perfected, it could possibly result in circuits 500 times smaller than those on today's silicon chips.

Tubes on a Chip Just when everyone thought that it was dead and buried, vacuum electronics—popular in the 1940s and 1950s—is making a comeback. Scientists are now talking about the very real possibility of putting up to ten billion microscopic tubes on a five-inch wafer. Why vacuum tubes? Electrons can travel much faster when placed in a vacuum. Unlike their predecessors, which needed heat to work, these new tubes work by an entirely different set of principles. Some researchers believe that tubes on a chip are capable of packing 1,000 times the power of today's silicon chips.

researchers have used such strategies as immersing circuits in helium "baths" to cool them. Helium baths are found in some supercomputers.

New Materials Most CPU chips today consist of metallic circuitry that is etched onto a silicon backing. Silicon-backed chips have been popular since the 1970s, when manufacturing technqiues to microminiaturize circuitry became widely available.

Today, because limits are quickly being reached on the number of circuits that can be packed onto a chip without heat damage, several other alternatives are getting considerable attention. Among these are gallium arsenide chips, superconductors, optical processing, biotechnology, and vacuum electronics (see the Tomorrow box).

Reduced Instruction Set Computers (RISC) To process data effectively, computers must be equipped with a variety of instructions, called the computer's *instruction set.* Each instruction in the set corresponds to a microcode instruction.

Studies have shown that computers are actually faster if they are given only a fraction of the instructions with which computers have traditonally been provided. (The old adage "too many cooks spoil the broth" applies in the world of computers, too.) The instructions that the computer doesn't need just get in the way of efficient and speedy processing.

In the mid-1970s, CPUs with limited instruction sets became available. These machines have aptly been named **reduced instruction set computers (RISC).** In certain test studies, RISC-based computers have been shown to be several times faster than conventional computers with larger instruction sets. Today, RISC devices are rapidly becoming the standard in engineering applications environments and in communications systems. The downside to RISC-based computers is that conventional software needs to be modified to work on them.

Reduced instruction set computing (RISC). A term referring to a computer system that gets by with fewer instructions than conventional computer systems.

Parallel Processing   Despite the astounding evolution of computer systems over the past 50 years, most are still driven by a single CPU. A single CPU can perform instructions only in serial, or one step at a time, whether working exclusively on one program or juggling several concurrently.

In the race to develop ever-faster computer systems for tomorrow, scientists are experimenting with ways to have two or more CPUs and memories perform tasks in parallel. For example, instead of relying on one processor to solve a lengthy calculation, a computer system using **parallel processing** assigns portions of the problem to several CPUs operating simultaneously. But just as it is difficult to coordinate two or more workers who are dedicated to completing a single job, so too is it difficult to integrate the parallel efforts of several processors working together at superhuman speeds. Nonetheless, many industry insiders see parallel processing as an unstoppable future reality. As it becomes harder and harder to make computers themselves faster—by, say, packing circuits closer together—parallel processing will become an increasingly important strategy for reducing the time it takes to do work.

Parallel processing. Refers to computing in which two or more CPUs share work and process pieces of this work simultaneously.

Today, several approaches to parallel-processing computer systems are observable in the marketplace. One popular approach is represented by the Cray-2, a supercomputer that carries a price tag of several million dollars. The Cray, like most other supercomputers, employs a common parallel design philosophy—namely, hooking up a small number of expensive, state-of-the-art CPUs. The Cray-2 uses four such processors, which carry out both parallel and serial processing. Another common tack is to design parallel machines with hundreds or thousands of relatively inexpensive, off-the-shelf microprocessors (see Feature 3-2). Although devices built this way are less versatile than conventional supercomputers, they can pack a respectable amount of power at the fraction of the cost.

Summary and Key Terms

In Chapter 3 we flip the lid off of a typical system unit and examine the function of the parts inside.

How the CPU Works   The CPU has two major sections. The **arithmetic/ logic unit (ALU)** performs arithmetic and logical operations on data. The **control unit** directs the flow of electronic traffic between memory and the ALU

F e a t u r e   3 – 2

Massively Parallel Processors

Supercomputing the microcomputing way

Today a lot of researchers are discovering that the best way to build extremely powerful computers is to buy microcomputers—a lot of them—and connect them all together in order to attack work in parallel.

The approach is called *massively parallel processing (MPP)*. Some computer-industry forecasters believe that MPP will eventually become the standard way to do supercomputing. The idea is to coordinate hundreds, thousands, or maybe even tens of thousands of powerful microprocessors into a single unit. Just as a dozen people can polish off a pizza faster than a single person, so, too, is it possible that a machine with scores of processors could knock off a problem faster than could just a single processor.

Not that it will be easy. A major problem is how to get the processors to do work efficiently without wasting a lot of time passing data back and forth between each other. In addition, complicated synchronizing techniques must be established to get the machines to share data. If, say, one processor is supposed to compute a result and supply it to another processor, you don't want the second processor trying to fetch anything from memory before the first processor has put it there. Nor do you want it to have to wait around too long for the first processor to complete its part of the job.

Because of such complexities, software for parallel processing machines has to be specially written. So far, only a narrow class of problems has been identified that can be handily split into independent pieces and run efficiently on a parallel processing machine. But progress is being made, and the rewards are gigantic.

Consider, for instance, modeling the global climate; that is, simulating the long-term effects of pollutants on the ozone layer, global-warming patterns, and acid-rain levels. Today's supercomputers can only accurately forecast about ten

Intel Touchtone Delta MPP Supercomputer. Hundreds of microcomputers under a single roof.

years into the future, which, because pollutants normally take decades to wreck their havoc, is hardly enough. But massively parallel processors may provide the quantum leap in computing power needed to predict environmental conditions a century or more into the future. Because the earth's atmosphere is logically divisible into many pieces, climate modeling falls into the category of problem that MPP handles best.

Massively parallel processors can also help out in the business world. Already, giant retailers such as Wal-Mart, K-Mart, and Mervyn's use MPP machines to identify sales patterns. Such supercomputing makes information on sales trends available within hours, instead of the days it would take a conventional mainframe. In retailing, faster information means staying competitive.

Today, the "holy grail" of MPP is the teraflops computer. Roughly described, the teraflops is a machine that can compute a trillion arithmetic operations per second. How fast is that? It's about 50 times more power than today's faster computer. Or, put another way, in one second a teraflops computer will be able to do a job that it would take a person 32,000 years to complete, working on a hand calculator every single second.

and, also, between the CPU and input and output devices. Both of these units work closely with memory to carry out processing tasks inside the system unit.

Memory—also called **primary (internal) storage**—holds the programs and data that have been passed to the computer, the results of intermediate processing, and output that is ready to be transmitted to secondary storage or an output device.

Registers are high-speed staging areas within the CPU that hold program instructions and data immediately before they are processed. The part of a program instruction that indicates what the ALU is to do next is placed in the **instruction register;** the part showing the address of the data to be used in the operation is placed in the **address register.** Before data are processed, they are taken from memory and placed in the **storage register.** The **accumulator** is a register that temporarily stores the results of ongoing operations.

The processing of a single, machine-level instruction is called a **machine cycle.** Each such instruction is broken down further into subinstructions called **microcode,** and each piece of microcode corresponds directly to a set of the computer's circuits. The computer system has a built-in **system clock** that synchronizes the processing of microcode.

A machine cycle has two parts: an **I-cycle** (instruction cycle), in which the control unit fetches and examines an instruction, and an **E-cycle** (execution cycle), in which the instruction is actually executed by the ALU under control unit supervision. A computer may need to go through thousands, millions, or even billions of machine cycles to fully process a single program. Computer cycle times generally are measured in **milliseconds** (thousandths of a second), **microseconds** (millionths of a second), **nanoseconds** (billionths of a second), or **picoseconds** (trillionths of a second).

Data and Program Representation

The electronic components of digital computers work in a two-state, or **binary,** fashion. It is convenient to think of these binary states as the 0-state and the 1-state. Computer people refer to such 0s and 1s as **bits.**

The computer uses several binary-based codes to process data. Two popular codes are **ASCII** and **EBCDIC.** These fixed-length codes can represent any single character of data—a digit, alphabet character, or special symbol—as a string of seven or eight bits. This string of bits is called a **byte.** ASCII and EBCDIC allow for an additional bit position, called a **parity bit,** to enable computer systems to check for transmission errors.

The storage capacity of computers often is expressed in **kilobytes (K-bytes or KB),** or thousands of bytes; **megabytes (M-bytes or MB),** or millions of bytes; **gigabytes (G-bytes or GB),** or billions of bytes; and **terabytes (T-bytes or TB),** or trillions of bytes.

Machine language is the binary-based code used to represent programs. A program must be translated into machine language before the computer can execute it.

The System Unit

Almost all computer systems sold today use a modular hardware approach; that is, related circuitry is etched onto *processor chips* or *memory chips,* the chips are mounted onto carrier packages that are later fitted into boards, and the boards are positioned into slots inside the **system unit.**

Every microcomputer system unit contains a specific microprocessor chip as its CPU. This chip is put into a carrier package that is mounted onto a special board, called the **system board,** that fits inside the system unit. CPU chips differ in many respects; one difference is word size. A computer **word** is a group of bits or bytes that can be manipulated as a unit. Often the larger the word size, the more powerful the processor.

Working alongside the CPU chip in many system units are specialized processor chips, such as *numeric coprocessors* and *graphic coprocessors.*

The regular memory chips on microcomputer systems are commonly referred to as **RAM,** for **random access memory.** Memory chips that contain noneras-able programs are referred to as **ROM,** for **read-only memory.** ROM is an example of **firmware.** Other types of firmware include PROM (programmable read-only memory) and EPROM (erasable programmable read-only memory).

Many system units contain a limited number of internal expansion slots, into which **add-in boards** can be mounted by the user. These boards can be used to customize a computer system by supplying more memory, adding facsimile-machine (fax) capability, and so on. Also, many system units have external I/O **ports** into which peripheral devices may be plugged.

The CPU connects to RAM, ROM, and peripherals (interfaced by add-in boards and ports) through circuitry called an I/O **bus.** Some widely used bus architectures include *Micro Channel Architecture,* used on the high end of the IBM PS/2 line of computers; *NuBus,* used on the recent Apple Macintosh line of computers; *EISA,* used extensively on Compaq computers and those of many other vendors; and *ISA,* which is often used on 16-bit computers.

Making Computers Speedier   Over the years, a number of strategies have been used to make computers faster. Four of these are moving circuits closer together, finding new materials with which to make computers, developing **reduced instruction set computers (RISC),** and using **parallel processing.**

SECONDARY STORAGE

4

Why are hard disks so popular today? Compared with other forms of secondary storage, they are relatively fast and capacious—and reasonably inexpensive per character stored. But as Chapter 4 explains, newer forms of storage are chipping away at the hard disk's dominance.

LEARNING OBJECTIVES

After completing this chapter, you will be able to:

1. Name several general properties of secondary storage systems.

2. Identify a number of disk storage systems as well as describe how they work and where they are particularly useful.

3. Describe the roles of other secondary storage media and equipment.

4. Explain several types of data access and organization strategies, and identify situations in which each is appropriate.

FAVORITES

U s e r   S o l u t i o n   4 – 1

CD-Type Programming for Record Lovers

Problem: You have a large record collection and would like to have the ability to automatically listen to song tracks in any order, as you can on a compact disk (CD). *Solution:* Not to worry. A new high-tech record turntable will let you specify the sequence in which you wish to hear tracks on a particular side of a record. For example, if you want to listen to the third song followed by the fifth song, you just press the "3" button on the front panel, then the "5" button, and then "Play." The turntable, called Song Stalker, works with a laser mechanism in the tone arm that detects the position of an album's song tracks. The device can accommodate up to eight songs' tracks and 15 entries, enabling you to play songs more than once.

item number 988. In this case, you move back and forth randomly through the records to obtain information from this file.

User Solution 4-1 describes how CD-like access is now possible on turntables that play vinyl records.

Magnetic Disk

Magnetic disk.
A secondary storage medium consisting of platters made of rigid metal (hard disk) or flexible plastic (diskette).

Hard disk.
A rigid platter coated with a magnetizable substance.

Diskette.
A small, removable disk made of a tough, flexible plastic and coated with a magnetizable substance.

Today **magnetic disks** are undoubtedly the most widely used secondary storage medium for information processing. Because they allow direct access to data, disks permit much faster retrieval of information than do tapes, and at a reasonable cost as well. Without disk storage, many of the computer applications we see around us would not be possible. Banking with automatic teller machines and making airline reservations are just two of the many activities that depend on the rapid access to data that magnetic disks provide.

Two common types of magnetic disks are hard disks and diskettes. **Hard disks** are round, rigid platters. Because of their large storage capacities and fast data-retrieval capabilities, hard disks are indispensible for most types of commercial applications. Many types of hard-disk systems are in use today; the most common are those that use either a removable-pack or sealed-pack design.

The advantages of hard disks notwithstanding, inexpensive **diskettes,** which are packaged in small plastic cases, are still widely used—because of their low cost and removability—on many microcomputer systems today. Diskettes are ideal for transferring small amounts of data from one system to another and for storing small amounts of backup.

Every disk systems is *addressable.* This means that each data record or program may be stored and later accessed at a unique *disk address,* which can be automatically determined by the computer system. Procedures for locating records on disk are discussed later in the chapter in the section entitled "Data Organization."

In this section, we'll discuss disk systems for small computers first, focusing primarily on diskettes and hard-disk systems and, secondarily, on some alternative products. Next, we'll look at some methods for optimizing disk processing. Finally, we'll turn to disk systems on large computers.

Diskettes

Diskettes, or *floppy disks*, are small, round platters encased in a plastic jacket. The platters are made of a tough Mylar plastic coated with a magnetizable substance. Each side of the diskette contains concentric **tracks,** which are encoded with 0- and 1-bits when data and programs are written to them (see Figure 4-1). The jacket is lined with a soft material that wipes the disk clean as it spins.

Track.
A path on an input/output medium on which data are recorded.

Types of Diskettes   Dozens of types of diskettes are commercially available. If one were to cite a single property that most distinguishes one of these products from another, however, that property would probably be *size*.

Diskettes are widely available in two sizes (diameters)—3½ inches and 5¼ inches—as shown in Figure 4-2. Historically, the 5¼-inch diskettes came along before their 3½-inch counterparts. The 5¼-inch diskettes are encased in flexible, plastic-coated cardboard jackets, whereas the 3½-inch diskettes are contained in rugged plastic cases that can fit into a shirt pocket. Strange as it may seem, 3½-inch diskettes can store more data than 5¼-inch ones.

FIGURE 4 – 1

Surface of a disk. Unlike a phonograph record, which bears a single spiral groove, a disk is composed of concentric tracks. The number of tracks per surface varies among manufacturers. The disk shown here has 80 tracks. Hard disks commonly have hundreds of tracks.

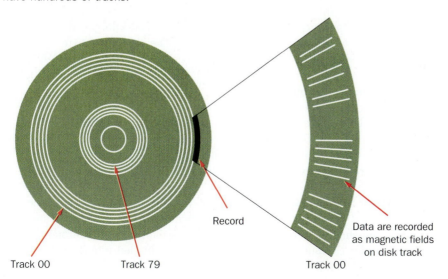

Record

Track 00   Track 79

Track 00

Data are recorded as magnetic fields on disk track

F I G U R E   4 – 2

Diskettes. Despite the fact 3¹/₂-inch diskettes (left) have become today's preferred standard on microcomputer systems, 5¹/₄-inch diskettes (right) continue to enjoy wide use.

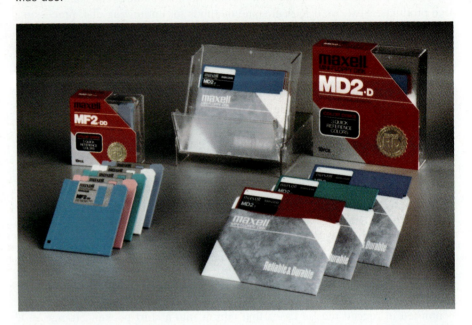

Despite their small size, diskettes can store a respectable amount of data. Common capacities are 360 kilobytes and 1.2 megabytes for 5¹/₄-inch diskettes, and 720 kilobytes, 1.44 megabytes, and 2.88 megabytes for 3¹/₂-inch diskettes. A 360-kilobyte diskette can store over 100 typewritten pages of information; thus, 1.44-megabyte diskettes can store up to 400 pages and 2.88-megabyte diskettes can store up to 800 pages. The 1.2- and 1.44-megabyte diskettes are often called *high-density* diskettes; the 360- and 720-kilobyte diskettes are called *double-density* or *low-density* diskettes. The 2.88-megabyte diskettes, which began being installed on some microcomputer systems in 1992, are sometimes referred to as *extra-density* diskettes. (Density refers to how tightly bits of data are packed on the diskette.)

To protect data, diskettes also contain a write-protect notch or square (see Figure 4-3). This prevents the user from accidentally writing on the disk. Covering the notch on 5¹/₄-inch diskettes makes it impossible to write on the surface. The convention on 3¹/₂-inch diskettes is the opposite: Exposing the notch or square makes writing impossible.

Sector.
An addressable pie-shaped area on a disk.

Sectoring on Diskettes   Computer systems differ in the number of **sectors** into which they divide, or *format*, a disk. Sectors divide a diskette into addressable, pie-shaped pieces. For example, 5¹/₄-inch diskettes formatted with IBM and similar computer systems commonly are divided into 8, 9, 15, 18, or more sectors, depending on the type of diskette and operating system used. Typically there are 512 bytes per sector (see Figure 4-4).

FIGURE 4 – 3

5¼-inch and 3½-inch diskettes compared. (a) In a 5¼-inch diskette, the recording window is always open, meaning that the disk surface is constantly exposed. (b) In a 3½-inch diskette, the recording window exposes the disk surface only when the shutter mechanism is slid to the left, which happens during reading and writing operations. In addition to offering this improved design feature, having a more rugged cover, and being more compact, 3½-inch diskettes can store more data than can 5¼-inch diskettes.

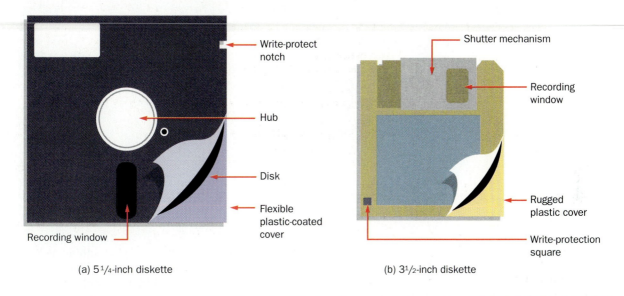

(a) 5¼-inch diskette   (b) 3½-inch diskette

FIGURE 4 – 4

Formatting a diskette. Formatting a diskette enables it to be divided into addressable, pie-shaped sectors. A diskette is not usable until it is formatted.

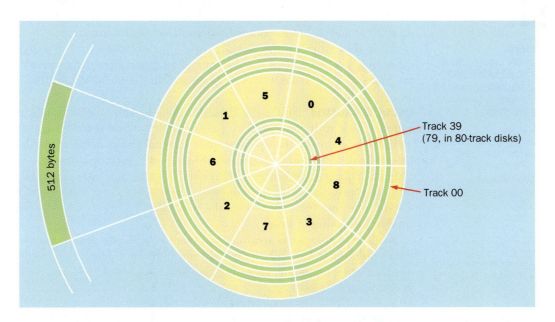

Inserting a diskette into a drive. Diskettes correctly fit into the drive only one way—with the label up and the recording window toward the drive door, as illustrated. Drive doors come in a variety of styles, as shown in Figure 4-6.

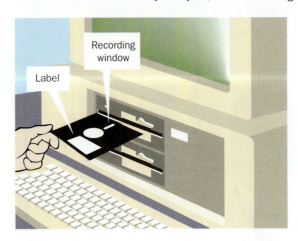

Recording window

Label

Formatting a diskette organizes it into addressable storage locations, as Figure 4-4 illustrates. For instance, let's assume that the diskette in Figure 4-4 has 40 tracks, as do low-density disks used with the IBM PC family and similar machines. Also, let's assume that the computer system divides the diskette into 9 sectors, as shown. Formatting the diskette causes it to be arranged into 9 pie-shaped sectors, 0 through 8. Because the diskette has 40 tracks, this results in $9 \times 40 = 360$ addressable storage locations per side. On many microcomputer systems, a FORMAT command is used to format the diskette, and a diskette is not usable for storage unless it has been formatted.

A **file directory** on the diskette, which the computer system automatically maintains, keeps track of the contents of each location. This directory shows the name of each diskette file, its size, and the sector at which it begins.

Using Diskettes   To use a diskette, the operator inserts it into a device called a **disk unit,** or *disk drive* (see Figures 4-5 and 4-6). When using 5¼-inch diskette drives, the operator must manually shut or latch the drive door before the diskette can be accessed. Drives for 3½-inch diskettes do not contain a manual door mechanism as such; instead, the operator just inserts the diskette into the appropriate slot. In both cases, there is only one correct way to insert the diskette into the drive—with the disk label facing up and the recording-window end going in first.

While the diskette is rotating, the read/write heads access tracks through the *recording window.* While the indicator light for a drive is on, meaning that the read/write heads are accessing the diskette in the drive, you must not try to remove the diskette.

Caring for Diskettes   Diskettes may look like unsophisticated pieces of plastic, but they are extremely sensitive items and must be cared for accordingly. Care of diskettes is covered in detail in Chapter 14.

File directory.
A listing on an input/output medium that provides such data as name, length, and starting address for each file on the medium.

Disk unit.
A direct-access secondary storage device that uses magnetic or optical disk as the principal medium.

Hard Disks for Small Computers

Small computers—such as microcomputers and low-end minicomputers—often employ nonremovable, sealed-pack Winchester disks. *Winchester* hard-disk systems consist of rigid metal platters that are tiered on a mounting shaft (see Figure 4-7, which shows a cutaway view). The term **disk pack,** or *pack,* is commonly used to describe the set of hard disks that are aggregated into such a modular unit. In the Winchester design, the pack is hermetically sealed in the storage unit along with the access mechanism containing the read/write heads. Because the pack is completely sealed and free from the air contamination that plagues removable-pack hard-disk systems, there are usually fewer operational problems.

Disk pack.
A group of tiered hard disks that are mounted on a shaft and treated as a unit.

FIGURE 4 – 6

Disk-drive doors. Drive doors for diskette units come in several varieties, the three most common of which are shown here. 5¼-inch drive doors have a latch mechanism that you push down to lock in an inserted disk, while 3½-inch doors have no such latch. To remove a disk from a 5¼-inch drive, you simply push up on the latch and remove the disk, while on a 3½-inch drive you must press the eject button.

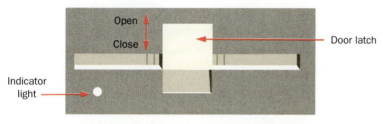

(a) 5¼-inch-drive door used on original IBM PC

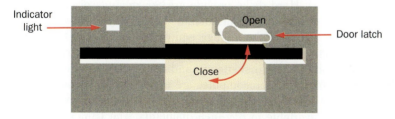

(b) 5¼-inch-drive door sold most widely today

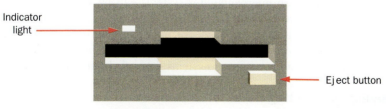

(c) 3½-inch-drive door

F I G U R E   4 – 7

A hard-disk unit. Hard-disk systems for microcomputers are most commonly found in capacities of 20 to several hundred megabytes. Featured here is an *internal* hard-disk system.

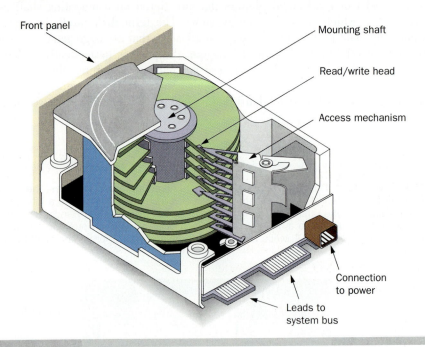

Front panel

Mounting shaft

Read/write head

Access mechanism

Connection to power

Leads to system bus

Although many microcomputer systems still use diskettes heavily, hard-disk systems are now a standard feature on virtually all computer systems sold for business purposes. Hard disks provide greater amounts of online storage and faster access to programs and data than diskettes. If you have a 160-megabyte hard-disk unit, you have the storage equivalent of about 400 double-density 5¼-inch diskettes online the minute you turn on the power. Also, you don't have to constantly shuffle diskettes in and out of disk drives.

Hard-disk units for microcomputer are most commonly found in capacities ranging from 20 to several hundred megabytes. For desktop micros, hard disks are most widely available in 3½-inch diameters. The IBM PS/2 Model 95 XP 486 computer, to cite just one example, comes with either an 80 MB, 160 MB, or 320 MB 3½-inch disk drive.

Hard-disk units on microcomputer systems can be internal or external. An *internal* hard-disk system, such as the one in Figure 4-7, is fitted into your computer's system unit in the space, or bay, normally occupied by one of the diskette drives. An *external* system is a detached hardware unit that has its own power supply. On large computer systems, hard-disk units are always external.

Reading and Writing Data   Most disk systems have at least one read/write head for each recording surface. These heads are mounted on a device called an **access mechanism.** Figure 4-7 shows how access is accomplished with a

Access mechanism.
A mechanical device in the disk pack or disk unit that positions the read/write heads on the proper tracks.

movable access mechanism. The rotating mounting shaft spins at high speeds, and the access mechanism moves the heads in and out *together* between the disk surfaces to access the required data. Movable devices are by far the most popular type of access mechanism.

A head never touches the surface of a disk at any time, even during reading and writing. Head and disk are very close, however—often millionths of an inch above the recording surfaces. A human hair or even a smoke particle (about 2,500 and 100 millionths of an inch, respectively), if present on a surface, will damage the disks and heads—an event known as a *head crash*. As Figure 4-8 shows, the results are like placing a pebble on your favorite phonograph album while playing it.

Disk Cylinders   In disk systems that use disk packs, an important principle for understanding disk storage and access strategies is the concept of **disk cylinders.** Consider the two-platter pack in Figure 4-9. There are 4 possible recording surfaces with 400 tracks per surface. One might envision the disk pack as being composed of 400 imaginary concentric cylinders, each consisting of 4 tracks, as illustrated in the figure. Outer cylinders fit over the inner ones like sleeves. Each cylinder is equivalent to a track position to which the heads on the access mechanism can move. With a movable access mechanism, all the read/write heads are positioned on the same cylinder when data are read from or written to one of the tracks on that cylinder.

Disk cylinder.
All tracks on a disk pack that are accessible with a single movement of the access mechanism.

Disk Access Time   In a removable-pack disk system with a movable access mechanism, three events must occur in order to access data.

First, the read/write head must move to the cylinder on which the data are stored. Suppose, for example, that the read/write head is on cylinder 5 and we wish to retrieve data from cylinder 36. For us to do this, the mechanism must

The space between a disk and a read/write head compared with a smoke particle and a human hair. A human hair or even a smoke particle, if present on a fast-spinning hard-disk surface, can damage both the surface and the read/write head.

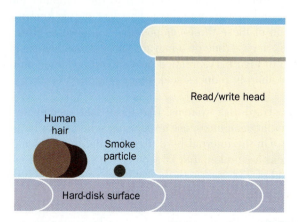

FIGURE 4-9

The cylinder concept. To imagine any particular cylinder, think of pushing an actual cylinder such as a tin can downward through the same track in each disk in the pack. In this example, cylinder 357 is made up of track 357 on surfaces 1 through 4.

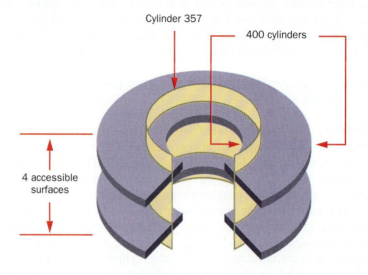

Cylinder 357

400 cylinders

4 accessible surfaces

move inward to cylinder 36. The time required for this task is referred to as *seek time*.

Second, when a read or write order is issued, the heads usually are not aligned over the position on the track on which the desired data are stored. So some delay occurs while the mounting shaft rotates the disks into the proper position. (The disks are always spinning whether or not reading or writing is taking place.) The time needed for completing this alignment is called *rotational delay*.

Third, once the read/write head is positioned over the correct data, the data must be read from disk and transferred to the computer (or transferred from the computer and written onto disk). This last step is known as *data movement time*. The sum of these three components is known as **disk access time.** To minimize disk access time on a movable-access-mechanism system such as the one depicted in Figure 4-7, related data should be stored on the same cylinder. This strategy sharply reduces seek time.

Disk access time.
The time taken to locate and read (or position and write) data on a disk device.

Sectoring Hard-disk systems, like those that accompany the IBM PC AT, PS/2, and similar computers, use a sectoring scheme similar to that for diskettes to store data. On the internal hard disks available with some PS/2 models, for instance, tracks are broken into 17 sectors. On each of the 4 recordable surfaces, there is a total of 732 tracks. In the language of hard disks, the tracks on these surfaces trace out 732 cylinders.

Subdirectories Because hard disks have large storage capacities, files commonly are organized hierarchically into *subdirectories*. As Figure 4-10 shows, at the top of the hierarchy is a "master" directory called the root directory. The *root directory*, among other things, contains a list of subdirectories on the hard disk. You can store all of your operating-system programs in one subdirectory, word-processed documents in another subdirectory, and so forth. Moreover, you can further divide these subdirectories. As shown in Figure 4-10, you can organize your word processing subdirectory by putting letters and school papers into two lower subdirectories. If you so wish, you can add several additional levels of subdirectories.

Later, when you want to access a file in any subdirectory, you must specify the *path* through the subdirectories to get to the file; for example,

```
C:\WORD\LETTER\MARY
```

Here the hard disk is the *C* drive and WORD and LETTER are the names of the two subdirectories on the path to a subdirectory of letters named MARY. On most microcomputer systems, the *A* and *B* drive designations are reserved for floppy drives.

Partitioning   *Partitioning* a hard disk enables you to divide a hard disk into separate disk drives, such as *D, E, F,* and so forth. You can change the number and size of the partitions at any time, although doing so will destroy any data

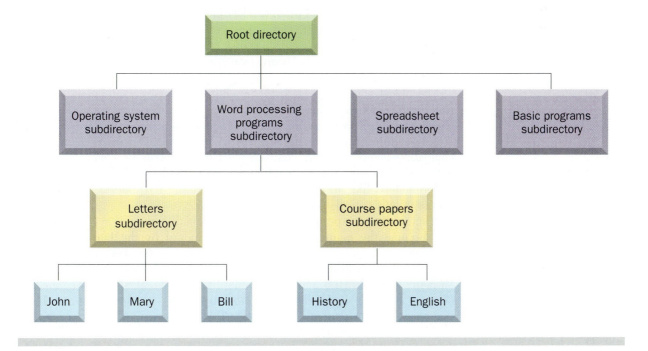

FIGURE 4 – 10

Organizing files into subdirectories. Shown here is a root directory and three levels of subdirectories. The subdirectory MARY, for instance, would contain all letters (files) written to Mary.

F I G U R E   4 – 11

A hard card. Hard cards, such as Plus Development's Hardcard, the original hard-disk-on-a-card product, are popular with users who are looking for a compact alternative to the conventional hard disk.

in the partitions. Thus, you have to download any affected data onto diskettes or tape first and then load the data back onto the repartitioned hard disk.

Partitioning a hard disk enables you to use different operating systems on it—say, MS-DOS, OS/2, and UNIX. Each operating system has its own method of formatting and managing disk space. By assigning each operating system to a different partition, you avoid the problem of having an operating system deal with a partition that works in a manner foreign to it.

Disk Standards   When buying a hard disk for a microcomputer system, it is easy to become confused when vendors throw around such acronyms as MFM, RLL, ESDI, IDE, and SCSI. These acronyms generally refer to the density with which data can be packed onto the disk, the speed of the disk, and the way the disk interfaces with the board (sometimes called the *disk controller*) that runs it.

The oldest standards are *MFM* (modified frequency modulation) and *RLL* (run length limited). These standards are commonly found on disks with a capacity of 40 or fewer megabytes. *ESDI* (enhanced small device interface) and *IDE* (integrated drive electronics) are widely used today by IBM and IBM-compatible computers with a hard-disk capacity of 60 or more megabytes. They both pack data more tightly than both the MFM and RLL formats and are faster. Unfortunately, like MFM and RLL, both ESDI and IDE interfaces allow users access to only two disk drives at one time.

Some industry experts predict that *SCSI* (small computer system interface) will become the main peripheral-device standard by the late 1990s. SCSI (pronounced "scuzzy") provides faster access speeds than both ESDI and IDE. It is now the prevailing standard for Apple Macintosh computers and is found on many high-end IBM and IBM-compatible systems. SCSI allows connection of up to seven devices—disks and other hardware—on one intelligent board that operates independently of the CPU. This independence allows you, say, to back up the contents of a hard disk onto tape while using the CPU for other tasks. SCSI, like ESDI and IDE, is widely used on disks with a capacity of 60 or more megabytes.

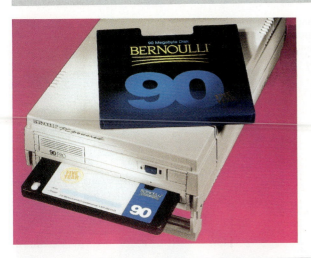

Microcomputer cartridge disk. Cartridge disk provides a storage alternative with the capacity and performance of a conventional hard disk and the removability of a diskette.

FIGURE 4 – 12

Other Types of Magnetic Disks for Small Computers

Although Winchester disks dominate the hard-disk scene for small computers, there are alternatives. Two of these are the hard card and the cartridge disk.

Hard Cards An alternative to the Winchester disk in the microcomputer hard-disk marketplace is the hard card (see Figure 4-11). **Hard cards** are hard disks that are configured onto an add-in board. As with any other board, the hard card fits into a slot in the computer's system unit. The card contains both the disk and the interface circuitry necessary for dealing with the CPU. Although relatively expensive, this type of hard-disk alternative is ideal for people who need hard-disk speed and capacity in a limited space.

Cartridge Disk Cartridge disk devices are commonly found on microcomputer and minicomputer systems. **Cartridge disk** devices used on microcomputer systems are external hardware units that accept small, removable high-capacity disk cartridges (see Figure 4-12). The high-capacity disk is packaged into a square case (i.e., the cartridge) to protect the disk's contents. The operator inserts a cartridge into a cartridge drive in a manner similar to inserting a diskette into a diskette drive. Cartridge disks commonly have a capacity of about 10 to 90 megabytes. Their biggest pluses are large storage capacity and, because of their removability, backup and security. The biggest drawback is cost—the disk unit can cost $2,000 to $3,000 and the cartridges up to $100 apiece.

RAM Disk and Cache Disk

RAM disk and cache disk are two strategies for creatively using RAM to compensate for the access-speed differences between memory and secondary storage. Both methods overcome the slow speeds involved with fetching instructions or data from disk, and both can be implemented inexpensively under

Hard card.
A hard disk that has been configured onto an add-in board.

Cartridge disk.
A magnetic disk in which a single disk platter is contained in a sealed plastic case.

F I G U R E   4 – 13

Removable-pack disks. Many larger computers use removable-pack disk units, onto which packs are manually mounted and removed by a computer operator. (a) A removable pack. (b) A disk unit that accepts removable packs.

(a)

(b)

certain conditions. On many computer systems sold today, RAM disk and cache disk are built-in features.

RAM disk.
A disk management system in which a portion of RAM is set up to function as a disk.

RAM Disk **RAM disk,** sometimes referred to as *electronic disk, E-disk,* or *disk emulation,* is a storage alternative in which the computer's operating system is "tricked" into thinking it is dealing with secondary storage when in fact it is dealing with memory.

When computer systems process programs or data files, typically only a limited number of program instructions or data records are in memory at any given time. When more instructions or data are needed, the operating system must fetch them from disk. However, if your system has enough RAM to store the entire program or data file, you can use an emulation package to load it into RAM and point the system to this part of RAM every time it would go to the disk to fetch additional program commands or data. Thus, the emulation software essentially tricks the system into thinking it's dealing with the disk drive when it actually is dealing with RAM. Such a technique can boost the speed of applications processing considerably.

Cache disk.
A disk management scheme whereby more data than are necessary are read from disk during each time-consuming disk fetch and are stored in RAM to minimize the number of fetches.

Cache Disk **Cache disk** refers to a strategy whereby, during any disk access, program or data contents in neighboring disk areas are also fetched and transported to RAM. For instance, if only a single data record needs to be read, a cache-disk feature may read the entire track on which the record is located. The theory behind cache disk is that neighboring program commands and data will likely have to be read later anyway, so one can save disk accesses by bringing those commands or data into RAM early so that they can be accessed more quickly. Thus, caching saves time as well as wear and tear on the disk unit. In portable computers, it can also extend battery life. Cache disk, is frequently implemented through the board that contains the disk controller.

Disk Systems for Large Computers

Disk systems on larger computers work by many of the same principles as microcomputer-based hard disks. However, some important differences do exist.

First, disk systems on larger computers sometimes have bigger-diameter platters, with many more tracks. It is not uncommon for the size of these platters to be as much as 14 inches in diameter, although the trend today is decidely toward smaller disks.

Second, not all disk systems on larger computers use a sealed-pack design, in which both disks and heads are permanently sealed as a unit. Many larger computers use instead removable-pack disk units, onto which packs are manually mounted or removed by a computer operator (see Figure 4-13). Because removable packs are not permanently sealed—the plastic disk covers are automatically separated from the packs when they are mounted so the heads can access the platters—removable-pack systems require an air-filtration system to keep disk surfaces free of dust. Despite this precaution, removable-pack disks are still vulnerable to dust and are therefore more prone to head crashes than sealed-pack disks. They are also slower and less reliable. However, removable-pack systems have one notable advantage: because packs can be removed from a unit, fewer drives are required.

The trend today in disk systems for larger computers and large networks of smaller computers is definitely toward sealed-pack disks (see Figure 4-14).

RAID The use of disk arrays—or *RAID* (for *redundant arrays of inexpensive disks*)—is a relatively new, sealed-pack disk-storage strategy that may signal

A sealed-pack disk unit. The IBM Direct Access Storage Subsystem featured here, targeted to business minicomputers, has a rack that can contain up to four disk units, each with its own pack. Sealed-pack disk systems are faster and more reliable than those that use removable packs.

RAID storage unit. StorageTek's Iceberg 9200 Disk Array Subsystem, which uses arrays of 5¼-inch disks, can store over 150 gigabytes of data when fully configured.

F e a t u r e   4 – 1

RAID

How a gang of small disks can team up to outperform a larger disk

It's a new and radical idea but one that experts say signals an important trend for disk technology in the near future. It's called RAID—for *redundant arrays of inexpensive disks*. It refers to a set of several small disks that work together as a unit.

Preliminary findings have shown that disk arrays made up of 5¼-inch hard disks can outperform a single 14-inch disk of the same capacity. Performance increases of several orders of magnitude have been observed in five critical areas: cutting access times, increasing reliability, reducing power consumption, slicing the cost of storing each byte, and reducing the physical size of storage hardware.

Several reasons account for the initial success of disk arrays. First, small disks theoretically can spin faster than larger ones. The larger a disk gets, the greater the potential for wobble at the outer edge of the disk, which causes reading and writing problems. (The more the wobble, the farther away from the disk surface the read/write heads must be positioned to prevent a head crash.) Second, data retrieved from a single disk is read from a track serially, one character after another. When several disks work together, they can be hooked up so that data are drawn off simultaneously—that is, in parallel—speeding up processing considerably.

One of the most-talked-about RAID products in recent years in StorageTek's Iceberg 9200 Disk Array Subsystem (see Figure 4-15). The minimum configuration of this system is 100 gigabytes, spread over 32 disks. If a disk in any array fails, the system has the ability to reconstruct data on a spare disk so that operations can continue uninterrupted.

The switch to disk arrays is likely to cause the greatest upheaval in the mainframe disk marketplace. Currently, more than $12 billion is spent annually on mainframe disk products.

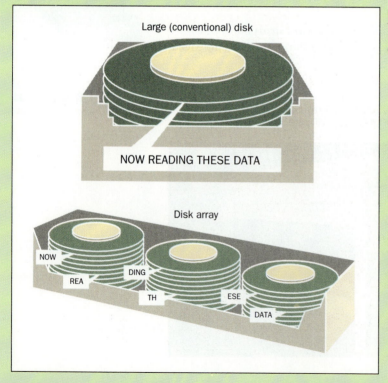

Disk arrays. By reading and writing track data in parallel rather than serially, access times can be sharply reduced.

a new trend in disk technology. RAID, which involves using several smaller disks hooked up in parallel to do the job of a larger disk, is discussed in detail in Feature 4-1. An example of RAID, StorageTek's Iceberg system, is shown in Figure 4-15.

Magnetic Tape

For years, **magnetic tape** has been one of the most prominent secondary storage alternatives. Although less popular than disk, it is still widely used on all sizes of computer systems. The tapes often are stored either on detachable reels or in cartridges. Figure 4-16 shows a tape cartridge compared with a conventional, detachable-reel tape.

    Detachable-reel tapes are commonly ½-inch wide and are made of plastic Mylar coated with a magnetizable substance. A standard reel diameter is 10½ inches, although smaller "minireels' are also quite common. A typical 2,400-foot reel can pack data at densities as high as 6,250 bytes per inch. When such a tape is read, it can transfer more data in one second than many secretaries could type in a month—and error free.

Magnetic tape.
A plastic tape with a magnetic surface for storing data as a series of magnetic spots.

Detachable-reel tape.
Magnetic tape that is wound onto a single reel, which in turn is mounted onto a tape unit with an empty take-up reel.

FIGURE 4 – 16

Magnetic tape. Shown here are two tape cartridges and, underneath, a conventional tape reel.

Cartridge tape.
Magnetic tape in which the supply and take-up reels are contained in a small plastic case.

Cartridge tapes are housed in a small plastic casing. On microcomputer systems, cartridges are commonly used to back up the contents of a hard disk (see Figure 4-17). These tapes can have huge capacities and work very fast. A ¼-inch tape up to 1,000 feet long can often hold 100 or more megabytes of data and copy the contents of a disk in a matter of minutes. Recently cartridges using *helical-scan* recording methods, which store data at an angle to the edge of the tape rather than perpendicular to it, have permitted storage capacities in the gigabyte range. Cartridge tapes designed specifically for disk backup are sometimes referred to as *streaming tapes.*

The IBM 3480 and 3490 tape storage systems, which are used with IBM mainframe computers, also use cartridge tapes. These tapes have twice the number of tracks as traditional detachable-reel tapes and a storage capacity of hundreds of megabytes. In contrast to streaming tapes, which are intended solely for backup, the IBM 3480 and IBM 3490 cartridges are designed for general use, including both regular input/output processing operations and backup.

The discussion that follows in this section is based principally on the nine-track, detachable-reel tapes that have been used with mainframes and minicomputers for years. These tape systems are still the most prevalent in the marketplace. Nonetheless, many of the principles described here apply to cartridge tapes as well.

FIGURE 4 – 17

Microcomputer cartridge tape. On microcomputer systems, cartridge tapes are commonly used to back up the contents of a hard disk. Featured here are two *internal* tape units (left), which fit into the computer's system unit, and an *external* tape unit (right).

Magnetic tape units for large computers. On large computers, magnetic tape is often used for backup and for many types of batch processing. (Background) In conventional detachable-reel systems, any reels of programs or data to be run must be selected manually from an offline tape library and mounted on the tape unit. (Foreground) In cartridge systems, several high-capacity cartridges can be loaded into hoppers for automatic processing.

Detachable-
reel tape units

Detachable-
reel tape

Cartridge
tape units

Cartridge
tapes

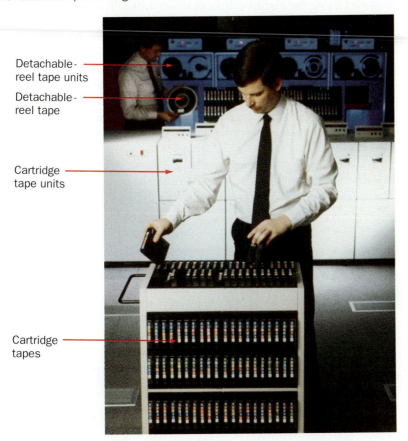

Processing Tapes

A tape must be mounted onto an online **tape unit** (see Figure 4-18) to be processed. Detachable-reel tape units are often the size of a common household refrigerator. The *supply reel* on the unit contains the tape that is to be read from or written to by the computer system. The *take-up reel* collects the tape as it unwinds from the supply reel. As it is processed, the tape passes by a read/write head, which reads data from the tape or records data on it. On many devices, the tape is allowed to droop in a vacuum chamber so that it will not break if the two reels move at different speeds. After processing, the tape is rewound onto the supply reel and removed from the unit. The take-up reel never leaves the unit. On cartridge tape units, because both reels are contained in the cartridge, the handling of supply and takeup reels is eliminated. Better

Tape unit.
A secondary storage device on which magnetic tapes are mounted for processing.

yet, it may be possible to stack several cartridges into an input hopper for automatic processing.

Storing Data on Tape

Figure 4-19 shows how data are stored on nine-track magnetic tape. Data may be coded using the eight-bit byte of either EBCDIC or ASCII-8, depending on the equipment used. Magnetized spots of iron oxide represent 1s; nonmagnetized spots represent 0s. The tape contains a track for each bit of information in a character, plus an additional parity track to allow the computer system to check for transmission errors. The tape unit reads across the nine tracks to identify the character represented in each column. Recall from Chapter 3 that in odd-parity machines, all 1-bits add up to an odd number and in even-parity machines to an even number. An incorrect sum indicates an error. The parity bit is included with the byte representation of each character when it is placed onto tape.

A magnetic tape is basically a long, narrow strip. Thus, when the records in a data file are stored on it, they must be alongside one another in sequence. The sequence often is determined by a **key field,** such as customer ID number,

Key field.
A field used to identify a record.

FIGURE 4 – 19

Storing data on nine-track magnetic tape. Shown here is the number 6 represented in EBCDIC (11110110, or 111110110 with the odd-parity track). In the shaded cross section of the tape, the magnetized spot representing the 1-bit is shown by a vertical mark in the appropriate track. The 0-bit is characterized by the absence of a mark.

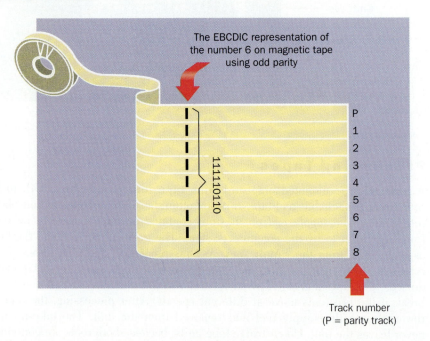

The EBCDIC representation of the number 6 on magnetic tape using odd parity

111110110

P
1
2
3
4
5
6
7
8

Track number
(P = parity track)

which can be ordered numerically. Every record's key field generally has a different value.

If you want to read a particular record from a tape, you can't go directly to it. Instead, you must pass through all the records that precede it. In a sense, this is similar to the fast forwarding you do on a music tape when the tune you want to hear is in the middle of it. Retrieving records in the order in which they are stored is called *sequential access*, and organizing data in sequence by a key field is called *sequential organization*. We will talk more about data access and organization later in the chapter.

Protecting Tapes

Tape reels are equipped with safety features that prevent operators from accidentally destroying the contents of the tape. One such device is the *file-protection ring* (see Figure 4-20). When tapes are stored offline, these rings are not mounted on the reel. To write onto any part of the tape, thereby destroying any data already stored there, the operator must insert this ring into the center of the reel. The tapes can be read, however, whether or not the ring is present.

Another device designed to protect tapes is the *internal header label*. This label appears at the beginning of the tape and identifies it. The identifying information in the label is usually generated automatically by the computer system or data-entry device. Thus, if you commanded the computer system to process tape AP-601 and the operator accidentally mounted tape AR-601 instead, no processing would occur. Also, the operator would receive a warning message.

Optical Disk

An emerging technology that is having a profound impact on storage strategies in the 1990s is the **optical disk.** With this technology, laser beams write and read data at incredible densities, thousands of times finer than the density of a typical magnetic disk. Data—which can consist of text, graphics, voice, or video images—are placed onto optical disks with high-intensity laser beams that burn tiny holes into the disk's surface. Then a lower-intensity laser beam reads the data inscribed.

Today 3½-inch optical disks can store almost 1 gigabyte of data. Roughly translated, that's close to 1 million pages of text or, alternatively, the contents of approximately 2,500 low-density, 5¼-inch diskettes. So-called *optical jukeboxes*, which offer online access to scores of optical disks, also have become available. These devices can store 300 or more billion bytes of data (see Figure 4-21).

Optical disk systems are used on computer systems of all sizes—and most of all, on microcomputers. Most optical disk units are of the *CD-ROM* (Compact Disk/Read-Only Memory) type; that is, you buy a prerecorded disk and "play" (read) it on the optical disk unit attached to your computer. You cannot write new data to the disk in any way. CD-ROM optical disk units are now available for microcomputers for less than $1,000.

Systems also are available that will let you write once to the disk; once written, the data cannot be erased. These are called *WORM* (Write Once, Read

Optical disk.
A disk read by laser beams rather than by magnetic means.

Optical disk units and their optical disks. (a) Optical disk units targeted to ordinary microcomputer users often accept only a single disk at a time. (b) Optical jukeboxes targeted to commercial users often chain several disk units together. Each disk unit accepts a cartridge (magazine) of several disks. The jukebox shown here has online access of up to 42 optical disks.

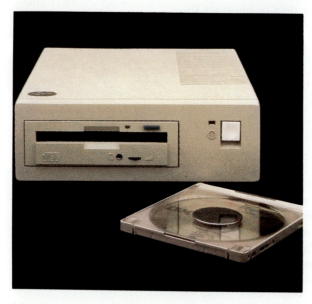

(a)

(b)

Many) disk systems. Since optical disks have very large storage capacities, most users can write to the disk for a year or more before using it up. Optical disk systems that allow you to erase unwanted data—called *fully erasable systems*—have also recently become available.

Uses of optical disk technology abound, and there are far too many applications to name here. One major applications area is learning. IBM's *Illuminated Books and Manuscripts,* for instance, is an optical-disk-based educational product that contains text, pictures, and video clips from several historical events and book classics (see Figure 4-22a). Another major applications area is reference. DeLorme Mapping's *Street Atlas USA,* which contains more than a million detailed maps on a single CD-ROM, is an excellent example (see Figure 4-22b). Users of this package can view the whole United States or zoom down to a state, region, neighborhood, or street anywhere in the country. Optical disks are also used in a variety of other environments, as illustrated in User Solution 4-2 and the Tomorrow box.

Despite the excitement over optical disks, hard magnetic disks still have two important advantages. First, hard disks are much faster; 10 to 20 times faster is not unusual. Second, there's a great deal of software written for hard disks that will have to be modified to work on optical disks.

Optical disk applications. Optical disks enable microcomputer users to have online access to close to a billion bytes of secondary storage. (a) IBM's *Illuminated Books and Manuscripts* is an interactive educational product. (b) DeLorme Mapping's *Street Atlas USA* provides maps showing U.S. states, regions, neighborhoods, and streets.

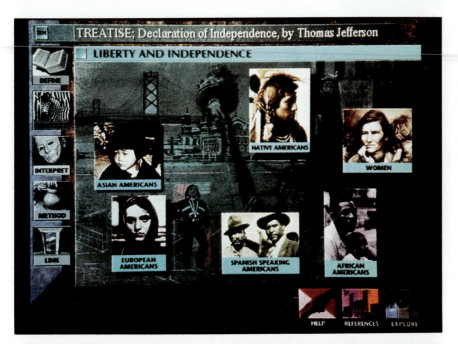

(a)

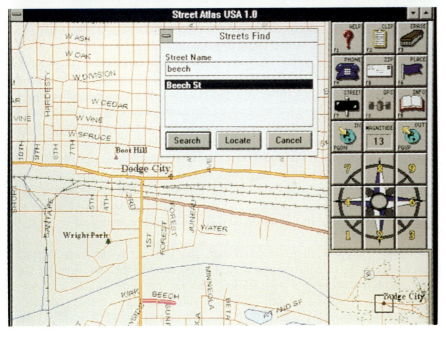

(b)

User   Solution   4 – 2

Optical Disks for Customer Support

When home-appliance manufacturer Whirlpool looked around for a more efficient way to handle the 1.6 million service calls it gets from customers annually, it opted for an optical-disk-based imaging system. Mounted on a centralized optical-disk system are page images of 20 years worth of service and product manuals, which can be accessed by about 100 service agents from desktop workstations. In the past, agents had to browse by hand through printed materials and microfiched records to get information. That same information is now available to them in less than two seconds. Whirlpool also has a software-based "expert system" integrated into this service application that helps agents diagnose the cause of equipment failure and recommend a solution.

Data Organization

Data access.
Fetching data from a device either sequentially or directly.

Data organization.
The process of setting up a data file so that it may subsequently be accessed in some desired way.

When a computer system is instructed to use data or programs residing in secondary storage, it first must be able to find the materials. The process of retrieving data and programs in storage is called **data access.** Arranging data for efficient retrieval is called **data organization.**

As we have seen, a major difference between, say, tape and disk is that data on tape can be *accessed* only sequentially, whereas data on disk can be retrieved both sequentially and in a direct (random) fashion. With sequential access, the records in a file can be retrieved only in the same sequence in which they are physically stored. With direct, or random, access, the time needed to fetch a record is relatively independent of its location in secondary storage.

The need for certain data access methods necessarily dictates the choice of ways to *organize* data files. Let's consider a practical example. Most book libraries are organized with card indexes ordered by title, author, and subject, so you can retrieve books directly. To locate a particular book, you simply look under the book's title in the index, find its call number, and go directly to the appropriate shelf.

However, suppose there were no card indexes and books were organized alphabetically by title on shelves from the first shelf to the last (say, the 758th shelf). With this sequential organization of books, it would take you much longer to retrieve the title you wanted—although you would get a lot of exercise. As you can see, sequential organization does not permit straightforward access to a specific book.

Data organization on computers works in a similar fashion. First, you decide on the type of access you need—direct, sequential, or both. Then you organize

T O M O R R O W

Photo CDs

Will They Become a Hot Item?

Photo CDs are a relatively new technology in which ordinary photographs are stored on compact (optical) disks, where they can be viewed and edited. The disks can be played in special photo-CD players that connect to TV sets like a VCR and in CD-ROM drives that connect to computer systems.

How does the technology work in practice?

One way is to have film that was shot with a conventional camera processed onto a photo CD instead of prints or slides. Today's photo CD is capable of holding about 100 images—the output from four boxes of 24-exposures film. Currently, the processing cost per image is more expensive than processing by conventional means, but the cost could drop sharply as more people use the technology.

Photo CDs can also be used to make prepackaged optical-disk products. Recently, Kodak—the most bullish advocate of photo CD technology—has been working with outdoor-apparel maker L.L. Bean to place apparel catalogs onto disk. A person receiving a photo CD catalog reads it on a TV or computer screen, where it is accompanied by a sound track. Computer users would be able to find items quickly by typing in key words, such as "green" and "sweater" to pull up all green sweaters.

Another possible application for photo CDs is to have users access remote CDs with their home or office computers. As computer networks become more popular and readily available, it's a good bet that a lot of people will be doing their shopping electronically. But how far out in the future this will be is anyone's guess.

Depending on the equipment they have available, users of photo CD technology have a wealth of high-tech options available to them. Once photos are in a high-resolution digital form, they can be blown up and cropped, manipulated with computer tools such as airbrushes and paint-

Photo CDs. The potential market is enormous.

boxes, and combined with sound effects and narration. If you thought your parents' carousel projector was neat, you'll be dazzled by what you can do with this new technology.

When you think about it, the potential market for photo CD products is enormous. Just consider the photography market. By Kodak's estimate, about 50 billion snapshots are taken annually by 250 million cameras. The U.S. alone can account for 15 billion snapshots and 100 million cameras.

But while design professionals are generally excited about photo CDs, severe hurdles face the new technology at the consumer level. Are average consumers, many of whom cannot program their VCRs, sophisticated enough to use such a product? Will people be willing to let go of the slide and print media they've grown accustomed to for images they can only see through a TV or computer screen? Does the average home entertainment cabinet have room for another electronic gadget?

Over the next few years, we will find out.

the data in a way that will minimize the time needed to retrieve them with the access method selected.

There are many ways to organize data. Here we will describe three—sequential, indexed-sequential, and direct organization.

Sequential organization.
Arranging data on a physical medium either ascendingly or descendingly by some key field.

Sequential Organization   In a file having a **sequential organization,** records follow one another in a predetermined sequence. Sequentially organized files generally are ordered by a key field or fields, such as ID number. Thus, if a four-digit ID number is the key field being used to order the file, the record belonging to, say ID number 0612 will be stored after number 0611 but before number 0613 (see Figure 4-23).

Now that you have an idea of what sequential organization is, let's see how it is used in information processing. Many companies update customer balances and prepare bills at the end of the month. Such an operation is known as a *sequential update.* Two data files are used. The *master file* normally contains the customer's ID number, the amount owed at the beginning of the month, and additional information about the customer. This file is sorted by the key field, customer ID number, and records are arranged in ascending sequence—from the lowest ID number to the highest. The *transaction file* contains all the transactions made during the month by old customers, who appear in the master file, and by new customers, who do not. Transactions might include purchases and payments. Like the master file, the transaction file is ordered in ascending sequence by customer ID number.

In a sequential update, the two files are processed together in the manner shown in Figure 4-24. The sequential-update program reads a record from each file. If the key fields match, the operation specified in the transaction file is performed. Note that in Figure 4-24, the key fields of the first records in each file match. Thus, record 101 is updated to the updated customer master file. For example, if the transaction file shows that customer 101 bought a toaster, data on this purchase are added to the master file. Next, both files are "rolled forward" to the next records. Here the program observes that customer 102 is not in the master file, since the next master file record after 101 is 103. Therefore, this must be a new customer, and the program will create a new record for customer 102 in the updated master file. At this point, only the transaction file will be rolled forward, to customer 103. The program now observes that this

F I G U R E   4 – 23

Sequential organization of records on tape.

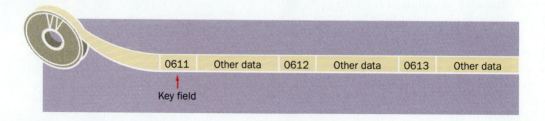

| 0611 | Other data | 0612 | Other data | 0613 | Other data |

Key field

FIGURE 4 – 24

A sequential update of a master file. Each customer record in the original master file might contain the customer's ID number (the key field), name, address, amount owed, and credit limit. For simplicity, only the key field is shown in the illustration. The transaction file contains a record of each customer transaction. Each record in this file might contain the customer's ID number (the key field), the amount of the purchase or payment, and the type of transaction involved (update, add, or delete). Only the key field and type of transaction are shown in the illustration. As both files are processed together, an updated master file is produced, as well as a printed listing of records that couldn't be processed because of some discrepancy.

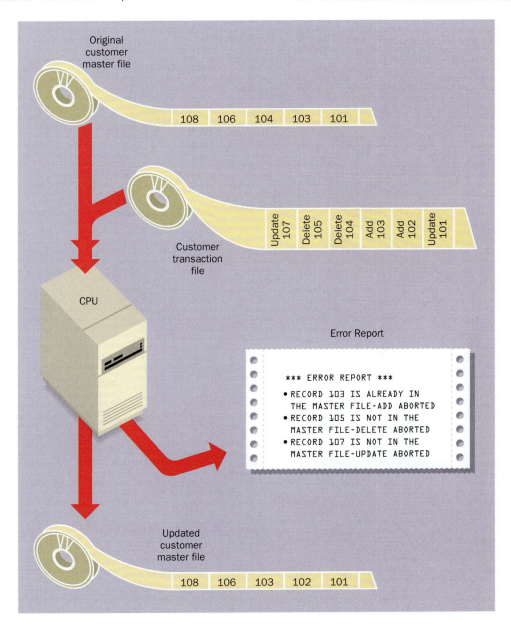

FIGURE 4 – 25

Indexed-sequential organization. Records are ordered on disk by key, and all record addresses are entered in an index. To process a request to find a record—say, record 200—the computer system first searches a cylinder index and then a track index for the record's address. In the cylinder index, it learns that the record is on cylinder 009. The computer system then consults the track index for cylinder 009, where it observes that the record is on track 2 of that cylinder. The access mechanism then proceeds to this track to locate the record.

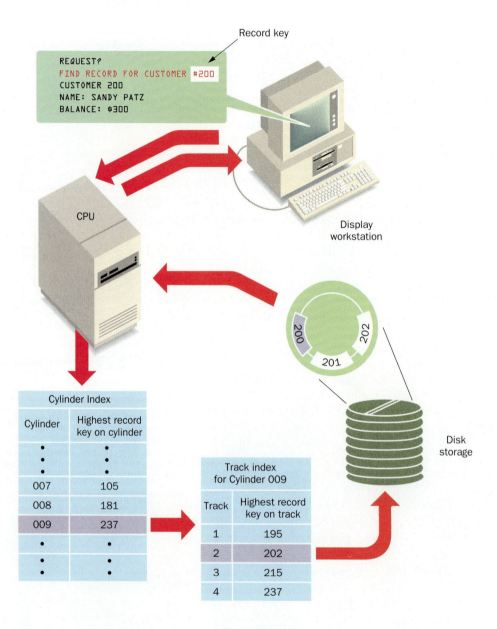

Record key

REQUEST?
FIND RECORD FOR CUSTOMER #200
CUSTOMER 200
NAME: SANDY PATZ
BALANCE: $300

CPU

Display workstation

Disk storage

Cylinder Index

Cylinder	Highest record key on cylinder
⋮	⋮
007	105
008	181
009	237
⋮	⋮

Track index for Cylinder 009

Track	Highest record key on track
1	195
2	202
3	215
4	237

record matches the one to which it is currently pointing in the master file. However, the transaction file indicates that 103 is a new customer. Hence, there appears to be an inconsistency, since the master file contains only old customers. The program makes no entry in the updated master file but sends information about this transaction to the error report.

The processing continues in this manner until both files are exhausted. The processing is sequential because the computer processes the records in both files in the order in which they physically appear.

Indexed-Sequential Organization Indexed-sequential organization is a way of organizing data for both sequential and direct access. This type of organization requires disk, since tapes can't provide direct access. Records are ordered on the disk by key field. Also, several indexes are created to locate these records later. These indexes work similarly to those in a phone book. For example, if the top of a phone book page reads "Alexander—Ashton," you'll know to look for the phone number of Amazon Sewer Service on that page. When implemented on a computer, as Figure 4-25 shows, such indexes permit rapid access to records.

Many computer systems have systems programs that help programmers set up indexes and indexed-sequential-organized files painlessly. As records are added to or deleted from a file, the systems software automatically adds them or deletes them from the disk and updates the index. Because the records remain organized sequentially on the disk, the file can be processed sequentially at any time.

Direct Organization Although indexed files are suitable for many applications, the process of finding disk addresses through index searches can be time consuming. Direct-organization schemes have been developed to provide faster direct access.

Direct organization eliminates the need for an index by translating the record's key field directly into a disk address. This is done with the use of mathematical formulas called *hashing algorithms.* Several hashing procedures have been developed. One of the simplest involves dividing the key field by the prime number closest to, but not greater than, the number of records to be stored. A prime number can be divided evenly by itself and 1 but not by any other number. The remainder of the division by the prime number (not the quotient) becomes the address of the relative location in which the record will be stored.

Let's consider an example. Suppose that a company has 1,000 employees and therefore 1,000 active employee numbers. Also suppose that all employee identification numbers (the key field) are four digits long. Therefore, the possible range of ID numbers is from 0000 to 9999.

Assume that this company wants to place the record of employee number 8742 onto disk. The hashing procedure will be as follows. The prime number closest to 1,000, the number of records to be stored, is 997. Figure 4-26 shows that the hashed disk address computes to 766. After the record has been placed at an address corresponding to this number, the computer can retrieve it as needed by applying the hashing procedure to the key field of the record again. Calculation of an address in this manner usually consumes much less time than would a search through one or more indexes.

Indexed-sequential organization.
A method of organizing data on a direct-access medium so that they can be accessed directly (through an index) or sequentially.

Direct organization.
A method of organizing data on a device so they can be accessed directly (randomly).

FIGURE 4 – 26

Hashing illustrated. The CPU follows a hashing procedure to assign a record to a disk address. In this case, the hashing procedure involves dividing the key field by the prime number closest to 1,000—997. The remainder corresponds to an actual disk address.

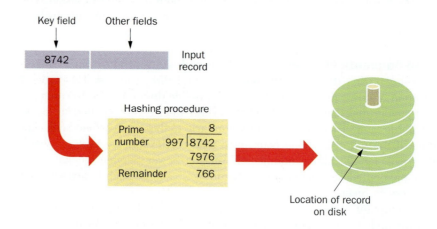

Hashing procedures are difficult to develop and pose certain problems. For example, it is possible for two or more records to be hashed to the same relative disk location. This, of course, means they will "collide" at their common disk address. When this happens, one record is placed in the computed location and assigned a "pointer" that chains it to the other, which often goes in the closest-available location to the hashed address. Good hashing procedures result in few collisions.

The disadvantage of direct organization is that, since records are not stored sequentially by key, it is usually impractical to process the records sequentially.

Summary and Key Terms

Secondary storage technologies make it economically feasible to keep several programs and sets of data online to the CPU. The most common types of secondary storage media are magnetic disk and magnetic tape.

Properties of Secondary Storage Systems   Any secondary storage system involves two physical parts: a peripheral device and an input/output medium. In most systems, media must pass by a **read/write head** in the peripheral device to be read from or written to.

Secondary storage media are **nonvolatile**—that is, when the power to the peripheral device is shut off, the data stored on the medium remain intact. This contrasts with most types of memory, which are **volatile.** Also, media on secondary storage devices can be either *removable,* meaning they must be mounted onto the peripheral device every time they are used, or *fixed,* meaning they are permanently mounted, or nonremovable.

Two basic access methods are used on secondary storage systems: sequential and direct. With **sequential access,** the records in a file can be retrieved only in the same order in which they are physically stored. With **direct access** (or **random access),** records can be retrieved in any order.

Magnetic Disk   **Magnetic disk** is most commonly available in the form of hard disks and diskettes. **Hard disks** are rigid platters. **Diskettes,** or *floppy disks,* in contrast, are flexible platters.

Diskettes are commonly used with microcomputers and small minicomputers. Each side of a diskette contains concentric **tracks,** which are encoded with 0- and 1-bits when data and programs are written to them. Diskettes are available in a number of sizes (diameters) and densities. **Sectors** divide a diskette into addressable, pie-shaped pieces. The disk's **file directory,** which the computer system maintains automatically, keeps track of the contents at each disk address. To use a diskette, the operator inserts it into a **disk unit,** or *drive.* A disk drive works only when the appropriate type of diskette is inserted correctly.

Sealed-pack hard-disk units are today a standard item on microcomputer systems. Hard disks are faster and have greater data-carrying capacity than diskettes.

In a hard-disk system, disks are tiered into units called **disk packs.** A read/write head is assigned to each recordable disk surface. The heads are mounted onto an **access mechanism,** which can move them in and out among the concentric tracks to fetch data. All tracks in the same position on the tiered platters of a disk pack form a **disk cylinder.**

Three events determine the time needed to read from or write to most disks. *Seek time* is the time required for the access mechanism to reach a particular track. The time needed for the disk to spin to a specific area of a track is known as *rotational delay.* Once located, data must be transferred to or from the disk, a process known as *data movement time.* The sum of these three time components is called **disk access time.**

Hard cards and **cartridge disk** devices are two other hard-disk alternatives for microcomputer systems.

Two strategies for reducing the number of time-consuming disk accesses are RAM disk and cache disk. **RAM disk** is a storage strategy whereby the computer's operating system is "tricked" into thinking it is dealing with secondary storage when in fact it is dealing with memory. **Cache disk** refers to a strategy whereby during any disk access, program or data contents in neighboring disk areas are also fetched and transported to RAM.

Disk systems on larger computers work by many of the same principles as microcomputer-based hard disks. Most disk systems for larger computers use either a sealed-pack or removable-pack design. Recently, *RAID* (for *redundant arrays of inexpensive disks*) technology has infiltrated the disk market for larger computers.

Magnetic Tape   **Magnetic tape** consists of plastic Mylar coated with a magnetizable substance and wound on a reel. Each character of data is represented in byte form across the tracks in the tape. Many **detachable-reel tapes** contain nine tracks—eight corresponding to the eight bits in a byte and an additional parity track to check for transmission errors. **Cartridge tapes,** in which both supply and take-up reels are enclosed in a plastic case, are also widely available.

Bit mapping.
A graphical output technique in which each of the dots in the output image may be individually operator controlled.

Bit mapping   The earliest display devices were strictly *character addressable;* that is, only text could be output. Every character sent to the screen was the same size and was fitted into a specific block of pixels in a predesignated grid. As demand for graphics devices grew, manufacturers developed techniques to make displays multipurpose—that is, capable of both graphics and standard text output.

Display devices that produce graphics output often use a technique called **bit mapping.** With bit-mapped graphics, each pixel on the screen (rather than simply a block of pixels) can be individually controlled by the computer operator or the software package in use. Bit mapping enables the operator or software to create virtually any type of image on the screen. Figure 5-4 features a variety of graphics applications.

One of the largest markets for graphics display devices today are in the engineering, science, and art fields. Powerful devices called *technical workstations* are used for mapping, circuit design, mechanical and engineering design (see Figure 5-4a), drafting, art, advertising, and other graphics-intensive tasks. Such applications collectively fall under the heading of *computer-aided design (CAD).* We will discuss CAD in greater detail in Chapter 11.

Another large market for computer graphics is in the business sector. Managers can easily become overwhelmed as they try to make decisions from piles of raw data. A possible solution lies in the old adage "A picture is worth a thousand words." Using a graphics image, a decision maker can more easily spot problems, opportunities, and trends. Many business applications of computer graphics fall into the general category of *presentation graphics*, which we'll cover in Chapter 9 and Window 6. With presentation graphics, computer images are used to increase the effectiveness of presenting data to others (Figure 5-4b).

Recently, computer graphics techniques have brought many businesses squarely into the age of *electronic document handling,* in which digital images of

FIGURE 5 – 4

Common graphics applications. (a) Engineering design. (b) Business presentation graphics. (c) Electronic document handling.

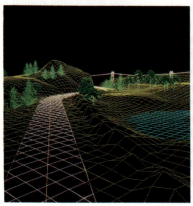
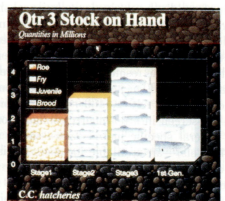

(a)   (b)   (c)

VGA versus Super VGA (SVGA). Because an SVGA screen (right) contains over twice the number of pixels as a VGA screen (left) of the same size, it can contain over twice the amount of information. SVGA is ideal for applications in which users wish to squeeze more information onto a single screen.

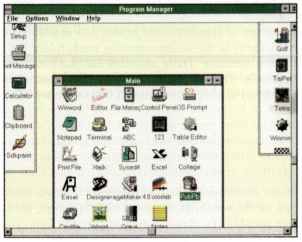

(a)

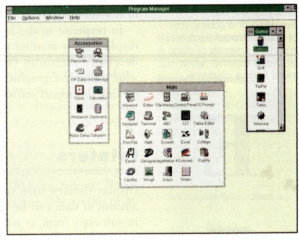

(b)

paper documents and photographs are electronically maintained by organizations and processed by workers at their display workstations (see Figure 5-4c). The paper documents and photographs are initially read into the computer system with a scanner. Once in electronic form, the images are stored on a high-capacity optical disk system. Workers having access to the system can summon documents to their workstations, where they can cull, sort, summarize, or repackage the information to their heart's content. Workers may also be authorized to annotate certain documents with comments or approvals and send them to other workers who are hooked into the system.

Graphics Standards   A number of standards for display devices are currently in effect. In the IBM microcomputing world, standards such as Hercules monochrome, Monochrome Display Adapter (MDA), Color Graphics Adapter (CGA), Multi-color Graphics Array (MCGA), enhanced Graphics Adapter (EGA), are widely found on display devices made before 1987. Video Graphics Array (VGA), the current standard, has been dominant over the last several years. VGA is available in three principal variants—in order of finer screen-resolution they are the original VGA standard (VGA), Super VGA (SVGA), and Extended VGA (XVGA). The Apple Macintosh line has a similar set of graphics standards.

Graphics standards specify "modes" in which the display device can run. For example, VGA can run in 17 different modes. One mode, for instance, divides the screen into a matrix of 320 by 200 pixels and allows 256 colors to be displayed simultaneously; another divides the screen into a matrix of 720 by 400 pixels and permits monochrome display only. SVGA and XVGA allow even larger pixel matrices than these. An SVGA display, for instance, shows

Overstriking on a dot-matrix printer. (a) Single striking. (b) Overstriking with multiple passes produces denser characters.

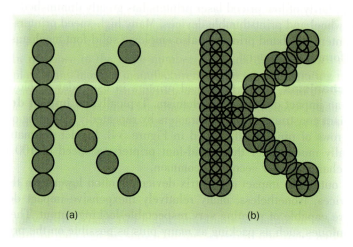

(a)   (b)

head, overstriking by making multiple passes on a line, and blending overstrike dots into previous dots by shifting the paper very slightly (see Figure 5-9). Top-of-the-line impact dot-matrix printers have 24 pins on their print heads, configured in two 12-pin rows. Generally, these printers can create characters that are virtually indistinguishable from those produced by solid-font printers. In the world of impact dot-matrix printing, low-quality output is often referred

Impact dot-matrix printer. Often costing only a few hundred dollars, impact dot-matrix printers are popular in microcomputing environments where draft-quality output is acceptable.

FIGURE 5 – 11

Thermal-transfer printers. Thermal-transfer technology is used for both (a) small portable printers and (b) situations where high-quality color output is required.

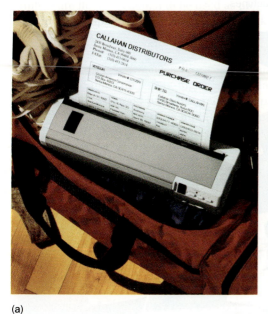

(a)

(b)

to as *draft-quality* printing and presentation-quality output as *near-letter-quality (NLQ)* printing. Many impact dot-matrix printers can also be used to produce graphical or color output.

An impact dot-matrix printer is featured in Figure 5-10.

Nonimpact Printing

Nonimpact printing, which most often employs dot-matrix characters, does not depend on the impact of metal on paper. In fact, no physical contact at all occurs between the printing mechanism and the paper. The most popular nonimpact methods today utilize electrothermal, thermal-transfer, ink-jet, and laser technologies.

In *electrothermal printing,* characters are burned onto a special paper by heated rods on a print head. Electrothermal printers are available at a very low cost, but they have the disadvantages of poor output quality, requiring special paper (which some people find unpleasant to touch), and being unable to produce color output. Electrothermal printing is the technology most used by fax machines, which are covered in Chapter 6.

Thermal-transfer printers, which represent a relatively new technology, thermally transfer ink from a wax-based ribbon or transfer dye onto plain paper (see Figure 5-11). The wax-based printers can produce text output that rivals a daisywheel's and, because they use a dot-matrix print head, can support high-quality graphics as well (see Figure 5-11a). The more-expensive dye-based printers, which have just recently become available, can produce images of near-photographic quality (see Figure 5-11b).

Nonimpact printing.
The formation of characters on a surface by means of heat, lasers, photography, or ink jets.

of them utilize an electrophotographic process similar to that used by the copying machines found in many offices. The printing commonly occurs on 8-by-11-inch paper, which is cheaper than the larger, sprocket-fed paper line printers typically use. The smaller-size paper is cheaper to file and mail as well. Some page printers can print in color and on both sides of the page.

A useful feature of page printers is their ability to output digital images of forms and letterheads. Forms can be filled out by users at display devices and automatically printed. Thus, page printers offer considerable savings over line printers, which require changing of paper and printing elements when output dictates a new form or format.

Page printers generally cost considerably more than line printers. Line printers range from $3,000 to $50,000, whereas page printers for large computers may cost between $50,000 and $300,000. In general, an organization that produces over a million lines of output per month should investigate the feasibility of acquiring one of these machines.

Source Data Automation

Often data must be translated from handwritten form into machine-readable form so that they can be processed, a procedure that sometimes consumes thousands of hours of duplicated effort and that can result in many mistakes and delays. Data must be hand-entered on documents or forms, keyed into machine-readable form on a data preparation device, verified, and read into the computer. Usually, several people will be involved in this process, complicating matters further.

Source data automation.
The process of making data available in machine-readable form at the time they are collected.

Source data automation eliminates much of this duplicated effort, delay, extra handling, and potential for error by making data available in machine-readable form at the time they are collected. Because ready-to-process transaction data are collected by the people who know most about them, source data automation is rapidly becoming the dominant form of data entry today.

Source data automation has been applied to a number of tasks. For example, many orders taken over the phone today are entered directly into display workstations, so they don't have to be recorded twice. Source data automation has also been used to speed up checkout lines and inventory taking at supermarkets, quality control operations in factories, and processing of checks by banks.

In the next few pages, we will discuss several technologies that can be used to achieve source data automation: optical character recognition (OCR), magnetic ink character recognition (MICR), digitizing, image scanning, voice input, handwriting recognition, and smart cards.

Optical Character Recognition (OCR)

Optical character recognition (OCR).
The use of light reflectivity to identify marks, characters, or codes.

Optical character recognition (OCR) refers to a wide range of optical-scanning procedures and equipment designed for machine recognition of marks, characters, and codes. These symbols are transformed into digital form for storage in the computer. Most symbols designed for OCR can be read by humans as well as by machines. Optical recognition of hand-printed characters is also technically possible but is still in its infancy. OCR equipment is among the

A selection of characters from an optical character set.

FIGURE 5 – 16

ABCDEFGHIJKLMN
OPQRSTUVWXYZ
1234567890

most varied and highly specialized in the information processing industry. A scanner that can read one type of document may be totally unable to read another.

FIGURE 5 – 17

An informative cash register receipt made possible by a local memory.

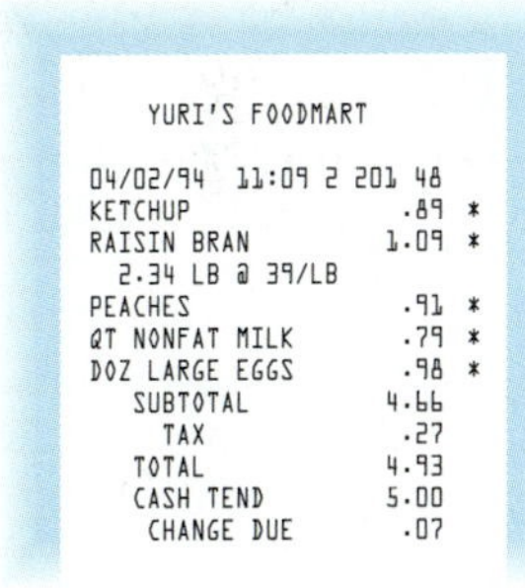

Optical Marks   One of the oldest applications of OCR is the processing of tests and questionnaires completed on special forms using *optical marks*. Take the case of grading a test in which the student darkens the bubbles on the answer sheet to indicate the answers to multiple-choice questions. An optical document reader scans the answer sheets offline. This machine passes a light beam across the spaces corresponding to the set of possible responses to each question. The light is reflected where a response is penciled in, and the machine tallies that choice.

Optical Characters   *Optical characters* are characters specially designed to be identifiable by humans as well as by some type of OCR reader. Optical characters conform to a certain font, such as that shown in Figure 5-16. The optical reader reflects light off the characters and converts them into electronic patterns for recognition. The reader can identify a character only if it is familiar with the font used.

In the early days of optical character reading, fonts differed widely among OCR manufacturers. As the years passed, however, a few fonts became industry standards. Today many machines are designed to read several fonts even when these fonts are mixed in a single document.

Probably the best-known use of optical characters is in **point-of-sale (POS) systems,** which are employed widely in retail stores. POS systems allow a store to record a purchase at the time and place it occurs. A sale is often automatically recorded from machine-readable information on a price tag attached to the product. The information on the tag is input to a special cash register. Today many cash registers are equipped with local, direct-access memories containing descriptions of stocked items, so they can print what each item is along with its price on the customer receipt (see Figure 5-17 and the Tomorrow box).

```
       YURI'S FOODMART

04/02/94  11:09 2 201 48
KETCHUP              .89 *
RAISIN BRAN         1.09 *
   2.34 LB @ 39/LB
PEACHES              .91 *
QT NONFAT MILK       .79 *
DOZ LARGE EGGS       .98 *
     SUBTOTAL       4.66
          TAX        .27
        TOTAL       4.93
    CASH TEND       5.00
   CHANGE DUE        .07
```

Point-of-sale (POS) system.
A computer system, commonly found in department stores and supermarkets, that uses electronic cash register terminals to process sales transactions.

Retailing in the 21st Century

How Much Will Technology Change the Way We Shop?

Like a lot of other industries, retailing has turned into a dog-eat-dog affair. If a supermarket or a department store doesn't have price, quality, convenience, or some type of curiosity factor going for it these days, it probably doesn't have much of a future.

Retailing has undergone many changes in the recent past. Warehouse stores and factory outlets have sprouted up to appeal to the price conscious. More and more companies are selling by catalog to professionals who don't have time to shop. And for customers who have both time and money but savor convenience, the competition among retailers to provide the best-quality service has reached heights that probably few dreamed of just a couple of decades ago. In all cases, the bottom line in the retailing business has come down to maintaining a competitive advantage in some key area.

Many companies are turning to technology for new ways to provide such an advantage. Some ideas are now getting a serious look:

■ **Self-service checkout aisles.** This service would allow grocery shoppers to scan their own bar codes at the checkout counter. "Smart" hardware and software products will be available to make sure no one cheats. For instance, each product scanned must be put on an intelligent scale before it's sent to the section where it can be packaged. That would prevent a $12.45 rump roast from being declared a 59-cent head of lettuce.

■ **Shopping by computer network.** Some futurists say that as computer networks become ever more popular people will begin doing more of their shopping by remote computer. Someday you might be able to call your local supermarket on your home or office computer, electronically select the items you want to buy, and show up at a distribution center where the items are all bagged and ready to take home.

■ **Signature systems.** The cost of handling signed paper receipts amounts to a large expense for any retail firm. Recently, pen-based handwriting systems have come to the fore that eliminate the need to file hard copies of signatures. The customer signs a digitizing pad that has a paper receipt on it; the customer then receives the paper copy, while the store logs the electronic copy into its record system.

■ **Information kiosks.** In supermarkets, you would be able to go up to a kiosk—a booth that looks like an automatic-teller machine at a bank—and get recipe information. Not only that, you would also be able to find the aisles where the ingredients for the recipe can be found and check to see if the items you want are in stock. In department stores, you could also use a kiosk to see how sweaters or shirts look on photorealistic models—in any color or style available.

■ **Tracking systems.** While many stores know what's selling and what's not, they desperately need information on *how* people shop. Some companies are now using computer-based sensor systems to count the number of shoppers visiting various areas of their stores. Kiosks can also be used to monitor the number of times requests of a certain type are made.

■ **Multifunction cash registers.** The first generation of cash registers merely rang up each sale. Then, in the 1960s, point-of-sale (POS) terminals came along to process sales electronically. The most recent crop of cash registers are multifunctional workstations that also make it possible for store personnel to check inventory at member stores, if a demanded item is not in stock (see photo).

■ **Video information.** Now in the test stage at several stores are videocarts—weather-

proof, flat-panel displays that attach onto the backs of supermarket carts (see photo). When the cart enters a particular aisle, the screen picks up data from a transmitter and displays information about nearby products. At the checkout counter, the video cart also provides information on news and sports to keep shoppers from getting bored. Electronic, flat-panel shelf tags are now also being tried out in a number of stores to keep prices up to date and, at the push of a button, provide such data as cost per serving and coupon discounts.

■ **Virtual reality.**   Perhaps the ultimate in shopping—though still many years away—is the virtual-reality store. The customer will don a special pair of goggles and gloves and will then be sent through a magical-mystery tour of a shopping experience without ever leaving home. Virtual reality was covered in the Chapter 2 Tomorrow box.

Magnetic ink character recognition (MICR). MICR is a technology confined almost exclusively to the banking industry, where it is used for processing checks in high volume. (a) A MICR-encoded check. (b) An electronic sorter capable of processing 2,400 checks a minute.

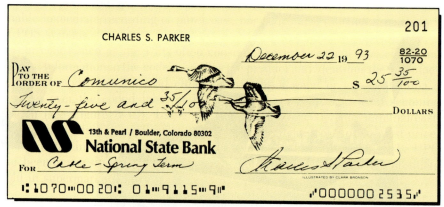

(a)

(b)

The characters are written on the check with a special magnetic ink. As with OCR readers, a machine called a MICR reader/sorter senses the identity of a MICR-encoded character on the check by recognizing its shape. But in contrast to OCR, the characters must be magnetized in order to be sensed by the reading device; no optical recognition is used. With MICR, checks can be quickly sorted, processed, and routed to the proper banks (see Figure 5-21b).

Digitizers

A **digitizer** is a device that converts a measurement into a digital value. By being moved along a surface or, alternatively, staying stationary and having another device move along them, digitizers determine position, distance, or speed and move the cursor on the display screen accordingly. Digitizers aid source data automation because they directly collect data on events in machine-readable form. Six common types of digitizers are the mouse, light pen, joystick, trackball, crosshair cursor, and digitizing tablet.

Mouse   Many people supplement keyboard operations with a **mouse,** the most widely used digitizing device (see Figure 5-22). When the mouse is moved along a flat surface, the cursor on the display screen moves correspondingly. Mice are very useful for moving the cursor rapidly from one location to another on a display screen, and for dragging images from one part of the screen to another. Using a mouse often is much faster than pressing combinations of cursor-movement keys on keyboard. Mice are especially handy when pointing to **icons** on the screen—small graphics symbols that represent commands or program options. When you use the mouse, say, to move to an icon on the display screen, you select or activate that icon by clicking a button on the mouse once or twice.

Light Pen   A **light pen** contains a light-sensitive cell in its tip. When the tip of the pen is placed close to the screen, the display device can identify its

Digitizer.
An input device that converts a measurement into a digital value.

Mouse.
A device used to rapidly move a cursor around a display screen.

Icon.
A graphical image on a display screen that invokes a particular program action when activated by the operator.

Light pen.
An electrical device, resembling an ordinary pen, used to enter input.

FIGURE 5 – 22

Mouse input. When the mouse is moved along a flat surface, the cursor on the display screen moves correspondingly.

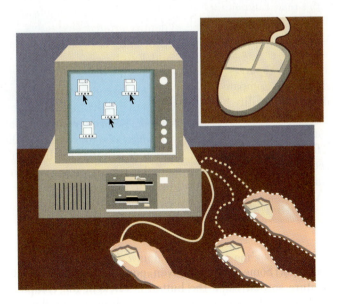

Plotters. Plotters are designed to produce charts, drawings, maps, and other forms of graphical hard copy. (a) Flatbed pen plotter. (b) Electrostatic drum plotter.

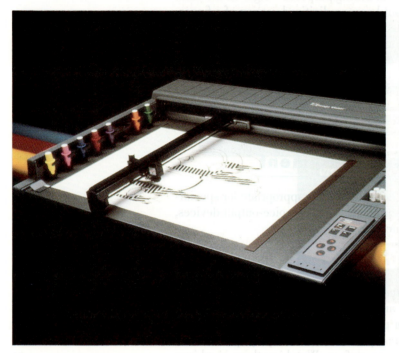

(a)

(b)

Voice-output device.
A device that enables the computer system to produce spoken output.

774-0202, is no longer in service," or "The time is 6:15 . . . the downtown temperature is 75 degrees"? **Voice-output devices,** the machines responsible for such messages, convert digital data in storage into spoken messages. These messages may be constructed as needed from a file of prerecorded words, or they may be synthesized using other techniques.

Computerized voice output is also used extensively at airline terminals to broadcast information about flight departures and arrivals, in the securities business to quote the prices of stocks and bonds, and in the supermarket industry to announce descriptions and prices of items as they are scanned. Voice output has great potential in any company with employees who do little else all day but, say, give out balances and status reports.

Currently one of the main shortcomings of this technology is that the number of potential messages is limited if the system must create them extemporaneously. Most voice-output devices have a vocabulary on the order of a few hundred words and a limited ability to combine words dynamically to form intelligible sentences. As a result, these devices are most useful when short messages are required—a telephone number, a bank balance, a price, and so on.

Film Recorders

Film recorders are cameralike devices that capture high-resolution, computer-generated images directly onto 35mm slides, transparencies, and other film media. Just a few years ago, film recorders served only large computers, with which they were used for applications such as art, medical imaging, and scientific CAD work. Today they are increasingly being used with PCs for applications such as spicing up corporate business meetings or client presentations with slide shows. Some experts predict that such computer-generated slides will soon account for a large percentage of all business slides made. Because film recorders, like cameras, are "dumb" and need not recognize an image in order to record it, they can easily transfer onto film virtually any image that can be captured on a display screen. Most of the images in Window 2 were produced on film recorders, which by far provide the highest resolution of any of the output devices discussed in this chapter.

Film recorder.
A cameralike device that captures computer output onto film.

Computer Output Microfilm (COM)

Computer output microfilm (COM) is a way of placing computer output on microfilm media, typically either a *microfilm reel* or *microfiche card*. Microfilming can result in tremendous savings in paper costs, storage space, the mailing of document images, and handling. For example, a 4-by-6-inch microfiche card can contain the equivalent of 270 printed pages. COM is particulary useful for organizations that must keep massive files of information that do not need to be updated. It's also useful for organizations that need to manipulate large amounts of data but find fast methods of online access too costly. In recent years, the near monopoly once held by COM for efficient document storage and retrieval has been seriously challenged by optical disks.

Computer output microfilm (COM).
A term that refers to reducing computer output to microscopic form and putting it on photosensitive film.

Summary and Key Terms

A wide variety of input and output devices is available in today's marketplace.

Input and Output   Input and output devices enable people and computers to communicate. **Input devices** convert data and programs into a form that the CPU will understand. **Output devices** convert computer-processed information into a form that people will comprehend.

Output devices produce results in either hard copy or soft copy form. The term **hard copy** generally refers to output that has been recorded into a *permanent* form onto a medium such as paper or microfilm. The term **soft copy,** in contrast, generally refers to display output, which is *temporary.*

Keyboards   For most people, a computer system would be useless without a **keyboard,** which is often the main vehicle for input. Keyboards vary tremendously in terms of such factors as number of keys, key arrangement, types of special keys, and touch. Most computer keyboards offer several *function keys*—labeled F1, F2, and so on—that can be used to activate single commands or entire computer programs. Usually a *numeric keypad* is also present that allows numbers to be keyed in faster.

Display Devices   **Display devices** are peripheral devices that contain a televisionlike viewing screen. Most display devices fall into one of two categories: monitors and display terminals. A **monitor** is an output device that consists of only the viewing screen. A **display terminal** is an input/output communications workstation that consists of a screen for output and a keyboard for input. As each key on the keyboard is depressed, the corresponding character representation of the key appears on the display screen at the **cursor** position.

One common way to classify display devices is according to whether they are monochrome or color. *Monochrome* display devices output using a single foreground color, whereas *color* display devices often are capable of outputting in eight or more colors.

Most display devices on the market today use a large picture-tube element similar to those found inside standard TV sets. These devices are called **CRTs (cathode-ray tubes).** Recently, slim-profile devices called **flat-panel displays** have also become available.

A key characteristic of any display device is *resolution,* or the sharpness of the screen image. On many display devices, resolution is measured by the number of dots, or **pixels,** on the screen. With **bit mapping,** the operator can control each pixel on the screen.

Printers   Unlike display devices, **printers** produce hard-copy output. *Low-speed printers* output one character at a time. Because of their relatively low cost, they are popular units for small computer systems. *High-speed printers,* which can output either a line or a page at a time, are popular for larger computer systems.

All printers use either an impact or a nonimpact printing technology. In **impact printing,** a hammer strikes the paper or ribbon to form characters. A **solid-font mechanism** is an impact device that produces fully formed characters like those a typewriter creates. Most low-speed printers in use today employ a print head that's an **impact dot-matrix mechanism,** which constructs printed characters out of a series of closely packed dots. **Nonimpact printing,** which outputs dot-matrix characters, uses a variety of techniques to form printed images. The most popular nonimpact printing methods today use *electrothermal, thermal-transfer, ink-jet,* and *laser* technologies.

The printers most commonly found on microcomputer systems are low-speed devices. Although impact-dot-matrix printers are still the most widely used devices, relatively high-speed laser printers have become especially popular in the last few years. Laser printers produce letter-quality output that rivals that of solid-font printers, quickly generate presentation graphics for reports and meetings, and enable certain publishing functions to be performed on a desktop.

Most of the printing done on large computer systems is accomplished by high-speed printers. High-speed printers fall into one of two major categories; **line printers,** which produce a line of output at a time, and **page printers,** which produce a page of output at a time.

Source Data Automation   **Source data automation** refers to technologies for collecting data in machine-readable form at their point of origin. Among these technologies are optical character recognition (OCR), magnetic ink character recognition (MICR), digitizing, image scanning, voice input, handwriting recognition, and smart cards.

Optical character recognition (OCR) refers to a wide range of optical-scanning procedures and equipment designed for machine recognition of marks, characters, and codes. *Optical marks* are most frequently used in test-taking situations in which students darken bubbles on special forms to show responses. Probably the best-known use of *optical characters* is in the **point-of-sale (POS) systems** widely used at checkout stations in stores. In many of these systems, the characters on the price tag are coded in a special font readable by both machines and humans. Some POS systems use *optical codes*, such as **bar codes.** The most widely used bar code is the *universal product code (UPC)*, which appears on the labels of most packaged supermarket goods.

An **image scanner** is used to input images such as photographs, drawings, and documents into computer storage. In the case of text documents, some image scanners are accompanied by software that enables the scanners to recognize the inputted characters.

Magnetic ink character recognition (MICR) is a technology confined almost exclusively to the banking industry. MICR characters, preprinted on bank checks, enable the checks to be rapidly sorted, processed, and routed to the proper banks.

A **digitizer** is an input device that converts a measurement into a digital value. One of the most widely used digitizers is the **mouse,** which, when rolled along a flat surface, moves the screen cursor accordingly. Mice are especially handy when pointing to **icons** on the screen. Some other widely used digitizing devices are the **light pen, joystick, trackball, crosshair cursor,** and **digitizing tablet.** Display devices that are designed to allow a finger rather than a light pen to activate the screen are commonly called **touch-screen devices.**

Voice-input devices enable computer systems to recognize the spoken word. Voice-input technologies have tremendous work-saving potential but have been slow to mature because of their relative complexity.

Handwriting recognition devices generally consist of a flat-screen display tablet and a penlike stylus. Practically speaking, handwriting recognition devices are still in the pioneering stage, and virtually all systems commercially available today can recognize only hand-printed characters.

Smart cards are credit-card sized pieces of plastic that contain a microprocessor chip and a memory.

Special-Purpose Output Equipment   A number of special-purpose output devices exist for a variety of information processing applications. Among these are plotters, voice-output devices, film recorders and computer output microfilm (COM) equipment.

A **plotter** is an output device that is used primarily to produce graphic output such as charts, maps, and engineering drawings. The two most common types of plotters are *pen plotters,* which use drawing pens to create images, and *electrostatic plotters,* which create images through electrostatic charges. Whether they employ pens or electrostatic charges, plotters are of either the flatbed or the drum type. A *flatbed plotter* uses a drawing surface that resembles a drafting table. A *drum plotter* draws on a cylindrically backed surface.

Voice-output devices enable computer systems to compose intelligible spoken messages from digitally stored words and phrases.

Film recorders are cameralike devices that are used to capture computer-generated images directly onto 35mm slides, transparencies, and other film media. Virtually any image that can be captured on a display screen can be output onto film.

Computer output microfilm (COM) is a way of placing computer output on microfilm media such as microfilm reels or microfiche cards. COM can result in savings in paper costs, storage space, and handling.

Review Exercises

Fill-in Questions

1. The term _____ generally refers to output that has been recorded onto a medium such as paper or film.

2. Resolution on a display screen is measured by the number of dots, or _____.

3. A highlighted position on a display screen indicating where the next character the operator types in will be placed is called a(n) _____.

4. A display device that outputs images in a single foreground color is known as a(n) _____ display.

5. High-quality dot-matrix printing is sometimes called _____ (NLQ) printing.

6. A(n) _____ printer heats ink from a wax-based ribbon onto paper.

7. A(n) _____ printer sprays small droplets of electrically charged ink onto paper to form images.

8. Two types of pen plotters are _____ and _____ plotters.

9. A display device in which all screen pixels can be controlled by the operator is called _____.

10. A(n) _____ is a cameralike device used to capture computer-generated images directly onto 35mm slides.

Matching Questions

Match each term with the description that fits best.

a. crosshair cursor   d. UPC   g. plotter
b. OCR   e. MICR   h. mouse
c. POS   f. COM

____ 1. Used almost exclusively by the banking industry.

____ 2. Refers to microfilmed output.

___3. A type of output device used to produce graphical images on paper with pens.

___4. Refers to a collection of different technologies used for optical recognition of marks, characters, and codes.

___5. A code that is prominent on the packaging of most supermarket goods.

___6. A device that would be useful for digitizing a map into computer storage.

___7. A device used to move the cursor rapidly around the display screen.

___8. Refers to the use of electronic cash registers, optical scanning devices, and so forth in retail establishments.

Discussion Questions

1. List several types of input and output devices. State whether each device is used for input, output, or both.

2. Identify several ways in which display devices differ.

3. Name some hardware devices that are used in conjunction with display devices for entering data into the computer system.

4. In what major respects do printers differ?

5. What is source data automation, and why is it significant?

6. How does MICR differ from OCR?

7. What are the limitations of voice-input and voice-output devices?

8. What is the difference between VGA and Super VGA?

Critical Thinking Questions

1. A page of typed text that is created and saved with a word processor takes up a different amount of storage than a copy of that same page read by a scanner. Why do you think this is so? Which would take up more space?

2. Some people predicted years ago that there would never be a significant market for color CRTs among office workers. This prediction proved dead wrong. What do you think motivated this prediction and why would you guess it proved wrong?

3. The president of J.C. Penney has stated that the leading retailers in the future will be those who make the best use of information processing technologies. Do you agree with this point of view? Explain why or why not.

2

2–3. Two watercolors produced with a painting package.

3

Special Effects

Many art packages have an assortment of drawing and/or painting tools that enable artists to imitate traditional art forms, creating images that look as if they were produced with pastels or watercolors, were sketched, or were painted with oils.

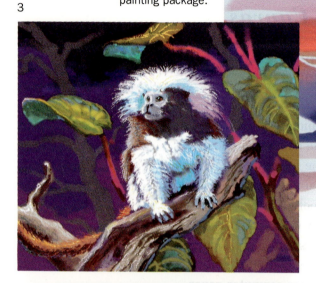

4. Using a painting package to impart an oil-painting effect.

5. Many painting packages come with a feature that generates a chalklike rendering of all or part of an art piece.

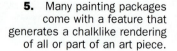

6

7

8

6–8. Airbrushing is a special effect commonly found in art packages. It allows a color gradient to be applied to a defined surface—like a background, sky, or snow bank—making it look more natural.

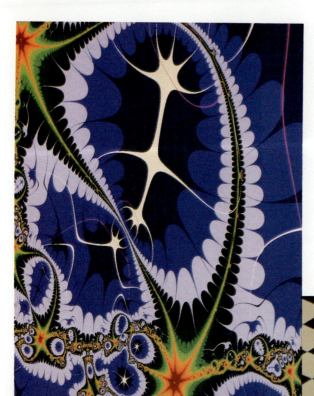

9

Algorithmic Art

Many forms of computer art are based upon complex mathematical algorithms. These algorithms allow the artist to specify formulas that create sophisticated geometric shapes and curious random patterns. Art pieces produced in this way are often somewhat "accidental," in that the artist has partly left the computer in charge of generating images.

10

9–11. The art of Clifford Pickover—of IBM's Thomas J. Watson Research Center—often mimics patterns and forms found in nature.

11

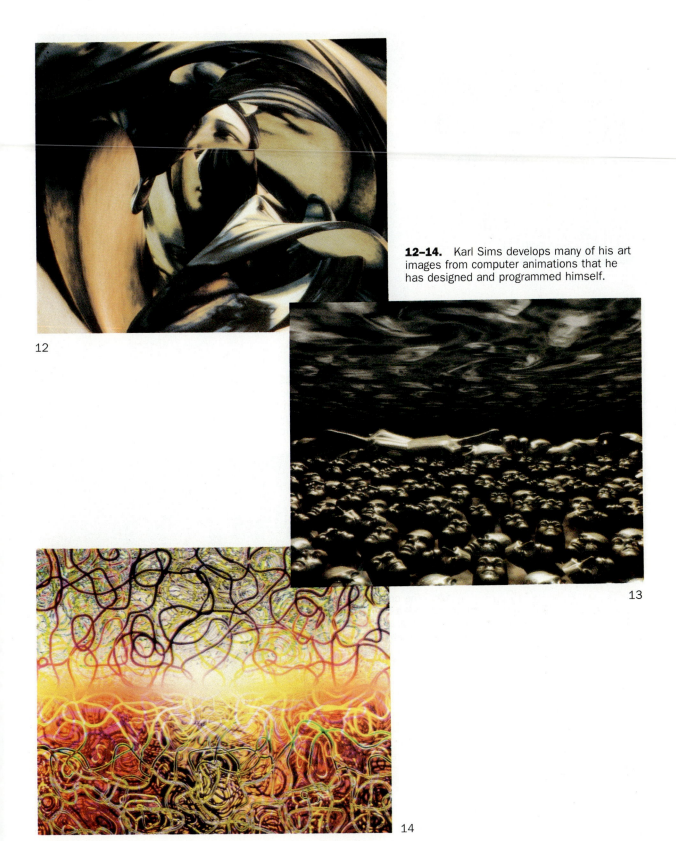

12

12–14. Karl Sims develops many of his art images from computer animations that he has designed and programmed himself.

13

14

15

16

15–17. Photorealistic images are often produced using special art packages that work in three dimensions and have natural-lighting tools. Many of the techniques used evolved from the movie industry.

17

18. The computer is often used as a tool to enhance photographs, making them more spectacular, as is done here to a background by artist David Rickerd.

Photorealism

Computers today are capable of creating very-high-resolution images that look as though they were captured with a camera.

18

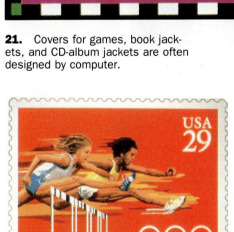

19

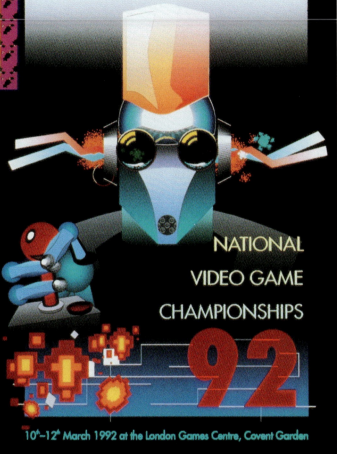

Commercial Art

Today, usually the most cost-effective way to produce art for commercial purposes is by computer. Shown here is just a small sampling of applications employed in the commercial art field.

19–20. Holiday cards and posters are natural outlets for computer-produced art.

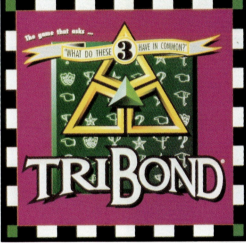

21. Covers for games, book jackets, and CD-album jackets are often designed by computer.

20

22–23. A set of stamps can be quickly developed and redesigned by computer technology.

22   23

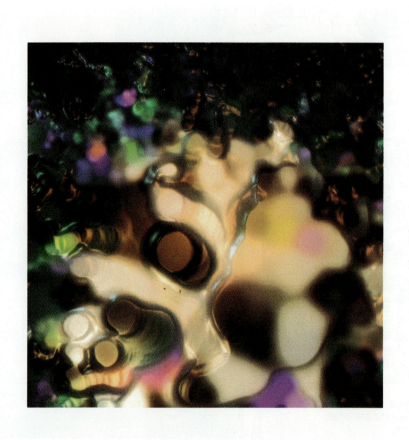

SUPPORT SYSTEMS

In this module we examine two areas that play support roles in a computer system—telecommunications and systems software.

Telecommunications, covered in Chapter 6, refers to applications that involve data traveling over distances, as well as the hardware and software that enable this to be done. For instance, special hardware devices send data over ordinary phone lines, and software is required to ensure that the receiving devices understand exactly what the sending devices are communicating. Because companies need to transmit and receive up-to-date information to operate successfully in today's highly competitive world, telecommunications is a top priority on managers' agendas.

Systems software, the topic of Chapter 7, refers to the programs that enable applications software to run on hardware devices. Systems software allows you to start up your computer system, summon applications programs so that you can work on them, recover lost files, reorganize disk storage, and translate applications software into the machine language native to your computer. Everybody who uses a computer system must in some way interact with systems software.

TELECOMMUNICATIONS

6

What's hot in the world of telecommunications? As discussed in Chapter 6, wireless technology, which enables electronic data to be sent from and received virtually anywhere. Wireless technology has changed the way many companies do business and made it possible for developing countries to compete economically.

LEARNING OBJECTIVES

After completing this chapter, you will be able to:

1. Describe several uses of telecommunications technology.

2. Identify the hardware and software components of a telecommunications system.

3. Describe various types of communications media and explain how messages can be sent over them.

4. Identify some types of communications services and network facilities that organizations may acquire.

5. Explain the conventions that devices use to communicate with one another.

6. Describe some of the strategies used to manage networks.

Overview

Telecommunications, or *telecom,* refers to communication over a distance—over phone lines, via privately owned cable, or by satellite, for instance. Today, telecommunications technologies are integrated in a variety of ways into many organizations' routine operations. Through telecommunications, for example, a marketing manager at company headquarters can instantly receive information on inventories from a warehouse at another location and then transmit that information to a division office across the country or even across the globe. Or a purchasing agent on the 25th floor of an office building can use a personal computer workstation to call up the status of a purchase order stored on the mainframe system located in the building's basement. Later, the agent can use

FIGURE 6-1

Distributed processing: trailing a VISA transaction. (a) In Chicago, a VISA card is used to pay for a $1,295 computer. (b) The transaction data travel by satellite or by ground to a processing center in New Jersey. (c) Because the transaction tops $50, it is routed to a computer in Atlanta for closer scrutiny. (d) The computer in Atlanta sends the transaction to California for processing. (e) The California computer finds that the card was issued by a Portland bank and checks that bank's computer system to see if the transaction request should be approved or denied. The answer retraces the same path back to the store. The total elapsed time of the transaction is 15 seconds.

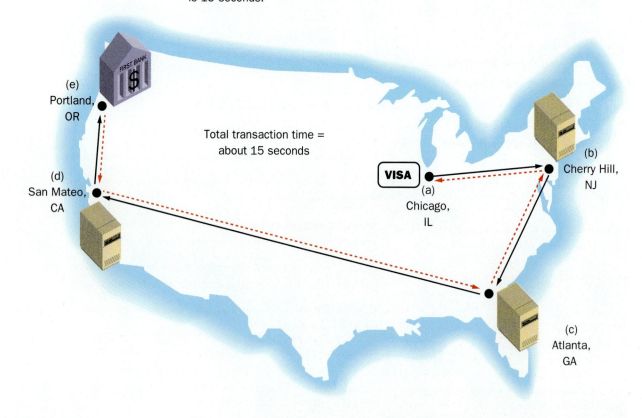

U s e r   S o l u t i o n   6 – 1

Speeding Products to Market with Networks

At TRW's Ross Gear Division, gears, linkages, and related components for trucks are designed and manufactured. A computer network enables professionals to electronically collaborate on engineering drawings, thereby getting work done faster and reducing the time between a product's conception and the day it goes on the market. Such speed often translates into a competitive advantage for TRW. The network now in place stores product designs on a mainframe-based system. Engineers can download the designs onto their local PC workstations. There, new drawings can be quickly cut and pasted out of old ones, sent back to the mainframe, and electronically accessed locally or remotely by co-workers and clients.

the same workstation to dial up a computer owned by a supplier, 1,000 miles away, and get a list of prices. User Solution 6-1 provides a good example of how companies are increasingly relying on telecommunications to keep competitive.

In this chapter, we'll look first at several business applications of telecommunications. Then we'll consider how data are sent over distances. We'll begin by describing the media that carry data, such as phone lines and microwaves, as well as the types of signals that encode the data. Next, we'll discuss the various ways in which people or organizations can get the resources they need to transmit data. Finally, we'll examine several issues concerning the management of telecommunications traffic.

Telecommunications Applications

Today a wide variety of important business applications involve telecommunications. Here we'll briefly discuss several.

Distributed Transaction Processing   At one time, transaction processing operations such as accounts receivable and order entry were totally centralized. As communications systems made it possible to *distribute* workloads to multiple sites, many organizations modified their systems accordingly. The airlines' passenger reservation system is one noteworthy example; thousands of agents located across the globe use display terminals or microcomputer workstations to tap into computerized databases located elsewhere that contain flight, hotel, and rental-car information. While a computer in, say, Chicago is processing a Cerritos, California, agent's request for flight information, that same agent may be processing a ticket for another client locally. Credit-card systems, such as the one for VISA shown in Figure 6-1, are also good examples of distributed

FIGURE 6 – 2

Electronic data interchange. Electronic data interchange enables companies to electronically exchange documents such as purchase orders and bills.

transaction processing. Once a store clerk inserts your credit card into a verification terminal, computers hundreds or thousands of miles away approve or deny the purchase.

Virtually every large organization today has several types of distributed transaction processing systems in place. For instance, chain stores often collect and process data locally, then transmit these data to a headquarters site for timely analysis. Mail-order firms frequently process orders at one site and then transmit transaction data to a warehouse site to initiate packing and delivery. The applications are virtually endless.

Strategic Alliances   Recently, many companies have gone a step further with their distributed transaction processing systems by creating *inter-organizational systems (IOSs)*, in which their computers are strategically linked to the computers of key customers and/or suppliers. For instance, many of the major automakers use their own computer systems to constantly monitor their suppliers' computer systems to ensure that proper inventory levels for critical parts are kept. They also may use the IOSs to shop electronically for the best prices.

Another widely used type of interorganizational information system used now by many companies is **electronic data interchange (EDI).** EDI enables standard business documents such as purchase orders and invoices to be exchanged from one company's computer system to the computer system of another company (see Figure 6-2). The company doing the purchasing often is able to electronically track its order's progress on the seller's computer system.

Companies that wish to exchange transaction documents through EDI must have compatible systems for this. If they don't, they can take advantage of EDI

Electronic data interchange (EDI). A computer procedure that enables standard business documents—such as purchase orders and invoices—to be exchanged electronically between companies.

by contacting an intermediary firm that has the hardware and software to take EDI transmissions from one company and recode them in a form that can be sent to the other company. Many large companies today order a sizable percentage of their supplies and raw materials through computer-to-computer order processing.

Electronic Mailboxes and Voice Mail   Electronic **mailboxes** are the computer-age equivalents of traditional mailboxes. They consist of files on hard disk, belonging to specific individuals or accounts, authorized to receive electronic messages. In one common application, a manager types a memo and electronically routes it to the electronic mailboxes of selected company employees (see Figure 6-3).

Voice mail, which involves voice data, is a telecommunications technology that takes electronic mailboxes one step further. In a voice-mail system, the sender's spoken messages are digitized by voice tone and stored in bit form on an answering device at the receiver's location. When the receiver presses a "listen" key, the digitized message is reconverted to voice data.

Bulletin Boards   Whereas electronic mailboxes usually consist of several individual files, each accessible by one specific person, an **electronic bulletin board** is a file that is shared by many people. Each person with access to the

Electronic mailbox.
A storage area used to hold messages, memos, and other documents sent to a person.

Voice mail.
An electronic mail system in which spoken phone messages are digitally recorded and stored in an electronic mailbox.

Electronic bulletin board.
A computer file that is shared by several people, enabling them to post or broadcast messages.

FIGURE 6-3

Electronic mailboxes. With an electronic mail package, users can create or summon electronic documents and route them to the electronic mailboxes of selected individuals.

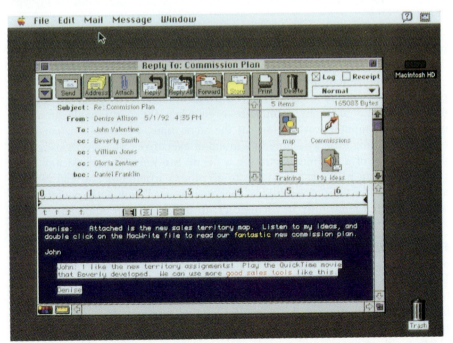

FIGURE 6-4

Fax transmission. A three-page memo can be sent from Kansas City to New York in less than a minute. In Kansas City, pages are placed in an input hopper in the back of the fax machine. As they are read, they exit out the front. The images are sent over the phone lines in electronic form, and when they reach New York, they are converted into natural-language form—identical to the originals—and output on continuous-roll fax paper.

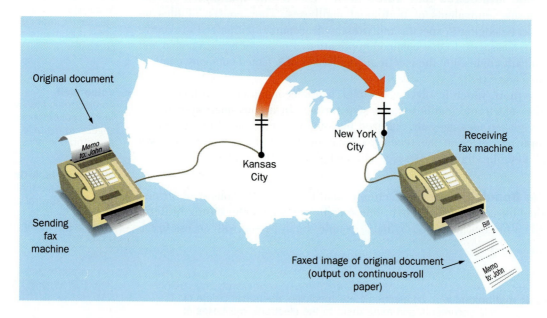

Original document

Sending fax machine

Kansas City

New York City

Receiving fax machine

Faxed image of original document (output on continuous-roll paper)

bulletin board can see the information "posted" on it, add information, and delete information.

Many organizations use in-house bulletin boards to carry out a high-tech phenomenon known as *computer conferencing*. Computer conferencing allows a meeting to take place by computer—even when the participants aren't all using their computer workstations at the same time. For instance, computer conferencing might be available to a group of executives who are investigating the feasibility of a big merger during a hectic two-week period. At any time, participants can broadcast messages to all other participants and can retrieve all or any part of the proceedings of the "conference." Computer conferencing will be covered more fully in Chapter 11, in the section on office automation.

Facsimile (fax) machine. A device that can transmit or receive hard-copy images of text, pictures, maps, diagrams, and the like over the phone lines.

Facsimile Machines   **Facsimile (fax) machines** enable hard-copy images of documents to be sent from one location to another over ordinary phone lines. For example, a secretary in Kansas City may place a short document containing both text and pictures into a fax machine, such as the one in Figure 6-4. The fax machine will digitize the page images and transmit them over ordinary phone lines to New York. In New York another fax machine will receive the electronic page images and reproduce them in hard-copy form. All of this may take place in less than a minute. Also, microcomputer systems can be equipped with *fax boards* that enable them to communicate with fax machines.

Facsimile machines have been in use for a long time. If you're an old-movie buff, you may remember the 1948 film *Call Northside 777*, in which a young Jimmy Stewart proves that a key trial witness has lied by summoning from across the country a timely fax image contradicting her testimony. It has only been since the recent development of both the microprocessor and improved manufacturing techniques, however, that inexpensive faxing—and the ensuing boom in persnal fax machines—has occurred.

Information Retrieval   The assortment of information you can get over the phone lines today is, in a word, amazing. Thousands of public databases are currently available for online *information retrieval*. Among these are services for recreational users, shoppers, businesses, researchers, travelers, and other microcomputer users with specialized information needs.

Businesspeople can summon a variety of corporate financial reports, such as those available from Moody's, Standard & Poor's, and Dun & Bradstreet. Also available is a never-ending stream of information from news wires such as those of Dow Jones and Reuters.

For researchers and others who read a lot, virtually every major general-interest or trade magazine, newspaper, and journal published worldwide is now online. Also, many regional newspapers in dozens of U.S. cities are available in electronic versions that can be "delivered" to your monitor screen. There are even clipping services that will scan publications for you and save articles in an electronic mailbox on subjects you designate.

Professionals such as lawyers and doctors also have databases targeted to their specialized needs. Mead Corporation, one of the largest electronic publishers, has been extremely successful with Lexis, a legal database. For the medical professional, there's Medis.

Most people get their online information through a particular services company, which works similarly to a pay-television network. When you subscribe to the services company, you gain access to the variety of participating databases to which it, in turn, subscribes. Prodigy and CompuServe, for instance, are targeted to information useful to the average person and they include news and weather, personal investing and money management, travel, and shopping (see Figure 6-5 and Window 3, which take an in-depth look at Prodigy). Many services companies have a one-time fee and, perhaps, an hourly hookup charge. They may also impose special charges for some types of services.

Cellular Phones   **Cellular phones** are mobile phones that do not need to be hooked up to a phone outlet in order to work. They can put two people into contact with each other anywhere, even if they are in motion.

Currently those who most benefit from the cellular phone boom are people who need to be in constant contact with the office or clients but must be on the move as well—such as a busy executive, salesperson, field worker, or real estate agent. Such a user might, for instance, take a cellular phone out of a briefcase and use it while waiting in line, sitting at a traffic light, or taxiing down a runway. People who work outdoors, such as farmers and refinery workers

Cellular phone.
A mobile phone that uses special stations called cells to communicate with the regular phone system.

Using Prodigy to fetch a stock quote. Shown here are the steps a user follows to make connections with Prodigy and request a quote.

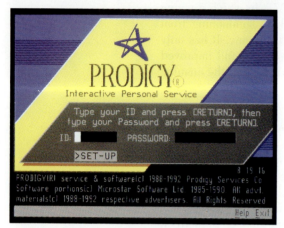

(a) The opening Prodigy screen.

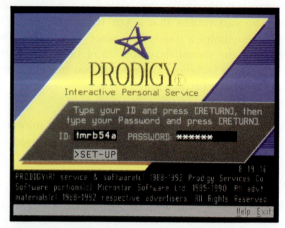

(b) User enters ID and password, with the password hidden. Prodigy is then automatically dialed.

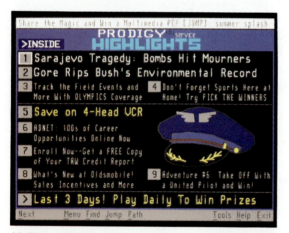

(c) The opening menu. User selects "Jump" (see bottom line) to access stock quotes.

(d) When the JUMP window box appears, the keyword "quote check" is entered at the cursor position.

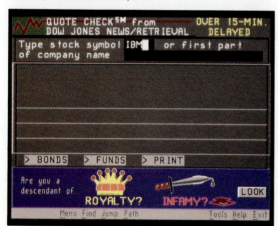

(e) When the Quote Check screen appears, the ticker symbol of a stock (e.g., IBM) is entered.

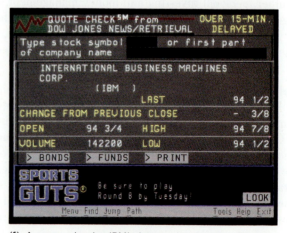

(f) A screen showing IBM's latest price appears. Other quotes can be retrieved similarly.

(see Figure 6-6), who may need to be in contact with others but can't afford the time it takes to get to a regular phone, are also reaping the benefits of cellular phone technology. You can even hook up a laptop computer with a cellular phone and gain access to huge databases of information while you are far from an office or a regular phone.

Cellular phones operate by keeping in contact with transmitter stations called *cell stations,* or *cells.* These stations, which resemble tall metal telephone poles, are strategically placed throughout a calling area. Cells perform two essential functions: (1) They provide an interface with the regular public phone network, and (2) they enable a moving vehicle with a phone to receive uninterrupted transmitting power by passing signals off to contiguous cells located in the zone into which the vehicle is moving.

Recently, allegations have been made that cellular-phone use—or overuse— may lead to brain cancer. To date, however, there is no proof that cellular phones are harmful.

Communications Media

Figure 6-7 shows a simple telecommunications system. Two hardware units that are distant from each other transfer messages over some type of **communications medium.** The hardware units may be a terminal and a computer, two computers, or some other combination of two devices. The medium may be privately operated, or it may use public phone lines, microwave, or some other alternative. When a message is transmitted, one of the hardware units is designated as the *sender* and the other as the *receiver.* There are several ways to send the message over the medium, as this section will demonstrate.

Types of Media

Communications media fall into one of two classes: physical lines and microwaves.

Physical Lines   Three types of physical lines are used in telecommunications systems today: twisted-pair wires, coaxial cable, and fiber optic cable.

Twisted-pair wires, in which strands of wire are twisted in twos, is the communications technology that has been in use the longest. The telephone

FIGURE 6-6

Cellular phones. Cellular phones are useful for people who are on the go, need to keep in contact with an office, or don't have access to a conventional phone.

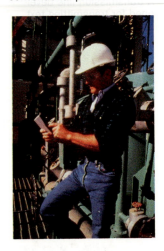

Communications medium. The intervening substance, such as a telephone wire or cable, that connects two physically distant hardware devices.

Twisted-pair wires. A communications medium consisting of pairs of wires twisted together and bound into a cable.

FIGURE 6-7

A simple telecommunications system. As complicated as telecommunications systems may seem, they reduce to simply one device being able to communicate effectively with another.

FIGURE 6 – 10

Communications satellites. Satellites move in correspondence to the earth's rotation, so they appear stationary to an observer on earth. Because each satellite can communicate effectively over slightly less than half the circumference of the earth, it takes a minimum of three satellites to provide worldwide service.

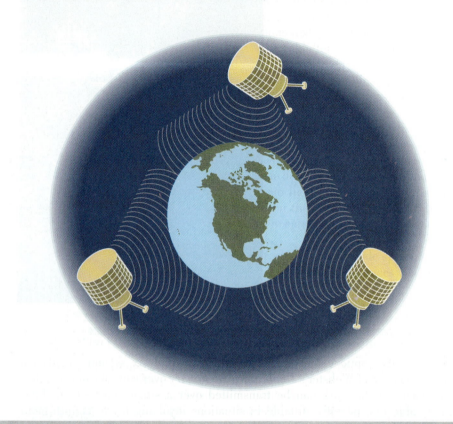

Communications satellite.
An earth-orbiting device that relays communications signals over long distances.

Communications satellites were developed to reduce the cost of long-distance transmission via terrestrial repeater stations as well as to provide a cheaper and better overseas communications medium than undersea cable. Communications satellites, such as the one shown in Figure 6-10, are placed into *geosynchronous orbit* thousands of miles above the earth. "Geosynchronous" means that, because they travel at a speed to keep pace with the earth's rotation, they appear to remain stationary over a given spot. During the 1991 Gulf War, satellites were deployed to pinpoint the positions of soldiers in the desert who carried small signaling devices about the size of paperbacks. This technology—called *global positioning*—is now being used in a variety of civilian applications, as the Tomorrow box explains.

Both communications satellites and terrestrial microwave stations are most appropriate for transmitting large amounts of data one way at a time. Thus, they are ideal for applications such as television and radio broadcasting. Because of the long transmission distances involved, they are often not feasible for rapid-response, interactive communications.

TOMORROW

Global Positioning Systems

Do You Know Where Your Truck Drivers Are?

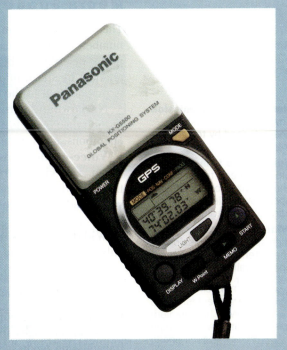

GPS unit. Small enough to be carried by back-country skiers and hikers.

Combine a technology that's been around for a couple of decades with a high-tech war and what do you get? A brand new technology and a better way of getting work done.

Global positioning systems (GPSs) were originally developed in the United States for military operations during the Persian Gulf War to pinpoint the position of troops. This new technology currently uses a squad of Department of Defense satellites that circle the earth, each in a different plane. When special hand-held devices, about the size of a paperback book, send signals to these satellites from earth, the exact latitude and longitude of the devices can be established within 45 feet. Not bad, considering satellites hover thousands of feet above the earth's surface.

Now that the Gulf War is history, GPS technology is enjoying a variety of civilian applications.

Take trucking—or any business that relies heavily on a vehicle fleet, such as the taxi trade or the overnight package business. In the past, it was often difficult for companies to tell exactly where a vehicle was at any given moment. Now, with the aid of GPSs, the home office can determine the location of all vehicles without requiring the driver to constantly call in. That means when an unanticipated passenger or package has to be picked up, the driver closest to the pickup location can be called. If the driver isn't available, a message can be left. Thus, companies can not only improve service, but they can manage their fleets in a more cost-effective manner.

In agriculture, GPSs are beginning to help with aerial crop spraying and—strange as it may seem—cutting down on pollution. Instead of relying on manual methods to determine where to take the next spray pass, pilots can use a GPS to pinpoint exactly where they are at all times. Consequently, planes can take the minimum number of passes and avoid overspraying. Even-

tually, say some advocates, GPSs will make it possible to speed up takeoffs and landings at commercial airports with increased reliability.

Scientists are also starting to benefit from GPSs. For instance, geologists can use global positioning to identify subtle changes in the earth's surface, thereby getting better advance warnings of earthquakes. It may someday also be possible to use satellites and computers to monitor the entire surface of the earth on a round-the-clock basis, thereby detecting even the tiniest environmental changes and their potential impact.

Affordable GPS devices would also be an ideal safety item for backpackers and backcountry skiers to carry with them on treacherous journeys. Additionally, the boating and automobile industries are anticipating the day when each boat or car comes equipped with a built-in GPS chip. Boats lost at sea would be a thing of the past. And just imagine how much more difficult it would be for anyone to steal your car.

As Figure 6-14 suggests, parallel transmission is much faster than serial transmission. However, because it requires many more channels, parallel transmission is also more expensive. Thus, parallel transmission usually is limited to short distances, such as computer-to-computer communications. Serial transmission is used to connect workstations to remote computer systems.

A common serial interface, the RS-232C, was developed to standardize remote computer-to-terminal connections. Modems, for instance, use this particular interface on many computer systems. An enhanced form of this interface, the RS-422, is widely used on the Apple Macintosh line of computers to connect modems, printers, and electronic musical instruments. These ports will also accept most RS-232C devices, which operate at higher voltages, without damage to the ports.

Of course, computers must communicate at high speeds with other nearby peripherals, such as disk and tape units. Since the distance involved is short, parallel transmission is feasible for this purpose. In many IBM microcomputer systems, nearby printers are connected in parallel to the computer's system unit with a popular standard known as the *Centronics* interface.

Asynchronous versus Synchronous Transmission

Asynchronous transmission.
The transmission of data over a line one character at a time.

Serial transmission can be further classified in terms of whether it's asynchronous or synchronous.

In **asynchronous transmission,** one character at a time is transmitted over a line. When the operator strikes a key on the terminal, the character's byte

---

FIGURE 6 – 15

Asynchronous and synchronous transmission. In asynchronous transmission, each byte is sent up the line as soon as it is generated. In synchronous transmission, bytes are collected in a buffer and sent in blocks.

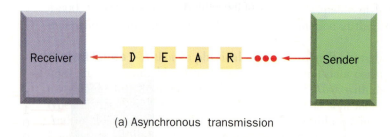

(a) Asynchronous transmission

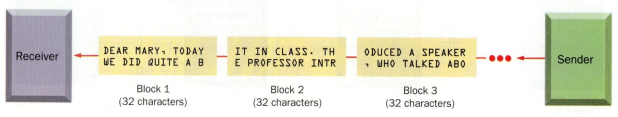

Block 1
(32 characters)

Block 2
(32 characters)

Block 3
(32 characters)

(b) Synchronous transmission

representation is sent up the line to the computer; striking a second key sends a second character; and so forth. But because even the fastest typist can generate only a very small amount of data relative to what the line can accept, a lot of idle time occurs on the line. Furthermore, each character sent must be packaged with a "start bit" and "stop bit," resulting in substantial transmission overhead.

Synchronous transmission corrects for this deficiency by dispatching data in blocks of characters rather than one at a time. Each block can consist of thousands of characters. Because no idle time occurs between transmission of individual characters in the block and less transmission overhead is required, the utilization of the line is much more efficient. Synchronous transmission is made possible by a *buffer* in the terminal—a storage area large enough to hold a block of characters. As soon as the buffer is filled, all the characters in it are sent up the line to the computer.

Figure 6-15 illustrates the differences between asynchronous and synchronous transmission. Synchronous transmission is commonly used for data speeds greater than 2,400 bps.

Synchronous transmission.
The transmission of data over a line one block of characters at a time.

Wide Area Networks and Local Networks

An organization generally has two choices for transmitting data: wide area networks and local networks.

Wide Area Networks

Wide area networks (WANs) are communications networks that encompass a relatively wide geographic area. Three common types of wide area networks are public-access networks, value-added networks, and private wide area networks.

Wide area network (WAN).
A network that covers a wide geographic area.

Public-Access Networks   **Public-access networks** are those maintained by phone companies, or common carriers. **Common carriers** are companies licensed by the government to provide wide area communications services to the general public. Although there are dozens of phone companies in the United States alone, virtually all are interconnected so that they appear to be a single, seamless network.

Among the most familiar common carriers are the Bell-system phone companies and firms such as US Sprint, MCI, and AT&T Communications. The Bell-system companies provide in-state and nearby-state communications services, and the other firms serve a wider area. Among the less familiar common carriers are the *specialized carrier companies*, such as those that provide satellite transmission facilities.

Public-access network.
A network—such as the phone system—that is designed to be used by the general public.

Common carrier.
A government-regulated private organization that provides communications services to the public.

Value-Added Networks (VANs)   **Value-added network (VAN)** vendors are firms that use the facilities of a common carrier to offer the general subscribing public additional services using those facilities. These services include information processing, information retrieval, electronic mail, and the like. Organizations that use the services are billed by both the common carrier (if toll charges are involved) and the VAN company.

One of the most popular types of VAN service is information retrieval, which we discussed earlier. Examples of firms that offer such services are Prodigy, CompuServe, Dow Jones News/Retrieval, and The Source. Once users make

Value-added network (VAN).
Use of the phone network by a firm other than the phone company to offer communications-related services over the network.

phone contact with the VAN company, the firm's software systems generally provide easy-to-use menus of available options. After users make a request from their keyboards, the selected services become available over the phone lines for use at the users' remote workstations.

In the United States, phone companies were for years blocked by law from offering information processing and related services over phone lines. That is, regional phone companies such as those that serve your area could not become VANs (ironically, by using the phone lines they lay themselves). In recent years, however—especially with the onslaught of competition from foreign organizations—the federal government has supported a strong deregulation movement regarding communications. Many of the phone companies want to enter the cable TV business; if the courts continue to back recent government rulings, this type of broadened access could eventually result in lower cable TV rates and better cable TV service.

One controversial type of VAN is the company with the 900-prefix phone number. Today, these firms are often collectively more famous for public abuses than for the useful services they actually do offer. While some companies may wrongfully charge teenagers hundreds of dollars for interacting with an alluring voice at the other end of the line, a number of other, reputable 900-line companies offer the public such useful information as technical support on computer products, legal and tax advice, and news. Considering the appetite of people for instant information, 900 lines seem to be an unstoppable business trend. The issue of what types of regulatory controls you think government should place on operators of 900 lines is the subject of a Critical Thinking question at the end of the chapter.

Private Wide Area Networks   Because many organizations today have such massive communications requirements, a number of them have set up their own exclusive **private wide area networks.** These networks are created by building certain facilities, leasing capacity on existing satellites, and generally stitching together a variety of cost-effective land- and air-based communications media dedicated to delivering a certain level of performance to the organization.

Private wide area network.
A wide area network that is built by an organization for its own use.

One such network has been built by Sears, the large Chicago-based retailer. The Sears network hooks up more than 50,000 workstations and terminals nationwide and supports the communications needs of the Sears merchandising group and Sears' member organizations. The network is hosted by an IBM mainframe in Chicago and handles both management information requests and transactions from the millions of users of the Sears Discover card. Sears has also set up a separate organization to sell excess capacity in the network as well as to sell the communications expertise it has acquired in building the network. In fact, Sears' networking expertise has been so extensive that, in recent years, it has joined forces with IBM to establish Prodigy Services Company and several other joint communications ventures.

Local Networks

Although wide area networks certainly are useful, many firms need communications facilities that connect local resources—say, computers and terminals located on the same college campus or several microcomputer workstations located in the same office. These types of networks are known as **local networks.**

Local network.
A privately run communications network of several machines located within a mile or so of one another.

Local networks often are acquired from communications media vendors—firms that sell or lease media for private rather than public use. These media

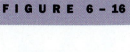

FIGURE 6 – 16

A local area network (LAN). The surge in microcomputer usage has made local area networking a particularly attractive solution for sharing resources.

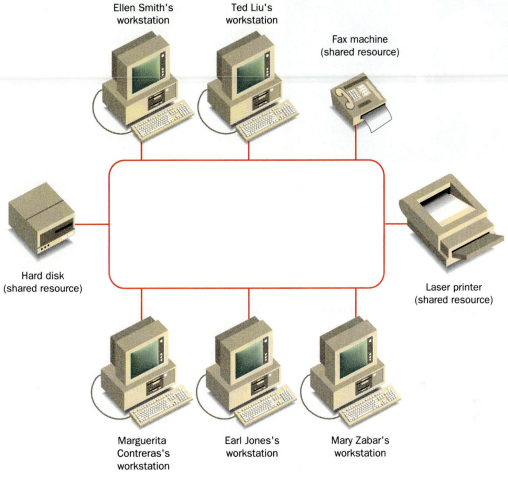

Ellen Smith's workstation

Ted Liu's workstation

Fax machine (shared resource)

Hard disk (shared resource)

Laser printer (shared resource)

Marguerita Contreras's workstation

Earl Jones's workstation

Mary Zabar's workstation

may consist of dedicated point-to-point lines, shared lines, switched lines that are unavailable for public use, or perhaps networks composed of a combination of these lines. Three common types of local networks are host-independent local area networks (LANs), private branch exchanges (PBXs), and hierarchical local networks.

Local Area Networks (LANs)   For many years, most networks consisted of a remote, central *host computer*—such as a mainframe—that controlled a large number of display terminals. With the arrival of inexpensive microcomputers, which could do their own local processing, local area networks (LANs) became possible.

Local area networks (LANs), such as the one in Figure 6-16, are local networks that do not utilize a host computer as such. Instead, computers within the network itself manage the devices as they demand the shared facilities. LANs are available principally as client-server LANs and peer-to-peer LANs.

Local area network (LAN).
A local network without a host computer that usually consists entirely of micro-computer workstations and shared peripherals.

F e a t u r e   6 – 1

Wireless LANs

Today's hot item in network computing

At Wright-Patterson Air Force Base in Dayton, Ohio, an all-too-familiar networking problem has surfaced. Thousands of PCs are used by base personnel, and many of the PCs are connected to LANs. However, the LANs keep changing. A thirty-person cabling crew is needed at the base that does nothing but adjust and install networks.

Wright-Patterson is learning something that many large corporations have already discovered—LANs often need to be rewired to meet changing needs. For instance, work units are frequently merged, new managers are hired, or assignments and locations are changed. Also, some LANs are just meant to be temporary, as those servicing retail stores that increase staff during peak selling seasons and insurance companies that need to form groups at emergency locations—such as in Florida after Hurricane Andrew hit.

When a LAN involves lots of wiring, a cabling specialist is often required to make adjustments.

Wireless warehousing. Radio communication with a mainframe makes inventory management a realtime affair.

However, when the LAN is basically wireless, this step is unnecessary. Wright-Patterson Air Force Base has recently joined the ranks of organizations that are now experimenting with wireless LANs.

conferences are run on LANs. And, *workgroup computing*—computing in which a common job, such as preparing a publication or solving a problem, is performed by people working simultaneously on a networked computer system—primarily uses LANs. Microcomputer-based LANs have a big advantage over systems based on larger computers: Organizations can inexpensively add small increments of extra computing power as their needs grow—say, by adding extra workstations or by adding more servers.

Some LANs—like those used to link soldiers in a battlefield and sports commentators at sporting events—are wireless (see Feature 6-1). Most, however, use coaxial cable or fiber-optic cable technology. Cable-based LANs usually employ either a baseband or broadband technology. *Baseband* products consist of a single, high-speed digital path over which text, graphics, voice, and video data can pass—but only one type of data can pass at a time. *Broadband* networks, in contrast, consist of several paths, thereby allowing transmission of many dissimilar types of data simultaneously. Broadband, which involves analog transmission, can also cover much longer distances than baseband.

Xerox's Ethernet is one of the most widely used baseband products. Wang's Wangnet is a prominent broadband product. Broadband, being more complex and powerful than baseband, is, as you might expect, more expensive as well.

Here's how a wireless LAN might work in an office environment. Each microcomputer workstation in the office is wired to a nearby device called a controller, which collects data from the workstation and later passes data back to it. Each controller, which can service several workstations, communicates by radio or infrared waves to a centrally located transmitter in the office. The transmitter then communicates to other controllers around the office that serve other workstations.

While the type of wireless LAN just described does not completely eliminate physical wiring, it does reduce the amount of it, making alterations relatively easy. This type of wireless LAN is expected to be very prevalent in offices during the next several years.

When a LAN needs to be set up outdoors or in places where wiring is infeasible, another approach is required. The U.S. Open Golf Championship turned to wireless LANs for the first time in 1992 to provide speedy information to television broadcasters and the news media. Operators carrying hand-held terminals, each with their own built-in transmitters, followed golfers around the course. Data on strokes and golfer progress were then beamed from the terminals to a mainframe at the course site where they were stored in a central database for authorized users. One consultant on the 1992 installation reported that hand-held terminals posted results quicker than it would take someone to gather the information by phone.

Warehousing is another application where wireless LANs offer appeal. A driver who is connected to the LAN can use a screen mounted on a mobile forklift truck to pull up the latest inventory information. As pallets of goods are loaded onto the truck and carried away for shipment, inventory records in remote databases can be updated in real time (see photo).

Wireless LANs are a compelling option for networks of the future. But the technology has not yet taken off, and some major problems still need to be worked out. For example, which design standard, or protocol, should be followed? A common standard would enable many distinct wireless LANs to communicate with each other easily. Another problem is health related. Are all of those waves zooming around the air going to be detrimental to people's health over the long term?

Private Branch Exchanges (PBXs)   The phone system consists of numerous switching stations that essentially are public branch exchanges. When a company leases or purchases a switching station for its own use, such a facility becomes known as a **private branch exchange (PBX).** Most PBXs are commonly referred to as "company switchboards"—you call a company's number and a private (company) operator routes you to the proper extension. In the world of computers, however, many PBXs need to deal with machine-to-machine communication. Thus, such PBXs are controlled by host computers that route machine-to-machine calls automatically and let the human operator deal with many of the interpersonal communications. Sometimes these computer-based private branch exchanges are referred to as *CBXs (computerized branch exchanges)* or *PABXs (private automatic branch exchanges).*

Private branch exchange (PBX).
A call-switching station that an organization acquires for its own use.

Hierarchical Local Networks   **Hierarchical local networks** are the oldest type of local network. At the top of the hierarchy is often a big host computer such as a mainframe or minicomputer. At the bottom are display terminals. Between the top and bottom are devices such as communications controllers, which manage exchanges between the host and the terminals.

Hierarchical local network.
A local network in which a relatively powerful "host" CPU is at the top of the hierarchy and communications terminals or less-powerful CPUs are at the bottom.

Downloading.
The process of transferring data or information from a large computer system to a smaller one.

Uploading.
The process of sending data from a small computer system to a larger computer system for storage or processing purposes.

Gateway.
An interface that enables two dissimilar networks to communicate.

Bridge.
An interface that enables two similar networks to communicate.

Star network.
A network consisting of a host device connected directly to several other devices.

Bus network.
A telecommunications network consisting of a line and several devices that are tapped into the line.

Ring network.
A telecommunications network in which machines are connected serially in a closed loop.

Files in hierarchical local networks can be either downloaded from or uploaded to the host. **Downloading** means that copies of existing files can be sent from the host to the microcomputer workstations. **Uploading** means that new data can be created at the microcomuter workstations and sent to the host. Both downloading and uploading usually require stringent organizational control. Downloading presents the danger that data will be retrieved for unauthorized use, whereas uploading entails the risk of garbage data corrupting other applications.

Gateways and Bridges   Local networks often must communicate with outside resources, such as those on wide area networks and on other local networks.

Let's look at an example. An executive working at a microcomputer workstation on a LAN may wish to access a financial database such as Dow Jones News/Retrieval. In this particular case, a facility known as a gateway is necessary for linking the two networks—here, the LAN and the WAN. A **gateway** is a collection of hardware and software resources that enables devices on one network to communicate with devices on another, *dissimilar* network.

When the two networks being linked—say, a LAN in one campus building and an identical LAN in another nearby campus building—are based on similar technology, a device called a bridge is used to connect them. A **bridge** is a collection of hardware and software resources that enable devices on one network to communicate with devices on another, *similar* network.

Network Topologies

Telecommunications networks can be classified in terms of their *topology*, or shape. Three common topologies are the star, bus, and ring.

Star Networks   A **star network** often consists of a host computer that's hierarchically connected to several display terminals in a point-to-point fashion. This configuration is illustrated in Figure 6-19a. In a common variant of this pattern, several microcomputer systems (the terminals) are connected to a larger host computer that switches data and programs between them. The private branch exchange (PBX), discussed earlier, is another example of a star network. Star networks are especially suited to an organization with several related plants or divisions, because each plant or division may need access to common centralized files but may also need to do its own local processing.

Bus Networks   A **bus network** works a lot like ordinary city buses in ground-based transportation systems. Moreover, the hardware devices are like "bus stops" and the data like "passengers." For example, the network in Figure 6-19b contains four terminal stations (bus stops) at which data (passengers) are "picked up" or "let off." Local area networks (LANs), discussed earlier, often use a bus topology. The bus line commonly consists of a high-capacity, high-speed coaxial cable, with inexpensive twisted-pair wires dropped off each terminal station. A bus network contains no host computer.

Ring Networks   A less common and more expensive alternative to the star and the bus is the **ring network,** in which a host computer is absent and a

FIGURE 6 – 19

Three network topologies. (a) Star. (b) Bus. (c) Ring.

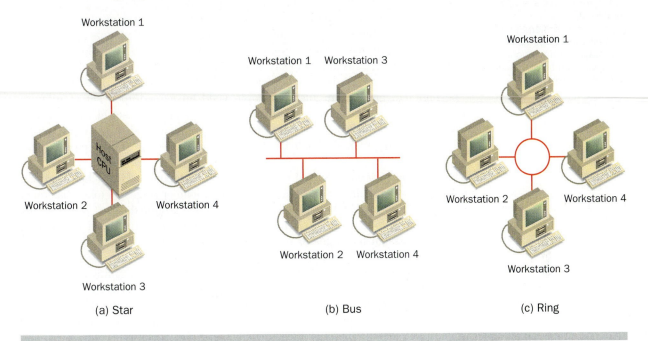

(a) Star   (b) Bus   (c) Ring

number of computers or other devices are connected by a loop. A ring network is shown in Figure 6-19c. One popular form of ring network is the *token-ring* local area network (LAN) pattern, which we'll discuss in the next section.

Communications Among Devices

In the last few sections, we covered various types of communications media and networks. In this section, we will discuss communications standards and special communications management techniques designed to optimize the flow of communications traffic.

Protocols

Because manufacturers have long produced devices that use a variety of transmission techniques, communications standards for the industry have been a major problem. Everyone recognizes the need for standardizing transmission methods, but the form such standards should take is still widely debated. What is needed is some common agreement on matters such as communications protocols.

The term *protocol* originates from the areas of diplomacy and etiquette. For instance, at a dinner party in the elegant home of a family on the social register, the protocol in effect may be formal attire, impeccable table manners, and

Protocol.
A set of conventions used by machines to establish communication with one another in a telecommunications environment.

remaining at the table until beckoned to the parlor by the host or hostess. At a backwoods country barbeque, a different protocol will probably exist. In the communications field, protocols have comparable rules.

A communications **protocol** is a collection of procedures used to establish, maintain, and terminate transmission between devices. Protocols specify how devices will physically connect into a network, how data will be packaged during transmission (e.g., asynchronously or synchronously), how receiver devices will acknowledge sender devices (a process called *handshaking*), how errors will be handled, and so on. Just as people need an agreed-upon set of rules to communicate effectively, so do machines need a common set of rules to help them get along with one another. Protocols are found in all types of networks. Two common protocols found in LANs, for instance, are token passing and CSMA/CD.

Token passing often is used with a ring network topology. Here's how it works: A small packet called a *token* is sent around a loop or ring. The token has room for messages and addresses. As the token is passed around the ring, workstations either check to see if the token is addressed to them or try to seize it so that they can assign messages to it. A token traveling around the ring contains a control area, which specifies whether the token is free or carries a message. When a sender device captures a free token, it changes the status of the token from "free" to "busy," adds a message, and releases it. The message then travels around the ring to the receiver location. The receiver copies the message, puts an acknowledgement on the token, and sends the token back to the sender station. The sender notes the acknowledgement message and changes the status of the token to "free."

CSMA/CD is an acronym for *carrier sense multiple access with collision detection.* With CSMA/CD, which is most commonly used in bus networks, workstations try to seize the network's attention whenever they are ready. The collision detection feature ensures that the devices don't interfere with each other as they compete.

Hardware for Managing Communications Traffic

Now that we've covered some of the basic elements of telecommunications systems, let's see how these systems have been made more efficient. As an example, we'll look at several types of devices that enhance the efficiency of wide area telecommunications networks. The most notable of these *communications management devices* are multiplexers, concentrators, and front-end processors.

Multiplexer.
A communications device that interleaves the messages of several low-speed devices and sends them along a single high-speed path.

Multiplexers   Communications lines almost always have far greater capacity than a single terminal can use. Many workstations can work adequately at speeds of 300 bps, and voice-grade lines can transmit up to 9,600 bps. Since communications lines are expensive, it is desirable that several low-speed devices share the same line. A device called a **multiplexer** makes this possible.

Figure 6-20 illustrates the use of two multiplexers servicing several workstations and a host CPU. The first multiplexes, or combines, the data from low-speed lines into a high-speed line. The second demultiplexes the incoming character stream so that the CPU appears to get the messages from the workstations individually. Recently, with the appearance of high-speed digital lines, devices called *T1 multiplexers* have arrived on the scene. These multiplexers have the capacity to carry as much voice and data traffic as 24 conventional (analog) phone lines.

Concentrators   A **concentrator** is a hardware device that combines control and multiplexing functions, among other things. Commonly it is a minicomputer with a facility that provides a store-and-forward capability. Thus, messages from slow devices such as asynchronous terminals can be stored at the concentrator until enough characters are collected to make forwarding to another device worthwhile.

In airline passenger-reservations systems, concentrators placed at key sites, such as Boston, New York, Los Angeles, and other transportation centers, allow several agents to share communications lines economically. Messages initiated by agents are sent to the concentrator, stored, multiplexed with messages from other agents, and transmitted at very high speeds over long-distance lines to a central processing site. Using the long-distance line in this fashion minimizes communications costs.

Concentrator.
A communications device that combines terminal control and multiplexing functions.

FIGURE 6 – 20

Multiplexing. Multiplexers enable several low-speed devices to share a high-speed line. Here multiplexer A combines the messages sent from four workstations. Multiplexer B "demultiplexes" the message for the CPU so that they look like standard local input.

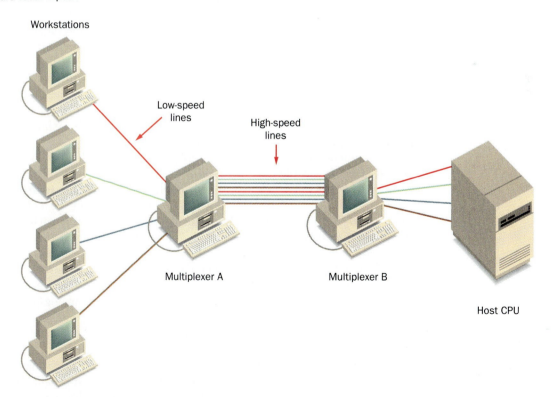

Front-End Processors The **front-end processor** is the most sophisticated type of communications management device. Generally it is a mainframe or minicomputer located at the site of the host CPU. It can perform all the communications functions of a concentrator as well as relieve the host of routine computational burdens. For example, a front-end processor can check for valid user account numbers and validate or change the format of incoming data.

Summary and Key Terms

Telecommunications refers to communications over a distance, such as over phone lines, via privately owned cable, or by satellite.

Telecommunications Applications A wide variety of important business applications involve telecommunications. Among these are distributed transaction processing, interorganizational systems (IOSs), **electronic data interchange (EDI), electronic mailboxes, voice mail, electronic bulletin boards,** computer conferencing, **facsimile (fax) machine, cellular phones,** and information retrieval.

Communications Media Messages transmitted in a telecommunications system are sent over some type of **communications medium.** Physical lines, such as **twisted-pair wires, coaxial cable,** and **fiber optic cable,** constitute one major class of media. Messages also are commonly sent through the air, in the form of **microwave** signals. **Terrestrial microwave stations** accommodate microwave transmission when either the sender or the receiver is on the ground. **Communications satellites** reduce the cost of long-distance transmission via terrestrial microwave stations and provide better overseas communications.

The *speed* of a data-communications medium is measured in **bits per second (bps).** The slowest speeds are referred to as **narrowband transmission.** Medium-speed lines, which are the type commonly found in the public phone network, are capable of **voice-grade transmission.** The highest speeds, referred to as **wideband transmission,** as possible only with coaxial cable, fiber optic cable, and microwaves.

Communications media can be in either the simplex, half-duplex, or full-duplex mode. In **simplex transmission,** messages can be sent only in a single, prespecified direction (such as with a doorbell). In **half-duplex transmission,** messages can be sent both ways but not simultaneously (for example, as with press-to-talk phones). **Full-duplex transmission** permits transmission in two directions simultaneously (as with traffic on a busy two-way street).

Signals sent along a phone line travel in an **analog** fashion—that is, as continuous waves. Computers and their support equipment, however, are **digital** devices that handle data coded into two discrete states—0s and 1s. For two or more digital devices to communicate with each other over analog phone lines, a **modem** must be placed between each piece of equipment and the phone lines. Modems perform digital-to-analog and analog-to-digital conversion. Modems can be bypassed when *digital lines* are used to interconnect devices.

To exchange data along a communications medium, two machines must "agree" on a mode of transmission and on a method of packaging data. Transmission between machines is done either in **parallel,** in which each bit of a byte is sent along a different path, or in **serial,** in which bits of a byte follow one another serially along a single path. Serially transmitted data are packaged either **asynchronously** (one byte to a package) or **synchronously** (several bytes to a package).

Wide Area Networks and Local Networks Wide area networks **(WANs)** are communications networks designed to encompass a relatively wide geographic area. Three types of WANs are public-access networks, value-added networks, and private wide area networks. **Public-access networks** generally are maintained by the phone companies, or **common carriers. Value-added network (VAN)** vendors are firms that use the facilities of a common carrier to offer the general subscribing public additional services using those facilities. These services include information retrieval, information processing, and electronic mail. Because many organizations today have massive communications requirements, some have set up their own **private wide area networks.**

Many organizations take heavy advantage of these and also build their own **local networks**—networks that link devices in a single building or at a single site. Three common types of local networks are local area networks, private branch exchanges, and hierarchical networks.

Local area networks (LANs) typically fall into one of two categories. The first, **client-server LANs,** consist of **server** devices that provide workstations services such as access to peripherals, database lookups, and computing. The second, **peer-to-peer LANs,** have the user workstations and shared peripherals in the network operating at the same level. A **private branch exchange (PBX)** consists of a central, private switchboard that links to devices by switched lines. A **hierarchical local network** typically consists of a powerful host CPU at the top level of the hierarchy and microcomputer workstations and display terminals at lower levels. Data used by the workstations can be either **downloaded** from the host or **uploaded** to it. Devices on two *dissimilar* networks can communicate with each other if they are connected by a **gateway.** Devices on two *similar* networks can communicate with each other if they are connected by a **bridge.**

Network Topologies Telecommunications networks can be classified in terms of their topology, or shape. Three common topologies are the **star network,** the **bus network,** and the **ring network.**

Communications among Devices A communications **protocol** is a collection of procedures used to establish, maintain, and terminate transmission between devices. Because there are so many ways to transmit data, many industry groups have pushed for certain protocols to become industry standards. These efforts notwithstanding, a number of incompatible guidelines remain in effect. Two major LAN protocols are *token passing* and *carrier sense multiple access with collision detection (CSMA/CD).*

Communications management devices enhance the efficiency of telecommunications traffic flow. Common devices are multiplexers, concentrators, and front-end processors. **Multiplexers** enable several low-speed devices to share one high-speed line. **Concentrators** perform multiplexing functions and can store and forward data as well. **Front-end processors** are the most sophisticated communications management devices. They can perform the concentrator's function as well as some of the tasks the computer normally does.

Review Exercises

Fill-in Questions

1. _____ (EDI) refers to sending electronic purchase orders and invoices from company to company.

2. A(n)_____ machine enables images of hard-copy documents to be sent over the phone lines.

3. _____, the communications medium employed by cable television, was developed primarily to provide interference-free video transmission.

4. In contrast to the continuous waves used to represent analog signals over phone lines, computers generate _____ signals.

5. _____ is a transmission medium that involves laser-generated light waves sent over transparent, hairlike strands.

6. Conversion from analog to digital and digital to analog is performed by a(n)_____.

7. _____ transmission involves sending data along a communications line in blocks of several characters at a time.

8. _____ are companies licensed by the government to provide communications services to the public.

9. _____ transmission is a type of serial transmission in which characters are sent along a line as they are generated.

10. A hierarchical local network is an example of a(n) _____ network topology.

Matching Questions   *Match each term with the description that fits best.*

a. front-end processor
b. modem
c. gateway
d. multiplexer
e. concentrator
f. protocol

_____ 1. A device that combines several low-speed lines into a high-speed line.

_____ 2. A hardware device that collects messages and forwards them in a transmission-efficient fashion.

_____ 3. A device that converts digital data for transmission over the phone lines.

_____ 4. The most sophisticated type of communications management device.

_____ 5. A standard used to make communications devices more compatible.

_____ 6. A device that enables two dissimilar networks to communicate with each other.

1. What is the difference between an electronic mailbox and a computer bulletin board?

2. What is the difference between a local area network (LAN) and a value-added network (VAN)?

3. What is the difference between a client-server LAN and a peer-to-peer LAN?

4. Name some types of communications media and explain how they differ.

5. What is the difference between uploading and downloading?

6. What is the difference between baseband and broadband transmission?

7. How do parallel and serial communications differ?

8. What is a protocol?

1. It has been said that advances in communications technology are collapsing the "information float"—the amount of time information spends in transit when being communicated from one point to another. Can you think of three business examples of collapsing information float? What is the benefit to a business in each example?

2. Identify two examples of computer applications that need the type of transmission that broadband cable provides.

3. You are asked by a teacher in your former high school to give a 45-minute presentation to her students on telecommunications. You are to prepare a list of the half-dozen things that every student today should know about telecommunications. What would be on your list?

4. EDI, its benefits notwithstanding, poses some new legal problems. One is that it's not clear who is at fault if transmission problems cause a miscommunicated transaction that results in a loss. Can you think of any ways in which an organization might protect itself from such legal headaches with EDI?

5. Should the government place special controls on operators of 900-prefix phone numbers? Defend your position by preparing a list of uses or practices you feel are not in the public interest and a list of uses or practices you feel are. If you believe there should be some controls, identify them.

6. In the section of VANs, the possibility of allowing phone companies to sell information over the phone lines is raised. What arguments can you present for and against letting the phone companies become VAN operators?

Inside Prodigy

A Closer Look at an Information Utility

Prodigy—created in 1988 as a joint venture between Sears and IBM—is an easy-to-use information-retrieval service that's targeted to the needs of the average person. It contains facilities for online shopping, banking, securities trading, news on a variety of topics, weather reports, mail, educational information, and dozens of other services. This window surveys types of potentially valuable information available through Prodigy and similar services.

1

1. Most Prodigy screens either provide information or, as shown here, ask users to make a selection from a menu of choices. The user highlights the choice and then presses the Enter key. Here, the "Race to Promontory" choice is highlighted; by pressing the Enter key the user will get information screens and further choices regarding this historical event.

2. News is available on a variety of topics, including current events, sports, and health. In this screen, the user can choose a subject area by pressing the arrow keys, typing in a number, or using a mouse.

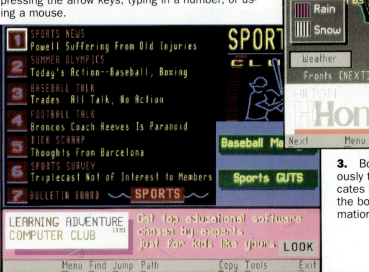

3. Both weather and news are updated continuously throughout the day. The weather map here indicates that by highlighting and selecting "Next" at the bottom of the screen, the user can pull up information about weather fronts.

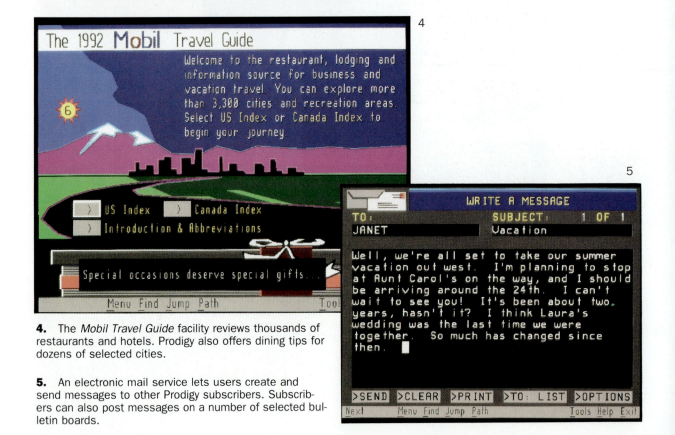

4. The *Mobil Travel Guide* facility reviews thousands of restaurants and hotels. Prodigy also offers dining tips for dozens of selected cities.

5. An electronic mail service lets users create and send messages to other Prodigy subscribers. Subscribers can also post messages on a number of selected bulletin boards.

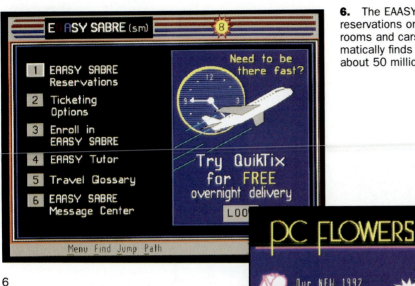

6

6. The EAASY SABRE system books and confirms reservations on all major airlines and reserves hotel rooms and cars worldwide. The system also automatically finds the lowest airfare from a database of about 50 million fares.

7

7. Hundreds of thousands of items are available for sale—occasionally at special discounts to Prodigy subscribers. Subscribers can buy anything from flowers to major catalog items to cruise packages. Payment can also be made online.

8

8. Prodigy offers a variety of financial services including automatic and manual price lookups for securities, financial news on specific companies, and market reports.

9

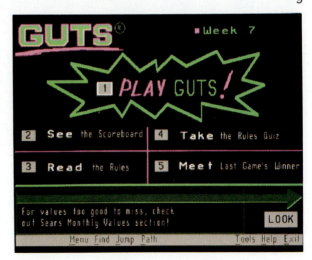

9. Games are available for subscribers to play alone or with other subscribers.

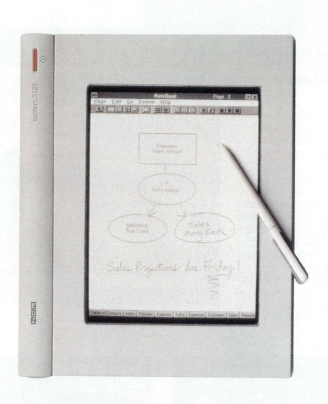

SYSTEMS SOFTWARE

7

Do pen computers have operating systems, too? You betcha. Shown here is Pen Windows, an operating system created so that pen computers can understand pen commands from applications software and, also, make selections from the Microsoft Windows interface. Chapter 7 covers the basics of operating systems.

OUTLINE

LEARNING OBJECTIVES

After completing this chapter, you will be able to:

1. Describe the types of systems software.

2. Explain the activities of an operating system and describe some of the differences between operating systems.

3. Describe several ways in which computer systems interleave operations to process data more efficiently.

4. Explain the role of a language translator and describe several types of language translators.

5. Explain the role of a utility program and describe several types of utility programs.

Overview

Systems software.
Computer programs that enable application programs to run on a given set of hardware.

Systems software consists of programs that coordinate the various parts of the computer system to make it run rapidly and efficiently. They perform such tasks as formatting disks to that they are suitable for storing budgets or word-processed documents, copying program files or data files from one diskette to another, and enabling your brand of applications software to work on your printer or display device.

Most users aren't aware of what systems software is doing for them. On microcomputer systems, for example, issuing a save command to store a program onto disk requires that systems software look for adequate space on the disk, write the program onto "addresses" of this space, and update the disk's directory (indicating the addresses at which the program has been placed). And when users are having their systems communicate with databases on remote mainframes, they may not realize that systems software goes to work checking the validity of their ID numbers and, later, translating their database commands into machine language.

Systems software is available in three basic types: operating systems, language translators, and utility programs.

In this chapter, we'll first look closely at the *operating system*, which is the main piece of systems software in any computer system. Here we'll discuss what operating systems do and examine the various differences among them. We'll also take a closer look at a few of today's most talked-about operating systems.

Next, we will look at *language translators*. A language translator is a program that translates a program in BASIC, COBOL, or some other programming language into machine language.

Finally, we will cover *utility programs*, or utilities. Utilities typically perform less-frequent or less-critical types of control functions, such as allowing you to recover inadvertently erased disk files. These packages are often sold by third-party vendors as add-ons to specific operating systems.

The Operating System

Before the 1960s, human operators generally ran computers manually. For each incoming job needing processing, the operator had to reset a number of circuits on the computer by hand. In fact, every function of the computer system—input, output, processing, and storage—required substantial operator supervision and intervention.

On these early computers, jobs could be processed only in a serial fashion—one program at a time. As a result, the computers sat idle for long periods while operators took care of manual procedures between jobs.

Operating system.
The main collection of systems software that enables the computer system to manage the resources under its control.

The development of operating systems greatly improved the efficiency of computers. An **operating system** is the main collection of programs that manage the computer system's activities. Operating systems have eliminated much of the manual work formerly required to process programs. Many of today's operating systems enable processing of several jobs concurrently and permit the computer to be left completely unattended by the operator while programs are running.

The primary chores of the operating system are management and control. The operating system ensures that each valid incoming program is processed in an orderly fashion and that the computer system's resources are made available to run the programs optimally. For example, on a large computer system, the operating system checks to see that people trying to gain access to the computer system are authorized users. When a user's identification number is found to be valid, he or she is signed in, or "logged on." Next, the operating system determines which of the computer system's resources will be needed to do the user's job. Then it automatically assigns these resources to the work request if and when they are available.

Generally, the user will need to tap a number of the system's resources. For example, a typical job might need the number-crunching power of the CPU, a language translator that understands the BASIC programming language, primary storage for storing intermediate results, secondary storage for storing data and programs, and a printer for output. The operating system makes all these facilities available. Finally, when the user finishes with the computer system, he or she is logged off. In effect, the operating system is the go-between that meshes the user's applications program with the system's hardware resources.

Figure 7-1 depicts the hierarchical principle by which computer systems work. The operating system serves as the gateway to applications programs,

The gateway role of the operating system. The operating system makes computer system resources available to the user. Everyone using a computer system must interact with the operating system in some way.

FIGURE 7 – 1

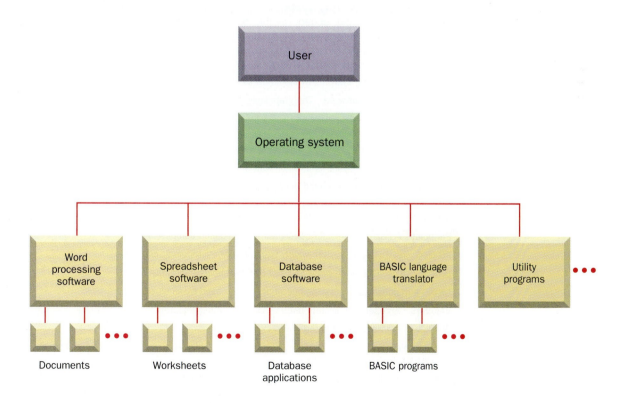

their data, and other system resources. As soon as you turn on your computer system or terminal, you are confronted with the operating system. From there, you choose the program with which you wish to work—say, word processor or spreadsheet—and the operating system retrieves it from disk for you. When finished, you generally must exit back to the operating system before you can invoke another program.

Because of the central role of the operating system in managing the computer system's activities, many consider the operating system to be the most critical piece of software in the computer system. Without an operating system, none of the other programs can run.

Differences among Operating Systems

The marketplace offers a wide selection of operating systems (see Figure 7-2). Like the executives who manage and control large corporations, the various operating systems differ in many important respects. For example, some operating systems are designed for only one "brand" of computer, whereas others are compatible with several. Other important differences concern ease of use, speed, number of features available, portability, and cost. Often these criteria conflict. For example, an operating system that's designed to be either easy to use or

FIGURE 7 - 2

Some popular operating systems. Operating systems can differ substantially with respect to ease of use, speed, number of features available, portability, and cost. Each operating system is targeted to one or more specific types of computers.

AOS, DG Operating systems used on Data General minicomputers

CPF, SSP Operating systems available on IBM's small business systems

Macintosh System Software The graphically oriented operating system used on Apple Macintosh microcomputers

MCP/AS, OS/1100 Operating systems used on Unisys mainframes

MS-DOS The most widely used operating system on IBM-compatible microcomputers

MVS, VM Operating systems used on IBM mainframes

NetWare The most widely used operating system on local area networks (LANs)

OS/2 The operating system designed for the high end of IBM's PS/2 line of microcomputers

Penpoint An operating system designed for pen-based computers

PC-DOS An operating system widely used on IBM microcomputers

UNICOS, COS Operating systems used by Cray supercomputers

UNIX A multiuser, multitasking operating system used by small computers

VAX/VMS An operating system used by DEC VAX minicomputers

Windows A graphically oriented operating environment.

Windows New Technology (Windows NT) Microsoft's high-end, graphically oriented operating system.

Xenix, Venix, Ultrix, A/UX Four UNIX-like operating systems

flexible generally isn't fast. In other words, the more overhead the operating system must carry, the slower it will be. And, as you might expect, a system that's packaged with an assortment of sophisticated or powerful features isn't likely to be inexpensive.

On large computers such as mainframes, operating systems can be quite powerful. Hundreds of users may be seeking access to the mainframe at more or less the same time. Many of those users will be running several programs concurrently. For instance, someone may be working on a set of database retrievals while having a 50-page report printed out. On large computer systems there are sophisticated facilities for interleaving users' work, for keeping the computer safe from unauthorized access, for bookkeeping, and for a number of other complex tasks. Because these systems often have huge memories, their operating systems can afford to be large and sophisticated.

Microcomputers, in contrast, have almost always been hampered by a limited amount of memory. For instance, the original IBM PC of 1981 came with only 128 KB RAM. Thus, PC-DOS, the flagship operating system of the IBM PC, was originally limited to this amount. Although later models of the IBM PC came with more RAM, allowing DOS to grow, 16-bit DOS—which is based on the primitive Intel 8088 chip—has a RAM limit of 640 KB. This situation has forced 16-bit DOS to become essentially just a partial operating system (by mainframe standards).

Now that powerful 32-bit chips such as the Intel Pentium and Motorola 68040 are available—and powerful operating systems such as OS/2, Windows NT, and UNIX are here to make use of them—we are beginning to see microcomputer operating-system environments that are approaching those of mainframes (see Tomorrow box).

Functions of the Operating System

Now that you have a general idea of what operating systems do and what some of the differences among them are, we can discuss their functions in greater detail. As we examine these functions, keep in mind that not all of them— especially functions that deal with more than one user or one program—will apply to the operating system on your computer.

Assignment of System Resources　When most computers are first activated, a major component of the operating system—a program called the **supervisor**—is also activated. On some systems, this program may be referred to as the *monitor,* the *kernel,* or something else. The supervisor will always be in memory when the computer is on. On many computers, other programs in the operating system are brought into memory from secondary storage only as they are needed. The supervisor mobilizes these other programs to perform system tasks for applications programs.

Once the supervisor activates any other program in the operating system, it relinquishes control to that program until the program has performed its role. At that point, control returns to the supervisor, which may then call up other systems programs that the job requires. The supervisor operates somewhat like a master of ceremonies, repeatedly introducing the next speaker on the program after the previous one has finished his or her talk.

Supervisor.
The central program in an operating system.

T O M O R R O W

The Battle of the 32-bit Operating Systems

OS/2, Windows NT, and UNIX Duke It Out

It's shaping up as possibly the biggest software war of all time. The stakes: coronation as the corporate operating system of choice for the new breed of high-end desktop computers—a crown that will probably be worn for at least the next decade. The main participants: OS/2, Windows New Technology (Windows NT), and UNIX— operating systems that are designed specifically for computer systems run by chips with 32-bit architectures.

What's so special about 32-bit chips? They have 4 GB or more of addressable memory on board as well as 32-bit-wide data paths to and from the CPU (see photo). With the ability to access only 640 KB RAM at a time, DOS hardly dents the power of these chips. The new breed of 32-bit operating systems do. Included among the most well-known 32-bit chips are the Intel '386, '486, and Pentium chips, the Motorola 68030 and 68040 chips, and several more advanced chips with greater power.

OS/2 has in its favor the sheer clout of being backed by the world's largest computer company, IBM. Also noteworthy is the fact that probably many desktop computers in the future will communicate with mainframes in corporate environments, two arenas where IBM has a long track record of experience and success.

Windows NT has a strong position because of the large base of Windows applications now already in use. Also, Microsoft Corporation, which produces Windows, has sold more software for microcomputers than anyone else. Its DOS software is the most widely sold piece of systems software of all time.

UNIX has been around the longest of any of the 32-bit operating systems and users have more experience with it than with any of its challengers.

32-bit chip. DOS hardly dents its power, but the new breed of operating systems does.

UNIX may also be the most flexible of all of the operating systems at sites where a diverse mix of hardware is used. Recently, Novell has made a major commitment to develop UNIX and to integrate it with its NetWare communications environmment.

Currently, most attention has focused on OS/2 and Windows NT, with UNIX running third. Critics observe that UNIX's current strength is in scientific rather than business applications. Also, many versions of UNIX are now in use, which inhibits it from developing into a standard platform for corporate applications.

But the real winner—if there is one—may not be decided for several years. If the past is any indication, companies will probably take a slow, cautious approach to making their decisions— especially with cost, compatibility of choices, and so many other factors riding on the line.

In addition to the supervisor, a number of other operating system programs have a hand in determining which parts of the computer system will be mobilized for any given job. One of these is the **command-language translator.** This program reads instructions to the operating system that the user or programmer initiates. These instructions, which often are coded in a **command language** (sometimes referred to as a *job-control language,* or *JCL*), permit the user and programmer to specify orders for retrieving, saving, deleting, copying, or moving files; which I/O devices are to be used; which language the user or programmer is employing; any customized requests for output format; and any other special processing needs of the applications program. The command language, in effect, gives the user or programmer a channel for communicating directly with the operating system.

Operating systems can differ significantly in how command-language instructions are invoked. Take deleting a file, for example. With operating systems such as MS-DOS and PC-DOS, which are used on many IBM microcomputers and similar machines from other manufacturers, you generally type in a command such as

ERASE FRED

to delete a file named FRED. Both MS-DOS and PC-DOS employ a *language interface,* meaning that users generally must know the syntax of a particular command language to communicate with these operating systems.

On the Apple Macintosh line of computers, icons representing operating-system commands have traditionally been used in conjunction with a mouse to carry out similar operations. So, to delete FRED, you can use the mouse to

Command-language translator.
Systems software that translates instructions written in a command language into machine-language instructions.

Command language.
A programming language used to communicate with the operating system.

Language interface versus graphical user interface. (a) A language command must be typed at the system prompt. (b) A graphical user interface lets users issue commands by selecting file and command icons with a mouse; here, the user is deleting a file named FRED.

FIGURE 7 – 3

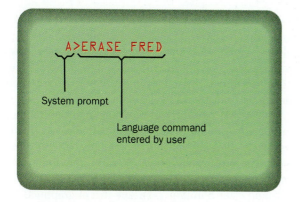

(a) Language interface

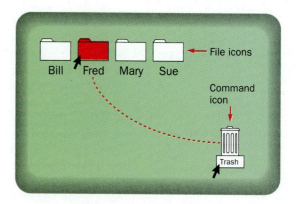

(b) Graphical user interface

F e a t u r e   7 – 1

Inside Windows

A closer look at Microsoft's popular operating environment

Microsoft Windows is an interconnected series of systems programs that supplies a graphical operating environment for your computer system. Most versions of Windows provide a graphical shell for the DOS operating system. They turn a display into an electronic desktop. Just as an ordinary desktop may be arranged with a calendar, clock, calculator, and notepads on top of it—along with papers stacked one on top of another or placed so that each is in full view—so, too, can the Microsoft Windows desktop be arranged. As with the conventional desktop, the electronic desktop gives you the freedom to rearrange items at will or to make them disappear from view.

Uses   Windows provides several advantages over "plain" DOS, including the following:

■ It replaces the DOS command line with a system of menus, boxes called "windows," and icons, eliminating the need to remember a command syntax. It lets users easily work on more than one program at a time; for exam-

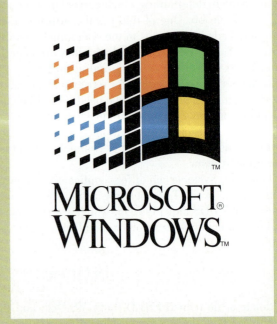

Microsoft Windows. A graphical operating environment with distinct advantages over "plain" DOS.

ple, you can temporarily abandon your word processor to work with a spreadsheet program and then return to the word processor at the same place you left off.

■ It lets users perform more than one task at a time; for example, you can be typing in

---

Graphical user interface (GUI).
Refers to the computer graphics screens that make it easier for users to interact with software.

Operating environment.
A term that refers to a graphical interface or to the combination of an operating system and graphical interface.

Windows.
A graphical operating environment created by Microsoft Corporation.

point first to a file-folder-shaped icon labeled FRED and then to a wastebasket-shaped icon to activate the delete operation. Operating systems such as Macintosh System Software employ a *graphical interface*—or **graphical user interface (GUI)**—meaning that users need only point to menus and graphical icons to issue commands rather than remember a specific syntax. Figure 7-3 illustrates the difference between a language interface and a graphical interface.

Virtually any operating system that naturally uses a language interface can be complemented with a graphically oriented "shell" program, thereby overlaying it with a graphical interface. These shell programs are commonly called **operating environments.** Probably the most well-known operating environment is Microsoft **Windows,** originally created to fit over the MS-DOS operating system (see Figure 7-4, Feature 7-1, and User Solution 7-1). The use of graphical user interfaces in software products is explored more fully in Window 4.

Although the trend in software today is to package GUIs into products, a person might not always choose to use one. While GUIs may encourage a novice to experiment with a new software package, they can slow down the experienced

one document while printing out another. It has built-in utilities that make it easier for users to share data among applications; that allows you to, say, prepare a graph with your spreadsheet program and store it in a word-processed document.

■ It encourages a consistent user interface; once you learn how to use one Windows program it becomes easier to learn others. It provides a variety of desk accessory programs—such as a card file, calendar, and calculator—that support doing work in a business environment.

■ It furnishes a cohesive system under which all applications can be managed.

Programs   To understand Windows' capabilities, it is important to know the names and duties of the systems programs that run within a Windows environment. Some of the most important of the programs and program groups are as follows:

■ **PROGRAM MANAGER**   Program Manager does exactly what its name suggests—it manages programs. You can use it to organize related programs into groups and to start programs. The Program Manager is also the gateway used to enter and exit Windows.

■ **MAIN PROGRAM GROUP**   Generally, when you start Windows, the Main Program Group is automatically displayed in a window. Each graphical symbol, or icon, within the Main window represents a program that you can run.

■ **FILE MANAGER**   This program, available through the Main Program Group, is principally used for managing disk files. It includes commands for formatting disks, copying and moving files, deleting files, finding files, and creating and removing directories, among other things.

■ **CLIPBOARD**   This feature, available through the Main Program Group, enables data from one program to be copied or moved to another program, thereby avoiding the need to deal with an external data-transfer utility.

■ **ACCESSORIES PROGRAM GROUP**   Windows also includes an assortment of desktop accessories and office applications that are available when you select the Accessories icon from the Main Program Group.

The basic elements of a Windows desktop are shown in Figure 7-4.

user who can type. Also, software normally takes longer to run under a graphical user interface. Many software products contain both a language interface and a GUI, so users can choose the approach that suits them best.

In the absence of special command-language instructions from the user—regardless of whether these instructions are invoked through written commands or via a graphical interface—the command-language translator makes some standard assumptions about how things are to be done. These assumptions are called **defaults.** However, you can often override the defaults. For instance, you can override the standard default of one printed copy of a document by asking for two, or you can change the way characters are displayed onscreen by asking for a higher or lower screen resolution.

Default.
The assumption a computer program makes when no specific choice is indicated by the user or programmer.

Scheduling Resources and Jobs   Closely related to the process of assigning system resources to a job is that of scheduling resources and jobs. The operating system helps decide not only which resources to use (assignment) but when to use them (scheduling). Scheduling can become extremely complicated when the system must handle a number of jobs at once.

Scheduling programs in the operating system determine the order in which jobs are processed. A job's place in line is not necessarily on a first-come, first-served basis. Some users may have higher priority than others, the devices needed to process the next job in line may not be free, or other factors may affect the order of processing.

The operating system also schedules the operation of parts of the computer system so that they work on different portions of various jobs at the same time. Because input and output devices work much more slowly than the CPU itself, millions of calculations may be performed for several programs while the contents of a single program are being printed or displayed. Using a number of techniques, the operating system juggles the various jobs to be done in order to employ system devices as efficiently as possible. Later in this section, we'll discuss some of the methods of processing a number of jobs at more or less the same time. These procedures are known collectively as *interleaved processing techniques.*

Monitoring Activities   A third general function of operating systems is monitoring, or keeping track of, activities in the computer system while processing is under way. The operating system terminates programs that contain errors or exceed their maximum storage allocations. It also sends an appropriate

---

F I G U R E   7 – 4

Microsoft Windows. Microsoft Windows provides computers running the MS-DOS and PC-DOS operating systems with a graphical user interface. Annotated in the figure are some of the principal elements of the Windows electronic desktop.

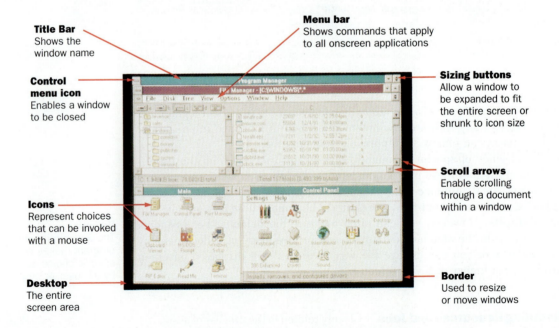

Title Bar
Shows the
window name

Menu bar
Shows commands that apply
to all onscreen applications

**Control
menu icon**
Enables a window
to be closed

Sizing buttons
Allow a window to
be expanded to fit
the entire screen or
shrunk to icon size

Scroll arrows
Enable scrolling
through a document
within a window

Icons
Represent choices
that can be invoked
with a mouse

Desktop
The entire
screen area

Border
Used to resize
or move windows

U s e r   S o l u t i o n   7 – 1

A Windows Solution at Fidelity

Boston-based Fidelity Investments is one of the world's largest financial-services companies. Account holders can choose among any of dozens of Fidelity mutual funds, scores of mutual funds from other companies, and thousands of stocks and bonds. A customer calling in with a query may first want information about one of his or her retirement accounts, then a balance from a second account, followed by the prices of several mutual funds, and ending with confirmation that paperwork sent two weeks ago was received. To keep up with such multiple transactions, the hundreds of service representatives at Fidelity's investment centers across the country must constantly be able to switch from one application to another while on the phone. To meet this need, Fidelity chose Microsoft Windows. The firm reports that information is better presented now than in the past and more of it is available on each rep's display screen.

message to the user or operator. Similarly, if any abnormalities arise in I/O devices or elsewhere in the system, the operating system sends a message to the user.

Bookkeeping and security are two other monitoring tasks of the operating system. Records may be kept of log-on and log-off times, programs' running times, programs that each user has run, and other information. In some environments, such records enable the organization to bill users. The operating system also can protect the system against unauthorized access by checking the validity of users' ID numbers and reporting attempts to breach system security. Moreover, it must protect memory so that an error in a program will not "crash" the computer system or, worse yet, corrupt vital data in other programs.

Interleaved Processing Techniques

In this section, we will examine some of the assignment and scheduling techniques that computers use to handle a large number of jobs at the same time. Sophisticated computers often take advantage of *interleaved processing techniques* such as multiprogramming, multitasking, time-sharing, virtual memory, and multiprocessing to operate more efficiently. These operating-system features enable computers to process many programs at almost the same time and, consequently, to increase the number of jobs the computer system can handle in any given period.

Multiprogramming.
The execution of two or more programs *concurrently* on the same computer.

Multiprogramming   Multiprogramming, a term that refers to multiuser operating systems, is somewhat similar to the operation of a busy dentist's office. The dentist *concurrently* attends to several patients in different rooms within a given time period. The dentist may pull a tooth in room 1, move to room 2 to prepare a cavity for filling, move back to room 1 to treat the hole created by the pulled tooth, and so forth. As the dentist moves from patient to patient, assistants do minor tasks.

In a computer system with a multiprogrammed operating system, several applications programs may be stored in memory at the same time. The CPU, like the dentist, works on only one program at a time. When it reaches a point in a program at which peripheral devices or other elements of the computer system must take over some of the work, the CPU interrupts processing to move on to another program, returning to the first program when that program is ready to be processed again. While the computer is waiting for data on one program to be accessed on disk, for example, it can perform calculations for another program. The systems software for the disk unit, like the dental assistants, does background work; in this case, it retrieves the data stored on disk.

Multiprogramming is feasible because computers can perform thousands of computations in the time it takes to ask for and receive a single piece of data from disk. Such disk I/O operations are much slower than computation, because the computer must interact with and receive communications from an external device to obtain the data it needs. It must also contend with the slower access speeds of secondary storage.

Multitasking.
The ability of a single-user operating system to enable two or more programs or program tasks to execute concurrently.

Multitasking   Multitasking refers to a multiprogramming capability on single-user operating systems. Thus, it refers to the ability of an operating system to enable two or more programs or program tasks from a single user to execute concurrently on one computer. This feature generally allows a user to do such things as edit one program while another program is executing and have two or more programs displayed on screen at the same time and modify them concurrently (see Figure 7-5). Remember, one computer, like one dentist, can attend to only one task at a time. But the computer works so fast that the user often has the illusion that it is doing two things at once.

One situation in which multitasking is very helpful occurs when a program has an exceptionally long processing time and the computer is needed for other work. For example, suppose that you want to search through a large employee file for all people between the ages of 25 and 35 with six years of service and some experience with computers. On a relatively small computer, such a search may take several minutes, during which time you may want to use the computer for other work. With multitasking, you can use your computer to perform another task, on the same or a different program, while the search is taking place in the background.

Time-sharing.
Processing in a multiuser environment in which the computer handles users' jobs in a round-robin fashion.

Time-sharing   Time-sharing is a very popular technique for computer systems that support numerous terminals. The operating system cycles through all the active programs in the system that need processing and gives each one a small time slice on each cycle.

For example, say there are 20 programs in the system and each program is to be allocated a time slice of 1 second (the time slice usually is much smaller than this, and all slices aren't necessarily equal). The computer will work on

FIGURE 7 – 5

Multitasking. A multitasking feature allows a user to edit one program while another is executing as well as to have two or more programs displayed onscreen at the same time and modify them concurrently.

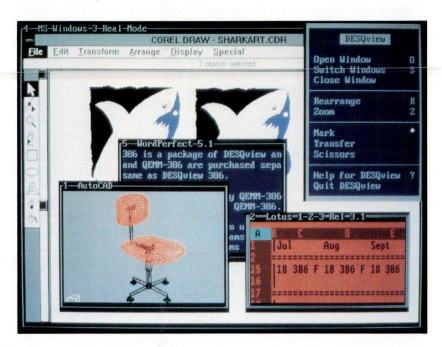

program 1 for one second, then on program 2 for one second, and so forth. When it finishes working on program 20 for one second, it will go back to program 1 for another second, program 2 for another second, and so on. Thus, if there is an average of 20 programs on the system, each program will get a total of 3 seconds of processing during each minute of actual clock time, or 1 second in every 20-second period. As you can see, in a time-sharing system it is difficult for a single program to dominate the CPU's attention, thereby holding up the processing of shorter programs.

Both time-sharing and multiprogramming are techniques for working on many programs concurrently by allotting short uninterrupted time periods to each. They differ in the way they allot time, however. In time-sharing, the computer spends a fixed amount of time on each program and then goes on to another. In multiprogramming, the computer works on a program until it encounters a logical stopping point, such as when more data must be read in, before going on to another program. Many computers today combine time-sharing and multi-programming techniques to expedite processing.

Virtual Memory In the early days of computing, users who had large programs faced numerous problems with loading them into memory. Often they had to manually split such programs into pieces so that only small portions of them resided in the limited memory space at any one time. In the early 1970s, a

Virtual memory.
An area on disk in which programs are "cut up" into manageable pieces so that they can be processed.

virtual-memory feature became available on some operating systems. It permitted users the luxury of writing extremely long programs that the operating system would automatically split up and manage.

Virtual memory refers to using disk to extend conventional memory, or RAM. This is the way it usually works: The operating system delivers programs to be processed to the virtual-memory area on disk. Here the programs generally are divided into either fixed-length *pages* or variable-length *segments*. Whether the programs are subdivided into pages or segments depends on the operating system's capabilities.

A virtual memory system using paging breaks a program into pages. If a program is 40 kilobytes long and the system divides programs into 4 kilobyte lengths, the program is divided into 10 pages. As the computer works on the program, it stores only a few pages at a time in RAM. As it requires other pages during program execution, it selects them from virtual memory and writes over the pages in RAM that it no longer needs. All the original pages, or modified ones, remain intact in virtual memory as the computer processes the program. So, if the computer again needs a page that has been written over in RAM, it can readily fetch it. This process continues until the program is finished.

Segmentation works somewhat like paging except that the segments are variable in length. Each segment normally consists of a contiguous block of logically interrelated material from the program. Some systems use a combination of segmentation and paging.

Not all operating systems on large computers use virtual memory. Although this technique permits a computer system to get by with a smaller RAM, it requires extra computer time to swap pages or segments in and out of RAM.

Multiprocessing.
The *simultaneous* execution of two or more program sequences by multiple computers operating under common control.

Multiprocessing   **Multiprocessing** refers to the use of two or more computers linked together to perform work at the same time. This, of course, requires systems software that will realize that multiple processors are in use and has the ability to assign work to them as efficiently as possible. Whereas multiprogramming involves processing several programs or tasks *concurrently* on a single computer, multiprocessing involves handling multiple programs or tasks *simultaneously* (at precisely the same instant) on several computers. There are many ways to implement multiprocessing; two common ones covered here are coprocessing and parallel processing.

With *coprocessing,* which we covered briefly in Chapter 3, the native CPU works in conjunction with specialized "slave" processors that perform dedicated chores. For instance, many microcomputer systems today have slave processors that handle tasks such as high-speed mathematical computation, display-screen graphics, and keyboard operations. At any point in time, two or more processors within the system unit may be performing work simultaneously. However, the time taken to perform an entire job will be largely constrained by the main CPU, which is at the top of the hierarchy.

In *parallel processing,* which is the most sophisticated and fastest type of multiprocessing, the multiple processors involved are full-fledged, general-purpose CPUs that operate at roughly the same level. They are tightly integrated so that they can work together on a job by sharing memory. This may sound simple, but there are many practical complications, and special software is often required.

Multiprocessing is closely related to *fault-tolerant computing,* in which computer systems are built with important circuitry duplicated. If a critical compo-

nent fails, an identical backup component takes over. Even though duplicate processors (or sets of processors) are involved, however, only one processor (or set of processors) will be in operation at any point in time. User Solution 7-2 describes the need for fault-tolerant computing in mission-critical applications.

A Closer Look at
Several Operating Systems

Here, we briefly cover several of the most widely used operating systems to give you a feel for their principal characteristics and to help you understand how they differ from each other. The operating systems we discuss in this section include MS-DOS and PC-DOS, Macintosh System Software, UNIX, OS/2, Windows NT, and NetWare.

MS-DOS and PC-DOS

During the 1980s, DOS* (for Disk Operating System) was the predominant microcomputer-based operating system for most businesses. Over 100 million copies of it have been sold to date, making it the most widely used software package ever developed. Even though it has been made technologically obsolescent by newer products, well over 50 percent of today's microcomputer systems still use DOS.

DOS is available in two forms: PC-DOS and MS-DOS. Both were originally developed by Microsoft Corporation of Redmond, Washington. Except for a few minor differences, these operating systems are virtually identical. **PC-DOS**

PC-DOS.
The operating system most widely used on IBM micro-computers.

---

*For simplicity, when used in this text, DOS refers strictly to MS-DOS and PC-DOS. DOS, however, is not a proprietary name, and other, lesser-known operating systems also use the name DOS—Radio Shack TRSDOS and Apple ProDOS, for instance.

MS-DOS.
The operating system most widely used by microcomputer systems similar to those made by IBM.

was created originally for the IBM PC, whereas **MS-DOS** was devised to operate on computer systems that look and work a lot like the IBM PC. All of these computer systems use the 16-bit Intel 8088 chip or the closely related 16-bit Intel 8086 chip. These chips support less than a megabyte of RAM.

Both the MS-DOS and PC-DOS operating systems have been revised many times since they were first developed. Each major revision is referred to as a *version.* All versions starting with the number 1 (such as 1.0 and 1.1) were designed for the earliest microcomputer systems, such as the original IBM PC, which used only floppy disk and cassette tapes for secondary storage. Today, DOS is up to Version 6 and has been extended to work with hard disks, networks, and the latest Intel microprocessors. Yet because it was originally designed around 16-bit chips—which supported limited amounts of RAM—16-bit DOS cannot take full advantage of the power of new chips.

Today, it is not clear whether the successor to DOS will be Windows NT, OS/2, UNIX, or some other multitasking operating system. Despite the fact that DOS has become technologically obsolescent, it is likely that DOS and DOS-based applications will be prevalent for a good part of this decade. So many DOS-based computers are around today that vendors of new software are still supplying—in force—DOS-based applications to the marketplace. Furthermore, products such as Microsoft Windows have extended the popularity of DOS. A sample of DOS commands is provided in Figure 7-6.

FIGURE 7 – 6

DOS. Even though DOS has been technologically obsolesced by sophisticated graphical environments and newer operating systems, most microcomputers still use DOS. Shown here are some of the most widely used DOS commands.

Command	Description	Example	Explanation
COPY	Copies individual files	COPY BOSS WORKER	Makes a copy of BOSS and stores it in WORKER
		COPY BOSS B:WORKER	Makes a copy of BOSS and stores it, on the B drive, in WORKER
DIR	Displays the names of files on a disk	DIR	Displays names of files on the default drive
		DIR B:	Displays names of files on the B drive
		DIR/W	Displays names of files on the default drive in a table format
ERASE (DEL)	Erases individual files	ERASE DOLLAR	Erases DOLLAR from the default drive
		ERASE B:DOLLAR	Erases DOLLAR from the B drive
REN	Renames individual files	REN SAM BILL	Renames SAM to BILL
DISKCOPY	Copies the contents of one disk to another disk	DISKCOPY A: B:	Copies the contents of the disk in drive A to the disk in drive B
FORMAT	Prepares a disk for use, erasing what was there before	FORMAT	Formats the disk in the default drive
		FORMAT B:	Formats the disk in the B drive

FIGURE 7-7

Macintosh System Software. Macintosh System Software sported the first commercially successful graphical interface for operating systems and it is still one of the most popular. Annotated in the figure are some of the principal elements of the Macintosh electronic desktop. Although the names and appearance of many of the features differ from the Windows desktop, the types of tasks that you can perform are virtually identical to those in Windows.

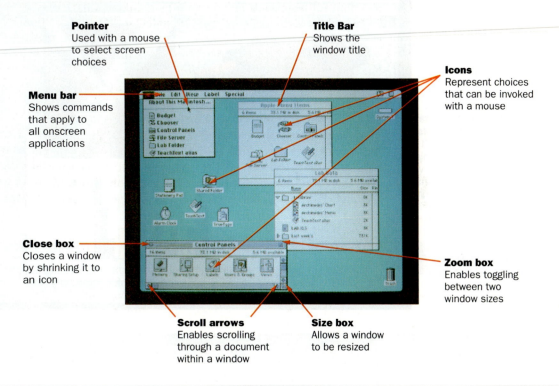

Pointer
Used with a mouse to select screen choices

Title Bar
Shows the window title

Icons
Represent choices that can be invoked with a mouse

Menu bar
Shows commands that apply to all onscreen applications

Close box
Closes a window by shrinking it to an icon

Zoom box
Enables toggling between two window sizes

Scroll arrows
Enables scrolling through a document within a window

Size box
Allows a window to be resized

Macintosh System Software

Macintosh System Software is the proprietary, icon-oriented operating system that comes with the Apple Macintosh line of computers. The Apple Macintosh, introduced in 1984, has set the standard for graphical user interfaces. Today, many operating systems are trying to copy what the Mac originally started.

Macintosh System Software has grown with the times, keeping pace with the increases in power made available with each new Motorola CPU chip and each new Macintosh computer system. The latest version of Macintosh System Software, Version 7, can be used on virtually all recent Macintoshes that have at least two megabytes of RAM. Some of the features it provides are typographic capabilities for display devices and printers, and multitasking.

Macintosh System Software is found, almost exclusively, on computers in the Apple Macintosh line. An example of the graphical user interface provided with the Macintosh is shown in Figure 7-7. Macintosh owners also frequently use UNIX, a flexible operating system that is not tied to any particular brand of computer.

Macintosh System Software.
The operating system that's primarily used on Apple's Macintosh line of computer systems.

2

2–3. The staple of the GUI is the *window,* a self-contained box of information. Windows can be arranged onscreen in either of two ways: by *tiling* them side by side (photo 2) or by *overlapping* them (photo 3). The active, or foreground, window often has a darkened title bar and/or a darkened border. The OS/2 windows shown here contain mostly *program icons.* The programs corresponding to these icons can be run when the icons are selected with a mouse or keyboard.

3

4–5. Selections in GUI choices are often made with *command buttons.* Buttons are chosen by clicking them with a mouse or, alternatively, by moving to them with a keyboard and pressing the Enter key. Usually the active choice will be darkened, as in photo 5. Photo 5 is also an example of a *warning box,* which pops up on the screen when a potential problem situation is unfolding.

4

5

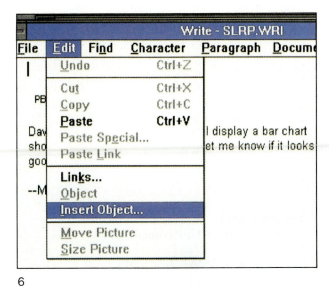

6

6. Many GUIs work with top-of-screen *menu bars* and *pull-down menus.* Here, when Edit is selected on the menu bar, the pull-down menu corresponding to it is unfurled onscreen and any of the choices on it can be accessed—unless they are shown in faded type (such as Undo and Cut). Current command choices are usually highlighted onscreen, such Edit and Insert Object, here. Pull-down-menu commands shown with an ellipsis (. . .) lead to other pull-down menus if selected. Underlined letters indicate keystrokes that can be used to access commands with a keyboard.

7

7. *Dialog boxes* prompt the GUI user for information. In the top left box shown here are round *radio buttons;* they work like push buttons on many radios in that only one choice in the panel can be active at a time. Below the radio buttons are square *check boxes;* any number of options in a check-box panel can be made active by placing an "X" in the appropriate box. At the top right are *text boxes;* they require the user to type in data.

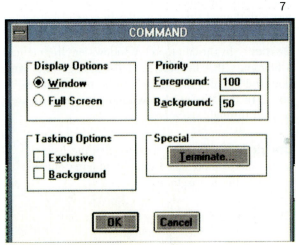

8

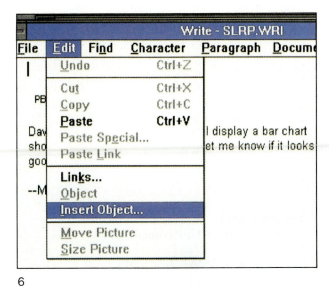

8. Many GUIs come with an *online help* feature, enhanced with diagrams. *Scroll bars* shown here in the right of the foreground window indicate that the diagram is larger than can fit in the window. By activating the scroll bar with a mouse or keyboard, the user can see the rest of the diagram. Alternatively, the window can be enlarged, so that the entire diagram or more of it fits onscreen.

A GUI Miniglossary

Defined below are several terms that users often encounter when working in a GUI environment. Most of the terms contained here can be found either in italic type in the photo captions for Window 4 or in the annotations that accompany Figures 7-4 and 7-7, which respectively illustrate the Microsoft Windows and Macintosh environments.

Active window   The window that represents the foreground application or document. This window is typically the topmost window on the screen and has a darkened title bar and/or darkened border.

Border   In the Microsoft Windows environment, a boundary that denotes the outside edge of a window and enables the window to be moved or resized. In the Macintosh environment, windows are resized through a *size box*.

Check box   A menu that enables the user to make one or more selections by placing check marks to the left of them.

Click   Refers to pressing the mouse button once, to highlight or select a choice.

Clipboard   A program feature that provides temporary storage for data you wish to transfer between applications.

Close box   In the Macintosh environment, a small box located at the top left of a window that enables the window to be closed. Works similar to the *control-menu icons* in Microsoft Windows.

Command button   In the Microsoft Windows environment, an icon representing a choice that can be activated or deactivated by clicking on it. Frequently used command buttons are "OK," "Cancel," and "Help."

Context-sensitive help   An online help feature that provides assistance relating to the type of operation the user is currently trying to perform.

Control panel   A feature that enables the user to customize the GUI environment.

Control-menu icon   In the Microsoft Windows environment, a small box located at the top left of a window that enables the window to be closed. Works similar to the *close box* on the Macintosh.

Corner   In the Microsoft Windows environment, the region where two adjoining edges of a border meet. The corner can be activated to shorten or lengthen two border edges simultaneously.

Desk accessory (DA)   A program—such as a clock or calendar—that provides a feature commonly found on a conventional office desktop.

Desktop   The area of the screen that is available for GUI applications. Usually, the desktop is the entire screen area.

Dialog box   A box that requires the user to supply information to the computer system about the task being performed.

Dimmed option   A faded-looking icon or command, indicating that the associated operation is not available in the current context.

Double-click   Pressing the mouse button twice in rapid succession, to open or activate an application or document.

Drag   A technique used to move icons on the screen or to resize windows. Dragging is normally performed by clicking on the desired screen item and moving the mouse while holding down the mouse button.

Drop-down list box   A list box through which the user scrolls to see all the choices available.

Font manager   A program feature that lets the user select and size typefaces.

Icon   A graphic symbol that can represent either a program or program group, a command, a file or file folder, a disk drive, and the like.

Linesize box   A box that enables the user to choose the thickness of lines for a drawing.

List box   A box that presents a list of choices. Often, the default or current choice is highlighted, and it can be changed using the mouse or keyboard.

Menu bar   A horizontal list of choices that appears on a highlighted line, usually below the window title. Often called the *main menu.*

Online help   A feature that enables the user to request help while on the computer. Online help is often *context sensitive.*

Paint program   A program that enables users to create drawings and to color the drawings.

Palette   A toolbox-type menu that enables users to select among various colors.

Pointer   The screen symbol showing where the mouse is currently pointing. Usually, the pointer is in the form of a small arrow, but the pointer often changes shape in various ways as the user performs such operations as typing text into a text box and resizing windows.

Pull-down menu   A menu of subcommands that drops down vertically from a horizontal menu bar or to the right of another pull-down menu.

Radio buttons   A set of choices that represents mutually exclusive options. Sometimes called *option buttons.*

Scroll bar   A horizontal or vertical bar along a side of a window indicating that the window is too small to display all the information involved. The user must activate the scroll arrows on the bar to see offscreen information.

Scroll arrows   Arrows on a scroll bar that enable users to see additional information.

Size button   In the Microsoft Windows environment, one or two small symbols that appear on the right edge of the title box and enable a window to be maximized to take up the full screen, minimized to icon size, or restored to its previous size. This feature is implemented in the Macintosh environment by a *zoom box.*

Size box   In the Macintosh environment, a box in the lower-right corner of the active window that enables the window to be resized. In the Microsoft Windows environment, this feature is implemented by clicking the mouse on the window border and dragging it.

Tear-off menu   A pull-down menu that can be kept visible and moved to a new location on the screen so that the user can refer to it while working.

Text box   A box that contains a space(s) for the user to type in text, such as a file's name.

Title bar   A horizontal bar, usually at the top of a window, that contains the window's name.

Toolbox   A menu in which icons are tightly arranged in a horizontal or vertical rectangular grid.

Warning box   A box that displays a warning when the user is trying to do something that is disallowed or is doing something that can result in a loss of data. Sometimes called an *alert box.*

Window   A box within an application that displays information or that contains an embedded application.

Zoom box   In the Macintosh environment, a small symbol that enables the user to toggle between two window sizes. This feature is implemented in Microsoft Windows by *sizing buttons.*

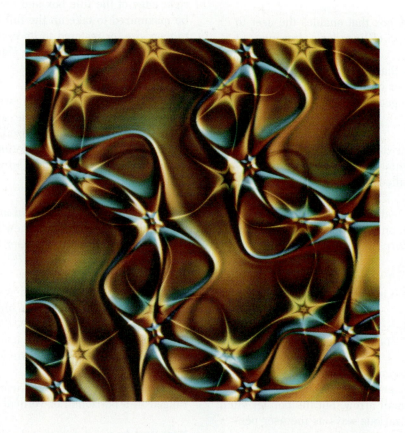

Productivity Software

Over the last decade or so, computers have completely transformed the workplace. Look at the desktops of many managers, analysts, designers, engineers, secretaries, and even corporate presidents today and you will usually see a computer system. Managers and analysts regularly use computers to crunch numbers, send and receive electronic-mail messages, and prepare presentation materials for meetings. Designers and engineers typically employ computers to create products. Secretaries use computers on a daily basis to prepare correspondence and reports. And corporate presidents rely on computers to access important facts about their organizations.

At the heart of this workplace transformation is productivity software. Productivity software refers to applications-software packages that enable end users to better perform their jobs. These packages help users save time, reduce costs, and perform types of work that couldn't possibly be done without the aid of a computer system.

Module D opens, in Chapter 8, with a look at word processors and desktop publishing systems, both of which assist in the development of documents. In Chapter 9 we cover spreadsheets and presentation graphics. Spreadsheets aid in the analysis of numbers, while presentation graphics packages help prepare graphs and charts showing numbers in a pictorial format. The module closes, in Chapter 10, with a discussion of file managers and database management systems. Both of these packages specialize in providing rapid access to electronically stored facts.

WORD PROCESSING AND DESKTOP PUBLISHING

8

Have you ever wanted to create and publish your own magazine or book? As you will learn in this chapter, word processing and desktop publishing systems enable you to do just that—at a cost you can probably afford.

LEARNING OBJECTIVES

After completing this chapter, you will be able to:

1. Describe word processing and name several ways in which it may be implemented on computer systems.

2. Identify the operations you must master to effectively use word processing software.

3. Explain the features common to many word processing packages.

4. Identify the software and hardware components found in many desktop publishing systems.

Overview

Word processing and desktop publishing are technologies that deal with the manipulation of words. *Word processing* enables a computer system to serve as a powerful typewriting tool. When using the computer in this way, one can quickly create, edit, and print documents and manage them as no ordinary typewriter can. *Desktop publishing,* available only since high-powered micro-computers entered the marketplace, carries word processing a step further. With desktop publishing hardware and software, one can create documents that look as though they were prepared by a professional print shop.

In this chapter, we'll first discuss word processors. We'll explore in detail some of the types of word processors currently available and many of the features that differentiate one word processor from another. We'll also look at some of the add-on packages that are available to make the word processing environment even more powerful. Then we'll turn to desktop publishing and the hardware and software found on desktop publishing systems.

Word Processing

Word processing.
The use of computer technology to create, manipulate, and print text material such as letters, legal contracts, and manuscripts.

When you use your computer to do the kinds of work you normally do on a typewriter, you're doing word processing. **Word processing** is the use of computer technology to create, manipulate, and print text materials such as letters, legal contracts, manuscripts, and other documents. Word processing is such a timesaver, in fact, that most people who learn to do it let their typewriters gather dust.

Types of Word Processors

You can perform word processing in several ways. Some common alternatives are discussed in the following subsections.

General-Purpose versus Special-Purpose Word Processing Packages
Most word processing software products in use today are *general-purpose word processing packages;* that is, they are designed to suit the needs of a variety of users, such as secretaries, authors, and average microcomputer users. Among today's best-selling general-purpose word processing packages are WordPerfect, Microsoft Word, Ami Pro, and WordStar. Word and WordPerfect are the undis-puted leaders in today's word processing marketplace, with close to a 75 percent combined market share. A number of *specialized word processors* are also commer-cially available to meet the unique demands of users in certain niche areas. For example, some word processors are designed to meet the unique needs of movie scriptwriters or musicians.

Dedicated Word Processing Packages versus Integrated Software Packages
Most people who do word processing use a *dedicated word proc-essing package*—that is, a package targeted exclusively to meeting various word processing needs. The packages most familiar to the general public—WordPerfect and Word, for instance—fall into this category. However, some software products combine the ability to process words with the ability to perform other, dissimilar functions, such as spreadsheeting and database management. This latter category of products—which includes Symphony, Works, and First

FIGURE 8-1

WYSIWYG versus embedded formatting codes. With WYSIWYG, what you see on the screen is exactly what you get in print. Most users of word processors today must, however, rely on some type of embedded formatting codes to tell them if text is to be given special treatment.

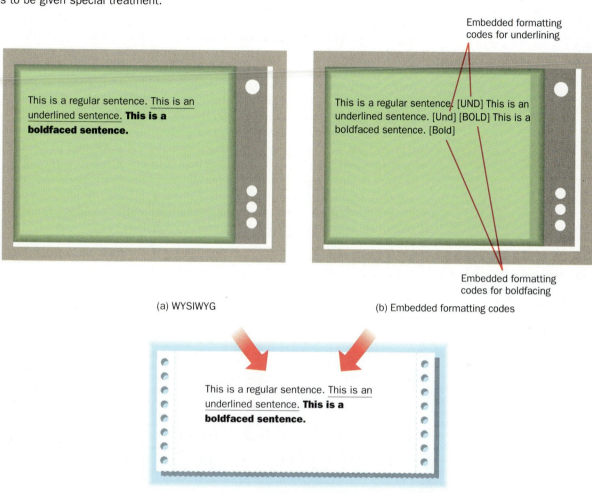

(a) WYSIWYG

(b) Embedded formatting codes

Embedded formatting codes for underlining

Embedded formatting codes for boldfacing

(c) Printed page

Choice—is most commonly referred to as *integrated software packages.* We'll discuss integrated software packages more fully in Chapter 9.

The remainder of this chapter will address dedicated, general-purpose word processing packages. These are the types of word processors most commonly encountered in practice.

Is What You See What You Get?

The vast majority of word processors in use today display on the screen an image that shows exactly, or almost exactly, how a document will appear before it's printed. Each screen line corresponds to a printed-page line, so you are rarely surprised at how the document looks when it's subsequently printed.

Ideally, the image on the screen and the image on the printed page correspond exactly. This feature is referred to as **WYSIWYG,** for What You See Is What You Get (see Figure 8-1a). WYSIWYG—which is pronounced "wizzy-wig"—most often occurs in desktop publishing applications, where the design of a page can be critical. There, users frequently employ high-resolution graphics monitors capable of simultaneously displaying a variety of type styles, sometimes scaled to different sizes. Users can experiment onscreen with several different page styles and inspect every document page in fine detail before committing anything to print.

Today, many word processors and monitors being used fall short of the full WYSIWYG ideal. In fact, boldface, italic, and underlined characters often do not display conveniently onscreen even though they will be output as such on the printed document. To apprise users of such print-formatting effects, many word processors use *embedded formatting codes.* Typically, the user places these codes before and after a word or phrase that is to be output in a special way (see Figure 8-1b). The code placed before the word or phrase alerts the printer to turn on a formatting feature; the code following the word or phrase alerts it to turn off the feature. Some word processors display these codes onscreen at all times, whereas others reveal them only on demand.

FIGURE 8 – 2

Preview feature. Most word processors enable users to inspect a document prior to printing by looking onscreen at a full page image, facing-page images, and close-up views.

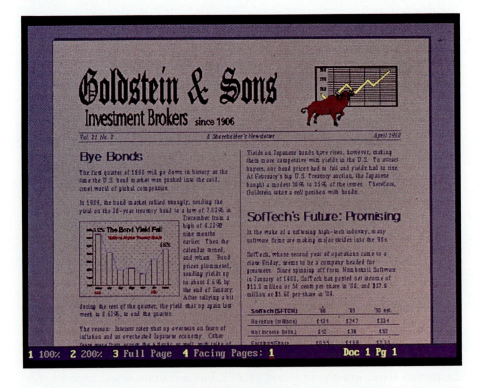

FIGURE 8 – 3

General operations needed for operating any productivity software package.
Depending on the package you use, the file that you work on may contain a word-processed document, a worksheet, a graph, a collection of database records, or something else.

- **Accessing** your package from the operating system
- Informing the package that you either want to **create** a new file or **retrieve** an old one from disk
- Commanding the package to **save** a file onto disk
- Commanding the package to **print** a file
- Commanding the package to **delete** a file that's on disk
- Indicating to the package that you want to **quit** working on your current file and do something on another file
- **Terminating** your work on the package and getting back to the operating system

In recognition of the usefulness of WYSIWYG, many word processors also have a *preview feature* (see Figure 8-2) that enables users to inspect an onscreen version of what the document will actually look like when printed. To employ the feature—which typically provides such options as a complete page image to be viewed on a single screen, facing pages to be viewed, or a piece of the document to be blown up—the user will usually have to leave the normal text-editing mode. Because the computer system must work in a bit-mapped, graphics mode to provide previewing and because painting each individual screen pixel is computationally intensive, a powerful processor is recommended to take full advantage of this feature.

WYSIWYG screens are but one example of the strong trend among word processors to sport graphical user interfaces (see the Tomorrow box).

Learning to Use a Word Processor: The Basics

Even though many word processing packages have hundreds of features, usually only a handful of them account for 90 percent or more of what you will do during the course of word processing a typical document. This basic set of word processing operations can be divided into three groups: general operations, entering and editing operations, and print-formatting operations.

General Operations To use virtually any type of productivity software package—word processor, spreadsheet, or whatever—you need to know how to carry out a number of general tasks. These are listed in Figure 8-3 and are functionally equivalent to activities like starting and stopping when operating a car.

Entering and Editing Operations Every word processor contains an assortment of entering and editing operations for keying in text and manipulating text on the screen. Among the most common of these operations are moving the cursor, scrolling, making a line return, inserting and deleting, moving and copying, and searching and replacing.

Graphical Word Processors

How Fast Will They Catch On?

During the last several years there has been a growing trend toward software that sports a graphical user interface (GUI). For a long time, this trend barely touched word processing, an applications area that is predominantly text based. But as computer hardware systems have become more powerful, word processing companies have taken advantage of the additional bytes and faster cycle times available on the new machines. As a result, word processors have leapt into the world of graphics.

In word processing, the graphics features being incorporated are generally of three principal types: a graphical command interface, improved WYSIWYG features, and drawing capabilities.

Graphical command interfaces refer to such features as mouse pointing and moving, onscreen windows and icons, and the ability to make choices from menus. Many of these features were covered in Window 4. Word processors that come with graphical interfaces include such Windows-based products as WordPerfect 6.0, WordPerfect for Windows, Microsoft Word for Windows, and Ami Pro (see photo). At a minimum, a graphical command interface lets you use a mouse to select screen icons and choices from menu bars and pull-down menus. You may also be able to move text by "dragging and dropping" it with a mouse. And to save extra keystroking, you may even be able to define your own screen icons and have them perform customized functions.

Although most high-end word processors allow you to preview text in some sort of *WYSIWYG* mode, graphically oriented word processors often go a step or two further. For instance, many will let you edit the text you are previewing directly on the WYSIWYG screen rather than making you switch back and forth between WYSIWYG and standard-text modes. Also, some packages are making a greater selection of built-in fonts and automatic-styling features available, so documents can look even more like they were professionally typeset.

Several word processors are now also packing in a greater number of *drawing* features. Among other things, these features allow you to import art from other software packages and size, rotate, and crop it. Some word processors even provide a drawing capability within documents.

In addition to providing features such as those just named, some graphical word processors also integrate such non-word-processing features as spreadsheet and database capabilities and fax and electronic-mail routines.

Reaction to this new breed of graphical products has been mixed. Most heavy users of word processing packages are touch typists who pro-

■ **MOVING THE CURSOR**   Many word processors offer well over a dozen ways to move the cursor around the screen. Usually you can move the cursor a character, a word, a line, or a screen at a time, as well as to the beginning or the end of a document. You can usually move the cursor either by typing in a short command or by depressing one of several function keys or cursor-movement keys. Many word processing users acquire a mouse to obtain additional cursor-movement capabilities.

■ **SCROLLING**   Scrolling lets you move contiguous lines of text up and down on the screen similarly to the way the roll on a player piano unwinds. When scrolling down, for example, as lines successively disappear from the top of the screen, new ones appear from the bottom. With many word processing packages, you can use the up-arrow and down-arrow keys to scroll a document line by line. By using the PgUp and PgDn keys, you can scroll even faster—page by page instead of line by line.

Word processing for the 1990s. Lotus' Ami Pro.

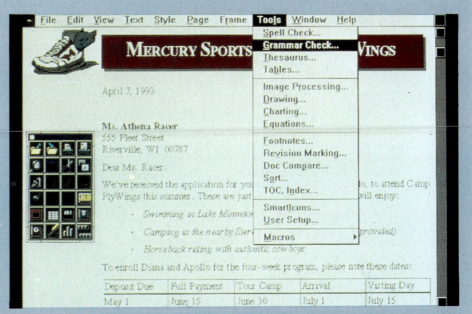

duce documents consisting of straight text—letters, memos, reports, and the like. Consequently, they don't have much need for WYSIWYG and drawing. Also, many touch typists dislike a graphical command interface because they feel it encourages them to use a mouse—forcing their hands off the keyboard. Moreover, a number of people complain that GUI word processors run slower than their non-GUI counterparts and that the graphical features word processors are now incorporating are best left to specialized support (add-on) packages, which do them better on the whole.

These drawbacks notwithstanding, the new breed of graphical word processors is drawing serious notice and appears to be an unstoppable trend. It's a good bet that as computers get ever more powerful, the word processing companies will be offering an even wider range of products from which to choose, including everything from full-blown desktop publishing with lots of typesetting and imagesetting features to watered-down packages aimed at folks who like to write an occasional letter to Mom and Dad.

■ **MAKING A LINE RETURN** With a conventional typewriter, you generally must press the Return key every time you finish typing in a line. Not so with a word processor. Word processors provide an automatic line return when the cursor reaches a certain column position at the right-hand side of the screen. This return is called a **soft return,** and the built-in feature that provides soft returns is called a **wordwrap** feature (see Figure 8-4).

Word processors also allow you to key in **hard returns** by hitting the Enter key. Normally, you will use hard returns between paragraphs or blocks of text or after typing in titles. You should not hit the Enter key after every line as you would on a normal typewriter. Hitting the Enter key will deny you any chances of reformatting the document later on.

■ **INSERTING AND DELETING** Inserting and deleting are two of the most basic editing operations.

Soft return.
An automatic line return carried out by word-processing software.

Wordwrap.
The word processing feature that automatically produces soft returns.

Hard return.
The use of the Enter key to provide line spacing in a document.

Wordwrap. Wordwrapping produces a soft return when the cursor reaches a certain position at the right-hand side of the screen.

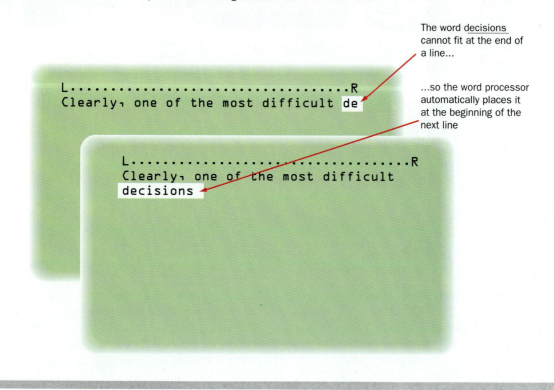

The word decisions cannot fit at the end of a line...

...so the word processor automatically places it at the beginning of the next line

Virtually all word processors have an *insert mode* that lets you insert characters at the cursor position on the screen. Often, you enter the insert mode by depressing the Insert key on the keyboard. When you are not in the insert mode, you are automatically in the *typeover mode,* in which case every character you type into an already existing line replaces the character at the cursor position. On most systems, the Insert key is a *toggle key*—depressing it once activates the insert mode, and depressing it again deactivates the insert mode.

Word processors will generally allow you to delete a character, word, line, or block of characters at a time. Deleting one character at a time is normally done through either the Delete or Backspace key. Deleting one word or line at a time is generally done by positioning the cursor on the word or line to be deleted and depressing one or two keys. When you want to delete a block of characters, you normally must first identify the beginning and end of the block, an operation called *block marking,* and then invoke a delete command. Block marking, illustrated in Figure 8-5, is also necessary when you want to move, copy, boldface, or underline text.

■ **MOVING AND COPYING**   Moving and copying are operations that allow you to "cut and paste" text with a word processor. *Moving* means identifying a specific block of text and physically relocating it in a new place in the document. *Copying* is similar to moving except that a copy of the block remains in the original place as well.

■ **SEARCHING AND REPLACING** Searching and replacing are extremely useful features. They enable you to search automatically for all occurrences of a particular word or phrase and change them to something else. For example, let's say you've typed out a long document that should repeatedly refer to a person named "Snider." If you've misspelled this name as "Schneider," you can instruct the word processor to look up all occurrences of "Schneider" and change them to "Snider."

Some people take dangerous shortcuts in searching and replacing. For example, suppose you ask the word processor to change all occurrences of "chne" to "n." This will change all "Schneider" occurrences to "Snider," but it will also change a name such as "Schneymann" to "Snymann," which you probably did not intend to do.

Figure 8-6 shows a document before and after a searching and replacing operation.

Print-Formatting Operations Print-formatting operations tell the printer how to output the text onto paper. These operations include adjusting line spacing, indenting, justifying, establishing a page format, reformatting, centering, tabbing, paginating, setting up headers and footers, selecting typefaces, putting text into multiple columns, and footnoting.

■ **ADJUSTING LINE SPACING** Adjusting line spacing is an important word processing operation. Suppose that you've single-spaced a paper, but your English 101 instructor wants all the essays you hand in to be double-spaced. Virtually all word processors will enable you to adjust the line spacing to

FIGURE 8–5

Marking a block of text. A block is usually marked by highlighting it onscreen (as shown here) or by marking its beginning and end with special characters. Once a block has been marked, it can be moved, copied, formatted, or deleted.

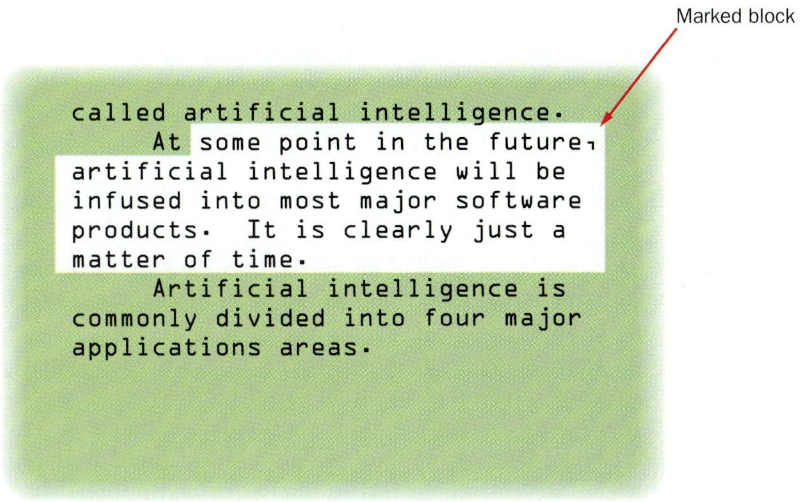

Marked block

```
called artificial intelligence.
    At some point in the future,
artificial intelligence will be
infused into most major software
products. It is clearly just a
matter of time.
    Artificial intelligence is
commonly divided into four major
applications areas.
```

Searching and replacing. In the figure, the operator wishes to search for all occurrences of the date March 27 and replace them with the date April 3. Such an operation is called a global search-and-replace. Many word processors will also stop at each occurrence of the search string, if desired, and provide the operator the option of changing each one individually.

Search string

```
On March 27, ABC Industries will
launch its biggest product line
ever. There will be seven new
display devices and fourteen new
printers announced. The March 27
announcement will be accompanied by
a series of big public-relations
events. Perhaps the most noteworthy
of these is a new ad campaign,
airing on TKKZ radio on March 27,
and the hosting of the Cherryvale Open
Golf Classic three weeks later.
```

Replaced text

```
On April 3, ABC Industries will
launch its biggest product line
ever. There will be seven new
display devices and fourteen new
printers announced. The April 3
announcement will be accompanied by
a series of big public-relations
events. Perhaps the most noteworthy
of these is a new ad campaign,
airing on TKKZ radio on April 3,
and the hosting of the Cherryvale Open
Golf Classic three weeks later.
```

a double space in a few second or minutes. Many packages will also permit triple-spacing, fractional blank lines between text lines, and several other line-spacing options.

■ **INDENTING**   Indenting, or adjusting margins, is useful when you are typing a paper with many quotations and want to set off these passages from the main text. Many word processors allow you to choose among several types of indenting styles. One of the most widely used of these is the *hanging indent,* which is used to indent text in numbered and bulleted lists (such as this list).

■ **JUSTIFYING**   Virtually all word processing packages enable a printed document to be formatted with either a ragged or smooth right edge. These style alternatives are respectively referred to as *left justification* and *full justification*. The text that you are reading at this instant has a fully justified right margin. The text inside the screens of Figure 8-6, in contrast, has a left-justified or ragged right margin. Users who create business documents often prefer left justification, as the extra blank spaces between words that often come with full justification can sometimes make documents too visually difficult to read. Full justification can look quite attractive, however, if the word processor and printer in use can handle proportional spacing (to be discussed shortly).

■ **ESTABLISHING A PAGE FORMAT**   Most word processors let you choose the way in which you would like your pages to be formatted. For instance, you can tell the word processor how many lines to print per page; the maximum number of characters to fit on each line; and the settings of the left, right, top, and bottom margins. A number of word processing packages will also automatically number lines for you—a useful feature if you are preparing legal documents or printer galleys. Having a number attached to each line makes it easy to identify text quickly and with less chance of error.

■ **REFORMATTING**   Reformatting normally is necessary when you insert text, delete text, change line spacing, readjust margins in your document, change justification, or change the basic page format. Reformatting places the document in a form suitable for output, for instance, by ensuring that the document is properly fitted within the margins after an insertion or deletion is made. After making the format change, you may need to issue one or more commands to reformat the sections of the document affected. Some packages reformat automatically after each edit.

■ **CENTERING**   Centering text is important for most users of word processors. Word processing packages usually require you to have the cursor on the line containing the text to be centered when invoking the centering command.

■ **TABBING**   Tabbing is a formatting feature that typists have relied on for years. Like typewriters, most word processors enable you to set your own tab stops. The tab-stop positions on the screen can normally be reached through the Tab key.

■ **PAGINATING**   A pagination feature lets you choose whether to number pages in a document. For example, you may want page numbers placed on class reports but not on short letters. Many word processing packages will place page numbers wherever you specify.

■ **SETTING UP HEADERS AND FOOTERS**   *Headers* are titles automatically printed at the top of every page; *footers* are titles automatically printed at the bottom. Some word processors give you a great deal of flexibility with respect to headers and footers. For instance, you can print both headers and footers on the same page and even alternate the title placed in a header or a footer. This textbook, like many other books, alternates headers; module letter and title are on the left-facing pages and chapter number and title are on the right-facing pages. Many word processors also allow page numbers to appear in a header or footer and give you several choices about where to place them.

■ **SELECTING TYPEFACES**   A **typeface** is a collection of characters that share a common design. Typeface selection features enable you to output

Typeface.
A collection of characters that share a common design.

FIGURE 8-7

Typefaces. A typeface is a collection of visually consistent characters. Shown here are the (a) Courier, (b) Helvetica, and (c) Times typefaces.

(a) Courier

(b) Helvetica

(c) Times

Point size.
a measurement used in the scaling of typefaces.

Font.
A typeface in a particular point size—for instance, 12-point Helvetica.

characters in a variety of typefaces and typeface sizes (called **point sizes**). A typeface in a particular point size is referred to as a **font;** for instance, 12-point Courier is a font. Figures 8-7 and 8-8 illustrate typefaces, point sizes, and fonts.

Many word processors will also let you create boldface, italic, underlined, subscript, or superscript characters. Both the word processor and the printer on your system must support a particular styling feature for you to be able to use it.

■ **PUTTING TEXT INTO MULTIPLE COLUMNS** Multiple-column formatting lets you print text in a columnar format similar to that used in newspapers and magazines. If you are doing multiple-column formatting, it is especially useful to have a feature that eliminates orphans and widows (discussed later in the chapter).

FIGURE 8-8

Point size. Point size refers to the size of type. A typeface in a particular point size is commonly called a font.

This is 10-point Helvetica

This is 12-point Helvetica

This is 18-point Helvetica

This is 24-point Helvetica

■ **FOOTNOTING** A footnoting feature allows you to create, edit, and delete footnotes in a document. Typically, the routine that manages the footnoting is designed to remember footnote references and automatically renumber footnotes if you insert or delete any.

Learning to Use a Word Processor: Advanced Operations

In addition to the basic operations we've just covered, the more sophisticated word processors enable you to do a number of other useful tasks. Some of these may be especially valuable if you are a professional typist or an author, or if your business requires a lot of correspondence. Among such tasks are using proportional spacing, spelling checkers and thesauruses, mailing list and mail merge operations, and a math feature; setting up macros; redlining; preparing an index and table of contents; eliminating orphans and widows; sorting; embedding codes for typesetters; embedding graphics into word processed text; and using style sheets.

Proportional Spacing On many printers, text is **monospaced;** that is, each character takes up the same amount of horizontal space. This textbook, however, like most others, was typeset on a system that proportionally spaces characters. **Proportional spacing** allocates more horizontal space on a line to some characters than to others. For example, a capital *M* takes up more space than a lowercase *i*. A microspacing feature may also be available. With

Monospacing.
A printing feature that allocates the same amount of space on a line to each character.

Proportional spacing.
A printing feature that allocates more horizonal space on a line to some characters than to others.

Proportionally spaced characters with microspacing. With proportional spacing, more horizontal space on a line is allotted to some characters than to others. Note, for instance, that a capital *H* takes up more space than the lowercase *t* and *i* combined. Microspacing inserts fractional spaces between characters to make a line appear more attractive to the eye.

FIGURE 8 – 9

How tight is tight?

How tight is tight?

How tight is tight?

How tight is tight?

Microspacing.
A technique used by some printers and software packages to insert fractional spaces between characters to give text a typeset look.

microspacing, fractions of a full blank space are inserted within each line in places where they aren't likely to be noticed so that the left- and right-hand margins are flush. Proportional spacing and microspacing are shown in Figure 8-9.

Both your word processor and your printer must support proportional spacing and microspacing for your documents to achieve a typeset look.

Spelling Checker Most leading word processing packages today include a routine that reads through a document and searches for misspelled words. This routine and its accompanying dictionary are collectively known as a **spelling checker.**

Spelling checker.
A program or routine that is often used with a word processor to check for misspelled words.

The capabilities of spelling checkers can vary dramatically. Some spelling checkers have dictionaries that contain around 50,000 words, whereas others have 130,000 or more. A particularly important feature is the ability to place additional words into a dictionary. A writer of a computer text or medical article, for example, uses very specialized terms, most of which aren't in the dictionaries of standard spelling checkers.

Many spelling checkers allow you to check for misspelled words either after you've finished typing or while you're typing a document. The latter feature, which is usually practical only if you have a hard disk, assist you as you type by beeping whenever you key in a word that it doesn't recognize. Spelling checkers usually also come with a feature that displays onscreen suggestions for how to properly spell a word they don't recognize (see Figure 8-10) and a feature that counts words.

Spelling checkers will not catch all spelling errors. For instance, if you misspell the word "their" as "there," which is also a word in the English

FIGURE 8 – 10

Using a spelling checker. Many spelling checkers stop to highlight words that they don't recognize when scanning a completed text document. Here the checker can't find "glossery" in its dictionary and, below the dotted line, offers the operator some replacement suggestions. Many spelling checkers automatically make a replacement when the operator depresses the assigned key—the *A* key, in this example.

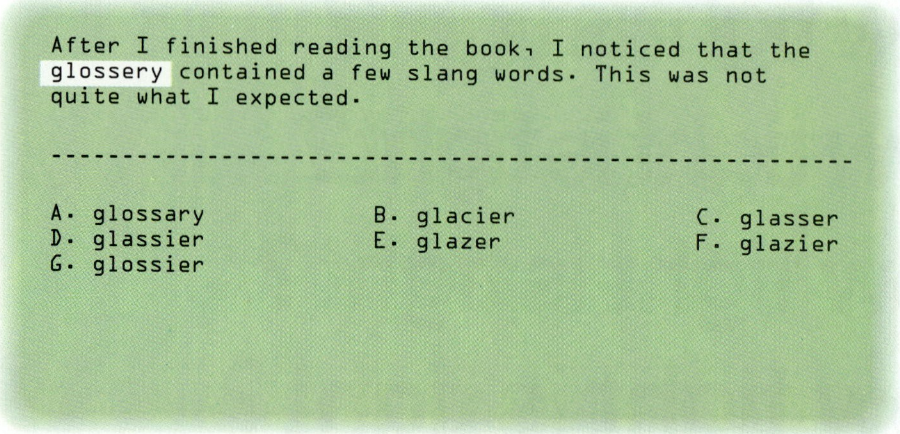

```
After I finished reading the book, I noticed that the
glossery contained a few slang words. This was not
quite what I expected.

--------------------------------------------------------

A. glossary         B. glacier          C. glasser
D. glassier         E. glazer           F. glazier
G. glossier
```

FIGURE 8 – 11

Using a thesaurus. In many word processors, the user points to a word to be "looked up" by positioning the cursor on it and then invokes the thesaurus feature. Here the operator has pointed to *want,* and the replacement suggestions in the middle of the screen have appeared. Many thesaurus routines automatically make a replacement when the key that corresponds to it is depressed.

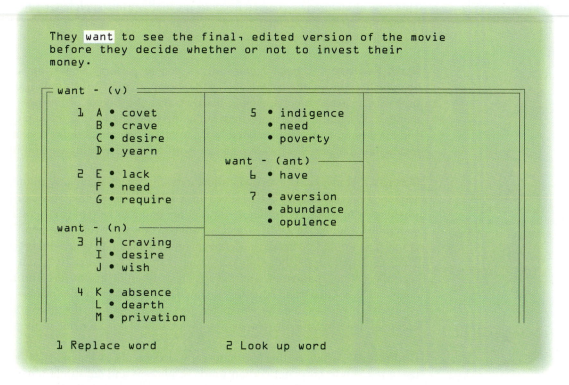

language, the spelling checker will not flag it. To root out errors of this sort you need a *style/grammar checker* (discussed shortly).

Thesaurus Feature A **thesaurus feature** allows you to check words for possible synonyms. To use a thesaurus, you first flag a word you wish to replace in your document. If the thesaurus feature recognizes the word, it will provide onscreen replacement suggestions in a form resembling that of a hard-copy thesaurus (see Figure 8-11). Often, when you see a word you like, you need only type in the key corresponding to it to perform the replacement. Many thesaurus routines automatically reformat text after replacing a word. In addition, several allow you to do word searches within other word searches, and many provide antonyms as well as synonyms. The thesauruses packaged with the leading word processors typically contain anywhere from 10,000 to 70,000 words. Some commercial-level electronic thesauruses used by newspapers and magazines have over a million words.

Thesaurus feature.
A word processing program or routine that enables electronic lookup of word synonyms.

Mailing list program.
A program that is used to generate mailing labels.

Mailing List/Mail Merge Programs   A **mailing list program** is used to generate mailing labels. With such a feature, you can usually sort records by specific fields (such as zip code) or extract records having special characteristics (such as all alumni from the class of 1975 living in San Francisco) prior to processing the labels. Mailing list programs are specialized versions of file managers, which we will discuss in Chapter 10.

Mail merge program.
A program that is specifically designed to produce form letters.

A **mail merge program** is specifically designed to produce form letters. This type of feature is so named because it usually prints such letters in volume by merging a file containing a list of names and addresses with a file containing the form letter.

Math Feature   A *math feature* allows you to perform modest amounts of computation during the course of word processing. Such a feature is useful for preparing expense reports, simple budgets, and other types of business documents that require little more than summing columns or rows of numbers. If you need to do more sophisticated forms of math, you might do well to acquire instead an integrated software package (with a spreadsheeting capability).

Macro.
A predetermined series of keystrokes or commands that can be invoked by a single keystroke or command.

Macros   Many word processors allow users to create macros. A **macro** is a sequence of keystrokes that is saved in a special file so that you can use it whenever you wish. For instance, say you are going to be typing several letters containing your home address and a canned, "we-wish-you-were-here" paragraph. You would first invoke a "define macro" command in your word processor. Then you would type the address, saving it in a macro file. Next you would type the canned paragraph and save it in a different macro file. During the course of preparing your letters, you would invoke either of the macros at the point where you wanted the associated text placed in your document. This is normally done by pressing one or two keys followed by the name of the macro.

Redlining.
A word processing facility that provides the electronic equivalent of the editor's red pen.

Redlining   When editing the hard-copy documents of others, many people use a red pen to cross out certain words or phrases and substitute others. This process is called **redlining.** After a document is redlined, the original author can see both what he or she originally wrote and the changes made by the editor. The redlining feature found in many word processors provides the electronic equivalent of the manual redlining process.

Index and Table of Contents Preparation   Many top-of-the-line word processors allow you to individually "tag" words or phrases so that you can later prepare an index or a table of contents. For instance, if you have tagged a few hundred words in a book for an index, you can later invoke an *indexing routine* that will arrange these words in alphabetical order and provide the page numbers on which the words appear. Most indexing routines also let you create index subheadings similar to the ones that appear in the index of this book.

Orphan.
The first line of a paragraph when it is separated from the rest of the paragraph by a page or column break.

Widow.
The last line of a paragraph when it is separated from the rest of the paragraph by a page or column break.

Orphan and Widow Elimination   Orphans and widows are aesthetically undesirable line breaks (see Figure 8-12). In document processing, the first line of a paragraph is called an **orphan** when it is separated from the rest of the paragraph by a page or column break. The last line of a paragraph is called a **widow** when it is separated from the rest of the paragraph by a page or column break. Many word processing packages allow you to eliminate widows

F I G U R E 8 – 1 2

Orphans and widows. Orphans and widows are aesthetically undesirable line breaks that many word processors can eliminate.

Widow

```
                    Page 1
     Babbage became obsessed
with the analytical engine
and devoted all his energy and
resources to creating it.  But
he was never able to complete
a working model, and he died
without knowing how his vision
was to shape the future of the
world.
     Born in 1792, Babbage died
```

```
                              Page 2
in 1871.
     Much of what we know
about Babbage's analytical
engine comes, not from Babbage
himself, but from the work of
his close friend and treasured
associate, Ada Augusta.  The
daughter of the poet Byron,
she has been called the first
programmer because of her work
on the kinds of instructions
```

Orphan

(a) Orphan

(b) Widow

and orphans by establishing a minimum number of lines that can be separated by a page or column break.

Sorting   A useful word processing feature is *sorting*—for example, arranging a list of names in alphabetical order or arranging addresses by zip code for mailing purposes. As handy as this feature may be, however, it is either unavailable, somewhat limited, or relatively cumbersome to use in many word processors.

Embedded Typesetting Codes   Sometimes word-processed text is sent directly to a professional compositor for typesetting. When this is done, considerable savings can result if *typesetting codes,* such as codes for special fonts or complex printing effects, are embedded into the document before it is sent to the typesetter. Many of the more powerful word processing packages targeted for commercial environments offer this feature.

Graphics   Many word processors have a *graphics feature* that enables users to create attractive boxes of information within text documents. An example of this feature is the boxed graph on the left side of the image shown in Figure 8-2. A graphics capability usually also lets users import art into a document—from other program files or from a library of art images—as well as do a limited amount of drawing.

Style Sheets   A feature that several leading word processors have begun incorporating—and that is standard fare in desktop publishing packages—is the style sheet. A **style sheet** is a collection of font and formatting specifications

Style sheet.
A collection of design specifications that can be saved as a file and later used to format documents in a particular way.

FIGURE 8 – 13

Microsoft Bookshelf. Users of this add-on package can summon any of the works shown on the screen with a couple of keystrokes.

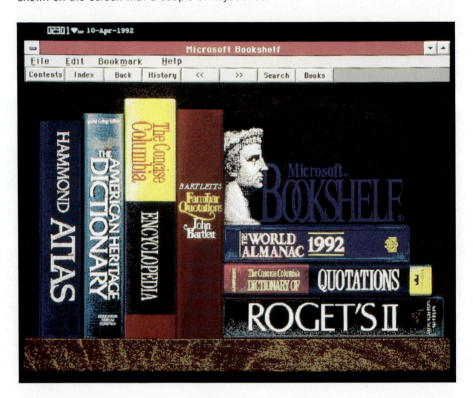

that is saved as a file and later used to prepare documents in a particular way. For instance, if your letters to clients are to conform to a certain letterhead style and to use a specific typeface and point size, you can declare all of these specifications in a style sheet that you invoke when preparing such letters. Reports, in contrast, would probably use a different style sheet.

Add-On Packages

When a word processor is missing a critical feature, chances are there's an aftermarket (third-party) vendor that offers such a feature as an add-on. Aftermarket vendors specialize in complementing a product made by another vendor with some type of "value-added" functionality. Four of the most widely used types of **add-on packages** are discussed in the following paragraphs.

Add-on package.
A software package that supplements the activities of a large software package, either by providing new functions or improving on already existing functions.

Reference Shelves *Reference shelves,* the most prominent of which is Microsoft Bookshelf (see Figure 8-13), provide a number of handy reference books online to the writer. For instance, Bookshelf packs electronic versions of the *American Heritage Dictionary,* a thesaurus, the *Chicago Manual of Style, Bartlett's Familiar Quotations,* an atlas, a zip-code directory, and a world almanac onto a single optical disk. Bookshelf enables any of its works to be summoned by a word processor with a couple of keystrokes. Once the computer system is pointing to a particular reference work on the "shelf," the work can be electronically searched for a particular block of text. When the block is found, it can be "cut and pasted" back into the document being word processed.

Bibliographic Databases   *Bibliographic databases* are specifically tailored to writers who prepare long reference lists or bibliographies. The programs use onscreen templates for entering information about references into specific fields and for entering lengthy notes. You can also select a style by which the entire bibliography will be automatically formatted.

Style/Grammar Checkers   *Style/grammar checkers* are designed to root out errors in grammar, punctuation, and word usage. They also analyze writing styles for specific weaknesses (such as overused words, overly long sentences, and words that are sexist or out-of-date). In addition, most packages will calculate some type of overall reading-level statistic for your written work. Unfortunately, good writing often depends on bending rules. So, although style/grammar checkers may help people write in an understandable fashion, they cannot turn a wretched writer into an instant Hemingway. Figure 8-14 shows a style/grammar checker at work.

FIGURE 8 – 14

Style/grammar checker. Style/grammar checkers are designed to root out errors in grammar, punctuation, and word usage. They will not, however, turn a wretched writer into an instant Hemingway.

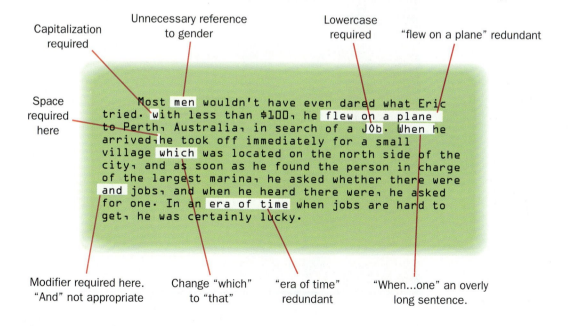

Capitalization required

Unnecessary reference to gender

Lowercase required

"flew on a plane" redundant

Space required here

Most men wouldn't have even dared what Eric tried. with less than $100, he flew on a plane to Perth, Australia, in search of a JOb. When he arrived,he took off immediately for a small village which was located on the north side of the city, and as soon as he found the person in charge of the largest marina, he asked whether there were and jobs, and when he heard there were, he asked for one. In an era of time when jobs are hard to get, he was certainly lucky.

Modifier required here. "And" not appropriate

Change "which" to "that"

"era of time" redundant

"When...one" an overly long sentence.

Font Libraries Even though many word processors come packaged with a variety of fonts, you can add others by acquiring a font library. A font library is a collection of fonts that supplements those packaged into your word processor. Font libraries are particularly useful for users who want to give their documents a "desktop publishing" look.

Desktop Publishing

The late 1970s introduced desktop computing—an entire computer system capable of fitting on a desktop. Thanks to other major improvements on the software and hardware fronts, we now have desktop publishing—microcomputer-based publishing systems that fit on a desktop.

What Is Desktop Publishing?

Desktop publishing.
A microcomputer-based publishing system that can fit on a desktop.

Desktop publishing systems are hardware/software systems that let you combine on a page such elements as text (in a variety of typefaces), art, and photos, thus creating attractive documents that look as if they came off a printer's press (see Figure 8-15). Desktop publishing systems are designed to replace many of the traditionally manual, labor-intensive tasks associated with cutting, arranging, and pasting elements onto a page. Because they make it possible for publishing to be done in-house, they also enable companies to save money, save time, and

---

FIGURE 8 – 15

Desktop publishing. Desktop publishing lets you combine on a page such elements as text, art, and photos, thus creating documents that look professionally prepared.

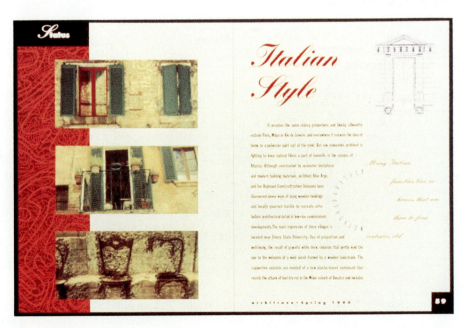

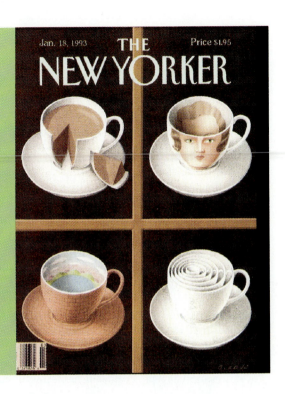

have more control over the look of finished documents (see User Solution 8-1). In the last decade or so, desktop publishing has rapidly evolved into a major applications area within the field of computers. Figure 8-16 lists several applications for desktop publishing.

As you can see from studying the image in Figure 8-15, the basic difference between word processing and desktop publishing is one of document "look." Whereas word processing deals mainly with straight, nontypeset text—and maybe a few simple fonts for emphasis—desktop publishing involves full-fledged typesetting and imagesetting. *Typesetting* implies full control over type styles and sizes as well as spacing between words, letters, and lines. *Imagesetting* involves combining on a page both type and such artwork elements as drawings,

---

FIGURE 8 – 16

Desktop publishing applications. Applications for desktop publishing run the gamut from business résumés and business cards to books and magazines.

- Advertisements
- Annual reports
- Books
- Brochures
- Business reports
- Catalogs
- Business cards
- Résumés
- Restaurant menus

- Magazines
- Newsletters
- Newspapers
- Posters
- Price lists
- Software/system documentation
- Stationery and business forms
- Training manuals
- Signs

Feature   8 – 1

A Crash Course in Typography

A look at some of the terms of the typographer's trade

At one time, most computer buffs cared little about the somewhat arcane terminology used in the publishing industry. Then, quite suddenly, came desktop publishing. Now, if you are going to wade through a trade book or a reference manual to understand how a particular desktop publishing package works, you'd better know your serifs from your ascenders.

Many professional graphic designers devote years to the study of typography. Fortunately for the part-time desktop publisher, such an immersion into the publishing field is hardly necessary. One can get by just by learning a few terms, most of which apply to type. Following is a miniglossary of some of the most useful terms to know:

Ascender   The portion of a lowercase character that falls above the x-height (see Figure 1).

Baseline   The imaginary line formed by connecting the bottommost parts of characters on a line, ignoring descenders (see Figure 1).

Body-copy typeface   The typeface used for the main text, or "body," of a document. Body-copy typefaces are chosen to guide the eye along comfortably on a page and are often serif.

Descender   The portion of a lowercase character that falls below the baseline (see Figure 1).

Display typeface   The typeface used in banners, headings, or decorative text on a page. Display typefaces usually are greater than 12 points.

Folio   A page number.

Font   Traditionally, a term that refers to the complete set of characters in a particular typeface and point size, for instance, 12-point Helvetica. In practice today, many people use the terms *font* and *typeface* interchangeably.

Greeking   Nonsense text used in a simulated layout to depict actual size, style, and placement of text.

Figure 1.

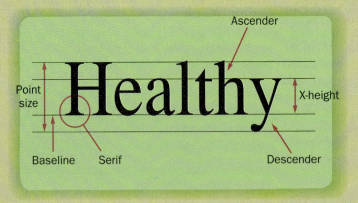

photographs, and color. Although there is a theoretical distinction that separates desktop publishing from word processing, many of the leading word processors are increasingly being packaged with desktop publishing features.

Desktop publishing systems have come a long way in providing individuals with the capability to produce documents that look as if they were professionally prepared, but they are still a far cry from professional-level publishing systems. Systems falling into this latter category are the preferred choice for producing large volumes of high-quality printed materials such as corporate annual reports and four-color books like this one.

Halftoning   The process of converting a continuous-tone photographic image into a series of dots.

Kerning   Adjusting the spacing between certain character combinations to create a more visually consistent image. For instance, the two letters *AW* naturally appear to have more space between them than the two letters *MN*, and a kerning feature can reduce the disparity.

Leading   The amount of vertical space between lines of a page; usually expressed in points.

Phototypesetting   The process of transferring a page image to film or photosensitive paper so that it can be printed out by a very-high-resolution output device called a *phototypesetting machine* (such as a Linotronic 300).

Pica   A unit of type measure commonly used to determine the depth of a set of lines, a paragraph, a photo, or a piece of art on a page. There are six picas to an inch.

Point   The smallest unit of type measure, commonly used when referring to the size of type on a page. There are 12 points to a pica and 72 points to an inch (see Figure 1).

Roman   Nonslanted type; often contrasted with *italic* type.

Rule   A line on a page; for instance, the vertical line that appears to the right of this column of type is an example of a rule.

Sans serif   A typeface without serifs, such as Helvetica.

Screen   A measure, usually expressed as a percentage, of grayscale or color intensity. For in-

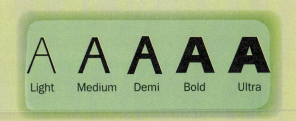

Figure 2.

stance, a 90 percent yellow screen translates into a bright yellow and a 10 percent yellow screen into a pale yellow. All of the artwork in this text is colored with screens, which consist of tightly or loosely packed dots. (You can see the dots under a magnifying glass.)

Script   A typeface that looks like handwriting or calligraphy.

Serif   Short lines used to finish off the main strokes of a character to give it a distinctive styling (see Figure 1).

Style   A variation within a typeface. For instance, a magazine article may be done in four styles of the Times typeface—roman, bold, italic, and bold italic.

Thumbnail   A miniature copy of an image, used for referencing or planning purposes.

Vertical justification   The ability to insert fractional lines within a page so that the top and bottom margins of all pages are even.

Weight   The relative thickness of type (see Figure 2).

X-height   The height of the lowercase letter *x* in a particular typeface (see Figure 1).

Components of a Desktop Publishing System

Naturally, not all desktop publishing systems are the same. You can spend a few thousand dollars for a system that produces simple newsletters, but you will pay several times that amount for one that creates stunning color artwork. Desktop publishing systems targeted for commercial applications often consist of several hardware and software components. These components are described in this section, and their use is covered in Window 5. Feature 8-1 offers a crash course in typography, covering some of the key terms.

Hardware   Hardware used to do high-end desktop publishing usually includes a high-end microcomputer system, a laser printer, a graphics-oriented monitor, and an image scanner. These devices were covered in depth in Chapter 5 of the text and are therefore addressed only briefly here.

■ **HIGH-END MICROCOMPUTER SYSTEM**   High-quality desktop publishing requires a microprocessor that packs plenty of power, a respectable amount of RAM, and a hard disk with plenty of storage. Manipulation of graphical fonts, photos, and art can be computationally intensive. A mere two-page newsletter, for instance, can require 200 KB of storage, a 30-point character set uses about 150 KB, and a half-page scanned image needs another 500 KB. Such work requires a system unit like those based on high-end Intel or Motorola chips. The systems should have at least 4 to 8 MB of RAM and at least 100 MB of hard-disk storage.

■ **LASER PRINTER**   Most laser printers for microcomputer-based desktop publishing applications cost anywhere from about $600 to $10,000. These devices have their own built-in microprocessors, about 1 to 3 MB RAM, and several ROM chips that carry popular fonts. Greater amounts of RAM allow you to output images of greater complexity. Many laser printers output at a resolution of either 300 dpi (dots per vertical and horizontal inch, or 90,000 dots to the inch) or 600 dpi. If you require higher resolution than this, you'll need professional typesetting equipment (which works at 1,000 dpi or more).

The laser printer in your computer system relies on a specific **page description language (PDL)** to carry out its work. The two most common PDLs are Adobe's *PostScript*, which is widely used in the fastest and most expensive laser printers, and Hewlett-Packard's *Printer Command Language (PCL)*, which is more popular on slower and less expensive laser printers.

■ **GRAPHICS-ORIENTED MONITOR**   Most monitors used with microcomputer systems contain a relatively small (13-to-15-inch) screen that can comfortably display about a third of a standard printed page at a time. On such screens, the resolution usually is adequate for text and some simple graphics. For desktop publishing applications, however, it generally is preferable to have a bigger screen with SVGA or XVGA resolution, both to fine-tune detailed graphics and to see without eyestrain, either a full-page or a two-page layout on the screen at one time. Monitors designed for these purposes often have screens up to 50 percent larger than the typical microcomputer display (see Figure 8-17).

■ **IMAGE SCANNER**   An image scanner (see Figure 5-20) allows you to scan photographs, drawings, or text and digitize them directly into computer memory. Later, you can edit the images with illustration software and hardware. Some image scanners also use optical character recognition (OCR) software, which enables them to recognize certain text characters instead of just digitizing them. Such a feature allows you to later edit any text that you enter with the scanner. Both color and grey-scale scanners are widely available.

Software   A variety of software and software-based products are used in desktop publishing environments. These include page-makeup software, word processing software, fonts, clip-art libraries, and art and illustration software.

Page description language (PDL).
A language used to communicate instructions to a laser printer.

FIGURE 8 - 17

Graphics-oriented monitor. Desktop publishing systems frequently use special monitors with oversized screens and the ability to output crisp images.

FIGURE 8 – 18

Page-makeup software. One of the best known page-makeup programs is Aldus Corporation's PageMaker. Because page makeup is the central function in desktop publishing, page-makeup programs are usually called desktop publishing packages.

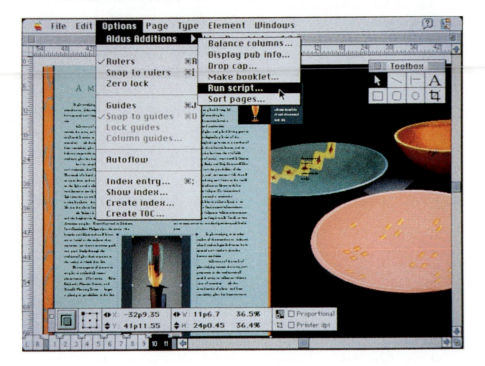

■ **PAGE-MAKEUP SOFTWARE** The programs that allow you to combine text, photos, and art elements into a finished page are collectively referred to as **page-makeup software.** Because page makeup is the central function in desktop publishing, page-makeup programs are often loosely referred to as "desktop publishing packages." Some of the leading page-makeup programs are Aldus Corporation's PageMaker (see Figure 8-18), Xerox Corporation's Ventura Publisher, and Quark Inc.'s Quark Xpress. Your page-makeup software must be compatible with the other desktop publishing products you use, such as fonts, clip-art libraries, and the software used to develop text or illustration files.

■ **WORD PROCESSING SOFTWARE** Because most users already have their own word processing software, such as WordPerfect or Word, the vendors of the leading desktop publishing packages have designed their products to accept text prepared with several of the leading word processors. Thus, when acquiring a desktop publishing system, it is always wise to check out which word processors it recognizes. Although most page-makeup programs do contain built-in word processing features, enabling you to modify any text that you import to them, it is important to recognize that their primary function is page makeup. Consequently, they are not as easy to use for word processing as your average word processor.

Page-makeup software.
Programs used to compose page layouts in a desktop publishing system.

FIGURE 8 – 19

Bit-mapped versus outline fonts. Bit-mapped fonts (left) are made up of a fixed pattern of dots, whereas outline fonts (right) are defined by a series of curves. Outline fonts can be resized to different point sizes; bit-mapped fonts can't.

■ **FONTS**   A variety of *fonts*—that is, typefaces conforming to a specific style and size—are available for desktop publishing applications. Some fonts are available as ROM chips that are packaged into the laser printer you buy. You can acquire additional fonts in disk form and load them into the laser printer's RAM. When choosing type for desktop-publishing work, most people need both large and small fonts. Large fonts are widely used for banners and titles; small fonts are commonly used for body copy.

Fonts are of two types: bit-mapped and outline (see Figure 8-19). *Bit-mapped fonts* are described by a fixed configuration of dots. While they are the least expensive kind of font, you cannot scale them to different sizes. *Outline fonts* consist of mathematical curves that describe how characters are shaped. They are more expensive than bit-mapped fonts, but you can scale them to virtually any size you want and also create your own fonts.

FIGURE 8 – 20

Clip art. Clip-art libraries are bundled into many illustration software packages and are also sold separately.

FIGURE 8 – 21

Illustration software. Illustration packages enable art images to be created and developed. Here, the palettes at the right enable the artist to select colors and styling effects.

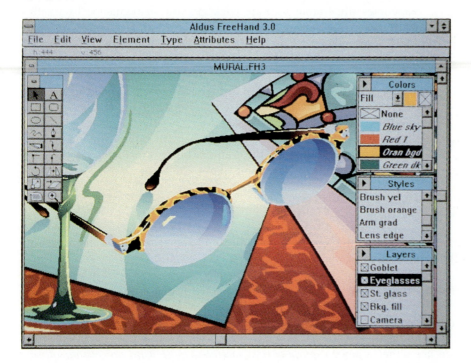

■ **CLIP-ART LIBRARIES** A **clip-art** library is a collection of prepared art images. You can use these images on their own or as building blocks to create other images. You can even modify them. A sample of clip-art pieces appears in Figure 8-20.

Clip-art libraries are bundled into many illustration packages and are also sold separately by third-party vendors. Vendors of illustration packages often use a proprietary format for their clip art, usually one that supports their other products, whereas third-party clip-art vendors typically make their clip art available in a variety of standard formats.

■ **ILLUSTRATION SOFTWARE** **Illustration software packages** enable artwork to be created from scratch. Also, they accept existing artwork as input and allow it to be modified using the software's image-manipulation facilities.

An image can be input to illustration software in several ways. If you have an image scanner, you can read a hard-copy image directly into RAM. If you have a digitizing tablet, you can trace over a hard-copy image with a stylus, thereby transferring the outline of the image to memory. Or, if the image is in a clip-art library, you can transfer the appropriate clip-art file directly to the illustration software if both use the same file formats.

High-quality illustration software enables you to size, rotate, flip, recolor, distort, and edit virtually any digitally stored drawing or photograph to your heart's content (see Figure 8-21). Because images are manipulated at

Clip art.
Prepackaged artwork designed to be imported into text documents or charts, say, by desktop publishing or presentation graphics software.

Illustration software package.
A program package that enables users to paint or draw.

electronically fast speeds, it is possible to try out dozens of possibilities in the time it would normally take to produce only a single image by manual means. Once an image is satisfactory, it can be imported to a desktop publishing (page-makeup) program.

Sometimes illustration software packages are distinguished by whether they are primarily oriented toward painting or drawing. *Painting packages* enable you to create bit-mapped images and to color them pixel by pixel. Usually, the images you create cannot be resized without loss of resolution. For instance, blowing them up may result in jagged edges, whereas reducing them may result in a blurry mess. In contrast, *drawing packages* enable you to create outlines that can be resized. Once properly sized, these outlines can be filled in with colors.

Many illustration software packages are available today. Among the best-selling packages are Adobe's Illustrator, Aldus's Freehand, Corel's Corel Draw!, Z-Soft's PC Paintbrush, and Claris's McDraw and McPaint.

Summary and Key Terms

Both word processing and desktop publishing are technologies that deal with the manipulation of words.

Word Processing　**Word processing** is the use of computer technology to create, manipulate, and print text materials such as letters, legal contracts, manuscripts, and other documents.

There are several ways you can perform word processing. For instance, you can use either a *general-purpose* or a *special-purpose word processing software package*. And, you can choose between a *dedicated word processing package* or an *integrated software package*. Most people today use general-purpose, dedicated word processing packages, such as WordPerfect and Microsoft Word.

Virtually all word processors today rely on *embedded formatting codes* rather than full **WYSIWYG** (What You See Is What You Get). Most packages have a *preview feature* that enables you to inspect what a document will look like in print before you print it out.

Using a word processor, or for that matter, any type of productivity software package, requires learning several general operations. These operations include accessing the package from the operating system, informing the package that you want to create a new file or retrieve an old one, commanding the package to save a file, commanding the package to print a file, commanding the package to delete a file, indicating to the package that you want to quit working on your current file and do something on another file, and terminating the package and getting back to the operating system.

Learning to use a word processor at a minimal level involves mastering a number of elementary editing operations as well as several print-formatting commands. Entering and editing operations include moving the cursor, scrolling, making line returns through either a **soft return** (the **wordwrap** feature) or a **hard return,** inserting and deleting, moving and copying, and searching and replacing. Among the print-formatting operations that one must learn are adjusting line spacing; indenting; justifying text; setting up page formats; reformatting body text; centering; tabbing; paginating; setting up headers and footers;

selecting **typefaces, point sizes,** and **fonts;** multiple-column formatting; and footnoting.

More sophisticated use of word processing packages often requires software and hardware that provide **proportional spacing** and **microspacing** so that they can produce typeset-quality output. Without these features, text will be **monospaced.** In addition, advanced applications often make use of such features as **spelling checkers, thesauruses, mailing list programs, mail merge programs,** a math feature, **macros, redlining,** index and table of contents preparation, **orphan** and **widow** elimination, sorting, embedded typesetting codes, graphics, and **style sheets.**

A wide variety of **add-on packages** can be acquired to enhance a word processing environment. Among such packages are reference shelves, bibliographic databases, style/grammar checkers, and font libraries.

Desktop Publishing   **Desktop publishing** systems go a step further than word processors. They let you combine on a page such elements as text (in a variety of fonts), art, and photos, thus creating attractive documents that look as if they came off a printer's press.

Whereas word processing deals mainly with straight, nontypeset text—perhaps using a few simple fonts for emphasis—desktop publishing involves full-fledged *typesetting* and *imagesetting*. But as much as desktop publishing systems have improved, they are still not capable of the document quality possible with professional composition systems.

Desktop publishing systems are commonly configured with some of the following hardware and software components. Hardware includes a high-end microcomputer system, a laser printer (which is used in concert with a specific **page-description language,** or **PDL**), a graphics-oriented monitor capable of WYSIWYG display, and an image scanner. Software components include **page-makeup software,** word processing software, fonts, a **clip-art** library, and **illustration software packages** such as *painting* and *drawing packages*.

Review Exercises

1. Most word processors have a(n) _____ feature that automatically produces a soft return.

   Fill-in Questions

2. _____ is a word processing feature that allocates more horizontal space on a line to some characters than to others.

3. A(n) _____ program is used to generate mailing labels.

4. A(n) _____ word processing system is a computer system exclusively designed for word processing applications.

5. WYSIWYG is an acronym for _____ .

6. The first line of a paragraph is called a(n) _____ when it is separated from the rest of the paragraph by a page or column break.

7. PDL is an acronym for _____

8. Prestored art images used in a desktop publishing environment are referred to as _____.

Matching Questions *Match each term with the description that fits best.*

a. copying   d. inserting
b. redlining   e. scrolling
c. proportional spacing f. moving

____ 1. Moving contiguous lines of text up and down on screen similarly to the way the roll on a player piano is unwound.

____ 2. A feature particularly useful when one person must edit another's written work.

____ 3. An operation that involves replication.

____ 4. An operation that entails physically relocating text so that it no longer appears in its original location.

____ 5. A word processing feature that gives text a typeset-quality look.

____ 6. An operation you would use on a word processor to quickly change the string MISSIPPI to MISSISSIPPI.

Discussion Questions

1. What is WYSIWYG and how do many word processors implement it?

2. What is the difference between monospacing and proportional spacing?

3. What are orphans and widows?

4. What is a reference shelf?

5. Identify the components of a desktop publishing system.

6. Why is it getting increasingly more difficult to distinguish word processing from desktop publishing?

Critical Thinking Questions

1. Spelling checkers are said to be of greatest utility to people who can spell reasonably well. Why do you think this is so?

2. Comment on this statement: "Now that desktop publishing is available, the professional typesetting and print shop is doomed."

3. Word processing and desktop publishing present undeniable benefits to organizations that can effectively use them. Can you think of any problems that these technologies pose to the average organizations?

Desktop Publishing

A Step-by-Step Look at What's Involved

During the last decade, the desktop publishing industry
has evolved from a dream to a highly sophisticated
reality—one characterized by powerful art and illustration systems, electronic darkrooms, and a spate of fonts
and clip art libraries to satisfy almost every need. In
this window, we'll look at some of the steps involved in
using a desktop publishing package—laying out pages,
handling type, manipulating art and photos, and refin-
ing pages so that the finished product looks just right.

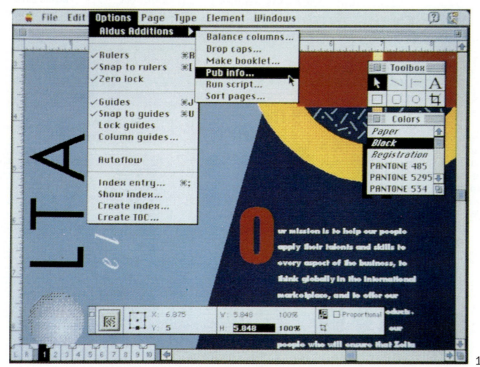

1. Desktop publishing packages enable finished pages consisting
of text and art to be composed onscreen. Illustrated here is the
zoom feature in Aldus' PageMaker, which enables pages to be
previewed in fine detail before they are approved for printing.

Page Layout

Desktop publishing generally begins after word processing ends. The first step in desktop publishing is designing the page layout.

2

2. Page layout is usually begun by creating or retrieving a page template. The template shows how the columns are to be formed on the page and where elements such as headings, art, and the main body of text are to go. Here, the areas shaded in blue will receive the text imported from a word processor.

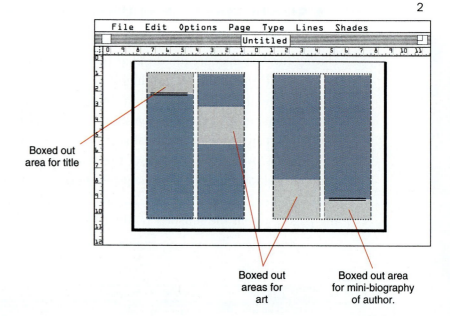

Boxed out area for title

Boxed out areas for art

Boxed out area for mini-biography of author.

3–4. The layout should be balanced so that it is pleasing to the eye. The piece at the left shows a good balance among the photo, heading, and body-copy text. The piece at the right, which has a "hole" in the middle, is unbalanced. Today, creating balance is largely a manual, judgmental process left to the talents of the user.

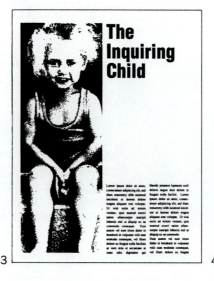

3

4

Type

A major element in any page layout is the typeface or typefaces used. In today's world of desktop publishing, hundreds of typefaces are available.

5

Times Bold Italic

Times Bold

Times Roman

Times Italic

HEALTH

HIGH ANXIETY

BY MICHAEL BAYLAND

Nearly forty years ago W.H. Auden termed our frenetic century "the age of anxiety." And that was before Three Mile Island and AIDS. Small wonder then that when the National Institute of Mental Health recently set out to see which mental problems most plagued Americans, anxiety disorders came in first. Eight percent surveyed in three sample cities reported phobic fears, panic attacks and extreme nervousness severe enough to interfere with normal life. That means over 13 million very anxious citizens–a number some experts even call conservative.

If you're human you know anxiety: tongue-tied embarrassment at the office Christmas party, sweaty palms before you sign the contract for your co-op, an inner thud when the phone rings in the middle of the night. Unpleasant perhaps, but useful. Anxiety is a mind/body signal wired into our brains to warn us of danger and gear us up to fight or flee. "It's the normal reaction to what we perceive as a threat to well-being," says Michael R. Liebowitz, M.D., director of the Anxiety Disorders Clinic at the New York State Psychiatric Institute. "It has real survival value."

For most people, the anxiety that appears before an event normally recedes once they gain confidence. But for others it does not. The pulse races faster, butterflies flutter more frantically, the voice quavers and the mind goes blank. For these people, who triple check the stove each time they go out, anxiety is a way of life. Dr. Liebowitz compares such anxiety to a burglar alarm that trips every time a door

It's enough to make a Chicken Little out of anyone

5. Typefaces are often available as a "family" that sports a variety of styles. Shown here is the standard roman style as well as the italic, boldface, and boldface italic styles for the Times typeface.

Tradition

Architectural **survival** in the south.

architrave • Spring 1990

6

6. Type is frequently wrapped around photos and diagrams, as shown here.

Centered Arc Text

Faded

Drop Shadow

7

7. Special effects for typefaces can be created with many illustration software packages.

8. Typeface selection, along with color, affect the mood of a document.

8

Typeface Sample	Mood Imparted
THE ELEGANT GOURMET	Elegant and formal
The Elegant Gourmet	Elegant and informal
The Elegant Gourmet	Playful
THE ELEGANT GOURMET	Serious
THE ELEGANT GOURMET	Action-oriented

Illustration Packages

Illustration packages are of two principal types: drawing and painting. Drawing packages enable users to create outlines that can be easily resized and filled in whereas painting packages enable users to create images pixel by pixel.

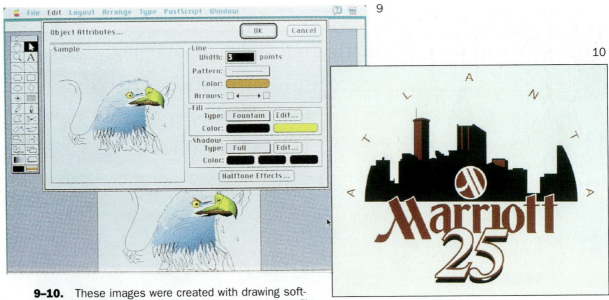

9

10

9–10. These images were created with drawing software. The finished art can be stored in independent files and later imported to a desktop publishing package to be merged with text.

11

12

11–12. Painting packages provide the most control over images. As shown in the pictures of the woman in the dress, images can also be readily recolored and configured with a variety of backgrounds.

Photographs

Photographs are either captured electronically or read with an image scanner into the computer system. Once they are digitized, they can be stored, touched up, or even distorted with photo-styling software.

13

13. This photo is being manipulated on a computer screen. With a zooming feature, photos can be inspected close up and color corrected using a palette such as the one at the right.

14. Photos stored on disk can be recalled to the screen in miniature or "thumbnail" form. In this form they can be easily organized and cataloged.

14

15

15. Here, a photo file is imported into a page-makeup program and cropped, so that it conforms to the narrow specifications of a newspaper column.

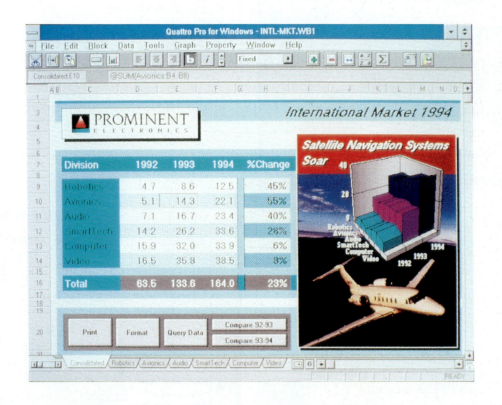

SPREADSHEETS AND PRESENTATION GRAPHICS

9

How do managers use computers to analyze data? As you will see in Chapter 9, analysis is often done with spreadsheet and presentation graphics software. These products make it easy for users to rapidly process business data into table form and graphs.

LEARNING OBJECTIVES

After completing this chapter, you will be able to:

1. Describe what spreadsheet packages do and how they work.

2. Identify the basic operations you must master to effectively use spreadsheet software.

3. Explain the use of several advanced spreadsheet features.

4. Describe how presentation graphics packages work, some of the differences among them, and the images they let you create.

Overview

Today, one of the most important software packages that *any* businessperson—whether he or she is a manager, an office worker, or a sales representative—should learn is the *electronic spreadsheet*. Spreadsheet software is to the current generation of end users what the pocket calculator was to previous generations: a convenient means of performing calculations. But while most pocket calculators can compute and display only one result each time you enter new data, electronic spreadsheets can present you with hundreds or even thousands of results each

FIGURE 9 – 1

Manually prepared and electronic worksheets. An electronic spreadsheet package produces computerized counterparts to the ruled, ledger-style worksheets with which accountants frequently work.

(a) Manually prepared worksheet

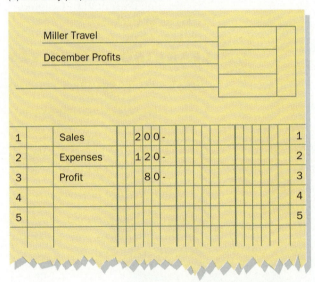

(b) Worksheet prepared by electronic spreadsheet package

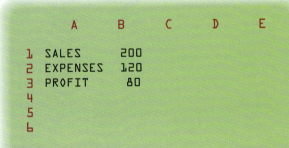

time you enter a single new value or command. What spreadsheets can do and how they work are two of the primary subjects of this chapter.

From our discussion of spreadsheets we'll move on to *presentation graphics software,* which is designed to present the results of business computations in a visually oriented, easily understood way. This class of business software is easy to learn and use. Today many spreadsheet packages are equipped with built-in presentation graphics features and tools. Also, many dedicated presentation graphics packages, which enable you to produce higher-quality presentation images than those possible with spreadsheet packages, are commercially available.

Spreadsheets

An **electronic spreadsheet** package produces computerized counterparts to the ruled, ledger-style worksheets with which accountants frequently work (see Figure 9-1). Electronic spreadsheets first came to public notice in the late 1970s when a Harvard Business School student named Dan Bricklin and a programmer friend produced a microcomputer package called VisiCalc ("The VISIble CALCulator"). Bricklin conceived of the idea while watching his accounting professor erase large chunks of blackboard computations every time a single number changed in an interdependent series of calculations. Awed by the amount of repetitive labor involved, Bricklin quickly saw the potential of computerized worksheets.

To call VisiCalc a huge success would be an understatement. It shattered sales records for applications software and made microcomputers valuable decision-making tools in business. It is also widely credited for moving Apple—the company that supported VisiCalc on its Apple II line of microcomputers—into the ranks of the computer-industry heavyweights. Both VisiCalc and the spreadsheet products that followed it have been easy to use and clearly made managers who mastered them more productive.

Today, although VisiCalc is gone from the scene, spreadsheet software for all sizes of computers abounds in the marketplace. Among the leading spreadsheet packages currently available for microcomputers are 1-2-3, Excel, SuperCalc, and Quattro, with 1-2-3 the pacesetter in sales. Technically speaking, most of these products are *integrated software packages;* they supplement spreadsheeting capabilities with one or more other functions (see Feature 9-1).

How Spreadsheets Work

Here we discuss some of the principles by which spreadsheets work.

The Anatomy of a Worksheet In electronic spreadsheets, the display screen is viewed as a *window* looking in on a big grid, called a **worksheet** (see Figure 9-2). Most major spreadsheet packages allow worksheets that consist of thousands of *rows* and a couple hundred *columns.* In Microsoft Excel, for instance, a maximum of 16,384 rows and 256 columns is available to create worksheets. Each of the 4,194,304 (16,384 × 256) **cells** formed by the intersection of a row and column may contain text, a number, or a formula. Each cell can be accessed through a **cell address,** such as B8 or E223.

Electronic spreadsheet.
A productivity software package that enables operators to develop tables and financial schedules quickly.

Worksheet.
The computerized counterpart to the ruled, ledger-style paper used by accountants.

Cell.
The part of the worksheet that can hold a single label or value; a cell occurs where a row and column intersect.

Cell address.
The column/row combination that uniquely identifies a spreadsheet cell.

F e a t u r e   9 – 1

Integrated Software Packages

When you need more than just a spreadsheet

For users who would like to tie together several applications under a single program "roof," an *integrated software package* may be the best choice.

An integrated software package bundles two or more relatively distinct productivity software functions into a single "megapackage." Symphony—which bundles together a spreadsheet, file manager, presentation graphics routine, word processor, and communications software—is an example of an integrated software product. So is Microsoft Works (see photo).

Integrated software packages give you the convenience of having to learn only a single command or menu structure rather than mastering the different software approaches of three or four vendors. In addition, a bundled package normally costs less than a system of individually purchased software components. Perhaps more important, you automatically are able to integrate data gener-

ated from any of the various package components—for example, it is not difficult to insert a graph into a word-processed document—because all the software components are fully compatible with one another.

On the negative side, integrated packages typically have one or two strong components and several weak ones. Thus, an author, who probably requires a top-of-the-line word processor, would be better off getting a dedicated word processing package than an integrated package that also caters to spreadsheet and database users. Another disadvantage of these packages is that some of the features may be of little or no use to the user. For example, users who don't need to communicate with a remote location certainly wouldn't get their money's worth out of a communications software feature. Also, because integrated packages let you have several productivity functions at your fingertips, they require a great deal of memory and result in extra processing overhead.

Closely related to conventional integrated software products are *office packages*—such as The Microsoft Office and Lotus' SmartSuite. Office packages provide a set of compatible, full-featured software products at a reduced price. For instance, The Microsoft Office assembles together the full-featured versions of Word, Excel, Powerpoint, and Mail at a price lower than it would cost to buy all the individual packages separately.

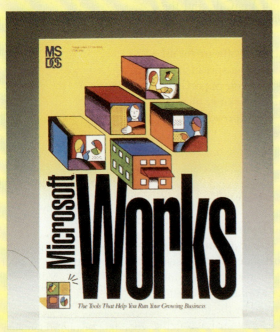

Microsoft Works Lets you build your applications under a single roof.

FIGURE 9-2

A worksheet and a window to the worksheet. Worksheets can be too large to view on the display screen at a single moment. The window allows users to see the worksheet in screen-sized chunks.

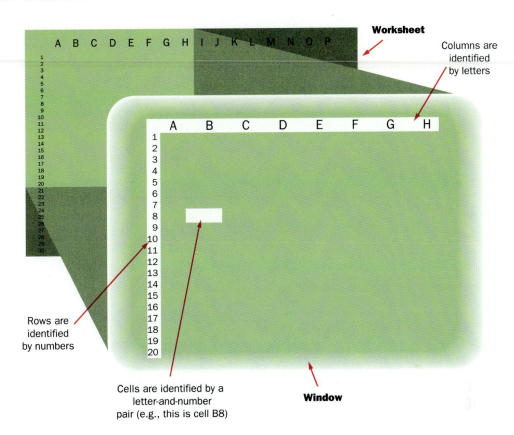

In most commercial spreadsheet packages, columns are identified by letters, rows by numbers, and each cell by a letter-and-number pair. For example, cell B8 is found at the intersection of column B and row 8. Of course, the display screen is too small to permit the viewing of more than a few rows and columns at any give time. However, users can press certain keys on the keyboard that will move the worksheet window around, letting them view other portions of the worksheet through it. After we've covered a couple of other important matters, we'll describe how to do this.

The discussion that immediately follows concerns two-dimensional spreadsheet applications. Later in the chapter, we'll look at the multidimensional capabilities rapidly being infused into most major spreadsheet packages.

The Spreadsheet's Screen   The format of a typical-looking screen from a spreadsheet package is shown in Figure 9-3. Each screen, such as the one shown here, is divided into two main areas: a control panel and a worksheet

F I G U R E   9 – 3

Elements of spreadsheet-package screen. Most screens are divided into two areas—a control panel, where cell contents are prepared, and a worksheet area, which holds the finished contents.

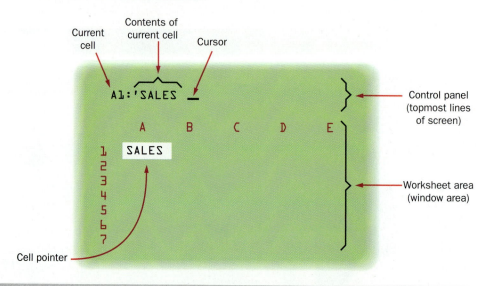

Control panel.
The portion of the screen display that is used for issuing commands and observing what is being typed into the computer system.

Current cell.
In spreadsheet software, the worksheet cell at which the highlight is currently positioned.

Cursor.
A highlighting symbol in the control panel that appears where the next character to be typed in will be placed.

Worksheet area.
The portion of the screen that contains the window onto the worksheet. Also called the **window area.**

area. In a nutshell, the *control panel* is where you prepare entries for the worksheet; the *worksheet area* contains the worksheet itself.

■ **THE CONTROL PANEL** The **control panel** in many spreadsheet packages consists of approximately three lines and is located in the top portion of the screen. The control panel serves several functions. Most important, it displays the address and contents of the current cell, as well as the spreadsheet's command menu.

The **current cell** is the cell to which the spreadsheet package is currently pointing. Spreadsheet packages point to one cell at a time; you can always tell which cell is current by looking at the control panel. In Figure 9-3, the current cell is A1.

To the right of the address of the current cell are its contents. If the cell is empty, nothing will be showing in this portion of the screen. As you type in the contents of the current cell or edit the contents of this cell, each keystroke you hit will appear at the **cursor** position in this part of the control panel. In Figure 9-3, the content of cell A1 is SALES.

Every spreadsheet package has a set of commands for activities such as inserting or deleting rows or columns, moving and copying cell entries, and saving and printing worksheets. All of these tasks are accomplished by selecting commands off of a menu that is displayed in the control panel. For simplicity, we have not shown this menu in Figure 9-3. Later in the chapter, however, we'll cover a number of operations that can be performed from the command menu.

■ **THE WORKSHEET AREA** The worksheet itself is displayed in the part of the screen called the **worksheet area,** or **window area.** One important element in the worksheet area is the **cell pointer,** sometimes referred to as the **highlight** or simply the *pointer.* The cell pointer highlights the current cell. As you can see in Figure 9-3, the current cell (as indicated in the control panel) is cell A1, and this is the cell at which the cell pointer is positioned. As each cell is filled in the control panel, its contents are not entered into the worksheet area until the Enter key is depressed.

Remember, the window area may not be large enough to show the whole worksheet at a single glance, but you can scroll the window about to see other parts of the worksheet if you desire. *Scrolling* is similar to moving a magnifying glass over a large map; the movable glass acts like the window, while the underlying map acts like the worksheet. We can scroll the worksheet a row or column at a time when the highlight is at the edge of the screen and we press one of the arrow keys. Keys such as Tab, PgUp, and PgDn let us scroll the worksheet in window-sized blocks.

Creating a Worksheet   Now that you are familiar with a few of the basic mechanics of spreadsheet-package use, let's learn how to create a worksheet. Refer to Figure 9-4. In the worksheet shown in the figure, we are computing a business income statement in which expenses are 60 percent of sales and profit is the difference between sales and expenses. Here we will show how to enter the text and numbers in the figure into the computer. We'll also look at some of the details that the spreadsheet software will take care of for you.

Into each worksheet cell the user can type either a label or a value. In the terminology of the spreadsheet world, a **label** is a cell entry that cannot be manipulated mathematically, whereas a **value** is an entry that can.

Cell pointer.
A cursorlike mechanism used in the worksheet area to point to cells, thereby making them active. Also called the **highlight.**

Label.
A cell entry that cannot be manipulated mathematically.

Value.
A cell entry that can be manipulated mathematically.

FIGURE 9 – 4

An electronic spreadsheet package at work. It's their *recalculation feature*—the ability to quickly rework thousands of tedious calculations—that makes spreadsheet packages so valuable to users.

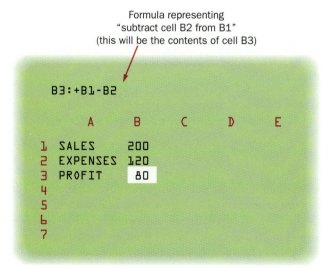

Formula representing
"subtract cell B2 from B1"
(this will be the contents of cell B3)

In the figure, we have entered—one at a time—the following six things into the control panel:

A1	SALES	(a label)
A2	EXPENSES	(a label)
A3	PROFIT	(a label)
B1	200	(a value)
B2	.6*B1	(a value)
B3	+B1-B2	(a value)

The spreadsheet package automatically assumes that each entry beginning with a letter (or a label-prefix character, which we'll cover shortly) is a label; otherwise, it's a value. (Incidentally, that's why we had to type the formula in cell B3 with a " + " in front of it.)

As we type each label or value into the control panel and enter it, that label or value is processed by the spreadsheet software, and the results are automatically transferred to the worksheet. For cells A1, A2, A3, and B1 in Figure 9-4, notice that a direct transfer occurs. For cells B2 and B3, the computer first makes the computation indicated by the *formulas* and then transfers the result to the corresponding worksheet cells.

The Recalculation Feature　Electronic spreadsheet packages are particularly useful for **what-if analysis.** For example, suppose we wish to know *what* profit will result in Figure 9-4 *if* sales are changed to $500. If we simply enter into cell B1 the value

$$500$$

the spreadsheet package automatically reworks all the figures according to the prestored formulas. Thus, the computer responds

SALES	500
EXPENSES	300
PROFIT	200

In seconds, electronic spreadsheets can perform recalculations that would require several hours to do manually or by writing a program in a regular programming language. In fact, it's this easy-to-use **recalculation feature** that makes spreadsheets so popular. You can learn to prepare budgets and financial schedules with them after only a few hours of training. User Solution 9-1 describes the use of what-if analysis in selling homes.

What-if analysis.
An approach to problem solving in which the decision maker repeatedly commands the computer system to recalculate a set of figures based on alternative inputs.

Recalculation feature.
The ability of spreadsheet software to quickly and automatically recalculate the contents of several cells, based on new operator inputs.

U s e r   S o l u t i o n   9 – 1

Selling Homes With What-If Analysis

At Old Town Builders in Visalia, California, 1-2-3 and what-if analysis are now being used as marketing tools. In the past, a home buyer had to wait endlessly for a salesperson to figure out with a calculator the cost of a changing list of customized building options and financing alternatives. Now, a customer can get answers instantaneously. After choosing a financing package, subdivision, lot, and various configuration options, the buyer is supplied with a variety of cash-requirement and monthly-payment information. Because the spreadsheet does all the recalculations, the buyer can easily change options to find the best house within budget. "It creates excitement," reports a member of the firm. "Buyers don't feel they're getting a tract home because they get a chance to make their own choices."

Blocks of Cells: The Range Concept   Often, users need to be able to manipulate data in a set of contiguous cells—say, in a row or column of several cells or in a rectangular-shaped block of cells. To enable you to do this, spreadsheet packages have you declare **ranges** of cells. Figure 9-5 shows four examples of valid ranges. You will generally have to declare ranges of cells when you want to print, move, copy, insert, delete, sort, or graph parts of the worksheet.

Range.
A set of contiguous cells arranged in a rectangle.

For instance, telling the spreadsheet package to print the range B4..C6 will result in the 3-by-2 block of cells in the southeast corner of Figure 9-5 being

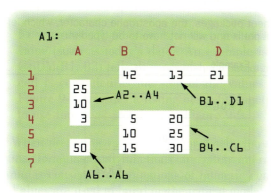

The range concept. A range is any contiguous *rectangular* block of cells. It may be as small as a single cell or as large as a grid with several hundred cells on each side.

F I G U R E   9 – 5

FIGURE 9 – 9

Using functions. Most functions represent prestored formulas, such as those that compute an average, count up cells, or find maximum or minimum values. The functions shown here, and others, are described in Figure 9–8.

	A	B	C	D
1	10	5	15	20
2	6	7	3	4
3	8	2	9	4
4	-1	0	3	15

@ MIN (B2..C3) = 2

@ MAX (A1..D4) = 20

@ MAX (A1..D4, 100) = 100

@ AVG (A1..D1) = 12.5

@ AVG (B1..B4, 2) = 4

@ ABS (A4) = 1

@ SUM (A1..D1) = 50

@ SUM (C1..C4) = 30

@ SUM (A1..D4) = 110

@ MIN (A1..D4) = -1

@ SQRT (C3..C3) = 3

@ COUNT (A1..D4) = 16

@ SQRT (@ COUNT (A1..A4)) = 2

@ IF (A4 < 0, 10, 20) = 10

FIGURE 9 – 10

Spreadsheet commands. In many spreadsheet packages, there are about a dozen or so basic commands. Each of these commands, in turn, corresponds to a hierarchy of options.

Command	Explanation
Worksheet	Allows you to perform a variety of operations that affect either the entire worksheet or parts of it. For example, it allows you to change the width of one or more columns and to insert or delete columns or rows.
Range	Allows you to perform operations on a portion of the worksheet.
Copy	Allows you to reproduce any portion of the worksheet in another place on the worksheet.
Move	Lets you relocate any portion of the worksheet in another place on the worksheet.
File	Enables you to access your disk to save, retrieve, or combine worksheets.
Print	Allows you to print all or any portion of your worksheet.
Graph	Enables you to create graphs from your worksheet.
Data	Enables you to sort data, group data, or retrieve records with specific characteristics.
System	Lets you temporarily leave your spreadsheet package in order to issue operating system commands.
Add-in	Lets you attach add-on routines and packages to the spreadsheet program.
Quit	Ends your spreadsheeting session and enables you to return to the operating system.

User Solution 9-2

Models That Motivate Motorcycle Merchants

Can a spreadsheet package be used as a motivational tool? At Harley-Davidson Inc., the motorcycle company, the answer would be a resounding "yes." Each regional sales manager at Harley has a microcomputer system and access to the company's mainframe at its Milwaukee headquarters. On each computer is a spreadsheet model designed to encourage dealers to sell more motorcycles and parts. The models download regional sales data and compute the dealer's sales ranking among other dealers in the region. The regional sales manager can then prepare a report that shows any dealer's position without revealing the other dealers' names—only their sales. Taking a report along on a sales call to a dealer who's lagging behind the pack can help the local sales representative assigned to the dealership apply peer pressure.

Commands and Menus   One of the most powerful features of any spreadsheet package is its command set. Commands enable you to save and print worksheets, copy the contents of one cell into other cells, sort data, erase worksheets, and so forth. Figure 9-10 shows a typical sample of spreadsheet commands. In this subsection, we'll look at a number of general principles governing commands. Later, in the section entitled "Basic Entering and Editing Operations," we'll examine in greater detail some of the types of tasks that can be done through commands.

Spreadsheet packages use a hierarchical series of menus from which users can select commands. The *main menu* (*command menu*)—usually in the form of a top-of-screen menu bar that appears in the control panel when a special key is depressed—shows the principal command set (see Figure 9-11). Subordinate to each command in the main menu are *submenus* that prompt users for finer and finer levels of detail. On either the main menu or submenus, selections are typically made by moving one of the arrow keys to highlight a choice and selecting it with the Enter key. That, or by typing in the first letter in the command name. As each selection is made by the user, successive submenus are presented onscreen until the spreadsheet package collects enough information to take a specific action.

Invoking spreadsheet commands can be thought of as a process of navigating through a *tree* of choices. Since you can point to the choices on the screen, there is no complicated command syntax to remember. Most packages are set up to enable ordinary users to apply their intuition, without constantly having to leaf through a reference manual. If you select the wrong option, you can, in most cases, easily void the choice and backtrack to where you were before.

F I G U R E 9 – 11

Main menu. The main menu, shown here on the second line of the control panel, provides the principal command set. Below the main menu is a description or set of options relating to the command that is active, or highlighted.

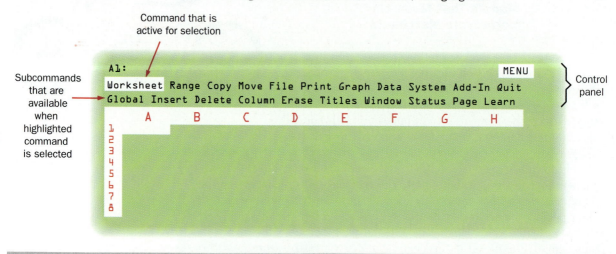

Graphical Interfaces   An increasing number of spreadsheet packages are gravitating toward *graphical user interfaces (GUIs)* that sport pull-down menus and pop-up (dialog) boxes for submenus, multitasked windowing environments, mouse pointer control, and simultaneous viewing of spreadsheet and graphical data. Many of these features were pioneered by Microsoft's Excel. With the success of Excel and with better graphics now available on all of the leading microcomputers, such interfaces are rapidly becoming an industry standard (see Figure 9-12).

Basic Entering and Editing Operations

Spreadsheet packages have numerous command options that help you enter and edit data. A sampling of the most important of these features follows.

Inserting and Deleting   Virtually all spreadsheet packages allow you to insert a new column or row in a worksheet. Also, you can delete a column or row that you no longer need. Generally, inserting or deleting involves moving the cell pointer to the appropriate position on the worksheet and issuing the proper command. Figure 9-13a illustrates inserting a blank row to make a worksheet more attractive.

Copying   Most spreadsheets have a command that enables you to copy the contents of one cell (or several cells) into another cell (or several others). The command usually works by prompting you for a *source range* that contains the data to be copied and a *destination range* that will receive the copied data.

If you are copying from cells that contain formulas, you generally will be asked to state whether you want the cell references in the formulas to be

FIGURE 9 – 12

Graphical interfaces in the leading spreadsheet packages. The current trend in spreadsheets is toward graphical user interfaces (GUIs), which provide multiple windows and pull-down menus, allow presentation graphics to appear onscreen simultaneously with worksheet data, and provide WYSIWYG features for styling worksheets for presentations.

(a) Lotus Development's 1-2-3

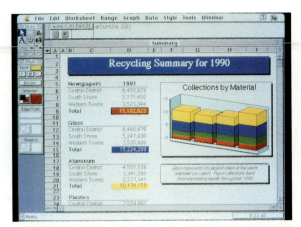

(b) Borland International's Quattro Pro

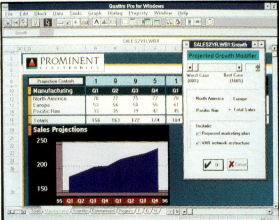

(c) Microsoft's Excel

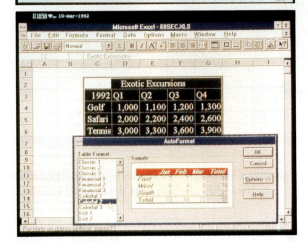

example, to change 90000 to $90,000.00). Generally, all you have to do is identify the range of cells that you want edited and select a Currency option that automatically inserts the proper symbols in the proper places. Adding percent signs (%) usually is an equally straightforward process.

Selecting Column Widths   Most packages allow you to change the width of columns on the worksheet. You can assign widths to each column individually, or you can select a single, global width that applies to all columns. Many spreadsheet packages have a spillover feature, which permits particularly long labels to spill over into adjacent columns, provided that those cells are empty.

Freezing Titles   Most spreadsheet packages have a Titles feature that allows you to keep a portion of the worksheet frozen in place on the screen when you are scrolling the rest of the worksheet. For example, if we used the Titles feature to freeze the first four rows of Figure 9-13f, we could use the down arrow key or PgDn key to scroll through data in the worksheet while the titles remained on the screen. When you freeze rows, you are working with a horizontally split screen. You can also freeze columns, resulting in a vertically split screen. You usually also have the option of freezing certain rows and certain columns at the same time.

Template.
A prelabeled onscreen form that requires only that the operator fill in a limited number of input values.

Using Templates   A **template** is a worksheet in which rows and columns are prelabeled and many cells already contain formulas. Only the data are missing. Thus, the work involved in setting up the worksheet has already been done, leaving you more time to enter and analyze data. A template is shown in Figure 9-13g. In many spreadsheet packages, it is also possible to protect cells, such as those that contain the template's labels and formulas.

Advanced Features

In addition to the basic operations we've just covered, many of the leading spreadsheet packages offer a rich variety of advanced features. In some cases, the spreadsheet package itself contains these features; in other cases, you have to buy the features from an aftermarket vendor that specializes in add-on routines.

Four features that advanced spreadsheet users find useful are data management, macro facilities, multidimensional spreadsheets, and presentation graphics. Here we discuss the first three features and defer discussing presentation graphics until the last section of the chapter.

Data Management   Most spreadsheets contain a facility for managing data. Two popular features in most spreadsheet programs' data management toolkits are sorting and searching (information retrieval).

■ **SORTING**   The ability to sort is a handy feature in almost any type of business software package. With a word processor, sorting enables you to prepare alphabetical listings of names as well as indexes, directories, and glossaries. With a spreadsheet package, you might find a sort facility handy for preparing phone and office directories, ordered listings of overdue accounts, and reports identifying fast-moving or high-selling products. Most spreadsheet packages allow you to sort on more than one field.

Many teachers use the spreadsheet's sort feature to keep grade books on students. Such a grade book can be maintained throughout the term in alphabetical order by student name, and at the end of the term, student records can be sorted according to final averages. Many spreadsheet packages also contain a *data distribution facility* so that a teacher can, among other things, quickly find the number of students with averages between 90–100, 80–89, 70–79, and so on.

■ **SEARCHING** Often each row in a worksheet represents some type of record. For example, if the worksheet stores company records, each row might contain a company name, a complete mailing address, a phone number, an employee record (see Figure 9-13e), and so on. If the worksheet is large (many can store thousands of records), it's handy to have a feature that will automatically extract records for you based on search criteria that you specify. For instance, you may wish to get a list of companies in Philadelphia, the address of Kane Publications, or a list of top employees. A search facility will enable you to gather this information rapidly and accurately.

Macro Facility One of the things you'll appreciate about spreadsheet packages is that they let you do a great deal of information processing without having to know how to program. However, if you do have the talent to write programs and if the spreadsheet package you are using has a macro facility, you can really put your worksheets into high gear.

A macro facility enables you to write programs within your worksheet. Each **macro** is, in fact, a program. It is identified by a name and consists of a series of keystrokes that the spreadsheet package executes every time you invoke the macro. In 1-2-3 and a number of other spreadsheet packages, for example, the macro shown in Figure 9-14 lets you automatically set column widths to 20 characters.

When you depress the Alt key followed by the name of the macro (C), seven keystrokes (/WCS20~) are automatically made for you. Roughly translated, these keystrokes mean invoke the command menu (/), pick the worksheet command off of this menu (W), select the column-width option (C), choose the set option (S), set the column width to 20 characters (20), and hit the Enter key (~).

Macros often are written in contiguous worksheet cells, as Figure 9-14 shows. Frequently the macro is written in a remote set of cells so it does not interfere

Macro.
A predetermined series of keystrokes or commands that can be invoked by a single keystroke or command.

FIGURE 9 – 14

Macro facility. This 1-2-3 macro, named C, lets you set a column width to 20 characters by merely depressing the Alt key and hitting the C key.

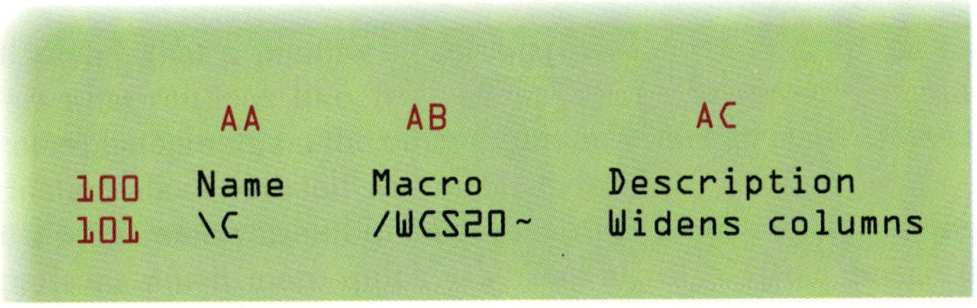

	AA	AB	AC
100	Name	Macro	Description
101	\C	/WCS20~	Widens columns

FIGURE 9 – 17

Types of presentation graphics. Any type of graphical image that enhances the impact of information as it is shown to people is a presentation graphic. Although packages vary with respect to the number and type of presentation graphics they produce, most allow you to create simple bar, pie, and line charts.

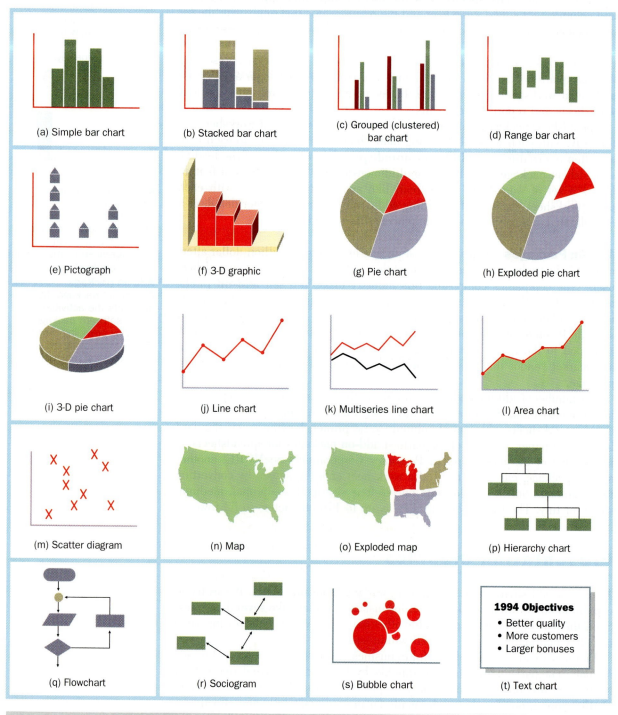

(a) Simple bar chart

(b) Stacked bar chart

(c) Grouped (clustered) bar chart

(d) Range bar chart

(e) Pictograph

(f) 3-D graphic

(g) Pie chart

(h) Exploded pie chart

(i) 3-D pie chart

(j) Line chart

(k) Multiseries line chart

(l) Area chart

(m) Scatter diagram

(n) Map

(o) Exploded map

(p) Hierarchy chart

(q) Flowchart

(r) Sociogram

(s) Bubble chart

1994 Objectives
- Better quality
- More customers
- Larger bonuses

(t) Text chart

Forms of Presentation Graphics

A **presentation graphic**—sometimes called a *presentation visual* or *chart*—is an image that visually enhances the impact of information communicated to other people. Presentation graphics can take many different forms, a number of which are illustrated in Figure 9-17 and Window 6. With the right types of software and hardware, the creation of presentation graphics is limited only by one's imagination.

There are several compelling reasons to use presentation graphics in business. Trends can be spotted or comparisons made much more quickly when data are in chart form. Presentation graphics can also be used to make a point much more convincingly or dramatically than plain text can. Recent studies have found that presentation graphics also make the presenter look more professional in the eyes of others.

Here, we'll discuss in detail three of the most widely used presentation graphics—bar charts, pie charts, and line charts. We'll also look at a number of ways in which these charts vary and examine where each is most appropriate. The best graphic in any given situation depends on the point you are trying to make.

Bar Charts **Bar charts** are especially useful for comparing relative magnitudes of items and for showing the frequency with which events occur. They can also be used to illustrate changes in a single item over time.

In a typical bar chart, one axis represents a categorical or *qualitative* phenomenon; the other represents a numeric or *quantitative* one. For instance, in Figure 9-18a, the horizontal axis (x-axis) represents months, the qualitative phenomenon, whereas the vertical axis (y-axis) represents price, the quantitative one.

A number of different types of bar charts are available, including the simple bar chart, stacked bar chart, grouped (clustered) bar chart, range chart, pictograph, and 3-D bar chart (see Figures 9-17a through 9-17f, respectively).

Each type of bar chart has strengths and weaknesses relative to prospective applications. A *range chart,* for instance, would be most useful for showing daily highs and lows of a particular stock in the stock market (see Figure 9-18a). A *grouped (clustered) bar chart,* on the other hand, would be more useful for showing something such as overall income comparisons for this year and last year by quarter (see Figure 9-18b). Grouped bar charts are especially effective when you want to emphasize a difference between two items over time. When one set of bars is consistently bigger than another set of bars, as is the case here, a *stacked bar chart* can also effectively show the differences between the two sets of bars (see Figure 9-18c). A *Gantt chart,* shown in Figure 9-18d, is particularly handy for showing when events in schedules begin and end.

When designing bar charts, it's a good idea to keep the total number of categories on the x-axis to a half dozen or less. Any more than this may be too much information to cram into a single visual.

Pie Charts **Pie charts** are commonly used to show how parts of something relate to a whole (see Figure 9-17g to 9-17i). Each slice of the "pie," or circle, represents a percentage of share of the total. One of the major advantages of the pie chart is that it is extremely easy to understand.

Presentation graphic.
A visual image, such as a bar chart or pie chart, that is used to present data in a highly meaningful form.

Bar chart.
A presentation graphic that uses side-by-side columns as the principal charting element.

Pie chart.
A presentation graphic in which the principal charting element is a pie-shaped image that is divided into slices, each of which represents a share of the whole.

T O M O R R O W

Intelligent Spreadsheets and Graphics

Automating Decision Support for Managers

Is it possible for computers to make decision support any easier than they already have?

Absolutely. Developers of spreadsheets and presentation graphics will be adding a variety of "intelligent enhancements" to their packages over the next several years. The enhancements are designed to help managers interpret the meaning of information, to perform for managers routine tasks that are time consuming, and to provide general support for decision environments.

Some of these enhancements are beginning to trickle into the market already. But by the turn of the century, it's possible that many of them may be standard fare in packages. Following is a list of three important enhancements we are likely to see.

Automatic Updates Often, managers need the same type of information every month. For instance, a presentation the manager makes in February might feature several worksheets and bar charts based on January data. In March, the worksheets and bar charts in the presentation would instead reflect what took place in February, and so on. An intelligent updating feature auto-matically updates each monthly worksheet and its associated presentation visuals as soon as new monthly data are entered into the computer system. Users on a network will be able to view new worksheets and graphs at their workstations as soon as data have changed.

Smart Files A smart file is a worksheet or presentation graphic that's not only "aware" of its own content, but has the ability to act on this content to make routine decisions. Here's how a smart file might work. A worksheet that you pull from your computer system shows that sales were dramatically low last month. But because you are now using a smart file, this month you get more than just a standard worksheet. The low figures automatically trigger the spreadsheet program to prepare a special report, complete with bar and pie charts that compare activity for the last several months. The program may even do analysis and provide an explanation. The report is then auto-matically routed to the electronic mailboxes of co-workers over your company's computer network. Also, since not everyone may be authorized to see the full set of data, the smart file customizes the report for each person.

Automatic Chart Selection and Styling With all of the graphics options available today, creating effective presentation visuals can become a mind-boggling challenge.

First, consider *selection*. Many users of presentation graphics packages are not skilled at choosing the most appropriate type of visual to present

In electronic spreadsheets, the display screen is viewed as a *window* looking in on a big grid, called a **worksheet.** The worksheet consists of *rows* and *columns* that intersect to form **cells,** each of which can be accessed through a **cell address.** Columns are labeled by letters, and rows are labeled by numbers, so, for instance, cell (cell address) B3 is located at the intersection of the second column and third row.

Spreadsheet software often divides the screen into two principal areas. The worksheet itself is displayed in the **worksheet area,** or **window area.** The **control panel** is the area of the screen where users perform tasks such as preparing text (called *labels*) or numbers (called *values*) that are to be placed in the worksheet cells. A **label** is a cell entry that cannot be manipulated mathematically, whereas a **value** is an entry that can. The control panel also

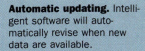

Automatic updating. Intelligent software will automatically revise when new data are available.

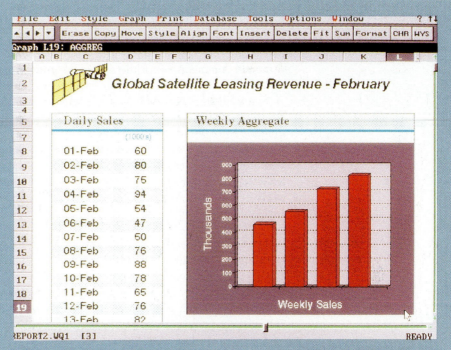

data. An intelligent graphics package will ask the user questions about the target audience and the data to be graphed. With these details out of the way, it will then automatically create the type of presentation visual that best depicts the data under consideration. The package will also have a modification feature that lets users point to any graph elements they want changed and correct them manually.

Now take *styling*. Styling involves such things as choosing colors, selecting fonts for titles and legends, balancing graphic elements visually, and scaling the axes and elements appropriately. A graphics artist may have the wherewithal to decide which colors out of a pallet of 256,000 are most appropriate, but the average user does not. An intelligent graphics package will automatically choose effective, compatible colors for visuals. It will also be programmed to avoid "rookie" design mistakes such as putting too many colors into a visual or making too many pie slices in a pie chart.

shows you the cell to which you are currently pointing, called the **current cell.** It is also the area used to display commands.

Most spreadsheet packages offer two pointing mechanisms: a cursor and a cell pointer (or highlight). The **cursor** is associated with the control panel, pointing to the place in that area where the next character typed in by the user will appear. The **cell pointer** (or **highlight**) is associated with the worksheet area, pointing to the current cell.

Spreadsheet packages are particularly valuable because they provide a **recalculation feature**—that is, they can perform recalculations in seconds that would require several hours to do manually or by writing a program in a regular programming language. It's this recalculation feature, and the **what-if analysis** it makes possible, that makes spreadsheets so popular.

A contiguous, rectangular block of cells is called a **range.** A range can be typed in explicitly or pointed to on the screen.

Most spreadsheet packages use a hierarchical series of menus from which users can select commands. The *main menu* (or *command menu*) shows the principal command set, while *submenus* prompt users for finer and finer levels of detail.

Spreadsheet packages have numerous features to aid in entering and editing data. Some of the basic entering and editing operations include inserting and deleting rows or columns, moving or copying the contents of cells from one part of the worksheet to another (through **relative replication, absolute replication,** or **mixed replication**), formatting dollar amounts and other values, selecting column widths, and freezing titles. Also, many packages have a **template** feature that permits the creation, saving, and protection of worksheets that have all of their rows and columns prelabeled, so that only the data need to be filled in.

A *data management* feature provides users with a variety of file-handling capabilities, including the ability to *search* for records with specific characteristics and to *sort* records on one or more fields.

A macro facility enables you to write programs within your worksheet. Each **macro** is, in fact, a program. It consists of a series of keystrokes that the spreadsheet package executes every time you invoke the macro.

Spreadsheet packages that allow you to develop worksheets with more than two cell dimensions are called **multidimensional spreadsheets.** A multidimensional feature allows a set of worksheets to be read like an "electronic book," with each page (worksheet) capable of adding detail to the one that precedes it.

During the last decade or so, a vigorous aftermarket industry has sprouted up to meet the continuing demands of spreadsheet users. The companies composing this industry make and sell **add-on packages**—utilities that enhance the major spreadsheet programs in the market. These packages allow you to print worksheets sideways, compress numbers on the screen so that you can see more of your worksheets, and so on.

Presentation Graphics   A **presentation graphic**—sometimes called a *presentation visual* or *chart*—is an image that visually enhances in some way the impact of information communicated to other people. A presentation graphic can take a large number of forms.

Probably the three most common types of charts used for presentations are bar charts, pie charts, and line charts. **Bar charts** are especially useful for comparing relative magnitudes of items and for showing the frequency with which events occur. Some common forms of bar charts are range charts, grouped (clustered) bar charts, stacked bar charts, and Gantt charts. **Pie charts** are commonly used to show how parts of something relate to a whole. **Line charts** are used to represent graph data in which both axes are used to represent quantitative phenomena. Also, because the line in the chart is unbroken, the effect on the eye can be far more dramatic than that of a bar chart.

Presentation graphics software lets you draw bar charts, pie charts, and the like. Presentation graphics packages are either dedicated or integrated. *Dedicated* packages provide the most sophisticated types of graphing capabilities, whereas *integrated* packages consist of modest graphics routines that support a particular spreadsheet.

Review Exercises

1. The principle behind electronic spreadsheets involves viewing the display screen as a(n) _____ looking in on a big grid, called a(n) _____.

2. Most spreadsheet packages provide two pointing mechanisms: a(n) _____ and a(n) _____.

3. Worksheet entries are created and edited in the _____.

4. Three types of copying operations available in many spreadsheet packages are _____, _____, and _____ replication.

5. A worksheet in which all rows and columns are prelabeled and formulas are supplied is called a(n) _____.

6. The spreadsheet feature that allows users to embed small programs in a worksheet is called a(n) _____ facility.

7. _____ packages are spreadsheet utilities commonly sold by after-market vendors.

8. Most presentation graphics packages fall into one of two categories: _____ packages and _____ packages.

Match each term with the description that fits best.

a. +B1-B2*C2   d. JOHN SMITH
b. @SUM   e. 200
c. D4   f. F18 . . F28

____ 1. A label.

____ 2. A range.

____ 3. A numeric constant.

____ 4. A formula.

____ 5. A cell address.

____ 6. A function.

1. What purposes are served by electronic spreadsheets?

2. What is the difference between a label and a value?

3. What purpose does a range serve?

Chart Types

Among the most popular types of presentation graphics are bar, pie, line, and text charts, along with their countless variations.

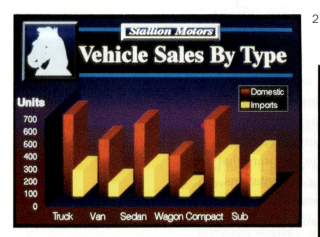

2

3

2–3. Bar charts are most useful for comparing the relative magnitudes of items in a given period (photo 2) and the frequency with which events occur over time (photo 3). A trend in bar charting today is to give graphs a three-dimensional look.

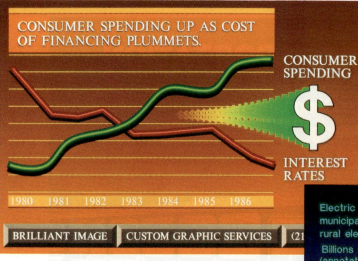

4

4–5. Line charts, where appropriate, can be more dramatic than bar charts because of the visual effect of the unbroken line. Because of their inherent simplicity, line charts are frequently accompanied with art elements.

5

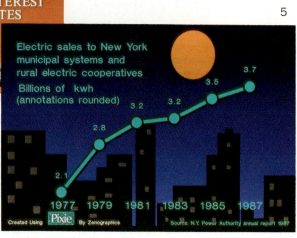

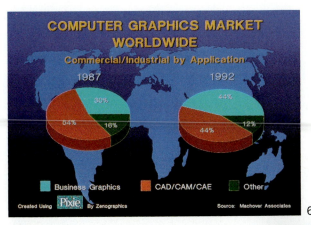

6

6. Pie charts are ideal for showing how individual parts relate to a whole. The visual shown here makes it obvious immediately which items constitute the biggest share of the action and that the activity represented by the blue pie slice has increased over the five-year period shown.

7. Text charts are often used to present a bulleted list of points. Often, as each point is discussed it is highlighted by a slide, as shown here. This type of presentation technique is called a *build.*

Image Preparation and Organization

In many presentations a series of slide images are shown in a certain order. Preparation and organization tasks involve choosing the most appropriate types of visuals, developing them from available data, choosing art elements that impart emphasis to the visuals, and deciding on the best order to show the visuals.

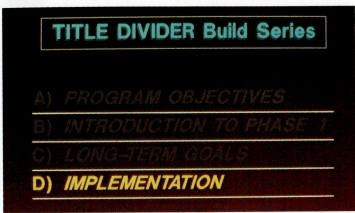

7

8

8. Dedicated presentation graphics packages typically have the widest selection of chart types from which to choose.

9

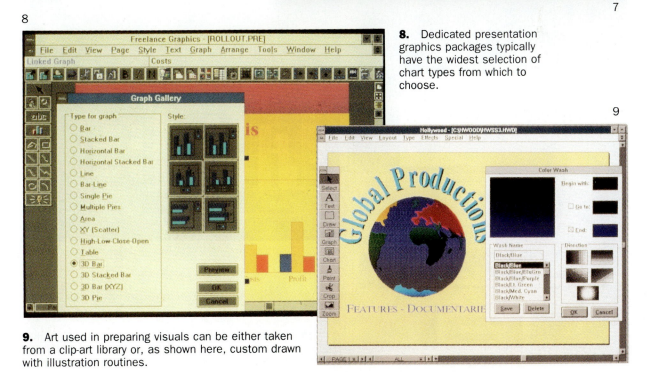

9. Art used in preparing visuals can be either taken from a clip-art library or, as shown here, custom drawn with illustration routines.

10. Borland International has been one of the leading companies to build advanced graphics techniques into its spreadsheet products. Shown in this Quattro Pro for Windows screen shot is a feature that lets users both create and rotate three-dimensional graphs. Note also the top-of-screen color palette for users to select colors for graph elements.

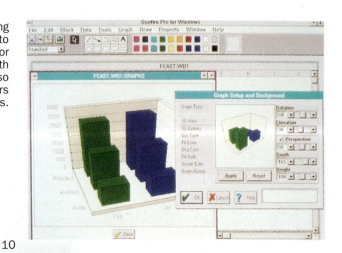

10

11–12. A presentation often looks more professional when its series of images has a consistent background. Dedicated packages enable you to create a "master slide" containing such a background and apply it to each visual you create.

12

11

13

13. Slide shows are often completely electronic, in that hard copies are never made of the slide images. When this is the case, it's handy to have a slide sorter that provides thumbnail sketches of the images and lets the user quickly reorder them onscreen.

14

Showtime

Once the visuals are created and organized, it's time for the final step: carrying out the presentation in front of a live audience. A number of hardware and software resources are available to make that presentation a stunning one.

14–15. Presentation hardware enables users to show hard- or soft-copy slide images on a monitor or projector screen. The hand-held gadget in photo 14 makes it possible for the user to preview the next image before showing it or to glance at electronic notes.

15

16–17. Dedicated graphics software often provides special transition effects—such as a diagonal wipe (photo 16) or vertical push (photo 17)—when the user changes images.

16

17

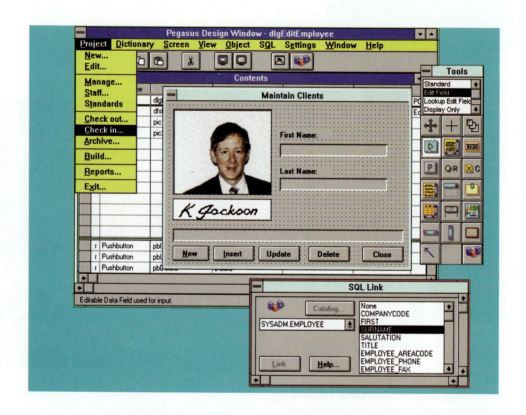

DATA MANAGEMENT

10

How do computers keep track of the thousands of facts needed to maintain business records? Often, it's through the use of data management software, which you'll be reading about in this chapter. In recent years, the electronic storage of picture and video data has revolutionized the data management function.

LEARNING OBJECTIVES

After completing this chapter, you will be able to:

1. Describe what file managers can do and how they work.

2. Explain what database management systems are and how they differ from file managers.

3. Identify some of the strategies used for database management on both large and small computer systems.

4. Identify the advantages and disadvantages of database management.

5. Appreciate the emerging importance of multimedia data management.

Overview

People often need to summon large amounts of data rapidly. An airline agent on the phone to a client may need to search through mounds of data quickly to find the lowest-cost flight path from Tucson to Toronto two weeks hence. The registrar of a university may have to swiftly scan student records to find the grade point averages of all students who will graduate in June. An engineer may need to test several structural design alternatives against volumes of complicated safety and feasibility criteria before proceeding with a design strategy.

In this chapter and the next, we'll cover the type of software used specifically for such data management tasks. This class of software is rapidly replacing the thick, hard-copy manuals that people have had to wade through to find the information their jobs require.

Data management software often is categorized into two major types: *file managers* and *database management systems.* As with other popular types of software products, numerous data management software packages are available for both small and large computer systems. File managers are easier to use and understand, so we'll discuss them first. Then we'll turn to database management systems. Finally, we'll consider the topic of multimedia data management, in which voice, graphics, and video data are combined into applications with the most traditional type of data—text.

In Chapter 10 we will frequently be using terms such as *fields, records,* and *files.* These were covered in Chapter 2; you should review them before reading this chapter.

File Management Software

File manager.
A productivity software package used to organize data into records and to access data a single file at a time.

A **file manager,** or *record management system,* is a software package that enables you to organize data into files and to access the data a single file at a time. For example, you might first use the package to search for and print out the names of all recipes in a recipe file in which kumquats are an ingredient. Minutes later, you may summon the same package to scan an employee file and total the number of employees in your organization whose birthdays are in April.

You can use a file manager to create and store as many files as you want. You may even be able to keep several files resident in RAM at the same time and switch among them with a keystroke or two. But because you can work on only one file at a time, file managers can be cumbersome to use for interrelating data located in different files. For example, you'd be unable to easily find the birthday of the employee in your employee file who gave you the candied kumquats recipe in your recipe file. To get such information, you would first have to look up the name of the employee in the recipe file; then, using the name you found, you would turn to the employee file to look up the birthday. With a database management system, which we'll be describing later in the chapter, you would be able to find the same information in a single step. In data management, files are sometimes referred to as **flat files,** meaning that they lack the multidimensionality imparted by the database structures.

Flat files.
A collection of related records that lack multidimensionality.

The one-file-at-a-time drawback aside, file managers are powerful and extremely useful. Besides enabling you to search for records with specific charac-

An onscreen form (template) representing an employee record. Such forms can be filled out while displayed on the screen.

```
            *EMPLOYEE FILE*
   NAME        [                        ]
   SOC-SEC-NUM   [                      ]
   STREET      [                        ]
   CITY    [        ] STATE [   ] ZIP [       ]
   HOME PHONE  [        ]  OFFICE EXT. [      ]
   DEPARTMENT CODE  [      ]
   SALARY     [        ]
```

teristics, most packages permit you to sort records and to produce both summary information and detailed reports from selected records. They also let you add, delete, and modify data.

How File Managers Work

Let's look at an example to get a feel for how file managers process data. Suppose an organization has 1,000 employees. The organization maintains a "form" on each employee like the one shown on the display screen in Figure 10-1. Such an *onscreen form,* or **template,** is commonly used for entering data into files or databases. Each file that needs to be created will have its own distinctive template.

As you place data into the records of a file, you start with an unfilled template for each record to be keyed in. Then you repeatedly fill the template images at the keyboard and save the records onto disk. At any later point, you can modify or delete records from the file and add new ones.

Setting Up a File   Before we examine some of the ways in which we can process the employee file, let's look more closely at the template in Figure 10-1. Notice that it contains ten fields: NAME, SOC-SEC-NUM (social security number), STREET, and so on.

With most file management packages, you can design your own templates. In creating a template for a recipe file, for example, a chef will probably set up a recipe-name field, an ingredients field, a directions field, and perhaps even a field for calories. Generally, the file management package will contain a CREATE FILE option that gives you tools to design whatever types of templates you need for your applications. The records in a given file usually must have the same format and conform to the template you make.

Template.
A prelabeled onscreen form that requires only that the operator fill in a limited number of entries.

FIGURE 10 – 2

A typical opening menu for a file management package. In the highlighted areas, you select the processing option you want and the file with which you wish to work.

```
            FILE MANAGEMENT PACKAGE
                 OPENING MENU

    1 CREATE FILE       5 PRINT/SORT

    2 ADD RECORDS       6 REPORT GENERATION

    3 COPY RECORDS      7 REMOVE RECORDS

    4 SEARCH/UPDATE     8 EXIT PACKAGE


         SELECTION NUMBER: 1
         FILE NAME: EMPLOYEE-FILE
```

To enable you to create templates or process file data, many file management packages provide you with an opening menu of choices, such as the one shown in Figure 10-2, as soon as you get into the package from the operating system. At this point, you must choose one of the given menu options and supply the name of the file you wish to process.

So, for example, if you were setting up a template for the 1,000-record employee file previously mentioned, you would select option 1, CREATE FILE, and create a name for the file—say, EMPLOYEE-FILE. Then the package would summon a routine that would ask you a series of questions about how you wanted to design the template for this file. Here you would name the fields, define the maximum length of the data in each field, and make some choices about how the template should look on the screen. Many packages will let you set up templates that require more than one screen.

After designing the EMPLOYEE-FILE template, you would go back to the opening menu and select option 2, ADD RECORDS, to fill out 1,000 copies of the form—one for each employee—and place them on disk.

File Maintenance   Once you have stored records on disk, you can add new records (opening menu option 2: ADD RECORDS) or delete records representing departed employees (option 7: REMOVE RECORDS). If a record contains outdated data, you can change them by requesting the update mode (option 4: SEARCH/UPDATE) on the menu.

Information Retrieval   Besides performing file maintenance operations, you can retrieve information for screen display and, if you desire, produce printed reports. For example, you might use the search/update feature on the opening menu to scan the file for the names of all employees in Department 544 or the names of all employees whose salaries exceed $40,000. You can direct any of this information to the screen and, if you wish, print it.

You may also want to produce mailing labels. You can extract the NAME, STREET, CITY, STATE, and ZIP fields from selected records by invoking opening menu option 5, PRINT/SORT. You can then sort these "reduced records" by zip code before sending them to the printer. (The postal service offers reduced rates for large mailings that are presorted by zip code).

Most packages also allow you to produce sophisticated written reports. For example, you may wish to produce a salary report on all employees in departments 212 through 214, sorted by department and totaled. Again you go back to the opening menu, select option 6, REPORT GENERATION, and identify

Using a file manager to produce a report. On the display screen, the user fills in blanks on a questionnaire that covers what the report is to look like. The file manager does the rest.

```
              FILE MANAGEMENT PACKAGE
           REPORT GENERATION QUESTIONNAIRE

    FIELDS USED? NAME, DEPARTMENT-CODE,
                 SOC-SEC-NO, SALARY

    RECORD SELECTION? DEPT = 212-214

    SORT FIELDS? DEPT

    TOTALS? SALARY

    HEADING? SALARY REPORT

    COLUMN TITLES? NAME, DEPT, SS#, SALARY

    OUTPUT? PRINTER
```

(a) Describing the report on the display screen

```
     4/22/94 SALARY REPORT PAGE 1

NAME        DEPT      SS#         SALARY
ABERNATHY   212    148-21-3224    $40,000
BENSON      212    146-48-6211    $35,000
GARRETSON   212    153-66-2150    $27,000
RIGGINS     212    140-32-3532    $12,000
COLES       213    139-64-3821    $52,000
GRETSKY     213    153-11-4121    $32,000
JACOBS      214    138-92-3005    $45,000

TOTALS.........................$243,000
```

(b) The report

FIGURE 10 – 4

Graphics data. Data management packages are increasingly being used for storage and retrieval of graphics-oriented data. Here, photographic data are included along with regular text data in an electronic insurance record.

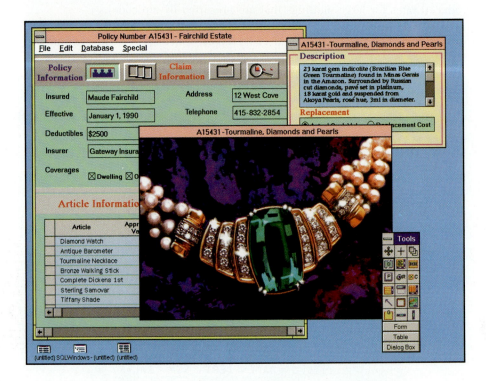

EMPLOYEE-FILE as the file you wish to process. Then the file management package is likely to present you with a report generation questionnaire, such as the one shown in Figure 10-3a, so that you can describe how to prepare the report. You merely fill out the questionnaire, hitting the Enter key after placing your responses into each field. The package will then produce the report (Figure 10-3b). In some cases, such as that in Figure 10-3, the file manager will automatically format the report, supply the current date, and number pages.

Increasingly, both file managers and database management systems are enabling storage and retrieval of information other than text, as shown in Figure 10-4, Feature 10-1, and User Solution 10-1.

Database Management Systems

A **database management system (DBMS)** is a software system that integrates data in storage and provides easy access to them. The data themselves are placed on disk in a **database,** which can be thought of as an integrated collection of related files. The three files shown in Figure 10-5, which we will discuss

Database management system (DBMS).
A software package designed to integrate data and provide easy access to them.

Database.
An integrated collection of data.

FIGURE 10 – 5

Using a relational database management system. Data in various files can be pulled together quickly by their common fields (shaded here).

(a) Product description file

Product name	Product number	Supplier	Price
Skis	A-202	Ellis Ski Co.	90.00
Boots	A-211	Ajax Bros.	60.00
Poles	A-220	Bent Corp.	25.00
Bindings	A-240	Acme Co.	15.00
Wax	A-351	Candle Industries	3.00

(b) Inventory file

Product number	Uncommitted stock	On order?
A-202	15	Yes
A-211	90	Yes
A-220	30	Yes
A-240	25	Yes
A-351	80	No

(c) Order file

Shipment date	Product number	Amount
1/8	A-202	30
1/8	A-240	15
1/9	A-211	50
1/9	A-202	40
1/10	A-220	35
1/12	A-211	60

(d) Information screen

Product number	Product name	Date	Total stock
A-211	Boots	TODAY	90
		1/9	140
		1/12	200

F e a t u r e   1 0 – 1

Geographic Information Systems (GISs)

Data management with maps

For hundreds of years, when information had to be recorded on a map, it was drawn right on the map surface. Transparency overlays, introduced later, were a more sophisticated development, allowing different types of data to be layered on a single map. Sometimes the overlays were used jointly, but use of two or more overlays could make the maps confusing. Then, in the late 1980s, GISs were created.

Geographic information systems (GISs) are computerized display maps that are backed by powerful database systems. Advances in database technology, large-capacity storage (optical disk) devices, and improved computer graphics techniques have made GISs possible. Stored in the database are map images and useful geographic data such as demographic breakdowns, sales data, store and warehouse locations, trends, and market research data. Anything you can put on a map—including data on animal populations, land use, foliage growth, traffic patterns, mineral deposits, or pollution—is fair game for a GIS database.

GISs are a promising new area within the computing field. Following is a sampling of their wide range of applications.

■ Oil companies such as Texaco, Shell, and Amoco use GISs to store exploration maps and data such as land-leasing arrangements, oil strikes, and terrain features. The systems have reduced the time needed to find promising places to drill and have made the process of locating drilling sites more accurate. GISs are also used by oil companies to locate profitable sites for gas stations.

■ GISs have helped environmentalists in their attempt to control the 1989 *Exxon Valdez* oil spill at Prince William Sound in Alaska. A desktop mapping program called GeoREF has been used to collect environmental data, display it, and plan a cleanup strategy. Moreover, the maps have provided a useful electronic journal of the disaster so that its long-term impact can be more accurately assessed.

■ Arby's uses GISs to assess the performance of its franchises and to select new sites. One of the key types of data it uses to select sites is traffic patterns. A spokesperson for the firm reports that GISs have dramatically reduced the number of bad decisions.

shortly, collectively form a database. In a nondatabase environment, these data would normally exist as flat files.

A database management system performs many of the same types of tasks as a file manager. For instance, the work that file managers are asked to do—retrieving information, updating data, arranging data in a specific order, and the like—is essentially the same work done by database management systems. Database management systems and file managers also employ the same tools, such as templates. A template is designed for each of the files in a database, and the template is repeatedly filled with data representing records.

However, database management systems differ from file managers in that they enable immediate, "seamless" access to related data in *different* files. Put another way, if a file manager did not have the one-file-at-a-time drawback, many people would consider it a database management system.

As a rule, because database management systems are technically more complex than file managers, they are also more expensive and usually more difficult to master.

GIS applications. Using technology to determine areas of maximum market penetration (left) and to reduce emergency response time (right).

■ The U.S. Geographical Survey (USGS) is planning to computerize its large collection of maps showing every town, river, lake, and highway in the country. These maps will be used for governmental planning purposes and also made available to GIS users in the private sector.

■ A feed company in Minnesota uses a GIS to estimate the amount of feed it can sell in a 12-state area. Data on animal populations and average consumption by each species by county are used to estimate demand.

■ A growing roster of companies—including Coca-Cola, UPS, and Federal Express—uses

GIS techniques to route trucks along the fastest routes. The city of Albuquerque, New Mexico, uses small display screens in ambulances that help drivers navigate to their destinations. Shaving minutes off driving time can be critical in emergency situations.

■ The city of Tacoma, Washington, is a leader in using GISs. The police department uses a GIS to track crimes, the fire department uses a GIS to cut response time in getting to a fire, city planners use a GIS to keep track of properties for tax assessment, and the water company uses a GIS to locate meters and valves.

Database Management on Microcomputers

The best way to understand what a microcomputer-based database management system does and how one works is to look at an example. Many different database management systems are commercially available. Not all of them work the same way nor are they all equally easy to comprehend. In the example that follows we'll look at **relational database management systems**—the type found on most microcomputers and probably the easiest type to understand.

A Simple Example   Imagine that you're a sales manager at a ski-equipment warehouse, and an order comes in for 160 pairs of ski boots. You first need to find out if the order can be filled from stock in inventory. If it can't, you next need to know how long it will be before enough stock is available. You have an impatient client on the phone and require an immediate response.

Because rapid access to more than one file's worth of data is required, this type of task is especially suited to a database management system. Traditionally,

Relational database management system.
A database management system that links data in related files through common fields.

Field descriptors. Most business applications require use of five field descriptors—character, numeric, logical, date, and memo.

Field Type	Description
Character	*Character* fields store data that cannot be manipulated arithmetically. You can, however, sort, index, or compare on these fields.
Numeric	*Numeric* fields, which store integer numbers or numbers that contain decimal points, are those that can be arithmetically manipulated. Numbers on which you do not need to do arithmetic—such as employee identification numbers and product identification numbers—should be stored in character rather than numeric fields.
Logical	*Logical* fields store a single character of data—a "T" (for "true") or an "F" (for "false") or, alternatively, a "Y" (for "yes") and an "N" (for "no"). Tests on logical fields can be used to select records from a file, as can tests on character, numeric, and date fields.
Date	*Date* fields store dates, provided that they are in the format MM/DD/YY (such as 12/31/94). You can sort or index on date fields, and you can also subtract them to calculate the number of days elapsing between two dates.
Memo	*Memo* fields are used to store text information. They cannot be arithmetically manipulated or compared, but they can be edited and output, as can any other field.

be hidden so that only certain users of the database, furnished with the proper password, are authorized to retrieve them. Also, only users with access to another password would be allowed to update these data.

Data Manipulation   The process of using the database in some hands-on fashion is called **data manipulation.** There are generally two ways to manipulate data in a microcomputer-oriented DBMS—through the retrieval/update facility that is provided with the DBMS and through an applications program developed with the programming-language facility.

Data manipulation encompasses a variety of activities. Here we briefly cover some of the most important of them.

Data manipulation.
The process of using language commands to add, delete, modify, or retrieve data in a file or database.

- ■ **CREATION OF DATABASE DATA**   This task consists of developing records for the database. Each template in the database is successively brought to the screen and filled with the records that pertain to it. In Figure 10-7, for example, you might first summon the template for the product-description file. Then you would type in the first record in that file and enter it. After you did this, a fresh template would appear on the screen. You would type in the second record, and so forth. When you had finished entering all the records for the product-description file, you would do the same thing for the next file—say, the inventory file.

- ■ **FILE MAINTENANCE**   File maintenance consists primarily of updating records. This involves adding new records from time to time, deleting records that are no longer needed, and making modifications to records. Modifications are necessary because data such as prices and delivery schedules can change and also because errors are sometimes made in entering data.

■ **INFORMATION RETRIEVAL (QUERY)**   The information on the screen in Figure 10-5d, where we needed to find out amounts and delivery dates of uncommitted stock, is an example of information retrieval, or query. Database queries can be simple or very complex. Figure 10-9 illustrates several queries from the database data described in Figures 10-5 and 10-7. Also

---

FIGURE 10-9

Examples of database queries. The queries given here can be directed to the database data described in Figures 10-5 and 10-7. Each of the queries conforms to SQL, the de facto standard for information retrieval from relational databases.

Query
```
SELECT   PRODUCT-NUMBER, PRODUCT-NAME
FROM     PRODUCT
WHERE    PRICE < 20.00
```

Selects all records in the product file that have a price of less than $20.00; outputs only the product number and product name on each selected record. That is,

Response
```
                      A-240  Bindings
                      A-351  Wax
```

Query
```
SELECT   PRODUCT-NUMBER, UNCOMMITTED-STOCK, ON-ORDER?
FROM     INVENTORY
WHERE    UNCOMMITTED-STOCK > 20   AND   ON-ORDER? = T
```

Selects all records in the inventory file that have an uncommitted stock level of over 20 and that are on order (i.e., the value of ON-ORDER is "T," for true); outputs all fields of each selected record. That is,

Response
```
                      A-211  90  T
                      A-220  30  T
                      A-240  25  T
```

Query
```
SELECT  SHIPMENT-DATE, PRODUCT-NUMBER
FROM    ORDER
WHERE   SHIPMENT-DATE > = 1/9 OR AMOUNT > = 30
```

Selects all records in the order file where the shipment date is 1/9 or beyond, amount is 30 or more units, or both. Outputs only dates and product numbers. That is,

Response
```
                      1/8   A-202
                      1/9   A-211
                      1/9   A-202
                      1/10  A-220
                      1/12  A-211
```

Query
```
SELECT   PRODUCT-NAME, ON-ORDER?
FROM     PRODUCT, INVENTORY
WHERE    PRODUCT.PRODUCT-NUMBER = INVENTORY.PRODUCT-NUMBER
```

Creates new records by linking the product and inventory files through their common field, PRODUCT-NUMBER. The new records show the name of each product and whether or not it is on order. That is,

Response
```
                      Skis       T
                      Boots      T
                      Poles      T
                      Bindings   T
                      Wax        F
```

FIGURE 10 – 10

Simplifying SQL with GUIs. The trend in database software today is toward graphical user interfaces (GUIs) that make it easier for ordinary users to construct SQL commands. Shown here are three different GUI approaches to the language interface illustrated in Figure 10–9.

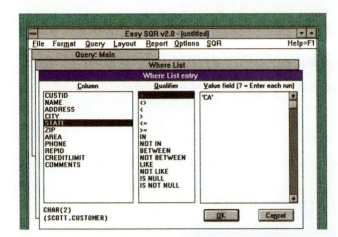

(a) Easy SQR lets users compose queries by placing search fields, search operators, and search criteria in separate windows.

(b) In Paradox's "Query By Example" feature, users simply check fields and include example elements to perform queries across multiple tables.

(c) Data Partner enables users to construct queries by connecting icons that symbolize access routines.

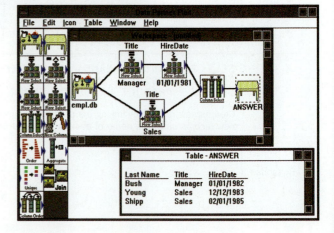

provided are the DBMS's responses to those queries. One important fact you should keep in mind is that if you can *manually* pull together the data you need, you should be able to get your database management system to pull these same data together *automatically*—and a lot faster, too.

Every database management system has its own way of letting users query the database for information. The style shown in Figure 10-9 is based largely on **SQL** (for **Structured Query Language**), which is recognized as today's de facto standard for information retrieval in relational databases. Recently, a number of tools have become available from both database vendors and vendors of add-on packages to make it easy for users to construct database queries without having to remember language syntax (see Figure 10-10).

Structured Query Language (SQL).
A popular language standard for information retrieval in relational databases.

■ **REPORTING** Reporting is the process of arranging the information you need in a formal report. Most database management systems require that you produce a *report form* for each type of report you need. The report form specifies what the report will look like when it is output—how the report title and column headings will look, which fields will be placed into which columns, the criteria used to select records for the report, how records are to be arranged in the report, and the like. Typically, a series of easy-to-use menus will guide users through report preparation (see Figure 10-11).

■ **SORTING** Sorting is the process of arranging records in some order. Most database management systems are equipped with the necessary tools to help you arrange records in virtually any sequence you desire. As with spreadsheets, you can choose several sort keys to do sorts within sorts.

F I G U R E 10 – 11

Developing a report form. Many database packages require you to use a series of menus to develop onscreen a mockup of what a report will look like in print. Here, in this Paradox screen, the mockup appears on the top half of the screen; the report is on the bottom.

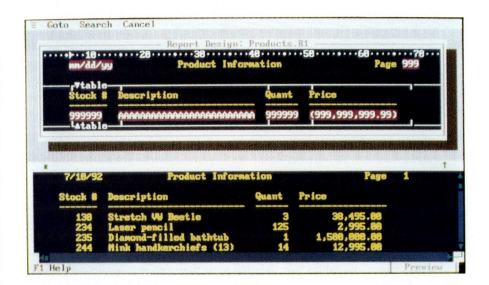

■ **CALCULATIONS**   Often it is necessary to compute sums for columns, take averages, count records, and so forth. Although spreadsheet software is especially suited to these particular applications, database management systems include such math features, too.

Database Management on Large Computers

On large computer systems, DBMSs perform exactly the same sorts of roles as they do on microcomputers, but they are necessarily more sophisticated, for several reasons. First, data are often organized in a more complex way to provide faster access. Second, DBMSs on large systems must deal with the problem of several users trying to access the database, perhaps simultaneously. Third, because database technology began evolving at a time when many organizations had thousands of dollars already invested in programs written in popular high-level languages, DBMS vendors had to design their products to interface with these languages.

Hierarchical and Network Data Models
The relational database model is particularly useful in managerial (decision-support) retrieval situations in which users are free to pose almost any sort of query to the database. In other situations, however, the types of queries that users need to make are highly predictable and limited. For instance, in banking, tellers usually have access only to the facts they need to perform their jobs, such as information on current customer account balances, deposits, and withdrawals. In these transaction processing environments, hierarchical and network database models are found more commonly than relational ones. Relational databases store data in tables, whereas hierarchical databases store data in trees and network databases store data in networks (see Figure 10-12). These models are explained below:

■ *Hierarchical databases* store data in the form of a tree, where the relationship between data elements is one-to-many. Note that each professor in Figure 10-12a is assigned to one and only one department. If Professor Schwartz were a member of two departments—say, marketing and MIS—she would have to be represented twice in the database to maintain the hierarchical structure, once under marketing and once under MIS. The database system would then treat Profesor Schwartz as two distinct individuals. She might even get two separate graduation invitations from the school's computer. Such an inefficiency can be tolerated, however, if it's relatively rare.

■ In *network databases,* the relationship between data elements can be either many-to-one (*simple* networks) or many-to-many (*complex* networks). The solid lines in Figure 10-12b depict many-to-one relationships; many courses can be handled by one professor and by one grader. The dotted lines, on the other hand, represent many-to-many relationships, where classes can be cotaught by two or more professors or have multiple graders. Complex networks are usually harder to deal with, but they can always be decomposed into simple networks. Sometimes this is done when, like in the earlier case of Professor Schwartz, some minor duplication can be tolerated.

■ In *relational databases,* as explained earlier, related data are placed into tables. Since the tables are independent, they can be dynamically linked

FIGURE 10 – 12

Database models. Most commercial databases are of the hierarchical, network, or relational type.

(a) Hierarchical

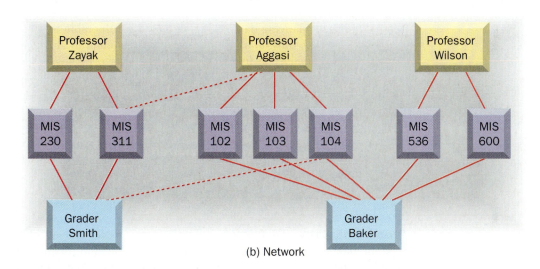

(b) Network

(c) Relational

by the user at program-execution time. This is in contrast to hierarchical and network databases, where data are prelinked.

Although further explanation of how hierarchical and network models work goes beyond the scope of this book, suffice it to say that these models store data in a way that makes access faster for predefined types of queries. Hierarchical and network databases have been around longer, too, so the security on these types of database systems is better than security on relational systems. Because hierarchical and relational databases are harder to set up and use, professionals known as *database administrators (DBAs)* are commonly hired to assist.

Setting Up the Database   Large DBMS packages usually have a special language dedicated to the data definition function. Such languages have generically come to be known as **data definition languages (DDLs).** Besides simply defining data, a major function of the DDL in these large packages is security— protecting the database from unauthorized use.

Because a large database management system in a firm is used by numerous people, the accompanying database is particularly vulnerable to security problems. For example, unscrupulous employees may attempt to alter payroll data, access privileged salary or financial account data, or even steal or erase data. To avoid these possibilities, the DBA may assign passwords when setting up the data dictionary, to determine which users access which data. This practice gives users only restricted views of the full database. For example, users working on a mailing list application that accesses an employee database will be locked out of access to data on employee salaries. Also, the DBA can allow some users to modify certain data and give other users of those data only retrieval privileges. For example, in an airline's passenger reservation database, a regular clerk or agent may not be allowed to rebook a special-rate passenger on an alternate flight, but a high-level supervisor, who knows the password, may be able to.

Processing Data   DBMSs targeted to larger computer systems often contain separate language packages to handle retrieval/update and programming tasks. Both sets pose their own array of problems that the typical microcomputer DBMS user doesn't encounter.

For example, on large computer systems (or microcomputer systems linked by a network), users often need to access the same data at more or less the same time. This can cause several problems. For example:

- Only one seat is available on a flight. Two agents seize it at the same moment and sell it to different customers.
- A program is tallying a series of customer balances in a database. When it is halfway finished, another program controlled by someone else transfers $5,000 from account 001 (which the first program already has tallied) to account 999 (which it hasn't). Thus, the first program will "double count" the $5,000 and obtain erroneous results.

To prevent such **concurrent access** problems, most database systems allow users to place a temporary "lock" on certain blocks of data to ensure that no other modifications to these data will be made during their processing.

Another problem unique to DBMSs on large computer systems relates to the need of these DBMSs to tie into programs coded in widely-used programming

Data definition language (DDL).
A language used to create, store, and manage data in a database environment.

Concurrent access.
A term that refers to two or more users attempting to interactively access the same data at more or less the same time.

languages. An interfacing feature known as a **data manipulation language (DML)** solves this problem, however. The DML is simply a set of commands that enable the language the programmer normally works with to function in a database environment. For example, if the programmer writes programs in COBOL, a COBOL DML must be used. The DML may consist of 30 or so commands, which the programmer uses to interact with data in the database.

Thus a COBOL program in a database environment consists of a mixture of standard COBOL statements and COBOL DML statements. The program containing this mixture of statements is then fed to the DBMS's COBOL **precompiler,** which translates this program into a standard COBOL program. This program then can be executed with the regular COBOL compiler available on the system.

High-level languages supported by their own DMLs are called **host languages.** Several host languages may be available on any particular system. Languages that a DBMS commonly employs as hosts are COBOL, C, PL/1, and BASIC.

Data manipulation language (DML).
A language used by programmers to supplement some high-level language supported in a database environment.

Precompiler.
A computer program that translates an extended set of programming language commands into standard commands of the language.

Host language.
A programming language used to code database applications.

Advantages and Disadvantages of Database Management

A DBMS can offer several advantages over traditional flat-file systems. Several of these follow.

- **BETTER INFORMATION**   Because many more data are integrated in a database environment than in a flat-file environment, information that otherwise might be difficult or impossible to pull together can be collected easily.
- **FASTER RESPONSE TIME**   Data that would otherwise require several flat files are integrated into a single database, so complex requests can be handled much more quickly.
- **LOWER OPERATING COSTS**   Because response time is faster, more work can be done by users in less time.
- **FEWER STORAGE REQUIREMENTS**   In a database system, integration often means that the same data need not appear over and over again in different files, thereby saving valuable disk space.
- **BETTER DATA INTEGRITY**   In a database system, integration often means that a data update need be made in only one place to be automatically reflected throughout the system, thereby avoiding the error that is often introduced when the same update has to be made manually in several independent files.
- **BETTER DATA MANAGEMENT**   Since more data are centrally stored in a database than in flat files there is better control over such matters as the data dictionary, security, and standards.

However, there is a downside to database processing that an organization or individual should consider. The major problem is *cost.* Significant expenses are normally incurred in the following areas:

- **DATABASE SOFTWARE**   Relative to other types of software, a DBMS is expensive. Microcomputer packages typically cost somewhere from $99 to $800. File managers, in contrast, are often priced much lower.
- **NEW HARDWARE**   A DBMS often requires a great deal of memory and secondary storage, and accessing records can be time consuming. Thus,

some users find it necessary to upgrade to a bigger, more powerful computer system after acquiring a DBMS.

■ **TRAINING**   Microcomputer-based database management systems are often considerably more difficult to master than file managers, spreadsheets, and word processors. Relating data in different files can be tricky at times. Also, if you want to custom design your own applications with the programming-language facility, prepare for a substantial investment in learning time.

■ **CONVERSION EFFORT**   Moving from a traditional, flat-file system to a database management system can entail considerable conversion expense. Data must be reorganized and programs rewritten. Fortunately, this is a one-time expense.

Cost is not the only problem. Database processing can increase a system's vulnerability to failure. Because the data in the database are highly integrated, a problem with a key element might render the whole system inactive. Despite the disadvantages, however, DBMSs have become immensely popular with both organizations and individuals.

Multimedia Data Management

So far in this chapter we've concentrated on data management applications that involve text data. But, as you saw in Figure 10-4, graphic data such as drawings and photographs also need to be managed systematically. Carrying this thought further, there is no reason why voice and video data couldn't be included within a data management application. Applications in which several types of data intermingle in "object-oriented" files or databases are known as **multimedia** data management, or *multimedia*, applications (see the Tomorrow box). Currently, this is still a very new applications area for computers.

The marriage by computer of text, graphics, sound, and video data in a single application is among the most exciting new technological frontiers we will explore in the 1990s. As many of the major hardware and software vendors jockey to position their products in what appears will soon be a multibillion-dollar market, one question remains unanswered: In which applications areas will multimedia take off?

A variety of applications are now being reported in the press. Three of these are discussed in the following paragraphs and several others in Window 7.

Multimedia.
A type of computing in which text, graphics, voice, and video are intermixed in applications.

Education and Training   Multimedia is increasingly being used as an educational and training tool. American French students, for instance, can now pull up an onscreen video that shows someone speaking French and see the spoken words spelled out nearby. Theoretically, if a word or phrase comes up that the student doesn't understand, the onscreen presentation could be halted by the press of a button, and the student could request an English translation. Figure 10-13 features a multimedia application at Rensselaer Polytechnic Institute in Troy, New York, in which engineering students have access to a system that shows with text and video clips how plumbing hardware works. A student can "click" (select with a mouse) on a designated icon to pull up windows of related topics or fetch a glossary by clicking on specific words embedded within the text. Education is seen today as a prime area for multimedia product develop-

T O M O R R O W

Managing Unstructured Data

A Look at Object-Oriented Databases

Traditionally, data management software has predominantly handled "structured" types of data, that is, those that fall neatly into rows and columns of text. Structured data are the type you've mostly been reading about in this chapter or working with in your computer lab. But new user needs and new trends in technology are creating other, more powerful possibilities that are putting an entirely new face on the data management function.

More types of data are being needed in applications today than ever before. In addition to text, the computer is now being widely used to store diagrams, still photographs, moving images, and voices. These multiple data types and the need to combine them into a multimedia format for applications have given rise to the possibility of *object-oriented databases*.

Here's how object-oriented databases and the objects they store work. In everyday life, various types of data naturally intermingle. A speech, for instance, consists of two types of data: a voice and a moving image of someone talking. Thus, we can consider the entire speech to be an "object," consisting of some voice and some moving-image data.

You can also combine other objects with the speech. If the speech is on the environment, for example, data such as pollution statistics and photographs of defoliated areas may also be useful to tack on to it. Each related batch of statistics and each related group of photographs may also be designated as objects. And, like the speech, any of these objects can be stored by the computer and given a name. All of these objects pertaining to the environment can then be assembled into an object-oriented database.

Just as with other types of databases, objects can be retrieved and cut and pasted as desired. This would enable you to create a customized

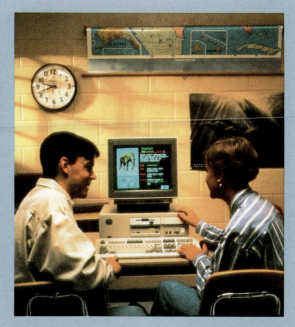

Object-oriented databases. Storing data as they exist in real life—intermingled.

presentation about the environment. Other people using the database would be able to prepare different presentations, targeted to different audiences.

Note that object-oriented databases go far afield of traditional text databases. The data they deal with are "unstructured" objects, which can be virtually anything—a moving image with people talking, a photograph with a narrative, text with music, and so on. Unlike the conventional text-only database in which each record has a similar format, little similarity may exist between the objects in this format.

Several companies are now in the process of developing their own object-oriented databases. Texas Instruments, for instance, is working on a database that computer manufacturers and other customers can access electronically. The objects contain several types of data on product designs—designs that are now published in catalogs sent to customers. Because the information will be stored on the computer instead of in printed-page form, the online catalog can also have voice and video segments that make it even more useful.

ment. Some people have gone so far as to say that multimedia will completely change the way most people learn. Several companies have already started using multimedia to train their employees.

Entertainment   Entertainment is another area where multimedia is almost guaranteed to be a success. As computer technology enables more and more types of information to be presented in new ways, a new breed of consumer product is beginning to evolve. One combines some of the best features of a TV show and a book. Say, for instance, you wanted to learn about a subject like the Amazon. You might go to a bookstore, where you would buy an optical disk containing all sorts of text, voice, and picture information about this endangered area. You could take a tour of the river, learn about the wildlife there, or watch a show about the risks posed by the cutting down of forests. The disk also might allow you to temporarily halt any of these shows to pull up statistical data about the things you were viewing or even maps of the area. Such "multimedia books" are just beginning to hit the market.

Live television is also likely to be packaged with a multimedia component in the future. Imagine watching a football game and being able to access football trivia or even another game in a window that you could blow up to any size. Multimedia may thus bring us to an age of "intelligent television." Who knows, being a couch potato might even become respectable.

Presentations   Organizations are increasingly turning to multimedia to make presentations to important clients and hot business prospects. Knowing that business leaders are used to slick presentations, the city of Aurora, Colorado,

F I G U R E   10 – 13

Multimedia in education and training. Multimedia is increasingly being used as an education and training tool. In the application featured here, college engineering students are provided access to a desktop multimedia system that shows with text and video clips how plumbing hardware works.

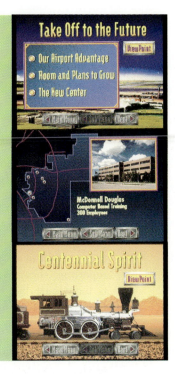

U s e r   S o l u t i o n   1 0 – 2

Wooing Execs With Multimedia

Aurora, Colorado, has chosen the high-tech route to marketing its strengths to new businesses. A suburb of Denver—a city in the process of building the world's largest airport—Aurora is expected to benefit enormously by its strategic location. Realizing that business executives react positively to professional-looking presentations by the cities that are courting their companies, Aurora's Economic Development Council used a multimedia approach to showcase its offerings. The menu-driven system contains text, voice, photographs, and videotaped testimonials from business and civic leaders. Information on the area's vital statistics, nearby colleges, and airport and growth plans is also available (see photos). The interactive nature of the presentation allows it to be customized to the specific needs of each audience.

recently turned to such an approach to woo new businesses to its area (see User Solution 10-2). Another popular use of multimedia as a presentation tool is in the design of self-guided tours. Texas A&M opted for this approach when it set up a new visitor center. The center features a multimedia presentation that lets visitors use mice at kiosk stations to get information about the school.

Summary and Key Terms

Database management software is often categorized into two major types: file managers and database management systems.

File Management Software   A **file manager** (*or record management system*) is a software package that enables users to organize data into files and to process the data a single file at a time. In data management, a "plain-vanilla" file is commonly referred to as a **flat file,** meaning that it lacks multidimensionality.

Many file managers employ an onscreen form, or **template,** to help users place data into the records of a file. At any later point, records can be modified or deleted from the file, and new records can be added.

Database Management Systems   A **database management system** (**DBMS**) is a software system that integrates data in storage and provides easy access to them. DBMSs differ from file managers in that they enable immediate access to data that could conceivably span several files.

The data in a DBMS are placed on disk in a **database,** which is an integrated collection of data.

Database management systems come in several types. **Relational database management systems** are the most common type found on microcomputer systems. These systems are so named because they relate data in various database files by common fields in those files.

Users gain access to the data they need through an easy-to-use *retrieval/ update facility* that accompanies the DBMS or through an applications program written with a *programming language facility.* DBMSs also contain *utility programs* such as a data dictionary and a help facility.

One task performed by anyone setting up a database is **data definition**—the process of describing data to the DBMS prior to entering them. The descriptions of these data are used to create **file structures** and a **data dictionary** for the application. Both the file structure and data dictionary contain a **field descriptor** for each field of data in the database.

The process of using the database in some hands-on fashion is called **data manipulation.** Data manipulation encompasses a variety of activities, including the creation of database data, file maintenance, information retrieval (query), reporting, sorting, and calculating. **SQL** (for **Structured Query Language**) is today's de facto standard for information retrieval in relational databases. Database systems are generally one of three common types: relational, hierarchical, and network.

Many microcomputer-oriented DBMSs come with only a single proprietary language that has commands for data definition, retrieval/update, reporting, and programming functions. Large computer systems that use sophisticated DBMSs usually have a special language dedicated to each of these tasks. For example, a **data definition language (DDL)** handles data definition chores, placing key data for applications development and security purposes into a *data dictionary.* A **data manipulation language (DML)** extends the language the programmer normally works with into a database environment. Languages supported by their own DMLs are called **host languages.** A program called a **precompiler** translates DML commands into host-language commands, which in turn can be executed on the regular compilers available at the computer site.

On large computer systems, DBMS packages must also deal with the problem of several users trying to access the database at the same time. To prevent such **concurrent access** problems, most database systems allow users to place a temporary "lock" on certain blocks of data to ensure that no other modifications to these data will be made during their processing.

A DBMS can offer several advantages over traditional flat-file systems. Among these advantages are better information, faster response time, lower operating costs, fewer data storage requirements, better data integrity, and better data management. The biggest disadvantage is cost. Costs are normally incurred in the areas of new hardware and software, training, and conversion. Still another disadvantage is greater vulnerability to failure, because database data are integrated and a problem with key element can render the whole system inactive.

Multimedia Data Management   **Multimedia** data management refers to data management in which a combination of text, graphics, voice, and video data are involved in a computing application. Three promising applications areas for multimedia data management are education and training, entertainment, and presentations.

Review Exercises

1. The two major types of data management packages are _____ and _____ .

Fill-in Questions

2. The onscreen form used to create records in a data management environment is often called a(n) _____ .

3. An integrated collection of data is called a(n) _____ .

4. _____ database management systems are the type of DBMSs typically found on microcomputers.

5. On hierarchical and network database management systems, a knowledgeable professional known as a(n) _____ often is called on to set up the database for users.

6. The problem of _____ access often arises when two or more people try to seize and modify data at the same time.

7. SQL is an acronym for _____ .

8. Applications in which several types of data are intermingled are known as _____ data management.

Match each term with the description that fits best.

Matching Questions

a. precompiler
b. data definition language (DDL)
c. data manipulation
d. retrieval/update language
e. host language
f. data definition

____ 1. A language used to describe database data.

____ 2. A language supported by a DML (data manipulation language).

____ 3. A translator used to translate DML commands into commands that can be input to a regular language translator.

____ 4. A database software product that permits programmers and nonprogrammers to easily retrieve, add, delete, or modify database data with simple, Englishlike commands.

____ 5. Organizing data in the database so that programmers and users have good access to them, data are stored as efficiently as possible, and the database's security is maintained.

____ 6. A task that can be performed through either a retrieval/update language or a programming language.

Discussion Questions

1. What is a file manager?

2. What is a database management system, and how does it differ from a file manager?

3. How do relational database management systems work?

4. What types of data are found in a file structure?

5. What is the difference between data description and data manipulation?

6. How do large database management systems solve the problem of concurrent access?

7. Identify the advantages and disadvantages of database management systems.

8. What is multimedia data management?

Critical Thinking Questions

1. An owner of a small personnel agency is about to purcase a well-known database package to manage a growing client list on a microcomputer system. One of her employees is a computer whiz and has suggested writing the database package himself, to make it better fit the agency's needs. What should the owner do in this situation—say yes, say no, or gather more information?

2. Many people believe that, to the average business, the choice of a particular database management system is much more important than the choice of a particular word processor or a spreadsheet package. What do you think?

3. In the multimedia world of the future, might it be difficult to differentiate a book from a movie? Comment.

Multimedia Computing

It May Revolutionize the Way We Deal with Information

Multimedia computing is a technology that might make an orchestra conductor envious of the ordinary user. Press a button, and screens full of information appear on a computer monitor. Press another, and related video images arise from an onscreen window. Press yet another, and related talk or music emerges out of an attached sound system. You control all of these media, each of which has a plethora of interesting information in the form of text, graphics, video, or sound ready at your beck and call. The possibilities of such a technology, which got started in earnest only in 1987, are almost endless and range from business to entertainment. In this window, we look at some of the environments in which multimedia is currently being applied.

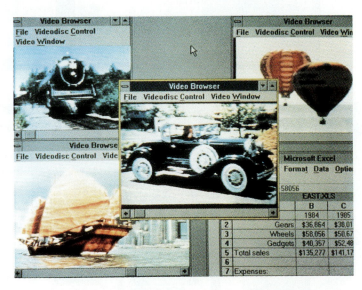

1. Multimedia products enable developers and users to combine the four principal types of data—full-video images, still images, text, and voice—into a single application or use.

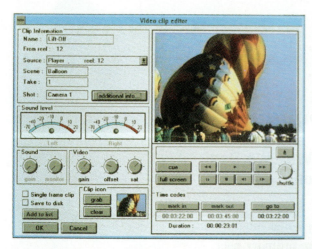

2

Authoring Software

Developers typically begin creating multimedia products with *authoring software*—a special program package designed to put presentations together quickly.

3

2.   Authoring software often contains control panels, like the one featured here, to enable developers to adjust settings as they interweave different types of data.

3–5.   Authoring software is frequently employed by in-house computer professionals—and even end users—to develop important business presentations. Unlike conventional slide shows, multimedia presentations can be customized in real time, enabling the presenter to field questions and explore audience interest areas.

4

5

Authoring Application

At Ben & Jerry's, the Vermont ice-cream maker, authoring software was used to prepare a presentation for an interactive, touch-screen kiosk, used by people who come to tour the plant facilities.

6–7. An early step in the kiosk-presentation development was the *storyboard*, which dictates the order in which images are to be run in a full-video sequence. Individual images can be chosen from a window and dragged to the storyboard with a mouse.

7

6

8. Special effects can be added to provide a smooth transition when a new scene sequence replaces another. In the photo here, the developer can choose between a crossfade, wipe, and a zoom.

8

9

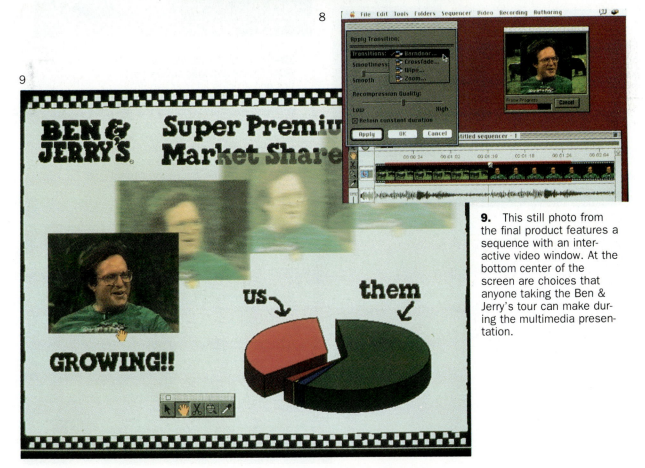

9. This still photo from the final product features a sequence with an interactive video window. At the bottom center of the screen are choices that anyone taking the Ben & Jerry's tour can make during the multimedia presentation.

BEN & JERRY'S® Super Premium Market Share

US them

GROWING!!

Books and Magazines

In the entertainment field, compact disks aren't just for music anymore. Now—if your computer has an optical-disk drive—you can read, watch, and listen to books and magazines on it.

10–13. The *Sports Illustrated CD-ROM Sports Almanac* covers statistics and articles on over two dozen sports, for both the most recent year and previous years. In the *Almanac* and most other interactive books and magazines you can access much more than just text and photos. Short audio and/or video clips kick in when you select certain screen buttons.

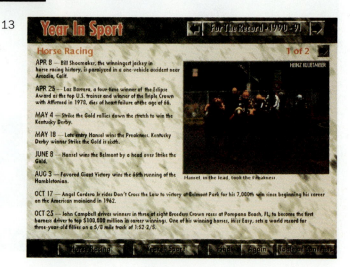

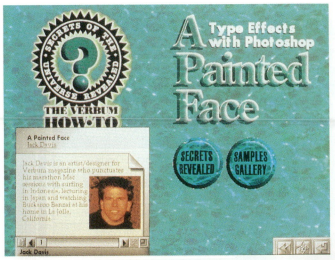

14

15

14–15. *Verbum* magazine is a CD-ROM product targeted to people interested in computer technology. Users can read about specific technologies, listen to roundtable discussions featuring industry authorities, pull up computer-generated art and animated features, listen to computer-generated music, and preview demonstration programs of major software products.

16

Travel and Tourism

In industries such as travel and real estate, multimedia computing provides potential clients the ability to take tours without ever leaving the host computer system.

16. Users can tour the Carribbean by selecting video, audio, and text segments.

INFORMATION SYSTEMS

This module integrates several concepts from earlier chapters, tying together the parts of a computer system that involve hardware, software, data, people, and procedures.

Chapter 11 looks at business information systems. Here you will learn about the principal types of information systems used in organizations today and the roles these systems play.

Chapters 12 and 13 cover systems development and program development in organizations, respectively. In the systems development chapter, we'll address the various ways in which organizations build systems, the types of activities performed in system building, and the kinds of people involved. In the program development chapter, we'll look in depth at applications software development and programming languages. Here, you'll learn about some of the tools used by computer professionals to design and code programs as well as gain an appreciation for what various programming languages do.

Chapter 14, on end-user computing, covers many of the things you should know about computer systems if you decide to acquire one for your own use. Today, unprecedented numbers of people are purchasing their own microcomputer systems or being assigned to use one, making knowledge in this area essential for virtually everyone.

BUSINESS SYSTEMS

11

How do businesspeople use computers to solve problems and spot opportunities? As you'll learn in Chapter 11, it's by building their own decision support systems—personalized information systems that are tailored to an individual's unique decision-making needs.

LEARNING OBJECTIVES

After completing this chapter, you will be able to:

1. Describe several types of computer systems commonly found in business and other environments.

2. Explain how a number of elements discussed in previous chapters fit together into a complete computer system.

3. Explain the role of artificial intelligence in improving the quality of applications software.

Overview

Now that we've covered various types of hardware and software, let's focus on how these combine into complete computer systems in businesses and other organizations. Undoubtedly you've encountered many types of computer systems. When you go to the supermarket, you may see electronic cash registers and various hand-held or laser scanning devices that obviously are parts of some supermarket system. Or, when registering for classes, perhaps you've observed someone at a display terminal checking to see whether a certain class that you want to take is still open or whether you've paid all your bills—apparently a procedure of a registration system. What's more, almost all organizations have accounting systems to help handle their business transactions, and many maintain manufacturing systems that assist in running their factories.

Perhaps hundreds of types of computer systems are in existence today. Many systems in businesses, nonprofit organizations, and government fall into one or more of four categories:

- **TRANSACTION PROCESSING SYSTEMS**   Systems in this category perform record keeping and other accounting tasks that many organizations handle regularly.
- **INFORMATION SYSTEMS**   These systems provide decision makers with predefined types of information on a periodic basis or with capabilities to meet customized information needs.
- **OFFICE SYSTEMS**   These systems cut down on the time-consuming paperwork normally generated in an office and help make office workers more productive.
- **DESIGN AND MANUFACTURING SYSTEMS**   This category of systems includes computers that are used to design and make products and to guide robots in factories.

In the following pages, we'll look more closely at each of these basic types of systems. We'll also explore *artificial intelligence*, which can lend each of these systems powers that we would normally attribute to humans.

Transaction Processing Systems

Virtually every company must support a number of routine operations, most of which involve some form of tedious recordkeeping. These operations, such as payroll and accounts receivable, were some of the earliest commercial applications of computers in organizations and are still among the most important. Because these systems heavily involve processing of business transactions—such as paying employees, recording customer purchases and payments, and recording vendor receipts and payments—they are called **transaction processing systems.** As you'll see in the following pages—and from taking a beginning accounting course—most transaction processing operations are highly interrelated (see also Figure 11-1).

Transaction processing system.
A system that handles an organization's business transactions.

Payroll   *Payroll systems* compute deductions, subtract them from gross earnings, and write paychecks to employees for the remainder. These systems also contain programs that prepare reports for managerial and taxing agencies of

FIGURE 11 – 1

Transaction processing. Transaction processing systems are the backbone of most businesses. They track goods being sold, record payments made for cash or credit, and monitor inventory levels and orders of stock.

the federal, state, and local governments. Many have links to bank systems, where direct deposits are made for firms' employees.

Order Entry   Many organizations handle some type of order processing daily. Customers either call in orders by phone, send in written orders by ordinary mail or by computer, or place orders in person. The systems that record and help manage such transactions are called *order-entry systems*.

For instance, mail-order-catalog firms such as Eddie Bauer, L. L. Bean, and Lands' End process orders daily from customers who want outdoor equipment or clothing. Retailers such as Sears and B. Dalton, who maintain shopping premises, also require order-entry systems, because goods must be ordered by their own stores. Even the airlines' passenger reservations systems have order-entry components, since air and hotel reservations often are made in advance.

Inventory Control   The units of product that a company has in stock to use or sell at a given moment are called its *inventory*. An *inventory control system* keeps track of the number of units of each product in inventory and ensures that reasonable quantities of products are maintained.

The term *inventory* may not necessarily refer to tangible merchandise on a shelf. For example, in airline passenger reservation systems, inventory refers to the seats available for sale on flights. In a college's course registration system, inventory refers to the slots for each class that are still open for enrollment.

User Solution 11–2

A GDSS Helps Insurers

In the insurance field, several photos and forms are often needed to process an accident claim. An adjuster may take a picture of a damaged car and prepare an adjustment form. An estimate and a claim form will also have to be filled out and filed. Gradually, a dossier on each accident will be developed. Many large insurance firms have turned to group decision support systems to make this complex process much simpler. All of these initial documents are read into the computer system with an image scanner and put into a form that can be annotated, processed, and shared electronically by people working over a network in the claims department. The claims-department employees can each in turn call up the file, sign off on certain documents, and add other documents. They can also "meet," using their workstations, to make joint decisions on particular cases. Processing claims in this way can be done faster and more cost effectively, with minimal chance of documents being lost, and with better service to the policyholder, too.

Group decision support system (GDSS).
A decision support system in which several people routinely interact through a computer network to solve common problems. Also sometimes called **workgroup computing.**

Group Decision Support Systems   A relatively recent development in the DSS area has been emergence of the **group decision support system (GDSS).** A GDSS is a decision support system in which several people routinely interact through a computer network in order to solve common problems. In fields such as newspaper publishing, architectural design, insurance, and banking, a GDSS allows workers to share ideas and collaborate on decisions through computer and communications technology. Workers can electronically route their outputs to other workers in the chain and even meet electronically when there is a bottleneck of some sort. An example of this computer-age phenomenon is described in User Solution 11-2. The GDSS is sometimes referred to by the term **workgroup computing.**

Executive information system (EIS).
A decision support system that is tailored to the needs of a specific, top-level individual in an organization.

Executive Information Systems   Executive information systems **(EISs)** are DSSs customized to meet the special needs of individual executives—those people at the highest organizational level. For many years, executives signed checks for billions of dollars worth of computer equipment but had been personally averse to using computers themselves. Now, as computer systems get easier to use and more and more types of information are stored in electronic form, things are changing. Executives in many industries are realizing that it is increasingly difficult to be effective without their own personal desktop systems.

As some executives see it, the business world today is so competitive and fast paced that they need instant access to fresh information. Among executives' favorite applications are using database management systems to access corporate and financial data, using electronic mail systems to streamline contact with subordinates, and using customized spreadsheet programs to display important ratios and trends in a graphical format. Because many executives can't type, many of them require easy-to-learn, easy-to-use graphical user interfaces (see Figure 11-7). With the right type of a system, it simply takes some pointing and, perhaps, a few keystrokes or mouse clicks to get executives what they want in exactly the form they require.

Office Systems

In recent years, computer technology has been applied to the task of increasing productivity in the office. The term **office automation (OA)** describes this trend. Office automation can be achieved through a wide variety of technologies and processing techniques, several of which we discuss in this section.

Word Processing and Desktop Publishing

By far the most widespread of the OA technologies is word processing. As stated in Chapter 8, **word processing** refers to technologies that enable computer systems to automate a variety of typing and document preparation tasks. Today most word processing is accomplished with general-purpose word processing packages used on general-purpose computer systems. Since we already have discussed word processing extensively, we will not go into the details here.

Office automation (OA).
The use of computer-based, office-oriented technologies such as word processing, desktop publishing, electronic mail, video teleconferencing, and the like.

Word processing.
The use of computer technology to create, manipulate, and print text material such as letters, legal contracts, and manuscripts.

FIGURE 11 – 7

Executive information systems (EISs). EISs are DSSs customized to meet the needs of executives, many of whom are not technologically sophisticated. Consequently, EISs are usually characterized by (a) easy-to-use graphic interfaces and (b) simplified procedures for making database queries.

(a)

(b)

Robotics.
The field devoted to the study of robot technology.

One type of CAM that seems to have caught the attention of people everywhere is **robotics,** the study of the design, building, and use of robots. Robots are machines that, with the help of a computer, can mimic a number of human motor activities to perform jobs that are too monotonous or dangerous for their flesh-and-blood counterparts (see Figure 11-12). Some robots can even "see" by means of embedded cameras and "feel" with sensors that permit them to assess the hardness, temperature, and other qualities of objects. The auto industry uses robots to weld and paint cars. Electronics firms employ robots to assemble calculators. Robots help mine coal and build other machines. Robots can represent substantial savings to a corporation, since they don't go on strike, don't need vacations, and don't get sick.

Computer-Integrated Manufacturing (CIM)

Computer-integrated manufacturing (CIM).
The use of technology to tie together CAD, CAM, and other business systems.

Over the last few years serious efforts have been afoot to implement **computer-integrated manufacturing (CIM)** systems. The idea behind CIM is to tie together CAD, CAM, and other business activities (see Figure 11-13 and Feature 11-1).

Here's how CIM might work: A large auto distributorship calls an auto manufacturer to check out the feasibility of changing a styling detail on 500 cars that are to be produced next month. The CAD part of the integrated system checks out the design change to see if it can be done and, also, what types of

F I G U R E   11 – 13

Computer-integrated manufacturing (CIM). CIM enables CAD, CAM, and other business activities to be tied together by computers. In the auto industry, CIM makes it possible to quickly check the effect of a design change on parts inventories, production schedules, and costs.

Virtual Corporations

A new form of business that meets new global challenges

People around the world are getting fussier about their products.

Take eyeglasses and cars. Consumers want to get a new pair of glasses within an hour and want a new car to be custom built and delivered to their dealer within a few days. Put another way, people want a quality product, want it targeted specially to their needs, and want it served up on the spot.

Today, with sophisticated computer systems around, companies can respond to such needs. However, to provide the speed with which consumers are increasingly demanding products, many firms are learning the benefits of forming virtual corporations.

Virtual corporations refer to companies that generally use modern information technology to its fullest and that forge temporary alliances with other state-of-the-art companies—ones established in a related business. The goal is to form a partnership—the virtual corporation, in essence—to deliver product rapidly to consumers. Each partner brings into the alliance the "thing" it does best. Since each firm doesn't have to spend time replicating what its partners are already doing well—foolishly letting the window for opportunity close—attention can be focused on tearing away certain organizational barriers and letting shared employees mingle freely. As soon as the market opportunity has run its course and each company has taken its profits, the partnership dissolves. Ideally, however, the partnership will last for years.

There are many ways that a virtual corporation could be put into use. For instance, a company wanting to produce a new type of vehicle might decide to merely organize and finance the venture, subcontracting all the manufacturing to a company located in a low-wage country. Taking

Virtual corporations. Will high-tech business partnerships be the norm in the 21st century?

such a course of action also saves the first company the cost of building an expensive new plant at home; it sends technology consultants to the low-wage country to advise how to build and/or equip the plant abroad, using less costly labor. Carried to its extreme, virtual corporations could result in countries becoming specialists in a particular phase of the product-development chain—say, design or manufacturing—or in certain industries.

Some experts have argued that virtual corporations may even be able to save manufacturing jobs in countries such as the United States and Canada. To a large extent, the U.S. auto industry has recently become more competitive through a related form of the virtual-corporation concept: computer-integrated manufacturing (CIM). Information technology has enabled auto makers to link up their factory-floor computers with those of their suppliers, dealerships, and engineering designers—thereby resulting in faster supply replenishment, lower inventory costs, quicker assessment of customer needs, and greater customization of product. In the future, the auto makers' design labs may even become independent companies, akin to advertising agencies. What's a car design but a creative concept, anyway?

F e a t u r e   1 1 - 2

Neural-Net Computing

Using artificial intelligence to recognize patterns

Most computing today is preprogrammed number crunching. Whether you are reformatting a document, doing spreadsheet computations, searching through a database, compiling a program, or coloring or rotating graphics images, you are simply executing a predetermined procedure at a high speed. Conventional computers are good at this type of thing. But if you ask them to recognize a handwritten letter, that's a different matter.

This is where neural nets come in. *Neural-net computing* refers to an artificial-intelligence technology in which the human brain's pattern-recognition process is emulated by a computer system. Neural-net systems aren't preprogrammed to provide predictable responses like conventional algorithms. Instead, they are designed to learn by observation.

Neural nets are usually software programs that work on conventional computers. Some research institutions have gone a step further, however, and have developed hardware-based neural nets—that is, computers with circuitry especially designed to solve pattern-recognition problems. This circuitry is often of analog design, in contrast to the digital (binary) circuitry that underlies conventional computers.

Technology taking a bite out of crime. Neural-nets are expected to help.

Neural-net computers translate pattern-recognition processes into small blocks of code that are processed in parallel. These computers simulate a network of hundreds or thousands of interconnected nodes, spanning several layers, that rapidly pass data among each other.

Although neural-net computing is largely a technology of tomorrow, several applications involving neural nets have already begun in earnest. These applications involve handwriting, speech, and image recognition; credit-risk assessment; crime analysis; and stock analysis.

Handwriting, Speech, and Image Recognition Recognition of a person's signature, voice, or face happens so quickly that you scarcely no-

would be expected of a human expert. Today expert systems are successfully used in many fields.

In medicine, for instance, an expert system might be used to incorporate the thinking patterns of some of the world's leading physicians. For example, a system might be given a configuration of symptoms exhibited by a patient. If these symptoms might lead to the diagnosis of a disease that the program knows something about, the program may ask the attending physician for information about specific details. Ultimately, through questioning and checking the patient's condition against a large database of successfully diagnosed cases, the program might draw conclusions that the attending physician might never have reached otherwise—and much more quickly as well.

Expert systems have enormous applications potential in business, where they can be used to capture the knowledge of expert business professionals into an

tice how the underlying process works. Neural nets attempt to emulate this process. Consider character recognition, for instance. The lower levels of the neural net may recognize that a character is composed of curves and straight lines. This information is passed to the next layer, which may attempt to determine the number of curves and lines and how they fit together. Finally, conclusions are passed to a third level, which may recognize the character as a capital "B." If the character can't be recognized, the neural net attempts to learn from the mistake. One financial-services institution is already using such an algorithm to recognize handwritten numerals on checks.

Credit-Risk Assessment Subtle patterns also exist in conventional text data, such as those found at financial institutions. If you were very sharp and studied the records of thousands of people who were granted and denied credit, you might eventually be able to discern which types of people were good credit risks and which types of people were poor ones. Of course, computers can work much faster than humans and can notice patterns that are hardly discernible. Neural nets are currently being applied to solve credit-risk assessment problems at American Express and other companies. Perhaps in the future, use of neural nets will help to avert catastrophes such as the recent U.S. savings and loan crisis.

Crime Analysis Neural nets are expected to offer some assistance in solving crimes. Many crimes, of course, display a pattern, and often this pattern is too subtle to be picked up without computer assistance. New York's Chase Manhattan Bank is currently using neural nets to examine hundreds of thousands of transactions daily and to look for fraudulent ones.

Stock Analysis One exciting neural-net application is a program that examines stock-market data for patterns and helps determine strategies for buying and selling stocks. At Boston-based Fidelity Investments, Brad Lewis—who manages the Disciplined Equity mutual fund—has outperformed the market consistently with a neural-net based computer model he began developing in business school. The model evaluates 180,000 pieces of data nightly to learn how the market is pricing stocks. It then reviews about a dozen characteristics of 2,000 target stocks to detect subtle patterns that are in line with current market valuations. Stocks are then selected by an "attractiveness rating."

Other applications for neural nets in the future abound. In medicine, neural nets may examine detailed records of patients having a specific disease and attempt to uncover an underlying pattern. In quality control, thousands of parts could be studied to uncover subtle structural problems. And, perhaps, the optimal mixture of glue, pulp, and water required to make top-quality paper can be determined with neural nets. Wherever there's a pattern to study, a neural-net application may be useful.

active form and can subsequently be employed to improve decision making within the firm or to train individuals (see Figure 11-14). Today the application of expert systems to the study of business problems is just beginning to be widespread.

Figure 11-15 shows a number of present and proposed applications for expert systems in business. Feature 11-2 describes an AI technology called neural networks, which is now widely used in building many expert systems.

Components of an Expert System Most expert systems consist primarily of two parts: a data part and a software part.

The data part is commonly called a *knowledge base*. The knowledge base is the part of the expert system containing specific facts about the expert area and any rules, or heuristics, the expert system will use to make decisions based

Techniques

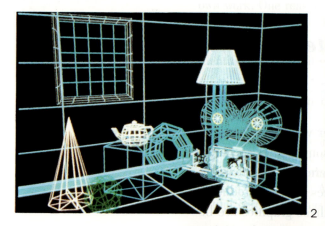

2

3

2–3. Three-dimensional computer graphics often start as wireframe models depicting geometrical shapes. These shapes are then rendered with color and shaded. Because the shapes are mathematically defined, they can easily be resized and rotated into different positions.

4

4. Computer graphics users frequently employ light sources that apply shadows and reflections to models.

5

5. Graphics artists often use the computer to impart special effects. Here, a balloon image is solarized.

6

7

8

9

6–9. Morphing is a technique in which two images are fed to the computer and other images are interpolated between them. Here, a car is morphed into a tiger for an Exxon ad. The opening image in this window is also a morph—between a face and a box—as was the villain-to-mummy sequence in photos 7–9 in Window 1.

10

Decision Support

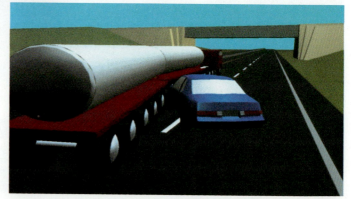

11

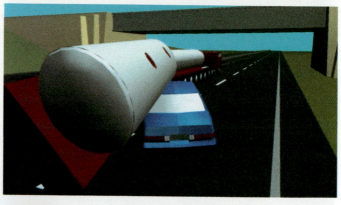

12

13

10–13. Computer graphics techniques are increasingly being brought into the courtroom to recreate accidents and help decide who was at fault.

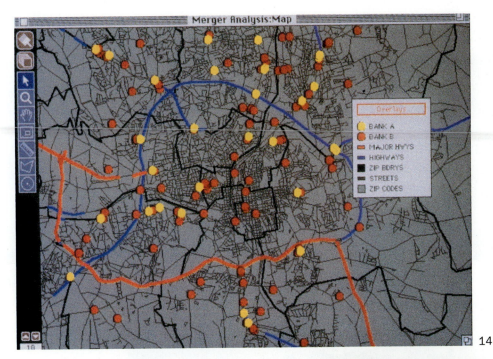

14

14–16. Mapping software is often used to help businesses make decisions. Here, maps are employed to assess the potential impact of two banks merging (photo 14), market penetration in salesperson territories (photo 15), and customer distributions by region (photo 16).

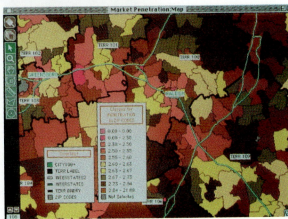

15

16

Architecture

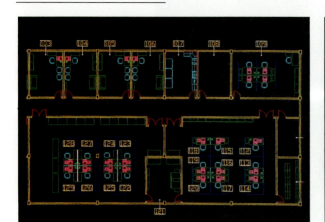

17

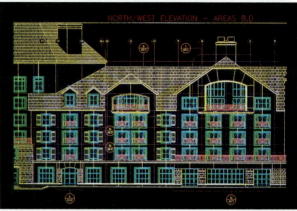

18

17–18. Simple, two-dimensional graphics can be employed for constructing floor plans and elevation drawings.

19

19–20. Site-visualization software enables clients of architectural firms to imagine what an undeveloped site will look like with the structure of their choice on it.

20

21

22

21–22. Because not only a building but also the sun and individual light bulbs can be modeled in three dimensions, architectural clients can see what their proposed home will look like in sunlight or at night—and even in fog or after a snowfall, for that matter.

23

23. Interior modeling, with realistic lighting effects, is a growing area of computer graphics applications. It is also an area where virtual reality is expected to make a big impact soon (see related story in the Tomorrow box in Chapter 2).

Computer Animation

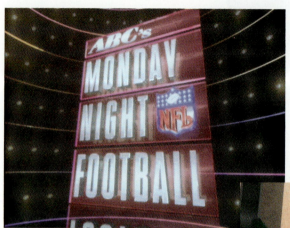

24

25

24. Three-dimensional computer logos that are "toured" in an imaginary space are a familiar sight to anyone watching football or basketball games.

25. Computers have become a popular, cost-effective tool for creating cartoon animations.

26

26–27. This computer-generated commercial for Quaker Oats shows how, through the "magic" of technology, cartoon characters can be photorealistically brought into lifelike settings.

27

28

28–30. Karl Sims' *Panspermia* is a computer animation that is halfway between science fiction and science. A computer model is used to cause intergalactic plants to move in natural ways and to grow and cull themselves based on evolutionary principles.

29

30

SYSTEMS DEVELOPMENT

12

How do organizations set up large computer systems for use in their factories and offices? As Chapter 12 will explain, it's through a process called systems development, in which computer professionals, end users, and management collaborate to methodically weigh alternatives.

OUTLINE

LEARNING OBJECTIVES

After completing this chapter, you will be able to:

1. Explain what a system is.

2. Define the roles of various people and departments in the systems development process.

3. Identify and describe the components of the systems development life cycle (SDLC).

4. Describe several approaches used to develop systems.

Overview

As you saw in Chapter 11, all organizations have various sorts of systems—for example, transaction processing systems, management information systems, office systems, and CAD/CAM systems. Such systems require considerable planning and follow-up effort. The process that includes the planning and implementation of any type of system, whether computerized or not, is called *systems development*.

Unfortunately, because no two organizations are exactly alike and ways of doing things differ among organizations, no sure-fire formula for successful systems development exists. A procedure that works well in one situation may fail in another. These facts notwithstanding, there is a set of general principles, that, if understood, will enhance the likelihood of the system's success. Those principles are the subject of this chapter.

The chapter opens with a general discussion of systems and systems development. From there we turn to the primary responsibilities of the computer professionals who are hired to develop systems in organizations. Then we look at the systems development life cycle—the set of activities that are at the heart of every serious systems-building effort. Chapter 12 concludes with a discussion of the major approaches to systems development.

On Systems

System.
A collection of elements and procedures that interact to accomplish a goal.

A **system** is a collection of elements and procedures that interact to accomplish a goal. A football game, for example, is played according to a system. It consists of a collection of elements (two teams, a playing field, referees) and procedures (the rules of the game) that interact to determine which team is the winner. A transit system is a collection of people, machines, work rules, fares, and schedules that get people from one place to another. Similarly, a computer system is a collection of people, hardware, software, data, and procedures that interact to perform information processing tasks.

The function of many systems, whether manual or computerized, is to keep an organization well managed and running smoothly. Systems are created and altered in response to changing needs within an organization and shifting conditions in its surrounding environment. When problems arise in an existing system or a new system is needed, systems development comes into play. **Systems development** is a process that consists of analyzing an applications environment, designing a new system or making modifications to an old one, acquiring needed hardware and software, and getting the new or modified system to work (see the Tomorrow box).

Systems development.
The ongoing process of improving ways of doing work.

Systems development may be required for many reasons. New laws may call for the collection of data never before assembled. The government may require new data on personnel, for example. The introduction of new technology, especially new computer technology, may prompt the wholesale revision of a system. Or, as is the trend today, a company may decide to convert certain applications into a global, networked environment. These and other kinds of pressure often can bring about major changes in the systems by which work is done in an organization.

T O M O R R O W

Re-Engineering

The High-Tech Equivalent of Putting the Horse before the Cart

In many ways, re-engineering is just old wine in a new bottle. But it's catching businesses and the information processing community by storm. And, who knows? It might become one of the big buzzwords of the 1990s.

Re-engineering is so simple it should have been obvious long ago. Here's the idea behind it: Instead of using computers to automate the way a process has always been performed, with re-engineering you first change the process to the way it really should work, applying computing power to the new system, if appropriate. In other words, rather than blindly going out and buying a new batch of hardware and software to help manufacture widgets faster on an assembly line, consider first that maybe you should be building widgets another way. That or be in the widget-design business instead.

Banc One Mortgage is one company that decided to re-engineer the way it performed its work before applying technology. In the 1980s, Banc One followed the traditional, assembly-line approach to processing loans. A loan application would move from one desk to another, then another, and so on, in a serial fashion. As the bank's mortgage business grew, the loan processing began to take longer and longer. But instead of hiring more people and bringing in more desks and computers, the bank began a team approach to process the loans instead. Today, groups of about 17 employees using networked computers

Re-engineering. The art of rethinking what you're doing before acquiring technology to do it faster.

convene electronically to process all aspects of a particular application at once. The bank says that not only is the job done faster, but workers also become cross-trained in each others' jobs.

On a larger scale, many companies have re-engineered across the board to deal with the new economics of the 1990s. IBM, which began restructuring in the late 1980s, is a prime example. The computer giant went to a "flatter" organization by cutting out layer upon layer of middle management. The move eliminated a lot of expensive beaureaucracy and provided IBM with an ability to respond much more quickly to customers and to changes in the business climate.

It's hard to call re-engineering a trend. Ideally, it should be Step One in every system-building process. No matter how you slice it, looking at re-engineering possibilities up front is the textbook way to think about systems development. Tomorrow's information system is not going to get you very far if you're trying to improve yesterday's process. Put another way, just running a race faster is not going to make you victorious if you're in the wrong race.

Responsibility for Systems Development

In large organizations—with thousands of employees and thousands of operational details to keep track of—there are usually thousands of systems, ranging from personal systems to systems that operate at an enterprisewide level. Deciding which systems best support the direction of the enterprise, and how much

FIGURE 12 – 3

Information center services. The principal goal of an information center is to help end users with their microcomputing needs.

- Training
- Advising and consulting
- System and applications software development
- System and software installation
- Ongoing support for systems and software
- Setting organizational microcomputing standards
- Serving as an information clearinghouse

up the team. Other people on the team might include users, programmers, an outside consultant, a cost accountant, and an auditor.

Information center.
A facility in an organization charged with developing small systems.

Information Center   The **information center** (IC) originally was conceived to help end users in the organization make intelligent choices about the microcomputer hardware and software they needed to perform their jobs better, as well as to promote an orderly acquisition of microcomputing resources within the organization as a whole. Many ICs are staffed primarily with *information center consultants* (systems analysts with special microcomputing skills) and with *trainers*.

ICs often are set up similarly to a typical microcomputer store. A user walks in and talks to a consultant about specific microcomputing needs. Perhaps the user is a sales manager who needs a small decision support system to coordinate the activities of a field sales force. The manager and consultant sit down at one or two computers and experiment with some appropriate, off-the-shelf software. Eventually, through trial and error, they put together a small system.

Figure 12-3 lists typical activities carried out by an information center.

Office automation (OA) area.
The group of computer professionals charged with managing office-related computer activities within the organization.

Office Automation (OA) Area   In many organizations, the **office automation (OA) area** is both the newest and the smallest group within the information systems department. The OA area is responsible for developing a cost-efficient, integrated approach to using office technologies such as electronic document prcessing and electronic mail. Typical duties, which resemble those of the IC, are arranging product demonstrations and helping end users and end-user departments select systems.

Outsourcing

Outsourcing.
The practice by which one company hires another company to do some or all of its information processing activities.

When an organization doesn't have the staff on hand to build or operate a system it needs, an outsourcing option is often chosen. **Outsourcing** involves turning over certain information systems functions to an outside vendor (see Figure 12-4). For instance, a paint manufacturer might have only a PC-based LAN at its headquarters to accept orders. The remote mainframes doing the processing workload are owned and operated by a third-party company skilled at high-volume transaction processing.

Why do companies outsource? A small firm might find it too expensive to keep in-house information systems personnel on hand, given its current work volume. Or a large company might not have the capacity or capital to expand its operations in house, so it may outsource some of them temporarily. And many firms have found it easier to outsource operations in areas in which it's too hard to find or too expensive to hire new personnel. Many firms also turn to an outsourcer when they think that the outsourcer could do the job better or cheaper than they.

Outsourcing may exist in a variety of different forms. In some cases, the outsourcer has its own computer center and supplies terminals and a network to the client. In other cases, the client firm has its own equipment and, needing

Outsourcing. At Andersen Consulting, a leading outsourcer, helping clients solve problems is a multimillion dollar business.

FIGURE 12 – 7

A data flow diagram for a mail-order firm. An order triggers the processes of verification and assembly of the goods ordered, and payment is recorded by accounts receivable.

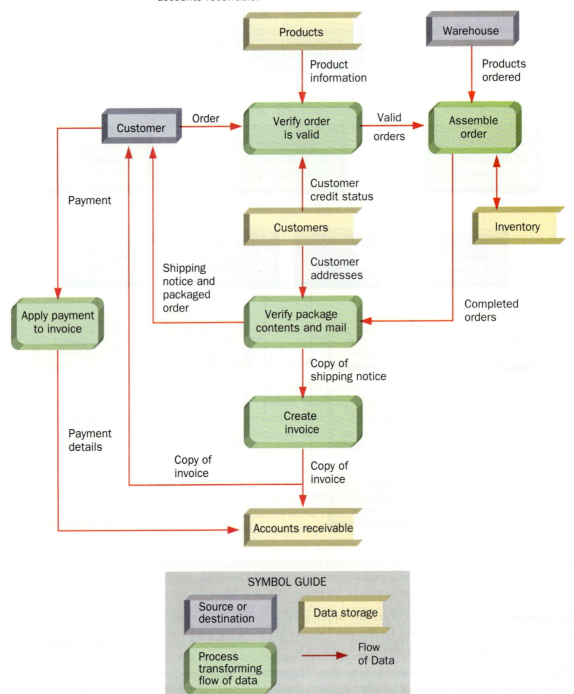

Logical design tools portray how a system works conceptually rather than how it is implemented in particular hardware. Premature commitments to certain types of hardware may limit how the analyst thinks about the system, and some promising possibilities may easily be overlooked. Also, *physical design* tools are available that can be used to show how subsequent hardware choices relate to one another.

■ **CHECKLISTS** *Checklists* are often developed for important matters such as the goals of the system and the information needs of key people in the system. An accounts receivable system, for instance, should have such goals as getting bills out quickly, rapidly informing customers about late payments, and cutting losses due to bad debts. On the other hand, a decision support system that helps teachers advise students should increase the quality of information and decrease the time it takes to develop suitable curricula for students.

Common sense eventually must dictate which type of checklist or diagram is most appropriate for the situation on hand. The principal purpose of these tools is to help the analyst organize thoughts so that conclusions can be drawn about what the system under study should do.

System Design

System design focuses on specifying what the system will look like. The system design phase primarily consists of developing a model of the new system and performing a detailed analysis of benefits and costs.

System design.
The phase of the systems development life cycle in which the parts of a new system and the relation-ships among them are formally established.

Developing A Model of the New System   Once the analyst understands the nature of the design problem, it is usually helpful to draw a number of diagrams of the new system. The data flow diagrams discussed earlier can show how data will flow through the new system.

When designing a system, the analyst must take into account output requirements; input requirements; data access, organization, and storage; processing; system controls; and personnel and procedure specifications. Figure 12-8 covers some of the issues that must be addressed in the design specification. Output considerations are almost always made first, because nothing else can be decided until the benefits and results the system will produce can be determined.

Analyzing Benefits and Costs   Most organizations are acutely sensitive to costs, including computer system costs. Costs include both the initial investment in hardware and software and ongoing costs such as personnel and maintenance. Some benefits can be computed easily by calculating the amount of labor saved, the reduction in paperwork, and so on. These are called *tangible benefits*, because they are easy to quantify in dollars.

Other benefits, such as better service to customers or improved information for decision makers, are more difficult to convert into dollar amounts. These are called *intangible benefits*. Clearly, the existence of intangible benefits makes it more difficult for management to reach firm decisions. On projects with a large number of such benefits, management must ask questions such as, "Are the new services that we can offer to customers worth the $100,000 they will cost us?"

FIGURE 12 – 8

Issues to cover during the system design specification. System design ultimately addresses all major elements of a computer system—hardware, software, data, people, and procedures.

Output Considerations

■ What types of information do users need?

■ How often is this information needed? Annually? Monthly? Daily? On demand?

■ What output devices and media are necessary to provide the required information?

■ How should output be formatted or arranged so that it can easily be understood by users?

Input Considerations

■ What data need to be gathered?

■ How often do data need to be gathered?

■ What input devices and media are required for data collection and input?

Storage Considerations

■ How will data be accessed and therefore organized?

■ What storage capacity is required?

■ How fast must data be accessed?

■ What storage devices are appropriate?

Processing Considerations

■ What type of functionality is required in the software?

■ What type of processing power is required? A mainframe? A minicomputer? A micro-computer?

■ What special processing environments must be considered? A communications network? A database processing environment?

System Controls

■ What measures must be taken to ensure that data are secure from unauthorized use, theft, and natural disasters?

■ What measures must be taken to ensure the accuracy and integrity of data going in and information going out?

■ What measures must be taken to ensure the privacy of individuals represented by the data?

Personnel and Procedures

■ What personnel are needed to run the system?

■ What procedures should be followed on the job?

System acquisition.
The phase of the systems development life cycle in which equipment, software, or services are acquired from vendors.

System Acquisition

Once a system has been designed and the required types of software and hardware have been specified, the analyst must decide from which vendors to buy the necessary components. This decision lies at the heart of the **system acquisition** phase.

RFPs and RFQs   Many organizations formulate their buying or leasing needs by preparing a document called a **request for proposal (RFP).** This document contains a list of technical specifications for equipment and software determined during the system design phase. An RFP may range from a few pages to hundreds, depending on the magnitude and complexity of the acquisition. The RFP is sent to all vendors who might satisfy the organization's needs. In the proposal they send back to the initiating organization, vendors recommend a hardware and/or software solution to solve the problem at hand and specify a price for that solution.

In some cases, an organization knows exactly which hardware and software resources it needs from vendors and is interested only in a quote on a specific list of items. In this case, it sends vendors a document called a **request for quotation (RFQ),** which names those items and asks only for a quote. Thus, an RFP gives a vendor some leeway in making system suggestions, while an RFQ does not.

Evaluating Bids   Once vendors have submitted their bids or quotes in response to the RFP or RFQ, the acquiring organization must decide which bid or quote to accept. Two useful tools for making this choice are vendor rating systems and benchmark tests.

■   **VENDOR RATING SYSTEM**   One system for rating vendors is illustrated in Figure 12-9. In many **vendor rating systems,** such as the one in the figure, important criteria for selecting computer system resources are identified and each is given a weight. In Figure 12-9, for example, the "60" for hardware and "30" for documentation may be loosely interpreted to mean that hardware is twice as important as documentation to this organization. Each vendor that submits an acceptable bid is rated on each criterion, with the associated weight representing the maximum possible score. Then the buyer totals the scores and chooses, if possible, the vendor with the highest

Request for proposal (RFP). A document containing a general description of a system that an organization wishes to acquire.

Request for quotation (RFQ). A document containing a list of specific hardware, software, and services that an organization wishes to acquire.

Vendor rating system. A point-scoring procedure for evaluating competing vendors of computer products or services.

A point-scoring approach for evaluating vendors' bids. Often, but not always, the vendor with the highest point total is the one selected.

Criterion	Weight (Maximum Score)	Vendor 1 Score	Vendor 2 Score
Hardware	60	60	40
Software	80	70	70
Cost	70	50	65
Ease of use	80	70	50
Modularity	50	30	30
Vendor support	50	50	50
Documentation	30	30	20
		360	325

Vendor 1 has highest total score

Feature 12-1

Developing International Systems

Risks to consider along with the incentives

It's no secret that commerce today is becoming an increasingly global affair. If a business is large, it's almost certain to have international branches, affiliates, or partners. And even if an organization is not directly involved in foreign trade, it's likely to somehow be impacted by events taking place in other countries.

Many incentives exist today for engaging in global trade. A company must look beyond national borders to invest its capital in the best markets, to manufacture goods at the lowest cost, and to sell goods and services where the demand or profits are strongest.

But along with the potential benefits an organization may realize with international expansion, a number of extra risks are introduced. Among those systems developers should be aware of are the following:

■ **Language Barriers** In countries where the native language is not English, English-speaking personnel may have difficulty intermingling with foreign nationals who cannot speak English. Fortunately, due to early computing developments in the United States and England in the 1950s and 1960s, English has become the de facto standard language in the global computing community.

■ **Culture** The importance of cultural differences between users and developers cannot be overestimated. People in different parts of the world often react differently to the same set of events. For instance, a system that depends on pinpoint timing and that works in a country with a sense of time urgency may not work in a slower-paced culture where immediacy is not a priority.

■ **Political Climate** In countries where the political environment isn't stable, security issues such as backup and disaster recovery must assume greater importance in the development of systems. Also to be taken into account is the possibility that the entire investment can be lost if a hostile government takes over.

■ **Hardware Availability** Some countries have very little hardware in place and the communications systems are poor. These are two reasons why systems development in the former Soviet Union and Eastern Bloc will probably creep along much slower than many people would initially expect.

■ **Standards** Communications standards vary considerably from one country to another as does the availability and support of specific hardware and software products. When a system spans several countries, it may have to consist of a variety of incompatible products with different replacement cycles.

■ **Laws and Customs** Virtually no two countries have the same sets of laws or customs. An especially knotty problem occurs when a country has laws regulating the flow of data that passes over its borders. For instance, in some countries laws require banks doing business within its borders to also process records locally.

■ **Nationalism** Citizens in many countries resent it when foreign companies bring in their own people to manage local facilities or

total. Although such a rating tool does not guarantee that the best vendor will always have the highest point total, it has the advantage of being simple to apply and relatively objective. If several people are involved in the selection decision, individual biases tend to be "averaged out."

■ **BENCHMARK TEST** After tentatively selecting a vendor, some organizations make their choice conditional on the successful completion of a "test

Workday differences. Time zones can pose a challenge to global systems in the financial-services sector.

key decisions are made from a headquarters that may be continents away. In one case, a South American country forbade a U.S. firm to bring in its own computers because the computers were not manufactured locally.

■ **Economic Differences** In some countries, a dollar will buy less than it does in others. Also, because exchange rates fluctuate, what seems like a good investment one year may come off as a bad one a year later. Communications costs can also vary widely from country to country.

■ **Staffing** Not every country has a ready pool of skilled computer professionals available to press into service. The Middle East and many Third World countries have a shortage of such professionals. Europe, Australia, India, and the former Soviet Union, however, maintain a healthy supply.

■ **Workday Differences** Many countries do not work on a 9-to-5 schedule or look at overtime work in the same way people do in North America. Also, time-zone differences can pose a challenge. In industries such as financial services, informations systems technology can be especially useful for monitoring worldwide operations and alerting people to events that have taken place while they were out of the office or asleep.

drive," or **benchmark test.** Such a test normally consists of running a pilot version of the new system on the hardware and software of the vendor under consideration. To do this, the acquiring organization usually visits the vendor's benchmark testing center and attempts to determine how well the hardware/software configuration will work if installed. However, benchmark tests are expensive and far from foolproof. It's quite possible that

Benchmark test.
A test used to measure computer system performance under typical use conditions prior to purchase.

the pilot system will perform admirably at the benchmark site but the real system, when eventually installed at the site of the acquiring organization, will not.

System Implementation

Once arrangements for delivery of computer resources have been made with one or more vendors, the **system implementation** phase begins. This phase includes all the remaining tasks necessary to make the system operational and successful.

To ensure that the system will be working by a certain date, the analyst must prepare a timetable. One tool for helping with this task is project management software, illustrated in Figure 12-10, which shows how certain implementation activities are related and when they must start and finish.

Implementation consists of many activities, including converting programs and data files from the old system to the new one, debugging converted and new applications programs, documentation, training and establishing ongoing support (see User Solution 12-1), appraising the new system's performance, and

FIGURE 12 – 10

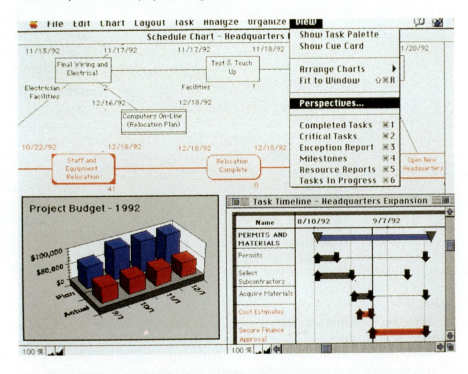

Project management. Large projects are often managed with the assistance of project management software, or "project managers." Many project managers, like the one featured here, provide a project timetable and graphs showing project costs and how pieces of the project fit together.

ongoing maintenance. If the system has been designed well, it should be flexible enough to accommodate changes over a reasonable period of time with minimal disruption. However, if at some point a major change becomes necessary, another system will be needed to replace the current one. At this point, the systems development life cycle—from the preliminary investigation to implementation—will begin all over again.

Approaches to Systems Development

In this section, we'll examine three approaches to systems development: the traditional approach, prototyping, and end-user development.

The Traditional Approach

In the **traditional approach,** the phases of systems development are carried out in a predetermined order: (1) preliminary investigation, (2) systems analysis, (3) system design, (4) system acquisition, and (5) implementation. Each phase is begun only when the one before it is completed. Often, the traditional approach is reserved for the development of large transaction processing systems. Because the traditional approach is usually expensive and extensive, it normally is carried out by knowledgeable professionals—that is, by systems analysts.

Traditional systems development requires system users to consider proposed system plans by looking at detailed diagrams, descriptive reports, and specifications of the proposed new system. The entire system is specified and built before

Traditional approach.
An approach to systems development whereby the five phases of the systems development life cycle are carried out in a predetermined sequence.

F I G U R E   12 – 11

Applications conditions that favor the traditional approach to systems development.

■ The system being developed is one with which there is a great deal of experience.

■ Data, program, and system requirements are easy to identify in advance.

■ Management wants the system completely "spelled out" before giving its approval.

■ The personnel developing the system are much more experienced at building systems using traditional approaches than those using prototyping approaches.

anyone gets to use it or test it. As each phase of development is completed, users "sign off" on the recommendations presented to them by the analyst, indicating their acceptance.

In some organizations, the traditional approach to systems development has recently fallen into disfavor for many systems projects. First, systems often take too long to analyze, design, and implement under the traditional approach. By the time a system is finally put into operation, important new needs that were not part of the original plan may have surfaced. Second, the system developed often turns out to be the wrong one. Managers almost always have difficulty expressing their information needs, and it is not until they begin to use a system that they discover what it is they really need.

Figure 12-11 lists several applications conditions that favor the traditional approach to systems development.

Prototyping

Prototyping.
A systems development alternative whereby a small model, or *prototype*, of the system is built before a full-scale systems development effort is undertaken.

To avoid the potentially expensive disaster that could result from completing every phase of systems development before users ever lay their hands on a system, many analysts have advocated prototyping as a means of systems development. In **prototyping,** the focus is on developing a small model, or *prototype*, of the overall system. Users work with the prototype and suggest modifications. The prototype is then modified, resulting in an improved prototype. As soon as the prototype is refined to the point where higher management feels confident that a larger version of the system will succeed, either the prototype gradually can be expanded or the organization can go full steam ahead with the remaining steps of systems development.

In prototyping, analysis and design generally proceed together in small steps that finally result in a completed system. The idea behind the prototyping process is virtually identical to the one described on page 418 for developing vacation plans. Prototyping is illustrated in Figure 12-12. Figure 12-13 lists several applications conditions that favor the prototyping approach to systems development.

End-User Development

End-user development.
Systems development carried out by the end user.

End-user development is a relatively new form of systems development—one that has evolved from the microcomputing revolution. It is defined as a systems development effort in which the end user is primarily responsible for

F I G U R E   12 – 12

Prototyping. Prototyping is an iterative process; after each prototype is built, the user and analyst try it out together and attempt to improve on it. Eventually, the prototype evolves into a finished system.

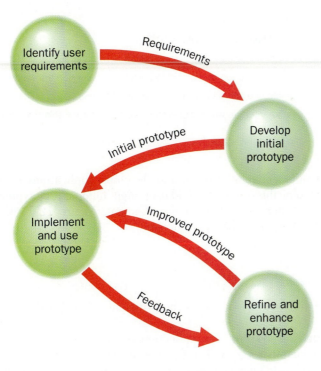

the development of the system. This is in contrast to other types of development discussed here, in which a qualified computer professional, such as a systems analyst, takes charge of the systems development process.

As you might guess, end-user development is feasible only when the system being acquired is relatively inexpensive. A good example is when an end user

F I G U R E   12 – 13

Applications conditions that favor the prototyping approach to systems development.

- Users do not really know what information they need to make decisions.
- User needs are evolving rapidly.
- The risks associated with developing the wrong system are high.
- The system must be developed quickly.
- There is little experience with the type of system being built.
- There are many design alternatives that need to be explored through experience.

FIGURE 12 – 14

Applications conditions that favor end-user development of systems.

- ■ The system affects only an individual or a small department (rather than, say, the entire company).
- ■ The system is relatively inexpensive.
- ■ High levels of security aren't necessary.
- ■ The potential damage associated with system failure is minimal.
- ■ Computer professionals are too overloaded to have time to develop the system.
- ■ The system is simple enough to be built and supported by end users.
- ■ The system does not interfere with other system-building efforts within the organization.

purchases a microcomputer system and develops applications on his or her own. In developing the system, the end user might follow a prototyping approach or a method similar to traditional development. Figure 12-14 lists several conditions that favor end-user development.

Summary and Key Terms

How organizations build systems is the principal subject of this chapter.

On Systems A **system** is a collection of elements and procedures that interact to accomplish a goal. The function of many systems, whether manual or computerized, is to keep an organization well managed and running smoothly.

Systems development is the process that consists of all activities needed to put a new system into place. Systems development may be required for many reasons—for example, changes in government regulations or new computer technology.

Responsibility for Systems Development The *chief information officer*, or someone with a similar title, holds primary responsibility for the overall direction of systems development. The technical details are the responsibility of individual areas—the **data processing area,** the **information center** (IC), and the **office automation (OA) area**—within the **information systems department. Systems analysts** are the people involved most closely with the development of systems from beginning to end. Often, the systems analyst is the **project manager** on the team assigned to the systems project. When a company lacks the in-house expertise, time, or money to do its own information processing, it often turns to an **outsourcing** company to provide system services.

The Systems Development Life Cycle Systems development is often divided into five phases: preliminary investigation, systems analysis, system design, system acquisition, and system implementation. These phases are often collectively referred to as the **systems development life cycle (SDLC),** because they describe a system from the time it is first studied until the time it is put into use. When a new business pressure necessitates a change in a system, the steps of the cycle begin anew.

The first thing the systems analyst does when confronted with a new project assignment is conduct a **preliminary investigation**, or *feasibility study*. This investigation addresses the nature of the problem under study, the potential scope of the systems development effort, the possible solutions, and the costs and benefits of these solutions.

Next, the **systems analysis** phase begins. During this phase, the main objectives are to study the application in depth (to find out what work is being done), to assess the needs of users, and to prepare a list of specific requirements that the new system must meet. These objectives are accomplished through fact collection and analysis. Four useful sources of factual information are written documents, questionnaires, interviews, and observation. A number of tools can help with fact analysis, including **data flow diagrams** and *checklists*.

The **system design** phase of systems development consists of developing a model of the new system and performing a detailed analysis of benefits and costs.

Once a system has been designed and the required types of software and hardware have been specified, the analyst must decide from which vendors to buy the necessary components. This decision lies at the heart of the **system acquisition** phase.

Many organizations formulate their buying or leasing needs by preparing a document called a **request for proposal (RFP).** This document lists the technical specifications for equipment and software determined during the system design phase. In some cases, an organization knows exactly which hardware and software resources it needs from vendors and is interested only in a quote on a specific list of items. In this case, it sends vendors a document called a **request for quotation (RFQ).**

Once vendors have responded to the RFP or RFQ, the organization must choose among the vendor alternatives. Two useful tools for making such a choice are a vendor rating system and a benchmark test. In most **vendor rating systems,** important criteria for selecting computer system resources are identified and weighted. Information systems personnel then rate each vendor on each criterion. A **benchmark test** normally consists of running a pilot version of the new system on the hardware and software of the vendors under consideration.

Once arrangements have been made with one or more vendors for delivery of computer resources, the **system implementation** phase begins. This phase includes all the remaining tasks that are necessary to make the system successfully operational, including conversion of files, debugging, training, and performance appraisal.

Approaches to Systems Development   In the **traditional approach** to systems development, the phases of the SDLC are carried out in a predetermined order—preliminary investigation, analysis, design, acquisition, and implementation. The focus in **prototyping** is on developing small models, or *prototypes*, of the target system in a series of graduated steps. **End-user development** is a systems development approach in which the user is primarily responsible for building the system. This is in contrast to other types of development, in which a qualified computer professional, such as a systems analyst, takes charge of the systems development process.

derived from these specifications must address all the tasks that programs must do as well as how to organize or sequence these tasks when coding programs. Only when the design is complete does the next stage—the actual program coding—begin.

Program Design Tools

Program design tools are essentially planning tools. They consist of various kinds of diagrams, charts, and tables that outline either the organization of program tasks or the steps the program will follow. Once a program has been coded and implemented, program design tools serve as excellent documentation.

Program Flowcharts

Program flowchart.
A visual design tool showing step by step how a computer program will process data.

Program flowcharts use *geometric symbols,* such as those in Figure 13-1, and familiar *relational symbols,* such as those in Figure 13-2, to graphically portray the sequence of steps involved in a program. The steps in a flowchart occur in

dustry tends to promote from within the technical ranks. So people who become managers often have only technical backgrounds and very few management skills. Says Yourdon, "Managing people wasn't such a big problem when, for example, Apple's software was being written by one guy in a garage. But if you look at Apple's System 7 [operating system], which consisted of some 200 people working together, you face the same kind of management challenge that Boeing does when managing a team of 200 engineers that are building a 747."*

One might also point a finger at management as regards the quality issue. The United States puts a premium on getting products out the door quickly and generating a steady stream of profits in the short term. Consequently, products are often knowingly released with a large number of bugs—bugs that perhaps should have been ironed out.

The greatest threat to U.S. software dominance may come from countries like India, the Philippines, and the Arab nations—places where salaries are comparatively low, where English is widely spoken, and where the potential for networking is strong. While countries in the former Soviet Union have excellent technicians, they have a shortage of hardware and the communications systems are poor. That makes it difficult to set up the LANs and WANs needed to become a software powerhouse. Also, the notions of business competition and capitalism are still relatively new in that part of the world.

All of these observations pose several interesting possibilities for the future. Will other countries grab the software mantle from the U.S.? Will domestic firms increasingly develop branches in foreign countries to write their software, taking even more jobs away from home?

Not to worry, say some skeptics. They claim that since the United States is still by far the dominant user of the world's software, it is unlikely that such an important resource will be ported overseas. Managers have suffered so many disappointments from software promises in the past, say some, that the idea that software can be developed more successfully thousands of miles away is too much to swallow. Others point out cultural differences and the enormous distances between users and foreign programmers as being insurmountable barriers. They argue it requires a giant leap of faith to assume, for instance, that a programmer in New Delhi will be able to respond effectively to system requests from a wholesaler in Des Moines.

What scenario will eventually evolve? Stay tuned to the year 2010.

*From an interview with Edward Yourdon reported in *Computer News Link*, Summer, 1992.

the same logical sequence that their corresponding program statements follow in the program. To help you understand what these symbols mean and see how to use them, let's consider an example.

Scanning a File for Employees with Certain Characteristics

A common activity in information processing is scanning an employee file for people with certain characteristics. Suppose, for example, a company's personnel department wants a printed list of all employees with computer experience and at least five years of company service. A flowchart that shows how to accomplish this task and also totals the number of employees who meet these criteria is shown in Figure 13-3.

This particular flowchart uses five symbols: start/stop, processing, decision, connector, and input/output. The lines with arrows that link the symbols are called *flowlines;* they indicate the flow of logic in the flowchart.

Every flowchart begins and ends with an oval-shaped *start/stop symbol.* The first of these symbols in the program contains the word *Start,* and the last contains the word *Stop.* The diamond-shaped *decision symbol* always indicates

FIGURE 13 - 5

Pseudocode for solving the employee file problem of Figure 13-3. The problem requires printing the names of all people in an employee file with computer experience and at least five years of company service. A count of the number of such people is also required as output.

```
Start
Counter = 0
Read a record
DOWHILE there are more records to process
   IF computer experience
      IF company service ≥ 5 years
         Print employee name
         Increment counter
      ELSE
         Next statement
      END IF
   ELSE
      Next statement
   END IF
   Read another record
END DO
Print counter
Stop
```

FIGURE 13 - 6

Some rules for pseudocode. In addition to the rules shown here governing program control structures, pseudocode often begins with the keyword *Start* and ends with the keyword *Stop*.

Sequence Control Structure

```
BEGIN processing task
   Processing steps
END processing task
```

The steps in the sequence structure are normally written in lowercase letters. If the steps make up a well-defined block of code, they should be preceded by the keywords BEGIN and END.

Selection Control Structure

```
IF condition
   Processing steps
ELSE
   Processing steps
END IF
```

The keywords IF, ELSE, and END IF are always capitalized and tiered. The condition and processing steps normally are written in lowercase letters. The processing steps are indented from the keywords in the manner illustrated.

Loop (DOWHILE and DOUNTIL)
Control Structures

```
DOWHILE condition        DOUNTIL condition
   Processing steps          Processing steps
END DO                   END DO
```

The keywords DOWHILE (or DOUNTIL) and END DO are always capitalized and tiered. The condition and processing steps follow the same lowercase convention and indentation rules as the selection control structure.

Pseudocode looks more like a program than a flowchart. In fact, it's often easier to code a program from pseudocode than from a flowchart, because the former provides a codelike outline of the processing to take place. As a result, the program designer has more control over the end product—the program itself. Also unlike a flowchart, pseudocode is relatively easy to modify and can be embedded into the program as comments. However, flowcharts, being visual, are sometimes better than pseudocode for designing logically complex problems.

There are no standard rules for writing pseudocode, but Figure 13-6 describes one set of rules that has a wide following. Note that all words relating to the three control structures of structural programming are capitalized and form a "sandwich" around other processing steps, which are indented. As Figure 13-5 shows, indentation is also used for readability. The keywords *Start* and *Stop* are often used to begin and end pseudocode, respectively.

Action Diagrams   Pseudocode is now being widely employed in the creation of **action diagrams,** a tool used to develop applications programs rapidly while online to the CPU. Action diagrams are composed of brackets into which pseudocodelike statements are written (see Figure 13-7). These statements,

Action diagram.
A programming tool that helps programmers code structured programs.

An action diagram. Action diagrams, which are created and modified with a special editor, are used to design and code pseudocodelike programs that are capable of being executed.

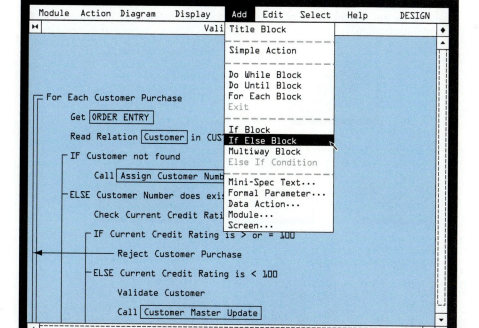

from which the computer is automatically able to develop executable code, are usually created with an *action-diagram editor.* Each control structure used in the diagram—sequence, selection, looping, or case—has its own set of brackets.

When the programmer signals that a particular control structure is to be used, the action-diagram editor creates both the appropriate pseudocode keywords and brackets. As programmers provide various conditions or field names at certain places within the brackets, the editor checks to see that the code is both valid and consistent with the existing code for the application. It does the latter by referring to the appropriate entries in the application's active data dictionary. If there is a problem, the editor will issue a warning or error message. Once an action diagram has been completed, it is automatically translated into executable code with a *code generator.* Action diagrams are an example of CASE tools, which are covered at the end of the chapter.

Structure Charts

Structure chart.
A program design tool that shows the hierarchical relationship between program modules.

Structure charts, unlike flowcharts and pseudocode, depict the overall organization of a program but not the specific, step-by-step processing logic. They show how the individual program segments, or modules, are defined and how they relate to one another. Each module may consist of one or more fundamental control structures.

FIGURE 13 – 8

Structure charts. This program-design technique subdivides a program into individual modules, each of which represents a well-defined processing task. The modules are then arranged hierarchically in a top-down fashion, as illustrated here for a payroll application.

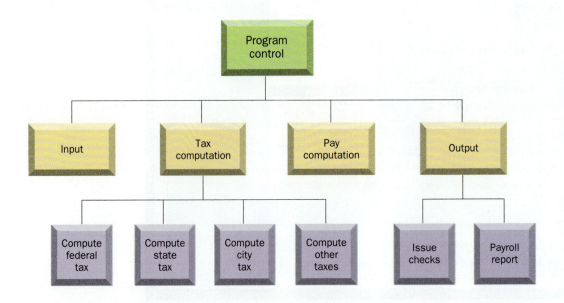

A typical structure chart, with its several rows of boxes connected by lines, looks like a corporate organization chart. Each box represents a program *module*—that is, a set of logically related operations that perform a well-defined task. The modules in the upper rows serve control functions, directing the program to process modules under them as appropriate. The modules in the lower boxes serve specific processing functions. These modules do all the program "work." The lines connecting the boxes indicate the relationship between higher-level and lower-level modules. Figure 13-8 is a structure chart for a payroll application.

Structure charts commonly embody a top-down design. **Top-down design** indicates that modules are conceptualized first at the highest levels of the hierarchy and then at progressively lower levels.

Top-down design.
A structured design philosophy whereby a program or system is subdivided into well-defined modules and organized into a hierarchy.

Programming Languages

An important decision that must be made during the development of a program is the selection of a programming language. A **programming language** is a set of rules used to write instructions to the computer. Many users and organizations code the bulk of their applications in one or two prespecified languages, so this decision normally is very straightforward.

Programming languages are commonly divided into three classes: low-level, high-level, and very-high-level (fourth-generation) languages.

Programming language.
A set of rules used to write computer programs.

Low-Level Languages

The earliest programming languages—machine and assembly languages—are called **low-level languages** because programmers who code in them must write instructions at the finest level of detail: the base level of the machine. In both machine languages and assembly languages each line of code corresponds to a single action of the computer system.

Virtually no one writes machine-language programs anymore, which consist of strings of 0s and 1s. Nonetheless, all programs must automatically be translated into machine language (by, say, a compiler or interpreter) before they are executed.

Assembly languages were developed to replace the 0s and 1s of machine language with symbols that are easier to understand and remember. The big advantage of assembly-language programs is executional efficiency: they're fast and consume little storage compared with their higher-level counterparts. Unfortunately, assembly-language programs take longer to write and maintain than programs written in higher-level languages.

Low-level language.
A highly detailed, machine-dependent programming language.

Assembly language.
A low-level programming language that uses mnemonic codes in place of the 0s and 1s of machine language.

High-Level Languages

High-level languages differ from their low-level predecessors in that they require less coding detail and make programs easier to write. Included in this class are what have come to be known as "third-generation" programming languages—BASIC, COBOL, Pascal, C, FORTRAN, PL/1, APL, and many others. A number of high-level languages that one commonly finds in computing environments are briefly discussed next.

High-level language.
The class of programming languages that includes BASIC, COBOL, C, FORTRAN, and Pascal.

FIGURE 13-9

A sample BASIC program and its output. This program is designed to accept as input the name of a product, its unit selling price, and the number of units sold and to output this information along with the total dollar value of sales.

(a) BASIC program

```
10      REM PROGRAM TO COMPUTE SALES
20      REM AUTHOR - C.S. PARKER
30      PRINT "    DESCRIPTION         PRICE        UNITS       TOTAL VALUE"
40      A$="\                  \    $###.##       #,###       $###,###"
50      READ ITEM$, PRICE, UNITS
60      WHILE ITEM$ < > "LAST RECORD"
70        VALUE = PRICE * UNITS
80        PRINT USING A$; ITEM$, PRICE, UNITS, VALUE
90        READ ITEM$, PRICE, UNITS
100     WEND
110     DATA "SMALL WIDGETS",150,100
120     DATA "LARGE SKY HOOKS",200,50
130     DATA "BLIVETS",100,3000
140     DATA "LAST RECORD",0,0
150     END
```

(b) Output from the program

```
DESCRIPTION                  PRICE         UNITS          TOTAL VALUE
SMALL WIDGETS               $150.00         100           $ 15,000
LARGE SKY HOOKS             $200.00          50           $ 10,000
BLIVETS                     $100.00       3,000           $300,000
```

BASIC.
An easy-to-learn, high-level programming language developed at Dartmouth College in the 1960s.

BASIC   BASIC (Beginner's All-purpose Symbolic Instruction Code) was designed to meet the need for an easy-to-learn beginner's language that would work in a "friendly," nonfrustrating programming environment. Over the years, it has evolved into one of the most popular and widely available programming languages. Because it is easy to learn and use, and because the storage requirements for its language translator are small, BASIC works well on almost all microcomputers. A BASIC program is illustrated in Figure 13-9.

Some experts think that BASIC's chief strength—ease of learning and use—is also its major drawback. Because beginners can get started quickly, they sometimes start off on the wrong foot by sacrificing good programming habits for quick results. Many versions of BASIC support unstructured, trial-and-error coding, so it's easy to write confusing, poorly organized programs.

COBOL.
A high-level programming language developed for transaction processing applications.

COBOL   COBOL (COmmon Business-Oriented Language) is the principal transaction processing language in use today. Currently, some 70 to 80 percent of transaction processing applications on mainframes in large organizations are coded in COBOL. Not too long ago, use of COBOL was restricted almost exclusively to large computer systems. Today, however, with many programmers developing mainframe-based applications on microcomputer workstations, microcomputer-based COBOL is a fast-growing trend. A COBOL program is shown in Figure 13-10. The use of a graphical user interface employed with microcomputer-based COBOL-program development is shown in Figure 13-11.

A sample COBOL program and its output. This program solves the same sales problem as the BASIC program in Figure 13–9.

FIGURE 13 – 10

(a) COBOL program

```
IDENTIFICATION DIVISION.
   PROGRAM-ID. SALES.
   AUTHOR. PARKER.

ENVIRONMENT DIVISION.
CONFIGURATION SECTION.
   SOURCE-COMPUTER. VS9.
   OBJECT-COMPUTER. VS9.
INPUT-OUTPUT SECTION.
   FILE-CONTROL.
      SELECT DISKFILE ASSIGN TO DISK-A1F2-V.
      SELECT PRINTFILE ASSIGN TO SYSLST.
DATA DIVISION.
FILE SECTION.
FD   DISKFILE
     LABEL RECORDS ARE STANDARD.
01   DISKREC.
     05 PART-DESCRIPTION-IN      PIC X(20).
     05 PRICE-IN                 PIC 999.
     05 UNITS-SOLD-IN            PIC 9(5).
FD   PRINTFILE
     LABEL RECORDS ARE OMITTED.
01   PRINTLINE                   PIC X(120).
WORKING-STORAGE SECTION.
01   FLAGS.
     05 WS-END-OF-FILE.          PIC X(3) VALUE 'NO'.
01   HEADING-LINE.
     05 FILLER                   PIC X(9)  VALUE SPACES.
     05 FILLER                   PIC X(11) VALUE 'DESCRIPTION'.
     05 FILLER                   PIC X(10) VALUE SPACES.
     05 FILLER                   PIC X(5)  VALUE 'PRICE'.
     05 FILLER                   PIC X(7)  VALUE SPACES.
     05 FILLER                   PIC X(5)  VALUE 'UNITS'.
     05 FILLER                   PIC X(4)  VALUE SPACES.
     05 FILLER                   PIC X(11) VALUE 'TOTAL VALUE'.
01   DETAIL-LINE.
     05 FILLER                   PIC X(5)  VALUE SPACES.
     05 PART-DESCRIPTION-OUT     PIC X(20).
     05 FILLER                   PIC X(4)  VALUE SPACES.
     05 PRICE-OUT                PIC $ZZ9.99.
     05 FILLER                   PIC X(5)  VALUE SPACES.
     05 UNITS-SOLD-OUT           PIC ZZ,ZZ9.
     05 FILLER                   PIC X(5)  VALUE SPACES.
     05 SALES-VALUE              PIC $ZZZ,ZZ9.

PROCEDURE DIVISION.
010-HOUSEKEEPING.
     OPEN INPUT DISKFILE
          OUTPUT PRINTFILE.
     READ DISKFILE
          AT END MOVE 'YES' TO WS-END-OF-FILE.
     PERFORM 020-HEADINGS.
     PERFORM 030-PROCESSIT
          UNTIL WS-END-OF-FILE = 'YES'.
     CLOSE DISKFILE
          PRINTFILE.
     STOP RUN.
020-HEADINGS.
     WRITE PRINTLINE FROM HEADING-LINE
          AFTER ADVANCING 1 LINE.
```

CONTINUED

FIGURE 13-10 (CONTINUED)

```
030-PROCESSIT.
    MULTIPLY    UNITS-SOLD-IN
         BY     PRICE-IN
         GIVING SALES-VALUE.
    MOVE PART-DESCRIPTION-IN TO PART-DESCRIPTION-OUT.
    MOVE PRICE-IN             TO PRICE-OUT.
    MOVE UNITS-SOLD-IN        TO UNITS-SOLD-OUT.
    WRITE PRINTLINE FROM DETAIL-LINE
         AFTER ADVANCING 1 LINE.
    READ DISKFILE
         AT END MOVE 'YES' TO WS-END-OF-FILE.
```

(b) Output from the program

DESCRIPTION	PRICE	UNITS	TOTAL VALUE
SMALL WIDGETS	$150.00	100	$ 15,000
LARGE SKY HOOKS	$200.00	50	$ 10,000
BLIVETS	$100.00	3,000	$300,000

Many features differentiate COBOL from other languages. Almost all of them—including machine independence, self-documentation, and detailed input/output specifications—relate to COBOL's business transaction processing focus. But because COBOL programs use long, Englishlike names and specify formats in fine detail, they tend to be lengthy. Since lengthy programs take time

F I G U R E   1 3 – 1 1

Microcomputer-based COBOL. Because display terminals connected to mainframes often lack color and graphical user interfaces, many programmers prefer developing mainframe-based COBOL applications on microcomputer workstations.

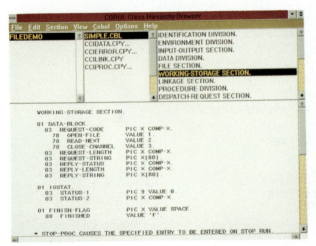
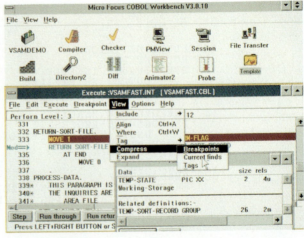

FIGURE 13 – 12

A sample Pascal program and its output. This program solves the same sales problem as the BASIC program in Figure 13–9.

(a) Pascal program

```
PROGRAM SALES (INPUT, OUTPUT);
(* PROGRAM TO COMPUTE SALES *)
(* AUTHOR -- C. S. PARKER *)

VAR   UNITS, INDEX        :INTEGER;
      PRICE, TOTAL        :REAL;
      PART                :ARRAY [1..20] OF CHAR;

BEGIN
WRITELIN ('     DESCRIPTION         PRICE        UNITS       TOTAL VALUE ');
FOR INDEX := 1 TO 20 DO
  READ (PART[INDEX]);
  READLN (PRICE, UNITS);
WHILE NOT EOF DO
    BEGIN
    TOTAL := PRICE * UNITS;
    FOR INDEX := 1 TO 20 DO
      WRITE (PART[INDEX]);
      WRITELIN ('       $', PRICE:6:2, UNITS:11,'      $', TOTAL:9:2);
    FOR INDEX := 1 TO 20 DO
      READ (PART [INDEX]);
      READLN (PRICE, UNITS);
    END;
END.
```

(b) Output from the program

DESCRIPTION	PRICE	UNITS	TOTAL VALUE
SMALL WIDGETS	$150.00	100	$ 15,000
LARGE SKY HOOKS	$200.00	50	$ 10,000
BLIVETS	$100.00	3,000	$300,000

to develop and maintain, COBOL is partly responsible for applications backlogs in many companies. In such firms, it often takes two to four years from the time an application is first approved until it is coded. (This has led some companies to adopt easier-to-code fourth-generation languages, which we'll discuss later in the chapter.) But with millions of dollars invested in COBOL programs and thousands of programmers versed in COBOL use, the language will likely endure for many more years. Despite the many complaints that COBOL is old-fashioned, cumbersome, and inelegant, if you're interested in making money as an applications programmer, COBOL is still clearly one of your best bets.

Pascal   Pascal, named after the mathematician Blaise Pascal, was created primarily to fill the need for a teaching vehicle that would encourage structured programming. Today, Pascal is widely used in academia as a model for how a programming language should be designed. A Pascal program is shown in Figure 13-12.

Although BASIC remains a strong favorite among beginners, Pascal is far superior to most versions of BASIC (and even COBOL) in its structured program-

Pascal.
A structured, high-level programming language that is often used to teach programming.

F e a t u r e   1 3 – 3

Beta Testing

How commercial developers get users into the act

Before the PC became a regular fixture, developing commercial software was a relatively simple process. A software vendor wrote a program, tested it internally, and then released it for general use. But times have changed.

In recent years, with the possible configurations of equipment numbering in the thousands, it is impossible to fully test software in house. So software developers have turned to the actual product users to serve as guinea pigs through a process commonly known as *beta testing*. To test Windows 3.1 and OS/2 Version 2.0, for instance, Microsoft and IBM each sent out preliminary copies of their respective software—called "beta versions"—to over 25,000 users.

Beta testing is usually done in waves. The first beta version may go to only a few dozen hard-

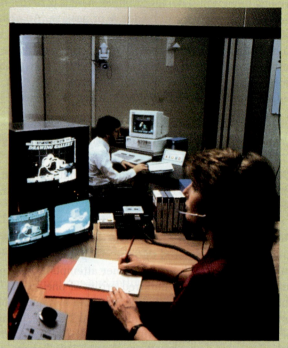

Usability lab. Observing users firsthand, before the software gets out the door.

releases, new equipment announcements, and changes in the way business is conducted.

Program maintenance is costly to organizations. It has been estimated that many organizations spend well over half of their programming time just maintaining existing applications programs. One of the major reasons why such tools as coding standards, fourth-generation languages, reusable code, and data dictionaries are so popular today is because these tools can result in lower maintenance costs.

Program Documentation

Documentation.
A detailed written description of a program, procedure, or system.

Program **documentation** includes manuals that enable users, maintenance programmers, and operators to interact successfully with a program. If you've ever had the frustration of trying to get something to work from poorly written instructions, you can appreciate how valuable good documentation can be.

User documentation normally consists of a user's manual. This manual should provide instructions for running the program, a description of language commands, several examples of situations the end user is likely to encounter, and a troubleshooting guide to help with difficulties.

Programmer documentation usually consists of any tools that will simplify maintenance of the program. These might include a program narrative, design

core users, the subsequent version may go to a couple of hundred users, and so on. Several thousand users may test the last version, since that's the one the developer goes with before making final adjustments to the product.

Beta testing serves a variety of purposes. First and foremost it samples the software over the numerous hardware platforms collectively owned by the user base. Beta testing can also save time and money when the final release is shipped, because the developer picks up valuable knowledge on how to inform users of upgrades. And—although few vendors would "fess up" to the fact—beta testing is a good vehicle for marketing a new product to consumers and for getting them excited about it prior to shipment.

Unfortunately for you interested testers out there, the compensation is small for beta testing while the expectations are large. Often, testers receive a free copy of the package when it's released and maybe some promotional items, such as a T-shirt and mug. The vendor, on the other hand, usually expects some type of reporting on a regular basis.

Beta testing is not in any way a substitute for in-house testing. Users are often busy people who have regular jobs. Understandably, they typically won't have the time to give the beta test their best shot. According to one industry consultant who specializes in new information technology, it is not unusual for only ten percent of the beta testers to actually load and use the programs they are sent.

Many companies will also test software long before the beta test. Some of the largest software developers have usability labs that first put the software through a "reality check," to see if users understand the package (see photo). The lab may contain one-way mirrors as well as experienced trainers and pyschologists that can recognize user confusion when they see it. Often, even programmers are invited in to see how users react to their work. Usually monitored are such indicators as the amount of time it takes to do a task, the number of keystrokes and errors made, the types of keystrokes and errors made, and if and how the user employed a mouse.

tools such as flowcharts and structure charts, a listing of the program, and a description of inputs and outputs. There should also be a set of procedures to help programmers test the program.

Operator documentation includes manuals that assist machine operators in setting up hardware devices, learning the ins and outs of successful hardware operation, and diagnosing machine malfunctions. Operator documentation is machine-dependent, and, unless you have a good grounding in computer fundamentals, it can be difficult to read through.

Quality Assurance

Quality assurance, as regards applications development, refers to the process of making sure quality programs are written in a quality way. The quality assurance function in many firms is carried out by a staff that's charged with making an independent, unbiased audit of program-development operations.

A major focus in quality assurance is on the outputs produced by programs. Not only are outputs checked for accuracy, but also for completeness, timeliness, relevance, and understandability. Furthermore, outputs are compared against original user requests to make sure programs are doing exactly what they are supposed to do—serving key user needs. System messages to the user are also evaluated to ensure programs are easy to use.

Quality assurance.
The process of making sure quality programs are written in a quality way.

User Solution 13–1

Developing A Small System in Record Time

To help its clients get an understanding of how quality is defined around the world, Ernst & Young, a New York-based accounting and consulting firm, sent hundreds of people a questionnaire to be filled out by hand. When the surveys were completed and returned, the firm out-sourced the work of keying the data into the computer and summarizing it. The outsourcer used Borland International's ObjectVision—a CASE product that has both a forms generator and a database—to quickly develop a screen form that looked like the ones that were mailed out and to report results. The form made it easy for the hefty task of inputting data to be done by temporary workers. ObjectVision can also be used to fill out forms directly on the computer, bypassing the need to rekey data and forcing survey participants to answer all survey questions.

Program development activities are another major target in the quality-assurance effort. Here, it is important to ascertain that programs have been developed using acceptable design and coding standards and that they have been properly tested and documented.

Quality-assurance specialists also look closely at program and system security. It is critical that programs and their data be secure from tampering and unauthorized use and that proper program controls be in place to safeguard against errors.

Computer-Aided Software Engineering (CASE)

Software development has never been an easy process. In fact, a partner at Arthur Andersen & Co. recently estimated that the average business applications program takes some 32,000 hours to develop from start to finish—an effort worthy of a team of three dozen programmers working for almost three years. And that represents only the programs that get finished! No wonder managers are looking for a better way to get programs developed.

In the last dozen years, a number of solutions have surfaced. Among the most promising are **CASE (computer-aided software engineering)** tools. The objective of CASE tools is automating one or more stages of applications software development. Although CASE is in its infancy now and has numerous bugs to be worked out, many people believe that most commercial software will be developed through a CASE-type approach at a not-too-distant future point.

Many of the CASE products now offered in the marketplace are called *software engineering workbenches.* Like a carpenter's workbench, which comprises a

Computer-aided software engineering (CASE). Program products that automate systems and program development activities.

number of the tools of the carpentry trade—hammers, saws, chisels, drill bits, and the like—software engineering workbenches contain a number of design, programming, and maintenance tools that get software products developed faster. For instance, such a workbench might consist of an action-diagram editor, a fourth-generation language, a code generator, a feature that facilitates the development of reusable code libraries, an active data dictionary, and tools that help turn unstructured programs into structured ones (see Figure 13-17). The specific tools included in the workbench vary from one vendor to another.

No company has yet developed an everything-but-the-kitchen-sink CASE package, the panacea that will cure every company's applications software development headaches. Consequently, an organization may have to shop around for several CASE products that will meet its needs collectively. This is easier said than done; many CASE tools are incompatible with one another and may not interface well with other proprietary software products that the organization is using. Fortunately, CASE vendors realize this and currently are attempting to forge alliances with other vendors to establish standards that will increase CASE applicability. Currently the most successful product in the CASE marketplace is Index Technology Corporation's Excelerator, a PC-based workbench product targeted primarily to systems analysis and design and to documentation. User Solution 13-1 describes one company's choice of Borland International's ObjectVision CASE tool to meet the needs of a particular application.

FIGURE 13 – 17

A CASE package. CASE products make it possible to develop applications software faster, with fewer coding mistakes.

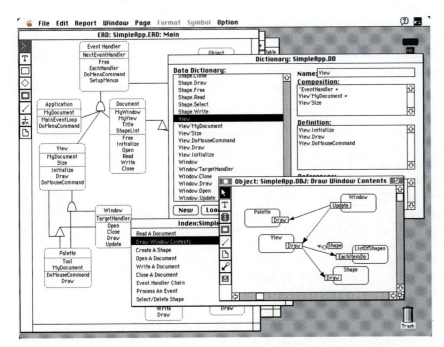

Summary and Key Terms

Like building a house, creating a successful applications program requires considerable planning.

Program Development Activities   The steps associated with creating successful applications programs are called **applications software development.**

In most large organizations, the development of applications software is the job of systems analysts and programmers. **Systems analysts** are the people who work with users to assess needs, translate those needs into a list of technical requirements, and design the necessary software specifications. The design is then handed to a **programmer,** who codes the program from it. Maintenance programmers monitor the software on an ongoing basis, correcting errors and altering the software as applications needs change.

The Make-or-Buy Decision   Many organizations choose to buy their software in the form of prewritten **applications packages** rather than creating it in house. The consideration to create software or acquire it from a vendor, which often takes place after the analysis and design stages of systems development, is frequently called the *make-or-buy decision.*

Program Design   Many tools are available to help the analyst design programs, including program flowcharts, pseudocode, and structure charts.

Program flowcharts use geometric symbols and familiar logical symbols to provide a graphic display of the sequence of steps involved in a program. The steps in a flowchart follow each other in the same logical sequence as their corresponding statements will follow in a program.

A group of techniques has evolved that has made program design more systematic and programs themselves easier to understand and maintain. These techniques are often grouped together under the term **structured programming.** Advocates of structured programming have shown that any program can be constructed out of three fundamental **control structures**—sequence, selection, and looping.

A **sequence control structure** is simply a series of procedures that follow one another. The **selection** (or **if-then-else**) **control structure** involves a choice: *If* a certain condition is true, *then* follow one procedure; *else*, if false, follow another. A **looping** (or **iteration**) **control structure** repeats until a certain condition is met. A *loop* can take two forms: **DOWHILE** and **DOUNTIL.** By nesting two or more if-then-else's, you can build a fourth control structure, known as a **case control structure.** All of these control structures follow the **one-entry point/one-exit-point rule**—that is, a structure can have only one way into it and one way out of it.

Pseudocode is a structured technique that uses Englishlike statements in place of the graphic symbols of the flowchart. Pseudocode is commonly employed in the creation of **action diagrams.**

Structure charts, unlike flowcharts and pseudocode, depict the overall, hierarchical organization of program modules and not the specific, step-by-step process logic involved. **Top-down design** indicates that modules are defined first at the highest levels of the hierarchy and then at successively lower levels.

Programming Languages   An important decision that must be made during the design phase is the selection of a **programming language.** Programming languages are either **low-level languages,** such as machine and **assembly languages; high-level languages,** such as **BASIC, Pascal, COBOL, C, FORTRAN,** PL/1, APL, Ada, Logo, RPG, Smalltalk (an **object-oriented language**), LISP, and Prolog; or *very-high-level* languages, which are also called **fourth-generation languages (4GLs).** Six types of 4GLs commonly used are report generators, retrieval and update languages, decision support system tools, graphics generators, applications packages, and applications generators. Interfaces that use **natural languages** are also available; they enable humans to communicate with the computer system in their own native language—whether it be English, Spanish, or Japanese.

Program Coding   Once analysts have finished the program design for an application, the next stage is to code the program. **Coding,** which is the job of programmers, is the process of writing a program from scratch from a set of design specifications. Among the techniques that have been developed to increase programmer productivity are coding standards, fourth-generation languages, **reusable code,** and **data dictionaries.**

Debugging And Testing Programs   **Debugging** is the process of making sure that a program is free of errors, or "bugs." Debugging is usually a lengthy process, sometimes amounting to over 50 percent of the total development time for an in-house program. Once preliminary debugging is complete, programs will also have to be *tested.* Good test data will subject the program to all the conditions it might conceivably encounter when finally implemented.

Program Maintenance   Program **maintenance** is the process of updating software so that it continues to be useful. Program maintenance is costly; it has been estimated that some organizations spend well over half of their programming time just maintaining existing applications.

Program Documentation   Program **documentation** includes manuals that enable users, maintenance programmers, and operators to interact successfully with a program. Although noted as the final stage of the program development cycle, documentation is an ongoing process that must be addressed throughout the life of the project.

Quality Assurance   **Quality assurance,** as it regards applications development, refers to the process of making sure quality programs are written in a quality way. Closely checked for quality are the outputs produced by programs, the program development process itself, and security.

Computer-Aided Software Engineering (CASE)   **Computer-aided software engineering (CASE)** refers to computer programs that assist in the development of other software. CASE packages differ widely, and no one vendor has produced a product that will cure every applications development headache.

Review Exercises

Fill-in Questions

1. _____ define the requirements that applications software must meet to satisfy users' needs.

2. _____ refers to the writing of computer programs.

3. The process of detecting and correcting errors in computer programs is called _____.

4. A program _____ uses geometric symbols and familiar relational symbols to provide a graphic display of the steps involved in a program.

5. _____ is a program design tool that uses Englishlike statements.

6. _____ is the principal transaction processing language in use today.

7. Report generators, retrieval and update languages, applications packages, and applications generators are all examples of _____ languages.

8. Program pieces designed to be "cut and pasted" into several programs are called _____.

Matching Questions

Match each term with the description that fits best.

a. Excelerator
b. sequence
c. debugging
d. documentation

e. flowchart
f. pseudocode
g. Pascal
h. program design tool

____ 1. A structure chart, for example.

____ 2. The process of ridding a program of errors.

____ 3. A graphical design tool with boxes and arrows showing step by step how a computer will process data.

____ 4. A program control structure.

____ 5. A technique for designing programs that uses Englishlike statements resembling actual program statements to show the step-by-step processing a program will follow.

____ 6. A high-level programming language.

____ 7. A written description of a program, such as a manual.

____ 8. A CASE tool.

1. What is done during applications software development?

2. What is an applications package? Provide two examples.

3. Name some advantages and disadvantages of applications packages relative to in-house systems development.

4. Why have structured techniques evolved as a major strategy in program design?

5. Name three fundamental control structures of structured programming and provide an example of each.

6. What is the difference between the DOWHILE and DOUNTIL control structures?

7. What is the difference between a flowchart and a structure chart?

8. What need is met by each of the following programming languages: BASIC, COBOL, FORTRAN, C, Pascal?

9. Identify several types of fourth-generation languages and the principal purpose each one serves.

10. Identify some ways to increase programmer productivity.

11. What is the purpose of program maintenance?

12. Why is program documentation important?

1. Most end users and programmers within organizations would prefer to work with a widely used applications package than a comparable software product developed in-house. Why is this so, and what benefits and/or problems does the widely used applications package present to the organization?

2. Computer programs have been created that distinguish people who are good credit risks from those who are not. How, would you suppose, do computer programs make this distinction?

3. With so many programming languages around today, why are new ones constantly being developed? Do any of these new programming languages really have a chance at wide acceptance, given the number of languages now is use?

4. Chapter 13 discusses the use of CASE tools in software development. If you had to justify the purchase of a $10,000 CASE package to your busy boss—who doesn't have even the vaguest notion of what CASE is—what would you say in that all-important first 60 seconds of your pitch?

5. India has recently become a major source of programmers to the world. How have both information technology and nontechnology-related conditions within India made it easier for programmers in that nation to compete in the global marketplace?

END-USER DEVELOPMENT

14

How do you go about buying a microcomputer system, keeping it up to date, and deciding when to call for help? Read Chapter 14 to find out. As people increasingly rely on microcomputers for their own use, it is becoming ever more important to be knowledgeable about developing and maintaining them.

LEARNING OBJECTIVES

After completing this chapter, you will be able to:

1. Identify some of the leading companies in critical market segments of the microcomputer industry, as well as the key sales and distribution alternatives for microcomputing products.

2. Explain how to select a microcomputer system for home or office use.

3. Name some practices designed to protect software, hardware, and data resources from damage, and list some important guidelines that you should follow when troubleshooting problems and having equipment repaired.

4. Describe some of the ways in which a computer system can be upgraded, and explain under what conditions an upgrade should take place.

5. Name several sources for learning more about microcomputer systems.

Laptop computers are currently the fastest-growing segment within the micro-computer marketplace. In laptops, three of the biggest names are Toshiba, GRiD, and AST.

Software Among the largest independent software producers (and their leading products) are Lotus Development Corporation (1-2-3 and Notes), Micro-soft Corporation (MS-DOS, Windows NT, and Windows operating-system software; BASIC language translators; Word; Excel; Access; and Works), Computer Associates International (SuperCalc), Borland International (Sidekick, Quattro, Paradox, dBASE and Turbo Pascal), and WordPerfect Corporation (Word-Perfect). At one time, many of these companies could have been characterized as single-product firms. Today, the leaders in this segment are in a period of aggressive diversification, internally developing new products and acquiring and partnering with other companies that have related product lines.

Monitors and Printers With the exception of a few U.S. companies such as IBM, Qume, Wyse, and Hewlett-Packard, these two segments are dominated

FIGURE 14 – 2

Who's who in the microcomputer marketplace. This list shows the products or product lines for which several leading companies are most famous.

Company	Principal Product(s)
Adobe	Assorted desktop publishing software products
Aldus	PageMaker desktop publishing program
Apple	Microcomputer systems
AST	A wide variety of hardware products
Autodesk	AutoCAD design software
Borland	A wide variety of software products
Canon	Printers and related products
Commodore	Amiga microcomputer system
Compaq	Microcomputer systems
Computer Associates	A wide variety of software products
Dell	Microcomputer systems
Gateway	Microcomputer systems
Hayes	Modems
Hewlett-Packard	Microcomputer systems and laser printers
IBM	A wide variety of microcomputing products
Index Technology	Excelerator, a CASE product
Intel	Chips for IBM and IBM-compatible computers
Lotus Development	1-2-3 spreadsheet package
Microsoft	A wide variety of software products
Motorola	Chips for Apple computers
NEC	A wide variety of hardware products
Novell	NetWare operating system
Packard Bell	Microcomputer systems
Quadram	A wide variety of hardware products
Qume	Printers
Seagate	Hard disks
Software Publishing	Harvard Graphics presentation software
Symantec	A wide variety of software products
Tandy/Radio Shack	A wide variety of microcomputing products
Toshiba	A wide variety of hardware products
WordPerfect	WordPerfect word processing package
Zeos	Microcomputer systems

by the Japanese. Some of the major players are Epson, Toshiba, Amdek, Brother, Fujitsu, Canon, NEC, and C. Itoh.

Computer and Memory Chips   The chip markets are ruled by Intel, Motorola, and Japanese companies. Intel makes CPU chips for most of the leading IBM and IBM-compatible system units, whereas Motorola makes chips for the Apple Macintosh line of computers.

Modems   Ten years ago, who would have thought that they'd someday watch a college football bowl game and see an award called the "Hayes Microcomputer Player of the Game"? Hayes is the dominant name in microcomputer modems today. Many other manufacturers are in the market of selling Hayes-compatible modems.

Add-In Boards   Hercules was one of the first big names in add-in boards. Like Hayes with its modems, Hercules's monochrome display board—which made possible monochrome graphics on a display screen—became somewhat of a de facto standard in the industry. Because there are many different products and specifications around today, a large variety of board products are now available (refer back to Figure 3-10 in Chapter 3). Two major manufacturers of boards are Quadram and AST.

Disk Systems   Some of the more familiar firms in the marketplace for diskette drives and hard-disk drives are Conner, Control Data, IBM, Seagate, and Tandon. In the optical-disk-drive marketplace, Canon and Philips are big names. Such companies as Iomega have done well with their hard-disk cartridges.

Diskettes   The competition in the diskette segment is among the fiercest imaginable, because there are not many important ways to differentiate diskettes. If the diskette "works" (that is, the quality level is sufficiently high—which is usually the case if you purchase a familiar brand), price is the only factor on which to compete. Most diskettes are sold by companies that don't make diskettes; instead they buy them from someone else and put their own labels on them.

A roster of some of the most familiar companies in the microcomputer marketplace appears in Figure 14-2, along with a description of the major product offerings that have made these companies famous. The popularity of U.S. packaged software in Japan is covered in Feature 14-1.

Sales and Distribution

Hardware and software microcomputing products are most often acquired from retail computer stores, mail-order houses, and manufacturers.

Retail Computer Stores   Organizations that need strong local support often turn to retail computer stores (see Figure 14-3). Generally, the salespeople at these stores are relatively knowledgeable about computers and help buyers try out hardware and software before making a commitment. If a purchased item does not work as advertised, some stores take great pains to resolve any problems. Typically, retail computer stores also offer consulting, repair, and other support services to users.

F e a t u r e   1 4 – 1

Selling Technology to Japan

The future outlook for PC software is strictly positive

For the past several years, a major complaint directed at Japan has been that it has created stiff trade barriers for foreign companies that want to do business within its borders. One industry, however—based largely outside Japan—has thrived under Japanese foreign policy. It is the microcomputer software industry, which consists mostly of packaged products made by companies in the United States.

Among the leading packaged applications-software products in Japan today are Lotus Development's 1-2-3, Microsoft's Excel and Works, Borland's dBASE and Paradox, and Autodesk's AutoCAD. To put Japan's reliance on foreign packaged software in better perspective, consider that U.S.-based Microsoft Corporation is over 30 times the size of Japan's biggest packaged-software company.

Outside venders currently control about half of Japan's packaged-software market. For a variety of reasons, some experts believe that this market could increase more than tenfold in size during the next decade. Why? For one, packaged software is increasing in popularity—by leaps and bounds—virtually everywhere in the world. Also, most software created in Japan is still custom made, and only recently has packaged software started to become popular there. By some estimates, per-capita packaged software use in Japan is only a fifth of that in the United States.

Ironically, many industry observers feel that Japan's protectionist trade barriers are exactly the

Microsoft. Over 30 times larger than nearest Japanese rival.

issue that has given foreign packaged-software vendors an edge. Barriers made it possible for Japanese companies to charge high prices for their products. This inevitably made those companies and products less competitive. Also, while the rest of the world was developing applications software that would run with widely used standard interfaces—such as Microsoft's Windows—Japanese companies were developing nonstandard products that were inherently more difficult to interconnect and use. Now these companies are far behind and playing catch-up.

Foreign versions of packaged software have to be carefully customized to meet the language restrictions in each user country. For example, Japanese versions of software rely on thousands of characters not found in the English alphabet. Also, foreign versions of software often must contain special features that appeal to local users. As a case in point, when Lotus Development Corporation first went to Japan, it customized 1-2-3 so that the Japanese version included on-screen grid lines in graphs.

Mail-Order Firms   Another source of computer products is mail-order firms. These companies regularly publish price lists in microcomputer journals and can ship products within 24 hours of a request (see Figure 14-4). Because these companies don't have to pay for a showroom and a large staff of knowledgeable salespeople, their prices are usually much lower than those of computer stores. Also, some mail-order firms have access to an enormous stock of goods and can get almost any item to buyers quickly via UPS or Federal Express. A disadvantage of mail-order shopping is that buyers need to know exactly what

Retail computer stores. Today, computer stores are a fixture at shopping malls everywhere. Some stores, like Egghead Software (pictured here), specialize in software, while others concentrate on hardware and repair services.

Mail-order houses. Mail-order houses like Mac-Connection (featured here) and PC Connection, which respectively specialize in Apple Macintosh products and IBM-compatible micro-computing products, regularly advertise their prices in the leading microcomputer journals.

they want, because many mail-order firms don't maintain showrooms or an informative staff.

Manufacturers   A third alternative for buying hardware and software is going directly to the manufacturer, although this is not always possible. Many manufacturers have exclusive selling arrangements with certain wholesalers and with buying consortiums such as schools and large computer clubs. Also, when manufacturers do sell directly to the general public, they usually sell only in large quantities—perhaps only *very* large quantities. Buying directly from the manufacturer usually means lower prices but often does not include ongoing support. Such support, if needed, must be purchased from another firm.

When buying a computer system, don't overlook used equipment. Ads for used equipment can usually be found in the classified section of local newspapers. If you take this route, ask to try out the equipment before you buy it. If the equipment functions properly during the trial period, it will probably work fine. Be especially careful to check how the monitor works over a period of a couple of hours, and evaluate the output quality of the printer as well. You should pay considerably less for a used system than you would for a new one.

Selecting a Computer System

Chances are good that at some point in your life you will need to select a microcomputer system to better perform your job. Selecting a microcomputer system for home or for business use must begin with the all-important question: "What do I want the system to do?" Once you've determined the purposes to which the system will be put, you must choose among the software and hardware alternatives available. Finally, you need a method to evaluate the alternatives and to select a system.

Analyzing Needs

With regard to computer systems, a *need* refers to a requirement that the computer system must be capable of meeting. For instance, at a videotape rental store, a computer system must be able to enter bar codes automatically from tapes being checked in and out, identify customers with overdue tapes, manage tape inventories, and do routine accounting operations. All four of these uses are needs.

A person owning a computer system will find dozens of ways to use it, but he or she may often justify the acquisition of a microcomputer system on the basis of only one or two needs. For example, many managers do so much financial planning that a spreadsheeting capability alone is enough to justify the entire computer-system cost. Many writers find word processing so indispensable to their livelihoods that it matters little what else the computer system can do. And sales personnel working out of the office can often justify a laptop computer simply on the basis of its usefulness as an account-closing tool at client sites. Figure 14-5 provides a list of potential needs that are met by microcomputer systems.

Microcomputer needs. Most users buy a microcomputer system on the basis of one or two of the needs listed here.

Word Processing

Word processing is the most common microcomputer application; many people have a need to create memos, letters, manuscripts, and other documents.

Spreadsheets

Business users find microcomputers handy for preparing budgets and other financial schedules and for analyzing information to improve decision making.

Organizing, Scheduling, Mailing, and Networking

Microcomputers are commonly being used as electronic desktops to coordinate office activities and to provide an environment in which people can communicate more effectively.

Desktop Publishing

Microcomputer systems are useful for preparing books and articles whose quality is comparable to that of products done on a professional printer's press.

Preparing Slides and Presentation Materials

35mm slides, automated slide shows, overhead transparencies, multimedia presentations, and handout materials are frequently produced on a microcomputer.

Retrieving Information from Local or Remote Databases

Users of all types find the microcomputer a handy device for looking up information.

Transaction Processing

Many database services let people use their microcomputer systems to shop, bank, and buy and sell stocks from the home—and businesses use microcomputers, too, to process these and other transactions.

Learning

An abundance of microcomputer software—some of it in multimedia form—is available today to provide instruction on virtually any subject.

Software Development

By using microcomputer systems with CASE tools and object-oriented interfaces, programmers are developing software for all sizes of computers.

Design

Artists and designers find the microcomputer indispensable for creating products that would be impossible or too expensive to do manually.

Games and Entertainment

Electronic games have always been popular on microcomputer systems; today, devices such as televisions, VCRs, and music synthesizers are teaming up with microcomputers to take entertainment potential further.

If you're not really sure what you want a system to do, you should think twice about buying one. Because computer systems that are specially configured to serve certain applications (say, games) are often poor at others (such as word processing), you can easily make some expensive mistakes if you're uncertain.

As part of the needs analysis, you should look closely at budgetary constraints. Every user has many needs, but it is their affordability that separates the real needs from the pipe dreams.

FIGURE 14 – 6

Product ratings. Software evaluations are a regular feature in *Infoworld*, a popular microcomputer journal. One week, six word processors might be compared; the next week, ten database management systems may be reviewed. Each multipage comparison is summed up in a "report card" (shown here for four workgroup scheduling packages) that provides an overall rating for each product evaluated.

REPORT CARD

INFO WORLD

Workgroup Scheduler/Mail Packages

	(InfoWorld weighting)	(Your weighting)	The Coordinator II Version 2.1	Office Works Version 2.0	Right Hand Man Version 5.1	Word Perfect Office Version 3.0
List price			$1,800 (10-user)	$495 (six-user)	$1,169 (10-user)	$495 (five-user)
Performance						
Scheduling	(125)	( )	Good	Good	Excellent	Good
Messaging features	(150)	( )	Excellent	Good	Very Good	Very Good
Archiving	(50)	( )	Excellent	Good	Good	Good
Printing/ word processing	(50)	( )	Good	Poor	Good	Very Good
Gateways	(125)	( )	Very Good	Satisfactory	Very Good	Excellent
Documentation	(50)	( )	Very Good	Good	Good	Excellent
Ease of administration	(75)	( )	Very Good	Satisfactory	Very Good	Satisfactory
Ease of learning	(50)	( )	Good	Very Good	Very Good	Satisfactory
Ease of use	(100)	( )	Good	Good	Good	Good
Error handling	(50)	( )	Very Good	Very Good	Good	Very Good
Support						
Support policies	(25)	( )	Satisfactory	Good	Good	Excellent
Technical support	(25)	( )	Satisfactory	Very Good	Very Good	Very Good
Value	(125)	( )	Good	Good	Very Good	Very Good
Final scores			**7.3**	**5.9**	**7.4**	**7.3**
Use your own weightings to calculate your score						

GUIDE TO REPORT CARD SCORES

InfoWorld reviews only finished, production versions of products, never beta test versions.

Products receive ratings ranging from unacceptable to excellent in various categories. Scores are derived by multiplying the weighting (in parentheses) of each criterion by its rating, where:

Excellent = 1.0 — Outstanding in all areas.
Very Good = 0.75 — Meets all essential criteria and offers significant advantages.
Good = 0.625 — Meets essential criteria and includes some special features.
Satisfactory = 0.5 — Meets essential criteria.

Poor = 0.25 — Falls short in essential areas.
Unacceptable or N/A = 0.0 — Fails to meet minimum standards or lacks this feature.

Scores are summed, divided by 100, and rounded down to one decimal place to yield the final score out of a maximum possible score of 10 (plus bonus). Products rated within 0.2 points of one another differ little. Weightings represent average relative importance to *InfoWorld* readers involved in purchasing and using that product category. You can customize the report card to your company's needs by using your own weightings to calculate the final score.

Listing Alternatives

Once a set of needs has been established, the next step is to list some alternative systems that might satisfy those needs. You should almost always consider applications software first, then the computer and systems-software "platform" that best meet your applications-software requirements.

Platform.
A set of computer-system architecture and systems-software choices that limit the user to work in a certain way.

A **platform** is a set of computer-system architecture and system-software choices that limit the user to work in a certain way. For instance, an IBM-compatible 80486 system unit running under Microsoft Windows 3.1 is an example of a platform. With such a base, the user would be able to buy any software that could run under DOS 6.0 or Windows 3.1 (or earlier versions and releases of these products).

Applications software is selected first because it most closely relates to needs. For instance, if you want a computer system to perform desktop publishing, it would be wise to first look at the various desktop publishing packages available. It makes no sense to choose a system platform first and then find out that it doesn't support the type of desktop publishing package you prefer.

Often, in the world of microcomputers, decisions are highly interrelated, so that software and hardware must be selected jointly. A software product may work only with a specific set of hardware. For instance, a certain word processor might be available only for an Apple Macintosh computer system, and it might also require a laser printer to work most effectively. An illustration software package may function optimally only if a specific type of graphics interface hardware is used—say, a digitizing tablet and a cursor movement device. Also, most illustration packages require a capacious hard disk, because graphics images require large amounts of storage. Because of the interrelated nature of many software and hardware products, it sometimes helps to make a list of system alternatives, in which each alternative listed consists of the principal platform and other hardware and software elements that can be added to it— both now and over time.

You can get a list of software and hardware products from the leading microcomputer journals. (We'll discuss some of these journals later in the chapter.) Many of these journals also periodically describe the best and worst features of products and give each product an overall rating (see Figure 14-6). The ratings can be used as input for evaluating products, your next step in acquiring a microcomputer system.

Evaluating Alternatives

Alternative products are best examined by "test driving" them. You must keep in mind that when observing the performance of a software package, you are viewing its performance on a given configuration of hardware. A software package that runs smoothly on a Dell 80486-based computer system won't necessarily run as well on a Compaq 80386 system, which uses a slightly different architecture and a less powerful chip. Also, the look, feel, and performance of a software package on a computer in the Apple Macintosh line will be notably different than they are on an IBM or IBM-compatible machine. Sometimes it's quite difficult, when selecting a configuration of hardware and software, to see the entire system together, but it's certainly advisable to do this whenever possible.

Selection Criteria   In evaluating software and hardware products, a number of criteria will help you make your final selection.

The most important selection criterion is usually *functionality*—the type of work the product does. For many people, ease of learning and ease of use follow closely behind. Also, most people prefer widely used products rather than unknown ones, because the large user base with the popular products ensures that vendor support will be around for a long time. In addition, if you are considering using a microcomputer system in an office environment dominated by, say, Apple Macintoshes, choosing that type of computer would probably be more convenient from the standpoint of having local expertise available for support. Good written documentation showing how to use the hardware or software is also important; when a helping hand isn't readily available, documentation is often the best alternative for answering a tough question.

T O M O R R O W

Software Support

Tomorrow's Concern about Today's Purchase

Computer instructors and trainers often try to teach their students an economic lesson that sounds simple on the surface but frequently doesn't sink in. It goes something like this: If software product A costs $5 and software product B costs $300, and both software products serve essentially the same needs, which should you buy? Assume that your time is worth $100 per hour and that you will spend 20 extra hours figuring out how software product A works because the user manual that came with it isn't worth a darn.

If you understand that time is money and you've answered "software product B," congratulate yourself on a correct response. But if you're like a lot of people, you'll miss the underlying lesson here and wind up learning it the hard way later on, when you discover the true value of

OS/2 help desk. A major support issue is having vendor assistance only a phone call away.

support. In other words, saving pennies today can cost you a bundle tomorrow.

There are two main sources of support: vendors and other users.

Vendor support can come in a lot of ways. Probably the most visible is the documentation you get when you buy a product. Good documentation should include a comprehensive hard-copy reference manual, a context-sensitive online-help

A list of important criteria for selecting a microcomputer system is provided in Figure 14-7. The increasingly important issue of getting good support tomorrow from the vendor you choose today is the subject of the Tomorrow box.

Software and Hardware Specifics   Before looking over software or hardware, you should make a checklist of properties that the software or hardware should possess—and be sure to watch for these during the test drive. A rehearsed presentation made by a salesperson is likely to point out only the strengths of a product, not its weaknesses.

For instance, in examining word processors, you should consider the type of text they output (e.g., do they allow proportionally spaced characters, half lines, subscripts and superscripts, and so on?), see how easy it is to execute standard commands (such as moving the cursor, centering, moving and copying text, indenting, reformatting, or footnoting), check the quality of the spelling checker and thesaurus features, and find out what advanced features the word processors possess (e.g., graphics and desktop publishing features). Again, consider the entire system. For example, if you are planning to buy an inexpensive dot-matrix printer that can't handle proportional spacing, certain types of graphics, or subscripts and superscripts, it may make little difference that a

feature, and a learning module that gets you started using the software. Needless to say, the manual should be clearly written. Unfortunately, many of the people who write documentation for software products are technical folks without sufficient writing and organizational skills, which mean you may end up wasting valuable time trying to figure out how the product works.

Another major source of support is the vendor hotline. Many vendors provide 800-area-code phone numbers for users to call to get help with problems—often free of charge. When evaluating a software package it is important to check out how easy it is to reach the hotline and the quality of service provided.

Many vendors also provide their own in-house electronic bulletin boards. These make it possible for the vendor to announce new hardware drivers and product information and to post useful macros. Users making contact with the bulletin board can download information to their local computer systems, where it is immediately available for use. Many vendors also regularly supply CD-ROM optical disks to their commercial users—disks that have the same knowledge base to which their own support representatives have access.

The microcomputer journals periodically publish statistics about user satisfaction as regards vendor support. Some vendors may also be willing to send you the results of independent support-department audits.

As far as *user support* is concerned, usually Rule One is to buy into a package that's widely used. This way, when you have problems, there's a large base of people to tap into if you don't want to turn to the vendor. Help might just be a scream away if you are working in an office where several other people are using the package.

Also, many users post problems on public bulletin boards. The message you post might be read by literally hundreds of other users, and there's a good possibility that someone out there has encountered and solved the problem you are now wrestling with. If the problem is knotty enough, you might get a satisfactory answer much faster than by going through the vendor hotline.

With the more widely used packages, you will also find formal user groups. User groups enable you to meet other users in person and to talk about common problems and creative ways to use the software. Many large user groups even publish their own newsletters.

word processor supports these features. Some of the items that you should watch for particularly when buying specific types of software packages are enumerated in Feature 14-2.

Hardware items that usually will need to be considered when buying a microcomputer system are the system unit and RAM, diskette and hard-disk units, a monitor, a keyboard, and a printer. Some of the questions that need to be addressed when buying these types of hardware are shown in Feature 14-3.

FIGURE 14–7

Important selection criteria. Buyers generally select computer systems on the basis of some combination of these criteria.

- Product functionality
- Ease of learning and use
- Cost
- Vendor reputation
- Support
- Expandability
- Meets industry standards
- Speed
- Favorable reviews
- Delivery
- Documentation

F e a t u r e   1 4 – 2

Buying Software

Some important questions to ask

When buying applications software such as word processors, spreadsheets, and database management systems, be sure to get answers to the following questions:

Word Processing

Does the package contain all the features that you want? Make a list of features and check a reference manual, trade book, or product review to see what the package has or lacks.

Will the package work on your hardware configuration? Keep in mind that printing attractive fonts, proportionally spaced text, and graphics usually requires a laser printer. If the package lets you preview graphics outputs before printing them, you will need a graphics-oriented monitor. If you plan to use a spelling checker or thesaurus, you will almost certainly need a hard disk.

Will the package fit on your system? Look closely at the RAM and hard-disk requirements of the package to see if it fits.

Does the package implement word processing features in a way you find compatible with your work style? The best way to answer this question is to try out the system at a store, in school, or at a friend's house. Of course, don't forget to check that the package exists in a version that will work on your system.

Buying software. Because of the need for long-term support, business users often favor familiar product names.

Spreadsheets

Does the package contain all the features that you want, and does it implement them in a way that is comfortable with your work style? Most major spreadsheet packages are remarkably alike. They contain virtually the same types of commands and closely follow the user interface of Lotus Development Corporation's 1-2-3. Packages with graphics-oriented interfaces differ from the pack in terms of look and feel.

Choosing a System

After you have considered the alternatives, it's time to choose a system and purchase it.

People choose between system alternatives in a number of ways. For instance, some people make a formal list of selection criteria (such as those shown in Figure 14-7) and quantitatively rate each alternative on each of these criteria. They then select the alternative that scores the highest. This method was discussed in Chapter 12 (see Figure 12-9).

Will the package fit on your system? Consider the RAM and hard-disk requirements of the package.

Will the package work on your hardware configuration? Check the graphics requirements of the package. If you are going to be using a great deal of presentation graphics, you will probably want a fast CPU and a laser printer. Of course, check that the package exists in a version that will work on your system.

Database Management Systems and File Managers

Will you need to relate data appearing in different files? If the answer is yes, forget about a file manager. You will need a database management system.

Do you have a hard disk? Compared to other types of productivity software, database management systems and file managers are very data-intensive. If you need to relate files so that the contents of several files are available simultaneously, you will almost certainly need a hard disk.

Does the package contain all of the features that you want and implement them in a way that you find comfortable with your work style? Database management systems and file managers are like word processors, in that both a software package's features and its look and feel can vary tremendously from vendor to vendor. Before buying a package, make a checklist of the features that you need and see how each feature is implemented in the packages you are considering purchasing.

Will the package work on your hardware configuration? Check that the package exists in a version that will work on your system.

How easy is the package to learn and use? Data management is generally harder to master than word processing or spreadsheets. Some packages, in fact, are targeted more toward programmers than toward ordinary users. Make sure that the package you want to buy comes with documentation, demo disks, or learning manuals that you are able to read and understand. If the vendor learning and documentation tools are mediocre, look for some good trade books to help you get started.

How fast is the package? Because data management packages are data-intensive, the speed with which the package can retrieve information is extremely critical. It will probably be difficult for you to design a benchmark test to test speed yourself before you buy, so to judge the package under consideration, read closely the results of the comparative product tests published regularly in the computer journals.

What type of backup procedures do you plan to use? One of the worst of all computer nightmares is having a large database destroyed when a hard disk malfunctions and there is no backup. When considering buying a database management system, you should consider what backup options are available to you. A backup tape unit is most convenient for large databases but will add to the cost of having database management in your applications portfolio.

Others prefer to make their choices less formally. After thinking about needs and the criteria that they will use to evaluate alternatives, they select a computer system as soon as it "feels right." In fact, several researchers have found that a large number of microcomputers are acquired in small quantities and that very little formal analysis, if any, is undertaken before the purchase. Although such an acquisition process could be criticized for lack of thoroughness, many managers claim that they are too busy to spend the time researching choices with greater care. There is, of course, a negative side to rushed selections. Just

Feature 1 4 − 3

Buying Hardware

Some important questions to ask

When buying a system unit, storage, a monitor, a keyboard, or a printer, be sure to get answers to the following questions:

System Unit

What brand of system is best for your needs? Buy a system that runs the type of software with which you wish to work and that is widely supported. Buying a bargain-basement system could leave you completely on your own, and it could cost you more in the long run than you save on the purchase price.

Does the system unit have enough power to meet current and future applications needs? Most computers sold today are 32-bit machines and run at speeds of from 20 to 100 MHz or more. You should buy a system that will last for several years.

RAM

How much memory does your most memory-intensive application require? If you are planning to move up to OS/2 or Windows NT at some point in the future, for instance, applications will require several megabytes of RAM. Other sophisticated operating systems and operating environments can also be memory intensive.

Can memory be expanded later if you need more? Determine in what increments and to what maximum it can be extended. As an example, many machines allow memory expansion in 1-MB or 2-MB increments.

Secondary Storage

Will you need one or two diskette drives? What disk diameter and capacity will you need? Recall from Chapter 4 that drives accommodate either 3½-inch or 5¼-inch disks and that disk capacities usually run from 360 KB to 2.88 MB. Many

Buying hardware. Make sure the equipment you select meets both your present and continuing needs.

people today use systems that have one 1.44 MB 3½-inch diskette drive and one 1.2 MB 5¼-inch diskette drive.

Will you need a hard disk? Increasingly, business software requires a hard disk to run. If you do need a hard disk, what capacity and format will you choose? Recall from Chapter 4 that hard disks today range from 20 to a few hundred megabytes in capacity, and most use either an IDE, ESDI, or SCSI format. Computer professionals often advise that you figure out the minimum amount of storage you will need and at least double or triple that figure in order to meet future needs.

Monitor

Do you need a color or monochrome monitor? Most business software made today is optimized for use on desktop, CRT-type color monitors. Monochrome monitors are very popular on laptop computers and may display in either green, amber, or white foregrounds.

How readable is the screen? Always inspect the output of the monitor you are considering before making a purchase. Monitors often work in several different display modes, some suitable for text and others for graphics. You only have one pair of eyes, so, if you're going to be spending many hours at a monitor screen each day, a monitor choice can be extremely important

Which graphics standards (for example, VGA and SVGA) does the monitor support? If you are working in a graphical environment, consider an SVGA display or, alternatively, a larger-than-normal screen size. If the work you do requires especially fine resolutions, make sure that you evaluate how well the monitor produces such outputs.

Does the monitor have adjustable features? Especially important are an adjustable base, which helps ward off glare, and brightness and contrast controls.

Keyboard

Does the keyboard feel comfortable as you type on it? If possible, type on the keyboard before buying; notice especially the key spacing and how the keys feel to your touch.

Does the keyboard have an assortment of special keys and features? Many people like light indicators showing if certain keys are active.

Are the keys placed in an arrangement that you prefer? Even though most people use the QWERTY key arrangement, several other keyboard layouts are available. Also, make sure that the special keys are conveniently located.

Does the keyboard have adjustable features? It is especially important that the keyboard is detachable, enabling you to move it about to suit your comfort, and that it has an adjustable slope.

Printer

What type of printer (for example, impact dot matrix, laser, color thermal transfer) is best for your needs? For most people, the choice will be between an impact dot-matrix printer and a laser printer. If you are selecting a more exotic type of printer, make sure that the software you are planning to buy supports it.

How fast is the printer? Impact dot-matrix printers typically are rated at several hundred characters per second (cps), whereas most microcomputer-oriented laser printers print anywhere from two to eight pages per minute.

What types of outputs can the printer produce (e.g., text or both text and graphics)? Be sure to examine closely both the range and the quality of outputs. Some laser printers, for instance, will print large-point-size text with jagged contours. You should never buy a printer unless you first see its outputs—and as wide a range of outputs as possible.

Can the printer be run in several modes? Impact dot-matrix printers should be capable of being run in a fast, draft-quality mode and a slow, letter-quality mode. Many laser printers have an adjustment for darkness that enables you to get lighter copies for drafts, which extends the life of the toner cartridge. Check the output quality in each of the available modes.

Other Hardware

If you are buying other hardware, make sure that your system has enough ports and expansion slots to accommodate it.

If you are buying a modem, decide whether you want it to be internal or external, how fast it must be, and whether or not it meets the communications standards prescribed by the application for which you intend it.

If you are thinking about buying a mouse, consider also the possibility of getting a trackball. Many people dislike using a mouse because it must moved around a desktop; trackballs, in contrast, are stationary.

as a car owner can go through years of torture driving around in the wrong type of car, so too can a computer buyer wind up with years of headaches resulting from a poor computer-system choice. The expense of a computer-system mistake may be much greater, however.

Operating a Computer System

Once you've acquired a computer system, it is important that you develop a set of practices to protect your software, hardware, and data from damage and from costly mistakes. Three important areas in this regard are backup of programs and data, proper maintenance of hardware and I/O media, and troubleshooting and repairs. A fourth area, securing the data on your computer system, is covered in Chapter 16.

Backup

Virtually everyone who has logged months or years of his or her life on a computer system will swear to you that, sooner or later, you will lose some critical files. Maybe lightning will strike nearby, zapping your RAM. Or maybe a small brownout will cause the heads on your hard disk to drop out of orbit and crash onto the disk surface, carving a miniature canyon through the elec-

FIGURE 14 – 8

Good reasons for backing up files. Taking a few extra minutes to make duplicate copies of important files can avert a potential disaster.

Why Back up?

■ A disk sector goes bad, destroying part of a file.

■ A file that you thought you no longer had a need for and erased turns out to be important.

■ You modify a file in an undesirable way, and the damage done is irreversible.

■ You accidentally reformat a disk.

■ The disk suffers a head crash.

■ A power brownout or failure at the time of saving a file causes "garbage" to be saved.

■ You save a file to the wrong subdirectory, overwriting a different file that has the same name.

■ While rushing your work, you make a mistake that causes the wrong files to be erased.

■ You unwittingly destroy a file while working on it—say, by deleting parts of it erroneously and then saving the file.

■ Malfunctioning hardware or software causes files to be erased.

■ A computer virus enters your system and destroys files.

■ Your disk is physically destroyed—for instance, a diskette is left in the sun or the hard disk is given a jolt. Alternatively, a fire or flood may destroy the disk.

■ Someone steals your diskette or hard disk.

tronic version of a 45-page term paper that's due tomorrow. Computer veterans will also tell you that these file losses always seem to happen at the worst possible times.

Fortunately, there is a solution to most of these problems—backup. Creating **backup** means making a duplicate version of any file that you can't afford to lose so that, when the fickle finger of fate causes inadvertent erasure, you're confronted with only a minor irritant rather than an outright catastrophe. Theoretically, you can back up any file on your computer system. The backups you create—through, say, a file-copy, disk-copy, or backup command—can be on diskette, hard disk, optical disk, streaming tape, or virtually any other secondary storage medium.

One common form of backup is making a duplicate of a long file that is being developed in RAM. For instance, suppose you are word processing a paper for a class. About every half hour or hour, you should make sure that you save the current version of the document file onto disk. That way, if the power goes out on your system, you will have lost only what you have typed in since the last save command. Many commercial packages provide certain types of automatic backup of files, but unless you know for sure what is being backed up and when, it's safer to do it yourself.

There are many different strategies for backing up files on a hard disk or a diskette. One is to perform a **full backup,** in which you back up all of the files on disk several times throughout the day or at the end of a day or a session. The advantage to a full backup is that it is relatively straightforward, and, since it employs a "shotgun" approach to backup, it sometimes saves "treasures" that you neglected to copy previously. On the down side, a full backup takes longer than a backup in which selected files are targeted for copying. Also, you need more storage space to contain the copied files.

An alternative to the full backup is a **partial backup,** in which only files created or altered since the last backup are copied. Many people who have hard disks will perform a partial backup daily and a full backup weekly.

Whenever you make backup copies on a disk, make sure that the backup files are not stored on the same disk as the originals. In theory, they shouldn't even be in the same room or building. Then, if a serious accident such as a fire or flood occurs at one location, the files at the other location will be safe. A variety of accidents that can destroy programs and data—accidents that are all good reasons to do disk backup—are listed in Figure 14-8.

Proper Maintenance of Resources

Microcomputer systems consist of sensitive electronic devices, so they must be treated with appropriate care. In this section we discuss protecting your computer system with a surge suppressor; caring for disks; protecting your computer system from dust, heat, and static; and protecting printers and monitors.

Surge Suppression One of the best devices to have on your computer system to minimize the chance of unexpected damage is a surge suppressor. A **surge suppressor,** which is installed between your system unit and the electrical outlet providing the power, is a hardware device that prevents random electrical power spikes from causing damage to your system (see Figure 14-9).

Backup.
A procedure that produces duplicate copies of programs or data.

Full backup.
A procedure that produces a duplicate copy of all files onto a secondary storage medium.

Partial backup.
A procedure that produces a duplicate copy of selected files onto a secondary storage medium.

Surge suppressor.
A device that protects a computer system from random electrical power spikes.

FIGURE 14 – 9

Surge suppressor. The system unit and its support devices feed into the surge suppressor, which is plugged into a standard wall outlet. This permits you to turn on all of your equipment, as well as a nearby lamp or two, with the flick of a single switch.

The power going into most homes is uneven. Power spikes, such as those caused from electrical storms, and power brownouts caused by drops in power can damage data or your system. Probably the most common problem caused by a spike or brownout is loss of data in RAM. Cases have also been reported, however, of loss of data in secondary storage and destruction of equipment.

A surge suppressor cannot guarantee complete protection. If lightning strikes your house, even a top-of-the-line surge suppressor will probably fail to protect your equipment. If you live in an area prone to severe lightning storms, the best thing that you can do if you are working on your computer system when a storm hits is save to disk what you've been working on, turn off your system, and unplug the surge suppressor. Lightning can cause damage to electrical equipment—whether it's turned on or off—if it is plugged in.

Disk Care   Precautions taken with diskettes and hard disks will safeguard any data stored on them.

Diskettes may look like inert slabs of plastic, but they are extremely sensitive items and must be cared for accordingly. Never touch the exposed diskette surface or bend the diskette in any way. Also, keep the diskette away from magnetic objects, motors, stereo speakers, and extreme temperatures.

You should have the heads cleaned on your disk drives periodically, and at the same time, check to see that the heads haven't slipped out of alignment.

Misregistered heads can usually be adjusted easily. Of course, never insert a warped disk into a drive. With a hard disk, the most important precaution to take is ensuring that the disk is in a place where it is not likely to be bumped.

Dust, Heat, and Static   Each of the tiny processor and memory chips in your hardware units are packed tightly with hundreds or thousands of circuits. Dust particles circulating in the air can settle on a chip, causing a short circuit. Many people buy dust covers that fit snugly over each of their hardware devices to prevent foreign particles in the air from causing hardware failure.

System units that support add-in boards require cooling fans. These boards generate heat, and too much heat inside the system unit can cause all sorts of problems. When inserting add-in boards, you should place them as far apart as possible to avoid heat buildup. Also, most boards draw power off the system's main power unit (as do many internal hard disks), so be particularly careful about overtaxing the power unit.

Static electricity is especially dangerous because it can damage chips, destroy programs and data in memory, or disable your keyboard. So that those nasty little electrical discharges from your fingertips don't wreak havoc, you might consider buying an antistatic mat for under your workstation chair or an antistatic spray for your keyboard. Static electricity is more likely in dry areas and in the wintertime, when there's less humidity in the air.

Other Concerns   CRT-type monitors have a phosphorescent surface that is "lit up" by an electronic gun. If you keep your monitor at a high brightness level and abandon it for an hour or two, the phosphorescent surface will be "torched" rather than merely lit up. This means that ghosty character images will be permanently etched on the screen, making it harder to read. Software packages called **screen savers** are available that either dim your monitor or create random patterns on the screen when the display remains unchanged for a given number of minutes.

> **Screen saver.**
> A software product designed to protect the phosphor coating on the inside of a display screen from damage when the display is turned on but is not used for an extended period.

Printers are particularly prone to failure because they are electromechanical devices. If you have an impact dot-matrix printer, the most vulnerable mechanism in the unit is the print head. Like typewriter keys, these print heads will wear down over time. Still, you can take precautions to prevent rapid wear, such as making sure that the head is cleaned periodically, not using the printer excessively for graphics (which wear the head more rapidly), and making sure that the head is not adjusted for carbon copies (which makes the head strike harder) if you want only single copies.

Naturally, as with other electronic devices, you shouldn't switch hardware units on and off excessively.

Troubleshooting and Repairs

If you work with computers for any length of time, at some point you will probably have an experience when your hardware or software does not work properly. You may turn on your computer system one day and get no response. Perhaps your monitor screen will begin flickering badly every few seconds. Or maybe you will issue a familiar command in a software package that you work with regularly and the keyboard will lock up or the command will remain unexecuted. When such an event takes place, you will need to troubleshoot to isolate the underlying problem. If the problem is serious enough, repairs may be necessary.

Troubleshooting *Troubleshooting* refers to any actions taken to diagnose or solve a problem. Unfortunately, many problems are unique to specific types of hardware and software, so there's no simple troubleshooting remedy that works all of the time. Nonetheless, the following are some simple steps and guidelines that will help you out in a surprising number of instances.

■ Try again. An unusual number of procedures work when you try a second or third time. You may have pressed the wrong keys the first time, or not pressed the keys hard enough. If the problem persists, attempt to save your work, restart (reboot) your computer system, and try again.

■ Check to see that all of the equipment is plugged in and turned on and that none of the cables are detached or loose.

■ Recall exactly what happened between the time the system was operating properly and the time you began to encounter problems. There might have been an electrical storm outside, and your system was plugged in and damaged by lightning. Or perhaps you installed new systems software during your last session, and these changes are affecting the way your current application works.

■ Be observant. If strange noises came out of the disk drives when you unsuccessfully tried to boot the system up, those noises might be important. Even though solving the problem may be beyond your capabilities, you may be able to supply important facts to the people repairing your system. The faster the repair technicians can diagnose and fix your system, the less money you will spend in repair costs.

You should weigh the time that it takes to solve a problem yourself against the cost of outside repair. It's not a disgrace to have to give up if the problem is more than you can handle. It is simply an admission that your time is valuable and that you are wise enough to know when to call in a professional for assistance.

Repairs In some cases, a problem is simple enough that no repair is necessary or you can do repairs yourself. However, when the repair is beyond the scope of your capabilities, you will need to seek professional help. Likely sources of professional help are the party that sold you the defective hardware or software, retail computer stores in your area, and computer repair technicians listed in the Yellow Pages of your local phone book (see Figure 14-10).

Keep the following considerations in mind when thinking about having someone else diagnose or repair your system:

■ Is it better to repair old equipment or to buy new equipment? For instance, if the equipment to be repaired costs less than $100, it may be cheaper to buy new equipment.

■ Will the repair work be done under warranty? Most new equipment is sold with a **warranty** stating that the manufacturer will pay for certain repairs if the equipment fails within a given number of days or months after purchase. If the warranty hasn't expired, the repair may cost you nothing. Be aware

Warranty.
A conditional pledge made by a manufacturer to protect consumers from losses due to defective units of a product.

FIGURE 14 – 10

Repair. As technicians repair computer systems, many of them also field calls from users about problems.

that many manufacturers state in their warranty that the warranty becomes void if you attempt to repair the equipment yourself or if a repair is attempted by an unauthorized person or shop. Most equipment manufacturers publish a list of authorized repair shops.

■ Can you get an estimate before proceeding with the work? In many cases, repair technicians can provide a free estimate of what the repair will cost. If they can't, you might want them to diagnose the problem first and to call you when they are able to provide an estimate. You never, ever want to put yourself in a situation in which you are presented with an unexpected, outrageously expensive repair bill.

■ Is priority service available? People who use their computers as part of their jobs often need repairs immediately. Many repair shops realize this and will provide same-day or next-day turnaround for an extra fee.

When you buy a computer system, you often will have the option of buying a maintenance contract with it to cover certain types of repairs beyond those stated in the warranty. Figure 14-11 lists a number of the points covered by maintenance contracts.

Upgrading

Upgrading.
The process of buying new hardware or software in order to extend the life of a computer system.

Hardware and software generally need to be upgraded over time. **Upgrading** a computer system means buying new hardware or software components that will extend the life of your current system. The question you must ask when considering a costly upgrade is the same one that you would ask when considering costly repairs to a car: Should I be spending this money on my current system or start fresh and buy a completely new system? User Solution 14-1 looks at how one firm weighed these alternatives.

When you acquire a microcomputer system initially, it is extremely important to have an upgrade strategy. Ideally, you should buy a microcomputer system that adheres to a well-supported standard and that is flexible enough and powerful enough to be upgraded to meet reasonable future needs over the course of its lifetime. Of course, it is not possible to anticipate all of those needs, but not putting any thinking into system growth can invite disaster.

FIGURE 14 – 11

Maintenance contracts. A good maintenance contract should cover the clauses listed here.

Coverage
The contract should state clearly if both parts and labor are covered.

Contract Period
Many contracts cover a period of one or two years. Some vendors provide a "lifetime" guarantee on certain types of parts.

Repair Procedure
A procedure should spell out clearly what steps will be taken when a problem occurs. Often, the vendor will first try to diagnose the problem over the phone. If this fails, either you will have to bring or send the unit to an authorized repair center or a technician will be dispatched to your home or office within a certain number of hours or days. If you can't afford to be without your computer system for an appreciable period, this part of the contract may be the most critical. Some contracts will provide you with a "loaner" system while yours is being repaired.

Hotline
Many companies provide a hotline for you to call when you have a question or problem. Sometimes you can call toll free, and sometimes you won't be billed for the vendor's time. It's a good idea to check how easy it is to reach the hotline; some of them are so understaffed that it takes days for calls to be returned.

Other Clauses
Most maintenance contracts will be void if you attempt to repair the equipment yourself or let someone who's not an authorized repairperson do it.

U s e r   S o l u t i o n   1 4 – 1

An Upgrade Decision at Amoco

Amoco Corporation, the oil giant, is one of many companies that have a well-defined strategy for upgrading the hundreds of PCs that are in its employees' hands. The company primarily buys 486-based machines, as well as a number of 286s and 386s, from a variety of manufacturers. Each individual upgrade or new system is considered by the information systems department on a cost-benefit basis. If a user's application requires powerful software that's best met by a 486 machine, and the application is critical enough, the machine will often be purchased. The user's old machine—a 286 for sake of example—will then be redistributed, if it is still usable, to someone else within the company. Occasionally Amoco will also replace the system boards in machines with more powerful ones, although it tries to avoid that strategy because of the time it consumes. The company also reports that network upgrades are more difficult when new machines and old machines are intermingled.

Hardware   Some common types of hardware upgrades include adding more RAM to a system, installing a hard disk, adding boards to increase the speed of the CPU or to provide new types of functionality, and adding new input or output equipment such as an image scanner or a pen plotter.

Unless your system is big enough to handle growth, many upgrades will not be possible. For instance, if you have an Intel 8088-based processor, which limits RAM to a total of 640 KB, RAM-intensive hardware or software upgrades usually cannot be accommodated. Also, it's important to check both the number of expansion slots (used for add-in boards) and the power of the system unit. If new peripherals require add-in boards, and all of the expansion slots that allow such boards to communicate with the CPU are used up, upgrading is not possible. Also, some upgrades, such as installing an internal hard disk or a streaming tape unit, require extra power; thus, upgrading the power supply may also be necessary.

Today, some microcomputer systems sold in the marketplace are touted as *upgradable PCs*. These devices are designed with upgrading in mind, making it possible to swap out components—like the CPU chip—as more powerful ones become available. Upgradable PCs are not without their limits; they may not be able to take advantage of future technology that the PC designers didn't anticipate.

Software   Software vendors typically enhance their products in some major way every year or so. Each of these upgrades—which are called **versions**—is assigned a number, such as 1.0, 2.0, 3.0, and so on. The higher the number,

Version.
A major upgrade of a software product.

Release.
A minor upgrade of a software product.

the more recent and more powerful the version. Minor versions, called **releases,** are typically numbered in increments of 0.1—say, 1.1, 1.2, 1.3, and so on.

Each version of a software product is almost guaranteed to be more sophisticated and more complex and to require more RAM than its predecessors. For example, it's not unusual for a package that five years ago fit on one or two diskettes and worked with 256 KB to fit on eight or nine diskettes and require one or more megabytes of RAM today. The technical documentation accompanying the software is much more extensive than it was a few years ago and harder for the average person to understand. Fortunately, however, the quality of user training has increased dramatically and is geared to people at various levels of expertise.

Most software products tend to be *upward compatible.* This means that applications developed on earlier versions of the software will work on later versions of the software. Downward compatibility is generally rare.

Functional versus Technological Obsolescence

Functionally obsolete.
Refers to a product that no longer meets the needs of an individual or business.

Technologically obsolete.
Refers to a product that, although superseded by a newer version or release, still meets the needs of an individual or business.

Many microcomputer products serve needs for several years before they must be replaced. A product is said to be **functionally obsolete** when it no longer meets the needs of an individual or business. However, improvements to hardware and software products are continuous, and often a product is replaced on store shelves with a newer version or release before it is functionally obsolete. A product in this latter class is said to be **technologically obsolete.**

In upgrading, a common problem is that users believe the product they are using is functionally obsolete when it is merely technologically obsolete. Because of the rapid pace of technology, virtually anyone buying a computer system today will have at least one technologically obsolete component within a matter of months. Consequently, it's often not feasible to keep current with versions or releases of products as soon as they become available. The most valid reasons for switching from a technologically obsolete product to a newer version are that the older product is also functionally obsolete, the older product results in considerably higher operating costs than the newer one, or support is no longer available for the older product.

Learning More about Microcomputers

A wealth of resources is available to those who want to learn more about microcomputer systems and their uses. Classes, computer clubs, computer shows, magazines, newspapers, newsletters, books, and electronic media are all sources of information about microcomputers.

Classes A good way to learn any subject is to take an appropriate class. Many colleges, universities, and community colleges offer microcomputer-oriented courses for undergraduate and continuing-education students. Probably the fastest way to find out about such courses is to phone a local college and ask to speak to the registrar or to someone in a computer-related academic department.

Clubs Computer clubs are another effective way to get an informal education in computers. They are also a good place to get an unbiased and knowledgeable viewpoint about a particular product or vendor. Generally clubs are organized by region, product line, or common interests. Apple computer enthusiasts join clubs such as Apple-Holics (Alaska), Apple Pie (Illinois), or Apple Core (California). Clubs such as The Boston Computer Society serve the needs of a more diverse group of microcomputer buffs. Many clubs also function as buying groups, obtaining software or hardware at reduced rates. Computer clubs range in size from two or three members to several thousand.

Shows   Computer shows give you a firsthand look at leading-edge hardware and software products. Such shows typically feature numerous vendor exhibits as well as seminars on various aspects of computing. The annual West Coast Computer Faire, held in the San Francisco area, is one event specifically oriented toward smaller computers.

Periodicals   Periodicals are another good source of information about microcomputers. Magazines such as *Byte, Popular Computing, PC,* and *MacWorld* (see Figure 14-12) focus on microcomputers. Computer magazines vary tremendously in reading level. You'll probably find and be able to browse through these publications and more at your local bookstore or computer store.

F I G U R E   14 – 12

Microcomputer periodicals. One of the largest reader audiences consists of users who want information about specific types of hardware platforms. *PC Week, PC World,* and *PC Magazine* are targeted largely to users of IBM and IBM-compatible microcomputers, whereas *MacWorld* and *MacWeek* are for users of the Apple Macintosh. *Infoworld* caters to both IBM and Macintosh environments.

Books   One of the best ways to learn about any aspect of personal computing is to read a book on the subject. A host of softcover and hardcover books are available, covering topics ranging from the simple to the highly sophisticated. Included are "how-to" books on subjects such as operating popular microcomputer systems or productivity software packages, programming in microcomputer-based languages, and the technical fundamentals of microcomputers. You can find such books in your local library, computer stores, and bookstores.

Electronic Media   One easy way to learn a subject in our electronic age is to pick up a training disk or view a videotape or television show devoted to the subject. Today many microcomputer-oriented software packages are sold with training disks that provide screen-oriented tutorials, showing you which keys to press and the results. Also, a large selection of videotapes are available for standard videocassette players, so you can see how something works simply by watching your television. Television shows such as PBS's "The Computer Chronicles," which may feature a program on optical disks one week and a program on bus architectures the next, are targeted to microcomputer users.

Summary and Key Terms

The term **end-user development** is often used to describe such activities as end users acquiring their own computer resources, using and taking care of their own systems, and upgrading systems on their own.

The Microcomputer Marketplace   The microcomputer marketplace comprises a wide variety of firms that make hardware and software products. One important market segment, composed of microcomputer system units, is dominated primarily by IBM, Apple, and **IBM-compatible computers.**

Hardware and software microcomputing products are most often acquired by users from retail computer stores, mail-order houses, and manufacturers.

Selecting a Computer System   When selecting a computer system, the steps include analyzing needs, listing system alternatives, evaluating alternatives, and choosing a system. Although applications software is normally selected before a computer and systems-software **platform,** software and hardware choices for microcomputers are often interrelated so that you must consider them jointly.

Operating a Computer System   **Backup** refers to making a duplicate copy of valuable files. Two types of backup are **full backup** and **partial backup.** Microcomputer systems contain sensitive electronic devices, so they must be treated with care and protected from damage. A **surge suppressor** will prevent most random electrical spikes from entering your system and causing damage. Precautions taken with diskettes and hard disks will safeguard any data stored on them. Other practices can protect your system from dust, heat, and static. Software called **screen savers** can protect your monitor. Printer life can often be extended by taking precautions with the print head.

Although no two problems with a computer system are ever totally alike, some useful guidelines can be followed when troubleshooting problems and when having equipment repaired. For instance, just trying a procedure out a second time often solves a problem. When considering a repair, you should check first to see what protection is granted under **warranty.**

Upgrading **Upgrading** a computer system means buying new hardware or software components that will extend the life of your current system. When considering a hardware upgrade, you must consider such things as your current system's storage capacity, the number of expansion slots, and the power of the system unit. Software upgrades are often accomplished by acquiring a new **release** or **version** of the program that you are currently using. You need to ask yourself whether upgrading is better than starting fresh and buying a new computer system. You also must consider whether you are planning to replace a product that's only **technologically obsolete** instead of **functionally obsolete.**

Learning More about Microcomputers A wealth of resources is available to those who want to learn more about microcomputer systems and their uses. Classes, computer clubs, computer shows, magazines, newspapers, newsletters, books, and electronic media are all sources of information about microcomputers.

Review Exercises

Fill-in Questions

1. _____ development refers to users themselves taking responsibility in developing and maintaining computer systems.

2. A(n) _____ computer runs the same software as that targeted to IBM microcomputers.

3. A minor upgrade of a software package is called a(n) _____.

4. The most important selection criterion is _____, which refers to the type of work a hardware or software product does.

5. _____ refers to making, for security purposes, a duplicate copy of a file.

6. A(n) _____ is a hardware device designed to stop power spikes from damaging a computer system.

7. A(n) _____ usually states that a product manufacturer will pay for defective software or hardware for a given period of time under certain conditions.

8. A product that no longer meets the needs of a user is said to be _____ obsolete.

Matching Questions

Match each term with the description that fits best.

a. Compaq   e. Hayes
b. Toshiba   f. Motorola
c. Intel   g. Seagate
d. Microsoft   h. Lotus Development

____ 1. Makes CPU chips for the Apple Macintosh line of computers.

____ 2. A large U.S.-based maker of IBM-compatible computers.

____ 3. Produces primarily disk products.

____ 4. Famous for Windows and MS-DOS, as well as a wide variety of other software products.

____ 5. Makes CPU chips for IBM and IBM-compatible computers.

____ 6. Mostly known for its popular spreadsheet.

____ 7. Set the standard for microcomputer-based modems.

____ 8. A famous foreign-based maker of laptop computers.

Discussion Questions

1. In the world of microcomputers, what is an IBM-compatible computer?

2. Who are the three leading manufacturers of desktop system units?

3. Name three ways in which microcomputer products are usually acquired by users.

4. Name several criteria that are important to consider when evaluating alternative computer systems for purchase.

5. Provide several examples that show why it is important to back up files.

6. Give several guidelines that are useful when troubleshooting a problem with your computer system.

7. What is the difference between a version and a release of a software package?

8. What is the difference between technological obsolescence and functional obsolescence?

Critical Thinking Questions

1. Almost every other year, a major new microprocessor chip is introduced, and it leads to the development of a new "family" of faster, more capable computer systems. What problems does this pose for a typical corporation?

2. Why, do you think, are so many companies in the business of producing IBM-compatible computer systems?

3. A number of newer microcomputer systems have multiuser capabilities, allowing several users to share the system at once. For instance, a single

system unit, hard disk, and printer might be shared by four people, each with his or her own monitor and keyboard. But despite the multiuser capabilities of such systems, they are often bought for a single individual and are not shared. Why do you think this is so?

4. Four nations that have recently become a force on the microcomputing scene are Korea, Hong Kong, Singapore, and Taiwan. What are these nations doing well to have become such an important factor in the microcomputer industry?

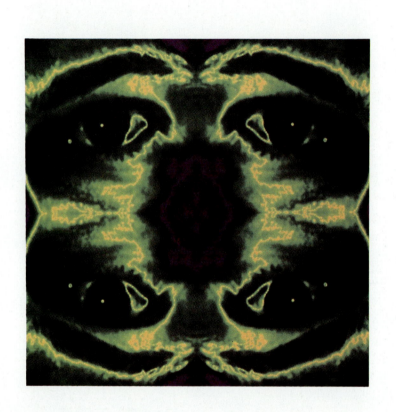

COMPUTERS IN SOCIETY

No study of computers is complete without a look at the impact these devices have had on the very fabric of our society. In the workplace, computers have created many jobs and careers but also have made others obsolete. Likewise, in society as a whole, they have created both opportunities and problems. Many people praise computers as a major source of progress. Others wonder if we are indeed any better off today than we were before the age of computerization.

Chapter 15 covers the important subject of computer-related jobs and careers. Chapter 16 discusses many of the opportunities and problems created by the proliferation of computers.

CAREER OPPORTUNITIES

15

What sorts of professional opportunities are available in the computer field? That's what we'll cover in Chapter 15. The rapid spread of technology has perhaps created more opportunities than ever before for talented computer professionals.

LEARNING OBJECTIVES

After completing this chapter, you will be able to:

1. Identify the various types of employment available to those seeking jobs in the computer field.

2. Understand the alternatives available to those seeking careers as computer professionals.

3. Describe the differences between computer curricula offered by colleges and universities.

4. Describe the resources available to computer professionals as they continue learning about computers.

Overview

If you're interested in obtaining computer-related employment, welcome to a relatively "hot" job market. The demand for computer professionals in government and industry has been booming over the past two decades, and this general trend is expected to continue well into the next century. Both the increasing dependence of organizations on computing and communications technologies and the rapid proliferation of technology products in the marketplace have created more opportunities for computer-related careers than ever before.

The explosive demand for computer professionals has been accompanied by an unusually acute shortage of qualified people. Thus, a degree in a computer field will probably land you several job offers and a good starting salary if your grades are high enough. But beware. Being a computer professional is not for everyone. If you have neither an aptitude nor an interest in computers—a field that involves grasping a relatively large number of technical concepts—you'd better try your hand at something else. As in other fields, high salaries generally are earned only by people with talent and dedication, and often only after many years of hard work.

We'll begin this chapter by looking at some of the jobs and careers possible in the computer field. Next, we'll cover the various educational paths to follow to prepare for entry-level jobs. Finally, we'll discuss finding a job and ways to maintain professional skills and develop new ones.

Jobs and Careers

So many jobs classify one as a "computer professional" that it's impossible to adequately cover them all in a single chapter. Here we'll consider only those that involve, either directly or indirectly, supplying end users with computer-generated information. These jobs require substantial training in a specific computer field. Included are equipment operators, programmers, systems analysts, and computer managers, as well as specialized jobs such as database administrator, EDP auditor, telecommunications specialist, and knowledge engineer. Excluded are computer salespeople, personnel engaged in manufacturing computer hardware, and service engineers.

In this section, we'll first look at some specific jobs that qualify one as a computer professional. Then we'll consider ways to combine jobs into various career paths. Finally, we'll look at some trends in the information-systems workplace and the effect that these trends have on jobs and careers.

Computer Jobs

Figure 15-1 shows how computer jobs are organized in a typical firm.

Computer Operations Personnel   Computer operations personnel include data-entry operators, computer equipment operators, system librarians, and managers who supervise the day-to-day running of computing centers. All these people perform a service for others working with large computer systems. Their responsibilities lie primarily in making the operating environment for company-wide information processing as efficient as possible.

An organization chart showing common computer jobs and their relation to one another.

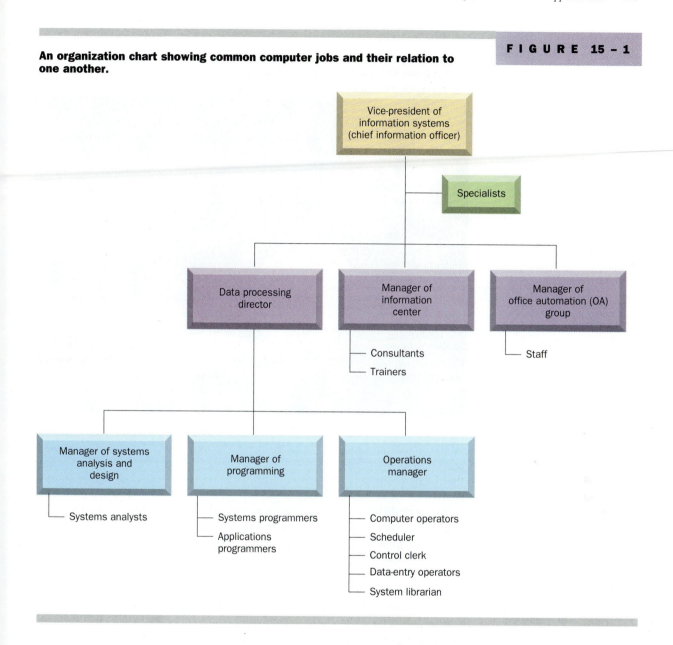

Computer operators are responsible for setting up equipment for various jobs, mounting and dismounting tapes and disks, and monitoring computer operations (see Figure 15-2). If a program is in an "endless loop," a terminal breaks down, a user is performing an unauthorized activity, or the computer "crashes," the operator is the one who initiates a solution to the problem. Because many commercial computers run nearly 24 hours a day, an operator's responsibilities extend over a single 8-hour shift. Entry-level personnel in this area should have at least an associate's degree from a community college or a certificate from a technical institute. Some companies train operators on the job, while others require experience with a particular system.

Computer operator.
A person responsible for the operation of the computer and its support devices.

Computer operator. Computer operators are responsible for setting up equipment, mounting and dismounting disks and tapes, and monitoring computer operations.

Scheduler.
The operations person hired to utilize system resources to peak efficiency.

Control clerk.
The person who monitors all work coming in and out of the computer center.

Data-entry operator.
A member of a computer operations staff responsible for keying data into the computer system.

System librarian.
The person in the computer operations area responsible for managing data files and programs stored offline on tapes, disks, microfilm, and other types of storage media.

The **scheduler** is the operations person whose job is to utilize system resources to peak efficiency. The scheduler allocates computer time for running and testing programs, data and file conversion, system maintenance, and downtime for equipment upgrades. Often, the scheduler has risen from the computer-operator ranks, after having gained experience with operations tasks.

The **control clerk** monitors all work coming in and out of the computer center. Incoming work from user departments is put into a form that can be handled properly by operations personnel. Outgoing work is checked for completeness and accuracy before going back to users.

Data-entry operators transcribe data files, programs, and other documents into machine-readable form. A high-school diploma and good typing skills are today the major requirements for a data-entry job. Increasingly, with advances in data-entry technology, many chores that were once performed by centralized data-entry departments are being shifted to the end-user level. Many companies with large data-entry burdens are today turning to offshore alternatives—like the Caribbean—for keyboarding work.

The **system librarian** is responsible for managing data files and programs stored offline on tapes, disks, microfilm, and all other types of storage media. These media may contain backup copies of important programs and data files, items that are stored offline because they are not needed on a day-to-day basis, and archival data kept for legal purposes. In addition, the librarian is also charged with managing books and journals, as well as program and system documentation. The librarian catalogs all the library items, purges materials no longer needed, and prevents unauthorized access to restricted material. A high-school education and some knowledge of information processing concepts generally are enough to qualify for an entry-level position as a system librarian.

The **computer operations manager** oversees the entire operation of the computer system. His or her duties include hiring and assigning operations personnel and coordinating operations to ensure that the system runs smoothly. This is not an entry-level position. Computer operations managers often must have at least three to five years of experience in the operations field.

Computer operations manager.
The person who oversees the computer operations area in an organization.

Programmers Programmers generally fall into one of two categories: systems programmers and applications programmers.

Systems programmers write and maintain systems software. Since this class of programs is very technical, systems programmers must have a good technical knowledge of computers. Often they have had rigorous training in subjects such as assembly languages and the C language, compiler design, operating systems, and computer system architecture. An entry-level job usually requires a college degree in a technically oriented field such as computer science.

Systems programmer.
A programmer who codes systems software.

Applications programmers write and maintain the programs that serve end users. Because there's still a shortage of people in this area in many parts of the country, entry-level requirements vary widely. Many applications programmers have computer-related degrees from four-year or community colleges. A business degree is also useful.

Applications programmer.
A programmer who codes programs that do the useful work—such as payroll, inventory control, and accounting tasks—for end users of a computer system.

Systems Analysts **Systems analysts** plan and implement computer systems. They form the critical interface between management and end users and, later, between end users and programmers. Management dictates the priority of the problems to be solved. Handed a problem, the analyst must work with users to find the best solutions. The analyst then translates these solutions into a system design and sets the technical specifications for applications programs to be written by programmers (see Figure 15-3). The general duties of the analyst were covered in detail in Chapters 12 and 13.

Systems analyst.
A person who studies systems in an organization to determine what actions need to be taken and how these actions may best be achieved with computer resources.

The role of the systems analyst. The systems analyst translates the business requirements of end users and management into a technical system specification that is passed on to programmers and other computer professionals.

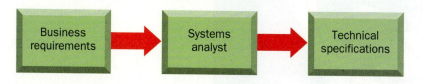

Feature   15 – 2

Job and Sales Opportunities Abroad

A miniguide to where the action is in the new global economy

As we move toward the 21st century, countries throughout the world are positioning themselves to be winners in the new, technology-driven global economy. Here's how the race is shaping up.

World Markets   The three largest markets in the world are shaping up to be North America, the Far East, and Europe. For the past couple of decades, the resident superpower in each of these markets has respectively been the United States, Japan, and Germany—with the United States both being the leading power among the three and having the largest market.

But how quickly things can change. The recent integration of European countries into the European Common Market has now made Europe both the largest potential market and the area that may have the most future economic clout. Meanwhile, the United States, Canada, and Mexico are scurrying into "borderless" trade agreements with one another, and China is just beginning to emerge

as a major factor—possibly giving neighboring Japan, Korea, Singapore, Taiwan, and Hong Kong a run for their future money.

Who will be the winner amid all this chaos is hard to predict. First of all, it's difficult to say for sure whether European countries—with the centuries they've spent fighting one another—will be able to integrate successfully into a unified power. Also, despite Europe's size and high rate of literacy, countries that were part of the former "communist bloc" have little spending power and a poor communications infrastructure. Communications technologies and skills are in particularly high demand in Europe these days, to link the more developed countries in western Europe with newcomers to capitalism farther east.

How much access "outsiders" might have to the three main markets is still a question mark, as well. For instance, will the European Common Market try to nuture its own answer to technology powerhouses such as Microsoft and Intel, capturing totally within European borders the profits made? If not, how much will it cost outsiders to do business in Europe? Nobody can answer questions like these for sure.

Leading Computer Companies   Most of the world's leading hardware, software, and comput-

---

systems department. Outsourcing is particularly desirable these days because the boom in technology products has caused many companies to need a wide range of skills that they can't afford to staff in house on a full-time basis. Also, the availability of inexpensive, high-quality packaged software has made it unnecessary for most firms to develop the same type of software in house. The outsourcing trend has made many more jobs available at firms that specialize in systems and program development and has taken many of those jobs away from firms in user industries.

Formal Education for Entry-Level Jobs

Going to school is one of the best ways to train for an entry-level position in computers. Many types of schools beyond high school offer some type of education in computers. These include four-year colleges and universities, two-year community colleges, and technical institutes. Course offerings vary widely among such schools. Some schools emphasize computer theory, whereas others focus on the more practical aspects of computing.

er-services companies are headquartered in either the United States, Japan, or Europe.

The accompanying figure shows the top ten technology companies worldwide—ranked by sales/service revenue—as reported in the June 1992 issue of *Datamation*. IBM Corporation, which has been the largest computer company in the world for the past three decades or so, took in over three times the revenue of its nearest competitor, NEC. Microsoft Corporation, the world's largest software company, ranked 24th. Intel was 47th. Virtually all the firms in *Datamation's* top 100 have operations worldwide.

Rank	Company	Area Headquartered
1	IBM	U.S.
2	Fujitsu	Japan
3	NEC	Japan
4	Digital Equipment	U.S.
5	Hewlett-Packard	U.S.
6	Hitachi	Japan
7	AT&T	U.S.
8	Unisys	U.S.
9	Siemens Nixdorf	Europe
10	Apple	U.S.

Worldwide top ten. The United States, Japan, and Europe house the lion's share of the most powerful computing firms.

Companies in the software and computer-services segments of the market showed the biggest gains from the year before. This suggests that two of the best bets for a career choice in today's global information-processing economy have to do with working with packaged software and building computer applications in organizations. Both of these areas include a variety of skills, such as training, programming, and systems development.

Independent of whether companies are able to finagle local government help to give them an edge within their home markets, it's hard to argue with the fact that there's a "home turf advantage" going to a company that both sells at home and is headquartered close to its customers. But there's another, perhaps more important factor in play here. Despite the fact that countries today are becoming engaged in an "economic war"—trying to gain favorable advantage for companies under their flag—history has shown that consumers have other ideas. No matter where a product comes from, people always seem to want to buy it if it meets their needs and if it satisfies certain price and quality requirements.

Maybe the most predictable fact about doing business on a global scale is that people everywhere are more alike than they are different.

Computer Curricula

If you're interested in pursuing formal academic study in computers, many curricula are available to you. Here we cover the most common of these. The specific names given to such programs vary widely among schools.

Computer Information Systems   The **computer information systems (CIS) curriculum** often is coordinated by a college or department of business. The primary emphasis is on directly providing services for end users, and many of the computer courses have a "business applications" flavor. These courses often include an introduction to computers, microcomputer fundamentals, COBOL programming, telecommunications, systems development and CASE tools, database processing, and information systems. Most schools also offer training in a variety of optional subjects, such as decision support systems, office automation, expert systems, and security.

Because the degree program is coordinated by the business school, students must also take several business courses. These courses can be particularly helpful to anyone aspiring to be a systems analyst or manager. Most graduates

Computer information systems (CIS) curriculum. A course of study, normally offered by business schools, that prepares students for entry-level jobs as applications programmers or systems analysts.

Can Users Manage Their Own Information Systems?

Decentralization is Not a Completely Free Ride

The relationship between end users and computer professionals has traditionally been a rocky one. Users have often complained that their needs are not being met and that the computer people just don't listen to them (see Feature 15-1). So when inexpensive microcomputers became available in the 1980s, many users jumped at the opportunity to bypass their information systems departments and acquire and manage their own computing resources.

Now, roughly a decade later, some of the short-comings of user-managed facilities are beginning to surface. While there have indeed been many success stories of users charging off on their own and doing splendidly, there have also been some horrifying tales of runaway buying, incompatible clusters of networks sprouting up, and a variety of other problems. So, many organizations are now beginning to rethink the question of whether

Users in charge. Acceleration in the pace of product introductions has caught many users off balance.

users should continue to manage their own information systems or if it's better to put this task back into the hands of qualified professionals.

Many of the problems that have beset end users have been in the areas of technology management, resource management, and personnel management.

---

of these programs assume entry-level work as applications programmers or programmer/analysts.

Two associations of computer professionals—the Data Processing Management Association (DPMA) and the Association for Computing Machinery (ACM)—have proposed model curricula for the CIS area. These curricula propose specific core and elective CIS courses as well as required business courses. Many schools adhere to one or the other model, although some have developed curricula independent of these models.

Computer science curriculum.
A course of study that includes all technical aspects of the design and use of computers.

Computer Science   The **computer science curriculum** often is coordinated by a college or department of computer science, mathematics, or engineering. The training provided is much more technical than that offered in a computer information systems program, because the primary emphasis is on software design. Graduates of these programs often find jobs as systems programmers, with responsibility for designing compilers, operating systems, and utility programs. They are also sought for the design of sophisticated software packages such as database management systems. A surprising number of graduates of

■ **Technology Management** Users aren't trained or paid to be technology experts, so it is highly unlikely that they have a good feel for new developments coming down the pike, not to mention the significance of those developments. The computing options available today far exceed those available just a decade ago, and the consensus among technology watchers is that even a greater number of choices will be offered by the year 2000, what with DOS, Windows, Windows NT, OS/2, UNIX, Macintoshes, and a spate of new chips, machines, and other options out there. The accelerated pace of product introductions has caught lots of users off balance, and many organizations are now realizing that the time has come for establishing formal acquisition strategies, setting standards, and ensuring compatibility across the board.

■ **Resource Management** Not too long ago, when users had their IBM PCs, Apple IIs, and homemade data that was for their personal use only, resource management was relatively simple. But times have changed. Microcomputers have grown in power and many are now networked. Also, users now regularly communicate with remote mainframes or servers to upload and download data. Consequently, there's a growing need to be concerned about matters such as security and backup as well as documenting and developing applications in an orderly fashion.

■ **Personnel Management** In many end-user departments, a resident computer person—called a *microcomputer specialist*—is hired by the department to assist users with buying resources and setting up applications. But such a position can become a dead end because there's no career path for the person hired to do the work. Also, whether the user group can adequately judge if it has hired the right person and whether it is qualified to assess that person's performance are two other questions that come to mind.

As a solution, many businesses today are keeping centralized information systems areas relatively intact and placing several computer professionals—called *department liaisons*—out into large user departments or groups. Thus, the liaisons are like missionaries, after a fashion. The user department or group has a certain amount of control over the person assigned to it, but the information-systems area ensures that the organization has a cohesive information-systems strategy, that uniform standards are developed and maintained, that a career path and new training is available for liaisons, and that performance can be adequately assessed.

these programs, however, take positions as applications programmers. Usually these students have prepared themselves by cross-registering for business-oriented courses such as COBOL, database processing, and systems development. Some have even taken an accounting course or two, because accounting generally is considered the language of business. Of course, cross-registration works both ways: Computer information systems majors often enroll in computer science courses—such as assembly-language programming, C-language programming, and operating systems—which help them sharpen their technical skills.

Computer Engineering Some schools also support a **computer engineering curriculum.** This degree program is intended primarily to prepare students to design computer hardware systems. Graduates of such programs usually are sought by hardware manufacturers.

Computer Operations In addition to their other computer offerings, community colleges and technical institutes typically provide practical training in **computer operations.** Students enrolled in these courses often plan to become

Computer engineering curriculum.
The field of knowledge that includes the design of computer hardware systems.

Computer operations.
A curriculum offered in many schools that is oriented toward training students to enter the computer operations field.

U s e r   S o l u t i o n   1 5 – 2

If You Want Diversity, Look at Fast Foods

At the headquarters of a fast-food company like a McDonald's or a Hardee's, any of a wide variety of computing skills can come in handy. Experience with point-of-sale (POS) systems is always useful because high-turnover, relatively inexperienced store personnel must be able to serve customers quickly. Microcomputer experience is becoming an important asset for new hires because most fast-food chains are now installing PCs in their stores to help local managers deal with such back-office functions as inventory and sales. Also, since these local PCs are typically tied into a corporate mainframe that polls them regularly for data, networking skills are also at a premium. Because most fast-foods businesses must identify attractive sites and then build their own stores, some knowledge of real-estate and construction software can also be just what you need to get your foot in the door.

computer or data-entry operators. These courses involve a great deal of hands-on, practical training, enabling students to quickly move on to entry-level positions in government and industry.

Many schools periodically have their curricula reviewed by representatives from national and local companies. This ensures both that curricula remain up to date and that graduates are being trained with marketable skills. Although there is no consensus about which specific type of academic training is best for entry-level programmer or analyst jobs in business, many companies prefer graduates with a strong technical or business background, a desire to learn the ins and outs of the particular organization, and an ability to identify with the users' needs.

Maintaining Skills and Developing New Ones

In the fast-paced computer field, retraining is a fact of life. If you want to keep your skills current and marketable, you must have some knowledge of the latest technologies. Various ways to effectively "retool" yourself or develop new skills include attending classes, seminars, and exhibitions; reading; using training disks and tapes; and participating in professional associations.

Attending Classes   Many universities, community colleges, and computer institutes offer courses on a nondegree or continuing-education basis. These courses are particularly visible in large cities, where a large market exists for such services. Many of the courses are taught at night to accommodate people who work during the day. Some companies also hold regular classes and even have schools for training employees in the latest computer technologies (see Figure 15-6). And, of course, there's graduate school. Most universities have master's and doctoral degree programs in areas such as computer information systems and computer science.

Attending Seminars   Many individuals and companies offer nationwide seminars on a variety of computer topics. An expert on telecommunications, for example, may travel the lecture circuit with an intensive, three-day seminar on the subject, charging, say, $650 per person. The speaker may present the seminar on January 11, 12, and 13 in Phoenix; on January 15, 16, and 17 in Los Angeles; then on to San Francisco; and so on. Some seminars, especially those conducted by hardware and software vendors, are offered free. Many computer trade publications maintain lists of seminars and details about them.

Classes. Computer classes are often run by companies for their employees or run by firms that specialize in computer training.

FIGURE 15 – 6

FIGURE 15 – 9

Organizations joined by computing professionals.

American Federation of Information Processing Societies   (AFIPS)

AFIPS is a consortium of several professional organizations, among which are the American Institute of Certified Public Accountants (AICPA), the American Statistical Association (ASA), and the Institute of Electrical and Electronics Engineers (IEEE). AFIPS represents the interests of its constituent organizations.

Association for Computing Machinery   (ACM)

The ACM is the largest professional association devoted specifically to the advancement of knowledge about computers and computer-related areas. Many of its members are from computer science faculty at colleges and universities. ACM has many special-interest groups (SIGs) in which its members may participate, such as SIGGRAPH (computer graphics), SIGS-MALL (small computers), and so on.

Association for Systems Management   (ASM)

The ASM is an international organization dedicated to the advancement of systems professionals in business and government. It publishes the *Journal of Systems Management,* a monthly journal that is widely read by information systems professionals.

Data Processing Management Association   (DPMA)

The DPMA is an organization dedicated to the advancement of knowledge in the areas of data processing and information systems. It publishes *Data Management,* a monthly journal that is widely read by computer professionals.

Society for Information Management   (SIM)

SIM is composed of information systems managers, systems analysts, and information systems educators. SIM cosponsors an annual International Conference on Information Systems, which provides a forum for new research ideas in the information systems area.

EDP Auditors Foundation

The EDP Auditors Foundation is an organization composed of professionals specializing in auditing computer systems. It regularly publishes a journal called *The EDP Auditor.*

Summary and Key Terms

The demand for computer professionals in government and industry has been booming over the past decade, and this trend is expected to continue well into the next century. Computer professionals include operations personnel, programmers, systems analysts, trainers, specialists, and managers.

Jobs and Careers   Computer operations personnel include data-entry operators, computer operators, system librarians, and computer operations managers. **Computer operators** set up equipment for various jobs, mount and dismount tapes and disks, and monitor computer operations. The **scheduler** is the operations person whose job is to utilize system resources to peak efficiency. The **control clerk** monitors all work coming in and out of the computer center. **Data-entry operators** transcribe data files, programs, and other documents into machine-readable form. The **system librarian** manages data files and programs stored offline on tapes, disks, microfilm, and all other types of storage media. The **computer operations manager** oversees the entire operation of the computer system, including hiring and assigning operations personnel and coordinating operations to ensure that the system runs smoothly.

Programmers generally fall into one of two categories: systems programmers and applications programmers. **Systems programmers** write and maintain systems software. **Applications programmers** write and maintain the programs that serve end-users' needs.

Systems analysts plan and implement computer systems. They form the critical interface between management and users and, subsequently, between users and programmers.

The information center is staffed primarily by consultants and trainers. The **information center consultant** is an analyst skilled in microcomputers and their applications who assists current and potential users with their personal computing needs. **Trainers** provide classes, often on some aspect of micro-computing.

Many firms have an OA group, consisting of about two to eight people, charged with strategy and implementation of OA technologies such as document processing and electronic mail. These people often perform many of the same analyst and trainer roles as people working in the data processing department or information center.

As the computer industry has expanded and become more sophisticated over the last two decades, a number of *specialist* positions also have evolved. For instance, many firms now employ specialists such as *microcomputer managers*, database administrators (DBAs), and telecommunications specialists.

At the highest level of computer management are positions such as data processing director, information center director, office automation director, and vice-president of information systems. The **data processing director** oversees all personnel involved with transaction processing, including programmers, systems analysts, and operations personnel. The **information center director** and the **office automation (OA) director** are in charge of all activities relating to the information center and the OA group, respectively. The **vice-president of information systems,** sometimes referred to as the **chief information officer (CIO),** oversees routine transaction processing and information reporting activities as well as planning in newer computer-related areas such as telecommunications, database processing, office automation, and the information center.

There are many ways to build computer-based careers. One possibility is to begin with an entry-level job and then move up the organizational ladder into positions of greater and greater responsibility. A second option is to specialize in a highly marketable "niche" area of computer processing where the demand for your services is likely to remain strong. Many people specialize by concentrating on a specific industry, technology, or function. A third possibility is to mold a career around a certain life-style.

During the last few years, several notable trends have evolved in the information systems workplace. Perhaps the three most important of these as they relate to jobs and careers are downsizing to smaller computer systems, decentralization of facilities, and outsourcing. These trends have involved a shift from mainframes to microcomputers and microcomputer-based LANs, the creation of new departmental positions such as **microcomputer specialist,** and the shifting of computer-related jobs to firms that specialize in systems and program development.

Formal Education for Entry-Level Jobs   Going to school is one of the best ways to train for an entry-level position in computers. Many types of schools offer some kind of education in computers. These include four-year colleges and universities, two-year community colleges, and technical institutes.

If you're interested in pursuing studies in computers, many curricula are available to you. The **computer information systems (CIS) curriculum** often is coordinated by a college or department of business. The primary emphasis is on directly providing services for end users, and many of the computer courses have a "business applications" flavor. The **computer science curriculum** frequently is coordinated by a college or department of computer science or engineering. The training provided is geared toward software design. Some schools also support a **computer engineering curriculum.** This degree program is aimed primarily at preparing students to design computer hardware systems. In addition to their other computer offerings, community colleges and technical institutes typically provide practical training in **computer operations.** Students enrolled in these courses often plan to become computer or data-entry operators.

Maintaining Skills and Developing New Ones   Retraining is a fact of life in the computer field. Various ways to maintain your skills and develop new ones include attending classes, seminars, and exhibitions; reading; using training disks and tapes; and participating in professional associations.

Review Exercises

Fill-in Questions

1. _____ transcribe data files, programs, and other documents into machine-readable form.

2. _____ are responsible for setting up equipment for various jobs, mounting and dismounting tapes and disks, and monitoring computer operations.

3. _____ are responsible for managing data files and programs stored offline on tapes, disks, microfilm, and all other types of storage media.

4. _____ oversee the entire operation of the computer system, including hiring and assigning operations personnel and coordinating operations to ensure that the system runs smoothly.

5. _____ write and maintain systems software.

6. _____ write and maintain the programs that serve end users.

7. _____ plan and implement computer systems. They form the critical interface between management and users and, subsequently, between users and programmers.

8. The _____ oversees all personnel involved in transaction processing, including programmers, systems analysts, and operations personnel.

Match each term with the description that fits best.

a. computer information   c. computer engineering
    systems curriculum   curriculum
b. computer science curriculum   d. computer operations curriculum

____ 1. The degree program tailored primarily for training students to design computer hardware systems.

____ 2. The degree program, often coordinated by a college or department of business, that trains students as applications programmers and systems analysts.

____ 3. The degree program, sometimes coordinated by a college of engineering or department of mathematics, that primarily trains students in the design of systems software.

____ 4. The degree program that trains students as data-entry operators, computer equipment operators, and the like.

1. Why is there such a big difference between the demand for computer professionals and the supply of qualified ones?

2. Discuss the types of work involved in performing each of the following jobs: data-entry operator, computer operator, system librarian, computer operations manager, systems programmer, applications programmer, systems analyst, information center consultant, data processing director, vice-president of information systems.

3. Describe some ways to build computer-based careers.

4. Are all academic computer curricula the same? Discuss.

5. Identify several ways in which you can effectively maintain your computer skills and develop new ones.

1. Many people think that programmers make poor systems analysts. What do you think accounts for this viewpoint?

2. Many industry experts say that for the most part, large, centralized data-entry departments will no longer be needed in the 21st century. How do you account for this?

3. A widely known and respected MIS scholar at Harvard Business School recently remarked that there is now a blurring of careers in information systems and in general business management. What do you think he means?

4. Many libraries stock both the current issue and past issues of *Computerworld,* a popular weekly computer periodical. Toward the rear of each issue, there's a list of job opportunities. Take a look at ads for jobs in five recent issues of *Computerworld* and determine both which foreign countries seem to have the most job opportunities and what types of job opportunities are most available.

COMPUTERS IN OUR LIVES: THE COSTS AND THE BENEFITS

16

How are computers impacting people outside the workplace? Perhaps in more ways than you would initially guess. In this chapter we'll look at the costs and benefits of living in the computer age.

LEARNING OBJECTIVES

After completing this chapter, you will be able to:

1. Describe some health-related concerns that people have regarding computers.

2. Explain the difference between crime and ethics, and describe several types of computer crime and ethical issues.

3. Appreciate that computer technology can encroach on people's privacy, and describe some of the legislation enacted to prevent such abuses.

4. Describe several applications in which computers affect the day-to-day life of the average person.

Overview

Since the early 1950s, when the era of commercial computing began, computers have rapidly woven their way into the fabric of modern society. In the process, they've created both opportunities and problems. Consequently, they've been both cursed and applauded—and for good reason.

So far in this book, we've focused on the opportunities. We've examined the impact computers have had in organizations and on the people who work there. Through the text and windows, we've seen how these devices have been put to work on routine transaction processing tasks, used to provide managers with better information for decision making, and employed to design and manufacture better products. In this chapter, we'll examine some of the effect that computer technology has had or is likely to have on our lives outside the workplace.

Before we look at these social benefits, let's examine some of the problems computers have created. Although the computer "revolution" has brought undeniable benefits to society, it has also produced some troubling side effects. Like any fast-paced revolution, it has been disruptive in many ways. Some jobs have been created, others lost, and still others threatened. In addition, an increasing variety of health-related concerns affecting people's working with computer-related technologies have surfaced. Computers have also immensely increased access to information, creating new possibilities for crime—even at the international level—and threatening personal privacy. Clearly some controls to limit the dangers that these awesome devices pose will always be needed. In this chapter, we highlight three important problem areas: computers and health in the workplace, computer crime and ethics, and computers and privacy.

Computers, Work, and Health

Computers have been said to pose a threat to our mental and physical well-being. Although the body of scientific evidence supporting this claim is far from conclusive, and is likely to be that way for many more years, we should all be aware of the major concerns raised about the possible effects of computers on our health.

Stress-related Concerns

Emotional problems such as financial worries, feelings of incompetence, and disorientation often produce emotional *stress*. This stress, in turn, may have been triggered by layoff or reassignment, fear of falling behind, or job burnout.

Layoff or Reassignment   One of the first criticisms leveled at computers upon their entry into the workplace was that their very presence resulted in job-related stress. When computers came in, many people were laid off and had to find new jobs. Clerical workers especially worried about job security. Many feared the full potential of computers in the office, never knowing when machines might replace them. These fears are still widespread today.

Even people who were not laid off found that their jobs had changed significantly and that they had no choice but to retrain. Airline agents, for example, had to learn how to manipulate a database language and to work with display terminals. Secretaries were pressured into learning word procesing (and perhaps electronic spreadsheets, electronic data management, and electronic mail) to keep in tune with state-of-the-art office work. Many workers never made the transition successfully.

A growing fact of life is that because of computers, fewer people are needed to do many types of work today. Computers are also regularly changing the way work is done—often, in ways that are difficult to predict. Even modern computer networks are posing a new threat to workers in that companies no longer have to physically staff each location as heavily with local expertise as in the past. Networks also mean that work can be transferred overseas more easily (see Feature 16-1).

Fear of Falling Behind   The microcomputing boom has placed computing power of awesome dimensions at almost everyone's fingertips. Some researchers perceive a widespread fear that failure to learn how to use these machines will make one "fall behind." One example is the numerous noncomputer-oriented executives, managers, and educators who see themselves being upstaged by their computer-knowledgeable colleagues. The surge of interest in micro-computers has even made many programmers who work in mainframe environments feel that they are somehow falling behind.

Burnout   Burnout is caused not by fear of computers (*cyberphobia*) but by overuse of them (*cyberphelia*). The infusion of microcomputers into home and office has raised new concerns about what will happen to children who withdraw into their computer systems, to computer-bound managers who have inadvertently been swept into the tide of the computer revolution, or to couples or families whose intimacy may be threatened by computer overuse in their homes.

To date, little research has been done on computer burnout. What makes this area so controversial is the compelling flip-side argument that most victims of computer burnout would burn out on something else if computers didn't exist.

Ergonomics-related Concerns

Ergonomics is the field that addresses such issues as making products and work areas comfortable and safe to use. With respect to technology, ergonomics covers the effects on workers of things such as display devices, keyboards, and workspaces. Let's consider some of the major fronts of ergonomic research.

Ergonomics.
The field that studies the effects of things such as computer hardware, software, and workspaces on employees' comfort and health.

Dangers Posed by Display Devices   For nearly a decade, large numbers of data-entry operators have reported a variety of physical and mental problems stemming from their interaction with display devices. The complaints have centered on visual, muscular, and emotional disorders resulting from long hours of continuous display device use. These include blurred eyesight, eyestrain, acute fatigue, headaches, and backaches. In response to these problems, several states and cities (such as San Francisco) have passed laws that curb display device abuse. In addition, vendors of these devices have redesigned their products with features such as tiltable screens and detachable keyboards to make them more comfortable to use.

F e a t u r e   1 6 – 1

Toward a National Technology Policy

When does government intervention help or hinder?

When people discuss the key industries that will determine the global competitiveness of nations in the next decade, technology is always a visible force. Widely regarded as being among the most critical industries as we move into the 21st century are computer systems and software, communications, microelectronics, robotics and machine tools, and biotechnology and new materials.

All the talk about key industries raises an important question: Should government protect these industries through favorable legislation or should it let them compete on their own steam, letting the chips fall where they may? As with most issues regarding government intervention, there is both a "for" side and an "against" side. Below we will consider each of these in turn.

The "For" Argument   Advocates for government intervention point to the case of Japan. In Japan, government and industry have collaborated during the last couple of decades in such industries as automobiles, consumer electronics, robotics, and microelectronics. Working together, they have fashioned one of the economic miracles of the century.

Government can be a big help to getting new industries launched in the United States, too, say the advocates. After all, had not the U.S. govern-

Keeping jobs at home. What role should government play?

ment been the first (and, for a long time, the only) consumer of the products of the U.S. computer industry in the 1940s and 1950s, the industry would not be where it is today. Who knows, maybe England would have been the world's information-technology powerhouse instead? Or Nazi Germany?

Dangers Posed by Keyboards   Years ago, computer keyboards frequently were built into display units, making it difficult for operators to move them about as freely as they could if the keyboards had been detached. Most claims that a computer keyboard could result in injury seemed to be put to rest after most keyboard manufacturers started making detachable keyboards—that is, until recently. Today, some people are experiencing a condition known as *carpal tunnel syndrome,* a painful and crippling complex of symptoms affecting the hand and wrist that has been traced to the repetitive finger movements routinely made when using a keyboard. The condition, which may not strike everyone who puts in long hours on a keyboard, and which can disappear in some cases,

Two areas in which the government might be able to play an important role now are fiber-optic cable and high-definition television (HDTV). As covered in Chapter 6, a fiber-optic backbone in the United States could bring unprecedented amounts of computing power within reach of almost every U.S. resident and business. Japan intends to be "all-fiber-optic" by the year 2015. HDTV—a technology that makes possible all-digital, flat-panel, large-screen TV sets that you can hang on a wall like a painting—has been identified by some technology futurists as the "next VCR." The market for such a product will be so large and so profitable, claim the futurists, that the country that captures HDTV leadership will be immediately rich and powerful.

The "Against" Argument   Those opposed to the government taking an active role in the technology race point out that government is ill suited to pick winners and losers in the private sector. When the government gets involved, they say, things often turn out worse. Governments are notoriously slow and inefficient, and their decision patterns are often harder for companies to predict than free-market forces.

Take the inexpensive flat-panel display screens that Japanese manufacturers were "dumping" on the U.S. market a few years ago. Most flat-panel screens are used to build laptop computers, and the Japanese companies were selling these screens to U.S. laptop companies at prices that were allegedly below their cost. Manufacturers of flat-screen devices in the United States were up in arms, claiming that Japanese firms were trying to put them out of business. Worse yet, they claimed, the predatory pricing would kill off the flat-panel-screen industry within the United States. If the United States lost its competitiveness in flat-screen technology, foreign powers could control pricing on U.S. products that use flat screens and could even gain an edge in the HDTV race.

But, laptop makers countered, by putting import tariffs on screens—thereby artificially making screens more expensive—the U.S. government would cause laptops to be that much more expensive to the U.S. consumer. (Almost half the cost of many laptops is in the price of the screen.) They also claimed that tariffs on Japanese screens would cause them, the U.S. laptop makers, to have to set up their own laptop manufacturing plants overseas in order to continue to give U.S. customers low prices. That would mean creating more jobs overseas—and losing more at home.

Those against government technology policy also argue that the United States does not have to be and cannot be the world leader in every single technology. Being a pioneer doesn't always translate into being the biggest winner. As a case in point, IBM let Apple and other companies be the pioneers in microcomputer systems, forcing them to pay the price of making learning mistakes. Finally, when the market ripened to an irresistable size and there was less risk to entry, IBM came out with its IBM PC—and walked away with the biggest share of the industry revenues. Of course, don't forget the VCR. While it was invented in the United States, it was the Japanese who made it into a successful consumer product.

makes it difficult to use a keyboard, drive long distances, and even hold up a book to read, among other things. Physicians recommend that to minimize the chance of such an injury, you take breaks every hour or so and relax your arms and hands so that blood flows freely throughout your body. Recently, a number of innovatively designed keyboards have come to the fore that attempt to reduce stress in the hands and wrists (see Figure 16-1).

Workspace Design   Display devices and keyboards are not the only things that can torture people at workstations. For example, the furniture may be nonadjustable, forcing the terminal user into awkward postures that are guaran-

behavior is involved, ethics play an important role in shaping the law and in determining how well we get along with other people. Some questions to ask when considering an action that might be ethically questionable are provided in Figure 16-4.

Today, there are a number of ethical concerns in the computer area. Several examples of these are listed below:

■ People tend to use computer resources casually in ways that, although not criminal, are ethically questionable. For instance, some people regularly use a software package that they don't own for personal purposes, claiming they are doing so just to "get the feel of it." Although most vendors encourage limited experimentation with their products, they frown on someone who hasn't bought the package using it regularly.

■ A student may casually eavesdrop on a university mainframe system on data not intended for his or her use. This may entail neither a prosecutable crime nor a major security threat, but that makes the act no less ethically reprehensible.

■ A computer professional working for one software company leaves and takes a job for a competing company. During the first few days with the new employer, the professional divulges product-development secrets that were entrusted in confidence by the former employer, putting the new employer at a distinct competitive advantage.

■ A large software company, hearing that a small competitor is coming out with a new product, spreads a rumor that it is working on a similar product. While the large company never provides a formal release date for its product, it leaves potential users with the fear that they will be taking a major risk

FIGURE 16 – 4

Ethical guidelines. When considering an action that bothers you from an ethical viewpoint, ask yourself these questions. Answering "yes" to certain key questions might be a tipoff that something you are considering doing is wrong. The propriety of an act must ultimately be a matter resolved in your own conscience.

■ Will you benefit in any way from the questionable action you are considering taking?

■ Are you not disclosing certain facts to others because you are afraid they will disapprove of the action?

■ Are you purposely coloring facts to portray a situation as being better or worse than it actually is to bias someone in a certain way?

■ If the same action that you are considering was instead done to you, would you feel taken advantage of, used, lied to, disrespected, or abused in any way?

■ Could anyone possibly object to the action as being unfair?

■ Will anyone be harmed by the action?

■ Do you feel yourself rationalizing your behavior in some way?

■ Could the action ultimately result in the evolution of a destructive practice or socially undesirable trend?

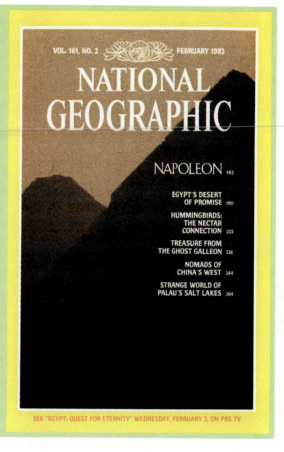

by adopting the small-competitor's product. (Incidently, software that exists more in people's imaginations than in actuality is sometimes referred to as **vaporware.**)

■ A magazine that you subscribe to sells your name to a company that develops marketing databases (see Tomorrow box). Soon, your mailbox is flooded with pesky junk mail and you are regularly getting calls at dinnertime from companies trying to sell you something you don't need or want.

Vaporware.
Software that exists more in people's imaginations than in actuality.

Many scholars think that educating people about ethical matters is being pushed aside today in the rush to achieve measurable results. A movement is afoot to change this, however. Several professional computer organizations—such as the Data Processing Management Association (DPMA) and the Association for Computing Machinery (ACM)—have established codes of ethics for computer professionals. Also, ethics is frequently a topic in computer journals and at professional conferences today.

Another interesting ethical issue that has surfaced in recent years involves using computers to manipulate photographs. As User Solution 16-1 asks, is the public being hoodwinked when images that are intended to disseminate fact are doctored for aesthetic emphasis?

T O M O R R O W

How Do They Know I Ski?

How Far Will Marketing Databases Go?

Advocates have called them necessary and effective. Detractors have called them dangerous and diabolical. They're marketing databases, and what you've seen of them today is probably only the beginning.

Marketing databases contain information about the consuming public. These databases record where people live, what they are inclined to do, and what they buy. Using this information, marketers attempt to determine the best way to promote specific products to specific people. Virtually any time you leave traceable information about yourself anywhere, there's a good chance that it will eventually find its way into somebody's marketing database.

When you buy a house, for example, your name, address, and the sales price are recorded in a county courthouse. These records are available to the public, including micromarketers. *Micromarketers* are companies that specialize in

Micromarketing. Is your name on someone's list?

creating marketing databases and selling them to companies that produce consumer goods and services. The micromarketer typically breaks down the neighborhoods in a region into several dozen categories. Consumers are placed into one of these categories according to their address. For instance, a "Blue-blood Estates" category might be a neighborhood in which the very wealthy live. A "Shotguns and Pickups" category, by contrast, might refer to a rural area where

Computers and Privacy

Almost all of us have some aspects of our lives that we prefer to keep private. These may include a sorry incident from the past, sensitive medical or financial facts, or certain tastes or opinions. Yet we can appreciate that sometimes selected people or organizations have a legitimate need for some of this information. A doctor needs accurate medical histories of patients. Financial information must be disclosed to credit card companies and college scholarship committees. A company or the government may need to probe into the lives of people applying for unusually sensitive jobs.

No matter how legitimate the need, however, once personal information has been made available to others, there is always the danger that it will be misused. Some of the stored facts may be wrong. Facts may get to the wrong people. Facts may be taken out of context and used to draw distorted conclusions. Facts may be collected and disseminated without one's knowledge or consent. People who are victimized may be denied access to incorrect or sensitive data. As it applies to information processing, **privacy** refers to how information about individuals is used and by whom.

Privacy.
In a computer processing context, refers to how information about individuals is used and by whom.

trailers are the likely abode. There are also categories for urban professionals, the elderly, and so on.

Each category is correlated in the micromarketer's computer system with certain buying preferences, a technique known as *geodemographics*. "Blueblood Estates" types are likely to buy expensive cars and take trips to places such as Aspen, St. Thomas, and Patagonia. Those of the "Shotguns and Pickups" sort are more likely to be interested in fishing equipment, chainsaws, and Elvis collectables. This information helps the micromarketer customize a direct mail (unaffectionately called "junk mail") campaign to consumers' specific tastes.

In addition to geodemographic data, micromarketers also collect data showing consumers' past purchasing behavior. Every time you make a computerized purchase, valuable data can be gathered about your purchasing tastes and entered into a computer system. Records kept by stores, credit-card companies, banks, the companies whose magazines you subscribe to, and other organizations are sold to the micromarketer. Even the government sells information.

A shift in marketing trends has necessitated micromarketing. Not long ago, consumer-prod-

ucts companies produced a small line of products that had little variation. If you wanted a pair of jeans, for instance, you'd better have liked the blue denim variety; it was the only type there was. Today, you can get your jeans in different colors, in different styles, in different fabrics, prewashed, stone-washed, regular or boot cut, with or without rivets, ad nauseum. You've probably noticed that other products seem to come in endless variations. Mass marketing is out; niche marketing, or micromarketing, is in.

Micromarketing, in order to work optimally, requires, in the words of the late Arthur Miller, a "womb-to-tomb dossier" on every consumer. As more and more transactions and records become computerized, it will be easier for the micromarketer to know how much you earn, the names and ages of your children, and where you went and what you did last week. And consider this: In the future, as cars and televisions become more computerized, electronic data may be gathered about exactly where you go, what you are watching, and how much time you spend doing things. How much will you be willing to let the micromarketer know?

The problem of how to protect privacy and ensure that personal information is not misused was with us long before electronic computers existed. But modern computer systems, with their ability to store and manipulate unprecedented quantities of data and to make those data available to many locations, have added a new dimension to the privacy issue. The greater the ability to collect, store, use, and disseminate information, the greater the potential for abuse of that information (see the Tomorrow box).

Privacy Legislation

Since the early 1970s, the federal government has sought to protect citizens' rights by passing legislation to limit the abuse of computer data banks. Some important laws enacted for this purpose are the Fair Credit Reporting Act, the Freedom of Information Act, the Education Privacy Act, and the Privacy Act.

The *Fair Credit Reporting Act (1970)* is designed to prevent private organizations from unfairly denying credit to individuals. It stipulates that people must have the right to inspect their credit records. If a reasonable objection about the integrity of the data is raised, the credit reporting agency is required by law to investigate the matter.

The *Freedom of Information Act (1970)* gives individuals the right to inspect data concerning them that are stored by the federal government. The law also makes certain data about the operation of federal agencies available for public scrutiny.

The *Education Privacy Act (1974)* protects an individual's right to privacy in both private and public schools that receive any federal funding. It stipulates that an individual has the right to keep matters such as course grades and evaluations of behavior private. Also, individuals must have the opportunity to inspect and challenge their own records.

The *Privacy Act (1974)* primarily protects the public against abuses by the federal government. It stipulates that collection of data by federal agencies must have a legitimate purpose. It also states that individuals must be allowed to learn what information is being stored about them and how it's being used and that individuals must have the opportunity to correct or remove erroneous or trivial data.

Most privacy legislation, as you can see, relates to the conduct of the federal government and the organizations to which it supplies aid. Some state governments have enacted similar legislation to protect individuals from abuses by state agencies. The federal government currently is developing private-sector privacy guidelines similar to those of federal and state agencies.

Privacy and Electronic Mail

The recent case involving Lieutenant Colonel Oliver North and the hearings on arms sales to Iran, in which electronic-mail messages between White House staffers were sought as evidence, raised a new issue concerning technology and right to privacy. Some people believe that the objective of electronic mail is to promote a free-flowing dialogue between workers—that is, to increase the effectiveness of organizational communication. They claim that electronic mail should be viewed as the modern-day version of informal chatting around the water cooler, and that electronic mail messages should not in any way be confused with official company records. Others claim that the law applies to hard-copy and soft-copy data in the same way, and that any business document created on the premises of an organization is not the property of the individual but of the organization. Currently under consideration is a *Communications Privacy Act,* which would address such issues, as well as the key matter of when it's appropriate to destroy government electronic-mail backups. Recently, a law professor at a leading university recommended that companies in the private sector should not keep backups on file longer than ten days.

Caller Identification

Caller identification.
Refers to the use of a telephone or answering device that displays the phone numbers of incoming calls.

Caller identification refers to a relatively new technology in which a telephone contains a microprocessor and a tiny display that will output the phone number of any incoming call. Thus, the party receiving the call can identify the caller before picking up the phone. Many people have praised caller identification systems as a good way of screening or cutting down on unwanted calls. Others have been less enthusiastic, seeing these systems as a potential invasion of privacy. For instance, a person living in an apartment or house in a dangerous neighborhood might be afraid to report a crime taking place outside, fearing that his or her identity could be leaked out and cause the criminal to take revenge at some point in the future.

Some companies have designed phone systems that connect caller identification systems to customer and vendor databases. Thus, for each incoming call, the recipient immediately knows the name of the caller or the company at the other end of the line. At the same time, the system can pull up and display certain types of information related to the transaction about to take place.

Computers in Our Lives: Today and Tomorrow

The number of uses to which computers have been put is so large and heterogeneous that it almost defies classification. As you've seen, computers are valuable, on-the-job tools whether you are a company executive, a manager, an engineer, a marketing research analyst, an accountant, a financial analyst, a lawyer, a doctor, a dentist, a real estate broker, an architect, or even a farmer or rancher. And although it may be hard to believe, the impact of the computer on those occupations and others is just beginning.

Outside the workplace, computers have also asserted their presence into our lives. Let's see how.

Computers for Home and Personal Use

When inexpensive microcomputer systems first became widely available in the late 1970s, many people predicted that soon there would be a computer system in every home. After all, computers are useful tools, and think about what happened in the case of other great inventions, such as the car, phone, and television. We are still far from being a society in which every home has a desktop personal computer system. However, those "brainy" little microcomputer and memory chips that are used to make desktop computers are finding their way into scores of other products purchased for personal use. Following are several examples.

Electrical Gadgets Today almost everybody in this country uses a variety of electrical gadgets—television sets, stereo systems, videocassette recorders (VCRs), washing machines, cameras, phones, kitchen appliances, and so on. Increasingly these products are coming packaged with built-in microprocessors and solid-state memories that provide a variety of special functions. The electronic components in your VCR, for instance, enable you to "program" the VCR to record television programs while you are away (see also Feature 16-3). Built-in components on your stereo system provide features such as "quartz tuning" and let you save your favorite radio stations in memory for easy access through push buttons. Electronic processors and memories in kitchen appliances can accept instructions, store them, and perform them according to a designated timetable.

Feature 16 – 3

VCR Programming Made Easy

Two entrepreneurs fill a niche missed by the electronic giants

Here's an interesting success story with a bit of the American Dream thrown in. It's about two guys in California who thought up something simple that a lot of people wanted, built it, and made millions of dollars in the process.

In the early fall of 1988, Henry Yeun and Daniel Kwoh, two naturalized Americans, were looking for a shortcut for taping baseball games on television. How convenient it would be, they thought, to not have to spend lots of time programming a videocassette recorder (VCR) to do this. After all, if you can operate a phone without typing in a person's complete name and address, why couldn't you just punch a single number to program your VCR to record a specific TV program?

Thus they developed a coding scheme—a "program generator"—and built it into a remote-control hardware device that works with a VCR. In this system, each television program translates into a single, unique number that, when keyed into the hardware device (see photo), programs the VCR to tape a show. These numbers are published in more than a hundred newspapers, several cable TV magazines, and some regional editions of *TV Guide*.

VCR Plus. Taking the "programming" out of VCR programming.

Yuen and Kwoh make money on two ends. They sell the hardware units—called VCR Plus—in stores for about $60. In addition, the television periodicals that carry their numbers pay Yuen and Kwoh for the exclusive rights to publish these numbers for several years in certain geographical markets.

VCR Plus is especially targeted to those who are confused by the button-packed front panel of their VCRs; that is, people who use their VCRs almost exclusively to play back rented movies. Recent industry surveys show that about 80 percent of Americans have never programmed their VCRs, and many don't even know how to do it. With more and more electronics being packed into consumer products and products requiring ever more user sophistication, the opportunities have never been greater for computer-savvy entrepreneurs who can find ways to simplify things.

Computerized Cars The car is one product that has been enhanced in a variety of ways through built-in microprocessors and memories (see Figure 16-5). Some of the earliest microprocessors were employed as control mechanisms—for instance, as regulators in electronic ignition systems. Lately they have been employed in more "exotic" applications, and it is not unusual for a car to have dozens of electronic chips of one form or another. In fact, creative use of microcomputing gadgets within cars is becoming a major selling point of cars themselves.

Computerized Homes Homes all over the world are being built today with computer-controlled devices that provide security, greet and identify visitors, monitor and water the lawn while the owners are away, and automatically regulate the temperature in the home. Although the potential for this type of microcomputer application seems far-reaching, it is limited by the reality that many people want their homes to reflect an ambience in which computers play no part.

Home Banking and Shopping   Electronic funds transfers (EFT) systems have long existed. The earliest systems enabled funds to be wired between banks. Later came the automatic teller machine. Most recent to the scene are home-computer-based communications packages and services that enable you to make transactions at banks, brokerage houses, travel agencies, and retail stores. The promise of home banking and shopping is yet to be fulfilled, although some industry observers see both of these applications as future giants.

Cottage Industries   We are living in an age in which information—the very thing that computers are best at producing—has become a highly salable commodity. As business-related computing products continue to drop in price, it is likely that many more of them will be used to create or enhance home-based businesses, or *cottage industries.* To some extent, this phenomenon has been observed with the availability of powerful desktop microcomputer systems. The feasibility of home-based businesses has also been fueled by technologies such as desktop publishing, personal copiers, inexpensive facsimile machines, modems, laptop computers, and satellite dishes.

FIGURE 16 – 5

Smart cars. Today, it's not unusual for a car to have dozens of processor chips of one sort or another.

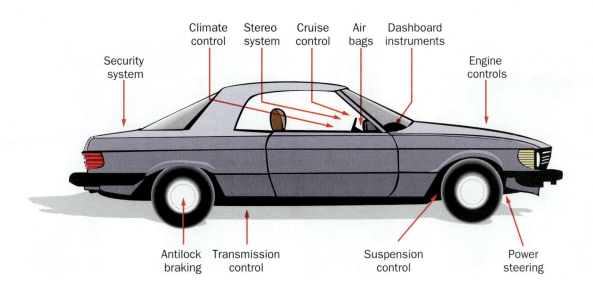

Climate control   Stereo system   Cruise control   Air bags   Dashboard instruments

Security system

Engine controls

Antilock braking   Transmission control   Suspension control   Power steering

Computers in Education

Some of the earliest electronic computers were installed in academic institutions in the 1940s and 1950s, where they were either studied as a curiosity in their own right or used to perform calculations rapidly. Thus, one of computers' earliest applications in education involved the training of engineers, who had to know how to build computers.

As computers found their way into businesses, data processing and information systems courses evolved in business schools. Some academic visionaries, such as John Kemeny at Dartmouth College in the 1960s, realized early on that computers would be useful for performing work in an ever wider variety of disciplines. And so BASIC was developed and rapidly became part of every student's life at Dartmouth.

Today computers and education are combined in many different ways.

Learning about Computers   Learning about computers involves taking courses that teach you general computer principles or hands-on use of a specific software package. As with other disciplines, learning about computers can be approached from several perspectives. Chapter 15 touched on a few of these—for example, *computer science* (a technically oriented perspective), *computer information systems* (a business perspective), and *computer operations* (a hands-on, operational perspective). In a large university, it's common to see 50 or more courses collectively devoted to covering such multiple emphases. Many large businesses and independent training firms also provide computer courses.

FIGURE 16–6

Education. Computers are widely used today to teach all types of courses at all levels of the educational system.

Computer-Enhanced Instruction   Computers are also widely used to assist in the process of teaching (see Figure 16-6).

With *computer-assisted instruction (CAI)*, the student and computer take part in an interactive dialog. For example, a high-school algebra student using a CAI package may be given a problem on the screen to solve. If the answer given is correct, the package poses another problem, perhaps one that's more advanced. If the answer is wrong, the package may go into a "remedial mode" in which it either gives hints, shows how to solve the problem, or provides another problem on the same level. Each student progresses at his or her own pace. At the end of the session, the student is graded. A "progress report" may also be provided.

New technologies such as *optical disk* and *multimedia* are just beginning to be used to assist in the educational process (see Window 7). These technologies enable students to access books and video clips on their computer systems. Of course, no computer-enhanced instructional tool has ever been recognized as a solution that will meet every teaching need. In many situations the computer may never seriously challenge the purely human, personal approach to education.

Problem Solving   One of the first applications of computers in education was for solving difficult problems. Today, students in diverse disciplines use computers to produce cash flow statements, develop business strategies through what-if scenarios, simulate product designs, plan facilities, test decision alternatives, compute mathematical curves, and produce course papers. The list is almost endless. Also, virtually every professor involved in research uses computers in one form or another to discover and organize new scientific facts or just to become more efficient at getting work done.

Computers in Entertainment and Leisure Activities

There are so many entertainment and leisure activities that support computer use that these applications are almost impossible to enumerate. Let's consider a few selected applications of general interest—sports, movies and television, music, and art.

Sports   Among the earliest applications of computers in sports were highly simplified computerized baseball games. The user would select opposing lineups and then issue a RUN command at the terminal. Subsequently the computer would use random numbers to simulate a ballgame and, within seconds, print out a box score. This may not seem very interesting, perhaps, but better things were to come. Today there are sophisticated products that enable users to "participate" in sports such as baseball, football, auto racing, and flying without ever leaving the comfort of their living rooms.

In televised sports broadcasting, the computer has added dazzle. Take those flashy graphics, for instance. There are attractive screens of scores and statistics, possibly a digitized freeze-frame of tennis or racing-car action that you saw live just seconds before, and sequences of fantasy flights over a basketball court or football field. Computer graphics and animation have made all of this possible.

FIGURE 16-7

Computers in sports. Today, computers are used in sports in a variety of ways. Two prominent applications are (a) to assist athletes preparing for the Olympic Games and (b) to help broadcasters keep track of vital statistics for professional sporting events.

(a)

(b)

In sports such as baseball, football, tennis, hockey, and basketball, as well as in Olympic competitions, coaches and managers are trusting computers to analyze player performances and game plans. What else but a computer could quickly determine that Kirby Puckett batted .314 against right-handers last month and .289 against left-handers? Some ballplayers even have their own laptop computers and personal databases to help them develop playing strategies.

Combine all of these applications with electronic scoreboards, computer-controlled ticketing, and all of the other computerized activities performed by any profit-making enterprise and you have an idea of the impressive array of computing power in the sports industry today (see Figure 16-7).

Movies and Films   Robots were among the earliest computer technologies to be worthy subjects of moviemaking. Then, with the 1950s and the ominous presence of the Cold War and atomic weapons, movies began to portray the computer as an infallible, Big Brother-type device that insensitive powermongers would use to rule the world. A major emphasis in movies today, of course, is the notion that computer systems are indeed fallible and that a human software oversight could cause some global diaster.

In the last several years, computers have figured prominently in the actual creation of movies and films (see Figure 16-8). For example, movies such as *Terminator 2: Judgment Day* would have been impossible without computers to keep track of and integrate the numerous special effects involved. Many scenes in that film used computers to combine live images, drawings, and dynamic electronic models. The colorized versions of old classics such as *The*

Maltese Falcon and *Yankee Doodle Dandy* would not have been possible without computers, nor would the restored versions of many old color films whose original prints have faded. At the 1989 Academy Awards, the computer virtually won an Oscar in its own right when the computer-generated film *Tin Toy* was the top vote getter in the animated short film category. Some people believe that the day is now in sight when the motion-picture industry will be able to release films that can be customized by viewers.

Music   Although creating music may be an art, sound is a matter of physics. Musicians frequently use computers called *electronic synthesizers* to store sounds, recall them from memory to have them played, and distort them in new and unusual ways. The use of computer technology in creating music is widespread today, and artists ranging from Stevie Wonder (popular music) to Herbie Hancock (jazz) to Pierre Boulez (classical music) have accepted technology as an important force in the creation of their works. Musicians use the computer as writers use a word processor, but instead of words, they store, edit, cut, and paste sounds. Today many musical pieces are so rich with electronically produced sounds that it's difficult for a nonexpert to tell what came directly from an acoustic instrument and what was electronically enhanced.

The computer plays many other important roles in the music industry today. For example, DJs and their staffs use computer-controlled equipment to edit and organize music for their radio shows. Also, written musical scores are prepared with desktop publishing systems that use specialized fonts, document preparation software, and laser printers.

FIGURE 16 – 8

Computers in film. Computers often assist in the creation of (a) cartoons and (b) special effects.

(a)

(b)

Art   At one time the only way an artistic image could be created was for someone to paint, draw, weave, or sculpt it completely by hand. Then the Gutenberg press arrived, and images could be mass produced. Although that event probably created panic among people contemplating a calligraphy career, the would-be Renoirs and Van Goghs had little to worry about.

The industrial revolution gave rise to the so-called industrial arts, and machines such as the Jacquard loom (see Appendix B), which could weave under program control, appeared. When photography was invented in the mid-1800s, it threatened the painters of the day, but it later evolved into an art form of its own, with a different set of standards.

Now that the computer has arrived, there are new perceived threats to artists on all levels—but there are also great opportunities. With a computer, images of virtually any shape can be created, colored in any of thousands of colors, enlarged, rotated, blended, combined with other images, illuminated by one or more shadow-casting light sources, and so forth. Also, colors, positions, and shapes of objects can be changed at electronically fast speeds to create new images. For example, a computer was used to generate the images in Figure 16-9 as well as the stunning images in Windows 2 and 8. A computer enables the artist to see a variety of images and store the most promising of them, all in a span of time that would be impossible with only canvas and brush.

Nonetheless, painters are still far from being replaced. Like photography, computer art has evolved into an art form in its own right. So, too, has computer-enhanced photography (see Figure 16-10).

FIGURE 16 – 9

Computer art. The computer is a useful tool for artists of all types—most of whom are not computer professionals. Computer art has rapidly evolved into a form in its own right, with its own shows and contests.

FIGURE 16 – 10

Computers and photography. Computers are widely used to both (a) enhance photographic images and (b) produce photorealistic art. Today, most publishers convert photographs into digital form for printing purposes.

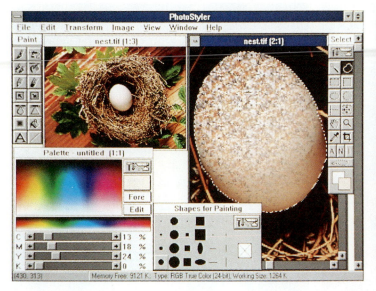

(a)

(b)

Computers in Science and Medicine

Science and medicine account for myriad computer applications. In this section, we'll look specifically at how computers are used for weather forecasting, environmental simulations, patient diagnosis, life-support systems, and to assist handicapped people.

Science   One of the earliest applications of computer power in a scientific field was weather forecasting. To predict the weather accurately, data on current weather conditions must be input to the computer, which then analyzes mounds of data on past conditions. Because predicting weather is often a round-the-clock chore that requires supercomputer-sized computational and storage capacity, it is usually done at a national level at places such as the National Center for Atmospheric Research (NCAR) in Boulder, Colorado.

Today, computer applications in the field of science virtually defy enumeration. Computers are used to control scientific experiments, uncover significant trends or properties in data, and perform various types of research functions. One popular tool is simulation. *Simulation* involves building a mathematical model of a real-life object or situation and thoroughly testing it with "dummy" data before the object is built or the situation encountered. A car may be modeled on a computer screen. Then, before the car is actually built, the

F I G U R E   16 – 11

Computers in medicine. Computers are used in the health-care industry today for virtually everything from patient management to assisting with the diagnosis of illnesses.

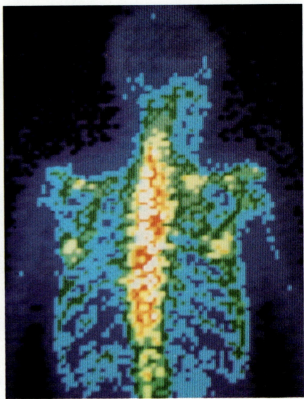

computer simulates real-life events such as accidents and stresses. Simulation is also useful to governments and businesses for predicting economic changes in society, the environmental impact of new policies, and consumer reaction to the effects of price changes.

Medicine   It is indeed comforting to know that computers are hard at work helping health-care professionals ensure that you remain healthy and live longer (see Figure 16-11).

Computer-assisted diagnosis refers to a number of hardware or software technologies that assist physicians in diagnosing patients' conditions. One example is inputting data about a patient's condition to a software program that compares the condition to previously diagnosed ones in a large patient database. The program then outputs relevant statistics to help the attending physicians diagnose the ailment. Many of these programs are expert systems; they employ artifical intelligence techniques that enable them to actually draw some conclusions for the physician.

Computer-assisted tomography, sometimes referred to as CAT or PET scanning, is another computer-assisted diagnosis technique. It employs X-ray hardware and computer technology to provide physicians with three-dimensional pictures of the organs in a person's body. Thus, the physicians have more information on which to base a diagnosis than they would from a traditional two-dimensional Xray.

Computerized life-support systems provide nursing support, although they usually bear no resemblance to their human counterparts. These systems monitor bedridden patients, freeing human nurses from the need for uninterrupted observation. A system might continuously monitor signs such as heart rate, temperature, and blood pressure and activate a silent alarm if something goes outside an acceptable range.

Today computers are being used in many ways to help the handicapped (see Figure 16-12). Computer-aided instruction (CAI), for example, has been used successfully to provide assistance to people with special learning needs. Computers have been used to artifically simulate the human voice, enabling cerebral palsy victims to "speak." The United States recently passed into law the Americans with Disabilities Act (1990), which requires U.S. organizations as of 1992 to make "reasonable accommodations" for handicapped workers. Although the law is vague, accommodations would likely include such aids as visual interfaces for the deaf and audio interfaces for the blind. Workers who feel that their employers are adopting a take-me-to-court attitude can file a civil lawsuit or a complaint with the Equal Employment Opportunity Commission.

Summary and Key Terms

Since the early 1950s, when the era of commercial computing began, computers have rapidly woven their way into the fabric of modern society. In the process, they have created both opportunities and problems.

FIGURE 16 – 12

Technology and the handicapped worker. Most assistive technologies fall into one or more of the categories given here.

Category	Examples
Magnified output	Large-screen displays that make reading easier
Audio/Voice output	Hardware and software that can read words aloud and provide audio rather than visual outputs
Alternative input	Voice-input devices, oversized-key keyboards, and devices that can accept input from mouth-held wands or from eye movements
Environmental control	Devices that activate appliances, change television channels, and turn lights on and off
Word aids	Tools that can anticipate words or commands, thereby making expression easier
Instructional aids	Software that provides special accommodations for the learning impaired

Computers, Work, and Health One of the first criticisms leveled at the entry of computers into the workplace was that their presence resulted in stress. Stress-related concerns triggered by the so-called computer revolution include fear of layoff or reassignment, fear of falling behind, and job burnout. In addition to these problems, other concerns related to **ergonomics**-related issues, such as display device usage and workspace design, have surfaced. Many people also worry about our society's apparent overreliance on computers.

Computer Crime and Ethics **Computer crime** is loosely defined as the use of computers to commit unauthorized acts. Some states have laws that address computer crime directly; others do not. In practice, however, computer crime is hard to pin down even in states that have such laws. It is hard to decide when an unauthorized act is really a crime, judges and juries often are bewildered by the technical issues involved, and companies frequently are reluctant to press charges.

Computer crime may take many forms. Types of computer crime include data diddling, the Trojan horse technique, salami-shaving methods, unauthorized use of superzap and trapdoor programs, logic bombs, **computer viruses,** scavenging, data leakage, wiretapping, **software piracy, hacking,** and counterfeiting.

Organizations can combat computer crimes in many ways: hiring trustworthy people; taking precautions with malcontents; separating employee functions; restricting system use; limiting access to programs and data with **passwords, access cards,** and **biometric security devices; site licensing;** devising staff controls; disguising particularly sensitive programs and data through **encryption;** using **callback devices;** monitoring important system transactions; conducting regular **audits;** and educating employees.

Ethics refers to standards of moral conduct. Today one of the most important concerns in the ethics area as regards computers is using someone else's property in an unauthorized way. Another is leading people to believe something that's more fiction than fact when it works to one's advantage—such as the case with **vaporware.**

Computers and Privacy Most people want some control over the kinds of facts that are collected about them, how those facts are collected and their accuracy, who uses them, and how they are used. Modern computer systems, with their ability to store and manipulate unprecedented quantities of data and make those data available to many locations, have added a new dimension to the personal **privacy** issue. Recently, two relatively new technologies—electronic mail and **caller identification** phone systems—have created further concerns about invasion of privacy.

Computers in Our Lives: Today and Tomorrow Today the number of uses to which computers have been put is so large and heterogeneous that it almost defies classification. Most of this text has examined the uses of computers in the ordinary business workplace. Outside this workplace, computers of some sort are found in the home, in educational institutions, in entertainment and leisure activities, and in science and medicine.

Review Exercises

1. Fear of computers is known as _____.

2. _____ is the field that covers the effects of factors such as equipment and computer workspaces on employees' productivity and health.

3. _____ refers to standards of moral conduct.

4. The unauthorized copying or use of computer programs is known as software _____.

5. The _____ Act was designed to prevent private organizations from unfairly denying credit to individuals.

6. _____ refers to phone systems that can display the phone numbers corresponding to incoming calls.

Match each term with the description that fits best.

a. computer virus
b. data diddling
c. salami shaving

d. hacking
e. trapdoor
f. superzap

____ 1. The deduction of small amounts from a large number of randomly selected accounts.

____ 2. Refers to a program that can bypass all system controls.

____ 3. Is transmitted through a copy operation.

____ 4. A diagnostic tool that allows viewing of computer storage.

____ 5. The altering of an organization's production data.

____ 6. Using a terminal or microcomputer system to illegally break into a larger computer system.

1. Identify some specific problems caused by the rapid spread of computer use in society.

2. Describe some ways in which computers may affect our health or well-being.

3. Why is computer crime so difficult to pin down?

4. Name some of the forms computer crime can take.

5. How does a computer virus work?

6. Provide some examples demonstrating unethical behavior related to the use of computers.

7. Name some rights of individuals that computer privacy laws have tried to protect.

8. Identify some ways in which computers affect our daily lives.

Critical Thinking Questions

1. A clerk in a steel company uses a company-owned desktop computer, on company time, to keep track of baseball statistics. Is a crime being committed?

2. A defense lawyer gets a computer researcher to electronically enhance photographs taken at the scene of an accident to prove that her client wasn't completely at fault. The enhanced photographs appear to show that there was some prior damage to the plaintiff's car, which, if true, would contradict statements made by the plaintiff. What problem might the lawyer have in presenting the case?

3. In a recent editorial in *Computerworld*, a software consultant touched off a flood of fiery protest by remarking that software piracy is overblown as an issue. He argued that:
   a. Most people who pirate software wouldn't have bought the software in the first place, so pirated software doesn't necessarily represent lost revenue.
   b. Pirates who like a product often buy future releases of it to access new features, so pirating often has a positive effect on future sales.
   c. The estimate of the value of stolen software—which ranges from $170 million to $4 billion a year—overstates the real drain on profits because it multiplies the number of illegal copies times sales price.
   Please comment.

4. A software developer creates a program to protect against computer viruses. To finance the advertising campaign for this product, the developer decides to call several computer executives at large firms and try to get them to put up $5,000 each. This, the developer believes, will both produce the funds needed and make the executives more likely to buy the product. Does this strategy seem sound to you from both a business and an ethical standpoint?

5. As hinted in the Tomorrow box, there is considerable fear that marketing databases can be used to invade a person's privacy. What important issue areas do you feel should be addressed by the government to ensure the privacy of individuals isn't invaded by micromarketers? For instance, one critical issue area concerns *access*; that is, who will have access to the marketing data and under what circumstances will access be granted?

 6. United States Labor Secretary Robert B. Reich once pointed out that it is difficult these days to tell whether some businesses are domestic or foreign. For instance, say that Company A is headquartered in your country and virtually all its owners and directors are fellow citizens. However, most of

its employees and all of its manufacturing facilities are located on foreign soil. Company B is just the opposite; while most of its employees and plant are in your country, virtually all of its owners and directors are foreign based. Which company would you say is domestic and which is foreign? Which company should your country's economic policy favor?

NUMBERING SYSTEMS

A

LEARNING OBJECTIVES

After completing this appendix, you will be able to:

1. Describe how the decimal, binary, and hexadecimal numbering systems work.

2. Convert values in one numbering system to those of another.

3. Add and subtract with the binary and hexadecimal numbering systems.

In Chapter 3, you learned that fixed-length codes such as ASCII and EBCDIC are often used to represent numbers, letters of the alphabet, and special characters. Although these codes are handy for storing data and transporting them around a computer system, they are not designed to do arithmetic operations. For this type of use, numbers must be stored in a "true" binary form that can be manipulated quickly by the computer.

This appendix covers several fundamentals of numbering systems. The two primary systems discussed are the decimal numbering system (used by people) and the binary numbering system (used by computers). Also discussed is the hexadecimal numbering system, which is a shorthand way of representing long strings of binary numbers so that they are more understandable to people. The appendix also covers conversions between numbering systems and principles of computer arithmetic.

Numbering Systems

A *numbering system* is a way of representing numbers. The system we most commonly use is called the *decimal*, or base ten, system (the word *decimal* comes from the Latin word for *ten*). It is called *base 10* because it uses ten symbols—the digits 0, 1, 2, 3, 4, 5, 6, 7, 8, 9—to represent all possible numbers. Numbers greater than nine are represented by a combination of these symbols.

Because we are so familiar with the decimal system, it may never have occurred to most of us that we could represent numbers in any other way. In fact, however, nothing says that a numbering system has to have ten possible symbols. Many other numbers would do as a base.

We saw in Chapter 3 that the *binary*, or base 2, system is used extensively by computers to represent numbers and other characters. Computer systems can perform computations and transmit data thousands of times faster in binary form than they can using decimal representations. Thus, it's important for anyone studying computers to know how the binary system works. Anyone contemplating a professional career in computers should also understand the *hexadecimal* (base 16) system. Before we examine some of the numbering systems used in computing—and learn how to convert numbers from one system into another—let's look more closely at the decimal numbering system. Insight into how the decimal system works will help us understand more about the other numbering systems.

The Decimal Numbering System

Decimal.
A numbering system with ten symbols—0, 1, 2, 3, 4, 5, 6, 7, 8, and 9.

All numbering systems, including the decimal system with which we work in our everyday lives, represent numbers as a combination of ordered symbols. As stated earlier, the **decimal*** (or base 10) system has ten acceptable symbols—the digits 0, 1, 2, . . . , 9. The positioning of the symbols in a decimal number is important. For example, 891 is a different number than 918 (with the same symbols occupying different positions).

The position of each symbol in any decimal number represents the number 10 (the base number) raised to a power, or exponent, that is based on that

---

*Boldfaced terms used in this appendix can be found in the Glossary at the end of the book.

FIGURE A-1

How the decimal (base ten) system works.

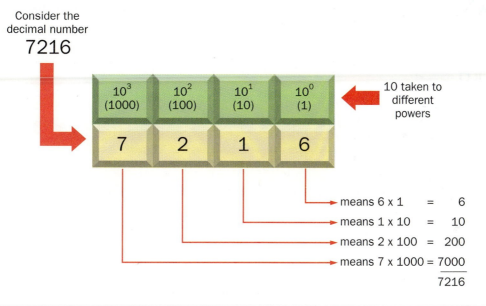

Consider the decimal number
7216

10 taken to different powers

means 6 x 1 = 6
means 1 x 10 = 10
means 2 x 100 = 200
means 7 x 1000 = 7000

7216

position. Going from right to left, the first position represents 10^0, or 1; the second position represents 10^1, or 10; the third position represents 10^2, or 100; and so forth. Thus, as Figure A-1 shows, a decimal number like 7,216 is understood as $7 \times 10^3 + 2 \times 10^2 + 1 \times 10^1 + 6 \times 10^0$.

The Binary Numbering System

The **binary,** or base 2, system works in a manner similar to the decimal system. One major difference is that the binary system has only two symbols—0 and 1—instead of ten. A second major difference is that the position of each digit in a binary number represents the number 2 (the base number) raised to an exponent based on that position. Thus, the binary number 11100 represents

$$1 \times 2^4 + 1 \times 2^3 + 1 \times 2^2 + 0 \times 2^1 + 0 \times 2^0$$

which, translated into the decimal system, is 28. Another example of a binary-to-decimal conversion is provided in Figure A-2.

Converting in the reverse direction—from decimal to binary—is also rather easy. A popular approach for doing this is the *remainder method.* This procedure employs successive divisions by the base number of the system to which we are converting. Use of the remainder method to convert a decimal to a binary number is illustrated in Figure A-3.

To avoid confusion when different number bases are being used, it is common to use the base as a subscript. So, referring to Figures A-2 and A-3, for example, we could write

$$89_{10} = 1011001_2$$

Binary.
A numbering system with two possible states—0 and 1.

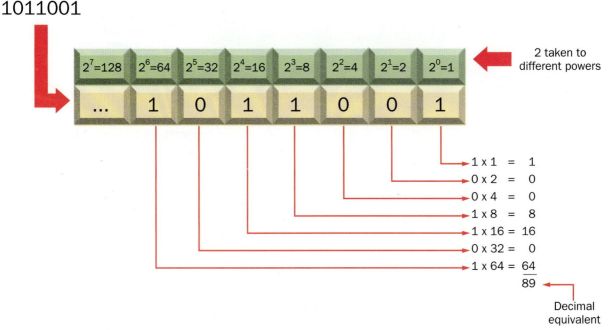

Binary-to-decimal conversion. To convert any binary number to its decimal counterpart, take the rightmost digit and multiply it by 2^0 (or 1), the next-to-rightmost digit and multiply it by 2^1 (or 2), and so on, as illustrated here. Then add up all the products so formed.

In addition, when we are using numbering systems other than the decimal system, it is customary to pronounce each symbol individually. For example, 101_2 is pronounced "one-zero-one" rather than "one hundred one." This convention is also used with other nondecimal systems.

The binary system described here is sometimes referred to as *true-binary representation*. True-binary representation does not use a fixed number of bits, as do ASCII and EBCDIC, nor is it used to represent letters or special characters.

The Hexadecimal Numbering System

Often diagnostic and memory-management messages are output to programmers and technically oriented users in hexadecimal (or *hex*) notation (see Figure A-4). Hex is a shorthand method for representing the binary digits that are stored in the computer system. Because large binary numbers—for example, 11010100010011101_2—can easily be misread by programmers, binary digits are often grouped into units of four that, in turn, are represented by other symbols.

Decimal-to-binary conversion using the remainder method. In this approach, we start by using the decimal number to be converted (89) as the initial dividend. Each successive dividend is the quotient of the previous division. We keep dividing until we've reached a zero quotient, whereupon the converted number is formed by the remainders taken in reverse order.

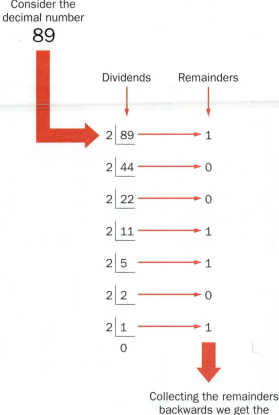

Consider the decimal number
89

Dividends   Remainders

2 | 89   ⟶   1

2 | 44   ⟶   0

2 | 22   ⟶   0

2 | 11   ⟶   1

2 | 5   ⟶   1

2 | 2   ⟶   0

2 | 1   ⟶   1

0

Collecting the remainders backwards we get the binary number 1011001.

Hexadecimal means base 16, implying that there are 16 different symbols in this numbering system. Since we have only ten possible digits to work with, letters are used instead of numbers for the extra six symbols. The 16 hexadecimal symbols and their decimal and binary counterparts are shown in Figure A-5.

Hexadecimal is not itself a code that the computer uses to perform computations or to communicate with other machines. It does, however, have a special relationship to the 8-bit bytes of ASCII-8 and EBCDIC that makes it ideal for displaying messages quickly. As you can see in Figure A-5, each hex character has a 4-binary-bit counterpart, so any combination of 8 bits can be represented by exactly two hexadecimal characters. Thus, the letter *A* (represented in EBCDIC by 11000001) has a hex representation of C1.

Let's look at an example to see how to convert from hex to decimal. Suppose you receive the following message on your display screen:

PROGRAM LOADED AT LOCATION 4F6A

This message tells you the precise location in memory of the first byte in your program. To determine the decimal equivalent of a hexadecimal number such

Hexadecimal.
Pertaining to the numbering system with 16 symbols: 0, 1, 2, 3, 4, 5, 6, 7, 8, 9, A, B, C, D, E, and F.

FIGURE A – 4

Hexadecimal display. Programmers often rely on the hexadecimal numbering system to give them information about where programs and data are stored in memory. Here, Quarterdeck's Manifest—a diagnostics and resources-management software package—tells how the first megabyte of memory is allocated by the DOS operating system.

FIGURE A – 5

Hexadecimal characters and their decimal and binary equivalents.

Hexadecimal Character	Decimal Equivalent	Binary Equivalent
0	0	0000
1	1	0001
2	2	0010
3	3	0011
4	4	0100
5	5	0101
6	6	0110
7	7	0111
8	8	1000
9	9	1001
A	10	1010
B	11	1011
C	12	1100
D	13	1101
E	14	1110
F	15	1111

as 4F6A, you can use a procedure similar to the binary-to-decimal conversion shown in Figure A-2 (refer to Figure A-6).

To convert the other way—from decimal to hex—we again can use the remainder method, this time dividing by 16. A decimal-to-hex conversion using the remainder method is illustrated in Figure A-7.

To convert from base 16 to base 2, we convert each hex digit separately to four binary digits (using the table in Figure A-5). For example, to convert F6A9 to base 2, we get

$$\begin{array}{cccc} F & 6 & A & 9 \\ 1111 & 0110 & 1010 & 1001 \end{array}$$

or 1111011010101001_2. To convert from base 2 to base 16, we go through the reverse process. If the number of digits in the binary number is not divisible by 4, we add leading zeros to the binary number to force an even division. So, for example, to convert 1101101010011_2 to base 16, we get

$$\begin{array}{cccc} 0001 & 1011 & 0101 & 0011 \\ 1 & B & 5 & 3 \end{array}$$

or $1B53_{16}$. Note that three leading zeros were added to make this conversion.

One final word before we close. In Chapter 3 we mentioned that 32-bit computer chips, such as the Intel 80386 and 80486, are capable of addressing

---

FIGURE A – 6

Hexadecimal-to-decimal conversion. To convert any hexadecimal number to its decimal counterpart, take the rightmost digit and multiply it by 16^0 (or 1), the next-to-rightmost digit and multiply it by 16^1 (or 16), and so on, as illustrated here. Then add up all the products so formed.

Consider the
hexadecimal number
4F6A

$16^3 = 4096$	$16^2 = 256$	$16^1 = 16$	$16^0 = 1$
4	F	6	A

means A x 1 or 10 x 1   =   10
means 6 x 16   =   96
means F x 256 or 15 x 256 =   3,840
means 4 x 4096   = 16,384

                             20,330

Decimal equivalent

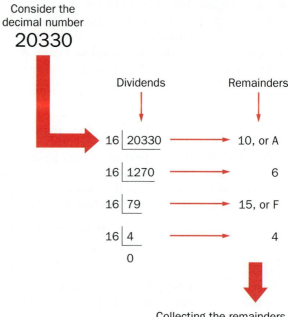

FIGURE A-7

Decimal-to-hexadecimal conversion using the remainder method. To convert 20330_{10} to a hexadecimal number, we start our successive divisions by 16 using 20330 as the initial dividend. Each successive dividend is the quotient of the previous division. As in Figure A-3, we divide until we've reached a zero quotient and form the converted number by taking the remainders in reverse order.

Consider the decimal number
20330

Dividends | Remainders

16 | 20330 ⟶ 10, or A

16 | 1270 ⟶ 6

16 | 79 ⟶ 15, or F

16 | 4 ⟶ 4

0

Collecting the remainders backwards we get the hexadecimal number 4F6A

about 4 billion bytes (4 gigabytes) of memory. You may have then wondered at that time, "Why 4 billion bytes?" Note that the maximum address in a 32-bit computer is a string of 32 1-bits, or

$$11111111111111111111111111111111$$

which, expressed in hex, is

$$FFFFFFFF$$

Note that the decimal equivalent is 4,294,967,296—or roughly 4 billion bytes.

A table summarizing all of the conversions covered in this appendix is provided in Figure A-8.

Computer Arithmetic

To most of us, decimal arithmetic is second nature. Addition and subtraction have been part of our education since kindergarten or first grade. Addition and subtraction using binary and hexadecimal numbers is not much harder than the same operations with decimal numbers. Practically the only difference is in the number of symbols used in each system.

Figure A-9 provides an example of addition and subtraction with decimal, binary, and hexadecimal numbers. Note that, as in decimal arithmetic, you carry to and borrow from adjacent positions as you move from right to left.

Summary of conversions.

From Base	To Base 2	To Base 10	To Base 16
2		Starting at rightmost digit, multiply binary digits by 2^0, 2^1, 2^2, etc., respectively. Then add products.	Starting at rightmost digit, convert each group of four binary digits to a hex digit.
10	Divide repeatedly by 2; then collect remainders in reverse order.		Divide repeatedly by 16; then collect remainders in reverse order.
16	Convert each hex digit to four binary digits.	Starting at rightmost digit, multiply hex digits by 16^0, 16^1, 16^2, etc., respectively. Then add products.	

Instead of carrying or borrowing 10, however—as you would in the decimal system—you carry or borrow 2 (binary) or 16 (hexadecimal).

Summary and Key Terms

This appendix covers several fundamentals of numbering systems.

Numbering Systems   A *numbering system* is a way of representing numbers.

The Decimal Numbering System   The number system we most commonly use is called the **decimal**, or base 10, system. It is called base 10 because it uses ten symbols—the digits 0, 1, 2, 3, 4, 5, 6, 7, 8, 9—to represent all possible numbers. The position of each symbol in any decimal number represents the number 10 (the base number) raised to a power, or exponent, which is based on that position.

Adding and subtracting with the decimal, binary, and hexadecimal numbering systems.

	Decimal	Binary	Hexadecimal
Addition	142 +47 189	10001110 +101111 10111101	8E +2F BD
Subtraction	142 -47 95	10001110 -101111 1011111	8E -2F 5F

The Binary Numbering System   The **binary**, or base 2, system works in a manner similar to the decimal system. One major difference is that the binary system has only two symbols—0 and 1—instead of ten. A second major difference is that the position of each digit in a binary number represents the number 2 (the base number) raised to an exponent based on that position.

The Hexadecimal Numbering System   Because large binary numbers can easily be misread by programmers, binary digits often are grouped and represented by other symbols. The **hexadecimal,** or base 16, system is used to represent a grouping of four binary digits. There are 16 different symbols in this system. Since we have only ten possible digits to work with, the letters A–F are used instead of numbers for the extra six symbols. The position of each digit in a hexadecimal number represents the number 16 raised to an exponent based on that position.

Computer Arithmetic   It is a relatively straightforward process to convert any value in one numbering system into a value in another system and to perform computer arithmetic on these values.

Exercises

1. Convert the following binary numbers to decimal numbers:
   a. 1011_2 _____
   b. 101110_2 _____
   c. 1010011_2 _____

2. Convert the following decimal numbers to binary numbers:
   a. 51_{10} _____
   b. 260_{10} _____
   c. 500_{10} _____

3. Convert the following binary numbers to hexadecimal numbers:
   a. 101_2 _____
   b. 11010_2 _____
   c. 111101000010_2 _____

4. Convert the following hexadecimal numbers to binary numbers:
   a. $F2_{16}$ _____
   b. $1A8_{16}$ _____
   c. $39EB_{16}$ _____

5. Convert the following hexadecimal numbers to decimal numbers:
   a. $B6_{16}$ _____
   b. $5E9_{16}$ _____
   c. $CAFF_{16}$ _____

6. Drawing on techniques you've learned in this appendix, provide an expression to convert the base 6 (yes, six) number 451_6 to a decimal number: _____.

7. Adding the binary numbers 11011001 and 1011101 yields _____.

8. Adding the hexadecimal numbers 8E and 5D yields _____.

9. Subtracting the binary number 1011 from 101110 yields _____.

10. Subtracting the hexadecimal number B6 from F2 yields _____.

A Brief History of Computers and Information Processing

B

LEARNING OBJECTIVES

After completing this appendix, you will be able to:

1. Name some of the key pioneers and describe some of the events that have influenced today's computers.

2. Understand how hardware and software have evolved over the past half-century.

3. Explain the differences between the first, second, third, fourth, and fifth generations of computers.

4. Appreciate how fast the computer revolution is progressing, and speculate intelligently about what might evolve during your lifetime.

Many people dismiss the need to learn about our technological heritage. But a subject's history gives us insight into why things are the way they are today and sharpens our ability to predict future events.

Electronic computers as we know them were invented about 50 years ago. The history of computers actually goes back much further than that. Since the beginning of civilization, merchants and government officials have used computing devices to help them with calculations and recordkeeping. The abacus, invented thousands of years ago, is an example of such a device.

In the first part of this appendix, we will discuss the early advances that gave birth to today's electronic computer, beginning with the invention of the first mechanical calculating machines in the 1600s. Next, we will cover the development of commercial computer systems from the 1950s to the present. Finally, we turn to developments that are likely to hold a key to the future of computing in the near term.

From Gears and Levers to Circuits and Tubes

In the 1600s, people found it remarkable that a process such as arithmetic could be carried out by a machine.

Pascal and Leibniz Blaise Pascal, the French mathematician, is credited with inventing the first *mechanical calculating machine* around 1642. Pascal got the inspiration for his invention at age 19, after spending many hours poring over columns of figures and painstakingly adding them up. Pascal realized that this tedious chore could be done faster and more accurately with a machine. After much effort, he built a mechanical device that was powered by levers and gears. This machine, which could add and subtract automatically, was named the **pascaline,*** after its inventor.

Pascaline.
A mechanical calculating machine developed by Blaise Pascal in the 1600s.

Later in the 1600s, Gottfried von Leibniz, the German philosopher and mathematician, went one step beyond Pascal and devised a machine that could multiply and divide as well as add and subtract. Like Pascal's, this device was run by levers and gears.

Jacquard's Loom One important event in the development of the computer might seem unrelated at first glance. In the early 1800s, a weaver named Joseph Jacquard invented a loom that produced patterned cloth automatically. The remarkable thing about this loom was that it used punched cardboard cards to control the pattern in the cloth. The holes in the cards determined which rods in the loom were engaged at any given time.

Jacquard's loom introduced two concepts that proved important to the future development of the computer. The first concept was that information could be coded on *punched cards*. Punched cards, as we'll see, were to become the main input/output medium for the first modern computers. The second concept was that the information stored in the cards could serve as a series of instructions— in effect, a *program*—when the cards were activated.

---

*Boldfaced terms used in this appendix can be found in the Glossary at the end of this book.

Babbage and His Engines   One of the most noteworthy figures in the history of computers was the nineteenth-century English mathematician Charles Babbage. About 150 years ago, he designed a machine with an amazing similarity to the first modern computers.

Babbage first became interested in mechanical computing devices while studying mathematical tables. These tables contained many errors because they had been hand-set into print. Babbage realized that a machine that could automatically calculate the numbers and print the results would produce much more reliable tables.

Babbage was able to get funds from the British government to build such a machine, which he called the **difference engine.** He succeeded in building a small prototype (Figure B-1). His attempts to build a larger version failed, however, because the technology for creating the parts that he needed did not yet exist.

While working on the difference engine, Babbage conceived another, much more powerful machine, which he called the **analytical engine.** It is this machine that is so similar in concept to the modern computer. Like the difference engine, it would consist of gears and shafts run by a steam engine. It was to be general-purpose, capable of many kinds of computing work. The analytical engine would be directed by instructions on punched cards, contain a memory for storing instructions and results, and automatically print results.

Difference engine.
A mechanical machine devised by Charles Babbage in the 1800s to perform computations automatically and print their results.

Analytical engine.
A device conceived by Charles Babbage in the 1800s that is considered the forerunner of today's modern electronic computer.

FIGURE B-1

The Babbage difference engine. Babbage was constantly at odds with the British government in getting funding for his projects. In 1833, he wrote in frustration, ". . . of all countries England is that in which . . . the governing powers are most incompetent to understand the merit either of the mechanical or mathematical."

Babbage became obsessed with the analytical engine and devoted all of his energy and resources to creating it. But he never was able to complete a working model, and he died without knowing how his vision would shape the future.

Much of what we know about Charles Babbage's analytical engine comes not from Babbage himself but from the work of his close friend and associate Ada Augusta, Countess of Lovelace, the daughter of the poet Byron. She has been called "the first programmer" because of her work on the kinds of instructions that would have been fed into the analytical engine to make it work.

Hollerith and the Census   Another milestone on the way to the modern computer was passed during the tabulation of the 1890 U.S. census. Until 1890, census figures had been tabulated manually. The 1880 census took seven years to complete, and officials worried that if something weren't done, the results of the 1890 census would not be completed before it was time to begin tabulating the 1900 census.

The government commissioned a man named Herman Hollerith to build a machine to aid in the tabulation of the 1890 census. The machine Hollerith built (Figure B-2) used punched cards and was powered by electricity. With its help, the tabulation of the census was finished in three years.

Hollerith later founded the Tabulating Machine Company to develop punched-card equipment to sell to business and government. Hollerith's company merged with several others in 1911, and in 1924, this new company changed its name to International Business Machines (IBM) Corporation (see Figure B-3).

FIGURE B-2

Hollerith and his census tabulator. Trained as an engineer, Hollerith began work with the U.S. Census Office in 1879. Shortly thereafter, Hollerith later recalled, the head of the division of vital statistics remarked to him ". . . there ought to be a machine for doing the purely mechanical work of tabulating population and similar statistics." The rest is history.

IBM circa 1924. IBM president and founder, Tom Watson, shown greeting some of the "Go Getters," the stars of the firm's sales force, on the boardwalk in Atlantic City, New Jersey. Watson stressed the role of marketing computer systems to users—selling business solutions rather than just electronic boxes—a strategy that eventually made IBM the world's top producer of computers.

IBM rapidly became the leader in the manufacture of punched-card equipment. By the mid-1930s, the mechanical machines of the nineteenth century had been replaced by electromechanical devices such as the one Hollerith pioneered. **Electromechanical machines** are mechanical machines driven by electricity. But although these devices were a vast improvement over their hand-cranked ancestors, they had some serious drawbacks. For example, the moving parts were slow to align themselves, which limited their speed. Also, the repeated movement of those parts caused wear, making the machines failure-prone.

Electromechanical machine.
A device that has both electrical and mechanical features.

Aiken, IBM, and the Mark I   The age of electromechanical computing devices reached its zenith in the early 1940s with the work of Howard Aiken of Harvard University. Aiken had long been interested in developing ways to use these machines for scientific calculations. IBM and other manufacturers had designed machines with business users in mind, but during the late 1920s and early 1930s, many scientists began to use them for their work as well. Aiken had the important insight that the technology of these machines could be adapted to create a *general-purpose computer*—one that could be programmed to do a variety of computing tasks.

With the support of a $500,000 grant from IBM and the help of four of IBM's top engineers, Aiken started work on his machine in 1939. Its official name was the "Automatic Sequence Controlled Calculator," but it came to be called

Minicomputer pioneer.
Kenneth Olsen, the founder
of Digital Equipment
Corporation.

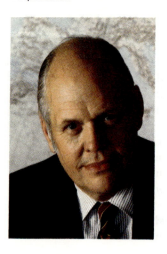

need for a programming lanugage that was easy to learn and use. The development of *RPG* (Report Program Generator) in the mid-1960s signaled a new trend in programming languages. It enabled users to input the specifications for reports and have the computer generate those reports automatically.

The Rise of the Minicomputer In the mid-1960s, the first successful *minicomputer* was built. The mini—a scaled-down version of larger computers of the day—was largely the brainchild of an electrical engineer named Kenneth Olsen (Figure B-11). Olsen saw early on the need for a small, rugged, inexpensive computer, one that didn't need to be housed in a computing center and tended to by a staff of trained operators. Together with his brother and another engineer, Olsen founded Digital Equipment Corporation (DEC). Their first successful mini, a refrigerator-sized computer called the PDP-8, cost about $18,000. It became widely used in both small and large companies. Following DEC's success, other companies soon started to manufacture minis. Data General, Wang, Prime, and Perkin-Elmer soon joined DEC as major players in the minicomputer marketplace.

Word Processing *Word processing* refers to using computer technology to assist in the typing of documents. IBM coined the term in 1964, when it first marketed the Magnetic Tape Selectric Typewriter (MT/ST). This machine enabled secretaries to store "canned" portions of documents on a tape unit connected to the typewriter and to interweave fresh text with preprepared materials. Today, of course, the tape units are gone and word processing has been enhanced by disk units, display screens, and large electronic memories. Word processing initiated the widespread use of computers in office settings, a phenomenon that people refer to today as *office automation (OA)*.

The Fourth Generation (1971–Present): Enter the Microcomputer

Fourth generation.
The fourth era of commer-
cial computing (1971–
present), which is characterized by microminiaturiz-
ation and the rise of microcomputing.

The earliest electronic computers reached fruition largely through the creative efforts of established scholars and the sponsorship of blue-chip corporations, prestigious academic institutions, and the federal government. In contrast, the beginning of the microcomputer industry—perhaps the singular most important event of the **fourth generation**—is absolutely grass roots. The history of microcomputers is a collage of interesting stories about bright teenagers, high-school dropouts, after-hours hobbyists tinkering in their garages or basements, shoestring budgets, speculative venture capital, and rags-to-riches enterprises.

The Microcomputer Revolution

A good place to begin the story of microcomputers is in 1969, when an ambitious, though now defunct, Japanese company contracted with Intel, a small California firm, to build programming logic into an ordinary calculator. The project was assigned to Marcian E. ("Ted") Hoff, whom many called an "engineer's engineer." Hoff developed a general-purpose logic chip, the Intel 4004, which became known as the first microprocessor, or "computer on a chip" (See Figure B-12). Intel later became the world's leading producer of microprocessor chips.

F I G U R E   B – 12

The Intel 4004. On November 15, 1971, *Electronic News* carried the first advertisement for the Intel 4004. With only 2,250 transistors—which is less than 1 percent of the elements on most of today's microprocessors—the 4004 was an adequate processor for simple electronic devices such as calculators and cash registers. Only a year later Intel introduced the 8080 microprocessor, the first device capable of supporting a complete microcomputer system.

Now that a computer on a chip was available, the next logical step was to develop it into a complete microcomputer system that the average person could use. One of the first noteworthy efforts in this direction came from a small group of Air Force personnel operating out of an Albuquerque garage in their off-hours. The name of their firm was Micro Instrumentation and Telemetry Systems (MITS). MITS initially made electronic calculators. In the early 1970s, when the bottom fell out of the calculator market, MITS turned its attention to making a kit computer to keep itself afloat. This machine was called the **Altair 8800,** and it became the world's first microcomputer system.

Most firsts in the history of computing were crude devices, and the 8800 was no exception. Users had to be knowledgeable enough to build it themselves from a kit. Moreover, it required users to code their own programs—in machine language, no less. MITS subsequently hired Bill Gates, a Harvard freshman, to install the BASIC programming language on the 8800. This attempt was successful, but MITS went bankrupt a few years later. Gates (see Figure B-13) subsequently dropped out of Harvard and formed Microsoft Corporation, today the largest software producer in the world.

The Rise of Apple   Enter Stephen G. Wozniak, or Woz to his friends. A talented California computer enthusiast, he had dropped out of college. Fortunately for the history of microcomputing, Woz like to build computers.

Altair 8800.
The first microcomputer system to achieve some degree of commercial success.

FIGURE B – 13

Bill Gates. The ultimate entrepreneur, Gates rode the crest of the micro-computer revolution and became a billionaire in the process. He is the founder and head of Microsoft Corporation, one of the world's largest and most successful software firms.

Now enter Steven Jobs, another brilliant college dropout. Jobs saw the potential in Wozniak's work and was able to raise thousands of dollars of venture capital to support it. Thus, Apple Computer, one of the biggest success stories in modern corporate history, was born. But Apple, which introduced its first computer in kit form in 1977 (see Figure B-14), wasn't an immediate success. It needed another event to take place in computer history before it would see its biggest triumphs.

On the East Coast, Harvard Business School student Dan Bricklin studiously watched his accounting professor erase large chunks of calculations on the blackboard every time a single number changed in an interdependent series of calculations. Astonished by the labor involved in the recalculations, Bricklin and Bob Frankston, a programming friend from MIT, went to work developing *VisiCalc* (VISIble CALCulator). Introduced in 1978, VisiCalc was the first spreadsheet package. It was easy to use and could do repetitive, accounting-type calculations in a snap.

With the availability of spreadsheets, businesspeople (who routinely prepare time-consuming budgets and profit-and-loss statements) suddenly had a compelling reason to buy microcomputers. The first computer manufacturer to adopt VisiCalc was Apple, which had just recently introduced its first preassembled computer, the Apple II. Apple II computers started selling wildly.

Enter IBM In 1981, IBM entered the microcomputing market with the IBM Personal Computer (IBM PC). This highly successful product immediately cut into sales of the Apple II as well as those of the two other premier microcomputer systems of the day—the Tandy/Radio Shack TRS-80 Model I and the Commodore Pet. Although the IBM PC was a widely hailed product and was more powerful than its competitors, many people attribute the PC's success largely to the fact

FIGURE B – 14

Apple Computer in the 1970s. (a) Steve Wozniak and Steve Jobs, Apple's founders, holding the original Apple I board. (b) The board in a homemade wooden "system unit." The Apple I, priced at $666.66, consisted of a single board with 4K RAM. Although less powerful than the Altair 8800, it was cheaper and less complicated.

(a)   (b)

that many businesspeople suddenly took microcomputers seriously when IBM, one of the world's largest corporations, became a player. Meanwhile, another new firm, Lotus Development Corporation, which today is one of the world's biggest software producers, created a spreadsheet product, 1-2-3, which became widely used on the IBM PC (see Figure B-15). Just as VisiCalc had helped sales of the Apple II, 1-2-3 helped sell the IBM PC.

During the early 1980s, a spate of firms entered the burgeoning microcomputer marketplace. So-called *clone manufacturers* came along to nip at the heels of IBM and Lotus, offering functionally identical products at bargain-basement prices. *Aftermarket vendors* sprouted up like weeds, offering add-in or add-on products that would enhance existing major products with new features. *Niche vendors* also entered the picture, providing specialized products targeted to narrow ranges of needs. Today microcomputers compose the major market segment in the computer industry, outpacing all other types of computers.

Attributes of the Fourth Generation

Many developments characterize the fourth generation, which is still very much in progress. In addition to the microcomputer, these include microminiaturization, semiconductor internal storage, further improvements in software, decision support systems, and information resource management (IRM).

Microminiaturization   The technological hallmark of the fourth generation is **microminiaturization.** Over the years, more and more circuits have been packed into less and less space, and integrated circuits have become increasingly smaller, faster, and cheaper. The terms *large-scale integration (LSI)* and later *very-large-scale integration (VLSI)* have been coined to describe this process. A single silicon chip smaller than the size of a fingernail now can contain over a million circuit elements. Future systems, experts predict, will contain billions of circuits in the same space.

Semiconductor Internal Storage   During the course of the third generation, core storage slowly gave way to MOS (metal oxide semiconductor) memory. By the fourth generation, MOS memory, which is faster, smaller, and cheaper than core planes, had become a common fixture. **Semiconductor memories,** as MOS devices are usually called, are similar to microprocessors in that the memory is etched onto a small silicon-backed chip. Also like microprocessors, these chips are commonly mounted onto metal carriers, which plug into boards that reside in the computer's system unit.

Further Improvements in Software   Many people are intimidated by computers and especially by programming languages. Yet computer technology is a powerful tool in the hands of the right users, and many people would be more productive in their jobs if the right computer tools were available. In response to such demands, a number of software vendors have developed *fourth-generation-language (4GL)* software products that are specifically targeted to the on-the-job needs of people in virtually every field. These products, which include database retrieval languages, report generation languages, spreadsheets, object-oriented interfaces, and the like, are much easier to work with than BASIC, FORTRAN, COBOL, RPG, and other third-generation languages.

F I G

Lotus's fo
Kapor. In
Kapor—a s
"intellectua   who had
been a disk jockey, piano
teacher, mental-health
counselor, and meditation
instructor—followed his
"karma" and crafted 1-2-3.
Today, Kapor is chairman of
a new company and is also
a vocal spokesperson for
rights on public networks.

Microminiaturization.
A term that implies a very
small size.

Semiconductor memory.
A memory whose components are etched onto small
silicon chips.

Decision Support Systems The 1970s and 1980s gave rise to a new type of information system—the *decision support system (DSS)*. Whereas the MISs of the 1960s provided managers with information in the form of preplanned, hard-copy reports, the DSSs that later evolved offered managers microcomputer systems—tools that gave them the power to satisfy their own information needs.

Information Resources Management (IRM) In recent years, rather than seeing computers merely as a means of mechanically processing transactions, many organizations perceive information technology as a *strategic force* that will largely determine their survival in the 1990s. For instance, firms such as banks, brokerage firms, and insurance companies sell products and services that depend critically on how information is collected, packaged, and disseminated. The growing philosophy that information is a critical asset that must be properly planned for and managed rather than just a necessary cost to be controlled is known as *information resources management (IRM)*.

The Fifth Generation: Integrating Intelligence into Computer Systems

No one has a crystal ball that can predict the future. Predictions about technology are especially risky, because one must look into the future through eyes that focus heavily on the world as it is today.

In the 1940s, for instance, the director of the Harvard Computational Laboratory predicted that the computer industry would never amount to much, since no more than a half-dozen machines (such as the one used at Harvard at the time) could handle the world's demand. As things turned out, a half-century later, tens of millions of microcomputers that sell for several hundred dollars or less are widely available—and these tiny machines can run circles around that gargantuan Harvard computer. The telephone, too, was at one time seen as a device that would receive limited use, because, as many said, there could never be enough telephone operators to handle any sort of widespread demand.

These cautions notwithstanding, there does seem to be relatively widespread agreement among industry onlookers that the upcoming **fifth generation** of computing will be characterized by artificial intelligence applications. **Artificial intelligence** refers to the ability of computers to perform tasks once considered to be the exclusive domain of humans. This means that we will be able to speak to tomorrow's computer systems in our own *natural languages* (e.g., English or Spanish), as we would to human beings. In turn, these computers will be able to understand us—in spite of our use of slang, dangling participles, lack of proper connective words, and regional accents. It also means that intelligent computers will be able to second-guess our intentions, calling to our attention actions that seem to be inconsistent or incorrect. Ultimately, the fifth generation may pave the way for *androids*—robotic computer systems that are virtually indistinguishable from humans themselves.

Fifth generation.
The coming era of computing, which is expected to be characterized largely by artificial intelligence applications.

Artificial intelligence (AI).
The ability of a machine to perform actions that are characteristic of human intelligence, such as reasoning and learning.

Summary and Key Terms

While computers as we know them today were invented about 50 years ago, the world's oldest computing device, the abacus, dates back thousands of years.

From Gears and Levers to Circuits and Tubes   The first *mechanical calculating machine,* the **pascaline,** was developed by Blaise Pascal in the early 1600s. This device could only add and subtract. Later in the 1600s, Gottfried von Leibniz devised a calculator that could also multiply and divide.

In the early 1800s, weaver Joseph Jacquard invented an automated loom that introduced two concepts important to the development of the computer: *Data* could be recorded on punched cards, and a sequence of cards could act as a *program.*

The first computing device bearing a resemblance to today's computers was proposed by Charles Babbage in the 1800s. He initially conceived a machine called the **difference engine,** which would both compute and print results. Later he developed a more ambitious machine called the **analytical engine,** which embodied the principles of input, processing, output, and storage found in today's modern computers. Unfortunately, Babbage died without seeing either machine completed.

The first **electromechanical machine** to perform computing was built by Herman Hollerith to aid in tabulating the 1890 census. Hollerith went on to become a pioneer in the development of business-oriented electromechanical tabulating machines.

Howard Aiken, with the help of IBM, designed and built the first large-scale, general-purpose electromechanical computer. It was completed in 1944 and called the **Mark I.**

While Aiken was constructing his machine, John Atanasoff was at work in the Midwest with a technology that would make the Mark I obsolete almost as soon as it was completed. With the assistance of Clifford Berry, Atanasoff created the **ABC (Atanasoff-Berry Computer),** the first **electronic machine** to do computing. In 1946, J. Presper Eckert and John Mauchly created the world's first large-scale, general-purpose electronic computer, the **ENIAC.** Later in the 1940s, mathematician John Von Neumann developed the concept of *stored programs.*

The Computer Age   The era of commercial computing is commonly divided into five distinct generations.

The First Generation (1951–1958)   The first generation began when the **UNIVAC I** computer was completed and delivered to the U.S. Bureau of the Census in 1951. **First-generation** computers used **vacuum tubes** as the main logic element. They also relied heavily on the use of punched cards and magnetic drum internal storage. Programs were written in **machine language** or, later, **assembly language.** Most first-generation commercial computers were limited to transaction processing applications, because these were relatively easy to justify in terms of labor savings.

The Second Generation (1959–1964)   In **second-generation** computers, **transistors** replaced vacuum tubes as the main logic element. Other noteworthy developments included the use of magnetic tapes and disks for secondary storage, **magnetic-core** internal storage, modular hardware design, **high-level programming languages** (such as FORTRAN and COBOL), airline passenger reservations systems, communications satellites, and management information systems.

The Third Generation (1965–1970)

In **third-generation** computers, **integrated circuits (ICs)** replaced transistors as the main logic element. Other major developments were the family concept of computers, **operating systems,** improvements in programming languages (such as BASIC and RPG) and applications software, minicomputers, and word processing.

The Fourth Generation (1971–Present)

Three concepts sum up the **fourth generation:** "small," "smaller," and "even smaller." This generation has been a period of **microminiaturization,** perhaps the single most important event being the development and acceptance of microcomputer systems. From such crude devices as the **Altair 8800,** circa 1970, the microcomputer industry boldly surged forward to become the major market segment of the entire computer industry. Other major developments for which the fourth generation will be remembered are tiny but powerful microprocessors and **semiconductor memories,** fourth-generation languages, decision support systems (DSSs), and information resources management (IRM).

The Fifth Generation

There is relatively widespread agreement among industry onlookers that the upcoming **fifth generation** of computing will be characterized by **artificial intelligence** applications. Artificial intelligence refers to the ability of computers to perform tasks once considered to be the exclusive domain of humans.

Exercises

1. The world's first large-scale, general-purpose electronic computer was called the _____.

2. The device Pascal developed in the 1600s that could add and subtract was called the _____.

3. The first calculating machine to be developed by Charles Babbage was called the _____.

4. The electromechanical computer that was developed jointly in the 1940s by Harvard and IBM was called the _____.

5. The first electronic computer was known by the initials _____.

6. The name of the first electronic computer to be widely used in business was the _____ I.

7. The name of the company that produced the first minicomputer was (is) _____ Corporation.

8. The first widely used microcomputer system, developed in an Albuquerque garage, was called the _____.

G L O S S A R Y

The terms shown in boldface are presented in the text as key terms. The number(s) in parentheses at the end of the definition of each term indicates the page (or pages) on which the term is boldfaced in the text. The terms shown in boldface italic are other commonly used and important words often encountered in information processing environments. The italic number in parentheses after the definition of each term indicates the page on which the term is first mentioned.

ABC.
See Atanasoff-Berry Computer. (B-6)

Absolute replication.
In spreadsheets, copying verbatim the contents in one range of cells into another range of cells. (311)

Access card.
A plastic card that, when inserted into a machine and combined with a password, permits access to a system. (542)

Access mechanism.
A mechanical device in the disk pack or disk unit that positions the read/write heads on the proper tracks. (102)

Accumulator.
A register that stores the result of an arithmetic or logical operation. (70)

Action diagram.
A programming tool that helps programmers code structured programs. (447)

Ada.
A structured programming language developed by the Department of Defense and named after Ada Augusta Byron, the world's first programmer. *(456)*

Add-in board.
A board that may be inserted into the computer's system unit to perform one or more functions. (81)

Add-on package.
A software package that supplements the activities of a larger software package, either by providing new functions or improving on already existing functions. (274, 315)

Address.
An identifiable location in storage where data are kept. Primary storage and direct-access secondary storage devices such as disk are addressable. *(68)*

Address register.
A register containing the memory location of data to be used. (69)

AI.
See Artificial intelligence. (390)

Altair 8800.
The first microcomputer system to achieve some degree of commercial success. (B-15)

ALU.
See Arithmetic/logic unit. (67)

American National Standards Institute (ANSI).
An organization that acts as a national clearinghouse for standards in the United States. *(75)*

Analog transmission.
The transmission of data as continuous-wave patterns. (190)

Analysis.
In program and systems development, the process of studying a problem area to determine what should be done. *(420)*

Analytical engine.
A device conceived by Charles Babbage in the 1800s to perform computations. This machine is considered the forerunner of today's modern electronic computer. (B-3)

ANSI.
See American National Standards Institute. *(75)*

APL.
An acronym for A Programming Language. APL is a highly compact programming language popular for problem-solving applications. *(456)*

Applications generator.
A fourth-generation-language product that can be used to quickly create applications software. *(459)*

Applications package.
A fourth-generation-language product that, when the user sets a few parameters, becomes a finished applications program ready to meet specific end-user needs. (439)

Applications programmer.
A programmer who codes programs that do the useful work—such as payroll, inventory control, and accounting tasks—for end users of a computer system. Contrasts with systems programmer. (511)

Applications software.
Programs that do the useful work—such as payroll, inventory control, and accounting tasks—for end users of a computer system. Contrasts with systems software. (48)

Applications software development.
The process of designing, coding, debugging and testing, maintaining, and documenting applications software. (438)

Arithmetic/logic unit (ALU).
The part of the computer that contains the circuitry to perform addition, subtraction, multiplication, division, and comparison operations. (67)

Architecture.
The underlying design of a computer system. Architecture is largely a function of the CPU and bus in use. (83, 482)

Artificial intelligence (AI).
The ability of a machine to perform actions that are characteristic of human intelligence, such as reasoning and learning. (390, B-18)

ASCII.
An acronym for American Standard Code for Information Interchange. ASCII is a fixed-length, binary-based code widely used to represent data for processing and communications. (74)

Assembler.
A computer program that takes assembly-language instructions and converts them to machine language. (238)

Assembly language.
A low-level programming language that uses mnemonic codes in place of the 0s and 1s of machine language. (449, B-10)

Asynchronous transmission.
The transmission of data over a line one character at a time. Each character is preceded by a "start bit" and followed by a "stop bit." Contrasts with synchronous transmission. (194)

Atanasoff-Berry Computer (ABC).
The world's first electronic digital computer, built in the early 1940s by Dr. John V. Atanasoff and his assistant, Clifford Berry. (B-6)

Audit.
An inspection used to determine if a system or procedure is working as it should or if claimed amounts are correct. (543)

Backup.
Making duplicate copies of programs or data. (491)

Bar chart.
A presentation graphic that uses side-by-side columns as the principal charting element. (317)

Bar code.
A machine-readable code consisting of sets of bars of varying widths. The codes are prominently displayed on the packaging of many retail goods and are commonly read with special reading equipment. (150)

BASIC.
An acronym for Beginner's All-Purpose Symbolic Instruction Code. BASIC is an easy-to-learn, high-level programming language developed at Dartmouth College in the 1960s. (450)

Batch processing.
Processing transactions or other data in groups at periodic intervals. Contrasts with realtime processing. (53)

Benchmark test.
A test used to measure computer system performance under typical use conditions prior to purchase. The test is analogous to a rigorous "test drive" taken with a car before buying it. (427)

Binary.
A number system with two possible states. The binary system is fundamental to computers because electronic devices often function in two possible states—for example "on" or "off," "current present" or "current not present," "clockwise" or "counterclockwise," and so forth. (71, A-3)

Biometric security device.
A device that, upon recognition of some physiological or learned characteristic that is unique to a person, allows that person access to a system. (543)

Bit.
A binary digit, such as 0 or 1. The 0- or 1-states are used by computer systems to take advantage of the binary nature of electronics. Bits often are assembled into bytes and words when manipulated or stored. (72)

Bit mapping.
A term, used with certain display devices and dot-matrix printers, that means that each of the dots in the output image may be individually operator-controlled. (136)

Bits per second (bps).
A measure of the speed of a communications device. (190)

Board.
A hardware device into which processor chips and memory chips are fitted, along with related circuitry. *(77)*

Bps.
See Bits per second. (190)

Bridge.
An interface that enables two similar networks to communicate. Contrasts with gateway. (202)

Bug.
An error in a program or system. *(463)*

Bus.
A set of wires that acts as a data highway between the CPU and other devices. (82)

Bus network.
A telecommunications network consisting of a line and several devices that are tapped into the line. The network is so named because data are picked up and dropped off at devices similarly to the way in which passengers are picked up and dropped off at bus stops. (202)

Byte.
A configuration of seven or eight bits used to represent a single character of data. (75)

C.
A programming language that has the portability of a high-level language and the executional efficiency of an assembly language. (454)

Cache disk.
A disk management scheme whereby more data than necessary are read from disk during each time-consuming disk fetch and are stored in memory to minimize the number of fetches. (108)

CAD.
See Computer-aided design. (386)

CAD/CAM.
An acronym for *computer-aided design/ computer-aided manufacturing*. CAD/ CAM is a general term applied to the use of computer technology to automate design and manufacturing operations in industry. *(386)*

CAI.
See Computer-assisted instruction. *(553)*

Callback device.
A device on the receiving end of a communications network that verifies the authenticity of the sender by calling the sender back. (543)

Caller identification.
A term that refers to a telephone or answering device that displays the phone numbers of incoming calls. (548)

CAM.
See Computer-aided manufacturing. (387)

Cartridge disk.
Magnetic disk in which a single disk platter is contained in a sealed plastic case, which in turn is mounted onto a disk unit when data are to be read from or written to the disk inside. (107)

Cartridge tape.
Magnetic tape in which the supply and take-up reels are contained in a small plastic case, which in turn is mounted

onto a tape unit when data are to be read from or written to the tape inside. (112)

CASE.
See Computer-aided software engineering. (466)

Case control structure.
A control structure that can be formed by nesting two or more selection control structures. (445)

Cathode-ray tube (CRT).
A display device that contains a long-necked display-tube mechanism similar to that used in television sets. (134)

Cell.
In spreadsheet software, an area of the worksheet that holds a single label or value. (295)

Cell address.
The column-row combination that uniquely identifies a spreadsheet cell. (295)

Cell pointer.
In spreadsheet software, a cursorlike mechanism used to point to cells on the display screen. (299)

Cellular phone.
A mobile phone that uses special stations called cells to communicate over the regular phone system. (183)

Central processing unit (CPU).
The piece of hardware, also known as the *computer*, that interprets and executes program instructions and communicates with input, output, and storage devices. (8, 40)

Chief information officer (CIO).
See Vice-president of information systems. (514)

CIM.
See Computer-integrated manufacturing. (388)

CIO.
See Chief information officer. (514)

Client.
A device designated to receive service in a client-server network. (198)

Client-server LAN.
A LAN that is comprised of *client* devices, which receive service, and *server* devices, which provide service. (198)

Clip art.
Prepackaged artwork designed to be imported into text documents or charts, by desktop publishing or presentation graphics software. (283)

Coaxial cable.
A transmission line developed for transmitting data at high speeds. (186)

COBOL.
An acronym for Common Business-Oriented Language. COBOL is a high-level programming language developed for transaction processing applications. (450)

Coding.
The writing of instructions, in a programming language, that will cause the computer system to perform a specific set of operations. (462)

COM.
See Computer output microfilm. (161)

Command language.
A programming language used to communicate with the operating system. (221)

Command-language translator.
Systems software that translates instructions written in a command language into machine-language instructions. (221)

Common carrier.
A government-regulated private organization that provides communications services to the public. (195)

Communications medium.
The intervening substance, such as a telephone wire or cable, that connects

two physically distant hardware devices. (185)

Communications satellite.
An earth-orbiting device that relays communications signals over long distances. (188)

Compiler.
A computer program that translates a source program written by a user or programmer in a high-level or very-high-level programming language into machine language. The translation takes place before the translated program is executed. Contrasts with interpreter. (236)

Computer.
See Central processing unit. (8, 40)

Computer-aided design (CAD).
A general term applied to the use of computer technology to automate design functions in industry. (386)

Computer-aided manufacturing (CAM).
A general term applied to the use of computer technology to automate manufacturing functions in industry. (387)

Computer-aided software engineering (CASE).
Program products that automate systems and program development activities. (466)

Computer-assisted instruction (CAI).
The use of computers to supplement personalized teaching instruction by providing the student with sequences of instruction under program control. The progression through the instructional materials in such a system enables students to learn at their own rate. *(553)*

Computer crime.
The use of computers to commit unauthorized acts. (537)

Computer engineering curriculum.
The field of knowledge that includes

the design of computer hardware systems. Computer engineering is offered as a degree program in several colleges and universities. (521)

Computer information systems (CIS) curriculum.
A course of study, normally offered by business schools, that prepares students for entry-level jobs as applications programmers or systems analysts. (519)

Computer-integrated manufacturing (CIM).
The use of technology to tie together CAD, CAM, and other business systems. (388)

Computer operations.
(1) The functions related to the physical operation of the computer system. (2) A curriculum offered in many schools that is oriented toward training students to enter the computer operations field. Computer operations curricula often train students to become computer or data-entry operators. (521)

Computer operations manager.
The person who oversees the computer operations area in an organization. The computer operations manager is responsible for tasks such as hiring operations personnel and scheduling work that the system is to perform. (511)

Computer operator.
A person responsible for the operation of the computer and its support devices. The operator is responsible for tasks such as mounting and dismounting tapes and disks and removing printouts from the line or page printer. (509)

Computer output microfilm (COM).
A term referring to equipment and media that reduce computer output to microscopic form and put it on photosensitive film. (161)

Computer science curriculum.
A course of study that includes all tech-

nical aspects of the design and use of computers. Computer science is offered as a degree program in many institutions of higher learning. (520)

Computer system.
When applied to buying a "computer system," the term generally refers to the equipment and programs being sold. When applied to a computer-based operation in an organization, it is commonly defined as all the equipment, programs, data, procedures, and personnel supporting that operation. (8)

Computer virus.
A small block of unauthorized code, transmitted from program to program by a copy operation, that performs destructive acts when executed. (539)

Concentrator.
A communications device that combines control and multiplexing. Concentrators have a store-and-forward capability that enables them to store messages from several low-speed devices before forwarding them at high speeds to another device. (205)

Concurrent access.
A term that refers to two or more users attempting to interactively access the same data at more or less the same time. (352)

Control-break reporting.
A term that refers to "breaks" in the normal flow of information in a computer report that periodically occur for subtotals and totals. *(52)*

Control clerk.
The person who monitors all work coming in and out of the computer center. (510)

Control panel.
In spreadsheet software, the portion of the screen display that is used for issuing commands and observing what is being typed into the computer system. (298)

Control structure.
A pattern for controlling the flow of logic in a computer program. The three basic control structures are sequence, selection (if-then-else), and looping (iteration). (445)

Control unit.
The part of the CPU that coordinates the execution of program instructions. (68)

Coprocessor.
A dedicated processor chip that is summoned by the CPU to perform specialized types of processing. *(80)*

CPU.
See Central processing unit. (8, 40)

Crosshair cursor.
A digitizing device that is often moved over hard-copy images of maps and drawings to enter those images into the computer system. (156)

CRT.
See Cathode-ray tube. (134)

Current cell.
In spreadsheet software, the worksheet cell at which the highlight is currently positioned. (298)

Cursor.
A highlighting symbol that appears on a display screen to indicate the position where the next character (or group of characters) typed in will appear. (133, 298)

Daisywheel printer.
A low-speed printer with a solid-font printing mechanism consisting of a spoked wheel of embossed characters. Daisywheel printers are capable of producing letter-quality output. *(138)*

Data.
A collection of raw, unorganized facts. (8)

Data access.
Fetching data from a device either sequentially or directly. (118)

Database.
An integrated collection of data stored on a direct-access storage device. (47, 338)

Database administrator (DBA).
The person or group of people in charge of designing, implementing, and managing the ongoing operation of a database. *(352)*

Database management system (DBMS).
A software package designed to integrate data and provide easy access to them. (338)

Data definition.
The process of describing the characteristics of data that are to be handled by a database management system. (345)

Data definition language (DDL).
A language used by a database administrator to create, store, and manage data in a database environment. (352)

Data dictionary.
A facility that informs users and programmers about characteristics of data or programs in a database or a computer system. (345, 462)

Data-entry operator.
A member of a computer operations staff responsible for keying data into the computer system. (510)

Data flow diagram.
A graphically oriented systems development tool that enables a systems analyst to logically represent the flow of data through a system. (421)

Data manipulation.
The process of using language commands to add, delete, modify, or retrieve data in a file or database. (346)

Data manipulation language (DML).
A language used by programmers to supplement some high-level language supported in a database environment. (353)

Data organization.
The process of establishing a data file so that it may subsequently be accessed in some desired way. Three common methods of organizing data are sequential organization, indexed-sequential organization, and direct organization. (118)

Data processing area.
The group of computer professionals within the information systems department who are charged with building transaction processing systems. (415)

Data processing director.
The person in charge of developing and/or implementing the overall plan for transaction processing in an organization and for overseeing the activities of programmers, systems analysts, and operations personnel. (514)

Data processing system.
See Transaction processing system. *(372)*

DBA.
See Database administrator. *(352)*

DBMS.
See Database management system. (338)

DDL.
See Data definition language. (352)

Debugging.
The process of detecting and correcting errors in computer programs or in the computer system itself. (463)

Decimal.
A number system with ten symbols— 0, 1, 2, 3, 4, 5, 6, 7, 8, and 9. (A-2)

Decision support system (DSS).
A system that provides tools and capabilities to managers to enable them to satisfy their own information needs. (378)

Default.
The assumption that a computer pro-

gram makes when no specific choice is indicated by the user or programmer. (223)

Design.
The process of planning a program or system. Design is normally undertaken after a problem has been thoroughly analyzed and a set of specifications for the solution established. *(423, 439)*

Desk accessory.
A software package that provides the electronic counterpart of tools commonly found on a desktop—a clock, calendar, notepad, and rolodex file, for instance. Also called a *desktop organizer.* (382)

Desktop computer.
A microcomputer system that can fit on a desktop. Some familiar examples are computers in the IBM PS/2 and Apple Macintosh II lines. *(15)*

Desktop publishing.
A microcomputer-based publishing system that can fit on a desktop. (276, 382)

Detachable-reel tape.
Magnetic tape that is wound onto a single reel, which in turn is mounted onto a tape unit with an empty take-up reel when data are to be read from or written to the tape. (111)

Device driver.
A utility program that enables an applications program to function with a specific hardware device. (243)

Difference engine.
A mechanical machine devised by Charles Babbage in the 1800s to perform computations automatically and print their results. (B-3)

Digital transmission.
The transmission of data as discrete impulses. (190)

Digitizer.
An input device that converts a measurement into a digital value. (153)

Digitizing tablet.
A digitizer that consists of a flat board and also a device that traces over the board, storing the traced pattern in computer memory. (156)

Direct access.
Reading or writing data in storage so that the access time involved is relatively independent of the location of the data. (95)

Direct organization.
A method of organizing data on a device so that they can be accessed directly (randomly). (123)

Disk access time.
The time taken to locate and read (or position and write) data on a disk device. (104)

Disk cylinder.
All tracks on a disk pack that are accessible with a single movement of the access mechanism. (103)

Disk drive.
A mechanism within the disk storage unit on which disk packs, diskettes, or disk cartridges are placed to be accessed. *(22)*

Diskette.
A small, removable disk made of a tough, flexible plastic and coated with a magnetizable substance. (96)

Disk pack.
A group of tiered hard disks that are mounted on a shaft and treated as a unit. A disk pack must be placed on a disk unit in order to be accessed. (101)

Disk unit.
A direct-access secondary storage device that uses magnetic or optical disk as the principal I/O medium. (100)

Disk utility.
A program that assists with such disk-related tasks as backup, data compression, space allocation, and recovering from accidental data destruction. (239)

Display device.
A peripheral device that contains a viewing screen. (132)

Display terminal.
A communications workstation that consists of a display device and a keyboard. (132)

DML.
See Data manipulation language. (353)

Documentation.
A detailed written description of a program, procedure, or system. (464)

Dot-matrix character.
A character composed from a rectangular matrix of dots. *(139)*

DOUNTIL control structure.
A looping control structure in which the looping continues as long as a certain condition is false (i.e., "do until true"). (445)

DOWHILE control structure.
A looping control structure in which the looping continues as long as a certain condition is true (i.e., "do while true"). (445)

Downloading.
The process of transferring data or information from a large computer system to a smaller one. Contrasts with uploading. (202)

Drum plotter.
An output device that draws on paper that is rolled along a cylindrically shaped drum. *(159)*

DSS.
See Decision support system. (378)

EBCDIC.
An acronym for Extended Binary-Coded Decimal Interchange Code. EBCDIC is a fixed-length, binary-based code widely used to represent data on IBM mainframes. (74)

E-cycle.
The part of the machine cycle in which data are located, an instruction is executed, and the results are stored. (70)

EDI.
See Electronic data interchange. (180)

EFT.
See Electronic funds transfer. *(551)*

Electromechanical machine.
A device that has both electrical and mechanical features. (B-5)

Electronic bulletin board.
A computer file that is shared by several people, enabling them to post or broadcast messages. (181)

Electronic data interchange (EDI).
A computer procedure that enables standard business documents, such as purchase orders and invoices, to be exchanged from one company's computer system to the computer system of another company. (180)

Electronic funds transfer (EFT).
Pertains to systems that transfer funds by computer from one account to another, without the use of written checks. *(551)*

Electronic machine.
A device that contains electronic components. (B-6)

Electronic mail.
A facility that enables users to send letters, memos, documents, and the like from one hardware device to another. (382)

Electronic mailbox.
A storage area used to hold a recipient's electronic mail. (181, 382)

Electronic spreadsheet.
A productivity software package that enables operators to create tables and financial schedules quickly by entering labels and values into cells on a display-screen grid. (295)

Encryption.
A method of disguising data or programs so that they are unrecognizable to unauthorized users. (543)

End user.
A person who needs computer-produced results in his or her job. (13)

End-user development.
Systems development activities carried out by the end user. (430, 474)

ENIAC.
An acronym for Electronic Numerical Integrator and Calculator. Unveiled in 1946, ENIAC was the world's first large-scale, general-purpose computer. (B-7)

Ergonomics.
The field that studies the effects of things such as computer hardware, software, and workspaces on employees' comfort and health. (533)

Ethics.
A term that refers to standards of moral conduct. (543)

Executive information system (EIS).
A decision support system that is tailored to the needs of a specific, top-level individual in an organization. (380)

Expert system.
A program or computer system providing the type of advice that would be expected of a human expert. (391)

Expert system shell.
A prepackaged expert system that lacks only a knowledge base. (395)

External disk.
A disk unit that is not housed within the computer's system unit. Contrasts with internal disk. *(102)*

External storage.
See Secondary storage. (11)

Facsimile (fax) machine.
A device that can transmit or receive hard-copy images of text, pictures, maps, diagrams, and the like over the phone lines. (182, 382)

Fiber optic cable.
A cable composed of thousands of hair-thin, transparent fibers along which data are passed from lasers as light waves. (186)

Field.
A collection of related characters. (46)

Field descriptor.
A code used to describe the type of data—say, numeric, character, or logical—that occupy a given field in a data record. (345)

Fifth generation.
The coming era of computing, which is expected to be characterized largely by artificial intelligence applications. (B-18)

File.
A collection of related records. (46)

File directory.
A directory on an input/output medium that provides data such as file name, length, and starting address for each file on the medium. (100)

File manager.
A productivity software package used to manage records and files. (334)

File structure.
A collection of information about the fields of a file, including the names, lengths, and types of the fields. (345)

Film recorder.
A cameralike device that captures computer output on film. (161)

Firmware.
Software instructions that are written onto a hardware module. (81)

First generation.
Usually refers to the first era of commercial computers (1951–1958), characterized by vacuum tubes as the main logic element. (B-8)

Flatbed plotter.
An output device that draws on paper that is mounted on a flat drawing table. *(159)*

Flat file.
See File. (334)

Flat-panel display.
A slim-profile display device. (134)

Floppy disk.
See Diskette. *(96)*

Flowchart.
See Program flowchart. *(440)*

Font.
A typeface in a particular point size—for instance, 12-point Helvetica. (268)

FORTRAN.
An acronym for FORmula TRANslator. FORTRAN is a high-level programming language used for mathematical, scientific, and engineering applications. (455)

Fourth generation.
Usually refers to the fourth era of commercial computing (1971–present), characterized by microminiaturization and the rise of microcomputing. (B-14)

Fourth-generation language (4GL).
An easy-to-learn, easy-to-use language that enables users or programmers to code applications much more quickly than they could with third-generation languages such as BASIC, FORTRAN, and COBOL. (458)

Front-end processor.
A computer that is positioned in a network to screen messages sent to the main computer and that also relieves the main computer of certain computational chores. (206)

Full backup.
A procedure that produces a duplicate copy of all files onto a secondary storage medium. (491)

Full-duplex transmission.
A type of transmission in which messages may be sent in two directions simultaneously along a communications path. (190)

Functionally obsolete.
Refers to a product that no longer meets the needs of an individual or business. (498)

Function key.
A special keyboard key that executes a preprogrammed routine when depressed. *(131)*

Gateway.
An interface that enables two dissimilar networks to communicate. Contrasts with bridge. (202)

GB.
See Gigabyte. (75)

GDSS.
See Group decision support system. (380)

General-purpose computer.
A computer capable of being programmed to solve a wide range of problems. *(9)*

Gigabyte (GB).
Approximately 1 billion bytes. (75)

Graphical user interface (GUI).
Refers to the use of computer graphics screens that make it easier for users to interact with software. (222)

Group decision support system (GDSS).
A decision support system in which several people routinely interact through a computer network to solve common problems. (380)

Hacking.
A term that, when used with computers, often relates to using a micro-computer system or terminal to break into the security of a large computer system. (539)

Half-duplex transmission.
Any type of transmission in which messages may be sent in two directions—but only one way at a time—along a communications path. (190)

Handwriting recognition device.
A device that can identify handwritten characters. (158)

Hard card.
A hard disk that has been configured onto an add-in board. (107)

Hard copy.
A permanent form of usable output; for example, output on paper or film. Contrasts with soft copy. (130)

Hard disk.
A rigid platter coated with a magnetizable substance. (96)

Hard return.
In word processing, the use of the Enter key to provide line spacing. Contrasts with soft return. (263)

Hardware.
Physical equipment in a computing environment, such as the computer and its support devices. (12)

Hashing.
A key-to-disk mathematical transformation in which the key field on each record determines where the record is stored. *(123)*

Heuristic.
An intuitively appealing "rule of thumb" that is often used as part of a trial-and-error process to find a workable solution to a problem. *(391)*

Hexadecimal.
Pertaining to the number system with 16 symbols: 0, 1, 2, 3, 4, 5, 6, 7, 8, 9, A, B, C, D, E, and F. (A-5)

Hierarchical local network.
A star-shaped local network in which a relatively powerful CPU is at the top of the hierarchy and communications terminals or less-powerful CPUs are at the bottom. (201)

High-level language.
See High-level programming language. (449)

High-level programming language.
The class of programming languages used by most professional programmers to solve a wide range of problems. Some examples are BASIC, COBOL, FORTRAN, and Pascal. (449, B-12)

Highlight.
See Cell pointer. (299)

Host computer.
In telecommunications, a computer that is used to control a communications network. *(197)*

Host language.
A programming language used to code applications within a specific software system, such as a database environment. (353)

HyperTalk.
A fourth-generation language that enables text, graphics, voice, and video data to be stored in a cardlike format and manipulated. *(460)*

IBM-compatible computer.
A computer that can run the same software as IBM computers run. (474)

IC.
See Integrated circuit. (B-13)

Icon.
A graphical image on a display screen that invokes a particular program action when selected by the operator. (153)

I-cycle.
The part of the machine cycle in which

the control unit fetches an instruction from memory and prepares it for subsequent processing. (70)

If-then-else (selection) control structure.
See Selection control structure. (445)

Illustration software package.
A program package that enables users to paint or draw. (283)

Image scanner.
A device that can "read" into digital memory a hard-copy image such as a text page, photograph, map, or drawing. (150)

Impact dot-matrix mechanism.
A print head that forms dot-matrix characters through impact printing. (139)

Impact dot-matrix printer.
A printer whose print head is an impact dot-matrix mechanism. *(141)*

Impact printing.
The information of characters by causing a metal hammer to strike a ribbon into paper or paper into a ribbon. Contrasts with nonimpact printing. (139)

Indexed-sequential organization.
A method of organizing data on a direct-access medium so that it can be accessed directly (through an index) or sequentially. (123)

Information.
Data that have been processed into a meaningful form. (9)

Information center.
A facility in an organization that develops small systems. (416)

Information center consultant.
A systems analyst, assigned to an information center, who helps end users develop their own systems. (513)

Information center director.
The person in charge of an information center. (514)

Information processing.
Pertains to computer operations that transform data into meaningful information. (9)

Information reporting system.
An information system whose principal outputs are preformatted, hard-copy reports. (377)

Information retrieval.
Online inquiry, through a display terminal or microcomputer workstation, to computer files or databases. (52)

Information system.
A system designed to provide information to managers to enable them to make decisions. (375)

Information systems department.
The area in an organization that consists of computer professionals—managers, analysts, programmers, operations personnel, trainers, specialists, and the like. (414)

Input.
Anything supplied to a computer or computer-system process or involved with the beginning of such a process, such as the data to be keyed in. Contrasts with output. (7)

Input device.
A machine used to supply data to the computer. Contrasts with output device. (7, 42)

Input/output (I/O) media.
Objects used to store data or information before or after processing. Examples include magnetic disk, magnetic tape, and paper. (8, 45, 130)

Instruction register.
The register that holds the part of the instruction indicating what the computer is to do next. (69)

Integrated circuit (IC).
A series of complex circuits that are etched onto a small silicon chip. (B-13)

Integrated software package.
A software package that bundles two or more major software functions into a single package. *(259)*

Internal disk.
A disk unit that is housed inside the computer's system unit. Contrasts with external disk. *(102)*

Internal storage.
See Primary storage. (10)

Interpreter.
A computer program that translates a source program written by a user or programmer in a high-level or very-high-level language into machine language. The translation takes place on a line-by-line basis as each statement is executed. Contrasts with compiler. (238)

I/O media.
See Input/output media. (8)

Issuance.
The use of computers to produce transaction processing documents such as paychecks, bills, and customer reminder notices. (52)

Iteration control structure.
See Looping control structure. (445)

Joystick.
An input device, resembling a car's stick shift, that often is used for computer games and computer-aided design (CAD) work. (155)

KB.
See Kilobyte. (75)

Keyboard.
An input device composed of various typewriterlike keys, arranged in a configuration similar to that of a typewriter. Computer keyboards also have a number of special keys that initiate preprogrammed routines when activated. (131)

Key field.
A field used to identify a record. (114)

Kilobyte (KB).
Approximately 1,000 (1,024, to be exact) bytes. (75)

Label.
In spreadsheet software, a cell entry that cannot be manipulated mathematically. (299)

LAN.
See Local area network. (197)

Language translator.
A systems program that converts an applications program into machine language. (236)

Laptop computer.
A portable computer light enough to be operated while it rests on one's lap. *(7, 16)*

Large-scale integration (LSI).
The process of placing a large number of integrated circuits on a single silicon chip. *(B-17)*

Laser printer.
A nonimpact printer that works on a principle similar to that for a photocopier. *(143)*

Light pen.
An electrical device, resembling an ordinary pen, used to enter input by pointing to a display screen. (153)

Line chart.
A presentation graphic in which the principal charting element is an unbroken line. (319)

Line printer.
A high-speed printer that produces output one line at a time. (145)

Linkage editor.
A systems program that binds together related object-module program segments so that they may be run as a unit. (238)

LISP.
A language widely used for artificial intelligence applications. *(458)*

Load module.
A complete machine-language program that is ready to be executed by the computer. Also called a *load program.* (238)

Local area network (LAN).
A local network, without a host computer, that usually consists entirely of microcomputer workstations and shared peripherals. (197)

Local network.
A privately run communications network of several machines located within a mile or so of one another. (196)

Logic element.
The electronic component used to facilitate circuit functions within the computer. *(B-8)*

Logo.
A programming language often used to teach children how to program. *(457)*

Looping (iteration) control structure.
The control structure used to represent a looping operation. Also see DOUNTIL control structure and DOWHILE control structure. (445)

Low-level language.
A highly detailed, machine-dependent programming language. Included in the class of low-level languages are machine and assembly languages. (449)

LSI.
See Large-scale integration. *(B-17)*

Machine cycle.
The series of operations involved in the execution of a single machine-language instruction. (70)

Machine language.
A binary-based programming language that the computer can execute directly. (77, B-10)

Machine-readable.
Any form in which data are represented so that they can be read by a machine. (8)

Macintosh System Software.
The operating system that's used primarily on Apple's Macintosh line of computer systems. (231)

Macro.
A predetermined series of keystrokes or commands that can be invoked by a single keystroke or command. (272, 313)

Magnetic core.
A tiny, ring-shaped piece of magnetizable material capable of storing a single binary digit. Magnetic cores were popular as memories in second- and third-generation computers. (B-11)

Magnetic disk.
A secondary storage medium consisting of platters made of rigid metal (hard disk) or flexible plastic (diskette). (96)

Magnetic ink character recognition (MICR).
A technology, confined almost exclusively to the banking industry, that involves the processing of checks inscribed with special characters set in a special magnetic ink. (151)

Magnetic tape.
A plastic tape with a magnetic surface for storing data as a series of magnetic spots. (111)

Mailing list program.
A program used to generate mailing labels. (272)

Mail merge program.
A program specifically designed to produce form letters. (272)

Mainframe.
A large, transaction-processing-oriented computer capable of supporting powerful peripheral devices. (19)

Main memory.
The computer system's primary bank of

memory; contrast with memory products such as ROM and flash memory. *(10)*

Maintenance.
A term that refers to making minor modifications and upgrades to systems or software over time to ensure that they continue to meet the needs of an organization. (463)

Maintenance programmer.
A programmer involved with keeping an organization's existing programs in proper working order. *(439)*

Mark I.
Completed in 1944 by Harold Aiken of Harvard University, the Mark I was the first large-scale electromechanical computer. (B-6)

Master file.
A file containing relatively permanent data, such as customer names and addresses. (47)

MB.
See Megabyte. (75)

Megabyte (MB).
Approximately 1 million bytes. (75)

Memory.
See Primary storage. (68)

Menu.
A set of options, provided at a display device, from which the operator makes a selection. *(24)*

MICR.
See Magnetic ink character recognition. (151)

Microcode.
Instructions that are built into the CPU to control the operation of its circuitry. (70)

Microcomputer.
See Microcomputer system. (15)

Microcomputer specialist.
A computer system user who is very knowledgeable in both microcomputer

systems and a particular applications area. (517)

Microcomputer system.
The smallest and least expensive type of computer system. Also called a *personal computer system.* (15)

Microfiche.
A sheet of film, often 4 by 6 inches, on which computer output images are stored. *(161)*

Microminiaturization.
A term that implies a very small size. (B-17)

Microprocessor.
A CPU on a silicon chip. *(15)*

Microsecond.
One millionth of a second. (70)

Microspacing.
A technique used by some printers and software packages to insert fractional spaces between characters to give text a typeset look. (270)

Microwave.
An electromagnetic wave in the high-frequency range. (187)

Millisecond.
One thousandth of a second. (70)

Minicomputer.
An intermediate-size and medium-priced type of computer. (17)

Mixed replication.
In spreadsheets, copying formulas in one range of cells into another range while varying some cell references and leaving others constant. (311)

Modem.
A contraction of the words MOdulation and DEModulation. A communications device that enables computers and their support devices to communicate over ordinary telephone lines. (191)

Monitor.
(1) A video display. (2) The supervisor program of an operating system. (132)

Monochrome.
A term used to refer to a display device that operates in a single foreground color. *(134)*

Monospacing.
A printing feature that allocates the same amount of space on a line to each character. Contrasts with proportional spacing. (269)

Mouse.
A device used to rapidly move a cursor around a display screen. (153)

MS-DOS.
An operating system widely used by microcomputer systems similar to those made by IBM. (230)

Multidimensional spreadsheet.
A program package that allows the construction of worksheets in which cells are referenced by more than two coordinates. (315)

Multimedia.
A type of computing in which text, graphics, voice, and video are intermixed in applications. (354)

Multiplexer.
A communications device that interleaves the messages of several low-speed devices and sends them along a single, high-speed transmission path. (204)

Multiprocessing.
The *simultaneous* execution of two or more program sequences by multiple computers operating under common control. (228)

Multiprogramming.
The execution of two or more programs, possibly being run by different users, *concurrently* on the same computer. (226)

Multitasking.
The ability of a single-user operating system to enable two or more programs or program tasks to execute concurrently. (226)

Nanosecond.
One-billionth of a second. (71)

Narrowband transmission.
Low-speed transmission, characterized by telegraph transmission. (190)

Natural language.
Refers to languages such as English, Spanish, and Japanese that are used by people in everyday conversation. (459)

NetWare.
The most widely used operating system on local area networks (LANs). (235)

Network.
A system of machines that communicate with one another. *(195)*

Nonimpact printing.
The formation of characters on a surface by means of heat, lasers, photography, or ink jets. Contrasts with impact printing. (141)

Nonvolatile storage.
Storage that retains its contents when the power is shut off. Contrasts with volatile storage. (94)

OA.
See Office automation. (381)

Object module.
The machine-language program that is the output from a language translator. Also called an *object program.* (238)

Object-oriented programming language.
A language that works with objects and messages rather than with separate instructions and data. (457)

OCR.
See Optical character recognition. (146)

Office automation (OA).
The use of computer-based, office-oriented technologies such as word processing, desktop publishing, electronic mail, video teleconferencing, and the like. (381)

Office automation (OA) area.
The group of computer professionals within the information systems department that is charged with managing office-related computer activities within the organization. (416)

Office automation (OA) director.
The person in charge of the office automation (OA) area. (514)

Offline.
Anything not in or prepared for communication with the CPU. Contrasts with online. (46)

One-entry-point/one-exit-point rule.
A rule stating that each program control structure will have only one entry point into it and one exit point out of it. (445)

Online.
Anything ready for or in communication with the CPU. Contrasts with offline. (46)

Operating environment.
A term that refers to a graphical interface or the combination of an operating system and graphical interface—for instance, MS-DOS running under Microsoft Windows. (222)

Operating system.
The main collection of systems software that enables the computer system to manage the resources under its control. (216, B-13)

Optical character recognition (OCR).
The use of light reflectivity to identify marks, characters, or codes and the subsequent conversion of such symbols into a form suitable for computer processing. (146)

Optical disk.
A disk read by laser beams rather than by magnetic means. (115)

Orphan.
The first line of a paragraph when it is

separated from the rest of the paragraph by a page or column break. Contrasts with widow. (272)

OS/2.
An operating system designed by IBM for high-end IBM and IBM-compatible microcomputers. (233)

Output.
Anything resulting from a computer or computer-system process or involved with the end result of such a process, such as information. Contrasts with input. (7)

Output device.
A machine used to output computer-processed data, or information. (7, 42, 130)

Outsourcing.
Refers to a company hiring another company to do some or all of its information processing activities. (416)

Page description language (PDL).
A language used to communicate instructions to a laser printer. (280)

Page-makeup software.
Programs used to compose page layouts in a desktop publishing system. (281)

Page printer.
A high-speed printer that delivers output one page at a time. (145)

Parallel processing.
A computer system that operates with two or more CPUs, which share work and process pieces of this work simultaneously. (86)

Parallel transmission.
Data transmission in which each bit in a byte has its own path and all of the bits in a byte are transmitted simultaneously. Contrasts with serial transmission. (193)

Parity bit.
An extra bit added to the byte representation of a character to ensure that

there is always either an odd or an even number of 1-bits transmitted with every character. (76)

Partial backup.
A procedure that produces a duplicate copy of selected files onto a secondary storage medium. (491)

Pascal.
A structured high-level programming language that is often used to teach programming. (453)

Pascaline.
A mechanical calculating machine developed by Blaise Pascal in the 1600s. (B-2)

Password.
A word or number used to provide selected individuals access to a system. (542)

PBX.
See Private branch exchange. (201)

PC-DOS.
The operating system most widely used on IBM microcomputers. (229)

PDL.
See Page description language. (280)

Peer-to-peer LAN.
A LAN in which all of the user workstations and shared peripherals in the network operate on the same level. (199)

Peripheral equipment.
All the machines that make it possible to get data and programs into the CPU, get processed information out, and store data and programs for ready access to the CPU. (7, 40)

Personal computer.
See Microcomputer system. (15)

Personal computer system.
See Microcomputer system. *(15)*

Picosecond.
A trillionth of a second. (71)

Pie chart.
A presentation graphic in which the principal charting element is a pie-shaped image that is divided into slices, each of which represents a share of the whole. (317)

Pixel.
On a display screen, a single dot used to compose dot-matrix characters and other images. (135)

Platform.
A set of computer-system architecture and systems-software choices that limit you to work in a certain way. (482)

Plotter.
An output device used for drawing graphs and diagrams. (159)

PL/1.
An acronym for Programming Language/1. PL/1 is a structured, general-purpose, high-level programming language that can be used for scientific, engineering, and business applications. *(456)*

Point-of-sale (POS) system.
A computer system, commonly found in department stores and supermarkets, that uses electronic cash register terminals to process and record sales transactions. (147)

Point size.
A measurement used in the scaling of typefaces. (268)

Port.
An outlet on the computer's system unit through which a peripheral device may communicate. (81)

Portable computer.
A microcomputer system that is compact enough to be carried about easily. *(15)*

POS system.
See Point-of-sale system. (147)

Precompiler.
A computer program that translates an extended set of programming language

commands into standard commands of the language. (353)

Preliminary investigation.
In systems development, a brief study of a problem area to assess whether or not a full-scale systems project should be undertaken. Also called a *feasibility study*. (418)

Presentation graphic.
A visual image, such as a bar chart or pie chart, that is used to present data in a highly meaningful form. (317)

Presentation graphics software.
A program package used to prepare line charts, bar charts, pie charts, and other information-intensive images. (320)

Primary storage.
Also known as *memory* and *internal storage*, a section of the computer system that temporarily holds data and program instructions awaiting processing, intermediate results, and output produced from processing. (10)

Printer.
A device that places computer output onto paper. (138)

Privacy.
In a computer processing context, refers to how information about individuals is used and by whom. (546)

Private branch exchange (PBX).
A call-switching station that an organization acquires for its own use. (201)

Private wide area network.
A wide area network that is built by an organization for its own use. (196)

Processing.
See Information processing. (7)

Productivity software.
Fourth-generation-language-based software—such as word processors, spreadsheets, presentation-graphics packages, file managers, and database management systems—designed to make workers more productive at their jobs. *(48)*

Program.
A set of instructions that causes the computer system to perform specific actions. (8)

Program flowchart.
A visual design tool showing step by step how a computer program will process data. (440)

Programmer.
A person whose job is to write, maintain, and test computer programs. (13, 439)

Programming language.
A set of rules used to write computer programs. (9, 449)

Project manager.
(a) A systems analyst who is put in charge of a team that is building a large system. (b) A software package that is used to manage projects. (415)

Prolog.
A language widely used for artificial intelligence applications. *(458)*

Proportional spacing.
A printing feature that allocates more horizontal space on a line to some characters than to others. (269)

Protocol.
A set of conventions used by machines to establish communication with one another in a telecommunications environment. (204)

Prototyping.
A systems development alternative whereby a small model, or *prototype*, of the system is built before a full-scale systems development effort is undertaken. (430)

Pseudocode.
A technique for structured program design that uses Englishlike statements to outline the logic of a program. Pseudocode statements closely resemble actual programming code. (445)

Public access network.
A network, such as the phone system, that is designed to be used by the general public. (195)

Quality Assurance.
The process of making sure quality programs are written in a quality way. (465)

Queue.
A group of items awaiting computer processing. *(243)*

RAM.
See Random access memory. (80)

RAM disk.
A disk management system in which a portion of RAM is set up to function as disk. (108)

Random access.
See Direct access. (95)

Random access memory (RAM).
The computer system's primary storage. (80)

Range.
In spreadsheets, a set of contiguous cells. (301)

Read-only memory (ROM).
A software-in-hardware module that can be read but not written on. (81)

Read/write head.
A magnetic station on a disk access mechanism or tape unit that reads or writes data. (94)

Realtime processing.
Updating data immediately in a master file as transactions take place. Contrasts with batch processing. (54)

Recalculation feature.
The ability of spreadsheet software to quickly and automatically recalculate the contents of several cells based on new operator inputs. (300)

System a
The phase
life cycle i
or services
(424)

System b
A board th
Sometimes

System cl
The timing
puter that
instruction
cuitry. (70

System d
The phase
life cycle i
system and
them are f

System in
The phase
encompass
ing the col
and succes
vendor. (4:

System lil
The person
area respo
and progra
disks, mic
age media

System u
The hardw
puter and
ber of othe
boards and

Systems a
The phase
life cycle i
thoroughly
should be

Systems a
A person
organizatic
need to be
may best l
resources.

Record.
A collection of related fields. (46)

Redlining.
A word processing facility that provides the electronic equivalent of the editor's red pen. (272)

Reduced instruction set computing (RISC).
A term referring to a computer system that gets by with a fewer number of instructions than conventional computer systems, thereby reducing system overhead and, in many cases, decreasing the time needed to process programs. (86)

Register.
A high-speed staging area within the computer that temporarily stores data during processing. (68)

Relational database management system.
A database management system that supports relational databases—that is, databases in which data records are placed into files and the files can be interrelated by common fields (columns). (341)

Relative replication.
In spreadsheets, copying formulas in a source range of cells into a target range of cells relative to the row and column coordinates of the cells in the target range. (308)

Release.
A minor upgrade of a software product. (497)

Report Program Generator (RPG).
A report-generation language popular with small businesses. *(457)*

Request for proposal (RFP).
A document containing a general description of a system that an organization wishes to acquire. The RFP is submitted to vendors, who subsequently recommend specific systems based on the resources they are able to supply. (425)

Request for quotation (RFQ).
A document containing a list of specific hardware, software, and services that an organization wishes to acquire. The RFQ is submitted to vendors, who subsequently prepare bids based on the resources they are able to supply. (425)

Resolution.
A term referring to the sharpness of the images on an output medium. *(135)*

Retrieval/update language.
A fourth-generation language specifically tailored to information retrieval and updating operations. *(343)*

Reusable code.
Program segments that can be reused several times in constructing applications programs. (462)

RFP.
See Request for proposal. (425)

RFQ.
See Request for quotation. (425)

Ring network.
A telecommunications network in which machines are connected serially in a closed loop. (202)

RISC.
See Reduced instruction set computing. (86)

Robotics.
The field devoted to the study of robot technology. (388)

ROM.
See Read-only memory. (81)

RPG.
See Report Program Generator. (457)

SAA.
See Systems Applications Architecture. (233)

Scheduler.
The operations person whose job it is to utilize system resources to peak efficiency. (510)

Screen saver.
A software product designed to protect the phosphor coating on the inside of a display screen from damage when the display is turned on but is not used for an extended period. (493)

Secondary storage.
Storage, provided by technologies such as disk and tape, that supplements memory. Also called *external storage*. (11)

Secondary storage device.
A machine, such as a tape unit or disk unit, capable of providing storage to supplement memory. (42)

Second generation.
Usually refers to the second era of commercial computers (1959–1964), characterized by transistor circuitry. (B-10)

Sector.
A pie-shaped area on a disk. Many disks are addressed through sectors. (98)

Selection.
The process of going through a set of data and picking out only those data elements that meet certain criteria. (52)

Selection (if-then-else) control structure.
The control structure used to represent a decision operation. (445)

Semiconductor memory.
A memory whose components are etched onto small silicon chips. (B-17)

Sequence control structure.
The control structure used to represent operations that take place sequentially. (445)

Sequential access.
Fetching records in storage ascendingly or descendingly by the key field on which they are physically ordered. (95)

Sequential organization.
Arranging data on a physical medium either ascendingly or descendingly by some key field. (120)

Serial
Data tr
a byte
in succ
transmi

Server
A comp
vices, s
capacit
work (1

Simple
Any ty
messag
only a
(190)

Simula
A techi
life obj
tested
or enci

Site li
A right
that en
copy so
purpos

Smallt
An obj
guage.

Smart
A cred
contain
(158)

Soft c
A nonj
put—fi
trasts v

Soft r
In word
return
a typed
gin. Co

Softwa
Compu

Softwa
The un
comput

Touch-screen device.
A display device that can be activated by touching a finger to the screen. (155)

Track.
A path on an input/output medium on which data are recorded. (97)

Trackball.
A cursor-movement device that consists of a sphere, with only the top of the sphere exposed outside its case. (156)

Traditional approach.
An approach to systems development whereby the five phases of the systems development life cycle are carried out in a predetermined sequence. (429)

Trainer.
A person who provides education to end users about a particular program, system, or technology. (513)

Transaction file.
A file of occurrences, such as customer payments and purchases, that have taken place over a period of time. (47)

Transaction processing system.
A system that processes an organization's business transactions. Operations falling into the transaction processing category include payroll, order entry, accounts receivable, accounts payable, inventory, and general ledger. (372)

Transistor.
A circuit device that dominated second-generation computers. (B-10)

Twisted-pair wires.
A communications medium consisting of pairs of wires twisted together and bound into a cable. The public-access telephone system consists mainly of twisted-wire cabling. (185)

Typeface.
A collection of printed characters that share a common design. (267)

UNIVAC I.
The first commercial electronic digital computer. (B-8)

UNIX.
A multiuser, multitasking operating system. (232)

Universal product code (UPC).
The bar code that is prominently displayed on the packaging of almost all supermarket goods, identifying the product and manufacturer. A variety of optical scanning devices may be used to read the codes. *(150)*

UPC.
See Universal product code. *(150)*

Updating.
The process of bringing something up to date by making corrections, adding new data, and so forth. (53)

Upgrading.
The process of buying new hardware or software to extend the life of a computer system. Contrasts with replacement. (496)

Uploading.
The process of sending data from a small computer system to a larger computer system for storage or processing purposes. Contrasts with downloading. (202)

Upward compatible.
A computer system that can do everything that a smaller model in the line or the previous model can do, plus some additional tasks. *(B-12)*

Utility program.
A program used to perform some frequently encountered operation in a computer system. (239)

Vacuum tube.
The circuit device that dominated first-generation computers. (B-8)

Value.
In spreadsheet programs, a cell entry

that can be manipulated mathematically. Contrasts with label. (299)

Value-added network (VAN).
A term that most commonly refers to a service offered over the public-access phone network by a firm other than the phone company, thereby adding value to the network. (195)

VAN.
See Value-added network. (195)

Vaporware.
Software that exists more in people's imaginations than in actuality. (545)

Vendor rating system.
An objective point-scoring procedure for evaluating competing vendors of computer products or services. (425)

Version.
A major upgrade of a software product. (497)

Very-high-level language.
A problem-specific language that is generally much easier to learn and use than conventional high-level languages such as BASIC, FORTRAN, COBOL, and Pascal. (449)

Very-large-scale integration (VLSI).
The process of placing a *very* large number of integrated circuits on a single silicon chip. *(B-17)*

Vice-president of information systems.
The person in an organization who oversees routine transaction processing and information systems activities as well as other computer-related areas. Also called the *chief information officer (CIO).* (514)

Virtual memory.
An area on disk in which programs are "cut up" into manageable pieces and staged as they are processed. While the computer is processing a program, it fetches the pieces that are needed from virtual memory and places them into conventional memory. (228)

VLSI.
See Very-large-scale integration. *(B-17)*

Voice-grade transmission.
Medium-speed transmission characterized by the rates of speed available over ordinary telephone lines. (190)

Voice-input device.
A device capable of recognizing the human voice. (157)

Voice mail.
An electronic mail system in which spoken phone messages are digitally recorded and stored in an electronic mailbox. (181, 382)

Voice-output device.
A device that enables the computer system to produce spoken output. (160)

Volatile storage.
Storage that loses its contents when the power is shut off. Contrasts with nonvolatile storage. (94)

WAN.
See Wide area network. (195)

Warranty.
A conditional pledge made by a manufacturer to protect the consumer from losses due to defective units of product. (494)

What-if analysis.
An approach to problem solving in which the decision maker repeatedly commands the computer system to recalculate a set of figures based on alternative inputs. (300)

Wide area network (WAN).
A network that covers a wide geographical area. (195)

Wideband transmission.
High-speed transmission characterized by the rates of speed available over coaxial cable, fiber optic cable, and microwave. (190)

Widow.
The last line of a paragraph when it is separated from the rest of the paragraph by a page or column break. (272)

Winchester disk.
A sealed data module that contains a disk, access arms, and read/write heads. *(101)*

Window.
Refers to either (1) using the display screen as a "peek hole" to inspect contiguous portions of a large worksheet or (2) a box of information overlaid on a screen display. (295, 253)

Window area.
In spreadsheet software, the portion of the screen that contains the window onto the worksheet. Also called the *worksheet area.* (298)

Windows.
A graphical operating environment created by Microsoft Corporation. (222)

Windows NT.
A multitasking, multiprocessing operating system designed by Microsoft Corporation for 32-bit microcomputers. (234)

Word.
A group of bits or characters that are treated by the computer system as a unit. (80)

Word processing.
The use of computer technology to create, manipulate, and print text material such as letters, legal contracts, and manuscripts. (258, 381)

Wordwrap.
In word processing, the feature that automatically produces soft carriage returns. (263)

Workgroup computing.
A computer application in which a group of workers interdependently use the same set of software and data on a network. (384)

Worksheet.
In spreadsheet software, the grid that contains the actual labels and values. (295)

Worksheet area.
See Window area. (298)

WYSIWYG.
An acronym for "What You See Is What You Get," WYSIWYG shows on the display screen an output image identical or very close to the desired,

ANSWERS TO FILL-IN AND MATCHING REVIEW EXERCISES

Chapter 1

Fill-in Questions

1. processing
2. primary or internal
3. information
4. software
5. secondary or external
6. hardware
7. program
8. computer system

Matching Questions

1. e   2. f   3. a   4. c
5. b   6. d

Chapter 2

Fill-in Questions

1. input/output medium
2. master
3. online
4. Applications
5. Systems
6. field
7. Batch
8. realtime

Matching Questions

1. b   2. f   3. c   4. e
5. a   6. d

Chapter 3

Fill-in Questions

1. accumulator
2. thousandth
3. terabyte
4. read-only memory
5. parity
6. reduced instruction set computing
7. parallel

Matching Questions

1. b   2. d   3. g   4. e
5. h   6. a   7. f   8. c

Chapter 4

Fill-in Questions

1. volatile
2. disk pack
3. cylinder
4. hard card
5. small computer system interface
6. tracks
7. file-protection ring
8. write once read many

Matching Questions

1. d   2. a   3. c   4. f
5. e   6. b

Chapter 5

Fill-in Questions

1. hard copy
2. pixels
3. cursor
4. monochrome
5. near-letter-quality
6. thermal-transfer
7. ink-jet
8. flatbed, drum
9. bit-mapped
10. film recorder

Matching Questions

1. e   2. f   3. g   4. b
5. d   6. a   7. h   8. c

Chapter 6

Fill-in Questions

1. Electronic data interchange
2. facsimile (fax)
3. Coaxial cable
4. digital
5. Fiber optic cable
6. modem
7. Synchronous
8. Common carriers
9. Asynchronous
10. star

Matching Questions

1. d   2. e   3. b   4. a
5. f   6. c

Chapter 7

Fill-in Questions

1. Systems
2. operating system
3. multiprogramming
4. Time-sharing
5. Multiprocessing
6. NetWare
7. language translator
8. Utility

Matching Questions

1. e   2. d   3. a   4. c
5. f   6. b

Chapter 8

Fill-in Questions

1. wordwrap
2. Proportional spacing
3. mailing list
4. dedicated
5. what you see is what you get
6. orphan
7. page-description language
8. clip art

Matching Questions

1. e   2. b   3. a   4. f
5. c   6. d

Chapter 9

Fill-in Questions

1. window, worksheet
2. cursor, cell pointer (highlight)
3. control panel
4. absolute, relative, mixed

5. template
6. macro
7. Add-on
8. dedicated, integrated

Matching Questions
1. d   2. f   3. e   4. a
5. c   6. b

Chapter 10

Fill-in Questions
1. file managers, database management systems
2. template
3. database
4. Relational
5. database administrator
6. concurrent
7. Structured Query Language
8. multimedia

Matching Questions
1. b   2. e   3. a   4. d
5. f   6. c

Chapter 11

Fill-in Questions
1. artificial intelligence
2. accounts receivable
3. general ledger
4. computer-aided design
5. electronic mail
6. Teleconferencing
7. robotics
8. expert system shell

Matching Questions
1. c   2. a   3. f   4. e
5. d   6. b

Chapter 12

Fill-in Questions
1. chief information officer (CIO)
2. steering
3. prototype
4. End-user development
5. system design
6. tangible

7. vendor rating
8. benchmark test

Matching Questions
1. b   2. d   3. e   4. c
5. a

Chapter 13

Fill-in Questions
1. Systems analysts
2. Coding
3. debugging
4. flowchart
5. Pseudocode
6. COBOL
7. fourth-generation
8. reusable code

Matching Questions
1. h   2. c   3. e   4. b
5. f   6. g   7. d   8. a

Chapter 14

Fill-in Questions
1. End-user
2. IBM-compatible
3. release
4. functionality
5. Backup
6. surge suppressor
7. warranty
8. functionally

Matching Questions
1. f   2. a   3. g   4. d
5. c   6. h   7. e   8. b

Chapter 15

Fill-in Questions
1. Data-entry operators
2. Computer operators
3. System librarians
4. Computer operations managers
5. Systems programmers
6. Applications programmers
7. Systems analysts
8. data processing director

Matching Questions
1. c   2. a   3. b   4. d

Chapter 16

Fill-in Questions
1. cyberphobia
2. Ergonomics
3. Ethics
4. piracy
5. Fair Credit Reporting
6. Caller identification

Matching Questions
1. c   2. f   3. a   4. e
5. b   6. d

Appendix A

1. a. 11
   b. 46
   c. 83
2. a. 110011
   b. 100000100
   c. 111110100
3. a. 5
   b. 1A
   c. F42
4. a. 11110010
   b. 000110101001
   c. 0011100111101011
5. a. 182
   b. 1513
   c. 51967
6. $(4 \times 6^2) + (5 \times 6^1) + (1 \times 6^0) = 175$
7. 100110110
8. EB
9. 100011
10. 3C

Appendix B

Fill-in Questions
1. ENIAC
2. pascaline
3. difference engine
4. Mark I
5. ABC
6. UNIVAC
7. Digital Equipment
8. Altair 8800

CREDITS

Module A opening photo © 1991 Karl Sims, Thinking Machines Corp.

Chapter 1 opening photo Courtesy of International Business Machines Corporation.

Figure 1–1A Courtesy of International Business Machines Corporation.

Figure 1–1B Courtesy of GRID Systems.

Figure 1–1C Courtesy of International Business Machines Corporation.

Figure 1–3 Word Perfect v.5.1 screen shots reprinted under authorization from Word Perfect Corporation. All rights reserved.

Figure 1–4A Courtesy of Apple Computer, Inc. Photographer John Greenleigh.

Figure 1–4B Courtesy of International Business Machines Corporation.

Figure 1–4C Courtesy of Apple Computer, Inc. Photographer John Greenleigh.

Figure 1–4D Courtesy of Sharp Electronics Corp.

Figure 1–5, 1–6 Courtesy of International Business Machines Corporation.

Figure 1–7 Photo by Paul Shambroom, Courtesy of Cray Research, Inc.

User Solution 1–1 Reprinted with permission of Compaq Computer Corporation. All rights reserved.

Feature 1–1 Courtesy of International Business Machines Corporation.

User Solution 1–2 Created using the Arts & Letters Graphics Editor by Computer Support Corp.

Tomorrow Box 1A Courtesy of Sharp Electronics Corp.

Tomorrow Box 1B Courtesy of Skytel.

Feature 1–2 Courtesy of David Rickerd.

Window 1–1 Courtesy Time Arts Inc.

Window 1–2 Courtesy of International Business Machines Corporation.

Window 1–3 Reprinted with permission of Compaq Computer Corporation. All rights reserved.

Window 1–4 Photo courtesy of Hewlett-Packard Company.

Window 1–5 Courtesy of International Business Machines Corporation.

Window 1–6 Courtesy of W. Industries and Rock, Kitchen, Harris, Leicester, England.

Window 1–7, 1–8, 1–9 © 1989 Lucasfilm Ltd. Paramount Pictures Inc. All rights reserved. Courtesy of Industrial Light & Magic.

Window 1–10 Created by Marialine Prieur of Voire (Lyon, France) using TDI software.

Window 1–11 Image courtesy MK-Ferguson Company. "Brew Master" image of complex piping assembly. Rendered with ModelView.

Window 1–12 Courtesy of Package Design of America.

Window 1–13 Created by Renault (Paris, France) using TDI software.

Window 1–14 Pixar/Colossal Pictures 1991.

Window 1–15 Courtesy of David Rickerd/Super Studio.

Window 1–16 Perry Woodworth, created with Corel-Draw. Courtesy of Corel Corp.

Window 1–17, 1–18, 1–19 Courtesy of International Business Machines Corporation.

Window 1–20, 1–21 Courtesy of Evans & Sutherland Computer Corporation.

Window 1–22 Images by Richard Podolsky using GAIA Software on a Macintosh Computer.

Window 1–23 Courtesy of Rockwell International/David Perry.

Window 1–24 Courtesy of International Business Machines Corporation.

Window 1–25 Courtesy of Ford Motor Company.

Chapter 2 opening photo Image courtesy of Colgate-Palmolive, J. Crawford, "Irish Spring Deodorant."

Figure 2–1 Images supplied by Logitech, Inc.

Figure 2–2A Courtesy of NEC Technologies, Inc.

Figure 2–2B, 2–3A Courtesy of International Business Machines Corporation.

Figure 2–3B Photo courtesy of Hewlett-Packard Company.

Figure 2–3C Courtesy of International Business Machines Corporation.

Figure 2–3D Courtesy of Iomega Corp.

Figure 2–4A Courtesy of Nashua Computer Products.

Figure 2–4B Photo courtesy of Memory Media Products.

Figure 2–9A Photo courtesy of American Airlines.

Figure 2–9B, 2–11 Courtesy of International Business Machines Corporation.

User Solution 2–1 Courtesy of Pier I Imports.

User Solution 2–2 Photograph courtesy of Norand Corporation, Cedar Rapids, Iowa.

Tomorrow Box 2 "The Lawnmower Man" image courtesy Allied Vision Lane Pringle Productions, © 1992. CyberJobe animation by Angel Studios, California.

Module B opening photo © 1991 Karl Sims, Thinking Machines Corp.

Chapter 3 opening photo Courtesy of AT&T Archives.

Figure 3–8A, 3–8B Courtesy Intel Corporation.

Figure 3–9 Courtesy of Motorola.

User Solution 3–1 Courtesy of International Business Machines Corporation.

Feature 3–1 Courtesy Intel Corporation.

Tomorrow Box 3 Courtesy of International Business Machines Corporation.

Feature 3–2 Courtesy Intel Corporation.

Chapter 4 opening photo Courtesy of International Business Machines Corporation.

Figure 4–2 Courtesy of Maxell Corporation of America.

Figure 4–11 Courtesy of Quantum Corporation.

Figure 4–12 Courtesy of Iomega Corporation.

Figure 4–13A Courtesy of International Business Machines Corporation.

Figure 4–13B Photo courtesy of BASF.

Figure 4–14 Courtesy of International Business Machines Corporation.

Figure 4–15 Courtesy of Storage Tek.

Figure 4–16 Photo courtesy of Memory Media Products.

Figure 4–17 Courtesy of Everex.

Figure 4–18 Photo courtesy of BASF.

Figure 4–20 Images by Richard Podolsky using GAIA Software on a Macintosh Computer.

Figure 4–21A Courtesy of International Business Machines Corporation.

Figure 4–21B Courtesy of Pioneer Communications of America.

Figure 4–22A Courtesy of International Business Machines Corporation.

Figure 4–22B Maps from DeLorme Street Atlas USA℠, Freeport, Maine.

User Solution 4–1 Courtesy of James Dowlen Artworks.

User Solution 4–2 Courtesy of Whirlpool Corporation.

Tomorrow Box 4 Courtesy of PhotoDisc, Inc.

Chapter 5 opening photo Images supplied by Logitech, Inc.

Figure 5–2A, 5–2B Courtesy of International Business Machines Corporation.

Figure 5–2C Reprinted with permission of Compaq Computer Corporation. All rights reserved.

Figure 5–4A Courtesy Autodesk, Inc.

Figure 5–4B Screen captures from Harvard Graphics®, including text material, are used with the permission of Software Publishing Corporation, which owns the copyright to such product. Harvard Graphics® is a registered trademark of Software Publishing Corporation. The Harvard Graphics® program is a product of Software Publishing Corporation and has no connection with Harvard University. Windows is a trademark of Microsoft Corporation.

Figure 5–4C Courtesy of Cornerstone Technology 1993.

Figure 5–5A, 5–5B Reprinted from PC Computing, October 1991. Copyright © 1991, Ziff Communications Company.

Figure 5–7 Courtesy of Dataproducts Corporation.

Figure 5–10 Courtesy of OKIDATA, Microline® 320.

Figure 5–11A Courtesy of Citizen America Corporation.

Figure 5–11B Courtesy of Seiko Instruments USA.

Figure 5–12A Photo courtesy of Hewlett-Packard Company.

Figure 5–14, 5–15 Courtesy of International Business Machines Corporation.

Figure 5–19A Photo courtesy of NCR Corp.

Figure 5–19B Courtesy of International Business Machines Corporation.

Figure 5–19C Photo courtesy of Intermec Corporation.

Figure 5–20A Courtesy of International Business Machines Corporation.

Figure 5–20B Images supplied by Logitech, Inc.

A Beginner's Guide to BASIC

BASIC (Beginner's All-purpose Symbolic Instruction Code) is one of many programming languages in use today. A programming language is a set of rules used to create a computer program. The computer program is what you enter into the computer system to produce results.

A BASIC computer program is very similar to a recipe. It consists of a list of instructions the computer must carry out in a specified sequence to produce the desired result. Each of the instructions in a BASIC program must be written in strict accordance with the rules of the BASIC language. These rules are referred to as syntax. If you make a seemingly trivial syntax error in writing the program, such as misspelling a word or omitting a comma, the computer system will reject your program or give unexpected, incorrect results.

The purpose of this *Guide* is to teach you how to write useful, simple BASIC programs. Of all the major programming languages, BASIC is among the easiest to learn. You should be able to create programs for business use, game playing, and performing difficult, repetitive computations after reading this *Guide* and practicing on a computer.

Many versions of the BASIC language are available today. *A Beginner's Guide to BASIC* has been written to conform to several of the most common BASIC usages, such as the BASICA, GWBASIC, and QBASIC translators that accompany the MS-DOS and PC-DOS operating systems. Also, an appendix containing additional commands is provided for users of QBASIC. In the pages that follow, program outputs are distinguished from programs and their inputs by highlighting in color.

The need to practice BASIC on a computer can't be emphasized enough. Programming, like driving a car or playing a sport, is a skill that is mastered mostly by practice. Since it is easy for a beginner in any endeavor to make mistakes at the beginning, practicing can initially be very frustrating (can you remember your first day with a musical instrument?). However, if you really want to learn BASIC, and if you start by writing simple programs rather than complicated ones, you will find BASIC to be relatively easy. So, be patient—and start playing with your computer as soon as possible.

A BASIC PRIMER

A Simple Example

Let's get into BASIC immediately by looking at a relatively simple problem and developing a BASIC program to solve it. The example given in Figure 1-1 will show you both some of the rules of BASIC and the manner in which computers carry out instructions in a logical, step-by-step fashion.

The problem is to write a BASIC program that adds the numbers 8 and 16. We want the computer to print the answer like this:

THE ANSWER IS 24

There are many ways to solve this problem, including the one shown in Figure 1-1.

The six numbered instructions in the figure make up a *BASIC program*. In most cases, you will be typing in instructions such as these at a keyboard hooked up to a computer. When you have finished typing in and entering the instructions (pressing the Enter key after each instruction), normally you then type the word RUN to command the system to execute (that is, to carry out) your program. You should study this program carefully before proceeding further. Sometimes the purpose of an instruction will be obvious. The comments that follow shortly should clarify the other instructions.

Before we go into detail about precisely how the program works, you should observe the following important points about the program in Figure 1-1:

1. Each of the six numbered instructions is a *BASIC program statement*. The computer completes the operation described in each statement. It then automatically moves on to another statement.

   Each BASIC program statement begins with a key word that tells the computer what type of operation is involved—for example, REM, READ, LET, PRINT, DATA, and END. These key words may be thought of as the vocabulary of the computer system when you are writing BASIC programs. You must always stay strictly within this vocabulary. If, for example, you substitute DATUM or DATTA for DATA in line 50, the computer system will not know what you want to do.

2. Each program statement is identified by a *line number*—for example, 10, 20, 30, and so on. Line numbers are normally written in increments of 10 rather than 1, which makes it easy to insert new statements in the program later. All line numbers must be integers (whole numbers), and all lines must have different line numbers.

   The computer will always execute statements in the sequence specified by the line numbers unless instructed to do otherwise. Ways to do this are discussed later in this section. Because the line numbers specify the order

F I G U R E 1 – 1

A simple BASIC program.

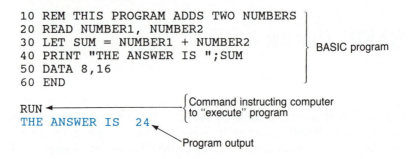

```
10 REM THIS PROGRAM ADDS TWO NUMBERS
20 READ NUMBER1, NUMBER2
30 LET SUM = NUMBER1 + NUMBER2                BASIC program
40 PRINT "THE ANSWER IS ";SUM
50 DATA 8,16
60 END

RUM ◄                          Command instructing computer
                               to "execute" program
THE ANSWER IS   24
                          Program output
```

of program statements, you can type in the lines in any order, such as 30, 60, 10, 50, 20, and 40. Before the computer system runs your program, it will automatically put all the statements in proper order by line number.

3. In this program, three *variables* (NUMBER1, NUMBER2, and SUM) are used. When the computer system begins to execute the program, it will set up separate storage locations for each variable. A storage location can be thought of as a "bucket" that can hold only one item (for example, a number) at a time.

    The storage locations represent the memory of the computer with respect to the program being run. For example, when we ask the computer in line 40 to print the value of SUM, the computer consults its memory to find the value.

    It is possible, as we will see in later programs, to change the values of variables such as NUMBER1, NUMBER2, and SUM several times during the execution of a program. It is because their values are allowed to change that they are known as variables. When NUMBER1, NUMBER2, and SUM are given new values, their old values are lost.

Now let's see, statement by statement, how the program works.

```
10 REM THIS PROGRAM ADDS TWO NUMBERS
```

The REM (remark) statement is actually ignored by the computer. However, even though the computer doesn't use it, the REM statement is very helpful. It allows you to place informative comments (such as the program title or description) in the body of the program.

```
20 READ NUMBER1, NUMBER2 and 50 DATA 8,16
```

The READ and DATA statements are always used together in BASIC. The READ statement instructs the computer to assign data to the specified variables. The DATA statement provides these data. Note that the computer assigns values one at a time and in the order in which they are typed in the READ and DATA statements. Thus, when the READ statement is executed, the computer sets NUMBER1 equal to 8 and NUMBER2 equal to 16.

```
30 LET SUM = NUMBER1 + NUMBER2
```

The computer system always reacts to a LET statement by computing the value indicated by the expression on the right side of the "=" sign and assigning it to the variable named on the left side. Thus, statement 30 will cause the following actions to be taken:

1. The computer system looks up the values of NUMBER1 and NUMBER2 in memory (finding 8 and 16, respectively).
2. The values of NUMBER1 and NUMBER2 are added (producing 24).
3. The value of the right side of the expression (24) is assigned to SUM.

```
40 PRINT "THE ANSWER IS ";SUM
```

The PRINT statement is used when we want the computer system to output something—for example, the results of a computation. The preceding PRINT statement consists of three elements:

1. A phrase appearing inside quotes (THE ANSWER IS). The computer system will print this phrase exactly as it appears. These *literal* phrases are handy in PRINT statements to label output.
2. A formatting character (;). The semicolon instructs the computer system to leave only one space between the literal phrase and the value of SUM.
3. A variable (SUM). The computer system will look up the value of SUM in memory and print its value.

If you are using a display device, PRINT instructs the computer to display results on the screen. You must use the command LPRINT in your program if you wish to direct output to your printer instead.

```
60 END
```

On many computer systems, the END statement physically must be the last statement in the program. It instructs the computer system that the program is finished.

At this point, you can start to see how BASIC works. Now is a good time to test your knowledge of some of the fundamental concepts just introduced by practicing on your computer system. The section that follows describes how to get started with BASIC on the particular computer system you are using.

Getting Started

To begin, your computer must be turned on and you must load, or "boot up," the operating system (either MS-DOS or PC-DOS).

Dual-Diskette Systems.   On a dual-diskette system, put the diskette containing the operating system in the A drive—that is, the leftmost or topmost disk drive—and turn on the power switch. Also turn on your monitor and printer.

When the date and time prompts appear, either enter a date and time where appropriate or press the Enter key to indicate that you wish to bypass the date and time settings. If it was 7:24 P.M. on December 15, 1994, for instance, you could enter the date and time in the form 12-15-94 and 19:24, respectively.

When the A> prompt is displayed, indicating that the operating system has been successfully loaded, or booted, replace the operating system disk with the disk containing BASIC and type BASICA, GWBASIC, or QBASIC, depending on the version(s) of BASIC available to your system.* Follow this by pressing the Enter key. At this point, the BASIC language translator will be loaded into memory, or RAM. You will see either a menu or the prompting message "Ok" on your screen, indicating that BASIC is ready for your first command.

Once BASIC is in memory, you no longer need to have the disk containing BASIC mounted on any of the disk drives as you use BASIC. The operating system will save programs to and retrieve programs from the default drive, A, unless you specify another disk drive in the filename. You will see how to name files a bit later.

Hard-Disk Systems.   On a hard-disk system, the date and time prompts sometimes display as soon as you turn on your computer system. If this is the case, follow the same instructions as dual-diskette users for responding to both the date and time prompts. Then, when the C> prompt is displayed, type in and enter BASICA, GWBASIC, or QBASIC, whichever is appropriate. This will load the BASIC language translator into memory, or RAM. You will see either a menu or the prompting message "Ok" on your screen, indicating that BASIC is ready for your first command. The operating system will save programs too and retrieve programs from the C drive unless you specify another disk drive in the filename. You will see how to name files a bit later.

Entering and Editing Programs

As you type in each line of your program, don't forget to enter the line by pressing the Enter key. It is only when you press Enter that the line is actually recorded in computer memory.

If you make a mistake as you are typing in a line, you can use either the Backspace or Delete keys to delete unwanted characters or the Insert key to insert new characters. Backspace deletes the character to the left of the cursor position, whereas Delete erases the character at the cursor position. Insert is a toggle key. Pressing it once makes insertion active (note that the cursor increases in size), and pressing Insert at any time when insertion is active makes insertion inactive.

You can use the arrow keys to move to any position in the line. BASIC has a full screen editor, meaning you can make a change to any line that appears on the screen and then enter the change by pressing the Enter key. The Enter key can be pressed with the screen cursor anywhere on the line. A more comprehensive list of useful BASIC keys is provided in Figure 1-2.

As you are entering lines of a program and making edits, it is usually important to ascertain exactly what BASIC is storing in memory. To get a listing of all lines of your program on the display screen, in ascending order by line number, type

```
LIST
```

*The BASIC language translator is often on the same diskette that contains the operating system, stored in a file that has "BASIC" as part of the filename. While QBASIC—the newest version of BASIC available with DOS—will load and run most programs developed under BASICA or GWBASIC, it also supports programs without line numbers and has several other new features (see Appendix 1).

Useful keystrokes for working in BASIC.

Keystrokes	Description
Arrow keys (← → ↑ ↓)	Used to move the cursor around the screen
Backspace	Used to erase the character to the left of the cursor position
Ctrl + Alt + Del*	Reboots DOS
Ctrl + Break	Interrupts a running program
Ctrl + Home	Clears the monitor screen
Ctrl + J	Used to continue a BASIC line on the next screen line
Ctrl + NumLock	Pauses a running program; hit any key to continue
Ctrl + PrtSc	Provides an echo of screen output to the printer; invoke keystrokes a second time to turn off this feature
Del	Used to erase the character at the cursor position
Enter	Used to enter a line of a program or to execute a command
Esc	Used to erase the line at the cursor position from the screen
Function keys	Used to quickly enter commands
Ins	Used to insert characters at the cursor position
Shift + PrtSc	Outputs whatever is on the screen to the printer

*Means holding down Ctrl and Alt keys while hitting Del key. The Ctrl, Alt, and Shift keys must always be held down when used in combination of another key. In this table and in this *Guide*, every key peceded by a "+" sign must be held down while striking another key(s).

Or, to send the same listing to your printer, type

```
LLIST
```

Remember, as soon as a line that you wish to edit is on the screen, you can move the cursor to it, edit it, and press Enter. If the line is really messed up, you can also reenter it from scratch. To get rid of a line completely, just type and enter its line number, with nothing else on the line.

There are several other versions of both the LIST and LLIST commands that we will cover later in Section 1.

Some Exercises

Now that you know how to load BASIC on your computer system and how to issue a few simple BASIC commands, you might try some of the following suggestions.

1. Type and run the BASIC program in Figure 1-1. Did you get the same result as in this guide?
2. Try altering the PRINT statement so that it produces fancier output. For example, to get the computer system to output

```
THE SUM OF 8 AND 16 IS 24
```

your PRINT statement should look like

```
PRINT "THE SUM OF ";NUMBER1;" AND ";NUMBER2;" IS ";SUM
```

3. Try making the expression in statement 30 more complicated to see what the effects are. For example, NUMBER1 and NUMBER2 could be multiplied by specifying NUMBER1 ∗ NUMBER2 instead of NUMBER1 + NUMBER2 in statement 30. Note that in BASIC, an asterisk is used to tell the computer to multiply. Multiplication is explained in more detail later.

4. Tinker with the DATA statement by changing the data values (try some negative numbers or numbers with decimal points). Also, experiment to see if it matters where the DATA statement appears. Try placing it as the first, second, or third statement of your program.

A Tougher Example

The program we just looked at was rather simple. The values of the variables didn't change, and the computer wasn't asked to execute a statement out of numerical order. In most programs, however, the values of the variables do change, and the computer is asked to branch to a statement other than the one that immediately follows.

Let's now consider a program that reflects these two added complications. We will write a program to compute and output the squares of 8, 16, and 12.

Designing an Algorithm

Before *coding* (that is, writing out) this problem in BASIC, let's consider what tasks are involved in solving this problem. In addition, let's think about the order in which these tasks must be presented to the computer. The tasks themselves, together with the order in which they are performed, are referred to as an *algorithm*. Designing an algorithm is not that different from building a house. You don't start putting the roof together before you've fully designed the whole structure and decided where the roof will go relative to other sections.

At first glance, it seems that the following algorithm is attractive for solving our problem:

1. Read a number.
2. Square the number.
3. Print out the result of step 2.
4. Return to step 1.

The fundamental structure involved here is called a *loop*. Thus, the computer system is to read 8, square it (producing 64), output the result (64), loop back to step 1, read 16, square it, and so on. There is one major problem with the four-step solution just described: Once the computer system fully processes the last number (12) and goes back to step 1, there are no more numbers to read. Thus, we need to instruct the loop when to stop. This problem is frequently solved by putting a *trailer* (or *sentinel*) *value* (such as -1) at the end of the data list and directing the computer to leave the loop immediately after this value is read. Thus, we could refine our algorithm as follows:

1. Read a number.
1.5. If the number $= -1$, go to step 5; otherwise process step 2.
2. Square the number.
3. Print out the result of step 2.
4. Return to step 1.
5. End the program.

Although this procedure is complete and produces correct results, many professional programmers include an extra "Read" step to make the procedure *structured*. Many programming languages (such as Pascal and COBOL) make it difficult to code satisfactory programs unless this extra step is taken. As you will learn later on, structured programs result in program logic that is easy to follow.

Inserting the extra Read step (step 3.5) and modifying step 4 so that it points back to step 1.5, we get

1. Read a number.	3. Print out the result of step 2.
1.5. If the number = −1, go to step 5; otherwise process step 2.	3.5. Read another number.
	4. Return to step 1.5.
2. Square the number.	5. End the program.

Once the algorithm is completely designed, coding it in BASIC becomes relatively straightforward, as you will see by observing the program in Figure 1-3. In this program, the WHILE and WEND statements form a loop that is executed *while* the value of the number is not (i.e. < >) −1. Thus, WHILE and WEND are, respectively, equivalent to steps 1.5 and 4 in the final algorithm just described. The program in Figure 1-3 has been liberally enhanced with

FIGURE 1-3

A program for computing and outputting the squares of several numbers.

```
10  REM    TITLE:   PROGRAM 1-3
20  REM
30  REM    DESCRIPTION:  THIS PROGRAM READS
40  REM       NUMBERS, SQUARES THEM, AND OUTPUTS
50  REM       THE RESULTS
60  REM
70  REM    AUTHOR: C.S. PARKER
80  REM    DATE: 10/5/94
90  REM
100 REM       NUMBER = THE NUMBER TO BE SQUARED
110 REM       SQUARE = THE SQUARE OF THE NUMBER
120 REM
130 REM    **********************************
140 READ NUMBER
150 WHILE NUMBER <> -1
160    LET SQUARE=NUMBER^2
170    PRINT "THE SQUARE OF ";NUMBER;" IS";SQUARE
180    READ NUMBER
190 WEND
200 DATA 8,16,12,-1
210 END

RUN
THE SQUARE OF  8   IS 64
THE SQUARE OF  16  IS 256
THE SQUARE OF  12  IS 144
```

| FIGURE 1-4 | | | | Steps the computer system must take to fully execute the problem in Figure 1-3. |

Step	Statement Executed	Value of NUMBER in Storage	Value of SQUARE in Storage	Action Taken
1	140	8		8 taken from data list and assigned to NUMBER
2	150	8		8 ≠ −1; therefore, proceed to next statement
3	160	8	64	SQUARE computed
4	170	8	64	Computer system prints THE SQUARE OF 8 IS 64
5	180	16	64	16 taken from data list and assigned to NUMBER
6	190	16	64	Computer directed to line 150
7	150	16	64	16 ≠ −1; therefore, proceed to next statement
8	160	16	256	SQUARE computed
9	170	16	256	Computer system prints THE SQUARE OF 16 IS 256
10	180	12	256	12 taken from data list and assigned to NUMBER
11	190	12	256	Computer directed to line 150
12	150	12	256	12 ≠ −1; therefore proceed to next statement
13	160	12	144	SQUARE computed
14	170	12	144	Computer system prints THE SQUARE OF 12 IS 144
15	180	−1	144	−1 taken from data list and assigned to NUMBER
16	190	−1	144	Computer direct to line 150
17	150	−1	144	−1 = −1; therefore, proceed to line 210
18	210	−1	144	The program ends

REM statements; remember, these are ignored by the computer. It will take the computer 18 steps to execute this program fully, as shown in Figure 1-4.

Saving and Retrieving

Programs such as the one in Figure 1-3 take some time to create and to successfully get in running order. Hence, when you are through, you may wish to *save* the program and, some time later, *retrieve* it.

Saving is done with the SAVE command. For instance, if we type the command

```
SAVE "SQUARES"
```

at any point when we are entering or editing the program in Figure 1-3, or after we've successfully run it, the computer system will take whatever lines of the program it has in memory and store them on the default disk in a file named SQUARES. The default disk is the one the operating system is currently pointing to, and it is the one identified in the operating system's prompt.

Tomorrow, if you wish to retrieve SQUARES, type

```
LOAD "SQUARES"
```

as soon as you're in BASIC. When the "Ok" message appears on the screen, type LIST to display SQUARES on the screen.

Filenames.   The name that you choose for your program can be any filename that's acceptable to DOS. For example,

```
B:SQUARES
B:SQUARES.DAT
A:SQUARES
C:SQUARES
SQUARES
SQUARES.DAT
```

are all acceptable filenames. DOS allows you to name a file with a one- to eight-character filename (the first character of which must be a letter of the alphabet), a one- to three-character filename extension (e.g., DAT), and a one-character disk-drive indicator (e.g., A, B, or C). Both the extension and disk-drive indicator are optional. If no disk-drive indicator is declared, the computer system will automatically go to the default drive to save or look for your file.

The characters allowed in the main part of the filename and the extension are the letters of the alphabet, the digits 0 through 9, and certain special characters. Any lowercase letters of the alphabet typed in a filename will be converted to uppercase characters.

If you do not save a filename with an extension, BASIC will automatically supply the extension .BAS (short for BASIC). You do not need to refer to this extension when you are under the control of BASIC. If you override this extension with one of your own, you must declare that extension whenever you do saving and retrieving operations in BASIC.

Statement and System Commands

You will use two major types of commands to write and run BASIC programs on your computer: BASIC statement commands and BASIC system commands.

Statement Commands.   Statement commands are the commands that are preceded by line numbers (unless you are in QBASIC and decide to override line numbers). The statement commands you've encountered so far are REM, LET, READ, DATA, PRINT, END, WHILE, and WEND. These commands instruct the computer what to do while it is executing your program. Subsequent sections of *A Beginner's Guide to BASIC* cover other important statement commands. A summary of statement commands covered in the *Guide* is given in Appendix 2.

System Commands.   System commands, in contrast, are designed to tell the computer system to do something before or after it executes a program. The system commands you've encountered so far are RUN, LIST, LLIST, SAVE, and LOAD. Some others that are particularly handy are NEW, RENUM, and SYSTEM. NEW erases memory so that you can work on a fresh program, RENUM renumbers lines of your program (changing all embedded references to these lines as well), and SYSTEM terminates BASIC and returns to the operating system prompt. A more comprehensive list of system commands and several examples of using them are provided in Figure 1-5.

FIGURE 1-5

Common usages of BASIC system commands.

AUTO

Automatically supplies the line numbers so that you don't have to type them in. Examples:

    AUTO   Numbers lines in increments of 10, starting with line 10 (i.e.,
                    10, 20, 30, . . .)
    AUTO 100   Numbers lines in increments of 10, starting with line 100
                    (i.e., 100, 110, 120,. . .)

To terminate automatic line numbering, press down the Control key while hitting the Break key.

DELETE

Used to delete lines of a program. Examples:

    DELETE 20   Deletes only line 20
    DELETE 20-100   Deletes lines 20 through 100
    DELETE 50-   Deletes from line 50 on
    DELETE -50   Deletes all lines up to and including 50

FILES

List the name of all files mounted on a particular disk drive. Examples:

    FILES "*.BAS"   Lists the names of all BASIC files on the default drive
    FILES "B:"   Lists the names of all files on the B drive

KILL

Used to erase a file from disk. Example: KILL "FRED" kills a file named FRED.BAS on disk.

LIST

Used to output the lines of the program on the display screen. Examples:

    LIST   Lists the entire program
    LIST 20   Lists only line 20
    LIST 20-100   Lists lines 20 through 100
    LIST 50-   Lists from line 50 on
    LIST -50   Lists all lines up to and including line 50

LLIST

Used to output the lines of a program on the printer. For examples, see the "LIST" command above. (Note: You must change the keyword LIST to LLIST to get these to work.)

Writing Acceptable BASIC Expressions

Now that we've covered some broad fundamentals concerning how BASIC works, let's consider more closely some rules for writing BASIC instructions. This subsection addresses allowable characters, formation of variables and constants, and the writing of mathematical and logical expressions.

BASIC Character Set

When you are typing in a program, you must use only those characters that are understood by the version of BASIC available to your computer system. Such characters are known as the BASIC *character set*. They fall into three groups:

- Alphabetic: ABCDEFGHIJKLMNOPQRSTUVWXYZ
- Numeric: 0123456789
- Special: . , + & ! < > / @ ( ) − * = (and so on)

LOAD

Used to retrieve a program from disk and place it into memory. Examples:

LOAD "JOHN"	Retrieves JOHN.BAS from the default drive
LOAD "JOHN.22"	Retrieves JOHN.22 from the default drive
LOAD "B:JOHN.22"	Retrieves JOHN.22 from drive B

NEW

Clears current program from computer memory, enabling a fresh program to be typed in. Example: NEW

RENUM

Used to renumber program lines. Examples:

RENUM	Renumbers in increments of 10, starting at 100 (i.e., 100, 110, 120, . . .)
RENUM 10	Renumbers in increments of 10, starting at 10 (i.e., 10, 20, 30, . . .)

RUN

Executes a program. Example: RUN PAYROLL runs a payroll called PAYROLL.BAS.

SAVE

Writes the program that is currently stored in memory onto disk. Examples:

SAVE "JOHN"	Saves program as JOHN.BAS on the default drive
SAVE "JOHN.22"	Saves program as JOHN.22 on the default drive
SAVE "B:JOHN.22"	Saves program as JOHN.22 on the B drive

SYSTEM

Automatically returns to the operating system. Example: SYSTEM

TRON and TROFF

Used for debugging purposes to trace the order in which lines have been processed in a program. Typing TRON before you run a program turns the trace feature on; typing TROFF anytime thereafter turns the feature off. Example: Typing TRON before you ran the program in Figure 1-1 would produce [10] [20] [30] [40] [60] as output.

Variables

Variables are of two fundamental types: numeric and string. *Numeric variables* can be assigned only numbers, whereas *string variables* can be assigned any combination of alphabetic, numeric, and special characters.

Numeric Variables.   The following program contains six numeric variables:

```
10 LET A = 6.5
20 LET B = 8.04
30 READ C1,C2,C3
40 LET FORMULA = A + B − (C1 + C2 + C3)
50 PRINT FORMULA
60 DATA 3,2,0.04
70 END
RUN
9.5
```

Each variable (A, B, C1, C2, C3, and FORMULA) is allocated a storage location by the computer at execution time. Each location may store a number while your program is executing.

Versions of BASIC vary somewhat in the way numeric variable names may be created by the programmer. In most versions of BASIC, variable names are made up of letters of the alphabet, the digits 0 through 9, and the decimal point. The following rules are in effect for naming numeric variables:

1. A variable name must begin with a letter of the alphabet.
2. A variable name cannot be more than 40 characters long.
3. The decimal point is used as a separator character in a variable name. Other characters used by other languages for this purpose, such as hyphens and underscores, are not allowed.
4. A variable name cannot be a reserved word. Reserved words are names that BASIC uses for its own needs. A complete list of reserved words is given in Appendix 3.

Some examples of acceptable variable names are:

```
TOM
AMOUNTDUE
AMOUNT.DUE
AMOUNT.DUE.NOW
DAYS.1
I
A1
```

Some examples of invalid names are:

```
$I              Does not begin with a letter
NAME            NAME is a reserved word
AMOUNT-DUE      The hyphen is not allowed
```

It is highly advisable to choose descriptive variable names so that you won't forget what they represent. The programs in the figures in the *Guide* generally use descriptive names. In the short example programs, however, we will often resort to shorter names so you can quickly see how a statement or function works.

String Variables.   A *string* is a collection of related characters; for example,

```
JOHN Q. DOE
1600 Pennsylvania Avenue
THX-1138
```

Strings may be assigned to variable names and manipulated by computer systems. Strings can contain uppercase and/or lowercase characters, and these characters are output exactly as they are entered. The following program contains only string variables:

```
10 LET A$ = "at this example"
20 LET B$ = "LOOK CAREFULLY "
30 PRINT B$;A$
```

```
40 END
RUN
LOOK CAREFULLY at this example
```

There are two string variables in this short program: A$ and B$. The computer allocates storage to string variables in much the same way it allocates storage to numeric ones. So the storage location set up for A$ contains the string

```
at this example
```

and the location set up for B$ contains the string

```
LOOK CAREFULLYb
```
      (b̸ represents a blank space)

Since A$ and B$ are variables, they can contain different strings throughout the course of the program but only one string at any given time. An important difference between numeric and string variables is that we can perform conventional arithmetic with numeric variables but generally not with string ones.

Names for string variables are formed under the same set of rules as numeric variables, with one exception. As you've probably already noticed, string variables always end with a $ sign.

Many computer systems require that the string assigned to a string variable be enclosed in quotes; for example,

```
10 READ A$
20 PRINT A$
30 DATA "EVERY GOOD STUDENT DOES FINE"
40 END
RUN
EVERY GOOD STUDENT DOES FINE
```

Constants

Like their variable counterparts, *constants* may be either numeric or string. Unlike variables, however, the value of a constant doesn't change (although constants can be assigned to variables, which can change).

Numeric Constants.   A *numeric constant* is simply a number—for example, 81, −54, .001. When creating arithmetic expressions in BASIC, it is often useful to assign numbers to or to use numbers in combination with numeric variables. Some examples are

- `10 LET A=5.0`   5.0 is a numeric constant
- `10 LET B=A+2`   2 is a numeric constant
- `10 LET C=.01*A+B`   .01 is a numeric constant

Although the numeric constant chosen can be an integer number or a number with a decimal point, the use of commas or dollar signs is not allowed as part of the constant itself. The following are invalid representations of numeric constants in a BASIC program:

- `10 LET A=2,000`   Comma invalid; LET A=2000 valid
- `100 DATA $6,$3.52` $ invalid; DATA 6,3.52 valid

In many cases we would like to precede a number by a $ sign. This can be done very simply, as the following short example suggests:

```
10 LET A=5.21
20 PRINT "$";A
30 END
RUN
$ 5.21
```

String Constants. A *string constant*, or *literal*, is simply any collection of allowable BASIC characters enclosed in quotes; for example,

```
"HELLO 12?"
"GOODBYE MY LOVELY"
"145-86-7777"
"Mr. William T. Jones"
```

String constants can be assigned to string variables, such as

```
10 LET A$="EVERY GOOD STUDENT DOES FINE"
```

or be declared independently of any variables, as in the following PRINT statement:

```
10 PRINT "The value of inventory is $";X
```

On many computer systems, string constants appearing in DATA statements need not be enclosed in quotes.

Expressions

Expressions in BASIC are one of two principal types—arithmetic and relational.

Arithmetic Expressions. Arithmetic expressions are combinations of arithmetic symbols, numeric variables, and numeric constants that evaluate to a numeric value. For instance, the expression

$$A+2$$

which consists of a numeric variable, the plus symbol, and the numeric constant 2, respectively, is an arithmetic expression. If $A = 1$, the expression has a value of 3. The following operations are permitted in arithmetic expressions:

Operation	BASIC Symbol Used
Addition	+
Subtraction	−
Multiplication	*
Division	/
Exponentiation	^

For example, suppose A = 1, B = 3, and C = 2. The following statements would produce the results indicated:

- `10 LET D=A+B−C`   D is assigned a value of 2. The previous value of D is lost.
- `10 LET C=B/2`   The right-hand side equals 1.5, which is assigned to C. The previous value of C is lost.
- `10 PRINT A*B`   A and B are multiplied, and the product, 3, is printed.

Now consider a more complicated expression, such as:

```
10 LET D=C−A+B/(C+4)^2
```

The question arises here as to which operation the computer will perform first. BASIC and many other languages recognize the following order of arithmetic operations:

1. All operations within parentheses are performed first, starting with the innermost set of parentheses.
2. Exponentiation is performed next.
3. Multiplication and division are performed next, and the computer executes these from left to right in the expression.
4. Addition and subtraction are performed last, also left to right.

Thus, the expression just given would be evaluated as follows under this set of rules:

Step	Operation Performed
1	(C+4) evaluated; result is 6
2	6^2 evaluated; result is 36
3	B/36 evaluated; result is .083333
4	C−A evaluated; result is 1
5	1 is added to .083333; result is 1.083333
6	D is assigned the value 1.083333; the previous value of D is lost

To be fully sure that you understand the order of arithmetic operations, you should study the following examples. Assume in the examples that W = 1, X = 2, Y = 3, and Z = 4.

EXAMPLE 1.   `10 LET A=Y/W*Z`
A would be assigned a value of 12, since division and multiplication, being on the same level of hierarchy are performed left to right.

EXAMPLE 2.   `10 LET B=(X+Y)*(W+1)^2`
B would be assigned a value of 20. Parenthetical expressions are evaluated first, then exponentiation, and finally multiplication.

EXAMPLE 3.   `LET C=((Z−W)*X)^2/2`
C would be assigned a value of 18. The computation in the innermost parentheses is performed first, yielding Z − W = 3. Then contents of the outermost parentheses are evaluated, yielding 3*2 = 6. After all of the parenthetical expressions

are evaluated, the 6 is squared. Finally, the result of all the previous operations, 36, is halved to produce 18.

Relational Expressions.   Relational expressions are combinations of variables, symbols called relational operators, and constants that evaluate to a value of "true" or "false." For example,

$$NUMBER = -1$$

is a relational expression that is true when NUMBER is -1 and false otherwise.
There are six relational operators that are used in relational expressions:

Relational Meaning	Operator
Equal to	$=$
Not equal to	$<>$ or $><$
Greater than	$>$
Less than	$<$
Greater than or equal to	$>=$ or $=>$
Less than or equal to	$<=$ or $=<$

Some examples of the use of relational operators follow. Assume in the examples that SEX\$ = "FEMALE" and X = 25.

- ```WHILE SEX$ = "MALE"```   Evaluates to false
- ```WHILE SEX$ = "Female"```   Evaluates to false
- ```WHILE SEX$ = "FEMALE"```   Evaluates to true
- ```WHILE SEX$ < > "MALE"```   Evaluates to true
- ```WHILE X >= 25```   Evaluates to true
- ```WHILE X > 25```   Evaluates to false

The WHILE and IF statements are two important statements in BASIC that use relational expressions. Later in this section you will learn how to use the IF statement.

Logical Connectives.   Relational expressions can be made more powerful through the use of the three reserved connective words: NOT, AND, and OR.
    Preceding a relational expression with the NOT connective negates the condition. So, for instance, the relational expression

$$NOT\ SEX\$ = "MALE"$$

is true if SEX\$ carries any value other than MALE, and the relational expression

$$NOT\ A = 6$$

is true if A is any value other than 6.
    The AND connective links two or more conditions in a compound expression. AND requires that all conditions be true for the entire expression to be true. It works as follows:

$$SEX\$ = "MALE"\ AND\ A = 6$$

means that *both* SEX\$ has to be MALE and A has to be 6 for the entire compound expression to be true. And,

```
A = 1 AND B = 6 AND C = 35
```

means that all three conditions have to be true for the compound expression to be true. If A = 1 and B = 6 but C = 34, the compound expression would be false.

The OR connective means that one or more of the conditions in a compound expression must be true in order for the expression to be true. For instance, the compound expression

```
A = 1 OR B = 6
```

is true if either one of the two conditions, or both of them, are true. Like AND, more than one OR can exist to link conditions that are part of a compound expression.

NOT, AND, and OR can be combined to form a compound expression. If you are doing this, it's advisable that you put parentheses around like subexpressions to minimize complexity. As with arithmetic expressions, whatever is in parentheses is evaluated first. For instance, the expression

```
NOT (TYPE = 1 OR TYPE = 2)
```

will be true if TYPE is not equal to 1 or 2. Similarly,

```
A = 6 AND (B = 4 OR C = 88)
```

will be true only if A is 6 and one of the following: (1) B is 4 but C is not 88, (2) C is 88 but B is not 4, and (3) both B is 4 and C is 88. In the absence of parentheses, the connectives are evaluated in the following order: NOT, AND, OR.

Hierarchy of Operations.   As you've learned here, expressions can be formed through a variety of symbols. When these are mixed, the following order is observed:

Order	Operation	Symbols
1	Parentheses	( )
2	Arithmetic operators	^ * / + −
3	Relational operators	= < > <> <= >=
4	Connectives	NOT AND OR

More on Elementary BASIC Statements

So far, we've informally shown the use of the REM, READ and DATA, WHILE and WEND, LET, PRINT, and END statements. Let's consider further the permissible usage of these statements.

READ and DATA Statements

As mentioned earlier, the READ and DATA statements are always used together. When a READ is executed, the computer will assign values appearing in the DATA statements to the respective variables named in the READ statement. The format of each of these statements is shown below:

> Line #   READ list of variables (separated by commas)
> Line #   DATA list of data items (separated by commas)

The DATA statements are never actually executed by the computer. Between the time the RUN command is issued and the program is executed, the computer system extracts all of the values from the DATA statements and prepares a "data list." It is this list that is referenced each time a READ is encountered. The DATA statement itself is ignored during program execution.

It is useful to think of a "pointer" attached to the data list. The pointer initially points to the first value in the data list. When this value is assigned, it then points to the second item, and so on. For example, consider the READ and DATA statements for the program in Figure 1-3. The pointer initially points to the 8. When statement 140 is executed, the 8 is assigned to NUMBER and the pointer moves to the 16; when the next READ (statement 180) is executed, 16 is assigned to NUMBER (the previous value, 8, being erased) and the pointer moves to the 12; and so on. When the -1 is finally assigned to NUMBER, the data list is exhausted.

There can be several DATA statements in a BASIC program, a fact that is observable in the solved review problems at the end of the section. In most implementations of BASIC, DATA statements can be placed anywhere before the END statement. It is critical to keep in mind that data are executed in the order in which they appear in the DATA statements, and if there are several DATA statements, the earliest of these will be used first.

LET Statement

The LET statement typically uses the following format:

> Line # LET variable-name = expression

An important requirement of this format is that only a single variable name is allowed to appear on the left-hand side of the $=$ sign. Thus,

```
10 LET A=6*B−C^(N−1)
10 LET D=O
```

are allowable, whereas

```
LET A+B=C
```

is not. A single variable must appear on the left-hand side because once the right-hand-side expression is computed down to a single value, a storage location (as represented by a single variable) must be declared to store this value. Remember, A, B, C, and so on are acceptable names for storage locations, whereas A + B is not.

The = sign of the LET statement is referred to as an *assignment* (or *replacement*) *symbol*. In a LET statement, = does not mean "is equal to," the relational operator. To understand the basis of this nomenclature, consider the perfectly acceptable BASIC statement

```
10 LET I=I+1
```

This statement makes absolutely no sense if we interpret the = sign as meaning "is equal to." However, if we interpret this statement as instructing the computer to determine the value of I + 1 and to assign the number obtained back to I, it does make sense. Thus, if the value 6 were initially stored in I, this statement would add 6 to 1 and assign the result, 7, back to I (erasing the 6 that was there previously).

In most versions of BASIC, the appearance of the word LET is optional in a LET statement. Thus,

```
10 I=I+1
```

is perfectly acceptable.

PRINT Statement

The PRINT statement, being the main vehicle for obtaining BASIC output, is so pivotal that a separate section in the *Guide* is devoted exclusively to its use (see Section 4). So far we have seen that one acceptable form of the PRINT statement is

$$\text{Line \# PRINT} \left\{\begin{matrix} \text{literal,} \\ \text{variable, or} \\ \text{expression} \end{matrix}\right\} ; \left\{\begin{matrix} \text{literal,} \\ \text{variable, or} \\ \text{expression} \end{matrix}\right\} ; \dots$$

Thus, the following statements are allowable:

- `50 PRINT "A=";A`
  If 6 is stored in A, the output is
  `A=6`
- `50 PRINT A;B;C*Z;M$`
  If 6 is stored in A, 72 in B, 16 in C, 2 in Z, and " ARE THE ANSWERS" in M$, the output is
  `6  72  32  ARE THE ANSWERS`
- `50 PRINT A$;B$`
  If "HIGH " is stored in A$ and "SCHOOL" in B$, the output is
  `HIGH SCHOOL`

Other versions of the PRINT statement are covered in Section 4.

WHILE and WEND Statements

WHILE and WEND are companion statements that form a loop. WHILE represents the beginning of the loop; WEND represents the end. For sake of program readability, statements within a loop are normally indented, as shown in Figure 1-3 (lines 160 through 180).

The formats of the WHILE and WEND statements are as follows.

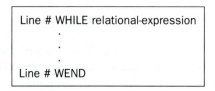

On each loop iteration, before execution of statements within the loop takes place, the computer system checks to see if the relational expression contained in the WHILE statement is true or false. If the expression is true, all of the statements within the loop are executed in the order suggested by the line numbers. Then the expression is checked again, before the next loop iteration. As soon as the relational expression returns a value of "false," control is passed to the statement that follows the loop (i.e., the statement that follows the WEND statement).

It is also possible to have loops within loops; that is, loops formed by WHILE and WEND statements can be nested. For example,

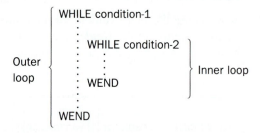

The rules for nesting WHILE/WEND loops are similar to those of FOR/NEXT loops, which we'll cover in Section 3.

IF Statement

The IF statement follows the format shown below:

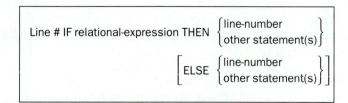

The computer executes an IF statement as follows:

1. The relational expression is evaluated as true or false.

2. In the case where there is no ELSE clause, if the expression is true, the computer does whatever action is specified after the THEN clause; otherwise, the computer advances to the next statement.
3. In the case where there is an ELSE clause, if the expression is true, the computer does whatever action is specified after the THEN clause, otherwise, it does whatever action is specified after the ELSE clause.

Sometimes, the two forms of the IF statement are differentiated by referring to the "IF without ELSE" version as the IF-THEN statement and the "IF with ELSE" version as the "IF-THEN-ELSE" statement. We will now consider each of these forms in turn.

IF-THEN. The following shows some acceptable forms of IF-THEN:

- ```
10 IF A > B THEN 170
20 . . .
```
The computer goes to statement 170 if A > B; otherwise, it goes to statement 20.
- ```
10 IF A > B THEN C = C + 1
20 . . .
```
If A > B, the computer calculates C + 1 and puts the value in C; then, it goes to statement 20. If A is not greater than B, the computer goes directly to statement 20, bypassing the calculation.
- ```
10 IF CUSTOMER$ = "LAST RECORD" THEN 50
20 ...
```
The computer goes to statement 50 if CUSTOMER$ has a value of LAST RECORD; otherwise, it goes to statement 20.

**IF-THEN-ELSE.** Below is an example of the IF-THEN-ELSE statement used to award a $50 bonus to salespeople selling $5,000 or more worth of merchandise:

```
20 IF S >= 5000 THEN B = 50
          ELSE B = 0
30 ...
```

In this statement, the relational expression S>=5000 is first evaluated. If the expression is true, then B is set to 50; otherwise, B is set to 0. Regardless of the value B assigned, after statement 20 is executed, the computer goes to statement 30.

While statement 20 could have been written in a single line, it is good programming practice to tier the THEN and ELSE clauses in the manner shown. To get to the second line of statement 20, use either the Line Feed key on your keyboard or press down the Control (Ctrl) key while pressing the J key. In either case, the screen cursor advances to the second line of statement 20, where you can type the ELSE clause. After finishing the second line, press the Enter key. Do not press Enter after the first line, because the computer will assume you are finished with it and will place it in memory.

In some programs that you write, you may want to execute two or more statements if the value of a relational expression is true or, possibly, two or more statements if the value is false. For example, suppose the salesperson selling $5,000 or more worth of merchandise is given both a bonus of $50 and
```

a watch (W$="YES"). We might then recode the statement given earlier to incorporate this information as follows:

```
100 IF S>=5000 THEN B=50:W$="YES"
            ELSE B=0:W$="NO"
```

On many computer systems, the colon character (:) is used, as shown above, to separate statements appearing on the same line.

Figure 1-6 provides a full program that shows how IF-THEN-ELSE is used. This program reads a series of numbers, determines whether each number is positive or negative, and outputs the result. In this program, a trailer value of 0 is used to indicate the end of the file.

REM Statement

The REM (remark) statement is a very important tool in BASIC, even though it is completely ignored by the computer when the program is executed. Its purpose is to allow you to put useful comments, or blank lines, in the program listing. The format of the REM statement is

FIGURE 1-6

Use of the IF-THEN-ELSE form of the IF statement.

```
10   REM     TITLE:  PROGRAM 1-6
20   REM
30   REM     DESCRIPTION:  READS A LIST OF NUMBERS
40   REM        AND TELLS WHETHER EACH NUMBER IS
50   REM        POSITIVE OR NEGATIVE
60   REM
70   REM     AUTHOR: C.S. PARKER
80   REM     DATE: 10/5/94
90   REM
100  REM     NUMBER = A POSITIVE OR NEGATIVE NUMBER
110  REM     SIGN$  = SIGN OF THE NUMBER
120  REM
130  REM     *************************************
140  READ NUMBER
150  WHILE NUMBER <> 0
160      IF NUMBER < 0 THEN SIGN$ = "NEGATIVE"          ◄── IF statement
                       ELSE SIGN$ = "POSITIVE"
170      PRINT NUMBER; "IS ";SIGN$
180      READ NUMBER
190  WEND
200  DATA 8,-16,-65,12,0
210  END

RUN
 8 IS POSITIVE
-16 IS NEGATIVE
-65 IS NEGATIVE
 12 IS POSITIVE
```

> Line # REM any remark

REMs can appear anywhere in a program. In many versions of BASIC, they must appear before the END statement.

END Statement

Generally the END statement is physically the last statement in the program; that is, it is the statement with the highest line number. When the computer encounters this statement, it terminates execution of your program. The format of the END statement is

> Line # END

Some versions of BASIC do not require an END statement; however, its use is highly recommended, because it leaves no doubt in anyone's mind about where the program ends. The END statement is frequently used in combination with the STOP statement. The STOP statement is discussed in Section 3.

Developing BASIC Programs

Now that we've covered how to write simple BASIC programs, it's time to consider how to develop them on your computer system.

Let's say you want to "try out" your computer system by typing in the squares program of Figure 1-3. You would type in all 21 lines, pressing the Enter key after finishing each line, as usual. Many versions of BASIC will check each statement for correct form (or *syntax*) when you press Enter. Thus, suppose you fumble at the keyboard while typing in the fourteenth line of your program, producing

```
140 READD NUMBER
```

Your keyboard has a set of arrow keys, a Delete key, and a Backspace key that will let you fix the error if you have not pressed the Enter key. If you have already pressed the Enter key to send the faulty line to the computer system, the following error message might be sent to the output device:

```
Syntax error in 140
```

At this point, list line 140 (if it isn't already on the screen), use the arrow and editing keys to go to and correct the error, and enter the change with the Enter key. The computer system will then replace the old line 140 with the corrected version.

When you have finished typing your program, you probably will be anxious for the computer to execute it immediately. Most systems require the user to type in the command

```
RUN
```

After you issue this command, one of the following will happen:

1. The program will run successfully, producing the correct answers.
2. The program will run but produce incorrect answers. This might happen if, for example, you typed in line 160 of the squares program as

```
160 LET SQUARE=NUMBER^3
```

The program would then produce cubes of numbers instead of squares! Thus, it is important that you look at your output carefully before you decide that your program works.

3. The program stops unexpectedly in the middle of a run. This would happen in the squares program if line 200 were typed in as follows:

```
200 DATA 8,16,"HELLO",12,-1
```

The program would complete the squares of 8 and 16 successfully, but it would stop (or abort) when it tried to assign the string "HELLO" to the numeric variable NUMBER. When BASIC runs into this situation while running the program, it is likely to display a message such as

```
Syntax error in 200
```

and halt. At this point you must correct the error, or *bug*, in the program and try again. Learning how to correct, or *debug*, faulty programs is one of the most important skills you must develop to program well. As unusual as it may seem, even a good programmer can easily spend 50 percent of the time it takes to develop a program in getting rid of bugs in it. This subject will be addressed in more detail later on.

Solved Review Problems

Example 1

A company has anywhere from five to twenty students employed on a part-time basis during the summer. This past week, five students were on the payroll. The students each worked different hours at different rates of pay, as shown in the following table:

Student Name	Hours Worked	Rate of Pay
John Smith	20	$5.40
Nancy Jones	15	$5.60
Bo Weeks	25	$5.00
Millicent Smythe	40	$4.80
Thu Duoc	20	$5.10

The company would like you to write a BASIC program to compute and print the total pay earned by each student.

Solution
The program must successively read a number of *records*. Consequently, a looping structure similar to the one in the program of Figure 1-3 will be required.

FIGURE 1-7

A program for computing the pay owed to employees.

```
10   REM     TITLE:   PROGRAM 1-7
20   REM
30   REM     DESCRIPTION: THIS PROGRAM
40   REM       COMPUTES EMPLOYEE PAY
50   REM
60   REM     AUTHOR: C.S. PARKER
70   REM     DATE: 10/5/94
80   REM
90   REM     EMPLOYEE$ = EMPLOYEE NAME
100  REM     HOURS     = HOURS WORKED
110  REM     PAY       = HOURLY PAY RATE
120  REM     PAYDUE    = PAY DUE
130  REM
140  REM********************************
150  READ EMPLOYEE$,HOURS,PAY
160  WHILE EMPLOYEE$ <> "LAST RECORD"
170     PAYDUE = HOURS * PAY
180     PRINT EMPLOYEE$;" HAS EARNED   $";PAYDUE
190     READ EMPLOYEE$,HOURS,PAY
200  WEND
210  REM ********DATA STATEMENTS*********
220  DATA "JOHN SMITH",20,5.40
230  DATA "NANCY JONES",15,5.60
240  DATA "BO WEEKS",25,5.00
250  DATA "MILLICENT SMYTHE",40,4.80
260  DATA "THU DUOC",20,5.10
270  DATA "LAST RECORD",0,0
280  REM *****************************
290  END

RUN
JOHN SMITH HAS EARNED  $ 108
NANCY JONES HAS EARNED  $ 84
BO WEEKS HAS EARNED  $ 125
MILLICENT SMYTHE HAS EARNED  $ 192
THU DUOC HAS EARNED  $ 102
```

Each record will contain a name, the hours worked, and a rate of pay—that is, a row of data from the preceding table. The number of records varies from week to week, so it will be convenient to employ a trailer record to enable the program to terminate. These considerations lead to the program in Figure 1-7, which you should study carefully.

Before we leave this example, let's consider some of the problems we might have run into if there were errors in the program. Also, we'll explore how we might correct such errors.

First, suppose we had mistyped line 170 as follows:

```
170 PAYDUE = HRS * PAY
```

When the computer encounters this statement, it has a value for HOURS and PAY. However, it doesn't have a clue as to what HRS is, since we never assigned a value to it. In most versions of BASIC, when the computer is asked to use the value of a variable that it has not yet encountered during execution, it assumes the value is zero. Naturally, this can lead to some very surprising results in your programs. In the current problem, your program would show that everyone has earned $0.

You should quickly be able to find an error like the one just described by making a few simple deductions. For example, since all the values of PAYDUE are printing as 0 and PAYDUE is supposed to be computed by HOURS * PAY, either HOURS or PAY (or both of these variables) is equal to zero.

As a second example, suppose we had mistakenly typed in line 250 as follows:

```
250 DATA 40,"MILLICENT SMYTHE",4.80
```

The computer would execute our program successfully until it had printed out

```
BO WEEKS HAS EARNED $125
```

Then we might receive a message such as the following:

```
Syntax error on line 250
```

These two lines of output give us a clue to the error. The computer successfully completed the processing of Bo Weeks's record but subsequently "bombed" on line 250. Thus, something must be amiss with the data in the next record. Now we would notice that the number 40 and "MILLICENT SMYTHE" are switched around, and BASIC cannot assign a string constant to a numeric variable.

Debugging programs is a skill that involves a lot of practice. You must learn to make deductions from the information given by the computer system (i.e., partial output, incorrect output, and error messages) to determine the source of errors.

Another technique that's recommended for particularly hard-to-find errors is the so-called dummy (diagnostic) PRINT statement. Suppose again that for line 170 you had typed

```
170 PAYDUE = HRS * PAY
```

You have deduced that either HRS, PAY, or both of these variables are zero, but you still can't put your finger on the error. However, you could now type the statement

```
175 PRINT "HRS = "; HRS;" PAY = "; PAY
```

The computer system would then respond with the following outputs after you typed RUN:

```
HRS = 0  PAY = 5.40
JOHN SMITH AS EARNED  $ 0
HRS = 0  PAY = 5.60
NANCY JONES HAS EARNED  $ 0
```

and so on. Now the source of the error is obvious: HRS is zero for every record in the program.

Once the dummy PRINT statement has served its purpose of uncovering the error and the error has been corrected, statement 175 should be deleted so that it won't interfere with the normal output of the program. The form for doing this is

```
DELETE 175
```

on your system, or you can type simply

```
175
```

and press Enter.

A selection program.

```
10   REM     TITLE:   PROGRAM 1-8
20   REM
30   REM     DESCRIPTION: THIS PROGRAM SELECTS FROM
40   REM       A FILE ALL FEMALE EMPLOYEES OVER 40
50   REM       WHO WORK IN THE ACCOUNTING DEPARTMENT
60   REM
70   REM     AUTHOR - C.S. PARKER
80   REM     DATE: 10/5/94
90   REM
100  REM     EMPLOYEE$ = EMPLOYEE NAME
110  REM     SEX$      = SEX
120  REM     AGE       = AGE
130  REM     DEPT$     = DEPARTMENT
140  REM
150  REM **********************************
160  READ EMPLOYEE$,SEX$,AGE,DEPT$
170  WHILE EMPLOYEE$ <> "LAST RECORD"
180     IF SEX$ = "MALE" THEN 220
190     IF AGE <= 40 THEN 220
200     IF DEPT$ <> "ACCOUNTING" THEN 220
210     PRINT EMPLOYEE$
220     READ EMPLOYEE$,SEX$,AGE,DEPT$
230  WEND
240  REM *********DATA STATEMENTS**********
250  DATA "JANE CRIBBS","FEMALE",25,"ACCOUNTING"
260  DATA "PHIL JONES","MALE",45,"ACCOUNTING"
270  DATA "ANNE WELLES","FEMALE",42,"ACCOUNTING"
280  DATA "MARY SMITH","FEMALE",41,"FINANCE"
290  DATA "LAST RECORD","MALE",99,"NONE"
300  REM **********************************
310  END

RUN
ANNE WELLES
```

Example 2
ABC Company has a file that keeps the following information on employees:

- Name
- Sex (M or F)
- Age
- Department

The file has approximately 1,000 employees, although the exact number is usually unknown. Write a BASIC program that will print out the names of all females over age 40 who work in the accounting department.

Solution
This program involves a series of three IF statements that pose the three conditions we wish to check in each record—in other words, female?, over 40?, and accounting? If a record passes all three checks, we print the associated name; otherwise we immediately read the next record.

   Since the data file is not given, we'll make up five test records (including a trailer record) to illustrate how the program works. The program is shown in Figure 1-8.

Exercises

Instructions: Provide an answer to each of the following questions.

1. Categorize the following variables as numeric, string, or invalid:

   a. A   b. 6F   c. D1   d. B$ e. $R   f. I

2. Write a valid LET statement for each of the following formulas:

   a. $C = A^2 + B^2$

   b. $A = \left(\dfrac{B + C}{D}\right)E$

   c. $R = \dfrac{S + T}{U - V} - Y$

   d. $A = \dfrac{3(B - 1)}{T + 2}$

3. Given A = 2, B = 5, and C = 6, determine the value of X in the following BASIC expressions:

   a. `X=(A+B)*C`
   b. `X=C/A*B`
   c. `X=(A+C/A+1)^2/2`
   d. `X=((3*A)*B)/C-4`

4. Identify the syntax errors, if any, in the following BASIC statements:

   a. `10 LET X+Y=Z`
   b. `98 IF X-Y<=C-D THEN 200`
   c. `20 LET F$=F+5.23`

5. In the expression

   $$X=(Y+Z)^2-2*B$$

   which operation does the computer do

   a. first?
   b. second?
   c. third?
   d. last?

6. Determine whether the following relational expressions are true or false. Assume that A = 1, B = 6, C = 2, CUSTOMER$ = "Smith", and TYPE = 3.

```
a.  A = 1 OR B = 2
b.  A = 2 AND B = 6
c.  NOT (TYPE = 1 OR TYPE = 2)
d.  A = 1 AND (B = 2 OR C = 2)
e.  CUSTOMER$ = "SMITH"
f.  A = 1 OR (B = 7 AND C = 1)
```

Programming Problems

Instructions: Write a BASIC program to do each of the following tasks.

1. Find the sum of each of the following pairs of numbers.

   6 and 8
   13 and 25
   14 and 33
   19 and 41

   Use trailer values at the end of your data list so that your program can sense when there are no more data.

2. Following are three sets of data. Each set of data has four variables: A, B, C, and D:

Set	Variables			
	A	B	C	D
1	8	15	10	4
2	6	5	3	2
3	4	0	5	2

   Plug the values in each set of data into the following formula, and print out the results:

   $$X = A - B \star C + A/D$$

3. Salespeople at XYZ Company are paid a base salary of $10,000. This salary may be augmented by commissions, which are equal to 10 percent of gross sales, and by a bonus of $500. The bonus is awarded only to salespeople with more than $80,000 in gross sales. Compute and output the amounts earned by each of these salespeople:

Salesperson	Gross Sales
Carlos Ortiz	$90,000
Jill Johnson	$70,000
Don Williams	$20,000
Dee Jones	$95,000
Al Ennis	$40,000

Your output should include the name of each salesperson and his or her earnings. Use trailer values at the end of your data list so that your program can sense when there are no more data.

4. Solve Problem 3 assuming that the commission is computed as follows:

If Gross Sales Are in the Range of	The Commission Rate Is
$ 1–$30,000	6%
$30,001–$60,000	8%
$60,001–$80,000	10%
$80,001 and above	12%

Assume also that the bonus is still in effect.

5. Grades in a course are awarded as follows: 90 and above = A, 80–89 = B, 70–79 = C, 60–69 = D, below 60 = F. Write a BASIC program that reads the following data and assigns letter grades:

Social Security Number	Score
182-66-1919	63
321-76-4344	81
821-66-0045	90
376-38-3202	54
802-11-1481	79
346-49-8911	75

Your output should include the social security number of each student and that student's letter grade. Use trailer values at the end of your data list so that your program can sense when there are no more items to be read.

6. A company running a copying service charges the following rates:

The first 500 copies are billed at 5 cents per copy
The next 500 copies are billed at 4 cents per copy
Any additional copies are billed at 3 cents per copy

Compute and output the amount each of the following customers is to be billed:

Customer	Copies
XYZ Amalgamated	1,200
ABC Industries	200
TR Systems Limited	800

Your output should include the name of each customer as well as the billing amount. Use trailer values at the end of your data list so that your program can sense when there are no more data.

7. Students at a university are billed as follows:

Tuition = $100 per credit hour
Activity fee = $30 for 6 hours or less
$60 for 7–12 hours
$75 for more than 12 hours

The total amount a student will be billed each semester is computed by the following formula:

Tuition fee + Activity fee − Scholarship

Compute the amounts due from the following students:

Student Name	Credit Hours This Semester	Scholarship Amount
Ed Begay	15	$700
Bill Mendoza	8	0
John Williams	3	0
Nancy Jones	12	500
Dennis Hall	6	0

Your output should include the name of each student as well as the billing amount. Use trailer values at the end of your data list so that your program can sense when there are no more data.

8. Workers at a factory receive "time and a half" for every hour worked over 40 hours in any week. That is, workers are paid 150 percent of their regular hourly rate for each hour worked beyond the 40-hour mark. Read the following employee records for the first week of January and compute the total pay owed to each employee.

Employee	Hours Worked	Rate Class
S. Akins	40	A
F. Baker	45	C
M. Chang	48	B
A. Faziz	35	A
J. Tate	40	C
L. Yev	42	B

Note that the following rate classes are in effect:

■ Class A workers make $14.00 per hour
■ Class B workers make $11.00 per hour
■ Class C workers make $10.00 per hour

Program Design Techniques

Introduction

As mentioned earlier, the design of computer programs requires considerable care. Programs used to help run businesses are usually in operation for several years, and they need to be constantly modified to meet changing business conditions. Thus, a program that is designed in a hasty fashion will often cause numerous maintenance problems over the years for programmers who have to keep it up to date. Simply stated, poorly designed programs are almost always expensive headaches. A few extra dollars spent on initial design may save hundreds of dollars later.

Many techniques have been employed over the years to design computer programs. Two of the most widely used techniques are flowcharts and pseudocode.

Flowcharts and Pseudocode

Program flowcharts, dating back to the 1940s, are among the oldest tools used to design programs. A program flowchart is a diagram that shows the flow of logic behind a computer program. For example, the flowchart in Figure 2-1 outlines the logic of the program shown in Figure 1-3. Shown with the program and flowchart is the corresponding pseudocode. Pseudocode is an alternate means of depicting the logic behind a computer program.

Flowcharts.   As you can see from the example, a *program flowchart* consists of geometric symbols and arrows. Each symbol contains an operation the computer must perform, and the arrows show the flow of the program logic (in other words, which operation is to be performed next).

As you have probably already noticed, not all of the symbols have the same shape. The shape of the symbol used depends on the type of operation being performed. The symbols used in this *Guide*, along with their program statement types, are shown in Figure 2-2.

You should note in Figure 2-1 that not every BASIC program statement will necessarily correspond to a flowchart symbol; conversely, not every flowchart symbol corresponds to a BASIC program statement. For example, there is no BASIC-program-statement counterpart to the flowcharting "START" symbol. The BASIC program shown actually begins with a REM statement. Also, there is no flowchart symbol for the DATA statement. The flowchart is intended to represent only the flow of program logic. This can be done without specifying actual values for the variables.

You should also note in Figure 2-1 that the flowchart need not contain every detail that will be specified in the program but only those that are important

Program, flowchart, and pseudocode for computing and printing the squares of several numbers (previously presented in Figure 1–3).

Program

```
10   REM    TITLE:  PROGRAM 1-3
20   REM
30   REM    DESCRIPTION:  THIS PROGRAM READS
40   REM      NUMBERS, SQUARES THEM, AND OUTPUTS
50   REM      THE RESULTS
60   REM
70   REM    AUTHOR: C.S. PARKER
80   REM    DATE: 10/5/94
90   REM
100  REM        NUMBER = THE NUMBER TO BE SQUARED
110  REM        SQUARE = THE SQUARE OF THE NUMBER
120  REM
130  REM    ************************************
140  READ NUMBER
150  WHILE NUMBER <> -1
160     LET SQUARE=NUMBER^2
170     PRINT "THE SQUARE OF ";NUMBER;" IS";SQUARE
180     READ NUMBER
190  WEND
200  DATA 8,16,12,-1
210  END
```

Flowchart

Pseudocode
```
Start
Read a number
DOWHILE there are more numbers to process
    Compute square of number
    Print square
    Read another number
END DO
Stop
```

for understanding the logical flow. Thus, the flowchart indicates the output as "Print square," whereas statement 170 of the corresponding program specifies in more detail:

```
170 PRINT "THE SQUARE OF ";NUMBER;" IS ";SQUARE
```

Pseudocode.   Whereas program flowcharts use graphical symbols to depict program logic, *pseudocode* uses English-like statements. Pseudocode is widely considered to be a better tool than flowcharts for designing structured programs. Although it is possible to create unstructured flowcharts, it is virtually impossible to create unstructured pseudocode.

All of the programs, flowcharts, and pseudocode represented in this text reflect a *structured* programming style. This style involves the strict use of three program structures: *sequence, selection,* and *looping* (shown in Figure 2-3). Virtually every programming problem that you encounter can be satisfactorily solved by using some combination of these—and only these—three structures. Note that the flowchart and pseudocode in Figure 2-1 involve a looping structure (DOWHILE) and, within the loop, a sequence of three statements. In a DO-WHILE structure, the procedure in a loop is performed *while* a condition is true, whereas in a DOUNTIL structure, the procedure in a loop is performed *until* a condition becomes true. Many versions of BASIC do not support the DOUNTIL looping structure, in which the procedure within a loop is always performed *at least once* and the test of the condition is performed at the bottom of the loop. In DOWHILE, by contrast, the loop procedure may not be performed at all (if the condition is initially false) and the test of the condition is performed at the top of the loop.

Flowcharting symbols.

FIGURE 2 – 2

Symbol	Name	Description
	Start/Stop	Used to begin and end every flowchart
	Input/Output	Used to represent the READ or INPUT statements on input, PRINT statement on output
	Assignment	Used to represent the LET statement
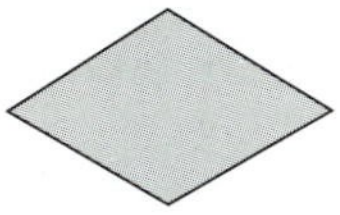	Decision	Used to represent the IF and WHILE statements
	Connector	Used to represent the NEXT statement or used to continue the flowchart when running out of room
	Loop	Used to represent the FOR statement

FIGURE 2-3

Flowchart and pseudocode forms of the three fundamental control structures—sequence, selection, and looping.

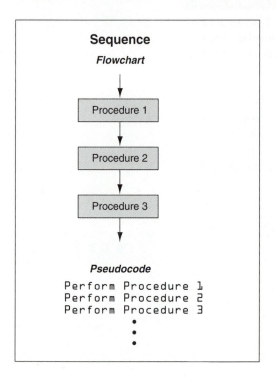

Sequence

Flowchart

Pseudocode

```
Perform Procedure 1
Perform Procedure 2
Perform Procedure 3
        •
        •
        •
```

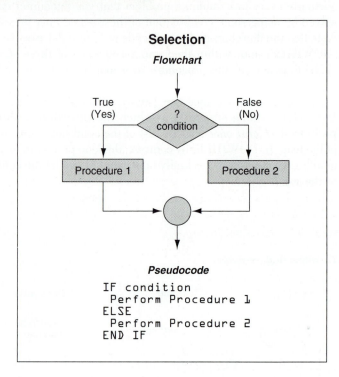

Selection

Flowchart

Pseudocode

```
IF condition
  Perform Procedure 1
ELSE
  Perform Procedure 2
END IF
```

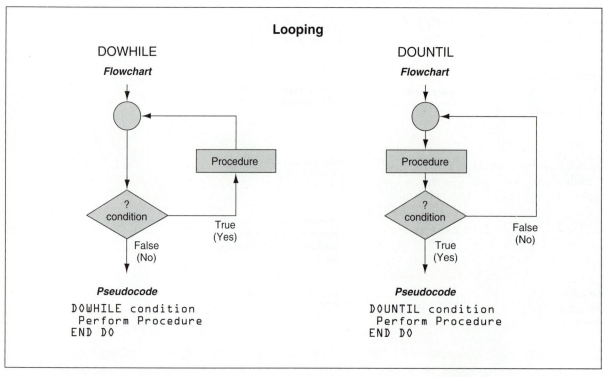

Looping

DOWHILE

Flowchart

Pseudocode

```
DOWHILE condition
  Perform Procedure
END DO
```

DOUNTIL

Flowchart

Pseudocode

```
DOUNTIL condition
  Perform Procedure
END DO
```

Just as there are many conventions used to construct flowcharts, so, too, are there many ways to develop pseudocode. The convention used in this text is to capitalize certain keywords, such as those shown in Figure 2-3, and to begin and end the pseudocode with the keywords "Start" and "Stop," respectively. Also, although it is not mandatory, the convention chosen in this *Guide* is to depict pseudocode at a very general level. Most professionals seem to prefer this style because if the pseudocode were too detailed, one might be better off just coding the program. While flowcharts can also be constructed at a general level, we've selected a detailed level here to give you better insight into how each corresponding BASIC program works.

Both flowcharts and pseudocode are useful as design tools for developing programs and, later, as program *documentation* aids. As a design tool, the flowchart or pseudocode lets the programmer "think through" the logical design of programs before writing them. This can be particularly helpful for the same reason a builder of a house consults a floor plan before constructing any individual room. Once a program is written, the flowchart or pseudocode becomes a documentation aid: it generally is easier for others to understand how a program works by studying the flowchart or pseudocode than the program itself. Also, because of their simplicity, flowcharts or pseudocode can often be understood by nonprogrammers.

Some Further Examples

Now that we've covered some of the fundamentals of flowcharting and pseudocode, we'll look at two further examples.

First, let's consider a simple problem involving the selection structure. Team A and Team B, crosstown rivals, played each other in baseball a total of five times during the course of a season. The results were as follows:

Game	Team A Score	Team B Score
1	8	5
2	6	7
3	2	0
4	0	1
5	5	4

Create a flowchart, pseudocode, and, finally, a BASIC program that will output, for each game, the team winning the game. The solution, which involves a simple selection structure within a loop, is shown in Figure 2-4.

As our second example, let's take another look at the problem solved in Figure 1-8 (page 29). There we were required to find all employees in a company who are female, over 40, and work in the accounting department. The associated program, flowchart, and pseudocode are shown in Figure 2-5. Note that the flowchart and pseudocode involve a looping structure and, within the loop, three selection structures. When selection structures are *nested* in pseudocode, as they are in the figure, every IF keyword is paired with an ELSE keyword, and there is an END IF terminating each structure.

Several other examples of flowcharts and pseudocode will be presented in later sections of this *Guide*.

FIGURE 2-4   Program, flowchart, and pseudocode for solving a simple baseball problem.

Program

```
10   REM   TITLE:  PROGRAM 2-4
20   REM
30   REM   DESCRIPTION:  THIS PROGRAM
40   REM     PICKS GAME WINNERS
50   REM
60   REM   AUTHOR: C.S. PARKER
70   REM   DATE: 10/5/94
80   REM
90   REM   GAME   = THE GAME NUMBER
100  REM   ASCORE = TEAM "A" SCORE
110  REM   BSCORE = TEAM "B" SCORE
120  REM
130  REM *********************************************
140  READ GAME,ASCORE,BSCORE
150  WHILE GAME <> 0
160     REM ASSUME NO GAMES END IN A TIE
170     IF ASCORE > BSCORE THEN PRINT "TEAM A WINS GAME";GAME
                           ELSE PRINT "TEAM B WINS GAME";GAME
180     READ GAME,ASCORE,BSCORE
190  WEND
200  REM ***********DATA STATEMENTS*******************
210  DATA 1,8,5
220  DATA 2,6,7
230  DATA 3,2,0
240  DATA 4,0,1
250  DATA 5,5,4
260  DATA 0,0,0
270  REM *********************************************
280  END

RUN
TEAM A WINS GAME 1
TEAM B WINS GAME 2
TEAM A WINS GAME 3
TEAM B WINS GAME 4
TEAM A WINS GAME 5
```

Flowcharting and Pseudocoding Problems*

Instructions: Write a flowchart and pseudocode to do each of the following tasks.

1. Three numbers (no two of which are equal) are to be read by the computer system and assigned to variables A, B, and C, respectively. Determine the largest, smallest, and middle number. (For example, if A is 3, B is 1, and C is 6, then 6 is the largest, 1 is the smallest, and 3 is the middle number.)

---

*For additional practice, try providing flowchart and pseudocode solutions to the problems described in Programming Problems 3–8 in Section 1 (pages 31–33). If you want to test your knowledge quickly, try Problems 4 and 7 first.

Pseudocode
```
Start
Read game number and score
DOWHILE there are more scores to process
    IF A's score > B's score
        Print "TEAM A WINS"
    ELSE
        Print "TEAM B WINS"
    END IF
    Read game number and score
END DO
Stop
```

Flowchart

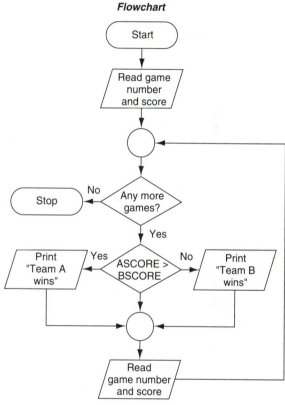

2. The following tax table is used to calculate the tax in a certain state:

Tax Rate Schedules
Table X
(Single Taxpayers)

If the Bottom Line Amount on Your Tax Return Is	Compute Your Tax as Follows:
$0–1,000	2% of the amount
$1,001–10,000	4% of the amount less $100
$10,001–50,000	6% of the amount less $300
Over $50,000	7% of the amount

Use this table to design a procedure to compute taxes due for a list of tax-payers.

FIGURE 2 – 5

Program, flowchart, and pseudocode for solving an employee selection problem (previously presented in Figure 1–8).

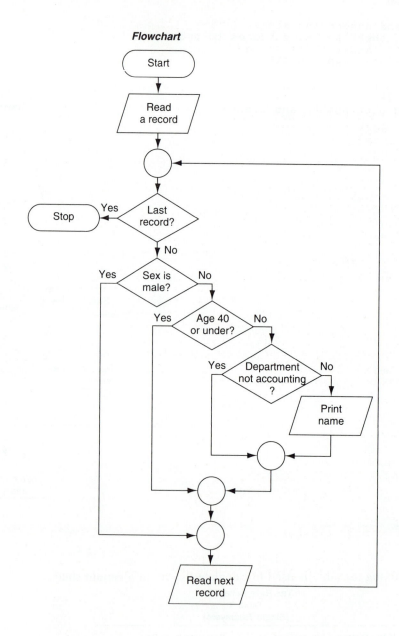

Program

```
10   REM     TITLE:   PROGRAM 1-8
20   REM
30   REM     DESCRIPTION: THIS PROGRAM SELECTS FROM
40   REM        A FILE ALL FEMALE EMPLOYEES OVER 40
50   REM         WHO WORK IN THE ACCOUNTING DEPARTMENT
60   REM
70   REM     AUTHOR - C.S. PARKER
80   REM     DATE: 10/5/94
90   REM
100  REM     EMPLOYEE$ = EMPLOYEE NAME
110  REM     SEX$      = SEX
120  REM     AGE       = AGE
130  REM     DEPT$     = DEPARTMENT
140  REM
150  REM ***********************************
160  READ EMPLOYEE$,SEX$,AGE,DEPT$
170  WHILE EMPLOYEE$ <> "LAST RECORD"
180     IF SEX$ = "MALE" THEN 220
190     IF AGE <= 40 THEN 220
200     IF DEPT$ <> "ACCOUNTING" THEN 220
210     PRINT EMPLOYEE$
220     READ EMPLOYEE$,SEX$,AGE,DEPT$
230  WEND
240  REM **********DATA STATEMENTS***********
250  DATA "JANE CRIBBS","FEMALE",25,"ACCOUNTING"
260  DATA "PHIL JONES","MALE",45,"ACCOUNTING"
270  DATA "ANNE WELLES","FEMALE",42,"ACCOUNTING"
280  DATA "MARY SMITH","FEMALE",41,"FINANCE"
290  DATA "LAST RECORD","MALE",99,"NONE"
300  REM ***********************************
310  END
```

Pseudocode
```
Start
Read an employee record
DOWHILE there are more records to process
  ┌IF sex is male
  │      Next statement
  │ELSE
  │    ┌IF age ≤ 40
  │    │    Next statement
  │    │ELSE
  │    │  ┌IF department < > "ACCOUNTING"
  │    │  │     Next statement
  │    │  │ELSE
  │    │  │     Print name
  │    │  └END IF
  │    └END IF
  └END IF
   Read next record
END DO
Stop
```

3. A state charges the following annual fees for fishing licenses:

	Resident	Nonresident
All species	$10.00	$22.00
All species except trout	$ 7.00	$15.00

Use this table to design a procedure to compute the fee to be charged for each person buying a license. Following are some sample data to test the correctness of your procedure.

Individual	Residency Status	License Wanted
Merlon Biggs	Resident	All species
Alexis Adams	Resident	All species except trout
Arlen Bixby	Nonresident	All species
Al Allen	Nonresident	All species except trout

EXPANDING ON THE BASICS OF BASIC

Counting and Summing

Now that we've covered a few fundamentals of how BASIC works, let's tackle a slightly more complicated problem. The example in Figure 3-1, a program to compute and print the average of a group of positive numbers, introduces two of the most fundamental operations in computing: counting and summing. You should observe the "mechanics" of both of these operations very carefully, because they occur in almost every large-scale programming problem.

Three important observations should be made about the program in Figure 3-1:

1. Statements 150 (LET COUNT = 0) and 160 (LET SUM = 0) establish *explicitly* the beginning values of COUNT and SUM. Establishing beginning values for variables is called *initialization*. Most versions of BASIC will *implicitly* initialize all variables to zero before the program is executed; thus, statements 150 and 160 are usually unnecessary. It is good practice, however, to explicitly initialize certain variables to zero whether or not it is necessary on your computer system. There are two reasons for this practice:

   a. Many programming languages will not automatically initialize variables to zero. This can lead to surprising results if you didn't explicitly initialize, because numbers from someone else's program may be lurking in the storage locations assigned to your variables. Thus, your variables will assume these arbitrary values.

   b. When you initialize explicitly, the intent of your program becomes more evident. In other words, initialization is good documentation.

   Only the variables COUNT and SUM require initialization to zero in this program. These are the variables for which the computer needs to "look up" the values on the right-hand side of the assignment symbol (=) in lines 190 and 200, respectively. The variables NUMBER and AVERAGE don't have to be initialized, since they never appear on the right-hand side of an assignment symbol before the computer has explicitly assigned them a value.

2. Statement 190 (LET COUNT = COUNT + 1) *counts* the number of numbers in the list. COUNT is initially assigned a value of zero. Each time a positive number is read into storage for NUMBER (so that the "NUMBER < > −1" condition is true in line 180 of the program), 1 is added to the current value of COUNT. Because only one number can be assigned to COUNT at any time, the previous value of COUNT is destroyed and lost forever.

3. Statement 200 (LET SUM = SUM + NUMBER) *sums* the numbers in the list. As with COUNT, SUM is initially zero. Each time statement 200 is executed, the current value of NUMBER is added to the current value of

FIGURE 3-1   **Computing the average of several numbers.**

Program

```
10   REM    TITLE:  PROGRAM 3-1
20   REM
30   REM    DESCRIPTION: THIS PROGRAM COMPUTES AND OUTPUTS
40   REM      THE AVERAGE OF SEVERAL POSITIVE NUMBERS
50   REM
60   REM    AUTHOR: C.S. PARKER
70   REM    DATE: 10/5/94
80   REM
90   REM    COUNT   = COUNT VARIABLE
100  REM    SUM     = SUM VARIABLE
110  REM    NUMBER  = A NUMBER IN THE LIST
120  REM    AVERAGE = AVERAGE OF ALL NUMBERS
130  REM
140  REM    ********************************
150  LET COUNT = 0
160  LET SUM = 0
170  READ NUMBER
180  WHILE NUMBER <> -1
190     LET COUNT = COUNT + 1
200     LET SUM = SUM + NUMBER
210     READ NUMBER
220  WEND
230  LET AVERAGE = SUM / COUNT
240  PRINT "AVERAGE IS";AVERAGE
250  DATA 7,23,33,15,42,-1
260  END
```

```
RUN
AVERAGE IS 24
```

Pseudocode
```
Start
Initialize count and sum
Read a number
DOWHILE there are more numbers to process
    Increment counter by 1
    Add number to sum
    Read next number
END DO
Compute average
Print average
Stop
```

Flowchart

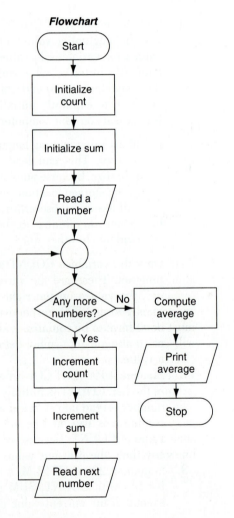

SUM. Thus, SUM can be seen as a "running total," as indicated in the following table:

When the Value of NUMBER Is	Statement 200 Does the Following
7	Adds 7 to the initial sum, 0, producing SUM = 7
23	Adds 23 to 7, producing SUM = 30
33	Adds 33 to 30, producing SUM = 63
15	Adds 15 to 63, producing SUM = 78
42	Adds 42 to 78, producing SUM = 120
−1	Statement 200 is not executed when NUMBER = −1

The INPUT Statement

The INPUT statement is one of the most useful statements in the BASIC language. It permits the program user to operate in a *conversational (interactive) mode* with the computer system. In other words, during the course of executing a program, the computer system asks the user for a response, and the user answers; then, based on the response given, the computer system asks the user for a response to another question, and so forth. The format of the INPUT statement is as follows:

Line # INPUT list of variables (separated by commas)

Figure 3-2 shows the program in Figure 3-1 rewritten with the INPUT statement. You should carefully note the following:

1. The READ statement in Figure 3-1 has been changed to an INPUT statement in Figure 3-2. With the READ statement, all data to be assigned to NUMBER are placed in an associated DATA statement; remember, READ and DATA statements are always used together. When we use INPUT NUMBER, no corresponding DATA statement is employed. Instead we supply data to the computer system as the program is running.
2. Data are supplied to the computer system as follows. Whenever an INPUT statement is encountered, a "?" is output by the system, and processing temporarily halts. At this point, we must enter as many data values as there are variables appearing after the word INPUT in the program. These values must be separated by commas. After we depress the Enter key, the system will assign the values to their corresponding variables and resume processing. If the same or another INPUT statement is encountered, the system will again respond with a question mark and await more input from the user.
3. In lines 170 and 220, just before the INPUT statements, are PRINT statements that provide instructions for the user of the program. When writing programs that include INPUT statements, it is always a good idea to include such a *prompting* PRINT statement before each INPUT so that the user will know both how to enter data into the computer and how to stop the program.

The major advantage of the INPUT statement over READ is that the user and computer system are involved in a dynamic dialog. In many cases, the user may not know the inputs in advance, since they depend on actions taken by the computer.

FIGURE 3-2   Program in Figure 3-1 rewritten with the INPUT statement.

```
10   REM     TITLE:   PROGRAM 3-2
20   REM
30   REM     DESCRIPTION: THIS PROGRAM COMPUTES AND OUTPUTS
40   REM         THE AVERAGE OF SEVERAL POSITIVE NUMBERS
50   REM
60   REM     AUTHOR: C.S. PARKER
70   REM     DATE: 10/5/94
80   REM
90   REM     COUNT   = COUNT VARIABLE
100  REM     SUM     = SUM VARIABLE
110  REM     NUMBER  = A NUMBER IN THE LIST
120  REM     AVERAGE = AVERAGE OF ALL NUMBERS
130  REM
140  REM *******************************
150  LET COUNT = 0
160  LET SUM = 0
170  PRINT "ENTER A POSITIVE NUMBER (OR -1 TO STOP)"
180  INPUT NUMBER
190  WHILE NUMBER <> -1
200     LET COUNT = COUNT + 1
210     LET SUM = SUM + NUMBER
220     PRINT "ENTER A POSITIVE NUMBER (OR -1 TO STOP)"
230     INPUT NUMBER
240  WEND
250  LET AVERAGE = SUM / COUNT
260  PRINT "AVERAGE IS";AVERAGE
270  DATA 7,23,33,15,42,-1
280  END
```

— Input statements

```
RUN
ENTER A POSITIVE NUMBER (OR -1 TO STOP)
? 7
ENTER A POSITIVE NUMBER (OR -1 TO STOP)
? 23
ENTER A POSITIVE NUMBER (OR -1 TO STOP)
? 33
ENTER A POSITIVE NUMBER (OR -1 TO STOP)
? 15
ENTER A POSITIVE NUMBER (OR -1 TO STOP)
? 42
ENTER A POSITIVE NUMBER (OR -1 TO STOP)
? -1
AVERAGE IS 24
```

The STOP Statement

Execution of a STOP statement in a program causes the program to halt execution, often by immediate transfer to the END statement. The STOP statement has the following format:

Line # STOP

Later, in Figures 3-6 and 3-9, you will see how the STOP statement works. In Figure 3-6, for instance, as soon as the STOP statement is executed, the message

```
Break in 200
```

is output and the program terminates immediately. At this point, BASIC's "Ok" prompt appears on the screen, indicating that you are free to do what you like.

FOR and NEXT Statements

The FOR and NEXT statements, which allows the programmer to loop (repeat a program section) automatically, are among the most important statements in BASIC. For example, consider the short program given in Figure 3-3.

The FOR and NEXT statements form a "sandwich," or loop. All statements inside the loop are executed the number of times determined in the FOR statement. (Note that these statements are indented, making the program easier to read.) In Figure 3-3, I is first set equal to 1. Then everything inside the loop (that is, statement 20) is executed; I is then set equal to 2 and statement 20 is executed again; and so forth. After I is set equal to 5 and the loop is executed for the fifth time, control passes to the statement that immediately follows the NEXT statement (in other words, statement 40).

FOR and NEXT statements are always used together. They physically establish the beginning and end of the loop. Like READ and DATA, one statement makes absolutely no sense unless the other is present. The format of these statements is:

```
Line # FOR loop-variable =  { Beginning value } TO { Ending value } STEP increment
        .
        .
        .
Line # NEXT loop-variable
```

Simple usage of FOR and NEXT statements.

FIGURE 3 - 3

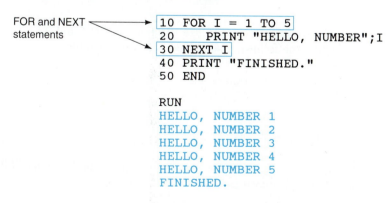

```
FOR and NEXT  ─────────▶  10 FOR I = 1 TO 5
statements                20    PRINT "HELLO, NUMBER";I
              ─────────▶  30 NEXT I
                          40 PRINT "FINISHED."
                          50 END

                          RUN
                          HELLO, NUMBER 1
                          HELLO, NUMBER 2
                          HELLO, NUMBER 3
                          HELLO, NUMBER 4
                          HELLO, NUMBER 5
                          FINISHED.
```

The use of the loop variable, beginning value, ending value, and increment will now be explained.

The variable I in the program of Figure 3-3 is an example of a *loop variable*. Note carefully that the chosen loop variable (which can be any acceptable BASIC numeric variable) must be included in both the FOR statement and its associated NEXT statement, as indicated in the figure.

In Figure 3-3, it was implicitly assumed that the loop variable was to be incremented by 1 each time the loop was executed. The increment could also have been explicitly declared in a STEP clause:

```
10 FOR I=1 TO 5 STEP 1
```

The results produced would be the same. If, on the other hand, we rewrote line 10 as

```
10 FOR I=1 TO 5 STEP 3
```

and ran the program, the computer system would respond

```
HELLO, NUMBER 1
HELLO, NUMBER 4
FINISHED.
```

Since the next possible incremented value, 7, exceeds the ending value of 5, the computer doesn't execute the loop for a third time but passes control to statement 40.

It is also possible to let the loop variable work "backwards." For example, if we changed line 10 to Figure 3-3 to read

```
10 FOR I=5 TO 1 STEP −1
```

we would obtain

```
HELLO, NUMBER 5
HELLO, NUMBER 4
HELLO, NUMBER 3
HELLO, NUMBER 2
HELLO, NUMBER 1
FINISHED.
```

BASIC also allows programmers to use variables in FOR and NEXT statements. For example, the following sequence is also acceptable:

```
30 FOR Z=J TO K STEP L
                .
                .
                .
70 NEXT Z
```

If J = 2, K = 10, and L = 3, the loop will be performed 3 times, with Z taking on values of 2, 5, and 8 as the loop is executed.

Let's now consider a more comprehensive example to further explore the concept of looping. Consider again the "averages" problem solved in Figure 3-1. How can we solve this problem using FOR/NEXT loops? The flowchart and program solution appear in Figure 3-4.

Note, in comparing the two programs, that because the number of times the FOR/NEXT loop is executed is predetermined before looping begins, no trailer

FIGURE 3-4

Solution to the problem in Figure 3–1 using loops.

Program

```
10   REM     TITLE:   PROGRAM 3-4
20   REM
30   REM     DESCRIPTION: THIS PROGRAM COMPUTES AND OUTPUTS
40   REM       THE AVERAGE OF SEVERAL POSITIVE NUMBERS
50   REM
60   REM     AUTHOR: C.S. PARKER
70   REM     DATE: 10/5/94
80   REM
90   REM     I       = LOOP VARIABLE
100  REM     SUM     = SUM VARIABLE
110  REM     NUMBER  = A NUMBER IN THE LIST
120  REM     AVERAGE = AVERAGE OF ALL NUMBERS
130  REM     TOTAL   = THE NUMBER OF NUMBERS
140  REM
150  REM **********************************
160  LET SUM = 0
170  READ TOTAL
180  FOR I = 1 TO TOTAL
190     READ NUMBER
200     LET SUM = SUM + NUMBER
210  NEXT I
220  LET AVERAGE = SUM / TOTAL
230  PRINT "AVERAGE IS";AVERAGE
240  DATA 5
250  DATA 7,23,33,15,42
260  END
```

```
RUN
AVERAGE IS 24
```

Pseudocode
```
Start
Initialize sum to zero
Read the list size
Set counter to 1
DOWHILE counter ≤ list size
    Read a number
    Add number to sum
    Add 1 to counter
END DO
Compute average
Print average
Stop
```

Flowchart

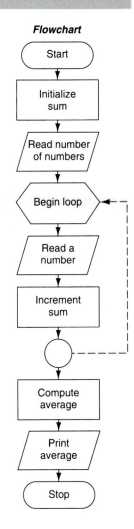

value is needed in the DATA statement. Also note that FOR/NEXT logic can be simulated in pseudocode through a DOWHILE looping structure. This requires a separate Set instruction before the loop to initialize the counter and a separate Add instruction at the end of the loop to increment the counter.

Finally, loops within loops, or *nested loops*, are allowed. Observe the short program below.

```
10 FOR I=1 TO 3
20    FOR J=1 TO 2
30       PRINT I;J
40    NEXTJ
50 NEXT I
60 END
RUN
   1     1
   1     2
   2     1
   2     2
   3     1
   3     2
```

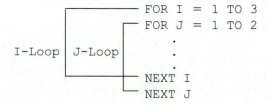

The program executes the PRINT statement a total of 3 * 2 = 6 times. The outer-loop variable (I) varies the slowest; the inner-loop variable (J) varies the fastest.

In writing nested-loop programs, it is always important to enclose the inner loop entirely within the outer loop. Thus, a program segment such as the one following,

```
                        ┌──── FOR I = 1 TO 3
                        │ ┌── FOR J = 1 TO 2
                        │ │      .
         I-Loop  J-Loop │ │      .
                        │ │      .
                        │ └── NEXT I
                        └──── NEXT J
```

would not work because the loops cross rather than nest.

Subroutines

BASIC *subroutines* are partial programs, or subprograms, that are contained within a BASIC program (called the *main program*). They are particularly effective when a series of statements in a program is to be performed numerous times or when a program is long and requires rigorous organization.

Subroutines enable programs to be organized in a modular, top-down fashion, as shown in the *structure chart* in Figure 3-5. The main part of the program, which is the topmost module, performs control functions. The modules at the

FIGURE 3 – 5

Structure charts. This technique subdivides a program into individual modules, each of which represents a well-defined processing task. The modules are then arranged hierarchically in a top-down fashion, as illustrated here for a payroll application.

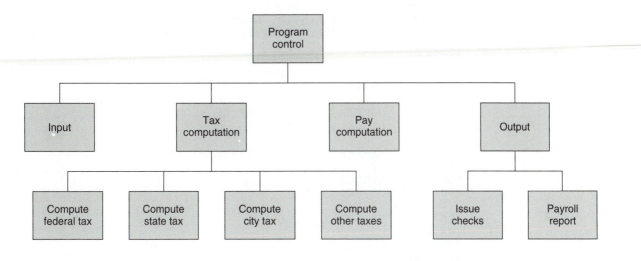

lower levels do the actual work. Anyone contemplating a career as a programmer is well advised to practice as much as possible writing programs in the modular, top-down fashion suggested by subroutines.

Each independent task should be done in a separate subroutine, making the main program logic much easier to follow. Such a modular programming style allows new programmers hired by a company to understand more quickly how existing programs work. It also makes debugging easier, since each subroutine can be tested independently with dummy variables.

Although the programs in the *Guide* are short enough that they are perhaps clearer in some cases without the use of subroutines, commercial-level programs usually require strict adherence to modularity. Unless programs that consist of thousands of lines of code are hierarchically organized into independent parts, as suggested in Figure 3-5, they become cluttered, tangled masses.

GOSUB and RETURN.   Subroutines introduce two new statements, GOSUB and RETURN, which have the following formats:

```
Line # GOSUB line-number
  .
  .
  .
Line # RETURN
```

The GOSUB statement causes immediate branching to the first statement in the subroutine. The RETURN statement causes branching back to the main

FIGURE 3-6   **Use of subroutines to solve the problem originally presented in Figure 1–6.**

```
10   REM      TITLE: PROGRAM 3-6
20   REM
30   REM      READS A LIST OF NUMBERS
40   REM         AND TELLS WHETHER EACH NUMBER IS
50   REM         POSITIVE OR NEGATIVE
60   REM
70   REM      AUTHOR: C.S. PARKER
80   REM      DATE: 10/5/94
90   REM
100  REM      NUMBER = A POSITIVE OR NEGATIVE NUMBER
110  REM      SIGN$  = SIGN OF THE NUMBER
120  REM
130  REM      ************************************
140  GOSUB 220
150  WHILE NUMBER <> 0
160     GOSUB 250
170     GOSUB 280                    ←———— Main part of program
180     GOSUB 220
190  WEND
200  STOP
210  REM
220  REM SUBROUTINE FOR INPUT
230     READ NUMBER
240  RETURN
250  REM SUBROUTINE TO FIGURE NUMBER'S SIGN
260     IF NUMBER < 0 THEN SIGN$ = "NEGATIVE"    ←———  Subroutines
                        ELSE SIGN$ = "POSITIVE"
270  RETURN
280  REM SUBROUTINE FOR OUTPUT
290     PRINT NUMBER; "IS ";SIGN$
300  RETURN
310  REM
320  DATA 8,-16,-65,12,0
330  END

RUN
  8 IS POSITIVE
 -16 IS NEGATIVE
 -65 IS NEGATIVE
 12 IS POSITIVE
```

program, to the statement that immediately follows the invoking GOSUB (that is, the GOSUB that caused the branching). Subroutines can also be nested.

An example of a program that uses subroutines and the output of this program are given in Figure 3-6. Figure 3-7 shows a structure chart for this program.

Note the use of the STOP statement in line 200. This statement is necessary so that, when the looping in lines 150 through 190 is finished, the program terminates immediately. If the STOP statement were taken out, the subroutines would be executed one more time between finishing the loop and reaching the END statement.

FIGURE 3-7

A structure chart for the problem solved in Figure 3-6.

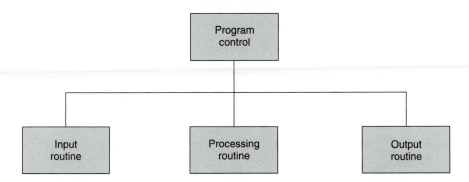

ON . . . GOSUB. Subroutines can also be employed effectively in a *case structure* by using the ON . . . GOSUB statement. This statement has the format:

> Line # ON case-variable GOSUB line-number, line number, . . .

A *case variable* is one that has values such as 1, 2, 3, and so forth that correspond to special situations, or "cases," that must be processed. If the case variable is equal to 1, the computer branches to the first line number after the GOSUB; if the case variable is equal to 2, it branches to the second line number; and so on. The case structure made possible by BASIC's ON . . . GOSUB is ideal for menu-selection programs as well as the Solved Review Problem that immediately follows in the next section. The case structure is a special case of a nested IF-THEN-ELSE, as shown in Figure 3-8.

Solved Review Problem

An auto rental company rents three types of cars at the following rates:

Car Type	Fixed Cost per Day	Cost per Mile
Compact	$10	$0.15
Intermediate	$20	$0.18
Large	$30	$0.22

Thus, for example, a person renting a compact car for 3 days and driving 100 miles would be charged $10 * 3 + .15 * 100 = \$45$.

Write an interactive BASIC program that will accept

- Customer name
- Car type
- Number of days car held
- Miles traveled

as input. It should output the charge for each customer. Use the sample data in the table at the bottom of page 56 to test your program.

FIGURE 3-8

A case structure. A case structure is a special case of a nested IF-THEN-ELSE structure. For instance, if the case-variable, TYPE, has a value of 1, Routine-1 is performed; if it has a value of 2, Routine-2 is performed, and so on.

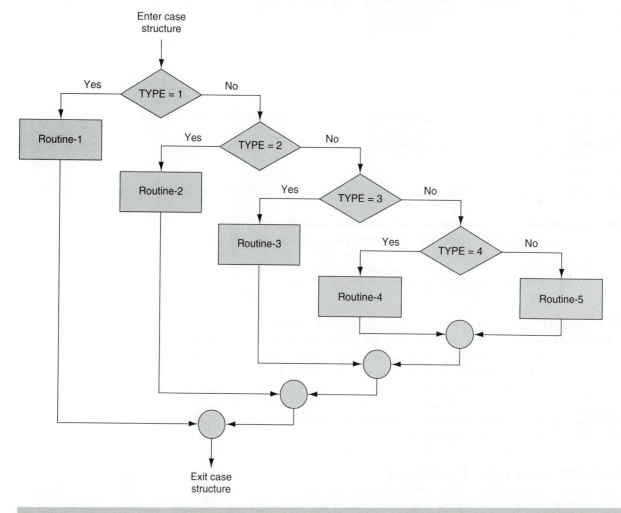

Customer Name	Car Type	Days Held	Miles Traveled
Jones	Large	6	500
Smith	Compact	17	3,000
Baker	Intermediate	8	250
Williams	Intermediate	4	1,000
Winston	Large	3	500

The solution to this problem is provided in Figure 3-9 (pages 57 and 58). You should note that the program will terminate if the user types in "GOODBYE" when asked to supply a customer name.

In Figure 3-9, pay particular attention to the error-trapping feature of the program. If the user keys in any car type other than TYPE 1, 2, or 3, line 260 sets TYPE = 4. Then, in line 270, the program is directed to a subroutine that processes the error.

FIGURE 3-9

An interactive program to determine auto rental charges.

```
10   REM      TITLE:   PROGRAM 3-9
20   REM
30   REM      DESCRIPTION: THIS PROGRAM COMPUTES THE CHARGES
40   REM         DUE ON RENTED AUTOMOBILES
50   REM
60   REM      AUTHOR: C.S. PARKER
70   REM      DATE: 10/5/94
80   REM
90   REM
100  REM      TYPE   = CAR TYPE (1=COMPACT)
110  REM                        (2=INTERMEDIATE)
120  REM                        (3=LARGE)
130  REM      CUSTOMER$ = CUSTOMER NAME
140  REM      DAYS      = DAYS CAR HELD
150  REM      MILES     = MILES TRAVELED
160  REM      CHARGE     = CHARGE FOR CUSTOMER
170  REM
180  REM ***************************************
190  PRINT "ENTER CUSTOMER NAME"
200  PRINT "   NOTE: ENTER GOODBYE TO STOP PROGRAM"
210  INPUT CUSTOMER$
220  WHILE CUSTOMER$ <> "GOODBYE"
230     PRINT "ENTER DAYS CAR HELD, MILES TRAVELED, AND CAR TYPE"
240     PRINT "   NOTE: 1=COMPACT  2=INTERMEDIATE  3=LARGE"
250     INPUT DAYS,MILES,TYPE
260     IF NOT (TYPE = 1 OR TYPE = 2 OR TYPE = 3) THEN TYPE = 4
270     ON TYPE GOSUB 350,400,450,490
280     PRINT "ENTER CUSTOMER NAME"
290     PRINT "   NOTE: ENTER GOODBYE TO STOP PROGRAM"
300     INPUT CUSTOMER$
310  WEND
320  STOP
330  REM **************SUBROUTINES*************************
340  REM COMPACT CAR CALCULATIONS
350     CHARGE = .15 * MILES + 10 * DAYS
360     PRINT CUSTOMER$;"     $";CHARGE
370     PRINT
380     RETURN
390  REM INTERMEDIATE CAR CALCULATIONS
400     CHARGE = .18 * MILES + 20 * DAYS
410     PRINT CUSTOMER$;"     $";CHARGE
420     PRINT
430     RETURN
440  REM LARGE CAR CALCULATIONS
450     CHARGE = .22 * MILES + 30 * DAYS
460     PRINT CUSTOMER$;"     $";CHARGE
470     PRINT
480     RETURN
490  REM ERROR ROUTINE
500     PRINT "YOU HAVE ENTERED AN INVALID CAR TYPE--TRY AGAIN"
510     RETURN
520  REM ****************************************************
530  END
```

CONTINUED

FIGURE 3-9 (CONTINUED)

```
RUN
ENTER CUSTOMER NAME
  NOTE: ENTER GOODBYE TO STOP PROGRAM
?JONES
ENTER DAYS CAR HELD, MILES TRAVELED, AND CAR TYPE
  NOTE: 1=COMPACT  2=INTERMEDIATE  3=LARGE
?6,500,3
JONES      $ 290

ENTER CUSTOMER NAME
  NOTE: ENTER GOODBYE TO STOP PROGRAM
?SMITH
ENTER DAYS CAR HELD, MILES TRAVELED, AND CAR TYPE
  NOTE: 1=COMPACT  2=INTERMEDIATE  3=LARGE
?17,3000,1
SMITH      $ 620

ENTER CUSTOMER NAME
  NOTE: ENTER GOODBYE TO STOP PROGRAM
?BAKER
ENTER DAYS CAR HELD, MILES TRAVELED, AND CAR TYPE
  NOTE: 1=COMPACT  2=INTERMEDIATE  3=LARGE
?8,250,6
YOU HAVE ENTERED AN INVALID CAR TYPE--TRY AGAIN
ENTER DAYS CAR HELD, MILES TRAVELED, AND CAR TYPE
  NOTE: 1=COMPACT  2=INTERMEDIATE  3=LARGE
?8,250,2
BAKER      $ 205

ENTER CUSTOMER NAME
  NOTE: ENTER GOODBYE TO STOP PROGRAM
?WILLIAMS
ENTER DAYS CAR HELD, MILES TRAVELED, AND CAR TYPE
  NOTE: 1=COMPACT  2=INTERMEDIATE  3=LARGE
?4,1000,2
WILLIAMS      $ 260

ENTER CUSTOMER NAME
  NOTE: ENTER GOODBYE TO STOP PROGRAM
?WINSTON
ENTER DAYS CAR HELD, MILES TRAVELED, AND CAR TYPE
  NOTE: 1=COMPACT  2=INTERMEDIATE  3=LARGE
?3,500,3
WINSTON      $ 200

ENTER CUSTOMER NAME
  NOTE: ENTER GOODBYE TO STOP PROGRAM
?GOODBYE
```

Exercises

Instructions: Provide an answer to each of the following questions.

1. Identify the syntax errors, if any, in the following BASIC statements:

    a. `10 FOR I=6 TO 1 STEP 2`   e. `10 FOR I=-5 TO 5`
    b. `10 INPUT N$,A,A1`   f. `10 FOR K=3 TO A STEP 2`
    c. `10 INPUT T=1, T=2, T=3`
    d. `15 IF N$="PHONY" THEN 25`

2. Consider the following FOR/NEXT loop:

```
10 FOR I=A TO B STEP C
        .
        .
        .
20 NEXT I
```

How many times will this loop execute if

a. A=1, B=7, and C=1?   c. A=5, B=17, and C=3?
b. A=1, B=7, and C=2?   d. A=5, B=1, and C=-1?

3. Consider the following program:

```
10 FOR I=1 TO 5
20 FOR J=3 TO 7
30 A=I*J
40 NEXT J
50 NEXT I
```

a. What is the first value assigned to A?
b. What is the value of A at the end of the program?
c. What is the value of A the 8th time statement 30 is executed?
d. What is the value of A the 12th time statement 30 is executed?
e. How many times will line 30 be executed?

Programming Problems

Instructions: Write a BASIC program to do each of the following tasks.

1. Read a list of positive numbers, sum all of the numbers greater than 10 in the list, and output that sum. Use the following list of numbers to check your program:

   32, 45, 6, 87, 4, 5, 17, 25

2. Sum all even numbers from 1 to 100 and output the square root of that sum. [*Hint:* The square root of any number X is $X^{1/2}$.]
3. Read a list of positive numbers, find the average of all numbers between 10 and 20 (inclusive) in the list, and output the average. Use the list of numbers given in Programming Problem 1 to check your results.
4. Write a program that will read in the 10 values

   -6, 8, 65, 4, 8, -21, 2, 46, -12, 42

   and identify the highest and lowest number. [*Hint:* Declare the first number in the list as both the highest and lowest value in the list. Then let each of the remaining nine numbers "get a shot" at competing for highest or lowest value. As each number is read, check it against the current high value and low value.]
5. The following data show the weather in a city on 10 successive days: Sunny, Cloudy, Rainy, Sunny, Sunny, Cloudy, Sunny, Sunny, Rainy, Cloudy.

   Write a program to read these 10 weather observations and then count and output the number of sunny days.

6. Use FOR/NEXT loops to compute the following sums (S):

$$S = 1 + 2 + 3 + 4 + \cdots + 10$$
$$S = 3 + 6 + 9 + 12 + \cdots + 30$$
$$S = 1 + 1/2 + 1/3 + 1/4 + \cdots + 1/1000$$

7. Write a program to convert several temperatures from Fahrenheit (F) to centigrade (C). Use the INPUT statement to supply each Fahrenheit temperature to the computer system for conversion. The following formula can be used to make the conversion:

$$C = (5/9) * (F - 32)$$

Use a trailer value, such as 9999 degrees, to stop your program.

8. The cost of sending a telegram is $2.80 for the first 20 (or fewer) words and 10 cents for each additional word. Write a program that will find the cost of a telegram after you have entered the number of words as input at a keyboard.

9. The population growth rate in a city has been projected at 5 percent per year for the next 10 years. The current population in the city is 31,840 residents. Write a program to find the population 10 years from now.

10. ABC Company has the following accounts receivable data:

Customer Name	Previous Balance	Payments	New Purchases
Clara Bronson	$700	$500	$300
Lon Brooks	100	100	0
Louise Chaplin	0	0	100
Jack Davies	50	0	0
Emil Murray	600	600	200
Tom Swanson	300	100	50
Lucy Allen	500	500	80

Write a subroutine that computes the new balance for each customer. Assume that unpaid portions of previous balances are assessed a 2 percent finance charge each month. The main part of your program should perform all the input/output functions necessary to support and supplement the subroutine.

11. Students in a class have taken a ten-question true/false exam. Below are the results and the correct answers:

Student ID Number	Questions									
	1	2	3	4	5	6	7	8	9	10
40033	F	T	F	F	T	F	F	F	T	T
40055	F	F	F	T	T	F	T	F	T	T
40058	F	T	F	T	F	F	T	F	F	T
40062	F	T	T	T	T	F	T	T	T	F
40066	T	T	F	T	T	F	T	F	F	T
40083	T	T	F	F	T	T	T	F	T	T
Correct answers	T	T	T	T	T	T	T	T	T	T

Score each exam. Assume scores are to be recorded as the percentage of right answers—in other words, 0, 10, 20, . . ., 100 are possible scores.

Formatted Printing

Spacing Output

Producing neatly formatted output is one of the prized skills of computer programming. A sloppy-looking report, even though it contains accurate information, often is not read. Readers of reports generally are favorably inclined toward well-presented output.

So far we have learned two formatting vehicles to use with the PRINT statement:

1. The semicolon. This generally leaves a space or two between printed items.* When it is the last character in the PRINT statement, it forces the next output from the computer system to begin on the same line.
2. The "blank" PRINT statement. This is used to produce blank output lines.

There are three other techniques discussed in this section that will aid in formatting output:

1. The comma (,).
2. The TAB function.
3. The PRINT USING statement.

Comma Print Control

The comma works in a manner somewhat similar to the semicolon, except that

1. It produces more space between the output data items.
2. The items are printed at fixed tab stops.

The fixed tab stops define so-called *print zones*. If you are on an output device that provides 80 characters per line, the zones might be fixed as follows:

Zone 1	Zone 2	Zone 3	Zone 4	Zone 5
Columns	Columns	Columns	Columns	Columns
1–14	15–28	29–42	43–56	57–80

In any case, you should check your output device to find out where the zones begin and end. With the zones just mentioned, the use of commas in a PRINT statement would have the effect shown in Figure 4-1, which features a simple program that inputs data and merely outputs the same data into zones. Positive

---

*The exception is that no spaces are provided between two strings separated by a semicolon (unless, of course, spaces appear within the string).

FIGURE 4-1

Use of comma in PRINT for spacing. This simple program reads in names of people along with associated pay rates and gross pay. This information is then output into print zones.

```
10   REM     TITLE:  PROGRAM 4-1
20   REM
30   REM     DESCRIPTION: THIS PROGRAM LISTS PAY
40   REM       RATES AND GROSS PAY OF EMPLOYEES
50   REM
60   REM     AUTHOR: C.S. PARKER
70   REM     DATE: 10/5/94
80   REM
90   REM     EMPLOYEE$  = EMPLOYEE NAME
100  REM     RATE       = PAY RATE
110  REM     GROSS      = GROSS PAY
120  REM     I          = LOOP VARIABLE
130  REM
140  REM  ***************************************
150  PRINT "NAME","PAY RATE","GROSS PAY"
160  PRINT
170  FOR I = 1 TO 3
180      READ EMPLOYEE$,RATE,GROSS
190      PRINT EMPLOYEE$,RATE,GROSS        ← Print statement
200  NEXT I                                  with zone spacing
210  DATA "JOHN DOE",6.30,200.15
220  DATA "MARY SMITH",7.20,316.40
230  DATA "ANN JONES",5.00,80.00
240  END

RUN
NAME              PAY RATE        GROSS PAY

JOHN DOE          6.3             200.15
MARY SMITH        7.2             316.4
ANN JONES         5               80
```

Zone 1   Zone 2   Zone 3

numbers printed in a zone are preceded by a blank space, negative numbers by a minus sign.

There are two other interesting features to note about the use of the comma for spacing in a PRINT statement:

1. If the number of items to be output in a PRINT statement is too large to fit on one line of the output device used, a "wraparound" effect will occur; for example:

```
10 FOR I=1 TO 12
20 PRINT I,
30 NEXT I
40 END
RUN
  1           2           3           4           5
  6           7           8           9          10
 11          12
```

Only five data items are printed per line because only five print zones are available on the output device used. If we tried running this program on a different output device, say, one with six zones, we would get six numbers per line.

2. If a particular data item is too large to occupy a single print zone, it will "overflow" into subsequent zones; for example:

```
10 PRINT "TODAY IS MAY 16, 1994", "HELLO"
20 END
RUN
TODAY IS MAY 16, 1994    HELLO
```
↑Begins in zone 1   ↑Begins in zone 3

(because the
first literal overflowed
into zone 2)

The TAB Function

The TAB function of BASIC permits us to "tab" over to any column to start printing. Thus, with the TAB function we don't have to begin printing at a zone boundary.

The following self-explanatory example will clarify how the TAB function is used in BASIC:

```
10 PRINT TAB(10);"HELLO"
20 PRINT TAB(15);"HELLO AGAIN"
30 PRINT TAB(20);"HELLO FOR A THIRD TIME"
40 END
RUN
         HELLO
              HELLO AGAIN
                   HELLO FOR A THIRD TIME
```
↑ Starts in column 20
↑ Starts in column 15
↑ Starts in column 10

Note that there must be no space between the word TAB in a statement and the opening parenthesis.

It is possible to use several TAB functions on one line. You can also specify tabbing for a single, long output line that spans two PRINT statements. For example:

```
10 PRINT "PART NUMBER";TAB(20);"NAME";TAB(30);
20 PRINT "AMOUNT IN STOCK";TAB(50);"UNIT PRICE"
30 END
   RUN
PART NUMBER    NAME        AMOUNT IN STOCK    UNIT PRICE
```
↑ Column 1   ↑ Column 20 ↑ Column 30   ↑ Column 50

Remember, the semicolon at the end of a PRINT statement (see line 10) will keep the output device on the same line.

In many versions of BASIC, you can use variable names as tab stops; for example:

```
10 F = 25
20 PRINT TAB(F);"GOODBYE"
30 END
RUN
```

```
                                          GOODBYE
                                          ↑
                                          Column 25
```

The PRINT USING Statement

The PRINT USING statement is the most powerful instruction in BASIC for formatted printing. The syntax of this statement varies considerably from system to system; however, the one presented here and in the examples to follow is used widely:

> Line # PRINT USING output-image-variable;
> list of variables (separated by commas)

A program employing the PRINT USING statement appears in Figure 4-2. This program reads in names (EMPLOYEE\$), pay rates (RATE), and hours worked (HOURS). It then computes and sums the amounts earned (AMOUNT = RATE * HOURS). You should examine this example carefully before reading further.

The program uses two PRINT USING statements. Each PRINT USING statement refers to a variable that specifies how to format, or *image*, the output when the PRINT USING is executed. The program in Figure 4-2 contains two such *output-image variables:* A\$ and B\$. The PRINT USING statement in line 260 references A\$, containing the output images of variables EMPLOYEE\$, HOURS, and AMOUNT. Similarly, statement 280 references B\$, containing the image of variable TOTAL. For both A\$ and B\$, the associated output image appears between quotation marks (see lines 190 and 200, respectively).

PRINT USING output images are formatted according to the following rules.

Numeric Variables. All numeric variable values are placed in the areas occupied by the pound (number) signs (#) of their associated output images, in the order in which the variable names appear in the PRINT USING. If the variable value contains a decimal point, you can specify where it must appear and the number of digits to the left and right of it. For example, an image such as

$$\#\#\#\#\#.\#\#$$

specifies that 1245.06 be printed as

        ƀ1245.06   (ƀ represents a blank space)

FIGURE 4-2

Use of PRINT USING statement.

```
10   REM     TITLE: PROGRAM 4-2
20   REM
30   REM     DESCRIPTION: THIS PROGRAM COMPUTES EMPLOYEE PAY
40   REM
50   REM     AUTHOR: C.S. PARKER
60   REM     DATE: 10/5/94
70   REM
80   REM     EMPLOYEE$    = EMPLOYEE NAME
90   REM     HOURS        = HOURS WORKED
100  REM     RATE         = PAY RATE
110  REM     AMOUNT       = AMOUNT EARNED BY EMPLOYEE
120  REM     TOTAL        = SUM OF ALL AMOUNTS EARNED
130  REM     I            = LOOP VARIABLE
140  REM     A$,B$        = OUTPUT-IMAGE VARIABLES FOR
150  REM                      PRINT USING STATEMENTS
160  REM
170  REM **************************************
180  TOTAL = 0
190  A$ = "\              \         ###        $##,###.##"
200  B$ = "SUM OF AMOUNTS                      $##,###.##"
210  PRINT "NAME                 HOURS       AMT EARNED"
220  FOR I=1 TO 3
230     READ EMPLOYEE$,RATE,HOURS
240     AMOUNT = RATE * HOURS
250     TOTAL = TOTAL + AMOUNT
260     PRINT USING A$;EMPLOYEE$,HOURS,AMOUNT
270  NEXT I
280  PRINT USING B$;TOTAL
290  DATA "JONES",6.5,160
300  DATA "SMITH",12.16,200
310  DATA "BAKER",5,100
320  END

RUN
NAME                 HOURS       AMT EARNED
JONES                160         $ 1,040.00
SMITH                200         $ 2,432.00
BAKER                100         $   500.00
SUM OF AMOUNTS                   $ 3,972.00
```

In many versions of BASIC, commas can also be automatically placed into numeric values. For example, an image such as

$$\#,\#\#\#.\#\#$$

specifies that 1245.06 be printed as

$$1,245.06$$

If a number to be output with the last image is smaller than 1,000, the comma is replaced by a ƀ. Thus, 154.68 is output as

ƀƀ154.68

You should note that the # is a special symbol when used to specify an output image.

String Variables.   The symbol pair \ \ is used to specify the maximum number of characters printed out for a string variable. The backslashes plus each space left between them represent the length of output. For example, a declaration such as

\ƀƀƀ\

will accommodate the full contents of any output strings of five characters or fewer.

Constants.   Generally any characters other than # (for numeric variables) and the backslashes (for string variables) will be printed as they appear. Thus, the dollar sign in lines 190 and 200 and the phrase SUM OF AMOUNTS in line 200 appear on the output exactly as they do in the output image.

As you can see by inspecting the program in Figure 4-2, a major advantage of PRINT USING is that it allows neat decimal-point alignment in columns. This is a must for reports used in business. The use of comma spacing or the TAB function does not provide this luxury, since variable values start printing in the zone boundary or tab stop indicated, leaving the decimal point to fall where it may. This can be seen in Figure 4-1; note that the gross pay for Ann Jones is not neatly lined up under the gross pay of the other individuals.

The values of string variables automatically begin at the far left (left-justified) within the \ \ symbol pair. The values of numeric variables are aligned with respect to the decimal point. The following example should make this clear:

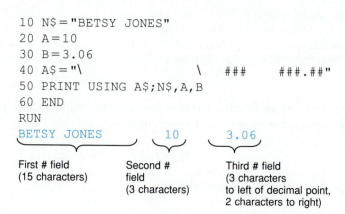

```
10 N$ = "BETSY JONES"
20 A = 10
30 B = 3.06
40 A$ = "\                \    ###     ###.##"
50 PRINT USING A$;N$,A,B
60 END
RUN
BETSY JONES              10       3.06
```

First # field
(15 characters)

Second #
field
(3 characters)

Third # field
(3 characters
to left of decimal point,
2 characters to right)

If the values of any of the variables are too large to fit within the specified \ \ or #-sign fields, either truncation, rounding, or output suppression (that is, spaces or nonnumeric symbols) may occur. Referring to the last example, if

```
N$ = "SHERIDAN P. WHITESIDE"
A = 10.6
B = 8321.46
```

the following output might be produced:

SHERIDAN P. WHI♭♭♭♭11♭♭♭******

Truncation   Rounding   Output suppression

Solved Review Problems

Example 1

Compute the square root ($I^{1/2}$), cube root ($I^{1/3}$), and fourth root ($I^{1/4}$) of all integers I in the range 1–10. The output should be neatly labeled and formatted.

Solution

The program and associated output are shown in Figure 4-3. You should note the use of the comma in lines 210 and 250, which keeps the output device printing on the same line. The blank PRINT statement in line 270 is extremely important; it negates the effect of the comma on line 250 when the fourth roots are printed and sends the output device to the next output line.

Example 2

Straight-line depreciation expenses are computed by the formula:

$$\text{Annual depreciation charge} = \frac{\text{Original cost} - \text{Salvage value}}{\text{Useful life}}$$

Provide a depreciation schedule for a car that originally cost $7,328 and will be worth approximately $600 at the end of its 10-year useful life. The depreciation schedule should show (for each year) the depreciation charge, total depreciation so far, and the (undepreciated) balance.

Solution

The program and associated output are shown in Figure 4-4.

The annual depreciation charge is computed in line 260. Because the charge for each year is the same, it is computed before the FOR/NEXT loop beginning in line 300. This loop is used to compute the total accumulated depreciation, compute the undepreciated balance, and produce most of the output lines for the report. The PRINT USING statement in line 330 aligns the output neatly in formatted columns.

A program for computing roots.

```
10   REM     TITLE: PROGRAM 4-3
20   REM
30   REM     DESCRIPTION: THIS PROGRAM COMPUTES THE
40   REM       SQUARE ROOT, CUBE ROOT, AND FOURTH ROOT
50   REM       OF ALL INTEGERS IN THE RANGE 1-10
60   REM
70   REM     AUTHOR: C.S. PARKER
80   REM     DATE: 10/5/94
90   REM
100  REM     I       = LOOP VARIABLE TO GENERATE 1-10
110  REM     N       = LOOP VARIABLE TO GENERATE EXPONENTS
120  REM     ROOT    = THE COMPUTED ROOT
130  REM
140  REM ************************************************
150  PRINT TAB(20);"COMPUTATIONS TABLE"
160  PRINT
170  PRINT "INTEGER","SQUARE ROOT","CUBE ROOT","FOURTH ROOT"
180  PRINT
190  FOR I = 1 TO 10
200     REM PRINT OUT ROW NUMBER
210     PRINT I,
220     FOR N = 2 TO 4
230        REM COMPUTE AND PRINT OUT THE REST OF THE ROW
240        ROOT = I ^ (1/N)
250        PRINT ROOT,
260     NEXT N
270     PRINT
280  NEXT I
290  END

RUN
```

COMPUTATIONS TABLE

INTEGER	SQUARE ROOT	CUBE ROOT	FOURTH ROOT
1	1	1	1
2	1.414213	1.259921	1.189207
3	1.732051	1.44225	1.316074
4	2	1.587401	1.414214
5	2.236068	1.709976	1.495349
6	2.44949	1.817121	1.565085
7	2.645751	1.912931	1.626577
8	2.828427	2	1.681793
9	3	2.080084	1.732051
10	3.162278	2.154435	1.778279

Example 3

The TAB function is extremely helpful for printing various types of geometric designs. The program in Figure 4-5 uses the TAB function to print a triangle.

The triangle in the figure consists of 11 lines of output. The top line of 21 asterisks and the bottom line of 1 asterisk are each produced by a single statement—statements 170 and 270, respectively. The nine middle lines of

FIGURE 4-4

A depreciation program.

```
10   REM    TITLE: PROGRAM 4-4
20   REM
30   REM    DESCRIPTION: THIS PROGRAM COMPUTES STRAIGHT-LINE
40   REM    DEPRECIATION CHARGES FOR AN AUTOMOBILE
50   REM
60   REM    AUTHOR: C.S. PARKER
70   REM    DATE: 10/5/94
80   REM
90   REM    COST      = ORIGINAL COST OF AUTO
100  REM    LIFE      = USEFUL LIFE
110  REM    SALVAGE   = SALVAGE VALUE AT END OF USEFUL LIFE
120  REM    ANNUAL    = ANNUAL DEPRECIATION CHARGE
130  REM    ACCUM     = ACCUMULATED DEPRECIATION
140  REM    UNDEP     = UNDEPRECIATED BALANCE
150  REM    I         = LOOP VARIABLE
160  REM    A$        = OUTPUT-IMAGE VARIABLE
170  REM
180  REM ****************************************************
190  A$=" ##      $#,###.##        $#,###.##        $#,###.##"
200  PRINT TAB(12);"AUTO DEPRECIATION SCHEDULE"
210  PRINT
220  PRINT "YEAR   DEPR CHARGE        ACCUM DEP      UNDEP BALANCE"
230  PRINT
240  READ COST,SALVAGE,LIFE
250  REM DEPRECIATION CALCULATION
260  ANNUAL = (COST - SALVAGE) / LIFE
270  ACCUM = 0
280  UNDEP = COST
290  REM PERFORM OTHER CALCULATIONS AND OUTPUT RESULTS
300  FOR I = 1 TO LIFE
310     ACCUM = ACCUM + ANNUAL
320     UNDEP = UNDEP - ANNUAL
330     PRINT USING A$;I,ANNUAL, ACCUM, UNDEP
340  NEXT I
350  DATA 7328,600,10
360  END

RUN
             AUTO DEPRECIATION SCHEDULE

YEAR   DEPR CHARGE      ACCUM DEP       UNDEP BALANCE

  1    $   672.80      $   672.80      $6,655.20
  2    $   672.80      $1,345.60       $5,982.40
  3    $   672.80      $2,018.40       $5,309.60
  4    $   672.80      $2,691.20       $4,636.80
  5    $   672.80      $3,364.00       $3,964.00
  6    $   672.80      $4,036.80       $3,291.20
  7    $   672.80      $4,709.60       $2,618.40
  8    $   672.80      $5,382.40       $1,945.60
  9    $   672.80      $6,055.20       $1,272.80
 10    $   672.80      $6,728.00       $   600.00
```

FIGURE 4-5

A program, flowchart, and pseudocode for producing a triangle.

Program

```
10   REM     TITLE: PROGRAM 4-5
20   REM
30   REM     DESCRIPTION: THIS PROGRAM MAKES A TRIANGLE
40   REM
50   REM     AUTHOR: C.S. PARKER
60   REM     DATE: 10/5/94
70   REM
80   REM     LEFT  = POSITION OF LEFTMOST ASTERISK
90   REM     RIGHT = POSITION OF RIGHTMOST ASTERISK
100  REM     I     = LOOP VARIABLE
110  REM
120  REM *****************************************
130  LEFT = 1
140  RIGHT = 21
150  REM
160  REM FIRST, PRINT THE TOP LINE OF ASTERISKS
170  PRINT "*********************"
180  REM
190  REM SECOND, PRINT THE MIDDLE LINES
200  FOR I = 1 TO 9
210      LEFT = LEFT + 1
220      RIGHT = RIGHT - 1
230      PRINT TAB(LEFT);"*";TAB(RIGHT);"*"
240  NEXT I
250  REM
260  REM THIRD, PRINT THE BOTTOMMOST ASTERISK
270  PRINT TAB(11);"*"
280  END
```

```
RUN
*********************
 *                 *
  *               *
   *             *
    *           *
     *         *
      *       *
       *     *
        *   *
         * *
          *
```

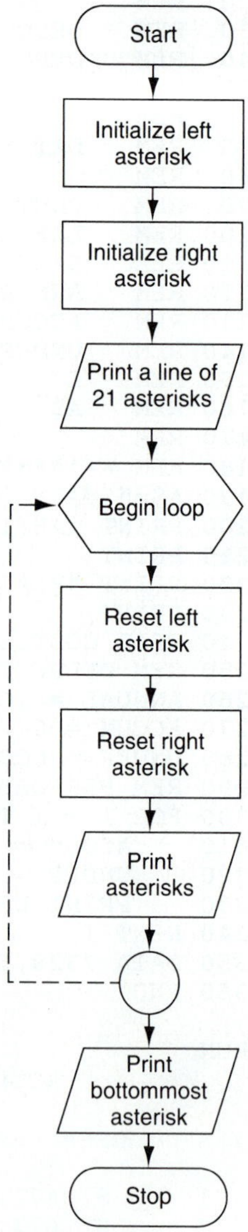

Pseudocode
```
Start
Initialize asterisk settings
Print a line of 21 asterisks
Set counter to 1
DOWHILE counter ≤ 9
   Reset asterisk settings
   Print asterisks at given settings
   Add 1 to counter
END DO
Print bottommost asterisk
Stop
```

Flowchart

Start

Initialize left asterisk

Initialize right asterisk

Print a line of 21 asterisks

Begin loop

Reset left asterisk

Reset right asterisk

Print asterisks

Print bottommost asterisk

Stop

output consist of two asterisks each and are produced in the FOR/NEXT loop, using the variables LEFT and RIGHT. As each pass is made in the loop, LEFT (which is initialized to 1) increases by one unit and RIGHT (which is initialized to 21) decreases by one unit, producing the collapsing sides of the triangle.

Example 4
The following table lists salespeople at XYZ Company, their branch affiliations, and the amount of their sales booked last week:

Name	Branch	Sales
M. Vincent	A	$1,020
T. Loux	A	$1,090
J. Jefferson	A	$1,400
A. T. Jones	A	$1,700
C. Smith	B	$1,100
L. Martinez	B	$1,400
M. Schurer	C	$1,550
G. Seaver	C	$1,090

Write a program that outputs salespeople (and their sales) by branch, subtotals sales by branch, and calculates a grand total over all branches.

Solution
The program and associated output are shown in Figure 4-6. The subtotals that "foot" each branch are examples of *control breaks*. In the program, variable BRANCH$ (branch) is referred to as the *control-break variable*. BRANCH$ "breaks" two times—when branch changes from A to B and later from B to C. At each break, a subtotal is printed. Before the program ends, it prints out the final subtotal and the grand total. The program uses a "holding variable" (HOLD$) to hold the value of BRANCH$ from the most recently processed record and uses a check (in line 260) to signal when a new record represents a change in branch. For this program to work, the data must be presorted by branch.

Exercises

Instructions: Provide an answer to each of the following questions.

1. Consider this program:

```
10 FOR I=1 TO 3
20 PRINT "HELLO NUMBER";I
30 FOR J=1 TO 4
40 PRINT X=I*J,
50 NEXT J
60 PRINT
70 NEXT I
```

   a. How many lines will be printed by this program?
   b. How many times will line 20 be executed?
   c. What will be the fourth line printed by this program?
   d. How many times will line 40 be executed?
   e. What will be the value of X at the end of the program?

F I G U R E   4 – 6   A control-break program and output (inset).

```
10   REM    TITLE: PROGRAM 4-6
20   REM
30   REM    DESCRIPTION: THIS PROGRAM COMPUTES BRANCH
40   REM       SUBTOTALS AND THE GRAND TOTAL
50   REM
60   REM    AUTHOR: C.S. PARKER
70   REM    DATE: 10/5/94
80   REM
90   REM    SUBTOTAL  = BRANCH SUBTOTAL
100  REM    GRAND     = GRAND TOTAL
110  REM    PERSON$   = SALESPERSON NAME
120  REM    SALES     = SALESPERSON SALES
130  REM    BRANCH$   = BRANCH
140  REM    HOLD$     = HOLDING VARIABLE FOR BRANCH
150  REM
160  REM ****************************************
170  SUBTOTAL = 0
180  GRAND = 0
190  PRINT TAB(10);"XYZ SALES REPORT"
200  PRINT
210  PRINT "NAME","SALES"
220  PRINT
230  READ PERSON$,BRANCH$,SALES
240  HOLD$ = BRANCH$
250  WHILE PERSON$ <> "LAST RECORD"
260     IF BRANCH$ = HOLD$ THEN 320
270         PRINT
280         PRINT "   SUBTOTAL - BRANCH ";HOLD$,SUBTOTAL
290         PRINT
300         SUBTOTAL = 0
310         HOLD$ = BRANCH$
320     GRAND = GRAND + SALES
330     SUBTOTAL = SUBTOTAL + SALES
340     PRINT PERSON$,SALES
350     READ PERSON$,BRANCH$,SALES
360  WEND
370  PRINT
380  PRINT "   SUBTOTAL - BRANCH ";HOLD$,SUBTOTAL
390  PRINT
400  PRINT "   GRAND TOTAL",GRAND
410  REM *********DATA STATEMENTS***************
420  DATA "M. VINCENT","A",1020,"T. LOUX","A",1090
430  DATA "J. JEFFERSON","A",1400,"A.T. JONES","A",1700
440  DATA "C. SMITH","B",1100,"L. MARTINEZ","B",1400
450  DATA "M. SCHURER","C",1550,"G. SEAVER","C",1090
460  DATA "LAST RECORD","Z",0
470  REM ****************************************
480  END
```

```
         XYZ SALES REPORT

NAME              SALES

M. VINCENT        1020
T. LOUX           1090
J. JEFFERSON      1400
A.T. JONES        1700

   SUBTOTAL - BRANCH A  5210

C. SMITH          1100
L. MARTINEZ       1400

   SUBTOTAL - BRANCH B  2500

M. SCHURER        1550
G. SEAVER         1090

   SUBTOTAL - BRANCH C  2640

   GRAND TOTAL         10350
```

2. How would your answers to Exercise 1 change if the following changes were made to the program?

```
 5 LET X=0
35 LET X=X+I*J
40 PRINT X,
```

3. Consider the following program:

```
10 READ A,B,C,D,E
20 PRINT . . .
30 DATA (data values)
```

Write a PRINT statement for line 20 that will do the following:

a. Place the values of A, B, and C in print zones 1, 2, and 3, respectively.
b. Place the value of A in all five print zones.
c. Place the values of C, D, and E in print zones 3, 4, and 5, respectively.
d. Place the values of A, B, and C in print zones 1, 3, and 5, respectively.

4. Assume X has a value of 2590.86. Show how this value would be output when assigned to the output-image fields below. (Use ƀ to represent a blank space.)

a. `####`   c. `$#,###`
b. `##,###.##`   d. `#.##`

5. Assume N$ has a value of JONES. Show how this value would be output when assigned to the output-image fields below. (Use ƀ to represent a blank space.)

a. `\ƀƀƀƀƀƀ\`   c. `\ƀ\`
b. `\ƀƀƀ\`   d. `#####`

Programming Problems

Instructions: Write a BASIC program to do each of the following tasks.

1. Students in a class are required to take three exams. The class performed as follows on the exams last semester:

Student Name	Scores		
	Exam 1	Exam 2	Exam 3
Jo Smith	70	80	90
Ed Lynn	40	65	59
Richard Johnson	86	93	72
Linda Harris	95	75	86
Wendy Williams	77	83	78
David Rudolph	55	83	78

Compute the average on each of the 3 exams, the average of each of the 6 students, and the overall average of the 18 scores. Print the table with these computed averages shown in their appropriate row and column positions.

Use trailer values at the end of your data list so that your program can sense when there are no more records to be read.

2. Solve Problem 1 by printing letter grades in place of the average score of each of the six students. Use the following formula to assign grades to numbers: 90 and above = A, 80–89 = B, 70–79 = C, 60–69 = D, below 60 = F.

3. Redo the following table so that all of the decimal points line up and each column of data is centered below its column title:

```
NAME                    GROSS PAY
----                    ---------

ZELDA SMITH             $ 1000
ZEB TSOSIE              $ 83.25
ZENON JONES             $ .50
```

4. If P dollars are invested in an account today at a compounded interest rate of R percent per period, the amount in the account at the end of N periods is given by

$$S = P(1 + R/100)^N$$

For example, $100 will be worth $129.15 on 12/31/94 if it was invested on 12/31/89 at an interest rate of 5.25 percent compounded annually; that is,

$$S = 100 (1 + 5.25/100)^5$$
$$= 100 (1.0525)^5 = 129.15$$

Produce a table showing the value of $1 at the end of 1, 2, 3, . . ., 10 years at interest rates of 10 percent, 10.5 percent, 11 percent, 11.5 percent, and 12 percent. The years should appear as rows of the table and the interest rates as columns. Make sure that your decimal points are lined up so that your output looks neat and professional.

5. Figure 4-5 shows how to use the TAB function to produce a triangle. Use the TAB function to produce a square with 10 asterisks on each side.

6. The program given in Figure 4-5 shows how to produce a hollow triangle. Revise this program so that the triangle is completely filled with asterisks.

7. Redo the program in Figure 4-4 using the sum-of-the-year's digits depreciation method, which works as the following example shows: Assume that an asset originally costs $4000, has a salvage value of $1000, and has a useful life of 3 years. The asset will be depreciated by $3000 ($4000 minus $1000) over the 3-year period. The sum of the year's digits for 3 years is $1 + 2 + 3 = 6$. The procedure to compute the depreciation charge for each of the 3 years is given below:

$$Year\ 1: (3/6) * \$3000 = \$1500$$
$$Year\ 2: (2/6) * \$3000 = \$1000$$
$$Year\ 3: (1/6) * \$3000 = \underline{\$\ 500}$$
$$\$3000$$

Note, in the computations above, that the fraction's denominator is always the sum of the year's digits. This is computed by the formula $n(n + 1)/2$, where n is the asset's useful life. The fraction's numerator is, for year i, equal to $n - i + 1$. The fraction is always multiplied by a constant amount, which is equal to the cost minus the salvage value.

Advanced Topics

Subscripting

Subscripting is one of the most useful tools in BASIC, enabling the programmer to build and store lists of numbers or strings. Such lists are commonly called *arrays*. A subscript is simply a number that refers to a position in the list or array. For example, suppose we wanted to place the data in the "averages" program of Figure 3-1 (page 46) in a list. If we decided to call the list X, it might look as follows:

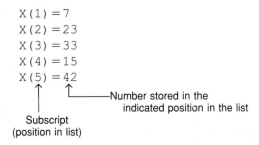

You should make certain that you fully grasp the difference between a position in the list and the number stored in that position before reading further. If, for example, you were asked if $X(3) < X(4)$, how would you respond? (*Note:* 33 is not less than 15, so the answer is no.)

A Simple Subscripting Problem

Let's again find the average of a set of numbers, expanding the problem to 12 values. Also, let's assume that we wish to output the difference of each of the numbers in the list from the average. A program for solving this problem is shown in Figure 5-1. As usual, study the problem carefully before reading the commentary that follows:

The first thing you may have noticed in Figure 5-1 is the DIM (dimension) statement in line 170. This statement instructs the computer to reserve 12* storage positions for array NUMBER. This is necessary because each number in the array is assigned to a different variable—that is, NUMBER(1), NUMBER(2), . . ., NUMBER(12)—and, as is the usual practice, each variable corre-

---

*Many versions of BASIC will also reserve a 13th storage location, for NUMBER(0). Many skilled programmers, however, choose to ignore this storage position, because other programming languages often prohibit a zero subscript.

FIGURE 5-1   **A program for computing differences of numbers in a list from the average of the list.**

```
10   REM     TITLE: PROGRAM 5-1
20   REM
30   REM     DESCRIPTION: THIS PROGRAM COMPUTES THE DIFFERENCES
40   REM        BETWEEN NUMBERS IN A LIST AND THE LIST AVERAGE
50   REM
60   REM     AUTHOR: C.S. PARKER
70   REM     DATE: 10/5/94
80   REM
90   REM     I        = THE LOOP VARIABLE
100  REM     NUMBER   = A NUMBER IN THE LIST
110  REM     LENGTH   = THE NUMBER OF NUMBERS IN THE LIST
120  REM     SUM      = THE SUM OF THE NUMBERS IN THE LIST
130  REM     AVERAGE  = THE AVERAGE OF THE NUMBERS
140  REM     DEV      = THE DEVIATION OF A NUMBER FROM AVERAGE
150  REM
160  REM ****************************************************
170  DIM NUMBER(12)
180  LET SUM = 0
190  READ LENGTH
200  REM
210  REM READ AND SUM NUMBERS
220  FOR I = 1 TO LENGTH
230      READ NUMBER(I)
240      LET SUM = SUM + NUMBER(I)
250  NEXT I
260  LET AVERAGE = SUM / LENGTH
270  PRINT "NUMBER","AVERAGE","DIFFERENCE"
280  PRINT
290  REM
300  REM RECALL VALUES, COMPUTE DEVIATIONS, AND OUTPUT RESULTS
310  FOR I = 1 TO LENGTH
320      LET DEV = NUMBER(I) - AVERAGE
330      PRINT NUMBER(I),AVERAGE,DEV
340  NEXT I
350  DATA 12
360  DATA 5,10,11,13,4,6,8,14,2,15,1,7
370  END

RUN
NUMBER          AVERAGE          DIFFERENCE

  5               8               -3
 10               8                2
 11               8                3
 13               8                5
  4               8               -4
  6               8               -2
  8               8                0
 14               8                6
  2               8               -6
 15               8                7
  1               8               -7
  7               8               -1
```

sponds to a single storage location. Thus, a total of 17 storage positions will be allocated to the variables in this program, as follows:

NUMBER(1), NUMBER(2), NUMBER(3), . . ., NUMBER(12)

Specified by the DIM
statement

SUM, LENGTH, I, AVERAGE, DEV

Nonsubscripted
variables
in program

Many versions of BASIC will allow you to omit the DIM statement if the length of the array stored is 10 positions or fewer. In other words, if there were 10 or fewer numbers in line 360, the computer would react as if you had specified

```
170 DIM NUMBER(10)
```

in your program if this statement is absent. This is called *implicit* dimensioning. Most skilled programmers, however, prefer *explicit* dimensioning, in which all arrays are declared in one or more DIM statements. The reasons for this are similar to the ones for explicitly initializing count and sum variables to zero: The intent is made clear, the opportunity for mistakes is minimized, and the practice is a good one to adopt if you program in other languages (BASIC is among a minority of languages permitting implicit dimensioning).

Since the array in our program has 12 positions, NUMBER must be dimensioned explicitly. If the DIM statement is absent, the computer will not automatically reserve space for NUMBER(11) and NUMBER(12). Thus, the program will "bomb" when the computer attempts to manipulate one of these variables. It is acceptable, however, to reserve more storage positions in a DIM statement than you will actually use.

The DIM statement, like the DATA statement, is not executed by the computer. Although there are several acceptable places to position it, it is good practice to put it at the beginning of the program to avoid potential problems.

If several arrays need to be dimensioned, it is possible to use one DIM statement or several. For example, both

```
10 DIM A(250),X(15),Y(20),Z(200),T(6)
```

and the combination

```
10 DIM A(250),X(15)
20 DIM Y(20),Z(200),T(6)
```

are acceptable to dimension the five arrays shown.

Another interesting feature of the program in Figure 5-1 concerns statements 230 and 240, which are contained in the first loop. Each time I is incremented, a single number is taken from statement 360 and assigned to the Ith variable in the NUMBER array. Thus, when I = 1, NUMBER(1) is assigned 5; when

I = 2, NUMBER(2) is assigned 10; and so on. When the computer exits the first loop and makes the computation in line 260, storage looks as follows:*

NUMBER(1) 5	NUMBER(2) 10	NUMBER(3) 11	NUMBER(4) 13
NUMBER(5) 4	NUMBER(6) 6	NUMBER(7) 8	NUMBER(8) 14
NUMBER(9) 2	NUMBER(10) 15	NUMBER(11) 1	NUMBER(12) 7
SUM 96	I 12	LENGTH 12	AVERAGE 8
DEV 0			

When the second loop is encountered (line 310), the computer has all the information it needs in storage to compute the 12 differences (DEV = NUMBER(I) − AVERAGE). Thus, all that needs to be done in this loop is to successively recall from storage NUMBER(1), NUMBER(2), . . ., NUMBER(12), subtract AVERAGE from each of these values, and compute the differences, DEV.

You should note that it would be extremely inconvenient to solve a problem like the one in Figure 5-1 without the use of subscripts. This is because we need to consider the values in the array twice—once to compute the average and again to compute the differences.

The general format of the DIM statement is as follows:

> Line # DIM list of arrays (separated by commas)

String Lists

The example provided in the previous subsections illustrated a list of *numbers*. BASIC also allows the programmer to form lists of *strings*. For example, suppose we wish to create a list of fruits (say, APPLES, ORANGES, BANANAS, PEACHES, and CHERRIES) and then output the list in reverse order. The program in Figure 5-2 does just this. Note that subscripted string variables are named in the same way as unsubscripted *(scalar)* ones—a string of characters followed by the dollar sign.

Double Subscripting

Data to be processed by the computer system are sometimes better represented in two-dimensional (table) form than in one-dimensional (list) form. For example,

---

*In some versions of BASIC, I would be set to 13 even though the loop was executed only 12 times. This is because the first time NEXT is encountered, I is set to 2; the twelfth and last time NEXT is encountered, I is set to 13. Some computer systems will "roll back" this value to 12 upon leaving the loop.

FIGURE 5-2

A program that manipulates a string list.

```
10   REM    TITLE: PROGRAM 5-2
20   REM
30   REM    DESCRIPTION:  THIS PROGRAM ILLUSTRATES HOW TO
40   REM       HANDLE STRING DATA IN AN ARRAY
50   REM
60   REM    AUTHOR: C.S. PARKER
70   REM    DATE: 10/5/94
80   REM
90   REM    I      = LOOP VARIABLE
100  REM    FRUIT$ = AN ARRAY STORING THE NAME OF FRUITS
110  REM
120  REM ***********************************************
130  DIM FRUIT$(5)
140  REM
150  REM READ A LIST OF FRUITS
160  FOR I = 1 TO 5
170     READ FRUIT$(I)
180  NEXT I
190  REM
200  REM PRINT OUT THE LIST IN REVERSE ORDER
210  FOR I = 5 TO 1 STEP -1
220     PRINT FRUIT$(I)
230  NEXT I
240  DATA "APPLES","ORANGES","BANANAS"
250  DATA "PEACHES","CHERRIES"
260  END

RUN
CHERRIES
PEACHES
BANANAS
ORANGES
APPLES
```

consider the following data, which show the vote distribution on a certain issue in different schools of a university:

	Voted Yes	Voted No	Didn't Vote
Business	205	152	38
Liberal arts	670	381	115
Engineering	306	251	47
Forestry	112	33	14

These data, which include four rows and three columns of numbers, exist naturally in the form of a table. It would be most convenient if we could give the table a name (ARRAY, for example) and store any number in the table with reference to its row and column position. For example, 115, which is in row 2 and column 3, would be referenced by the subscripted variable ARRAY(2, 3).

FIGURE 5-3

A program that reads a table, totals all the numbers in the table, and prints the fraction that each number is with regard to the sum.

```
10   REM    TITLE: PROGRAM 5-3
20   REM
30   REM    DESCRIPTION:  THIS PROGRAM OUTPUTS AN ARRAY OF
40   REM       NUMBERS, TOTALS IT, AND OUTPUTS EACH ARRAY
50   REM       VALUE AS A FRACTION OF THE TOTAL
60   REM
70   REM    AUTHOR: C.S. PARKER
80   REM    DATE: 10/5/94
90   REM
100  REM    ARRAY    = THE ARRAY OF NUMBERS
110  REM    I,J,M,N  = LOOP VARIABLES
120  REM    SUM      = THE SUM OF ALL NUMBERS IN THE ARRAY
130  REM    FRACTION = THE FRACTION OBTAINED
140  REM
150  REM ***********************************************
160  DIM ARRAY(4,3)
170  SUM = 0
180  REM
190  REM READ NUMBERS INTO ARRAY AND TOTAL THEM
200  FOR I = 1 TO 4
210     FOR J = 1 TO 3
220        READ ARRAY(I,J)
230        SUM = SUM + ARRAY(I,J)
240     NEXT J
250  NEXT I
260  REM
270  REM COMPUTE FRACTIONS AND OUTPUT RESULTS
280  FOR M = 1 TO 4
290     FOR N = 1 TO 3
300        FRACTION = ARRAY(M,N) / SUM
310        PRINT FRACTION,
320     NEXT N
330     PRINT
340  NEXT M
350  DATA 205,152,38
360  DATA 670,381,115
370  DATA 306,251,47
380  DATA 112,33,14
390  END

RUN
 .088210       .065405       .016351
 .288296       .163941       .049484
 .131670       .108003       .020224
 .048193       .014200       .006024
```

Fortunately, BASIC permits us to represent two-dimensional tables in the simple manner just described. Thus, we could store the table numbers in the following 12 variables:

ARRAY(1, 1) = 205	ARRAY(1, 2) = 152	ARRAY(1, 3) = 38
ARRAY(2, 1) = 670	ARRAY(2, 2) = 381	ARRAY(2, 3) = 115
ARRAY(3, 1) = 306	ARRAY(3, 2) = 251	ARRAY(3, 3) = 47
ARRAY(4, 1) = 112	ARRAY(4, 2) = 33	ARRAY(4, 3) = 14

It is relatively easy to create such a table in BASIC and to later access each number and process it as needed. To see how this might be done, refer to the program in Figure 5-3, which totals all of the numbers in the table and subsequently divides each number in the table by this total.

You should observe that in this program, as is the usual practice with subscripts, a DIM statement is immediately employed to declare the size of the table. Then nested loops are established in statements 200–250 to automatically generate the row (I = 1, 2, 3, 4) and column (J = 1, 2, 3) subscripts. Thus, the first time these nested loops are executed,

I = 1, J = 1, ARRAY(1, 1) is assigned 205, and SUM = 0 + 205 = 205

The second time,

I = 1, J = 2, ARRAY(1, 2) is assigned 152, and SUM = 205 + 152 = 357

and so forth.

In the nested loops in statements 280–330, we simply recall ARRAY(1, 1), ARRAY(1, 2), . . ., ARRAY(4, 3) successively from storage and, as we do so, divide each by the table sum and print out the fraction obtained. Note that the variables (M, N) used to represent the subscripts in the second set of nested loops are different than those (I, J) used in the first set. Although we could have used I and J again, the example illustrates that any choice of a subscript variable will do as long as the proper numbers are substituted by the computer to represent the row and column involved.

Two final points on the program in Figure 5-3 deserve your close attention. First, note that the PRINT statement in line 310 contains a comma. This keeps output belonging in the same row printing on the same line. Second, note the blank PRINT statement on line 330. This statement forces the output device onto a new line, where a new row of numbers is printed.

Functions

A *function* is a precoded formula that is referenced in a computer program. BASIC permits two types of functions: *library (built-in) functions* and *user-defined functions*. Two widely used library functions are INT and RND, which truncate numbers and generate random numbers, respectively. Since these functions are built into the BASIC language, the computer system knows exactly what type of action to take when it runs into one of them. Many other library functions are probably available with the version of BASIC used by your computer system. Following is a partial list of some of the more common ones:

Function	Purpose
ABS(X)	Return the absolute value of X
SQR(X)	Calculates the square root of X (X must be >=0)
RND	Returns a random number between .000000 and .999999
SIN(X)	Computes the sine of X (X must be in radians)
COS(X)	Computes the cosine of X (X must be in radians)
TAN(X)	Computes the tangent of X (X must be in radians)
LOG(X)	Calculates the natural logarithm of X (X must be positive)
EXP(X)	Calculates the term e^x, where e is approximately 2.718
INT(X)	Returns the greatest integer <=X

You can also define your own functions. This can be useful when there is a formula you need to use repeatedly that is not a library function. User-defined functions are specified with the DEF statement. For example, suppose we wanted to compute the commission earned by a salesperson as

- 15 percent of gross sales of brand-name items
- 10 percent of gross sales of nonbrand items

Thus, if DUMM1 represents gross sales of brand-name items and DUMM2 is gross sales of nonbrand items, the commission, C, may be calculated as

$$C = .15*DUMM1 + .10*DUMM2$$

A program that computes this commission for three salespeople is given in Figure 5-4. You should inspect this program carefully before proceeding further.

Note in the program that the formula for computing the commissions is defined in line 150. The formula must be defined (with a DEF statement) before it can be used (as in statement 180).

The format of the DEF statement is

```
Line # DEF FNx(y) = z
```

where x is a single alphabetic letter or string of letters chosen by the programmer, y is a list of arguments, and z is a valid BASIC expression. It is also permissible to use several DEF stastements in a single program. Note that the word DEF must be followed by a space and then FN. You must remember, however, to define the functions early in your program, *before* you reference them.

You should also note that the formula, or function, in the figure also contains two *dummy arguments*, arbitrarily named DUMM1 and DUMM2. The only significance of dummy arguments is that they demonstrate how the function will be computed. After reading in the salesperson information in line 170, the computer system prints out in line 180 the salesperson's name and total commission due. Before the computer calculates and prints the commission, it "refers" to line 150 and substitutes REAL1 for DUMM1 and REAL2 for DUMM2.

REAL1 and REAL2, also arbitrarily named, are called *real arguments*. Real arguments are always substituted for corresponding dummy arguments, according to their respective positioning within the parentheses, whenever the function is used in the program. The program could also have been written by using the same variable names as both dummy and real arguments.

This ability to define a function is one of the most useful and most powerful features of BASIC. It is also the capability most overlooked, even by many skilled programmers.

File Processing

Most business applications in real life involve the processing of enormous amounts of data. Typically, when such applications are coded in a language like BASIC, these data are stored in independent files, apart from the programs that use them. There are several reasons why this practice is followed. Three of the most important ones are the following:

■ **PROCESSING FEASIBILITY.**   Memory is often not large enough to store a complete set of data at one time. Consequently, it is easier to manage data independently from programs, bringing only specific pieces of data into memory on an "as needed" basis.

■ **LESS STORAGE.**   Most data serve multiple purposes; that is, they are used by more than one program. For example, data on customer purchases and payments can be used by both a program that prepares customer billings and by a program that determines which customers are delinquent in their payment (and must be sent a remainder). So, when data are stored separately from programs, several programs can access the same body of data, requiring less storage space.

■ **BETTER DATA INTEGRITY.**   When data are physically independent of their programs, the *integrity* of the data is higher. This means that when a change is made in any body of data, the change is reflected consistently in all of the applications that use it.

Versions of BASIC can differ substantially with respect to the way in which they process files. Here, to keep matters simple, we will cover only the convention

---

FIGURE 5-4

Use of a user-defined function to compute commissions.

```
10   REM    TITLE: PROGRAM 5-4
20   REM
30   REM    DESCRIPTION:   THIS PROGRAM COMPUTES SALES
40   REM       COMMISSIONS USING FUNCTIONS
50   REM
60   REM    AUTHOR: C.S. PARKER
70   REM    DATE: 10/5/94
80   REM
90   REM    I            = LOOP VARIABLE
100  REM    DUMM1,DUMM2  = DUMMY ARGUMENTS
110  REM    REAL1,REAL2  = REAL ARGUMENTS
120  REM    PERSON$      = SALESPERSON NAME
130  REM
140  REM    *********************************************
150  DEF FNC(DUMM1,DUMM2) = .15 * DUMM1 + .1 * DUMM2    ◄─── The function is defined here
160  FOR I = 1 TO 3
170     READ PERSON$,REAL1,REAL2
180     PRINT PERSON$,FNC(REAL1,REAL2)    ◄─── The function is executed here
190  NEXT I
200  DATA "JOE SMITH",700.00,1000.00
210  DATA "ZELDA GREY",600.00,1200.00
220  DATA "SUE JOHNSON",1000.00,500.00
230  END

RUN
JOE SMITH        205
ZELDA GREY       210
SUE JOHNSON      200
```

that works on IBM microcomputers and compatible machines and also we will cover only one type of file—*sequential files.*

Organizing Data into Files. When putting data into files, it is customary to first organize the data into fields and records. The terms "field," "record," and "file" each have a precise meaning in a computing environment, and you should use them with care.

A *field* is a collection of characters (a character is a single digit, letter of the alphabet, or special symbol such as the decimal point) that represents a single type of data. A *record* is a collection of related fields, and a *file* is a collection of related records. Files, with their associated records and fields, are normally stored on input/output media such as disks and tapes.

A college, for example, probably would have a file on disk of all students currently enrolled. This file would contain a record for each student. Each record would have several fields—one each for the student's ID number, name, street, city, state, local address, local phone number, major subject area, and so on. Types of programs that would access such a file are the program that produces the campus phone directory, the program that provides a listing of dormitory residents to each dormitory advisor, the program that provides listings of departmental majors to each department chairperson, and so on.

Types of File Access. There are two principal ways to access data—sequentially and directly. With the *sequential access*, the records in a file can be retrieved only in the order in which they physically appear on the storage medium. A music tape provides an example of sequential access; when you play the tape, the tunes play in the order in which they are physically recorded on the tape. With *direct access*, by contrast, records can be accessed in any order. A vinyl phonograph album and a compact disk are examples; you can easily play the tunes in any order you like, and you can play them in sequential order as well.

Sequential files can only be accessed sequentially, whereas direct files can be accessed both directly and sequentially.

Creating a Sequential File. The program shown in Figure 5-5 illustrates how to create the sequential file shown in Figure 5-6. The OPEN statement in the program indicates that the data file is to be given the name PAYFILE and stored on the disk in drive B.

You've seen most of the statements in Figure 5-5 before; however, the OPEN, WRITE, and CLOSE statements are new.

■ OPEN STATEMENT. Every BASIC file must first be opened by an OPEN statement. The OPEN statement makes the file available for processing, sets a pointer to the beginning of the file for writing or reading records, and establishes a buffer in memory through which records are passed between the program and disk.

The general format for the OPEN statement for sequential files is

```
                                    ┌OUTPUT┐
Line # OPEN "filename" FOR  ⎰INPUT ⎱  AS # file-number
                                    └APPEND┘
```

A program that creates a sequential file.

```
10   REM     TITLE:   PROGRAM 5-5
20   REM
30   REM     DESCRIPTION: THIS PROGRAM CREATES A
40   REM        SEQUENTIAL FILE
50   REM
60   REM     AUTHOR: C.S. PARKER
70   REM     DATE: 10/5/94
80   REM
90   REM     EMPLOYEE$  = EMPLOYEE NAME
100  REM     RATE       = PAY RATE
110  REM     GROSS      = GROSS PAY
120  REM
130  REM *************************************
140  OPEN "B:PAYFILE" FOR OUTPUT AS #1
150  READ EMPLOYEE$,RATE,GROSS
160  WHILE EMPLOYEE$ <> "LAST RECORD"
170     WRITE #1,EMPLOYEE$,RATE,GROSS
180     READ EMPLOYEE$,RATE,GROSS
190  WEND
200  CLOSE #1
210  DATA "JOHN DOE",6.30,200.15
220  DATA "MARY SMITH",7.20,316.40
230  DATA "ANN JONES",5.00,80.00
240  DATA "LAST RECORD",0,0
250  END
```

The filename that you choose for your data file can be any filename that's acceptable to DOS. For example,

```
B:PAYFILE
B:PAYFILE.DAT
A:PAYFILE
C:PAYFILE
PAYFILE
PAYFILE.DAT
```

are all acceptable filenames.

In the OPEN statement's FOR clause, you must use one of the keywords OUTPUT, INPUT, or APPEND. When you are creating a file, meaning that

The sequential file created by the program in Figure 5–5.

```
"JOHN DOE",6.3,200.15
"MARY SMITH",7.2,316.4
"ANN JONES",5,80
```

you are writing data to it, use the word OUTPUT. When you are reading from a file, use the word INPUT. The keyword APPEND is used when you want to add records to the end of an existing file. If, for instance, there are currently 15 records in the file, APPEND will write the first record it encounters to the 16th record position in the file. Incidentally, opening a file for OUTPUT always creates a new file, so if the filename declared in the OPEN statement already exists and you want to output to it, the contents of the file will be erased and the file will be opened again as an empty file.

The file number (#1, in Figure 5-5) in the OPEN statement is used as a shorthand way to represent the filename (B:PAYFILE) in subsequent statements. You'll see this file number referenced in statements 170 and 200. If you want your program to process several files concurrently, you must use several OPEN statements and several file numbers, each of which corresponds to a particular file. For example, the statements

```
10 OPEN "B:NAMEFILE" FOR OUTPUT AS #1
20 OPEN "B:PAYFILE" FOR OUTPUT AS #2
30 OPEN "B:RATEFILE" FOR OUTPUT AS #3
```

open three files for processing.

- **WRITE STATEMENT.**   The WRITE statement in line 170 is used to write data to the file. Also, it puts commas between each item (field) in each record, enabling the file to later be read by the INPUT# statement, which will be described shortly. If you are writing BASIC programs that will process several files concurrently, make sure that the file number you are referencing in the WRITE statement corresponds to the name of the file to which you want to write.
- **CLOSE STATEMENT.**   The CLOSE statement is used to close files. All open files must be closed before the program terminates. Also, a file must be opened before it can be closed. Once a file is closed, its file number can be assigned to another file.

Below are some acceptable forms of the CLOSE statement:

```
100 CLOSE #1           Closes file #1
100 CLOSE #1, #2       Closes files #1 and #2
100 CLOSE             Closes all open files
```

READING A FILE.   Once a sequential file is established in the manner just described, it can be read and processed. Before you attempt to process a file, however, you should make sure that it exists in the proper form, with commas separating data fields and each record occupying a new line. For example, if you've established PAYFILE on the B drive, as shown in Figure 5-6, get into DOS and enter

```
TYPE B:PAYFILE
```

at the A> prompt. What appears next on your screen is a listing of the contents of the file. You should inspect the file carefully before proceeding.

After you're satisfied that the file you've created does exist and is correct, it's time to develop a program to read and process it in some way. The program in Figure 5-7 reads and prints the file in Figure 5-6. The OPEN and CLOSE statements should be rather self-explanatory at this point. Files must be opened and closed when they are read just as when they are being created. Note carefully that the OPEN statement in line 140 uses the keyword INPUT, indicating that the PAYFILE is to be opened for reading.

The EOF argument in line 170 and the INPUT statement in line 180 warrant further explanation.

- **EOF.** In sequential file processing, EOF tests to see if the end of a file has been reached. The "1" in parentheses in line 170 means file #1; a "2" would mean file #2, and so forth. As soon as a record is read (by the INPUT statement), EOF automatically advances the file pointer to the next record.

- **INPUT.** In sequential file processing, the word INPUT followed by a file number has a meaning different from a conventional INPUT statement. The statement in line 180 does the reading of records for the program. It works like the familiar READ statement in that, every time it executes, the next three values from file #1 are respectively assigned to the named variables.

The programs in Figures 5-5 and 5-7 have been made very simple to enable you to focus on how file processing works. You could, if you wish, make them much more sophisticated by using subroutines, the PRINT USING statement, and the like. Virtually all of the BASIC programming tools you've encountered earlier in this *Guide* also work in a sequential file processing environment.

FIGURE 5-7

A program that reads a sequential file.

```
10   REM     TITLE:   PROGRAM 5-7
20   REM
30   REM     DESCRIPTION: THIS PROGRAM READS A
40   REM        SEQUENTIAL FILE
50   REM
60   REM     AUTHOR: C.S. PARKER
70   REM     DATE: 10/5/94
80   REM
90   REM     EMPLOYEE$   = EMPLOYEE NAME
100  REM     RATE        = PAY RATE
110  REM     GROSS       = GROSS PAY
120  REM
130  REM ****************************************
140  OPEN "B:PAYFILE" FOR INPUT AS #1
150  PRINT "NAME","PAY RATE","GROSS PAY"
160  PRINT
170  WHILE NOT EOF(1)
180     INPUT #1,EMPLOYEE$,RATE,GROSS
190     PRINT EMPLOYEE$,RATE,GROSS
200  WEND
210  CLOSE #1
220  END

RUN
NAME           PAY RATE      GROSS PAY

JOHN DOE       6.3           200.15
MARY SMITH     7.2           316.4
ANN JONES      5             80
```

FIGURE 5-8

A program for cross-classifying sales data.

```
10  REM     TITLE: PROGRAM 5-8
20  REM
30  REM     DESCRIPTION: THIS PROGRAM CALCULATES PRODUCT SALES
40  REM        ATTRIBUTABLE TO VARIOUS SALESPEOPLE IN A COMPANY
50  REM
60  REM     AUTHOR: C.S. PARKER
70  REM     DATE: 10/5/94
80  REM
90  REM     PERSON$     = THE SALESPERSON NAME
100 REM     NUMBER      = THE NUMBER OF SALESPEOPLE
110 REM     PRICES      = THE ARRAY OF PRODUCT PRICES
120 REM     UNITS       = THE UNITS SOLD BY A SALESPERSON
130 REM     ROWS        = THE ARRAY SAVING PRODUCT SALES
140 REM                       IN EACH ROW BEFORE THEY ARE OUTPUT
150 REM     FOOTINGS    = THE ROW TOTALS
160 REM     COLUMNS     = THE ARRAY SAVING THE COLUMN TOTALS
170 REM     GRAND       = THE GRAND TOTAL OF ALL SALES
180 REM     I,J         = LOOP VARIABLES
190 REM     A$,B$       = OUTPUT-IMAGE VARIABLES FOR PRINT USING
200 REM
210 REM **********************************************************
220 DIM ROWS(3),COLUMNS(3),PRICES(3)
230 PRINT "   NAME         PRODUCT1   PRODUCT2   PRODUCT3      TOTAL"
240 PRINT
250 READ NUMBER
260 REM INITIALIZATIONS
270 FOR I=1 TO 3
280    COLUMNS(I) = 0
290    READ PRICES(I)
300 NEXT I
310 GRAND = 0
```

Solved Review Problems

Example 1

A company that produces three products currently has eight salespeople. The sales of each product by each salesperson are given in the following table:

		Units Sold	
Salesperson	**Product 1**	**Product 2**	**Product 3**
William Ing	100	50	65
Ed Wilson	500	0	0
Ann Johnson	200	25	600
Edna Farber	150	30	500
Norris Ames	600	80	150
Elma Jace	100	410	800
Vilmos Zisk	300	30	60
Ellen Venn	400	0	0

The latest unit prices on products 1, 2, and 3 are $1.00, $1.25, and $.85, respectively.

Figure 5-8   *continued*

```
320 A$ = "\                \    #,###.##    #,###.##    #,###.##    #,###.##"
330 B$ = "TOTALS                #,###.##    #,###.##    #,###.##    #,###.##"
340 REM
350 REM MAIN COMPUTATIONS
360 FOR I = 1 TO NUMBER
370      FOOTINGS = 0
380      READ PERSON$
390      FOR J = 1 TO 3
400         READ UNITS
410         ROWS(J) = UNITS * PRICES(J)
420         COLUMNS(J) = COLUMNS(J) + ROWS(J)
430         FOOTINGS = FOOTINGS + ROWS(J)
440         GRAND = GRAND + ROWS(J)
450      NEXT J
460      PRINT USING A$;PERSON$,ROWS(1),ROWS(2),ROWS(3),FOOTINGS
470 NEXT I
480 PRINT
490 PRINT USING B$;COLUMNS(1),COLUMNS(2),COLUMNS(3),GRAND
500 REM *****************DATA STATEMENTS*********************
510 DATA 8
520 DATA 1,1.25,.85
530 DATA "WILLIAM ING",100,50,65
540 DATA "ED WILSON",500,0,0
550 DATA "ANN JOHNSON",200,25,600
560 DATA "EDNA FARBER",150,30,500
570 DATA "NORRIS AMES",600,80,150
580 DATA "ELMA JACE",100,410,800
590 DATA "VILMOS ZISK",300,30,60
600 DATA "ELLEN VENN",400,0,0
610 REM *********************************************************
620 END
```

Use the preceding data to produce the following table. Use subscripted variables to represent the totals associated with the three products and the eight salespeople.

NAME	PRODUCT1	PRODUCT2	PRODUCT3	TOTAL
WILLIAM ING	100.00	62.50	55.25	217.75
ED WILSON	500.00	0.00	0.00	500.00
ANN JOHNSON	200.00	31.25	510.00	741.25
EDNA FARBER	150.00	37.50	425.00	612.50
NORRIS AMES	600.00	100.00	127.50	827.50
ELMA JACE	100.00	512.50	680.00	1,292.50
VILMOS ZISK	300.00	37.50	51.00	388.50
ELLEN VENN	400.00	0.00	0.00	400.00
TOTALS	2,350.00	781.25	1,848.75	4,980.00

Solution
A program solution to this problem is given in Figure 5-8.

F I G U R E   5 - 9

A menu-selection program using subroutines. The program's output is in the inset at the bottom right.

```
10   REM    TITLE: PROGRAM 5-9
20   REM
30   REM    DESCRIPTION: THIS PROGRAM DEMONSTRATES THE
40   REM      USE OF SUBROUTINES AND MENUS
50   REM
60   REM    AUTHOR - C.S. PARKER
70   REM    DATE: 10/5/94
80   REM
90   REM    EXPENSE$    = ARRAY TO HOLD EXPENSE CATEGORIES
100  REM    AMOUNT      = ARRAY TO HOLD AMOUNTS
110  REM    RECORDS     = NUMBER OF RECORDS
120  REM    MENU        = MENU-SELECTION VARIABLE
130  REM    HOLD,HOLD$ = HOLDING VARIABLES FOR LARGEST
140  REM                        EXPENSE AND CATEGORY
150  REM    TOTAL       = TOTAL EXPENSES
160  REM
170  REM ******************************************
180  DIM EXPENSE$(100),AMOUNT(100)
190  REM
200  REM DATA ENTRY
210  READ RECORDS
220     FOR I=1 TO RECORDS
230        READ EXPENSE$(I),AMOUNT(I)
240     NEXT I
250  REM MENU AND SELECTION
260  MENU = 0
270  WHILE MENU <> 4
280     PRINT
290     PRINT "PROGRAM OPTIONS"
300     PRINT
310     PRINT "   1 - THE LARGEST CATEGORY"
320     PRINT "   2 - TOTAL COST"
330     PRINT "   3 - ALL CATEGORIES EXCEEDING $1000"
340     PRINT "   4 - END PROGRAM"
350     PRINT
360     PRINT "WHICH OPTION DO YOU WISH TO TAKE (TYPE IN NUMBER)";
370     INPUT MENU
380     IF NOT (MENU = 1 OR MENU = 2 OR MENU = 3 OR MENU = 4) THEN MENU = 5
390     ON MENU GOSUB 420,540,630,740,790
400  WEND
410     STOP
420  REM ************LARGEST COST SUBROUTINE**************
430     HOLD = AMOUNT(1)
440     HOLD$ = EXPENSE$(1)
450     FOR I=2 TO RECORDS
460        IF AMOUNT(I) <= HOLD THEN 490
470           HOLD = AMOUNT(I)
480           HOLD$ = EXPENSE$(I)
490     NEXT I
500     PRINT
510     PRINT "LARGEST EXPENSE:";HOLD$;"   (AMOUNT =";HOLD;")"
520     PRINT
530     RETURN
```

```
540 REM **************TOTAL COST SUBROUTINE***************
550     TOTAL = 0
560     FOR I=1 TO RECORDS
570         TOTAL = TOTAL + AMOUNT(I)
580     NEXT I
590     PRINT
600     PRINT "TOTAL COST IS...$";TOTAL
610     PRINT
620     RETURN
630 REM ***********$1000-OR-MORE SUBROUTINE**************
640     PRINT
650     PRINT "CATEGORIES EXCEEDING $1000"
660     PRINT
670     PRINT "CATEGORY","EXPENSE"
680     FOR I = 1 TO RECORDS
690         IF AMOUNT(I) < 1000 THEN 710
700             PRINT EXPENSE$(I),AMOUNT(I)
710     NEXT I
720     PRINT
730     RETURN
740 REM **********TERMINATION ROUTINE********************
750     PRINT
760     PRINT
770     PRINT "YOU HAVE CHOSEN TO END THE PROGRAM--GOODBYE"
780     RETURN
790 REM *************ERROR ROUTINE*******************
800     PRINT
810     PRINT
820     PRINT "YOU HAVE INPUT AN INCORRECT CHOICE--TRY AGAIN"
830     PRINT
840     RETURN
850 REM **************DATA STATEMENTS*****************
860 DATA 8
870 DATA "SALARIES",8500,"RENT",2000,"ADVERTISING",1100
880 DATA "UTILITIES",590,"SUPPLIES",200,"DEPRECIATION",1200
890 DATA "INSURANCE",300,"TAXES",150
900 REM *********************************************
910 END
```

```
          PROGRAM OPTIONS

              1 - THE LARGEST CATEGORY
              2 - TOTAL COST
              3 - ALL CATEGORIES EXCEEDING $1000
              4 - END PROGRAM

          WHICH OPTION DO YOU WISH TO TAKE (TYPE IN NUMBER)?2

          CATEGORIES EXCEEDING $1000

          CATEGORY       EXPENSE
          SALARIES         8500
          RENT             2000
          ADVERTISING      1100
          DEPRECIATION     1200

          NEXT MENU SELECTION (TYPE IN NUMBER)?
```

The output loop (lines 360–470) is used to read each salesperson's record. The inner loop (lines 390–450), which executes three times for each iteration of the outer loop, is used to multiply sales of each of the three products by its price, accumulate the row totals, and accumulate the column footings.

Example 2

The program in Figure 5-9 processes accounting expenses for the past month. Users of the program have several options—for example, finding the category with the greatest expense, computing total expenses (over all categories), or listing all categories with an expense exceeding $1,000. The options are presented to the user in the form of a *menu*. Once the user selects a choice on the menu, either a 1, 2, 3, or 4 is typed in, corresponding to the options in lines 310–340. Given the choice, the computer then branches to the appropriate subroutine to be processed, goes to an error-trapping routine, or ends the program. If, for example, the user selects option 2 (total cost), the computer branches to line 540 and proceeds from that point until line 620 (RETURN) is encountered. It then goes back to the main part of the program and redisplays the menu.

Exercises

Instructions: Provide an answer to each of the following questions.

1. Consider the following program:

```
10 DIM A(5)
20 FOR I=1 TO 5
30 READ A(I)
40 LET A(I)=A(I)+1
50 NEXT I
60 DATA 35,18,-6,42,27
```

   What is the final value of

   a. A(1)?   b. A(2)?   c. A(3)?   d. A(4)?   e. A(5)?

2. Consider the following program:

```
10 DIM A(6)
20 A(1)=0
30 FOR I=2 TO 6
40 READ A(I)
50 LET A(I)=A(I-1)
60 NEXT I
70 DATA 35,18,-6,42,27
```

   What is the final value of

   a. A(1)?   b. A(2)?   c. A(3)?   d. A(4)?   e. A(5)?

3. Consider the following program:

```
10 DIM A(4,4)
20 FOR I=1 TO 4
30 FOR J=1 TO 4
40 READ A(I,J)
50 NEXT J
60 NEXT I
70 DATA 12,2,0,3,1,4,2,7,6,10,9,0,11,3,8,7
```

What is the final value of

a. A(1,3)?   b. A(2,2)?   c. A(3,4)?   d. A(4,3)?

4. What does the following program do?

```
10 DIM A(20), B(20)
20 FOR I=1 TO 5
30 READ A(I), B(I)
40 A(I)=A(I)-B(I)
50 NEXT I
60 DATA 6,8,4,5,7,1,0,2,8,3
```

5. What are the values of all variables in the C array when the following program has finished executing?

```
10 S=0
20 FOR J=1 TO 5
30 READ A(J)
40 S=S+A(J)
50 NEXT J
60 FOR I=1 TO 5
70 C(I+1)=S-A(I)
80 NEXT I
90 DATA 10,4,1,6,8
```

Programming Problems

Instructions: Write a BASIC program to do each of the following tasks.

1. The following is a list of salaries of the six employees in a certain company:

Name	Salary
T. Agasi	$43,000
F. Smith	$31,000
K. Johnston	$22,000
P. Miner	$18,000
C. Altman	$27,000
A. Lu	$19,000

Calculate and output the average salary for the company as well as the names of all people whose salaries exceed the average.

2. Read the 10 numbers in the following list, and then output the list in reverse order (that is, 12, 43, 6, etc.):

$$31, 15, 85, 36, 22, 81, 70, 6, 43, 12$$

3. The following list contains names and sexes of people at XYZ Company: Janice Racza (female), Bill Smith (male), Debra Parks (female), Chantelle Johnson (female), William Anderson (male), Art James (male), Bill Finley (male), and Ellen Woo (female).

    Read the list into the computer in the order given. Then prepare and output two separate lists—one composed of all of the males and the other composed of all of the females.

4. Write a program that reads the following matrix,

$$\begin{bmatrix} 8 & 7 & 3 \\ 2 & 4 & 1 \\ 6 & 5 & 8 \end{bmatrix}$$

    adds the number 5 to each element (number) of the matrix, and prints the result.

5. Refer to Programming Problem 7 on page 32 of the *Guide*. Write a program to enter the five student records into a file. Then write another program to produce student bills in the manner described in the problem statement.

Appendix 1: QBASIC Guide

Starting with Version 5.0 of DOS, Microsoft introduced its QBASIC translator. QBASIC supports most programs created under earlier versions of BASIC available with DOS—BASICA and GWBASIC—and adds several new features. The most important of these features with respect to material presented in this *Guide* are described below.

Optional Line Numbers.   QBASIC supports BASIC programs written with or without line numbers.

DO Loops.   "DO loops" allow programmers to include both DOWHILE and DOUNTIL loops in their programs. Figure 1 shows a sample loop that uses the DOUNTIL control structure. With a DO loop, looping continues either until (DOUNTIL) or while (DOWHILE) the condition in the LOOP statement is met. Then, program control is passed on to the statement immediately following the loop.

SELECT CASE Construct.   The SELECT CASE construct enables users to code case control structures more straightforwardly into their programs. Figure 2 provides a simple, self-explanatory example of how SELECT CASE works.

FIGURE 1

The SELECT CASE statement.

```
INPUT "Enter desired level of risk (1-5): ",RISK
SELECT CASE RISK
      CASE 1
            PRINT "Small risk, small return"
            PRINT "Buy CD or government-backed security"
      CASE 2 TO 4
            PRINT "Moderate risk, moderate return"
            PRINT "Buy into a mutual fund"
      CASE 5
            PRINT "High risk, potentially high return"
            PRINT "Buy stocks"
END SELECT
```

FIGURE 2

SUBs and FUNCTIONs.

```
(a) SUB
        SUB CALCULATION (PI, RADIUS, AREA, CIRCUMFERENCE)
            AREA = PI*RADIUS^2
            CIRCUMFERENCE=2*PI*RADIUS
        END SUB


(b) FUNCTION
        FUNCTION AREA (RADIUS)
            AREA = 3.14159*RADIUS^2
        END FUNCTION
```

FIGURE 3

A DO loop.

```
DO
    INPUT "Name the capital of New York", NYCAPITAL$
    IF NYCAPITAL$ = "Albany" THEN PRINT "Right"
                                    ELSE PRINT "Guess aga
LOOP UNTIL NYCAPITAL$ = "Albany"
```

Enhanced Subprogramming Capabilities. QBASIC enables you to develop two new types of subprograms, called procedure "SUBs" (for subprograms) and "FUNCTION" procedures. Not to be confused with conventional GOSUBs or DEF FN functions, respectively, which are embedded into the main BASIC program, these two new types of subprograms are freestanding and can be submitted for translation along with any compatible programs. Furthermore, each can use either variables in the main BASIC program (called global variables) or its own variables (called local variables).

Both SUBs and FUNCTIONs can accept parameters from the main program and can pass parameters or a value back. Typically, SUBs are used when several parameters are exchanged; FUNCTIONs are used when only a single value is passed back. Shown in Figure 3 are examples of their typical usage. Each type of procedure can be summoned by the main program by merely invoking its name. For instance, regarding the SUB, a reference in the main program such as

```
CALL CALCULATION (PI, RADIUS, AREA, CIRCUMFERENCE)
```

will cause the values of PI and RADIUS in the main program to be passed to the SUB, the SUB to be executed, and the values of AREA and CIRCUMFERENCE passed back to the main program. Similarly, with the FUNCTION, any time AREA is referred to in the main program, say,

```
PRINT AREA
```

the FUNCTION named AREA will be passed the value of RADIUS and executed, and the value of AREA returned to the main program.

Appendix 2: BASIC Statement Commands

Statement	Description	Example
CLOSE	Closes a file (86)	`100 CLOSE #1`
DEF	Sets up a user-defined function (82)	`90 DEF FNC (A,B) = .15*A+.10*B`
DIM	Dimensions an array (75)	`120 DIM X(12)`
END	The last statement in a program (25)	`250 END`

FOR/NEXT	The beginning and ending statements in a loop (49)	`160 FOR I=1 TO N`
		`.`
		`.`
		`.`
		`190 NEXT I`

GOSUB/RETURN	Branch to a subroutine; Return to main program from subroutine (53)	`120 GOSUB 150`
		`.`
		`.`
		`.`
		`190 RETURN`

IF/THEN	A conditional branch (23)	`110 IF A=-1 THEN 160`
IF/THEN/ELSE	A conditional branch (23)	`110 IF S>5000 THEN B=500` `             ELSE B=0`
INPUT	Enables data to be entered interactively (47)	`80 INPUT X`
INPUT#	Enables a file to be read (87)	`100 INPUT #1, EMPLOYEE$, RATE`
LET	An assignment (replacement) statement (20)	`30 LET C=A+B`
ON . . . GOSUB	Branches to a specific case (55)	`100 ON M GOSUB 300,400,500`
OPEN	Opens a file (84)	`100 OPEN "INVTY" FOR OUTPUT AS #1`
PRINT	Displays or prints program output (21)	`160 PRINT N$`

PRINT USING	Enables neatly formatted output (64)	`100 A$ = "###.##"`
		`.`
		`.`
		`.`
		`200 PRINT USING A$;X`

READ/DATA	Assigns values to variables from a list of data (20)	`20 READ A,B`
		`.`
		`.`
		`.`
		`50 DATA 8,16`

REM	A program remark (24)	`100 REM THIS IS A REMARK`
STOP	Stops a program (48)	`80 STOP`

WHILE/WEND	The beginning and ending statements in a loop (22)	`150 WHILE X>0`
		`.`
		`.`
		`.`
		`200 WEND`

WRITE#	Enables a file to be created (86)	`100 WRITE #1, EMPLOYEE$, RATE`

Note: Numbers in parentheses in the second column are the pages on which the statement is described.

Appendix 3: Reserved Words

ABS	DELETE	INT	OPEN	SOUND
AND	DIM	INTER$	OPTION	SPACE$
ASC	DRAW	IOCTL	OR	SCP
ATN	EDIT	IOCTL$	OUT	SQR
AUTO	ELSE	KEY	PAINT	STEP
BEEP	END	KILL	PEEK	STICK
BLOAD	ENVIRON	LEFT$	PEN	STOP
BSAVE	ENVIRON$	LEN	PLAY	STR$
CALL	EOF	LET	PMAP	SRIG
CDBL	EQV	LINE	POINT	STRING$
CHAIN	ERASE	LIST	POKE	SWAP
CHDIR	ERDEV	LLIST	POS	SYSTEM
CHR$	ERDEV$	LOAD	PRESET	TAB
CINT	ERL	LOC	PRINT	TAN
CIRCLE	ERR	LOCATE	PRINT#	THEN
CLEAR	ERROR	LOF	PSET	TIME$
CLOSE	EXP	LOG	PUT	TO
CLS	FIELD	LPOS	RANDOMIZE	TROFF
COLOR	FILES	LPRINT	READ	TRON
COM	FIX	LSET	REM	USING
COMMON	FNxxx	MERGE	RENUM	USR
CONT	FOR	MID$	RESET	VAL
COS	FRE	MKDIR	RESTORE	VARPTR
CSNG	GET	MKD$	RESUME	VARPTR$
CSRLIN	GOSUB	MKI$	RETURN	WAIT
CVD	GOTO	MKS$	RIGHT$	WEND
CVI	HEX$	MOD	RMDIR	WHILE
CVS	IF	MOTOR	RND	WIDTH
DATA	IMP	NAME	RSET	WINDOW
DATE$	INKEY$	NEW	RUN	WRITE
DEF	INP	NEXT	SAVE	WRITE#
DEFDBL	INPUT	NOT	SCREEN	XOR
DEFINT	INPUT#	OCT$	SGN	
DEFSNG	INPUT$	OFF	SHELL	
DEFSTR	INSTR	ON	SIN	